THE ESSENES, THE SCROLLS, AND THE DEAD SEA

The Essenes, the Scrolls, and the Dead Sea

JOAN E. TAYLOR

OXFORD
UNIVERSITY PRESS

OXFORD
UNIVERSITY PRESS

Great Clarendon Street, Oxford, OX2 6DP,
United Kingdom

Oxford University Press is a department of the University of Oxford.
It furthers the University's objective of excellence in research, scholarship,
and education by publishing worldwide. Oxford is a registered trade mark of
Oxford University Press in the UK and in certain other countries

British Library Cataloguing in Publication Data

Data available

Library of Congress Cataloging in Publication Data

Data available

ISBN 978-0-19-955448-5

Printed in Great Britain by
MPG Books Group, Bodmin and King's Lynn

For Fergus Millar, Geza Vermes, and Martin Goodman,
with thanks

Preface

More than 60 years after their first discovery in 1947, the Dead Sea Scrolls remain a mystery. Were they written by the Essenes? Why were they hidden? What are they, exactly?

While it has been supposed they are part of an Essene library, secreted away when the Romans advanced, there is today some nervousness among scholars about linking the Dead Sea Scrolls with the Essenes. For a long time the 'Qumran-Essene' hypothesis, as it is called, seemed to reflect a consensus view: the Essenes were responsible for the writing and hiding of the Scrolls, and they lived in the small site of Qumran by the Dead Sea from the late second century BCE to the year 68 CE. But the hypothesis is now questioned widely, meaning that many Scrolls scholars focusing on the fine details of these remarkable Hebrew, Aramaic, and Greek writings are cautious about locating them within a wider cultural environment.

Currently, in order to avoid a simple assumption that the Scrolls were produced by Essenes, many Scrolls scholars avoid language that presupposes endorsement of the Qumran-Essene hypothesis. Using definitions such as the 'Qumran Community/ies', '*Yaḥad* community/ies' or even 'Scrolls community/ies', scholars aim to define identities from the Scrolls' salient features, across time. The history of the people responsible for the Scrolls is sought within the texts themselves, without much reference to descriptions of named groups within Second Temple Judaism, or to the archaeology of Qumran and the Dead Sea region.

Among those who have supported the Qumran-Essene hypothesis, the historical sources on the Essenes have long been studied in order to identify features of the Essenes that can be compared with the communities evidenced in the literature of the Scrolls corpus itself. The Essenes have been seen as a marginal, isolated group, and their literature is likewise configured as peripheral to the main currents of Judaism. The contents of the Dead Sea Scrolls are largely then peculiar and particular, not representative of the centre. Aspects of the ancient Essenes that have received most scholarly attention have been their identity as 'sectarian', their location beside the Dead Sea, communality, separation from other Jews, negative attitude to the Temple, asceticism, pacifism, allegorical scriptural exegesis, and special concern with purity. In placing these characteristics next to the evidence of the Scrolls, however, various anomalies have come to light. There are issues of method that then arise. There can be a circularity of interpretation of the Scrolls: if one begins with an initial presupposition that the Scrolls are 'Essene', do we then interpret them in the light of what we think we know about the Essenes? Without such an *a priori* position, might different interpretative possibilities arise? Hence the current focus on close readings of the Dead Sea texts in isolation.

In addition, there has been a reconfiguration of the archaeology of the site of Qumran. It has been explored and contextualized by archaeologists as being a site situated in a regional context in which the Essenes played a very minor role. The question of whether Qumran was a community centre for those Essenes writing the Scrolls has been answered with a firm 'no'. The Scrolls, it is argued, might have nothing at all to do with Qumran: it is a mere accident of history that they are lying next to it.

Because of the strength of such scholarly 'de-bunking', at the present time, it is not surprising that many Scrolls scholars shy away from issues of identity, history, and cultural context. However, for a historian, the mysteries remain a tantalizing taunt. It is not satisfying to place a question-mark over such a stunning archaeological discovery as the Dead Sea Scrolls and to assume that historical contextualization is impossible, or that our historical sources are so rhetorical that elements of historical actuality must surely disappear in 'spin'. In ancient history overall, historicity and rhetoricity are interwoven partners: there is no plain corpus of simple data. Yet we know a great deal about the world of the past, because historians have probed evidence in various ways and continue to do so. Can we then probe again here?

Given the current testing of the Qumran-Essene hypothesis, with its emphasis on features of either the Scrolls or the site of Qumran that do not cohere with the Essenes of the classical sources, it is fundamental that we define who exactly the Essenes were. This can only be done by working through ancient literature, to ensure that what we think we know is consistent with what is actually stated. The historical sources on the Essenes, a variety of works written in Latin and Greek by different authors mainly in the first century of the common era (CE), are key to the Essenes' identity. In the present study, the examination will be broader than any hitherto undertaken, in that it will consider also whether the Essenes may appear under other names in Christian and Jewish material from the first centuries.

We will tackle the vexing question of whether the Dead Sea Scrolls and the site of Qumran can be related to the Essenes only after the Essenes themselves are defined and situated on the basis of this literary evidence, which will constitute the project of the first part of this investigation. Subsequently, in the second part, the classical sources on the Dead Sea and its resources, and the archaeological context, will be explored. The Dead Sea Scrolls are the central focus of this entire project, but they will be considered primarily as archaeological objects, and thus their material nature and context will be paramount. They are, after all, among the most important archaeological discoveries ever made. They will at times be called upon in textual analysis, but more than anything they are *things* of a bygone age: they were placed in caves at certain times, for certain reasons.

We will explore a case for why the inhabitants of Qumran lived in this harsh and hot location, by a salty lake, and placed the Scrolls in caves nearby. The approach is contextual, in looking widely at features of the environment and our historical evidence for changes of occupation and resource utilization.

The Scrolls are also seen as cultural artefacts, and this study looks at the wider culture in which they belong. Where the Scrolls are probed, it is with a view to seeing this culture. The results will, I hope, illuminate Second Temple Judaism, through to the second century CE, with its rich blend of diversity and unity. This study will shine a light on the situation of the ancient Dead Sea, and provide a sound historical context for the Dead Sea Scrolls. We will encounter both the secretive world of medicine and healing, and the economic worlds of the Hasmonean and Herodian dynasties. We will be concerned with the historical development of the Dead Sea as a centre of lucrative resources and also consider its role in literature as a 'paradoxical marvel'. There will be close literary analysis of works written in ancient languages and also detailed archaeological examinations, as the scope is ultimately a broad one and the aim is to gain a holistic historical understanding. The scrutiny of details is done in order to find the big picture in which the Scrolls can be situated. I hope this study will, at least, be interesting, as it synthesizes evidence and adopts cross-disciplinary approaches to solve the questions of who the historical Essenes really were, who wrote the Dead Sea Scrolls, who lived at Qumran, and why the Scrolls were placed in caves close to this site.

Acknowledgements

I wish to thank the many people who have discussed various matters with me over the past seven years that I have been working on this book, in particular Fergus Millar, Geza Vermes, Martin Goodman, Jodi Magness, Jean-Baptiste Humbert, Michael Knibb, Charlotte Hempel, Shimon Gibson, Dennis Mizzi, Daniel Stökl Ben Ezra, John J. Collins, Nigel Hepper, Yuval Peleg, Michael Stone, Steve Mason, George Brooke, Konstantinos Politis, Greg Doudna, David Stacey, Douglas Finkbeiner, Sidnie White Crawford, Maxine Grossman, Bart Wagemakers, Ida Fröhlich, Gideon Hadas, Robert Kraft, Shani Tzoref, the late Yizhar Hirschfeld, and the late Hanan Eshel. This work is dedicated to the first three names on this list, as esteemed historians and Schürer associates. Geza Vermes and Martin Goodman are well-known for their volume that collects together the classical sources on the Essenes for an English-reading audience, but also because they now have different points of view on the underlying questions addressed here. That two such eminent Oxford scholars can take different positions on key issues indicates just how intractable the problems have become.

I am grateful to the Palestine Exploration Fund, the Wellcome Foundation, the British Society for the History of Pharmacy, and the International Society for the History of Pharmacy for their financial assistance as I have completed parts of this study. The support from those bodies promoting the exploration of the history of medicine has been very helpful in enabling research towards Part II in particular. I have spent some time at the Dead Sea, travelling over the areas around its circumference and learning of its many geographical, botanical and archaeological features.

I thank also the Studia Philonica Annual, and Brill Academic publishers, for permission to update and use material that has previously been published with them. In Part I, the following articles have been expanded and revised here: Chapter 2: 'Philo of Alexandria on the Essenes: A Case Study on the Use of Classical Sources in Discussions of the Qumran-Essene Hypothesis,' *Studia Philonica Annual* (2007): 1–28; Chapter 5, parts of my article: 'On Pliny, the Essene Location and Kh. Qumran,' *DSD* 16 (2009): 129–49; Chapter 6: 'Dio on the Essene Landscape,' in Charlotte Hempel (ed.), *The Dead Sea Scrolls: Texts and Context* (Leiden: Brill, 2010), 467–86. In Part II, I have updated in Chapter 2: 'Buried Manuscripts and Empty Tombs: The *Genizah* Hypothesis Reconsidered,' in Aren Maeir, Jodi Magness and Lawrence Schiffman (eds), *'Go out and study the Land' (Judg 18:2): Archaeological, Historical and Textual Studies in Honor of Hanan Eshel* (Supplements of the Journal for the Study of Judaism; Leiden: Brill, 2011), 269–316. With these pieces, it is not a case of a simple reprint of previously published material, as the articles were essentially work in progress for this book, and much further development has been done since their publication. The reader should therefore reference the present discussion, within its total argument. Most of this volume is hitherto unpublished.

As always, I also thank my family—Paul, Emily, and Robbie—for their love and support.

Contents

List of Illustrations

Maps

Plates

1. The first-century synagogue of Kiryat Sepher, near Modin, which is only 9.6 square metres, has the typical form of a central area with stone benches around it. Only the lower benches were in fact made of stone and a platform would have supported tiered wooden benches above it.

2. Remains of monumental stairs running up to where there was once a gate leading into the Herodian palace complex on the western side of Jerusalem (see Map 1). Shimon Gibson (in the distance with a BBC film crew) has identified the stairs as leading to the Gate of the Essenes. A. remains of stairs; B. remains of Hasmonean wall; C. remains of lower part of surrounding architecture of the gate posts, partly built up on natural stone; D. outline of the approximate dimensions of the gate interior (author's suggestion; Gibson has a slightly different form). The line of steps culminates in a flat pavement just before the gate (where people are standing).

3. As noted by Hieronymous of Cardia, palms grow wild around the Dead Sea, wherever water sustains them.

4. The Hasmonean fortress of Hyrcania. The edge of the Buqeia (Judaean wilderness) region that falls away to the trough of the Dead Sea basin is seen in the distance, to the right.

5. The mount of Masada, south-west of the Dead Sea. A Hasmonean fort was built by Alexander Jannaeus, in the early first century BCE, but it was Herod the Great who developed it into a formidable palace-fortress.

6. Rujm el-Bahr, a Hasmonean anchorage that served Jericho. This site continued in use through the early Roman period.

7. Khirbet Mazin, a Hasmonean anchorage which continued in use through the early Roman period.

8. En Gedi: ancient agricultural terraces to the north of Tel Goren, where there was a Hasmonean fort.

9. Chemical mining on the south-eastern side of the Dead Sea.

10. One of the many warm springs of Callirhoe, providing irrigation. The oasis is lush (burnt trees notwithstanding).

it lasted to the end of the first century and even into the second, when it was badly damaged by an earthquake (in *c*.115 CE).

26. Qumran. Remains of kiln in Locus 84, where there was a pottery workshop. Behind it the sloping area of the cemetery, with the lower Dead Sea shores and lake in the distance.

27. View south from Qumran to Ain Feshkha Oasis.

28. One of the spring-fed pools of Ain Feshkha: a natural *miqveh*.

29. Ain Feshkha: ruins of a building of the Herodian period, looking west.

30. The Ain Feshkha water channels leading to large pools from a spring now dried up, on the northern side of the ruins.

31. En Boqeq stream, flowing from a spring higher up in the valley. The site of the Herodian *officina* complex (further to the left of this photograph) has been partially filled in for its protection, given the proximity of tourist hotels. There is another spring further up the hill to the north, irrigating a small oasis, the water of which was harnessed in later centuries for a Roman fort.

32. Cylindrical jar on display at the Jordan Archaeological Museum, Amman, J.19416.

33. View of artificial marl caves from the Wadi Qumran, with natural caves of hills behind. Cave 8Q is the semi-circular collapsed cave on the right spur, and collapsed cave 7Q lies to the right of it, slightly higher, while cave 4Q (a and b) openings are seen on the left spur.

34. Plan of Qumran and its occupation zone: marl caves, aqueduct, wall, and cemetery.

35. Plans of caves surveyed in 1952 drawn by Jack Ziegler (courtesy of Jean-Baptiste Humbert, EBAF).

36. View of openings of artificial cave 4Q (a and b) from the Qumran plateau above caves 7Q–9Q. The view is looking up the Wadi Qumran to natural caves in the hills behind. Cave 6Q is just hidden (courtesy of Daniel Gibson).

37. Plate 6: Mohammed ed-Dhib and Ahmed Mohammed outside cave 1Q. Photo 13011 from the de Vaux-Qumran archives, supplied and printed with permission of Jean-Baptiste Humbert, EBAF.

38. Box of linen in the Qumran stores, Rockefeller Museum, Jerusalem, with the bitumen impregnated into the fabric. Photo supplied and printed with permission of Jean-Baptiste Humbert, EBAF.

39. Box of linen in the Qumran stores, Rockefeller Museum, Jerusalem, with the bitumen impregnated into the fabric. Photo supplied and printed with permission of Jean-Baptiste Humbert, EBAF.

40. Asphalt fragment from the Dead Sea.

41. The Kidron stream (Wadi en-Nar), flowing through the Judaean wilderness from Jerusalem, west of Kh. Mazin.

List of Abbreviations

ADSS	Roland de Vaux, *Archaeology and the Dead Sea Scrolls* (London British Academy/Oxford: Oxford University Press, 1973).
ANRW	Wolfgang Haase and Hildegard Temporini (eds), *Aufstieg und Niedergang der römischen Welt: Geschichte und Kultur Roms im Spiegel der neueren Forschung* (Berlin/New York: Walter de Gruyter).
BA	*The Biblical Archaeologist*
BAIAS	*Bulletin of the Anglo-Israel Archaeological Society*
BAR	*Biblical Archaeology Review*
BASOR	*Bulletin of the American Schools of Oriental Research*
BDAG	Frederick W. Danker (ed.), *A Greek-English Lexicon of the New Testament and Other Early Christian Literature,* 3rd ed., based on Walter Bauer, *Griechisch-deutsches Worterbuch zu den Schriften des Neuen Testaments und der fruhchristlichen Literatur,* 6th ed., ed. Kurt Aland and Barbara Aland, with Viktor Reichmann and on previous English editions by W. F. Arndt, F. W. Gingrich, and F. W. Danker (Chicago/London: University of Chicago Press, 2000).
BZNW	Beihefte zur Zeitschrift für die neutestamentliche Wissenschaft
CBQ	*Catholic Biblical Quarterly*
CIJ	Jean-Baptiste Frey, *Corpus Inscriptionum Iudaicarum*, 2 vols (Rome: Pontifical Institute, 1936–52).
CPJ	*Corpus Papyrorum Judaicarum*, ed. Victor A. Tcherikover and Alexander Fuks (Cambridge, MA: Harvard University Press, 1957–64).
CUP	Cambridge University Press
DJD	Discoveries in the Judaean Desert, 40 vols (Oxford: Oxford University Press, 1955–2008).
DSD	*Dead Sea Discoveries*
HTR	*Harvard Theological Review*
HUCA	*Harvard Union College Annual*
IG	*Inscriptiones Graecae* (Berlin: George Reimer, 1873)
IGR	*Inscriptiones Graecae ad res Romanus pertinentes* (Paris: Leveux, 1911–27).
IEJ	*Israel Exploration Journal*
IES	*Israel Exploration Society*
Jastrow	Marcus Jastrow, *Dictionary of the Targumim, the Talmud Babli, and Yerushalmi, and the Midrashic Literature* (New York: Title Publishing, 1943; repr. Peabody, MA: Hendrickson, 2005).

JBL	*Journal of Biblical Literature*
JJS	*Journal of Jewish Studies*
JNES	*Journal of Near Eastern Studies*
JQR	*Jewish Quarterly Review*
JRA	*Journal of Roman Archaeology*
JRS	*Journal of Roman Studies*
JSJ	*Journal for the Study of Judaism in the Persian, Hellenistic and Roman Periods*
JSOT	*Journal for the Study of the Old Testament*
JSP	*Journal for the Study of the Pseudepigrapha*
JSS	*Journal of Semitic Studies*
LSJ	Henry George Liddell, Robert Scott, and H. Stuart Jones, *A Greek–English Lexicon*, 9th ed. with suppl. (Oxford: Oxford University Press, 1968).
LXX	The Greek Septuagint
NT	*Novum Testamentum*
NTS	*New Testament Studies*
OGIS	*Orientis Graeci Inscriptiones Selectae*, ed. Wilhelm Dittenberger (Leipzig: S. Hirzel, 1903–5).
OUP	Oxford University Press
PEFQST	*Palestine Exploration Fund Quarterly Statement*
PEQ	*Palestine Exploration Quarterly*
PG	Jacques-Paul Migne (ed.), *Patrologia Graeca* (Paris: Migne, 1844–).
PGM	K. Preisendanz and Albert Henrichs, *Papyri Graecae Magicae. Die Griechischen Zauberpapyri*, 2 vols 2nd ed. (Stuttgart: Tübner, 1974).
RB	*Revue Biblique*
RQ	*Revue de Qumran*
SBL	Society of Biblical Literature
SPA	*The Studia Philonica Annual*
SUNY	State University of New York
TDNT	Gerhard Kittel (ed.), *Theological Dictionary of the New Testament*, transl. and ed. Geoffrey W. Bromiley (Grand Rapids: Eerdmans, 1964–76).
USQR	*Union Seminary Quarterly Review*
VC	*Vigiliae Christianae*
VT	*Vetus Testamentum*
WUNT	Wissenschaftliche Untersuchungen Zum Neuen Testament
ZAW	*Zeitschrift für die alttestamentliche Wissenschaft*
ZDPV	*Zeitschrift des Deutschen Palästina-Vereins*

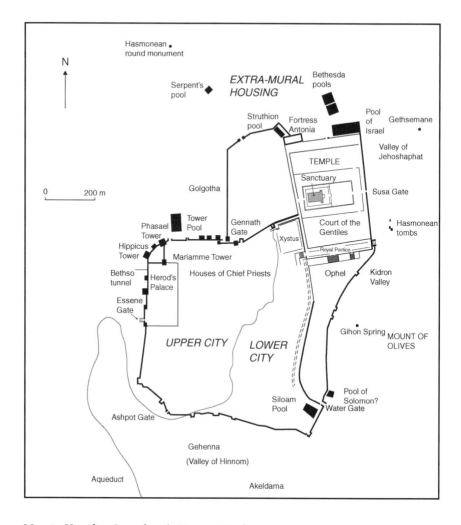

Map 1. Herodian Jerusalem (*c.*31 BCE–40 CE).

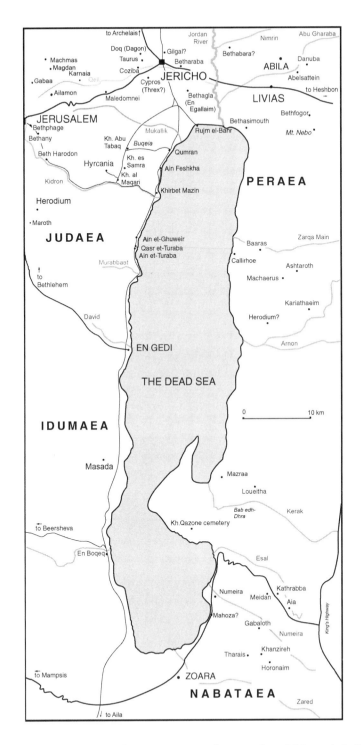

Map 2. The Dead Sea in the first century CE, with some identifiable roads indicated.

Part I

The Essenes in Ancient Literature

1

'A Peculiar Problem': A Short History of Scholarship on the Essenes

The nature of the Essenes attested in ancient literature was considered in scholarship long before the discovery of the Dead Sea Scrolls, since the Essenes appeared to be a mystery within the corpus of material about Judaism at the time of Jesus. However, it is important to note at the outset that the study of Judaism was, in Christian scholarship, dominated throughout the nineteenth and early twentieth centuries by the paradigm of Pharisaic hegemony, in that the rabbis' supposed antecedents, the Pharisees, were believed to have been the principal party that dictated law and governance. In addition, Christian scholarship portrayed the type of Judaism led by the Pharisees as narrow, rigid, legalistic, and unspiritual. Into this pre-formed notion of Second Temple Judaism the Essenes were inserted as a peculiar anomaly.

That Judaism was created as a foil to the Christian proclamation was already explored almost a century ago by George Foot Moore, who looked to Johan Andreas Eisenmenger, and his book *Entdecktes Judenthum*, published in 1700, as a damaging explication of Judaism that fitted a tendentious goal, namely the defamation of the Talmud and Jewish 'superstitions'.[1] Despite its intrinsic anti-Semitism, Eisenmenger's work was republished as late as 1893.[2] But more deeply rooted was the simple and repeated notion of a dominant 'Pharisaic' and unspiritual 'legalism' within Judaism: rabbinic material was read back into Second Temple times, and then it was interpreted to indicate a severe construction that fitted into the Lutheran dichotomy of 'faith' versus 'works of the law'.[3] In short, the presentation of Judaism was founded on the underlying understanding that Judaism was antithetical to Christianity.[4]

---

[1] George Foot Moore, 'Christian Writers on Judaism,' *HTR* 24 (1921): 197–254, at 214–33.

[2] Johan Andreas Eisenmenger, *Entdecktes Judenthum* (Schierferl: Dresden, 1893).

[3] See E. P. Sanders, *Paul and Palestinian Judaism* (Philadelphia: Fortress, 1977), 2–6, 33–59; Geza Vermes, 'Jewish Studies and New Testament Interpretation,' *JJS* 31 (1980): 1–17.

[4] Ferdinand Weber, *System der altsynagogalen palästinischen Theologie aus Targum, Midrasch und Talmud* (Leipzig: Dörfling und Franke, 1880), and also Wilhelm Bousset, *Die Religion des Judentums im neutestamentichen Zeitaiter* (Berlin: Reuther, 1903).

The scholarly analysis of the Essene question from its post-Renaissance beginnings to the beginning of the twentieth century, done excellently by Siegfried Wagner and Jean Riaud,[5] therefore needs to be understood against this larger cloth.[6] The Essenes—as known from the descriptions by Philo of Alexandria, Josephus, and Pliny—muddied the waters of the Christian portrayal of Judaism. In order to accommodate the significantly 'other' type of more mystical Judaism that Essenism apparently represented, the Essenes had to be explained. Given their communality and allegorical interests, they could be appropriated for Christianity: it was suggested that Jesus either was an Essene or took Essene tenets into his own teaching,[7] though this was a view most thoroughly refuted by A. Regeffe.[8] The Essenes could be seen as mutating into Christian groups, as if it was within Christianity that the Essenes truly belonged. For example, both F. C. Baur and Albrecht Ritschl saw the early Jewish–Christian Ebionites as deriving from Essene roots.[9]

On the other hand, the Essenes could be conflated with the Therapeutae, described by Philo of Alexandria in his treatise *De Vita Contemplativa*, thereby creating a larger mystically minded, quasi-Pythagorean or even Buddhist brotherhood standing apart from the Pharisaic–rabbinic mainstream.[10] In this, they were very marginal, and destined to become extinct.

This Christian scholarly definition of the alien and marginal quality of Essenism stands in marked contrast to many of the studies of the Essenes taking place within Jewish scholarship at the same time. Jewish scholars of the

---

[5] Siegfried Wagner, *Die Essener in der wissenschaftlichen Diskussion vom Ausgang des 18. bis zum Beginn des 20. Jahrhunderts* (Berlin: Töpelman, 1960) and Jean Riaud, 'Les Thérapeutes d'Alexandrie dans la tradition et dans la recherche critique jusqu'aux découvertes de Qumran,' *ANRW* 2: 20: 2 (Berlin and New York: Walter de Gruyter, 1987), 1189–295. For a review of literature from the 19th century, see Adolph S. Shutz, *The Essenes: A Brief Historical Review of the Origin, Traditions and Principles of the Order* (New York: Occult Press, 1897) and see too Charlotte Hempel, 'The Essenes,' in Dan Cohn-Sherbok and John M. Court (eds), *Religious Diversity in the Graeco-Roman World. A Survey of Recent Scholarship* (The Biblical Seminar 79; Sheffield: Sheffield Academic Press, 2001), 65–80.

[6] Rather than repeating the surveys of others, here a few key authors only will be noted in considering this issue.

[7] See, among others: G. F. W. Lippert, *Jesus der Essener-Meister dargestellt nach dem Traumgesicht seiner Mutter Maria bei Matth. Cap. IV, V. 1–11* (Nuremberg: Wilhelm Schmid, 1857); Arthur Lillie, *Buddhism in Christendom or Jesus the Essene* (London: K. Paul, Trench and Co, 1887); Edward Planta Nesbit, *Christ, Christians and Christianity: Jesus the Essene* (London: Simpkin, Marshall, Hamilton and Kent, 1895).

[8] A. Regeffe, *La Secte des Esséniens. Essai critique sur son organization, sa doctrine, son origine* (Lyons: Emmanuel Vitte, 1898).

[9] Ferdinand C. Baur, *De Ebionitarum origine et doctrina, ab essenis repetenda* (Tübingen: Hopferi de l'Orme, 1831); Albrecht Ritschl, *Die Entstehung der altkatholischen Kirche. Ein kirchen- und dogmengeschichtliche Monographie*, 2nd ed. (Bonn: Marcus, 1857), 204–20.

[10] For a review of the scholarship on this, see Riaud, *Thérapeutes*, and also James C. VanderKam, 'Identity and History of the Community,' in Peter Flint and James C. VanderKam (eds), *The Dead Sea Scrolls After Fifty Years: A Comparative Assessment* (Leiden: Brill, 1999), 2: 487–533, at 490–9; Hempel, 'The Essenes,' 66–7.

nineteenth century had also found the Essenes of Philo, Josephus, and Pliny interesting, but, rather than reaching to Hellenistic philosophy, Buddhism, or even nascent Christianity to explain them, there was a concern to see the Essenes within the context of groups mentioned in rabbinic texts. Jews, of course, never accepted the branding of pre-rabbinic Judaism as essentially unspiritual and had no need to 'explain' Essenism as anomalous. Jewish scholarship on the question of the Essenes had begun long before with Azariah de Rossi, in 1567.[11] De Rossi did indeed equate the Essenes and the Therapeutae, but only to link both of these named groupings with the rabbinic Boethusians. By the mid-nineteenth century there was, overall, a different analysis to that of Christian scholarship, with a stress on the Essenes being essentially a phenomenon entirely understandable within the milieu of Judaism. Still, the difficulty lay in fitting them together with a concept of the mainstream proto-rabbinic Judaism that was believed to have led the nation. Various obscure non-rabbinic groups mentioned in the Mishnah and Talmuds were considered key.

In Heinrich Graetz's monumental history of the Jews, published from 1853 to 1875, the Christian model of the Essenes as being somewhat isolationist was adopted. They were separated from the Pharisaic Judaism to which Graetz traced the rabbis and his own conservative Judaism, and yet, importantly, not that much. Graetz claimed that the Pharisees and the Essenes were essentially part of the same phenomenon. Graetz's work was highly influential among Jewish scholars, not only in its original German but via the five-volume English edition of his eleven-volume *Geschichte der Juden*,[12] translated as *History of the Jews*,[13] and by means of a French edition of volume 3 of this work.[14]

Graetz identified the origins of Essenism as being among the Ḥasidim mentioned in 1 Macc. 2: 42; 7: 13; 2 Macc. 14: 6, a party (*Partie*, rather than a 'sect') from which the Pharisees split, despite a fundamental similarity. The Essenes were extremists, more rigid than the Pharisees in terms of Sabbath rules, with a different understanding of Fate. They were highly fastidious in terms of living priestly purity, while their asceticism was due to lifelong Nazirite practices,[15] but they were by no means alien to Judaism, even though Graetz too could wonder whether Christianity (following John the Baptist)

---

[11] See Azariah de Rossi, *The Light of the Eyes*, trans. from the Hebrew with an introduction by Joanna Weinberg (New Haven: Yale University Press, 2001).

[12] Heinrich Graetz, *Geschichte der Juden: Von den ältesten Zeiten bis auf die Gegenwart. Aus den Quellen neu bearbeitet*, 11 vols (Leipzig: Leiner, 1853–75).

[13] Heinrich Graetz, *History of the Jews*, 5 vols, trans. by Bella Lowy, with Phillipp Bloch (Philadelphia: Jewish Publication Society of America, 1891–98).

[14] Trans. by Maurice Hess as *Sinaï et Golgotha, ou Les origines du judaisme et du christianisme, suivi d'un examen critique des évangiles anciens et modernes* (Paris: Michel Levy, 1867). The discussion of the Essenes among the sects of Judaism is found at pp. 131–58.

[15] Graetz, *History*, 2: 16–31; *Geschichte*, 3: 83–99.

sprung from their ranks.[16] The paradigm for the Essenes was nevertheless one of isolationism, which was that of the Ḥasidim themselves:

> The strict religious party of Assidaeans withdrew from the scene of passing events, and, in order to avoid mixing in public life, they sought a secluded retreat where they could give themselves up to undisturbed meditation. In this solitude they formed themselves into a distinct order, with strange customs and new views, and received the name of Essenes.[17]

For Graetz, the Pharisees were the national party, concerned with the nation's affairs, at the centre of religio-political life. After this came the Sadducees, and only the Pharisees and Sadducees had any powerful influence on events, with most people inclining to Pharisaism, the party that comprised the learned body who correlated with the rabbinic sages. In this supposition, Graetz's views were not so different from those of Christian scholars. But Graetz continually stressed how fundamentally close the Essenes were to the Pharisees; they were no anomaly. Graetz did not read them as objecting in principle to the Temple, but only to laxer purity standards than those they insisted upon, so that their own purer offerings were sent without any Essenes appearing in person. They were a 'higher grade' of piety, not alien to Judaism and not deeply hostile to other parties. Their isolationism and communality were designed to preserve purity only. For Graetz there was no underlying dichotomy between an apparent 'mainstream' and 'marginal' Judaism.

Graetz's view dominated Jewish scholarship, and was synthesized into the entry in the *Jewish Encyclopaedia* published in 1902, where the exasperation of Jewish scholars in regard to the theories of their Christian colleagues—who posited outside influence on the Essenes to 'explain' their difference from other (rigid, unspiritual, legalistic) Jews and who took Josephus on face value—was clearly evident. Kaufman Kohler, the leading scholar of Reform Judaism who wrote the entry, states:

> Accordingly, the strangest theories have been advanced by non-Jewish writers ... who found in Essenism a mixture of Jewish and pagan ideas and customs, taking it for granted that a class of Jews of this kind could have existed for centuries without leaving a trace in rabbinical literature, and, besides, ignoring the fact that Josephus describes the Pharisees and Sadducees also as philosophical schools after Greek models.

Following Graetz, the evidence for the Essenes was sought and found in the party of the Ḥasidim, among numerous others scattered throughout the corpus of rabbinic literature, indeed 'the line between the Pharisees ("Perushim") and

---

[16] Graetz, *History*, 2: 142, 145, 219–20.
[17] Ibid. 2: 16 cf. 24: 'they avoided the glare and tumult of public life'; *Geschichte*, 3: 83, 91.

Essenes was never very clearly drawn', noted Kohler, and 'there is little in Essene life which does not find its explanation in rabbinical sources'.[18]

Despite all this extensive research from Jewish scholars, undoubtedly the most influential work in terms of defining the Essenes at this point remained that of the German Protestant scholar Emil Schürer, whose five-volume *Geschichte des jüdischen Volkes im Zeitalter Jesu Christi* (1885–91) had been translated into English as *History of the Jewish People in the Time of Jesus Christ* in 1900,[19] and had become the standard reference. As with his predecessors, Schürer by no means considered Judaism positively, seeing it instead as a religion that relied on duty and legalism.[20] His section division heading (Division II, Book 2) 'Das Leben unter dem Gesetz', or 'Life under the Law' (Section 28), implicitly suggested that the Law was a heavy burden.[21] Jewish prayer itself, to Schürer, could be entrapped in 'external formalism … very far removed from true piety'.[22] Thus, when faced with the Essenes, Schürer confined them to the edges: the Essenes were a Jewish monastic institution. As many other Christian scholars before him, Schürer presented them as a radically different, alienated group to 'der grossen Heerstrasse des jüdischen Volkslebens': 'the great high road of Jewish life'.[23] Schürer defined the Essenes as:

> a religious community which, though it grew up on Jewish soil, differed essentially in many points from traditional Judaism, and … though it exercised no powerful influence upon the development of the people, deserves our attention as a peculiar problem in the history of religion.[24]

In trying to solve this peculiar problem, Schürer differentiated the Essenes from the Pharisees and Sadducees in terms of their place as a 'sect' within Judaism, stating that 'it scarcely needs the remark, that we have here to deal with a phenomenon of an entirely different kind', for while 'the Pharisees and Sadducees were large political *parties*, the Essenes might far rather be compared to a *monastic order*'.[25] Focusing on their purity and moral excellence, Schürer noted that Josephus stated

---

[18] Kaufman Kohler, 'Essenes,' *The Jewish Encyclopedia* (New York: Funk and Wagnalls, 1901–6), 5: 224–32.

[19] Emil Schürer, *Geschichte des judischen Volkes im Zeitalter Jesu Christi*, 5 vols (Leipzig: Hinrich, 1885–91); id. *History of the Jewish People in the Time of Jesus Christ*, 5 vols (New York: Charles Scribner, 1900). The Essenes are examined in Division II, Vol. 2, Section 30 of the work, 467–93 of the German edition and 188–218 in the English translation.

[20] For example, Schürer understood Jewish prayer as 'chilled into an external performance,' *History*, II.2: 118; *Geschichte* II.2: 410. See the critique by Israel Abrahams, 'Professor Schürer on Life Under the Jewish Law,' *JQR* (1899): 626–42; Claude G. Montefiore, 'Jewish Scholarship and Christian Silence,' *Hibbert Journal* 1 (1902–3): 335–46.

[21] As noted by Moore, 'Christian Writers on Judaism,' 239–40.

[22] Schürer, *History*, II.2: 115; *Geschichte*, II.2: 407.

[23] Schürer, *History*, II.2: 190; *Geschichte*, II.2: 468.

[24] Ibid.

[25] Ibid. The italics are in the English translated edition and the text is emphasized in the original German by spaced lettering.

that there was an order of Essenes who married, but 'these must have formed a small minority'.[26] Schürer did recognize that in the first place Essenism was superlative Pharisaism, but ultimately the Essenes went beyond their contemporaries in piety and behaviour, in that 'a surpassing of ordinary Judaism is apparent'.[27] But, ultimately, Schürer severed them from the rest of Judaism because they were purportedly separated and alienated from the Temple authorities, rejected animal sacrifices, and prayed towards the sun (rather than to the Temple), indicating that there was a 'complete *breach with Judaism proper...*' or '[t]hus Essenism would be a separation from the soil of Judaism proper'.[28] Foreign influences were indeed at work on the Essenes, namely Pythagoraeanism.[29]

In another great survey work, *The Beginnings of Christianity* (1920) by F. J. Foakes-Jackson and Kirsopp Lake, the Essenes are discussed under the title of 'the ascetic sects'. Unusually, Jackson and Lake did not trace any specific Neo-Pythagoraean influence on Essenism but noted that their asceticism was 'due to the wave of asceticism and of a tendency to abandon society in favour of a more secluded and simpler life, which was sweeping over the whole ancient world, rather than to the direct influence of any single cult, or of Hellenism in the strict sense'.[30] Still, the notion that the Essenes had abandoned society and separated themselves into removed, isolated societies was implicit.

In using the language of 'sect' to define groups that are understood to be marginal to the dominant and powerful 'centre', these concepts can be linked to the definitions of Max Weber,[31] though Weber's full study of ancient Judaism did not appear in its final form till 1921.[32] For Weber, all 'sects' required some degree of separation from the mainstream (defined universally

---

[26] Schürer, *History*, 200; *Geschichte*, II.2: 477.

[27] Schürer, *History*, 212; *Geschichte*, II.2: 'ein Hinaugeben über das gewöhnliche Judenthum zeigt'.

[28] Ibid. II.2: 213, 218; *Geschichte*, II.2: 'ein völliger *Bruch mit dem eigentlichen Judenthum* (488)...*Der Essenismus wäre demnach eine Separation von dem Boden des eigentlichen Judenthus'* (492). Likewise the emphasis is original. Schürer did not link the Essenes with the Therapeutae, as he was convinced that Philo's treatise *De Vita Contemplativa* was spurious, representing Christian monastics of a later era. For discussion of the authenticity of this treatise, see Riaud, 'Thérapeutes,' 1191–210; Joan E. Taylor, *Jewish Women Philosophers of First-Century Alexandria: Philo's 'Therapeutae' Re-considered* (Oxford: OUP, 2003), 32–3.

[29] For the Essenes as Pythagoraeans (cf. Josephus, *Ant.* 15: 371), see Schürer, *History*, II.2: 204–6, 216–18; *Geschichte*, II.2: 480–3, 491–3. Schürer noted that Jewish scholars in the main were comfortable about claiming Essenism for Judaism, seeing it as substantively not that dissimilar from Pharisaism, with Hasidic origins, a view which, by the time of Schürer, was gathering a few more adherents within Christian circles, though this was qualified by looking to either Pythagoraean or Zoroastrian influence on Judaism as a whole.

[30] F. J. Foakes-Jackson and Kirsopp Lake, *The Beginnings of Christianity: Part 1: The Acts of the Apostles* (London: Macmillan, 1920), 89. The other such sects are defined as Therapeutae and Covenanters evidenced by the Zadokite document, which 'represent some hitherto unknown movement in Judaism' (p.101).

[31] Max Weber, '"Kirchen" und "Sekten" I,' *Frankfurter Zeitung* (13 April 1906).

[32] Max Weber, *Gesammelte Aufsätze zur Religionssoziologie, Band 3: Das antike Judentum* (Tübingen: Mohr-Siebeck, 1921).

under the category of 'church'). In his study, *Das antike Judentum*, Weber did not himself find any problem in identifying even the Pharisees as a sect, despite their mainstream influence. Looking for his definition primarily in the rabbinic portrayal of the *Perushim*, 'separated ones', he noted that a Pharisee segregated himself from impure persons and objects and:

> [s]ince they lived in the same purity as the priests, its members claimed holiness equal to those who lived correctly and superior to that of incorrect priests. The charisma of the priest was depreciated in favor of personal religious qualification as proven through conduct. Naturally, this was brought about only gradually.[33]

For Weber, then, the Pharisees (*Perushim*) were a sect by means of a separation based on purity, which differentiated them from other Jews, a factor that endorsed Weber's own particular church/sect dichotomy. However, to Weber, after the fall of the Temple all Judaism became essentially Pharisaic. Thus, Essenism was 'merely a radical Pharisaic sect' or 'order', being in character 'strict and monk-like'.[34] Like many, Weber could not reconcile aspects of Essenism with conceptions of Judaism in general, so that he concluded:

> The true motive for the special Essenian way of life is apparently to be found in the gift of grace conveyed by the secret teaching and the quest for this reward. For this contains an element which can be distinctly recognized as alien to Pharisaism and Judaism generally.[35]

The implicit characterization of 'central' Judaism as being a religion antithetical to the Lutheran conception of Christianity as a religion led by 'grace' led Weber also to brush the Essenes towards the Christians over against the supposedly legalistic and 'grace-less' mainstream of Judaism.

The first challenge to this comfortable view among Christian scholars might have come with the momentous discovery and publication of documents identified as deriving from 'Jewish sectaries', found within the corpus of the Cairo Genizah in 1910, but in fact this discovery had no impact at all on the study of the Essenes.[36] No one connected the people responsible for what is now known as the Damascus Document (CD A and B) with the Essenes, since the location of the group was plainly stated in these texts to be 'Damascus', a

---

[33] Max Weber, *Ancient Judaism*, trans. and ed. by Hans H. Gerth and Don Martindale (Glencoe, Illinois: The Free Press, 1952), 386; id. *Gesammelte*, 402.

[34] Weber, *Ancient Judaism*, 406; *Gesammelte*, 423.

[35] Weber, *Ancient Judaism*, 408; *Gesammelte*, 425. 'In jenen Gnadengaben der Geheimlehre nun und dem Streben nach ihnen scheint das eigentliche Motiv der besonderen essenischen Lebensführung gefunden werden zu müssen. Denn an diesem Punkte liegt ein gegenüber dem Pharisäismus und dem Judentum überhaupt deutlich als Fremdkörper erkennbares Element.'

[36] Solomon Schechter, *Documents of Jewish Sectaries, edited from Hebrew MSS. in the Cairo Genizah collection, now in the possession of the University Library, Cambridge*, 2 vols, (Cambridge: CUP, 1910); see also the edition with prologomen by Joseph A. Fitzmyer, edited by Anan ben David (Jerusalem: Ktav, 1970).

place to which people had fled under the leadership of the apparent 'Star'.[37] Moreover, given the portrayal of the Essenes in Schürer and others, there seemed to be a different type of Judaism here to that of the 'monastic' Essenes: one in which people were married, Temple-attending, and animal-sacrificing. They were identified by Solomon Schechter as refugee 'Zadokites' (perhaps Dositheans) bothered by the Pharisees within Judaea.[38]

In his monumental work, *The History of Religions* (Volume 2: *Judaism, Christianity and Mohammedism*), published in 1919, the Presbyterian scholar George Foot Moore provided only a brief summary of the Essenes. He contested whether the term 'sect' should rightly be applied to the Pharisees—whom he saw as representative of normative Judaism, as noted above—and stated, instead, that there were 'several bodies to which the term sect may with greater propriety be applied, because they separated themselves more or less completely from the mass of their fellow countrymen in religious matters'. Such were the Essenes who, according to Moore, 'were a celibate order, living in monasteries' who had 'no antecedents in Judaism, and foreign influences are probably to be recognized in some of their peculiar rites and customs', though Moore rejected the supposition of Buddhist borrowings.[39] Moore simply gave a brief summary of Philo and Josephus' testimony and otherwise ignored the Essenes completely.

However, the people responsible for the Damascus Document of the Cairo Genizah made scholars such as Moore suppose that there were other small, unreported sects than those defined in the sources. In his three-volume work, *Judaism in the First Centuries of the Christian Era* (1927–8), a study that defined normative Judaism of the first century according to a Pharisaic–rabbinic model,[40] the 'sectaries in Damascus' were grouped with a category of Jewish 'others' little understood, and the Essenes were barely mentioned.[41] Moore's categories of analysis confidently differentiated between a main line of development in Judaism, which led from the Pharisees to the Rabbis, and 'sectarian' offshoots. In Volume 1 of Moore's study, for example, he reviews a single category comprising: 'Sectarian Writings: Testaments (of Moses, etc), Jubilees and Sectaries at Damascus', with the supposition that different writings indicated possible different sects. Perhaps it is here, with Moore, that we find the origins of what would become understood as 'sectarian Judaism' in the Second Temple Period, since if every variant theology evidenced in texts

---

[37] Schechter, *Documents*, I, xiii, in new ed. p. 45.

[38] Schechter, *Documents*, I, xvi–xxi.

[39] George Foot Moore, *The History of Religions: II: Judaism, Christianity and Mohammedism* (New York: Charles Scribners, 1919), 58.

[40] George Foot Moore, *Judaism in the First Centuries of the Christian Era: The Age of the Tannaim*, Vol. 1 (Cambridge, MA: Harvard University Press, 1927).

[41] Ibid. 209, n. 6. Concerning Josephus' *War* 2, Moore wrote: 'The long description of the Essenes is a question for itself.'

could indicate a variant sect, then clearly Judaism of this time was composed of a great number. This is ironic given that Moore himself asserted that Judaism's strength was in its overarching unity and universality (despite different small sects and variant opinions), based on a 'uniformity of observance'.[42] The halakhic character of the Damascus Document led Moore to consider that this Damascus group had affinities more 'with the Pharisees, not with any other variety of Judaism', and he differentiated them primarily by location: they lived in Damascus.[43]

In addition, two works promoted a kind of typology for understanding the Essenes within a wider phenomenon, and one that was defined in terms of its marginality to mainstream Judaism. Joseph Thomas,[44] following Wilhelm Brandt,[45] argued the case for there being a baptizing movement that functioned as a kind of counter-cultural, ultra-purist alternative to the mainstream. Within this movement were the Essenes, along with John the Baptist, Bannus, and a variety of second-century 'sects' referred to in patristic literature. The identification of this movement served to push the Essenes even further out to the extremities, and into a milieu from which Christianity itself was thought to spring.

In other words, the marginalization of the Essenes, their characterization anachronistically as an isolationist 'monastic' order, and their detachment from normative Judaism was all complete before the Dead Sea Scrolls were discovered.

When the Dead Sea Scrolls first began to come to light from 1947 onwards, scholars had long understood the region of the north-western Dead Sea as being an Essene locality, on the basis of Pliny, *Hist. Nat.* 5: 15 [73].[46] For example, already in August Neander's monumental history of the Church, published in 1825, we learn that the Essenes lived in the quiet region on the west side of the Dead Sea,[47] what Schürer could call 'the desert of En Gedi on the Dead Sea'.[48] Their isolation in terms of Judaism as a whole was paralleled in a model of physical isolation and a separation from the holy city of Jerusalem.

Thus, when Syrian Orthodox representatives from St. Mark's Monastery brought the first scrolls to scholars in Jerusalem, they had an awareness of the Essene location. As John Trever reports in his memoir of the discoveries:

---

[42] Ibid. 110–11.

[43] In fact, when parts of the Damascus Document were found within the Dead Sea Scrolls corpus, their existence posed one of the most serious issues to contend with in terms of the Qumran-Essene hypothesis, given the way the Essenes have been constructed on the basis of the classical sources.

[44] Joseph Thomas, *Le Mouvement Baptiste en Palestine et Syrie* (Gembloux: Duculot, 1935).

[45] Wilhelm Brandt, *Die Judischen Baptismen oder das religiose Waschen und Baden im Judentum mit Einschluss des Judenchristentums* (Giessen: Topelmann, 1910).

[46] See below pp. 248–51.

[47] '[I]n der stillen Gegend an der west-seite des todten Meeres,' August Neander, *Allgemeine Geschichte der christlichen Religion und Kirche* (Gotha: Friedrich Andrens Berthes, 1825), 24.

[48] *History*, II.2, 194; *Geschichte*, II.2, 470.

Ibrahim [Sowmy] remarked that while working at Allenby Bridge he had studied about the history of Jericho and the Dead Sea area. From his studies he had learned about the Essenes who lived in that region during the lifetime of Jesus, and as a result had become very interested in them. He had suggested to the Syrians at the Monastery that these documents might have belonged to that ancient sect of Jews . . . [49]

One wonders what scholar exactly Ibrahim Sowmy was reading, but it is clear here that the model of the ascetic and isolated Essenes was in the minds of those who looked at the first contents of Cave 1Q, some time before the excavation of the nearby site of Khirbet Qumran. Key texts, particularly the Community Rule (1QS or *Serekh*), were found to fit with what appeared in the descriptions of the Essenes by Josephus. The Essene identification was made almost the instant the scrolls arrived in Jerusalem: Millar Burrows recorded in his diary for 19 March 1948 that he worked on the 'Essene manuscript' at the American School.[50] The Essene hypothesis was most persuasively championed by André Dupont-Sommer, and became the standard view.[51]

The Damascus Document, however, remained contested and its relationship to the group evidenced in the *Serekh* has been (and continues to be) debated.[52] Elsewhere, when the classical sources and the Scrolls did not correlate, the simple explanation was offered that ancient authors such as Philo, Josephus, or Pliny did not necessarily know the whole story. As was pointed out by Millar Burrows, none of our classical authors was an Essene; each witness is located in the position of an outsider in relation to the group he describes.[53] The Scrolls then were seen to give a more accurate presentation of who the Essenes were than the classical sources, and yet the Scrolls were read with a fixed idea of what these classical sources actually indicated.

While the Qumran-Essene hypothesis—that the Scrolls and the site of Qumran are Essene—became the standard view,[54] different interpretations were also proposed, notably by Cecil Roth[55] and G. R. Driver,[56] who both advocated that the Scrolls should be associated with the 'Zealots' who ruled

---

[49] John C. Trever, *The Untold Story of Qumran* (Old Tappan, NJ: F. C. Revell, 1965), 25, cf. 76.

[50] Millar Burrows, *The Dead Sea Scrolls* (London: Secker and Warburg, 1956), 279.

[51] André Dupont-Sommer, *The Essene Writings from Qumran*, trans. by Geza Vermes of *Les Écrits esséniens découverts près de la Mer Morte* (Oxford: Blackwell, 1961).

[52] For the history of the identification and discussion see Charlotte Hempel, *The Damascus Texts* (Sheffield: Sheffield Academic Press, 2000), 54–6.

[53] Burrows, *The Dead Sea Scrolls*, 290–1 and also Roland de Vaux, *Archaeology and the Dead Sea Scrolls* (The Schweich Lectures of the British Academy; Oxford: OUP, 1973), 138.

[54] Jonathan Campbell, 'The Qumran Sectarian Writings,' in William Horbury, W. D. Davies, and John Sturdy (eds), *The Cambridge History of Judaism* (Cambridge: CUP, 1999), 3: 813–21.

[55] Cecil Roth, *The Historical Background of the Dead Sea Scrolls* (New York: Philosophical Library, 1959); idem, *The Dead Sea Scrolls: A New Historical Approach* (New York: Norton and Co., 1965).

[56] Godfrey R. Driver, *The Judaean Scrolls: The Problem and a Solution* (New York: Schocken, 1965).

Jerusalem during the revolt of 66–70 CE and also made their way to the Dead Sea, importantly to Masada and to various caves of refuge. As time has gone on, there have been more and more questions asked as to whether the Dead Sea Scrolls should be associated with the Essenes, given discrepancies between what the ancient sources state and what is found in the Scrolls, since not all discrepancies can be explained away by an 'insider' versus 'outsider' model.

Lawrence Schiffman has argued that some of the key 'sectarian' texts of the Scrolls indicate a group that corresponds far better to the rabbinic references to the *Tsedukim* (Sadducees) than to Josephus' Essenes.[57] Questions about whether Josephus' description of the Essenes naturally fits the group(s) evidenced in the Scrolls have also been raised by Steve Mason.[58] Norman Golb[59] has queried the plausibility of the Qumran-Essene hypothesis, strongly emphasising the discrepancies between the Scrolls and the classical sources on the Essenes, and noting that Qumran could have functioned as a fortress. Lena Cansdale, Robert and Pauline Donceel-Voûte, Yizhar Hirschfeld, Yizhak Magen, and Yuval Peleg have all sought to interpret the archaeological remains of Qumran without reference to the Essenes.[60]

---

[57] Lawrence H. Schiffman, 'The New Halakhic Letter (4QMMT) and the Origins of the Dead Sea Sect,' *BA* 53 (1990): 64–73; id. 'The Sadducean Origins of the Dead Sea Scroll Sect,' in Hershel Shanks (ed.), *Understanding the Dead Sea Scrolls* (London: SPCK, 1993); id. *Reclaiming the Dead Sea Scrolls: The History of Judaism, the Background of Christianity, and the Lost Library of Qumran* (Philadelphia: Jewish Publication Society, 1994).

[58] Steve Mason, 'What Josephus Says about Essenes in his Judean War,' in Stephen G. Wilson and Michel Desjardins (eds), *Text and Artifact in the Religions of Mediterranean Antiquity: Essays in Honour of Peter Richardson* (Waterloo, Ont.: Wilfred Laurier University Press, 2000), 434–67. Mason explores matters further in 'What Josephus Says about the Essenes in his Judean War,' online at http: orion.mscc.huji.ac.il/orion/programs/Mason00-1.shtml and orion.mscc. huji.ac.il/orion/programs/Mason00-2.shtml.

[59] Norman Golb, *Who Wrote the Dead Sea Scrolls? The Search for the Secret of Qumran* (New York: Scribner, 1995).

[60] Lena Cansdale, *Qumran and the Essenes: A Re-Evaluation of the Evidence* (Tübingen: J. C. B. Mohr, 1997), and Alan D. Crown and Lena Cansdale, 'Qumran: Was it an Essene Settlement?' *BAR* 20 (1994): 24–35, 73–4, 76–8; Robert Donceel and Pauline Donceel-Voûte, 'The Archaeology of Khirbet Qumran,' in Michael Wise, Norman Golb, John J. Collins, and Dennis Pardee (eds), *Methods of Investigations of the Dead Sea Scrolls and the Khirbet Qumran Site: Present Realities and Future Prospects* (New York, Annals of the New York Academy of Sciences 722, 1994), 1–38, and id. 'Poursuite des travaux de publication du matériel archéologique de Khirbet Qumrân: Les lampes en terre cuite,' in Z. J. Kapera (ed.), *Mogilany 1995: Papers on the Dead Sea Scrolls Offered in Memory of Aleksy Klawek* (Qumranica Mogilanensia 15; Enigma Press, Cracow, 1998), 87–104; Pauline Donceel-Voûte, 'Les ruines de Qumrân réinterprétées,' *Archéologia* 298 (1994): 24–35; ead. 'Traces of Fragrance along the Dead Sea,' *Res Orientales* 11 (1998): 93–124; Yizhar Hirschfeld, *Qumran in Context: Reassessing the Archaeological Evidence* (Peabody, MA: Hendrickson, 2004); id. 'Early Roman Manor Houses in Judea and the Site of Khirbet Qumran,' *JNES* 57 (1998): 161–89; Yizhak Magen and Yuval Peleg, 'Back to Qumran: Ten Years of Excavation and Research, 1993–2004,' in Katharina Galor, Jean-Baptiste Humbert, and Jürgen Zangenberg (eds), *Qumran, the Site of the Dead Sea Scrolls: Archaeological Interpretations and Debates* (Leiden: Brill, 2006), 55–113; id. *The Qumran Excavations 1993–2004: Preliminary Report* (Judea and Samaria Publications 6; Jerusalem: Israel Antiquities Authority, 2007).

Understandably, in the face of these challenges, in 1997 Martin Goodman rightly asked for a careful defence of the Qumran-Essene hypothesis to be made: 'it is up to proponents of the Essene hypothesis to make their case'.[61] The simple union of Qumran, the Dead Sea Scrolls, and the Essenes has since then been qualified with a nuancing of the Essene hypothesis. Notably, in the 'Groningen Hypothesis', as it is called, Florentino García Martínez and Adam van der Woude have sought to account for differences between the classical sources on the Essenes and the 'sectarian' Dead Sea Scrolls by suggesting a separation between a Qumran group and a broader Essene grouping, which is identified not as a small sect but a wide stream of Enochic Judaism, different from rabbinic Judaism, and opposed to a succession of Hasmonean priest-kings.[62] The origins of this wider Essenism/Enochic Judaism are placed within the late third or early second century BCE, just prior to the Maccabean revolt, in an apocalyptic tradition represented by the books of Enoch and Jubilees. Yet, Gabriele Boccaccini concludes that the Dead Sea Scrolls community—defined by the sectarian scrolls—was itself 'a radical and minority group within Enochic Judaism'.[63] Qumran then remains separated, small, and isolationist.

Over against this, however, is the important thesis of Hartmut Stegemann, who argued on the basis of his reading of the Scrolls that Qumran was not an alienated offshoot of the mainstream Essenes, but comprised one local settlement in a much larger entity. Stegemann pointed out that the Scrolls' critiques of those in power in Jerusalem and the Temple operations were aimed at the Hasmoneans, not at all other Jews. After the Hasmoneans seized power in the revolt of 167–4 BCE and created a new royal-priestly dynasty, the Essenes formed as a 'union' (*yaḥad*) opposed to them. They were led by the Teacher of Righteousness, the mysterious High Priest (159–2 BCE) Judas Maccabeus deposed, who at one point fled to Damascus with his supporters (see CD 7: 18–20), though the union was established in the heartland of Judaea. After the collapse of the Hasmonean dynasty, Herod the Great was their patron; they were thus known as 'Herodians', as in the Gospels (Mark 3: 6; 12: 13; cf. 8: 15; Matt. 22: 16).[64] Stegemann criticized

---

[61] Martin Goodman, 'A Note on the Qumran Sectarians, the Essenes and Josephus,' *JJS* 46 (1995): 161–6, at 164.

[62] Florentino García Martínez, 'Qumran Origins and Early History: A Groningen Hypothesis,' *Folio Orientalia* (1988): 113–36; Adam S. van der Woude, 'Wicked Priest or Wicked Priests? Reflections on the Identification of the Wicked Priest in the Habakkuk Commentary,' *JJS* 33 (1982): 149–59; id. 'Once again: The Wicked Priests in the Habakkuk Pesher from Cave 1 of Qumran,' *RQ* 17/90 (1996): 375–84, but see for a contrary argument Timothy Lim, 'The Wicked Priests of the Groningen Hypothesis,' *JBL* 112 (1993): 415–25.

[63] Gabriele Boccaccini, *Beyond the Essene Hypothesis: The Parting of the Ways between Qumran and Enochic Judaism* (Grand Rapids: Eerdmans, 1998), 162, and see too: id. *Enoch and Qumran Origins: New Light on a Forgotten Connection* (Grand Rapids: Eerdmans, 2005).

[64] Harmut Stegemann, *Die Essener, Qumran, Johannes der Täufer und Jesus* (Freiburg im Breisgau: Herder, 1993); id. *The Library of Qumran: On the Essenes, Qumran, John the Baptist, and Jesus* (Grand Rapids: Eerdmans, 1993); id. 'The Qumran Essenes—Local Members of the Main Jewish Union in Second Temple Times,' in Julio T. Barrera and Luis V. Montaner (eds),

the Qumran-Essene hypothesis not because of its identification of the Scrolls or the site of Qumran as Essene, but for its basic conceptualization of the Essenes as being a marginal and small sect, and disputed whether the tiny site of Qumran could be the Essene centre.

Importantly also, John J. Collins has reviewed the organization reflected in the Scrolls and read within the texts a wide concept, with the *yaḥad* functioning as a kind of umbrella over multiple groups. Against the concept of Qumran forming a centre and headquarters of Essene communities, Collins argues that there is no one defining centre, but rather an amalgam, a dispersion of groups united by a common ethos, which also developed over time. With this kind of study, any strictly monolithic entity evaporates, particularly any notion that Qumran was itself a defining locus for what is evidenced in the Scrolls.[65]

Recently, the Israeli philosopher Edna Ullman-Margalit has examined the history of scholarship since the discovery of the Dead Sea Scrolls,[66] and has rightly noted the elasticity of the Qumran-Essene hypothesis as it has responded to various criticisms. She has called for a separate analysis of each part of the hypothesis: 'arguments must be presented independently for each of the three sides of the Essenes-scrolls-Qumran triangle', though she concludes that the Essene hypothesis remains the most convincing solution.[67]

This is a wise suggestion. However, in approaching the first part of this triangle, in looking at the Essenes, we cannot proceed without a sharp awareness of the broader categorizations at work in the history of scholarship, especially in the scholarship which has found the Essenes to be a 'problem' in terms of a conceptualization of Judaism as a religion lacking those features Paul proclaimed within his churches. We need to be alert to the language that would compartmentalize Judaism for the sake of a Christian *kerygma*. We need to consider the Essenes within a holistic understanding of Second Temple Judaism that is very different from that formulated largely by Christian scholars of the nineteenth century. Despite scholarly critique of these antiquated conceptualizations, arguments both for and against the Qumran-Essene hypothesis have depended on pre-existing notions of who the Essenes actually were, or—all too often—rested on uncritical readings of the ancient

---

The Madrid Qumran Congress. Proceedings of the International Congress on the Dead Sea Scrolls, Madrid, 18–21 March, I (Leiden: Brill, 1992), 83–166.

[65] John J. Collins, 'Forms of Community in the Dead Sea Scrolls,' in P. M. Shalom et al. (eds), *Emanuel: Studies in Hebrew Bible, Septuagint, and Dead Sea Scrolls in Honor of Emanuel Tov* (Leiden: Brill, 2003), 97–111; id. '"The Yahad" and "The Qumran Community",' in Charlotte Hempel and Judith M. Lieu (eds), *Biblical Traditions in Transmission: Essays in Honour of Michael A. Knibb* (Leiden: Brill, 2006), 81–96; id. *Beyond the Qumran Community: the Sectarian Movement of the Dead Sea Scrolls* (Grand Rapids: Eerdmans, 2010).

[66] Edna Ullman-Margalit, *Out of the Cave: A Philosophical Enquiry into the Dead Sea Scrolls Research* (Cambridge, MA: Harvard University Press, 2006).

[67] Ibid. 64, 116.

sources that describe them, readings in which the legacy of tendentious scholarly judgements made over the past centuries can still play a part. Instead of discussions raising issues about the larger context of Judaism of the Second Temple Period, the image of the Essenes among contemporary Scrolls scholars and Qumran archaeologists alike, both Jewish and non-Jewish, can at times travel even further down the Schürer road of seeing the Qumran Essenes as a very isolated and small group, sharing much of their ideology with the Pythagoraeans, and withdrawing from not only Temple worship but the city of Jerusalem itself. The studies of nineteenth-century Jewish scholars that resulted in the synthetic analysis presented by Kohler in the *Jewish Encyclopedia* have been forgotten by many, with Stegemann being the most striking dissident in terms of the general view.[68]

So, for example, Yizhar Hirschfeld, in his re-presentation of Qumran's archaeology as having nothing to do with the Essenes, assumed a model of the Essenes as 'a small sect' against which to present aspects of the site of Qumran.[69] The Essenes were pacifist, and did not eat meat, being ascetic and veritably identical to Pythagoreans:

> Another important point concerns the presence of animal bones at what is purported to be an Essene site. Josephus (*Ant.* 15: 371) says that the Essenes lived 'a Pythagorean way of life,' which was ascetic and characterized mainly by vegetarianism. It is absurd to think that the inhabitants of Qumran, who were obviously meat eaters, could also have been Essenes.[70]

However, nowhere in the classical sources is it actually stated that the Essenes were vegetarians. For Hirschfeld, too, the presence of women's skeletons in the cemetery ruled out the identity of the population as Essene because 'according to Pliny, they shunned the company of women'.[71] In fact, 'shunned' is too strong a word for what Pliny actually states, as we shall see. The Essenes are described, according to Hirschfeld, 'as freely choosing poverty and a frugal life' and were a 'small sect living on the periphery of Jewish society, without access to the Jewish administrative establishment in Jerusalem'.[72] This builds considerably on what our sources tell us, but fits completely with the scholarly *tendenz* in constructions of the Essenes throughout the nineteenth and early twentieth centuries, in which the dominant paradigm was of a normative

---

[68] For a review of alternative theories see Magen Broshi and Hanan Eshel, 'Qumran and the Dead Sea Scrolls: The Contention of Twelve Theories,' in Douglas R. Edwards (ed.), *Religion and Society in Roman Palestine: Old Questions, New Approaches* (London/New York: Routledge, 2004), 162–9.

[69] Hirschfeld, *Qumran in Context*, 45.

[70] Ibid. 111.

[71] Ibid. 161.

[72] *Qumran in Context*, 231.

Judaism 'chilled' by strict Pharisaic legalism, against which the fire of the charismatic Christian proclamation could be contrasted.

A new perspective on Judaism came with the publication in 1977 of E. P. Sanders' *Paul and Palestinian Judaism*[73] and with Sanders' corresponding work, *Judaism: Practice and Belief 63 BCE to 66 CE*,[74] in which he set out a vibrant 'Common Judaism' based on covenantal nomism: adherence to the Jewish law, which was also the law of the land. This was a law that was essentially about community and deep devotion to God which was far from being narrow, legalistic, or unspiritual.

Yet Sanders, for all his awareness of the nature of the scholarship that preceded him, assumed at the very outset that the Essenes were:

> a small group . . . a tiny and fairly marginal sect . . . [and while] both the aristocrats and the Pharisees (in my view) need to be saved from misinterpretation . . . this is not true of the Essenes. They were not major players in politics and society, and no one says they were.

However, the model of Sanders' 'Common Judaism' itself is probably too simple. Beyond Judaea, Judaism becomes harder to define, since praxis could be variously followed. John J. Collins, in *Between Athens and Jerusalem*, concludes after an analysis of the diverse sources that 'there was no simple normative definition which determined Jewish identity in the Hellenistic Diaspora', and notes only some 'persistent tendencies', including what could be construed as 'covenantal nomism', but also ethnic pride 'with little regard for religious laws or for anything that could be called nomism', witnessed in the writings of the Alexandrian Artapanus. Collins notes there was also a moral system and code of conduct, loyalty to the Jewish community, the common thread coming from the reliance on the 'Jewish tradition'. This tradition, in the way Collins frames it, is Scripture.[75] Overall, among scholars of diverse backgrounds there is now a much greater awareness of Second Temple Judaism in all its rich *variety*, but still with a strong sense of internal cohesion founded on the *concept* of the Temple, the Law of Moses, and tradition.[76]

---

[73] Philadelphia: Fortress, 1977.

[74] London: SCM, 1992.

[75] John J. Collins, *Between Athens and Jerusalem: Jewish Identity in the Hellenistic Diaspora*, 2nd ed. (Grand Rapids: Eerdmans, 2000), 273–5. For example, Josephus notes that in the conversion of Helena Queen of Adiabene and her son Izates, *c*.30 CE, instruction in Scripture was an essential part of the process (*Ant.* 20: 34–53), but Izates gained two opinions from Jewish teachers on whether circumcision was absolutely necessary or not.

[76] Shaye Cohen, *From the Maccabees to the Mishnah*, 2nd ed. (Louisville: Westminster John Knox, 2006); Sean Freyne, *Galilee from Alexander the Great to Hadrian 323 BCE to 135 CE: A Study of Second Temple Judaism* (Wilmington: Glazier, 1980); Lester L. Grabbe, *An Introduction to First Century Judaism: History and Religion of the Jews in the Time of Nehemiah, the Maccabees, Hillel and Jesus* (Edinburgh: T & T Clark, 2010); Shemuel Safrai, Mordecai Stern, and

Wherever we look in the textual evidence from the first centuries BCE to the second centuries CE, from the Jewish historian Josephus, to the Jewish philosopher Philo of Alexandria, to the pseudepigrapha, to works of Jewish mysticism, to the Dead Sea Scrolls, we find diversity. Schürer's 'Proper Judaism' has disappeared; Sander's 'Common Judaism' appears not quite comprehensive enough. This has led some to talk not about 'Second Temple Judaism' but to 'Second Temple Judaisms'.[77] There are differences between Judaism in the Diaspora and the land of Israel, but also within Jewish groups within the land, fractures of class, regionality, and legal interpretation, differences between those who interpret scripture literally and allegorical readers. The range of mystical thought is being explored, with material from later times now connected with much earlier texts, and linked not with marginal groups but with the priesthood.[78] The old dichotomies no longer fit the model.

However, Michael Stone embraces the singular 'Judaism', as he reaches far to gather in all the material of the age that is deemed 'heterodox' by later orthodoxies. This is not a fragmented religion, but one that was thriving creatively, with all kinds of different spiritual, theological, and practical expressions. It just so happens that only those parts that fitted in with a standard imposed upon it by later orthodoxies, whether Christian or Jewish, were preserved.[79] The material Dead Sea Scrolls may appear unusual, but this is because we have lost most of the tapestry from which the texts are cut. Stone traces the survival of lost strands through the centuries, and presents a picture of Second Temple Judaism that completely overturns any sense of a rigid and legalistic tradition, or even a religion that one can sort out into 'orthodox' and 'heterodox' sections.

David Flusser, with Willem C. Van Unnik, *The Jewish People in the First Century: Historical Geography, Political History, Social, Cultural and Religious Life and Institutions*, 2 vols (Assen: Van Gorcum, 1974–6); Emil Schürer, with Geza Vermes, Fergus Millar, and Matthew Black (eds), *The History of the Jewish People in the Age of Jesus Christ*, revised edition, 3 vols (Edinburgh: T & T Clark, 1973–9); Joan E. Taylor, *The Immerser: John the Baptist Within Second Temple Judaism* (Grand Rapids: Eerdmans, 1997). I italicize 'concept' here because this avoids an insistence on the continuing existence of a physical Temple in Jerusalem, and destabilizes a supposition of approval of all aspects of this Temple and its operations.

[77] Following Jacob Neusner, 'Varieties of Judaism in the Formative Age,' *Formative Judaism. Second Temple* (Chico: Scholars, 1983), 59–83.

[78] See Rachael Elior, *The Mystical Origins of Hasidism*. trans. Shalom Carmy (Portland, OR: Littman Library of Jewish Civilization, 2006), 17–18, though this link with the priesthood is seen as too narrow by Peter Schäfer, *The Origins of Jewish Mysticism* (Tübingen: Mohr Siebeck, 2009), 14–16, 20–5, and see too id. *The Hidden and Manifest God: Some Major Themes in Jewish Mysticism* (New York: SUNY Press, 1992); see also James Davila, *Descenders to the Chariot: the People behind the Hekhalot Literature* (Leiden: Brill, 2001) and now the monumental Christopher Rowland and Christopher Morray-Jones, *The Mystery of God: Jewish Mysticism and the New Testament* (Leiden: Brill, 2009).

[79] See Michael Stone, *Ancient Judaism: New Visions and Views* (Grand Rapids: Eerdmans, 2011), 8.

In approaching the ancient sources on the Essenes, therefore, they need to be understood against this very different cloth. In reading these sources afresh, it is not necessarily the case that we will be able to slot the Essenes into a working model of Judaism that everyone can support; rather, the sources on the Essenes may provide a key to a better model of Second Temple Judaism as a whole.

In addition, there is greater awareness of the function of rhetoric—the art of persuasion—in studies of classical historiography from the latter part of the twentieth century and through to today.[80] As every ancient historian well knows, the writing of current affairs or history in antiquity could be openly polemical, propagandistic, selective, or exaggerated, and not intended to provide a coolly comprehensive, impartial body of evidence that can be used to create a coherent identity for either an individual or a group. One need only look at Strabo's summary of Jews and Judaism (*Geogr.* 16: 2: 35–9) for an example: all Jews are vegetarians and practise both male and female circumcision. Strabo's presentation shows the Jewish rulers and law as having a fundamentally tyrannical nature, and elements of his description are subsumed into this rhetorical end. If we only had Strabo's evidence for ancient Judaism, we would not have a simple window to history, since actuality is mixed with fabrication for the sake of convincing the readership of an implicit assertion.

The sources themselves may have been constructed from anecdotal evidence and what today would be termed 'urban myths'. It is not always possible to weed these out by comparative textual study. One cannot necessarily look to an earlier source for better information than a later one. Later authors could insert more reliable information into unreliable sources, rather than modify reliable sources for the sake of their own rhetoric. In other words, there could have been an 'invention' of the Essenes as a historical group, as a result of simple extrapolation from prior sources, as various features were seized upon to create an idea of who the Essenes were that would function within a particular literary piece, so the resulting presentation would become a selective representation of some aspects of previous texts (and possible oral traditions) that are now unknown to us.

Yet, this probably goes too far. In establishing the rhetoricity of historical texts, the danger is that modern scholars can despair of finding reliable factual data, so that to propose that the 'Essenes' might be *only* an imaginative construction with no substantial grounding in actuality assumes that ancient

---

[80] Emilio Gabba, 'True History and False History in Classical Antiquity,' *JRS* 71 (1981): 50–2; Anthony J. Woodman, *Rhetoric in Classical Historiography. Four Studies* (London and Sydney: Croom Helm, 1988); Christopher Gill and Timothy P. Wiseman (eds), *Lies and Fiction in the Ancient World* (Exeter: University of Exeter Press, 1993); T. James Luce, 'Ancient Views on the Causes of Bias in Historical Writing,' *Classical Philology* 84 (1988): 16–31.

historians were fantasists who did not care about reality.[81] As I have argued elsewhere, the rhetorical can also be historically true.[82] The way forward for a historian or archaeologist when faced with literary rhetoricity is not a simple one of either simply accepting all that is written as being entirely the truth, or viewing everything as the writer's imagination or selective summarizing of rumour: factuality and exaggeration, history and hearsay, are woven together, and only careful understanding of the contexts of the work in question and the grand themes within a writer's surviving corpus can lead us towards intelligent understanding.

It is to the extant ancient texts about the Essenes that we must now turn, in order that the Essenes can be clearly identified and understood. Moreover, it is a prerequisite in the exercise that we accept that these can tell us something historically true about the Essenes, or else there is no point in engaging with them at all. Methodologically, in this study, I am going to begin with a presupposition of truth within the texts, and remove elements of the presentations of the Essenes if necessary only after careful scrutiny. This is a random assertion rather than an epistemological position, because there is—fundamentally—very rarely any sure means of establishing the truth empirically. While in ancient history there are possibilities of multiple independent attestation for confirmation in terms of the lives of kings and generals, wars and political events, and different bodies of evidence (epigraphy and numismatics, and diverse histories), once we roam away from 'great history' our sources grant us no such luxury. In terms of the ancient evidence for the Essenes we cannot therefore reject any part of the information they provide—even if singly attested—without careful argument which would explain how an author came to present them in a certain way that is most probably inconsistent with historical reality. Almost nothing can be proven to be true, but it does not follow that in that case it must be false.

In these descriptions, it is fundamental to recognize that we are not in the realm of *simple* truth or falsehood; the truth our authors tell need not be whole. In other words, I will predicate a discussion on Essene identity with a conditional statement: *if* what the classical authors say is true, yet partial (selective) and shaped by their rhetorical interests, then what can we say about Essene identity? I read historical actuality as conditional on a resounding *if*. Given that much of the evidence from literature in antiquity is improvable in terms of its veracity, to take a sceptical view that it is therefore unknowable, or not worth trusting, is arbitrary, since equally it cannot be

---

[81] See Rachael Elior, *Memory and Oblivion: The Secret of the Dead Sea Scrolls* (Jerusalem: Van Leer Institute and Kibbutz haMeuchad, 2009) (Hebrew). Elior is doubtful given that the Essenes do not apparently appear in rabbinic literature, though by the same criterion of judgement one would assume that Christianity through the first five centuries was constituted by a tiny handful of persons. See the discussion in Part I, Chapter 7 below.

[82] See Taylor, *Jewish Women Philosophers*, 1–20.

proven to be untrue. In a discussion where no proof can be presented for or against historical actuality, and where rhetoricity does not invalidate historicity, the *if* prerequisite remains a given. Where, however, it becomes apparent that other evidence happens to cohere with the presentation of our ancient sources, then this creates a somewhat more persuasive picture in terms of history. Nevertheless, nothing proves the evidence, by empirical criteria of assessment.

The Groningen hypothesis and the work of Harmut Stegemann have both led the way in calling for a far more expansive understanding of ancient Essenism, though the old view of the Essenes as a small, marginal group remains very fixed. A fresh review of the ancient sources themselves—now that Second Temple Judaism is much better understood and there is no longer a dominant paradigm within the academy of a legalistic Judaism standing as a foil for 'liberating' Christianity—is the chief aim of the chapters that follow in Part I in this book.

The task of reviewing the classical sources on the Essenes is relatively straightforward, since the principal ancient writings on the Essenes have been collected and translated in the German edition of Alfred Adam,[83] and in a more concise English edition by Vermes and Goodman, both books having the Greek and Latin texts as well as a translation.[84] But we will look wider than these sources—to the New Testament, to other Christian material, and to rabbinic texts—in order to define as accurately as possible who the historical Essenes actually were and how they related to others within the world of ancient Judaea.

---

[83] Alfred Adam, *Antike Berichte über die Essener*, 2nd ed. (Kleine Texte für Vorlesungen und Übungen 182; Berlin: Walter de Gruyter, 1972).

[84] Geza Vermes and Martin Goodman (eds), *The Essenes according to the Classical Sources* (JSOT Press: Sheffield 1989).

2

Philo of Alexandria

Philo of Alexandria is the first author known to have written specifically on the Essenes, though not all his writing about them has been preserved. Philo was one of the most erudite and prolific Jewish thinkers of the ancient world. As a member of a rich and important family, and one of the most eminent leaders of the Jewish community in Alexandria during the late 30s and early 40s of the first century, Philo was contemporary to the Essenes and in a position to obtain reasonably accurate information about them, since he himself visited Judaea, as did many other Jews from Egypt.[1] He was also writing for a readership that would have included people who could verify what he was stating, and it would not have served his purposes to be accused of misrepresentation.

In writing to applaud Judaism, by the criteria of Graeco-Roman philosophy, Philo used the Essenes (Ἐσσαῖοι) as the prime example of the outstanding nature of the Jewish religion at least three times. One of these passages describing the Essenes has been preserved in full: *Quod Omnis Probus liber sit* ('Every Good Person is Free') 75–91. Also extant is a description in part of the *Apologia pro Iudaeis*, 'Apology for the Jews', or *Hypothetica*, found in Eusebius' *Praeparatio Evangelica* 8: 11: 1–18. Philo mentions the Essenes briefly also at the beginning of his treatise on the Therapeutae, *De Vita Contemplativa*: they are the subject of a preceding treatise on the active life of philosophy. This formed part of a work called *On Virtues*, designed to show the excellence of Judaism,[2] so he simply summarizes that he has already 'discoursed on the Essenes, who worked hard and excelled in active [philosophical] life in all—or rather to put it

[1] For a survey of the life and treatises of Philo, see Jenny Morris, 'The Jewish Philosopher Philo,' in Emil Schürer, ed. by Geza Vermes, Fergus Millar and Martin Goodman, *The History of the Jewish People in the Age of Jesus Christ (175 BC–AD 135)*, III/2 (Edinburgh: T & T Clark, 1987), 809–70, and for Philo as a leader of the Jewish community in Alexandria see Ellen Birnbaum, 'A Leader with Vision in the Ancient Jewish Diaspora: Philo of Alexandria,' in Jack Wertheimer (ed.), *Jewish Religious Leadership: Image and Reality*, I (New York: Jewish Theological Seminary, 2004), 57–90.

[2] See Joan E. Taylor, *Jewish Women Philosophers of First-Century Alexandria: Philo's 'Therapeutae' Re-considered* (Oxford: OUP, 2003), 49, 68–72.

more tolerably—in most respects . . .' (*Contempl.* 1). But we do not know where else, in his lost works, Philo used the Essenes.

For Philo, the Essenes were by no means a small, marginal, alienated group living on the fringes of Jewish society, or one that was not representative of the whole; they were the very opposite. The Essenes were among the most exemplary representatives of the best in all of Judaism, and thus he used them as an example several times in different rhetorical contexts. As such, while it is important to Philo's rhetorical success that his claims be true, or else his concrete example of excellence would be dismissed as imagination, he has no interest in giving us a warts-and-all introduction to the Essenes. Rather he presents them in ways that will strike positive chords of recognition in terms of the philosophically educated audiences he seems keen to impress.[3]

QUOD OMNIS PROBUS LIBER SIT (*c.*25 CE)

The treatise *Quod Omnis Probus liber sit* (*Every Good Person is Free*) is addressed to a certain 'Theodotos' (*Prob.* 1), meaning 'gift of God', which would translate Hebrew Nathaniel, but this was a relatively common Greek name and has no necessary Judaic association. Philo notes at the beginning of *Probus* that his treatise was originally the second part of a work, the first part being titled 'Every Bad Man is a Slave'. The issues of this treatise are philosophical, the paradoxical propositions being typically Stoic.[4] The internal evidence of the text strongly indicates that the addressee was non-Jewish, and probably Stoic, but he was also one who was very interested in Judaism: there are only five references to Jewish Scripture, but a large number to Greek literature, and Greek philosophers are highly esteemed.[5] For example, on the very first page, there is a reference to 'the most sacred company of Pythagoraeans' (*Prob.* 2) and later 'the most holy Plato' (*Prob.* 13). Sophocles' words are 'as any from the Pythian god' (*Prob.* 19), this being Apollo—the prophet-inspiring god of the oracle at Delphi. Anaxarchus and Zeno are 'heroes and from the gods' (*Prob.* 106). Moses gets a mention as 'the law-giver of the Jews' (*Prob.* 29), but—strangely—without quite the same dazzling compliments, and one senses that a youthful Philo is trying to impress, by wit, language,

---

[3] What follows is a revised and updated version of what first appeared as, 'Philo of Alexandria on the Essenes: A Case Study on the Use of Classical Sources in Discussions of the Qumran-Essene Hypothesis,' *Studia Philonica Annual* (2007): 1–28.

[4] See the introduction to the work in F. H. Colson (ed. and trans.), *Philo* (Loeb Classical Library; London/Cambridge, MA: Heinemann/Harvard University Press, 1941), IX, 2–9; Morris, 'Jewish Philosopher,' 856.

[5] Morris, 'Jewish Philosopher,' 856.

intelligence, and erudition, not only his ostensible addressee but a largely non-Jewish audience skilled in Stoic philosophy. Therefore, I consider that the work should probably be placed in his first phase of writing, around the middle 20s CE. It is therefore the earliest extant discussion of the Essenes.

In terms of the delivery of this treatise, Philo appears to suppose an audience hearing it read out: at certain points in *Probus* Philo anticipates a reaction. For example, regarding a statement of Zeno's, Philo describes certain (non-Stoic?) people here wrongly jeering and laughing (*Prob.* 54).

In keeping with its Greek philosophical themes, *Probus* on the whole does not contain many references to Essene particularities that are not immediately recognisable as examples of philosophical perfection within the Greek tradition.[6] Therefore, we would expect to hear that the Essenes love virtue, do not care about money or reputation or pleasure, that they are pious, ascetic, controlled, orderly, enduring, frugal, simple-living, content, humble, respectful of the law, steady, and humanity-loving (77, 83–4). We would also expect that they spurn property-ownership and hoarding of money (*Prob.* 76), and have a sense of communality. There is also the sense that Philo is describing what he knew of all pious Jews: going to synagogue on the Sabbath, studying the law, practising virtue, and so on (*Prob.* 80–1). Jews are, after all, for Philo an entire nation devoted to philosophy, instructed by the most holy Moses via customs and laws (*Virt.* 65), and educated in this in synagogues (*Mos.* 2: 16; *Spec.* 2: 62; *Opif.* 128; *Legat.* 155).[7] The Essenes represent the best of what all Jews do.

When we turn to look at how Philo introduces the Essenes, it is important to note that the specific description of the Essenes in *Probus* 75–91 is introduced by a geographical placement, which follows a reference to the fact that 'land and sea are full of wealthy, distinguished and pleasure-seeking people, but small is the number of the wise, righteous and decent' (*Prob.* 72).[8] The small number here is not meant to relate to the Essenes being a tiny sect *within* Judaea, but rather this smallness of the number of good people is in relation to the entire population of the world. It refers to a general principle that overall (within humanity, universally), those who follow an exemplary philosophical lifestyle are the few. Philo notes then examples of these few in Greece (the Seven Sages whose maxims are inscribed on the Temple of Delphi), Persia (the Magi), India (the Gymnosophists), and thereafter he expounds on the Essenes from Syria Palestine as being among this worthy

---

[6] Cf. Doron Mendels, 'Hellenistic Utopia and the Essenes,' *HTR* 72 (1979): 207–22, who has argued that the Essenes themselves may have modelled their society on Hellenistic utopia.

[7] Taylor, *Jewish Women Philosophers*, 112–13.

[8] My translation here follows the Greek text of Leopold Cohn and Paul Wendland (eds), Philo of Alexandria, *Philonis Alexandrini opera quae supersunt* Editio maior, Vol VI, *Quod omnis probus liber sit. De vita contemplativa. De aeternitate mundi. In Flaccum. Legatio ad Gaium* (Berlin: George Reimer, 1915), and Colson's edition in the Loeb Classical Library, as above.

group of exemplary sages. This links the description of the Essenes in Philo to a particular genre in antiquity. Graeco-Roman philosophers pointed to exceptional philosophers in other traditions to show that virtue, self-control, and philosophical excellence were found among the 'Barbarians' in geographical placements outside the ambit of Graeco-Roman culture (*Contempl.* 21, *Prob.* 92–7). These extraordinary models of excellence could include the Persian magi, the gymnosophists ('naked wise men') of India, the Sarmanae (Buddhist monks), Babylonian and Assyrian 'Chaldeans', and Celtic and Gallic Druids, the ultimate source discussions on these being Aristotle's lost *Magicus*, Sotion's *Succession of the Philosophers* (Diogenes Laertius, *Vitae* 1:1–11, cf. Clement of Alexandria, *Strom.* 1) and Megasthenes' *Indika* (cf. Strabo, *Geogr.* 15:1:59–60). Porphyry, in *De Abstinentia* 4, would gather together a collection of extraordinary ascetics, from Egyptian priests (from Chaeremon, *On the Egyptian Priests*) to Indian Brahmins and Sarmanae, including the Essenes of Josephus' *War* 2, as part of the illustrative package.[9]

In this genre, as the Magi or Gymnosophists are to Persia or India, respectively, the Essenes are to Judaea: they are the pinnacle of excellence representing the best of the philosophy of these nations. So Philo continues:

And also not devoid of goodness is Syria Palestine, which is inhabited by no small part of the very populous nation of the Jews. They refer to certain people among them, over 4000 in number,[10] by the name of *Essaioi*, in my opinion deriving from *hosiotēs*,[11] 'holiness', [though] this is not an accurate form of Greek language, since indeed[12] to them (viz. the Jews) they have become superlative ministers of God, not by sacrificing animals, but by being worthy to render their minds holy. (*Prob.* 75)

---

[9] Note that Christoph Burchard, 'Pline et les Esséniens: à propos d'un article récent,' *RB* 69 (1962): 533–69, at 560–4, does not think Pliny's description, by contrast, situated the *gens* of the Essenes within this paradigm, but rather within the context of other people identified by the word *gens* in his work, such as the Hyperboreans (*Hist. Nat.* 4: 12 [89–91]).

[10] The same number is given by Josephus, *Ant.* 18: 20.

[11] The two words at the end of the clause, παρώνυμοι ὁσιότητος, are slightly problematic: παρώνυμοι may be an adjective meaning 'derivative' or 'formed with a slight change from a word', but it appears in the masculine plural, and it does not really work to think that Philo is reflecting Ἐσσαῖοι in the plural: 'they are derivative of holiness'. It is usually translated, however, as if the word appears in Greek as a masculine singular, so the Loeb edition has: 'a variation . . . of ὁσιότης' to indicate that the word Ἐσσαῖοι derives from the word ὁσιότης· The alternative reading of παρώνυμοι is as an Optative Active form of the verb παρωνυμέω, third person singular, with the meaning of either 'it is synonymous with' or 'closely deriving from'. We find this very verb used elsewhere in Philo's corpus in the same way at *Her.* 97 where the Chaldeans' name in meaning 'is synonymous with equability' (ὁμαλότης), or in *Abr.* 271 where the names are almost identical in sound. In the case of the Essenes, the Optative would have been used by Philo to indicate hesitancy, introduced by the expression κατ᾽ ἐμήν δόχαν, 'according to my opinion'.

[12] I understand κἂν as being an intensification of καί so LSJ sense 3, p.873 and the Dative τοῖς.

So, within the extremely populous nation of the Jews, we meet people that the Jews themselves call Ἐσσαῖοι, a name which Philo associates with Greek ὁσιότης, a noun indicating a 'disposition to observe divine law, piety', or we might say 'holiness'.[13] Noteworthy here is that the Ἐσσαῖοι (Essenes) do not here call themselves by this name as a self-reference, but other Jews of Syria Palestine call 'certain people among them . . . by the name' (*Prob.* 75, so also in Philo, *Hypoth.* 11: 1 cf. Josephus, *War* 2: 119). Inherently, Philo assumes then that this is a name indicating great honour, bestowed on the Essenes from the wider Jewish community as a great endorsement. In relating it to the term for piety and holy observation, Philo strikes at the identity of the Essenes as being most representative of an essential quality of Jewish religious devotion. In *Mos.* 1: 190 Philo notes how a mind that has tasted ὁσιότης learns to gaze upwards to the divine heights and rejects earthly things as child's-play. Synagogues, for Philo, are 'schools of prudence, manly virtue, temperance, righteousness, piety as well as holiness and every virtue' (*Mos.* 2: 216). The Essenes are, according to Philo, named by means of an epithet that strikes at the heart of Jewish philosophy.

In terms of the name of the Essenes, Stoics in Philo's audience might well have gasped at the understatement regarding the inaccurate Greek etymology of the word Ἐσσαῖοι. Diogenes Laertius notes that there were five excellences of language: pure Greek, lucidity, conciseness, appropriateness, and distinction, and that among the vices of usage 'barbarism is the violation of the usage of Greeks of good standing' (*Vitae* 7: 59). To get from ὁσιότης to Ἐσσαῖοι, with only a *sigma* and an *iota* shared by both words, would have indicated some barbarian deformity, regardless of a similarity in pronunciation: a better comparison would have been ὅσιοι, 'holy ones'. Philo uses precisely this word later on, when he writes of τὸν . . . τῶν Ἐσσαίων ἢ ὁσίων ὅμιλον, 'the throng of the *Essaioi* or "holy ones"' (*Prob.* 91).[14]

It is Philo's own 'opinion' that links the name with ὁσιότης. In the *Hypothetica*, which we will consider below, he writes too that the *Essaioi* are called (καλοῦνται) by this name 'in my opinion' (παρά . . . μοι δοκῶ) because of their exceeding holiness (παρὰ τὴν ὁσιότητά 11.1).[15] In the *Hypothetica*, his

---

[13] LSJ 1261.

[14] Stephen Goranson, 'Others and Intra-Jewish Polemic as Reflected in Qumran Texts,' in Peter W. Flint and James C. VanderKam (eds), *The Dead Sea Scrolls after Fifty Years: A Comprehensive Assessment*, ii (Leiden: Brill, 1999), 534–51, has suggested that the authors of the sectarian scrolls called themselves *osei ha-torah*, 'doers of the Torah', but see Joseph B. Lightfoot, 'On Some Points Connected with the Essenes,' in id. *The Epistles of St. Paul iii. The First Roman Captivity. 2. The Epistle to the Colossians, 3. Epistle to Philemon* (London: Macmillan, 1875), 114–79, at 126–8.

[15] Note that Philo's Essenes do not call themselves Ἐσσαῖοι as a self-reference· In *Prob.* 75 it is the Jews in general that call 'certain people among them by the name': λέγονται τινες παρ' αὐτοῖς ὄνομα Ἐσσαῖοι. Likewise in *Hypoth.* 11.1 they 'are called' καλοῦνται, Ἐσσαῖοι, cf. Jos. *War* 2:119: Ἐσσηνοὶ καλοῦνται.

rhetorical strategy is simply to pass over the etymological problem in silence. In *Probus* he chose to make the issue explicit, and address it defiantly in the face of potential critics.

Thus in *Probus*, Philo seems to subvert negative reaction by stating his opinion couched in ironic understatement. At first sight it is a very poor card to play rhetorically to introduce a perfect example of goodness with a note that Jews got their Greek wrong. But Philo cleverly uses precisely this point again towards the close of his description of the Essenes. He writes: 'In such a way philosophy without over-exactness of Greek names turns out athletes of virtue' (*Prob.* 88). Philo then makes a virtue out of his concession to the Jews' laxity of Greek language; he turns an apparent negative into a positive, accepting a lack of Greek exactness in the name of the group only to emphasize that substance is more important than mere superficiality of language.

Philo clearly then thought the name he knew as Ἐσσαῖοι was inaccurate Greek, reflecting ὁσιότης, but here he was probably wrong. It may be that Philo is representing not a Greek word but a Hebrew one, in that he had heard that the Jews called this group *ḥasidim*, 'pious' (חסידים). But whether this term is actually a designation proper or simply language of approval is difficult to say, since *ḥasid*, 'pious', in general is used in rabbinic literature not to designate one group, but simply as an adjective: it is an endorsement of behaviour.[16]

In the later Aramaic dialect of Christian Syriac there existed a fairly common word which could reflect Jewish Aramaic usage of the preceding centuries (lack of attestation being accounted for by the fact that the surviving sources for Jewish Palestinian Aramaic of the appropriate time are thin). In Syriac a holy person may be called a *ḥasya'* (emphatic).[17] This word is translated Greek ὅσιος in the Syriac Peshitta (Acts 2: 27; 13: 35; Titus 1: 8).[18] Accordingly, it has been suggested that perhaps there was an equivalent Jewish Palestinian Aramaic form, even though it is not attested.[19] If this were the case,

---

[16] Jastrow, 487; b.Tem. 15b.

[17] Robert Payne Smith, *A Compendious Syriac Dictionary* (Oxford: OUP, 1903), 150.

[18] Lightfoot, 'On Some Points,' 118, thought this might explain the usage of Epiphanius, who is often thought to reflect some memory of Ἐσσαῖοι by the name of Ὀσσαῖοι, though the correlation is not exact, with different breathing and an additional sigma, and the text indicates that the name means 'strong people' (*stibaron genos*), i.e. it must come from Hebrew *ᵃtsomim* (*Pan.* 19: 2: 2); see Joan E. Taylor, 'The Classical Sources on the Essenes and the Scrolls Communities,' in Timothy Lim and John J. Collins (eds), *The Oxford Handbook of the Dead Sea Scrolls* (Oxford: OUP, 2011), 173–99, at 188. According to Epiphanius, the Ὀσσαῖοι—so-called—were Jews in Nabataea, Ituraea, Moabitis and Arielitis, and regions on the other side of the Dead Sea who became influenced by 'Elchasai' at the time of Trajan (*Pan.* 1:19:1:1–19:5:4; 30:1:3), after which some became known as Σαμψαῖοι (*Pan.* 19:2:2), a sect that continued to live in Nabataea and Peraea.

[19] For discussion see Marcel Simon, *Jewish Sects at the Time of Jesus*, trans. by James H. Farley of *Les sectes juives au temps de Jésus* (Philadelphia: Fortress Press, 1967), 49–50; Schürer, with Vermes, Millar and Black, ii, 558–9; Geza Vermes, 'The Etymology of "Essenes",' *RQ* 2 (1960): 427–43, has supported the suggestion that the word derives from Aramaic *ʿasayya*, 'healers',

then Philo would have heard it said that the Ἐσσαῖοι are called such because they are ὅσιοι, 'pious' or 'holy', but—being unfamiliar with Aramaic—he assumed it was an explanation of Greek etymology rather than meaning.

Philo then in *Probus* goes on to explain further the reason why he thinks that the Essenes are called by this designation. Here it is important to note the third person plural pronouns and tenses of the verbs throughout this long Greek sentence. After mentioning the Jews of Syria Palestine, Philo notes that λέγονται, 'they refer to', certain people παρ' αὐτοῖς, 'among them', by the name of Ἐσσαῖοι, a name deriving from ὁσιότης, 'piety' or 'holiness', since indeed τοῖς, 'to them', the Essenes γεγόνοσιν, 'have become', superlative ministers of God not by sacrificing animals, but by being worthy to construct their minds as ἱεροπρεπεῖς 'beseeming a holy place'.[20] Importantly, the very reason why the name is given to this group of people is explained as being because 'to them' (to the aforementioned Jews) the Essenes construct their minds as sacred, equivalent to holy edifices.

It cannot be that τοῖς refers to the Essenes only, since this would mean that Jews call the Essenes 'holy' because these Essenes think that they themselves have become superlative ministers of God; that may be, but why should any other Jews endorse that? Rather, the explanation Philo gives is entirely concerned with why these people are named *by Jews generally* in such a special way. Philo thereby reaches wide to show that his own endorsement of this group is shared by Jews within Syria Palestine. While people normally deemed to be 'ministers of God' are priests sacrificing animals in the Temple (see below), there are other people worthy to be called 'holy' or 'pious'—in the eyes of other Jews—because they superlatively sanctify their minds.

Are we to read from this that Philo here means to indicate that the Essenes as an entire group spurned animal sacrifices as a theological policy, contrary to Mosaic law? This passage is frequently interpreted to state precisely this, as part of a portrayal of the Essenes as standing apart from normative modes of Judaism.[21] This is read despite the fact that Philo uses the Essenes to champion Judaism, and simply cannot be right. Already some time ago a note of caution was voiced by Ralph Marcus, who noted that Philo's words did not mean that

---

though against this proposal see Frank M. Cross, *The Ancient Library of Qumran and Modern Biblical Studies*, rev. ed. (Garden City, NY: Anchor Books, 1961), 51–2 and, long ago, Lightfoot, 'On Some Points,' 116–17. This will be discussed further below.

[20] LSJ 822.

[21] For example, Geza Vermes, *The Dead Sea Scrolls in English*, rev. 4th ed. (Harmondsworth: Penguin, 1995), 21; Geza Vermes and Martin Goodman (eds), *The Essenes according to the Classical Sources* (JSOT Press: Sheffield, 1989), 5; Simon, *Jewish Sects*, 74–5; Per Bilde, 'The Essenes in Philo and Josephus,' in Frederick H. Cryer and Thomas L. Thompson (eds), *Qumran between the Old and New Testaments* (Journal for the Study of the Old Testament Suppl. Series 290; Sheffield: JSOT Press, 1998), 35; Lena Cansdale, *Qumran and the Essenes: A Re-Evaluation of the Evidence* (Tübingen: J. C. B. Mohr/Paul Siebeck, 1997), 29.

the Essenes disapproved of animal sacrifices at all; such a reading was based 'upon a fundamental misunderstanding'.[22] The relativizing of the sacrificial system in terms of moral law is common to the prophets (Isa. 1: 10–16; Amos 5: 21–3; Jer. 7: 21–6). Thus, Frank Moore Cross has written of Philo here:

> This may be taken to mean that the Essenes repudiated the sacrificial system. It need not be. The conviction that 'obedience is better than sacrifice, hearkening (to the voice of the Lord) than the fat of rams' (1 Sam. 15: 22) is shared by prophet and priest in old Israel, and might have been expressed by a pious Jew of the later period, whatever his party.[23]

Philo could not have thought that Jews as a whole gave such a very complimentary name—expressive of Judaism's highest aspirations—to a group of people who rejected the Temple: the institution which stood at the heart of Jewish religion and the land of Judaea itself.

If we look at Philo's text closely, it is apparent that the contrast that is made here is not between those who were active in the Temple and those who rejected it, but between two types of service offered by ministers of God. Philo (and the Jews who name the Essenes) distinguished between what priests do in the Temple (offer animal sacrifices) and what Essenes do in terms of their service (construct their minds as holy, cf. *Her.* 184). This makes the Essenes μάλιστα, 'superlative' ministers of God, in Philo's esoteric view, but it does not invalidate the need for sacrifices in the Temple, nor in fact does it mean that no Essenes were priests (cf. Josephus, *Ant.* 18:22; *War* 2:111, 131). We are here in the world of Philo's lush imagery: the Essenes are not in their daily living behaving as priests offering animal sacrifices to God in the Temple, and yet they are truly God's ministers by continually offering the spiritual sacrifice of their minds. This is what other Jews find so impressive.

So, in creating the Essenes as the prime example of excellence within Judaism, Philo could not have meant to state that the Essenes who are so exemplary spurned the entire sacrificial system of the Jerusalem Temple. While Philo agreed with much of the exegesis of the so-called 'extreme allegorizers' of Alexandria, who really did devalue the importance of Temple sacrifices and festivals, he did not accept their practice (*Migr.* 89–93). Instead, Philo believed there should be a balance between outward action and inner meanings and advocated both: 'we shall be ignoring the sanctity of the Temple and a thousand other things, if we are going to pay heed to nothing except what is shown us by the inner meaning of things' (*Migr.* 92), he wrote, against

---

[22] Ralph Marcus, 'Pharisees, Essenes and Gnostics,' *JBL* 63 (1954), 157–61 at 158, and see also Todd Beall, *Josephus' Description of the Essenes Illustrated by the Dead Sea Scrolls* (Cambridge: CUP, 1988), 118.

[23] Cross, *Ancient Library*, 100–1.

them.[24] The Temple system was necessary as a kind of training (*Her.* 123), and one should participate in it so as not to cause any offence to others (*Ebr.* 87), even though Philo accepted that the real and true sacrifice was bringing oneself to God (*Spec.* 1: 269–72) by piety (*Mos.* 2: 107) because 'God takes pleasure from altars on which no fire is burned, but which are visited by virtues' (*Plant.* 108). Philo's words in *Probus* 75 are therefore consistent with what we find elsewhere in his work, where true spiritual sacrifice is emphasized, but Philo never accepted that this meant invalidating the need for actual sacrifice.

In short, a reading that would have Philo indicating that the Essenes spurned animal sacrifices in the Temple is simply wrong, and is an interpretation resulting from a long tradition of scholarship that has wished to see the Essenes as anomalous to Second Temple Judaism, quasi-Christian and influenced by foreign philosophies, as we saw in the previous chapter. Philo instead asserts that Jews of Syria Palestine themselves gave the Essenes a name that indicated their exceptional holiness, a name that showed an appreciation that the minds of the Essenes were like sacred sacrifices, appropriate to the Temple which is here implicitly validated as the locus of sanctity.

It should also be noted here that the term θεραπευταὶ θεοῦ should not lead anyone to suppose that Philo is linking the Essenes here with the so-called Therapeutae of Alexandria described in *De Vita Contemplativa*, for which see below. In Philo's writings this term repeatedly refers to cultic ministers of a deity, generally to priests and Levites in the Jerusalem Temple (*Det.* 160, *Leg.* 3:135, *Sacr.* 13, 118–19, 127, cf. 120, *Ebr.* 126, *Contempl.* 11; *Fug.* 42, *Mos.* 2:135,149, 274, cf. *Mos.* 2:67),[25] but it was also very useful metaphorically given that θεραπευταί was a word with a double-entendre indicating healing.[26]

In the LXX the verb θεραπεύω has a limited employment, but is most frequently used in its core sense of 'serve', 'minister to', 'look after', with the object being God or human beings (1 Esdras 1: 4; Wisdom 10: 9; Sirach 32

---

[24] See David Hay, 'Putting Extremism in Context: The Case of Philo, De Migratione 89–93,' *SPA* 9 (1997): 126–42; Taylor, *Jewish Women Philosophers*, 143–5.

[25] Taylor, *Jewish Women Philosophers*, 55–9. Philo uses the verb θεραπεύω both literally and figuratively to mean 'minister to', 'serve', 'care for', or 'attend to' in *Sacr.* 44, 118; *Det.* 53–4; *Ebr.* 76, 86, 131; *Conf.* 94, 95; *Her.* 223; *Fug.* 89; *Somn.* 1: 35, 77, 218; *Somn.* 2: 90, 183; *Abr.* 125, 128, 130; *Ios.* 64, 76, 77, 242; *Mos.* 2: 5, 22, 67; *Decal.* 71, 129; *Spec.* 1: 31, 42, 2: 21, 167, 259, 3: 27, 4: 191; *Virt.* 185, 217; *Praem.* 56, 106; *Prob.* 35, 39, 43; *Legat.* 140. Comparatively, in Josephus there is repeated use of θεραπεύω in relation to serving with flattery or paying court, e.g. *War* 1: 222, 242, 289, 302, 460, 463, 464; 2: 4, 297, 350; 3: 8; 4: 249; 4: 365; *Ant.* 5: 189; 6: 341, see Louise Wells, *The Greek Language of Healing from Homer to the New Testament* (BZNW 83; Berlin/New York: Walter de Gruyter, 1998), 116, and her Appendix 6: 2. Though Josephus also uses the primary meaning of 'serve', 'attend to' (e.g. *War* 1: 187, 462; *War* 7: 424, etc.), including the action of the High Priest serving God in the Temple (*Ant.* 11: 62).

[26] Philo uses the verb to mean 'treat (therapeutically)' in *Leg.* 2: 87; 3: 36; 118; 127, 128; *Cher.* 105; *Det.* 43; *Post.* 141; *Deus* 66; *Her.* 299; *Congr.* 53; *Somn.* 1: 110; 2: 232; *Ios.* 10, 23; *Mos.* 2: 139; *Spec.* 2: 241; *Praem.* 19; *Legat.* 35; *Hypoth.* 11: 13; *Prov.* 2: 17. He also uses it in the sense of 'cultivate' (*Cher.* 105) and 'court' or 'flatter' (*Flacc.* 9, 108; *Legat.* 32, 260).

(35): 20; Esther 1: 1–13, 2: 19; 6: 10; Judith 11: 17; Tobit 1: 7; Isa. 54: 17; Baruch, Letter of Jeremiah 6: 25–6, 38; Daniel 7: 10).[27] Philo could then assume a usage known to Alexandrians.

Philo can also use the word ironically. When Gaius Caligula decks himself in the regalia of the Roman god Mars, Philo scoffs at how his minions had to be 'the θεραπευταί of this new and unknown Mars' (*Legat.* 97).[28] In epigraphy, literature, and papyri this meaning of 'ministers' is relatively common and attested as far back as Plato.[29] On the basis of this understanding of θεραπευτής as a '[cultic] attendant' or 'minister'—with a specific reference at times to priests and Levites—Philo can use the word θεραπευτής symbolically to refer to someone who 'attends' or 'ministers to' God by means of a good, ascetic, wise, and devoted life, one which (using the double-entendre) 'heals souls' (cf. *Plant.* 60; *Ebr.* 69; *Mut.* 106; *Congr.* 105; *Fug.* 91; *Migr.* 124; *Sacr.* 127; *Contempl.* 1; *Spec.* 1.309; *Virt.* 185–6; *Praem.* 43–4).[30] It is this sense that is found here. It is a metaphorical compliment, as if Philo is saying, 'Now there's a real servant of God.' It endorses piety and lifestyle.

As such, the Essenes are immediately placed in a category that Philo deems ultimately good in terms of the human relationship to the Divine. The language reflects Philo's imagery of using the processes of cult to point to alternate, more spiritual, methods of serving God. Philo did not mean to invalidate the importance of the Jerusalem Temple cult by this imagery, only to insist on the superiority of spiritual sacrifice (cf. *Ebr.* 87; *Her.* 123).[31]

Philo goes on to state in *Probus* that the Essenes spurn cities in order to avoid the sinful lifestyles there, and live instead in villages where they work on the land or, 'seeking out (μετιόντες)[32] crafts that work together with peace, they benefit both themselves and the people who are nearby (τοὺς πλησιάζοντας)' (76); that is, far from being inward-looking, their industry benefits the people who live closely around them. They are embedded in villages, as a force of good. This statement about only being village-dwelling is corrected by Philo in the *Hypothetica*, where he writes that the Essenes live in

---

[27] See Wells, *Greek Language of Healing*, 109, and her Appendix 6: 1. Accordingly, the word θεραπεία can relate to a group of attendants serving Pharaoh (Gen. 45: 16). It can be used also in an expanded sense, as meaning 'repair' (1 Esdras 2: 17), 'honour', 'flatter', or 'seek favour' (Prov. 14: 19; 19: 6; 29: 26) and in 2 Kingdoms 19: 24 it is used of Memphiboshthe not looking after his feet. The verb θεραπεύω is applied to pharmacological treatment in 4 Kingdoms 9: 15, 16–17, Wisdom 16: 12, Sirach 38: 1–8 and Tobit 2: 10.

[28] He can use the term to mean 'ministers' symbolically: the θεραπευταί of the intemperate and incontinent soul': gluttonies (*Ebr.* 210). The θεραπευταί of the sun, moon, and planetary powers are in grave error (*Decal.* 66).

[29] For examples, see Taylor, *Jewish Women Philosophers*, 57–9.

[30] Ibid. 59–61.

[31] Philo enhances moral excellence by comparisons with the Temple, see *Contempl.* 91–3.

[32] The word μέτειμι has the sense of 'questing after': LSJ 1119, 2b.

'many cities of Judaea and many villages' (11: 1, so Josephus, *War* 2: 124). The village setting of the Essenes in *Probus* nevertheless adds to their characterization: they are quietly focused on the spiritual life, avoiding any distraction. In Philo's personal view, expressed in *De Vita Contemplativa* 19, cities were not very beneficial to philosophy: 'For every city, even the best governed, is full of noise and innumerable disturbances which no one who has ever once been led by Wisdom can endure.' Therefore, Philo it seems creates an image of the Essenes living away from the cities in outlying villages. However, nothing in his account indicates that this choice of location should be read as meaning the Essenes were marginal or out of step with the rest of Judaism, or that they spurned Jerusalem. Their choice of a quiet location simply coheres with the superior philosophical mode, which involves detachment from the hurly-burly and vices of a normal city.

The Essenes do not try to acquire money or land, but only want what is necessary for life, so that they have become ἀχρήματοι 'moneyless' and ἀκτήμονες 'property-less' not by bad luck but by choice, because they think that they are rich when they practise frugality with contentment, choosing this lifestyle themselves (77). Continuing in the mode of superlative hyperboles, Philo writes in §78:

> You would not find one maker of arrows, spears, daggers, a helmet, breastplate, or shield among them, nor on the whole an armourer or engineer or one making business of anything for war, but the [professions listed] do not slip towards evil as much as [one making business] of those things for peace. For the [Essenes] do not dream of a trading market or retail business or ship-owning, eliminating the starting-line towards greed.

The verb that governs all this is ἐπιτηδεύοντα, 'one making business'. Philo is in full rhetorical mode here, in stating that the Essenes have nothing to do with making instruments of war,[33] but even less to do with specific products for peace, because they avoid the latter as inducements towards what seems to be a greater evil than war, namely greed. Here Philo qualifies what he has stated in § 76, where the Essenes seek out crafts that work together with (true) peace: this does not mean that they are engaged in making luxury goods or items that satisfy greed. The starting-line, ἀφορμή, of the race towards greed they remove entirely, ἀποδιοπομπούμενοι (cf. *Post.* 72).

That the Essenes aspire to peace is what everyone guided by philosophy would also aspire to as a moral position, as Plato defined (*Rep.* 628b), because peace and order is a prerequisite for excellence. The fundamental principle of justice within Nature is, in the words of Epicurus, 'neither to harm one

---

[33] As noted by Vermes and Goodman, *The Essenes*, 4 n. 34. Philo creates a visual image of a man decked with armour and weapons, using plural for the multiple weapons and singular, appropriately, for his helmet, breastplate, and shield.

another nor be harmed' (*Principle Doctrines* 31, cf. 32–5).[34] Extolling peace and promoting it was a common theme. But here Philo uses rhetoric that he employs elsewhere in *De Confusione Linguarum* 45–9 in which he defines peace—a universally recognized good—as paradoxically full of the dangers of war for someone who is devoted to philosophy. While everyone admires and praises 'coveted treasures of peace', people dishonour the 'valued beauty of peace' (*Conf.* 49) by engaging in the terrible abuses associated with war: they plunder, steal, kidnap, despoil, sack, torture, maltreat, rape, dishonour, and murder; each one aims 'for wealth and glory', spurning equality and κοινωνία (communality), lusting after money, hating, with any supposed benevolence being sheer hypocrisy. In this passage the rhetoric is fierce and condemning, but in *Probus* there is a lighter touch, and a certain wit or irony. While many might expect an ascetic philosopher beyond worldly concerns to spurn associations with war, these philosophers also spurn associations with peace. Philo makes war and peace counter-balance each other in dualistic imagery that is actually designed to emphasize the fact that the Essenes are not commercial businessmen. The point of all this is that they are disengaged from acquiring wealth. They are ignorant of commerce, they would not even dream of it (*Prob.* 78), literally, because it induces greed, which is the true enemy in the minds of the holy ministers of God who have made their minds holy.

Read with an awareness of Philo's rhetoric, evidence for Essene pacifism in this passage evaporates. Philo is making a different point: that the Essenes did not engage in any manufacturing industries for war, for profit or for luxury (the principle motivations for such enterprise), because they are entirely alienated from the world of commerce. In Philo's rhetoric in *Probus* they are detached from the world of money and land just as they are detached from the world of the city (*Prob.* 76), and yet one continually senses the role of the hyperbole. The Essenes were not in fact people who had no money or land, since later Philo indicates that individual Essenes did indeed earn money, which they would then deposit into a communal fund (*Prob.* 86; *Hypoth.* 11:4, 10). They had houses, but shared them (*Prob.* 85). From Philo's hyperboles it is easy to draw extreme conclusions: the Essenes totally avoid all cities, they are absolutely without money or land, they spurn completely everything to do with war or luxury. If we mute these, as we must to read Philo for actuality, we do not need to limit Essene work here very much, only Essene interest in the struggle for profit-making per se.[35] What Philo is stressing here is an attitude of detachment from material things, whether for war or peace. The dichotomy forms a neat whole.

---

[34] For further see Willem C. Van Unnik, '"Tiefer Friede" (1. Klemens 2,2),' *VC* 24 (1970): 261–79.

[35] Likewise, there is no reason to doubt that Philo thought that the Essenes could have been collectively quite prosperous.

Philo then stresses that all the Essenes are free; they denounce slave-owners for rejecting the law of Nature whereby all are born as siblings (*Prob.* 79). In this Philo links his ideas to the theme of the entire treatise 'Every Good Person is Free'; the moral goodness of freedom itself is stressed by the good. In this too there is finally a striking Essene characteristic, at variance with the rest of Judaism and the wider world, in that the Essenes adhere to a principle that all humanity is created free and equal and that slavery is a distortion of the ideal. Essenes refuse to own slaves.

Philo then uses this moral position in terms of humanity to the tripartite division of ancient philosophy, and notes that the Essenes are not concerned with logic and physical philosophy, but rather with ethics, in that their philosophy concerns God, creation, and morality (*Prob.* 80). In stating this Philo may indicate that the Essenes are not concerned about debating with other schools, since much of logic was concerned with argument (as he notes in *Agr.* 14–16), while physical philosophy is essentially the natural sciences determined by empirical study and theory, as defined by Aristotle and others. But in emphasizing that the Essene philosophy concerned ethics this is really emphasising the philosophy of Judaism itself, and Philo's own concerns. Like other Jews, therefore, the Essenes can be instructed on this anytime, but particularly on the seventh days at which times they rest, congregate in synagogues, where they sit according to age, and listen carefully. Someone reads the books, and another expounds, usually allegorically (*Prob.* 81–2). It is the allegorical exposition that is the only distinctive feature in these sections, and one that Philo would have particularly endorsed, since to him and to other Alexandrian allegorists it was the only way to properly understand Scripture.[36]

Philo continues in § 83:

> They [the Essenes] are educated (παιδεύονται) in piety, holiness (ὁσιότης), right-eousness, household law, city law, apprehension of what leads to truth (τῶν πρὸς ἀλήθειαν) of good, evil and moral indifference, choices which are by necessity indeed a flight from the opposite. They have for landmarks also these three [principles]: love of God, love of virtue and love of humanity.

Lists of virtues then follow that would be widely recognized as good in the ancient world, but particularly among Jews: after all, the Essenes here are educated from childhood: παιδεύονται implies this by integrating the word for child, παιδίον. The word 'holiness' (ὁσιότης) is repeated, and included with piety, righteousness, household law (οἰκονομία) and civil law (πολιτεία). Such instruction from childhood again was provided for all Jewish boys in syna-gogue schools, and continued in discourses in synagogues for adults, and thus Philo is using words that he uses frequently to extol Mosaic philosophy. Moses himself is the prime lover of virtue (φιλάρετος) (*Opif.* 128); and the Mosaic

---

[36] Taylor, *Jewish Women Philosophers*, 126–8.

laws concern love of humanity (φιλάνθρωπος) (*Mos.* 2: 9). In the *Special Laws* too Philo describes how synagogues are for the study of things pertaining to virtue; in terms of God one learns 'piety and holiness' and in terms of human beings 'love of humanity and righteousness'.

Philo then indicates how the Essenes demonstrate the Jewish triad of love of God, love of virtue, and love of humanity. They show their love of God in numerous ways, by the maintenance of purification, rejection of sworn oaths, truthfulness, and a belief in the goodness of God who causes all good and nothing bad. In stating that the Essenes demonstrated their love of God 'by continuous and repetitive purification (συνεχῆ καὶ ἐπάλληλον ἁγνείαν) the whole of life' (*Prob.* 84), however, Philo's language seems to stress a certain never-ending repetition of ablutions for the sake of this purity that would distinguish the Essenes from the practices of pious Jewish Alexandrians like himself, but keeping the purity laws were of course part of the requirements for all Jews, even if these laws and their applications could be interpreted differently.[37]

The Essenes demonstrate their love of virtue by detachment from the love of wealth, reputation/glory, or pleasure, by self-control, endurance, frugality, simple living, contentment, humility, respect for the law, steadiness, and so on: all standard Graeco-Roman philosophical ideals (*Prob.* 84), and all common to virtuous Jews everywhere.

They demonstrate their love of humanity by being well-disposed, equal, and by their remarkable communality, κοινωνία. Philo then explicates this further. The Essenes share their houses, so that they dwell in communities which are also open to others of their persuasion (*Prob.* 85). They have a common fund and disbursements, and share clothes and food through common meals (συσσίτια), for even wages they earn during a day go into the fund, and are not kept as private means (86). The costs of medical treatment are paid for out of the fund and old people are cared for by younger members like parents are cared for by their true offspring (87). This commonality of resources would have been met with approval by members of Philo's audience: the pooling of possessions was advocated by Plato for the guardians of the city (*Republic* 416d, 462c) and was practised by Pythagoraeans (Iamblichus, *De Pyth. Vita* 167–9). At this point too we have a more distinctive Essene characteristic, something that could be used as a differentiating marker.

The conclusion of the passage on the Essenes provides the most important proof example for his thesis: that every good person is free. Indeed, the Essenes have been given freedom even by the country's most heinous rulers. This argument is clinched by a conclusive proof (σημεῖον), namely that despite the evil violence of the country's rulers, they could never fault the throng of the

---

[37] For which, see E. P. Sanders, *Judaism: Practice and Belief 63 BCE–66 CE* (London: SCM Press, 1992), 213–30, and also Jonathan Klawans, *Impurity and Sin in Ancient Israel* (New York: OUP, 2000).

Essenes, and instead treated them as self-governing and free, even praising their common meals and lifestyle. This is an important and neglected section, containing as it does a rant at how truly appalling certain rulers of Judaea were in their atrocities, a passage which is here quoted in full so that the vehemence of Philo's words and the stark contrast he creates can be appreciated (§§ 89–91):

> As many rulers of the country have arisen over time, furnished with different natures and purposes, they have striven to seize [control] by force with the untameable savagery of wild animals, not avoiding any cruelty, slaughtering their subjects in herds, or also [not avoiding] a practice of butchering those still living into parts, and cutting off limbs. They did not stop, in order to leave behind the said offences under [the authority of][38] a justice that observes human affairs. (90) But the [rulers] adapted the perversion even into another mad form of evil. Practising indescribable acrimony, conversing gently with a very quiet voice in hypocrisy, exhibiting a character (ἦθος) of deep wrath, fawning in the manner of poisonous dogs responsible for incurable ills, they left behind throughout the cities a memory of their ungodliness and misanthropy: the suffering of unforgettable misfortunes.
>
> (91) But not one of the absolutely savage-hearted or treacherous and deceitful [rulers] had the capacity to accuse the aforementioned throng of the Essenes, or 'holy ones', but all became enfeebled approaching the goodness of the men who are just as autonomous and free by nature, singing every word [of praise] for their common meals or perfect and very happy life. It is a very clear example (ἐστι σαφέστατον δεῖγμα).

The 'clear example' is the point that needs to be made: somehow the Essenes were protected and 'free', preserved by their own goodness from the horrific abuses of the nation's past rulers, who were unable to find fault with them. The mention at the end of the rulers singing every word to praise the Essenes, may possibly indicate that Philo possessed some written piece, deriving from high places, which praised them. While accepting the veracity of this eulogy, Philo distanced himself from those who stated such things, considering these rulers to be evil hypocrites weakened before the Essenes.

Striking here are the details Philo furnishes of the appalling barbarity of the nation's former rulers, which is contrasted with the goodness of the Essenes. Whereas the Essenes work peacefully, avoiding crafts that lead to either war or the luxuries of peace, the evil rulers strive for power and engage in horrific acts of the worst forms of brutality in order to make gains. The specific atrocity of cutting up a living body seems to have been one that Philo found particularly dreadful; in *Flacc.* 189–90 it is the fate of the governor: Flaccus is essentially cut

---

[38] I read ὑπό here in line with its usage in LXX Prov. 6: 7, as meaning that the rulers should have been under the control of or in subjection to a higher authority; see LSJ 1875: II.

into pieces by his murderers. In *Probus*, then, Philo presents an image of a deeply traumatized nation.

These rulers are the antithesis of the image of the Essenes Philo has just presented, so that this passage comes as something of a shock. This description is replete with astonishing characterization, in presenting an image of a ruler who speaks softly in his hypocrisy, like a wolf in sheep's clothing. This contrasts with the simple honesty of the Essenes.

To which rulers is Philo referring? One may think of the client kings of Rome, the Herodian dynasty, especially given the bad reputation of Herod the Great, as described by Josephus,[39] but Philo himself had connections with this dynasty through his brother Alexander, the Jewish alabarch, who was the property manager for Antonia, Livia's daughter-in-law, with whom Herod Agrippa lived as part of the family. Agrippa, in 41 CE, gave his daughter Berenice as a wife for Alexander's short-lived son Marcus (Josephus, *Ant.* 18: 159–60; 259; 19: 276; 20: 100, cf. Acts 25: 13–14, 23; 26: 30–1), and Philo reports actions of Herod Agrippa positively in his *Legatio ad Gaium* 261–333 and *Flaccus* 25–35. To characterize the Herodians as ghastly murderers would not have been a very diplomatic move within the family, and does not fit the evidence.

Furthermore, the reference indicates a past age, given that many rulers of the country had arisen *over time* (πολλῶν κατὰ καιροὺς ἐπαναστάντων τῇ χώρᾳ δυναστῶν), who were struck with weakness when they approached the recognisably good Essenes. Philo writes in the past tense of 'rulers', δυνασταί, that are now gone, who had 'left behind' a terrible memory; and notably here they are not called 'kings'. The most likely candidates for Philo's vitriol are not the Herodians at all, who remained in power, but their predecessors: the Hasmonean dynasty that the Herodians (and Romans) felt entirely justified in overthrowing. Moreover, there was considerable opposition to Hasmonean rule among Egyptian Jews, both at the temple constructed by Onias in the nome of Heliopolis,[40] and also in circles responsible for 3 Maccabees, in which the Hasmonean festivals Hanukkah and Purim are rejected.[41]

The specific act of cutting someone up is in fact found in 2 Macc. 15: 29–36, and associated with the Hasmonean ruler Judas Maccabeus (d. 160 BCE), who cuts up Nicanor *after* he is dead, though we are lacking the full account of this, as written by Jason of Cyrene, since 2 Maccabees is an abridged version of part of his account. Moreover, this is pro-Maccabee, and other stories of the same event may not have been so kind. The anti-Hasmonean work of Nicolaus of

[39] See Colson, *Philo*, IX, 515.

[40] See my discussion in 'A Second Temple in Egypt: The Evidence for the Zadokite Temple of Onias,' *JSJ* 29 (1998): 1–25.

[41] See Philip Alexander and Loveday Alexander, 'The Image of the Oriental Monarch in the Third Book of Maccabees,' in Tessa Rajak, Sarah Pearce, James Aitken and Jennifer Dines (eds), *Jewish Perspectives on Hellenistic Rulers* (Berkeley: University of California Press, 2007), 92–109.

Damascus, Herod's supporter, has likewise been lost, apart from where it has been quarried by Josephus.[42] However, this history clearly contained accounts of numerous horrific actions, including bodily disfigurement: Antigonus Mattathias ripped off his uncle Hyrcanus' ear with his teeth so as to render him disqualified from being High Priest (*War* 1: 120; *Ant.* 14: 366). It is simply unknown what kinds of tales were told in anti-Hasmonean circles, but it is clear from the Qumran *pesharim* and other texts that the group(s) responsible for these also took a very dim view of Hasmonean rulers.[43]

In this important section of *Probus*, then, Philo writes of the Essenes as being given liberty, under the wicked Hasmoneans, to maintain a certain independence, in that they remained αὐτόνομος (*Prob.* 91). Where Philo uses this word elsewhere in his writings (*Somn.* 2.100, 293; *Jos.* 136, 242) it carries the sense of 'self-governing' or 'independent of outside rule' in terms of law (νόμος), and it is a very strong word to employ. This reminds us that—in contrast to Graeco-Roman philosophical schools of thought—in Judaism the focus of philosophical discussion and exegesis is the Law (Torah) and how it should be practised in everyday life. The Mosaic law was not only a guide for belief or morality or for what took place in the Temple, but the judicial basis of the law of the Land of Israel in operation throughout countless village and town courts.[44]

Had the Essenes then marked out areas of jurisdiction separate from others? Could one see it then as a school of law? Clearly in Judaism there were groups and individuals focusing on the correct interpretation of Mosaic law, which was far from theoretical. It was also the law of the land. There were practical ramifications for legal interpretations within the borders of Judaea—where the law was operational. We may be better served by looking forward in time to the schools of law within Sunni Islam—Malaki, Hanifi, Shafiʻi, and Hanbali—which have different interpretations that impact not only on jurisprudence but also lifestyle, including consumption of food. It is then extremely important that Philo identifies the Essenes as 'autonomous' in law. We will return to this issue again when reviewing Josephus.

Noteworthy also here is that Philo emphasizes at the end of the passage in *Probus* that the number of these he gives at the start (4,000) indicates to him a very large group within their class, since they are a ὅμιλος, a 'throng' (*Prob.* 91), the largeness of which is emphasized by reference to such virtue existing

---

[42] See Ben Z. Wacholder, *Nicolaus of Damascus* (Berkeley: University of California Press, 1962).

[43] See Hanan Eshel, *The Dead Sea Scrolls and the Hasmonean State* (Grand Rapids: Eerdmans, 2008).

[44] See Shemuel Safrai and Mordecai Stern, eds, *The Jewish People in the First Century: Historical Geography, Political History, Social, Cultural and Religious Life* (Compendia Rerum Iudaicarum ad Novum Testamentum; Assen: Van Gorcum, 1974), i, 377–419, and the discussion of private law 504–33.

'among large groups', ἐν τοῖς πλήθεσιν. Philo then contrasts this with the virtue of individuals (*Prob.* 92–109). This stress on large numbers of Essenes is found also in *Hypoth.* 11: 1. Philo writes that Moses trained μυρίους 'multitudes' of his pupils for a life of community, namely the Essenes, and 'they dwell in many (πολλὰς) cities of Judaea, and many (πολλὰς) villages, and in great and much-populated throngs (μεγάλους καὶ πολυανθρώπους ὁμίλους)' (*Hypoth.* 11: 1, cf. 11: 5). While Philo stated at the outset that there were few who were good in terms of humanity as a whole, there are now many Essenes when viewed against the backdrop of a class.

THE *HYPOTHETICA* (*c*.40 CE)

The *Hypothetica* is found only in a quotation in Eusebius, *Praeparatio Evangelica*, and therefore its accuracy as Philo's work is not entirely guaranteed.[45] *Praeparatio* formed part of Eusebius' *Apodeixis* (composed *c*.312/314–*c*.320/322 CE), and is designed to counter pagan accusations that Christians have abandoned ancestral religion for a barbarian innovation, and the Essenes are configured as an ancient philosophical elite who prefigured Christianity, especially by their use of allegorical interpretation.[46] Interestingly, this is not the only mention of the Essenes in *Praeparatio*; Eusebius elsewhere cites Porphyry's account of the Essenes (rather than his source, Josephus, since Porphyry was far more esteemed) to show how the Greeks admired the Jews (*Praep. Evang.* 9: 10: 6).

As a whole the *Hypothetica* seems to have been designed to make a case for the Jews against the 'Greek' lobby in Alexandria, who were determined to present Alexandrian Jews—and Judaism—in the foulest light. Both the 'Greeks' and the Jews of Alexandria sent delegations to Gaius Caligula, in 39 CE, and then again to Claudius, in 41 CE, in which they presented their cases before the emperors.[47] The apologetic elements of the work fit within this context. The passage about the Essenes in the *Hypothetica* differs from *Probus* in style and in content, and correlations with Josephus, *Ant.* 18: 18–22 have been used to argue that Philo and Josephus both used a common Hellenistic Jewish source.[48] However, the correlations are not very systematic and, in fact,

---

[45] Sabrina Inowlocki, *Eusebius and the Jewish Authors: His Citation Technique in an Apologetic Context* (Ancient Judaism and Early Christianity 64; Leiden: Brill, 2006), 290–3.

[46] Ibid. 127, 254–62.

[47] Morris, *Jewish Philosopher*, 866–8. The *Hypothetica* may have formed part of a dossier meant to counter the accusations of scholars such as Apion (see Josephus, *Ant.* 18: 259–60; Eusebius, *Hist. Eccles.* 2: 5: 2–5).

[48] Morton Smith, 'The Description of the Essenes in Josephus and the Philosophumena,' *HUCA* 29 (1958): 273–313, at 278–9; Roland Bergmeier, *Die Essener-Berichte des Flavius*

material in Josephus overlaps more with *Probus* than the extant parts of the *Hypothetica*. For example, we find this in the assertions that the Essenes do not own slaves, rejecting slave-owning as not consistent with the creation of all humanity as equal siblings (*Prob.* 79; cf. *Ant.* 18: 21); they practise allegorical exegesis, according to an ancient tradition (*Prob.* 82; cf. *Ant.* 18: 11, 20); they do not swear oaths (*Prob.* 84; cf. *War* 2: 135); and that they maintain exceptional purity (*Prob.* 84; cf. *Ant.* 18: 19; *War* 2: 129). The overlaps with both *Probus* and the *Hypothetica* are that they live in communities (*Prob.* 85; *Hypoth.* 11: 1, 5; *Ant.* 18: 21); they have common clothes and meals (*Prob.* 86; cf. 91; *Hypoth.* 11: 4–5, 10, 12; *Ant.* 18: 20; *War* 2: 122, 129–32); and they look after their sick and elderly (*Prob.* 87; *Hypoth.* 11: 13, cf. *Ant.* 18: 21). While a common source cannot be ruled out, it must be noted that since Josephus wrote *Antiquities* some fifty years after Philo, it is equally possible that he found useful material in Philo's treatises.[49] At any rate, if we consider Philo independently of potential sources, there are a few idiosyncrasies in terms of the identity of the Essenes that appear in *Hypothetica* and not in *Probus*.

Apart from its apologetic dimension, the rhetorical context of *Hypothetica*—which would furnish a reason to explain why this is important—is only partially understood. The extant work is fragmentary, comprising at most only two short extracts from a bipartite treatise.[50] However, it seems that various features of Mosaic law were identified, and illustrated, hence the relevant section on the

---

Josephus: Quellenstudien zu den Essenertexten im Werk des judischen Historiographen (Kampen: Kok Pharos, 1993), 66–107, and Randal A. Argall, 'A Hellenistic Jewish Source on the Essenes in Philo, Every Good Man Is Free 75–91 and Josephus, Antiquities 18.18–22,' in Randal A. Argall, Beverly A. Bow and Rodney A. Werline (eds), *For a Later Generation: The Transformation of Tradition in Israel, Early Judaism and Early Christianity* (Harrisburg, PA: Trinity Press International, 2000), 13–24. Given that Philo wrote about Essenes in a missing treatise preceding *De Vita Contemplativa* (see *Contempl.* 1), Josephus' source may have been this, for all we know.

[49] As suggested by Tessa Rajak, 'Ciò che Flavio Giuseppe Vide: Josephus and the Essenes,' in Fausto Parente and Joseph Sievers (eds), *Josephus and the History of the Greco-Roman Period. Essays in Memory of Morton Smith* (Leiden: Brill, 1994), 141–60; reprinted in ead. *The Jewish Dialogue with Greece and Rome. Studies in Cultural and Social Interaction* (Leiden: Brill, 2002), 219–40.

[50] See the introduction by Colson, *Philo IX*, 407–13. For an exploration of the relationship between Josephus and the *Hypothetica*, see Gregory E. Sterling, 'Universalizing the Particular: Natural Law in Second Temple Jewish Ethics,' *Studia Philonica Annual* 15 (2003): 64–80. Sterling identifies a common ethical tradition reflected in the *Hypothetica*, Josephus' *Against Apion* and in the *Sentences* of Pseudo-Phocylides. The similarities between the *Hypothetica* and *Against Apion* have been noted by several authors; see John Barclay, *Flavius Josephus, Against Apion. Translation and Commentary* (Josephus 10; Leiden: Brill, 2006), Appendix 5, who suggests that the section on the Essenes in fact comes from a different work altogether, the *Apologia*. Porphyry (*De Abstinentia* 4: 11) ascribes to Josephus a description of Essenes found in the second part of a work he names πρὸς τοὺς Ἑλληνας, To the Greeks. However, alternatively perhaps Porphyry here wrongly attributed Philo's *Apologia* (= *Hypothetica*) to Josephus; Philo's account of the Essenes (i.e. *Hypoth.* 11.1–13) is in the second part of the work Eusebius refers to as ἡ ὑπὲρ Ἰουδαίων ἀπολογία (*Praep. Evang.* 8:10:19), and adding πρὸς τοὺς Ἑλληνας to this title would not be inappropriate.

Essenes begins: 'Our lawgiver prepared (ἤλειψεν)[51] many of the pupils towards communality (κοινωνία)' (11: 1), implying ancient origins for the school and a deep devotion to Moses' law. As noted above, Philo states that the Essenes are numerous, and live in 'many cities of Judaea and many villages' (11: 1, cf. *War* 2: 124); this corrected the factual error made in *Probus*, made for the sake of rhetoric. Philo notes that the derivation of the name Essenes as coming from ὁσιοτης, 'holiness', is his opinion.[52]

While the Essenes are identified as being part of a tradition (i.e. Judaism) so ancient as to trace its origins to Moses, Philo notes that new members come into an Essene community because of 'a zeal for virtue and philanthropy' (11: 2). They are not born into it, but join by their own volition: 'for them the choice of life is not by birth—for birth is not of free will'. There are, therefore, no children or young men among them, but rather all are τέλειοι—mature—and, more than that, ἄνδρες καὶ πρὸς γῆρας ἀποκλίνοντες ἤδη, 'men indeed already inclining towards old age' (*Hypoth.* 11: 3).[53] Philo's reasons for insisting on the advanced age of Essenes fits with his own interests, since Philo himself was suspicious of people who endeavoured to live philosophically ascetic lives at an early age. In *De Fuga et Inventione* (30–38) Philo insists that you have to first prove yourself in business and ordinary life, noting that Levites have to work until they are 50 years old. People who are youthful and unready for a spiritual life will fail: 'we arrive at the court of divine service and turn away from this austere way of living more quickly than we came, for we are not able to bear the sleepless observance, the unceasing and relentless toil' (*Fug.* 40). Therefore, in *Hypoth.* 11: 3 Philo links the Essenes' sublimation of the body's desires with this advanced age, not with exceptional virtue, whereby 'they are no longer inundated (κατακλυζόμενοι) by the flood of the body nor led by the passions'. He assumes they come to this community from wider Israel, and does not imagine Essene schools for young persons (cf. *Prob.* 83, where the reference is simply to synagogue schools).

---

[51] The verb ἀλείφω literally means 'to anoint with oil', but in Philo's usage (e.g. *Prob.* 111, *Flacc.* 5) it may be translated as 'prepare' or 'train'. This metaphorical use of the word is derived from the fact that gymnasts would be anointed with oil in preparation for a contest. For the full list of instances of ἀλείφω in Philo's extant work, see Peder Borgen, Kåre Fuglseth and Roald Skarsten, *The Philo Index: A Complete Word Index to the Writings of Philo of Alexandria* (Grand Rapids: Eerdmans, 2000), 15.

[52] As we have seen, Philo's Essenes do not call themselves Ἐσσαῖοι as a self-reference. In *Prob.* 75 it is the Jews in general that call 'certain people among them by the name': λέγονταις τινες παρ' αὐτοῖς ὄνομα Ἐσσαῖοι· Likewise in *Hypoth.* 11: 1 they 'are called' καλοῦνται, Ἐσσαῖοι, cf. Josephus, *War* 2: 119: Ἐσσηνοὶ καλοῦνται.

[53] Philo reinforces their elderliness when he states: 'For they take whatever exercises they practice to be more useful and sweet to soul and body than those of [athletic] contests, not quite being in the prime of the body's youth' (*Hypoth.* 11: 7). This also continues athletic/gymnastic language already signalled by the word ἀλείφω.

Philo then discusses communality in terms of how it is manifested in an Essene group: 'None by any means continues to possess (ὑπομένει κτήσασθαι) his own things altogether—neither a house, nor a slave, nor a plot of land, nor herds (of cattle or sheep), nor anything other provided and furnished by wealth—but all things are placed publicly[54] in common at once, everyone reaping the benefits' (*Hypoth.* 11: 4). By means of this Philo provides an image of an older man who has acquired considerable wealth and property giving his possessions to the community for the entire body to benefit.[55] This endorses the impression that Philo sees Essene communities as being a choice for senior men later in life.

They live together (11: 5), but each one has a different manual job. They delight in various diverse occupations as much as gymnasts in competitions and so work hard (11: 6) as a kind of discipline or exercise even when they are past the age of vigour (11: 7), for example in agriculture, shepherding, cow-herding, animal husbandry, bee-keeping (11: 8), artisanal crafts, all for the necessities of life (11: 9). They give over their wages to the treasurer of the communal fund, who does the purchasing (11: 10). They live and eat together moderately (11: 11), sharing the same clothes: thick mantles for winter and light, cheap mantles for summer (11: 12). The sick are treated from the common resources, and the old are looked after as they would be by the young in a family (11: 13).

At this point during this eulogy of ideal κοινωνία Philo makes a grand exception, signalled by the word ἔτι, 'however, yet', with the strengthening particle τοίνυν (11: 14):

> However (ἔτι τοίνυν), most sharply seeing the very thing, alone or great, that was certain to shatter the communality, they beg off marriage (γάμον παρῃτήσαντο);[56] by means of this indeed to fashion self-control most excellently. For none of the Essenes has (lit: leads) a wife (Ἐσσαίων γὰρ οὐδεὶς ἄγεται γυναῖκα) . . . '[57]

The sense is that even with the pooling of possessions for the sake of the community life, previously stated, women are not included. The Essenes do not have wives, but it is not at all stated by Philo that these older men who have acquired property have *never* had wives. Their departure from married life is presented as positive, while the situation of a married man with children

---

[54] Here μέσον, literally 'in the middle'. Perhaps Philo is indicating a declaration in an assembly, as in Acts 5: 1–11; for further see Justin Taylor, 'The Community of Goods among the First Christians and among the Essenes,' in David Goodblatt, Avital Pinnick and David R. Schwartz (eds), *Historical Perspectives: From the Hasmoneans to Bar Kokhba in Light of the Dead Sea Scrolls* (Leiden: Brill, 2001), 147–64.

[55] What happens to any slaves is passed over here.

[56] The verb παραιτέομαι in Philo indicates that there is something one is released from by entreaty, e.g. *Flacc.* 31.

[57] 'For no Essene takes a wife,' translates Colson, *Philo IX*, 443.

is presented in very negative terms. Women are selfish, jealous, and distracting. Because of the importance of communality in this piece, the essentially problematic issue of women's objection to this life is stated: when women have children they object to κοινωνία, so that men become slaves rather than free (11: 16–17). This notion of the slavery of a man to a woman is found also in *Probus*, where a male master of a pretty little slave girl ends up fawning on her and, for all intents and purposes, becomes her slave (*Prob.* 38–40), thanks to her beauty and charming speech, which become weapons of mass destruction (ἑλεπόλεις[58]) against weak souls, 'mightier than all the machines which are constructed for the overturning of walls' (*Prob.* 38).

What Philo insists on here is that the Essenes did not have a 'community of wives', a frequently repeated motif in Greek philosophical systems, including Stoicism (Diogenes Laertes, *Vitae* 7: 131), ever since Plato advocated that there should be a community of wives and children held in common in the ideal philosophical city (*Rep.* 423e; 457d; 458c–d; 460b–d; 540; 543). This ideal appears also in the utopian description of the 'children of the sun' by Iambulus (Diodorus Siculus, *Bibl. Hist.* 2: 58: 1), where sharing of wives fits in with a sharing of property, eschewing of slavery, common meals, frugality, and uniformity of dress.[59] Such communality is not what the Essenes consider an ideal situation, and it is therefore important to state categorically in the case of the Essenes that women are not shared in the possessions of the community or kept individually by a member of a community. It is this, then, that the Essenes reject, despite their communal life, because of the discord or strife it may produce, which would 'shatter the community life'.

In directly addressing the issue of celibacy in a life of ascetic philosophy, Philo appears to have had an eye to a current debate in which the value of celibacy was increasingly advocated in Stoic circles. The first-century Stoic Musonius Rufus would not recommend marriage or the bearing of children for the ascetic life of philosophy (*On Training*, Discourse 6); sexual activity was allowed purely for production of offspring (*On Sexual Indulgence*, Discourse 12), a view expressed also by his fellow Stoic Epictetus, in *De Natura*. This position seems to have been arrived at after a long debate with the Cynics, who could advocate eschewing marriage altogether. Pythagoraeans could be equally renunciatory; the Pythagoraean Apollonius of Tyana, according to Philostratus, vowed lifetime celibacy and, in a late tradition, Pythagoras expresses the view that sex was not conducive to health (Diogenes Laertius, *Vitae* 8: 9). This particular ascetic practice can be traced back to Plato's later work (*Laws* 838a, 841b–c).[60]

---

[58] 'City-destroying'.
[59] Mendels, 'Hellenistic Utopia,' 211–15.
[60] See Will Deming, *Paul on Marriage and Celibacy: The Hellenistic Background of 1 Corinthians 7*, 2nd ed. (Grand Rapids: Eerdmans 2004), 47–104.

However, for Philo—as a Jew—celibacy was a qualified good.[61] Given the argument about the practice of celibacy taking place in Graeco-Roman philosophical circles, it was no wonder that a Jewish group might have been called upon as an illustration of how Judaism had anticipated the phenomenon and exceeded all, but while Philo could use the Essenes to illustrate self-control, ἐγκράτεια, Philo himself believed strongly that it was important for men to fulfil the commandment of God to multiply (*Det.* 147–8, cf. Gen. 1: 28; m.Yeb. 6:6; b.Yeb. 63a). He states outright in *Praem.* 108–9 that 'all genuine ministers (θεραπευταί) of God will fulfil the law of Nature for the procreation of children', as if it is an issue. In his description of the Essenes, he implies that the men have had an opportunity to fulfil this commandment.

Indeed, that most of the Essenes had produced children prior to their commitment to celibacy is implied in a conditional clause to address the case of certain men who may *not* have managed to do so: '*Even if* (κἂν εἰ) the older men, however, happen to be (τύχοιεν) childless . . . ' they are looked after as if they were fathers to the others in the community (*Hypoth.* 11: 13). He indicates then that these are exceptional. Practically speaking, all the Essenes he portrays live as if they are childless, in that they do not rely on their physical children but on others in the community for care. In his description of the Therapeutae in *De Vita Contemplativa*, Philo implies that the men who have joined this community have already fulfilled their divine duty to procreate, in that—on going off they 'abandon their belongings to *sons* or *daughters*' (*Contempl.* 13), and leave 'brothers/sisters, *children, wives, parents . . .*' (*Contempl.* 18). Likewise in the *Hypothetica*, read on its own terms, Philo means to provide a picture of men who have properly fulfilled their roles in the world—acquiring property in its fullest sense (including women and children)—prior to a celibate life in the community with other males alone. In other words, the comment of *Hypoth.* 11: 14, that 'none of the Essenes has/leads a wife', is relative to the community into which the man comes, in his maturity: a wife is not involved. For Philo, any married life (configured as appallingly fraught) these men tending to old age may have had prior to their celibate life in community is not classified as 'Essene' at all. New members join this κοινωνία as mature adults tending towards old age by choice, not by birth; it is not a case of raising children within the κοινωνία, within a family, but this does not imply at all that no Essene ever had children prior to being an Essene. The wider pool from which Essenes come is simply Israel.

What the implications are of this model are simply not explored by Philo and we are left to wonder what this must have been like for women and children if his description is indeed true. Did men live away from their wives

---

[61] See Taylor, *Jewish Women Philosophers*, 258–9.

and children, in community, while still remaining officially married and therefore responsible for family support? If so, did the Essene community as a whole support the women and children who remained in their previous abodes? Given complex patterns of ownership in the ancient world, especially in regard to land and property, as we see clearly demonstrated in the records of the Babatha archives,[62] the method by which property was held in common by any given Essene community could have been far more complex than we can imagine. Was this property only personal, individual property? Did the wives of men living within an Essene community gain a special status of their own, even if they did not live with their husbands any longer? The 'even if' of *Hypoth.* 11: 13 seems to indicate that if a member did have children then he would expect (additional?) care from his actual offspring. Were the wives of men living in the community part of a wider support structure? As I have explored in relation to the Therapeutae, Philo does not wish in *De Vita Contemplativa* to emphasize such support structures in focusing on his prime examples of excellence; Philo does not even wish to pay much attention to the junior members of the very community he describes, and barely lets slip the fact that these junior members indeed do all the servicing of the elite few, acting as servers (διάκονοι) in the meals and general workers in the rural estate where they all live together.[63] Philo shines a light only on what is useful to him.

Philo then moves quickly on to his conclusion. So wonderful are the Essenes that both ordinary people and great kings esteem this school by praising them and giving them honours (11: 18). This may remind us of what has been stated in *Probus* as a conclusion to this passage on the Essenes, but we have here something very different. Here there is no attack on past rulers for their atrocities; the concern is with the present. Those who esteem the Essenes are defined as being both 'great' kings and 'ordinary' (ἰδιῶται) people. The passage reads:

> Such then is their prized life, so that not only ordinary people but also great kings admire the[se] men, astonished, and still greatly give honours to their worthiness (τὸ σεμνὸν αὐτῶν[64]), receiving back approvals and honours.

As with the passage in *Probus*, this is a very important comment about the relationship between the Essenes and others: not only with rulers but also common people. The great kings (μεγάλοι βασιλεῖς) still (ἔτι) highly magnify (σεμνοποιοῦσι) the Essenes. What exactly do they do to praise the Essenes that gains favours and honours back? The verb σεμνοποιέω is used in eleven

---

[62] For explorations of various dimensions of how legal systems played out in regard to the complexities of Babatha's family and property, see Jacobine G. Oudshoorn, *The Relationship between Roman and Local Law in the Babatha and Salome Komaise Archives: General Analysis and Three Case Studies on Law of Succession, Guardianship and Marriage* (Leiden: Brill, 2007).

[63] Taylor, *Jewish Women Philosophers*, 99–103.

[64] See BDAG, 919.

other places in Philo's surviving works to mean magnifying the praise of someone or something, usually in a cultic sense, with at times the implication that this implies furnishing gifts, as laid before the image of a god in a temple.[65] For ordinary people, this means that people may have made donations to the Essenes in return 'for approvals and honours' (ἀποδοχαῖς καὶ τιμαῖς), but Philo does not explain what these might be. The plurals indicate more than specific states (i.e. being held in approval and honour).

As for the kings, now Philo is meaning to refer to the Herodian royal dynasty, for we have the present tense as opposed to the Aorist used in *Probus* in reference to the evil rulers of the past. Given that this is written in about 40 CE, one might immediately think of Herod Agrippa, but the plural indicates he is not alone: he was King of the Jews like Herod the Great. Both these kings and commoners received back from the Essenes approvals and honours, in return for their gifts. It is as if people at large and especially the current kings want to ensure that the Essenes are on their side. In *Hypothetica* there is no criticism of past evil rulers but an endorsement of present 'great kings' (this concept is good in Philo[66]) and likewise the present Jewish populace for rightly honouring the Essenes highly.

THE *THERAPEUTAE*

As noted above, Philo's description of the Therapeutae has caused considerable discussion as being a possible related group to the Essenes, from the very beginning of scholarship on the question, and it continues to be mooted today.[67] A group living outside Alexandria, people called θεραπευταί, 'ministers' (see above), are described by Philo as another example of Jewish excellence. In *De Vita Contemplativa*, Philo praises them as exemplifying the virtues of the simple, contemplative life in accordance with Stoic concepts.

---

[65] Borgen, Fuglseth, and Skarsten, *Philo Index*, 308. The cultic sense of the term is important, indicating a magnification of praise or honour in some way, including veneration. In *Det.* 4 people 'magnify' pride by means of costly clothing and property; *Det.* 71 great works of art are 'magnified and served' by costly embellishments; the word σεμνοποιία (*Dec.* 80) is actually 'veneration' connected with Egyptian animal worship; *Spec.* 1:20 describes the great veneration shown to images of gods; metaphorically, champions of the senses 'magnify' their importance in *Spec.* 1: 337; in different cities different gods are 'venerated and esteemed' (*Spec.* 2: 164); metaphorically myths and fables 'magnify' the worthless; vanity 'magnifies' the wrong things (*Virt.* 17); God 'magnifies and esteems' moral excellence (*Praem.* 126); in *Legat.* 136 it relates to the honouring of the emperor Gaius by setting up statues to him, and likewise in *Legat.* 153 and 207 σεμνοποιέω relates to honour given to the emperor in the imperial cult.

[66] See Philo on kingship in general, as discussed by Erwin Goodenough, *The Politics of Philo Judaeus: Practice and Theory* (New Haven: Yale University Press, 1938), 86–120.

[67] See Riaud, 'Thérapeutes,' 1241–64; Vermes and Goodman, *The Essenes*, 15–17, 75–99; Bilde, 'Essenes in Philo and Josephus,' 65–6.

This is probably not the only time he wrote about the so-called Therapeutae. He notes at the beginning of *Probus* that it was the second part of a work, with the first part being titled 'Every Bad Man is a Slave', presenting another exemplary group. Since Philo mentions the Essenes briefly also at the beginning of *De Vita Contemplativa* as being the subject of a lost, preceding treatise on the active life of philosophy, it is possible that the exemplary group described in 'Every Bad Man is a Slave' was the Therapeutae, with Philo keeping to the same pairing of *different* Jewish groups to describe different Stoic tenets.

While Philo uses language common to all Graeco-Roman philosophical schools in his descriptions, Philo's θεραπευταί of *De Vita Contemplativa*, who were living near Lake Mareotis, outside Alexandria, are very unlikely to be related to the Essenes. Both the Essenes and the people of the Mareotic group are 'ministers of God', by Philo's definition of philosophical excellence, but there are various features of Philo's Mareotic group that are distinctively different from what he states about the Essenes. The Therapeutae live a contemplative rather than an active life. They are situated in a completely different place to the Essenes of Syria Palestine, close to Alexandria on the shore of Lake Mareotis, and they are characterized as having women members, when Philo believed that the Essenes did not allow women. The Therapeutae seniors have left their families behind to live an ascetic, semi-communal, meditative, and spiritual existence, in which all active roles are taken by junior members of the group. They give away their belongings before coming into the group, rather than putting them into communal use, thereafter living in small huts in a solitary existence. The Essenes work in artisanal crafts, whereas the Therapeutae spend all their time inside these small huts meditating and studying scripture, apart from holding synagogue services (like all Jews) and a common meal every 49th day, when they spend the night in sacred singing and dancing. There are no purifications mentioned among the Therapeutae. As I have argued at length in a previous book, they are more likely to be a mystically minded ascetic community who are part of the allegorical school of exegesis in Alexandria.[68]

CONCLUSIONS

Overall, Philo's model of the Essenes creates a paradigm of the exemplary (mature/aged men devoted to community life and self-control) within the milieu of Judaism and the wider Graeco-Roman world. They are the most

---

[68] Taylor, *Jewish Women Philosophers*.

admirable of all Jews, at the top of the pyramid in terms of religious excellence, not marginal or isolationist but superior by means of their lifestyle, springing from their love of God, love of virtue, and love of humanity.

In other words, Philo's paradigm of 'entirely mature male celibate' Essenes is not a complete picture of a separate 'sect', but rather it is presented as a superior level of advancement within Judaism, a kind of elite group of men who could maintain autonomy and a very high standard of ethical and moral conduct within a communal lifestyle of great purity and frugality. They embraced a communality that rejected slavery and refused to pander to evil rulers, the Hasmonean dynasty. Under the Herodian dynasty, they are magnified by both rulers and common people. They serve as an illustration that is designed ultimately to reflect back on Judaism as a whole; they are a beacon of brilliance within the Mosaic system, illustrating the pinnacle of Moses' divine philosophy, as Philo saw it.

Philo's Essenes are given an honorific name that represents widespread admiration. The Essenes are older or mature men who leave their usual lifestyles in order to live a life of very great adherence to Essene principles within communities where they are autonomous. They conform to standard ideals of a virtuous and masculine life, working in artisanal crafts without any regard for advancement, living a frugal existence with complete detachment in regard to luxury, property, and wealth, maintaining a high degree of purity.

It is interesting what Philo does not say, or even remotely imply. He does not consider that there is some other mainstream form of Judaism against which the Essenes may be seen as an isolated sect, or some normative centre from which they are detached. Their opposition is indicated as being the Hasmonean rulers, who ultimately cowered before them, when faced with their goodness. Their support comes from the common people, and the 'great kings' of the present. Philo does not indicate that they adopted lifetime celibacy, but he is not interested in their families. Women are simply configured as unreliable and a distraction, and the model of sharing wives is rejected: the focus is entirely on the men and their lifestyle. Philo does not state that the Essenes are small in number, or that they eschewed Jewish practice by rejecting the Temple or by being pacifists. These interpretations of Philo are unwarranted, and were created in a scholarly context that could not understand the Essenes as being part of the Judaism that Christianity spurned, as we saw in Chapter 1. Philo's Essenes were heroes and models for all Jews. They were truly pious and good, ancient, hard-working, and moral. They proved the excellence of Mosaic law, as the best examples Philo knew.

3

Josephus

After Philo, the Essenes are mentioned again in our surviving historical material some thirty years later. The historian Josephus wrote two major works designed to explain aspects of Judaean history to a Graeco-Roman audience. *The Judaean War* was probably written around the year 76 CE, with a rhetorical aim to explain the causes of the Jewish revolt against the Romans in 66–73 CE. *Antiquities of the Jews* was completed around the year 93 CE, and would provide a summary of Judaean history from its origins to the present.[1] Along with these he composed the defence of Judaism against an attack by the Egyptian writer Apion, *Against Apion*, and also an autobiography, *Life of Josephus*. The mood of the time, in Rome, was a strongly negative one towards Jews and Judaism, and Josephus' works may be conceptualized overall as apologetic, in seeking to emphasize positive aspects of Judaean history and belief, differentiating what he perceived as the true heart of the nation from the dangerous rebels who incited revolt. Josephus was of wealthy priestly descent: his great-great-grandmother on his father's side was the daughter of Jonathan the High Priest, as he explains in his autobiography (*Life* 4).

THE THREE *HAIRESEIS* OF JUDAISM

Josephus discusses the Essenes as one of three Judaean αἱρέσεις and thus, at the very beginning of our review of his discussions, this word as used by Josephus should be understood. While it is common to translate αἵρεσις as 'sect', this

---

[1] See Emil Schürer, with Geza Vermes, Fergus Millar, and Matthew Black (eds), *The History of the Jewish People in the Age of Jesus Christ*, i (Edinburgh: T & T Clark, 1979), 43–63; Tessa Rajak, *Josephus: The Historian and his Society* (London: Duckworth, 1983). The standard Greek edition of Josephus is that of *Flavii Iosephi Opera*, ed. Benedict Niese. 7 vols (Berlin: Weidmanns, 1885–97), on which is based the edition and translation of H. St. J. Thackeray, Ralph Marcus, and Allen Wikgren, *Josephus*, 14 vols (Loeb Classical Library; London/New York: Heinemann/ G. P. Putnam's Sons, 1926–63). Note that I use 'Jews' and 'Judaeans' interchangeably, translating Ἰουδαῖοι (GK.) and *Yehudim* (Heb.).

may carry with it certain modern concepts.[2] Josephus states that he undertook instruction by the three αἱρέσεις (*Life* 10–12), which means these αἱρέσεις are conceived as being educative of wealthy young priests like himself. The education is provided with a view to him potentially adopting their principles and interpretations of the law. The basic meaning of αἵρεσις, deriving from the verb αἱρέω, is something 'grasped' or 'taken' (in the same way that 'apprehension' comes from 'apprehend' or 'tenet' comes from *tenere*, 'to hold'). In Greek literature it can then be a 'choice', especially in terms of a form of philosophy that is chosen, as well as a 'taking' or 'seizure' of a town in war.[3]

Philo had used αἵρεσις in *Probus* 83 with its basic meaning of 'choice' in the section that summarizes what all good Jews do: '[t]hey are educated in piety, holiness, righteousness, household law, city law, apprehension of what leads to the truth of good, evil and moral indifference, *choices* which are by necessity indeed a flight from the opposite.' Philo does know of the other use of this term as indicating a philosophical school, like the Stoics or the Pythagoraeans, since he uses it in this sense in *Contempl.* 29 (cf. 2, 17, 32, 67, 79) in reference to the Therapeutae, driven entirely to live the life of philosophy, but Philo never splits Judaism into three definitive philosophical 'choices' or 'schools' as Josephus does; Philo's language is different and looser, seeing that it can encompass the Alexandrian Therapeutae.[4]

As Steve Mason has explored, Josephus uses αἵρεσις in the non-technical, general sense of a 'grasping', 'taking', or 'seizure' in terms of towns being captured (*Ant.* 7: 160; 10: 79, 133, 247; 12: 363, etc.), and also in the sense of a 'choice' (as in *War* 1: 99; 6: 352; *Ant.* 1: 69; 6: 71, etc.), but in thirteen of the thirty-one occurrences within Josephus' extant corpus it seems to mean 'philosophical school' (*War* 2: 118, 122, 137, 142, 162; *Ant.* 13: 171–3; *Life* 10–12, 191, 197), with such usage interchanging with the word φιλοσοφία and its cognates (*War* 2: 119, 166; *Ant.* 18: 11, 23, 25),[5] though importantly Josephus can also use the term σύνταγμα, a 'contingent', or 'battalion', a militaristic—rather than a philosophical—term. The Pharisees are called a σύνταγμα in *War* 1: 110, and the Sadducees are τὸ δεύτερον τάγμα, 'the second order', in *War* 2: 164. In *War* 2: 122 αἵρεσις and τάγμα are used as synonyms. The word τάγμα is found also in *War* 2: 125 and in *War* 2: 160–2, where there

---

[2] The following discussion partly draws on what I have published previously in 'The Nazoraeans as a "Sect" in "Sectarian" Judaism? A Reconsideration of the Current View via the Narrative of Acts and the Meaning of *Hairesis*,' in Sacha Stern (ed.), *Sects and Sectarianism in Jewish History* (Leiden: Brill, 2011).

[3] LSJ 41–2.

[4] Joan E. Taylor, *Jewish Women Philosophers of First-Century Alexandria: Philo's 'Therapeutae' Re-considered* (Oxford: OUP, 2003), 106.

[5] Steve Mason, 'Josephus's Pharisees: The Philosophy,' in Jacob Neusner and Bruce Chilton (eds), *In Quest of the Historical Pharisees* (Waco, TX: Baylor University Press, 2007), 41–66, 433–6 at p. 434 n. 4; id. *Life of Josephus: Translation and Commentary* (Leiden: Brill, 2000), 15–16. The adherents of the school are αἱρετισταί (*War* 2: 119, 2: 124, 141).

is 'another order of Essenes' (ἕτερον Ἐσσηνῶν τάγμα). The language of marching into battle here is quite interesting, because it relates also to the militaristic use of the term αἵρεσις. The Essenes then constitute both a 'battalion' and a 'seizure': they are also a collective, a group of people holding the same philosophy, but they are also at the vanguard of Judaean religion.

That there are 'more than 4000' Essenes (*Ant.* 18: 20) agrees with Philo, *Prob.* 75. Josephus notes comparatively that there are 'over 6000' Pharisees (*Ant.* 17: 42), and 'a few' Sadducees (*Ant.* 18: 17), giving a total number of a little over 10,000 in the three entities.

It is usually understood that Josephus uses the word αἵρεσις as part of his general presentation of Judaism as a kind of philosophy,[6] and, just as Graeco-Roman philosophy was composed of various schools, so was Judaism, in Josephus' view, though there is no adequate explanation as to why Josephus should have limited them in number. Nevertheless, prior to the Revolt the αἱρέσεις are presented as being only three in total: the Pharisees, the Sadducees, and the Essenes (*Life* 10–12). We could suppose that Josephus wished to limit the diversity of Judaism by presenting three schools of thought in order to tidy things up and to make Judaism neat for his Graeco-Roman readers. However, this would be to assume that his readers would see complexity as bothersome in some way. In fact, to define αἵρεσις as referring to a philosophical choice or a 'school of thought' would be to create a loose definition for the term in Josephus and then interpret everything in the light of that. It is better to consider the word in its basic meaning, and to see how Josephus employs it, as above, so that his own usage and rhetoric can become clearer. Their identities as cohesive entities like battalions is important, and thus 'societies' would fit as a translation.

Moreover, we need to remember that Judaism in Josephus was primarily a system of religious *law*, founded on Torah (the five books of Moses, 'the law'), and another 17 authoritative texts (*Apion* 1: 8), by which the law of the land was governed. Given this, the different 'battalions' and 'apprehensions' cannot be anything but schools or societies of law. Once this is recognized, we move away from conceptualizing these groupings as different varieties of philosophical thought, by Graeco-Roman definitions, or even 'sects'. The philosophies of the Graeco-Roman world did not decide on legal interpretations. Law and philosophy were essentially different fields. Behind Josephus' rhetorical shaping, those who are part of the Judaean αἱρέσεις are men who promote varieties of praxis-based legal interpretation. As such, in the following discussion the word αἱρέσεις is rendered as 'choices', 'seizures', 'legal schools', or 'societies', but the term 'sects' is avoided.

---

[6] Steve Mason, '*Philosophiai*: Graeco-Roman, Jewish and Christian,' in John S. Kloppenborg and Stephen G. Wilson, *Voluntary Associations in the Graeco-Roman World* (London/New York: Routledge, 1996), 31–58.

That legal interpretation is actually the *raison d'être* of these societies in Josephus' writings is indicated by the comment that 'the Pharisees appear the most accurate in *interpreting the law*' (*War* 2: 163). Interpretation of the law is not just theoretical but practical: according to Josephus, since 'all [public] prayers and sacred rites' are performed according to Pharisaic instructions (*Ant.* 18: 15), the Sadducees had to submit to their rulings in public office (*Ant.* 18: 17). Arguing against the propositions of Morton Smith, who considered that the Pharisees withdrew from public life in the Herodian period, Mason notes that, after the hiatus of their jurisprudential authority under Hyrcanus I, their authority was reinstated by Queen Alexandra (*Ant.* 13: 408). Josephus avoids continually mentioning this not because he wished to devalue their significance, but rather because readers did not need to be constantly re-minded of it. As Mason states, 'he gives no narrative reason why their position waned appreciably through the period of his history'.[7]

Such a description strongly cautions against a notion that there were very many other societies of a similar nature that could claim the same kind of judicial reputation and status with the practical consequences of legal authority.[8]

As noted above, in *Life* 10–12 Josephus states that he as a young man investigated the three αἱρέσεις, before deciding to follow the rules of the Pharisees in his own role in public life.[9] Josephus is emphatic about the limited numbers of choices available to him. He investigated the αἱρέσεις: τρεῖς δ' εἰσὶν αὗται, Φαρισαίων μὲν ἡ πρώτη, καὶ Σαδδουκαίων ἡ δευτέρα, τρίτη δ' Ἐσσηνῶν: 'of which there are *three*: first: the Pharisees, second: the Sadducees, and third: the Essenes'. Josephus then decides which of them he will follow as a priest from a wealthy family with responsibilities to the nation. As with Philo, nothing in Josephus' *Life* implies Essene alienation from involvement with civic authority; they are the opposite, as they are presented as an option in terms of an affiliation appropriate for Josephus' own public life in Jerusalem.

Josephus explicitly counts them down: one, two, three. A young man in his position had to choose (αἱρήσεσθαι) the best, and thus they are, quite tech-nically, choices. The number three is repeated emphatically in this passage (in 10, 11, 12): these are all the choices he had. The three schools are even more strongly emphasized as a defined triad by a comparison with a variant Judaean

---

[7] Steve Mason, 'Josephus's Pharisees: The Narratives,' in Neusner and Chilton (eds), *Quest*, 3–40, 429–33, at 30.

[8] *Contra* Martin Goodman, 'Josephus and Variety in First-Century Judaism,' *The Israel Academy of Sciences and Humanities Proceedings* 7/6 (2000): 201–13.

[9] Mason has argued that this does not mean he became a Pharisee himself, but he simply follows their rulings as a necessity, id. *Pharisees*, 31–3 and id. 'Was Josephus a Pharisee? A Reconsideration of *Life* 10–12,' *JJS* 40 (1989): 31–45. The question is whether Josephus later in life wishes to detach himself from the Pharisees by expressing himself in a particular way in this text. See below, pp. 54–5.

lifestyle existing apart from them. As a young man, not content with being toughened up among the three schools, Josephus became a ζηλωτής (a 'devotee', or 'zealous disciple') of the alternative Bannus. It is Bannus who is the isolated and alternative entity, not the Essenes, and Bannus is not described as being a member of one of the three 'choices' proper. He is a kind of non-choice drop-out. He was a lifelong Nazirite (*Ant.* 20: 6) who managed to exist by means of clothing and food provided naturally, employing frequent purificatory immersions: a way of life very similar to that of John the Baptist, who is also described as a lifelong Nazirite.[10] Bannus' wilderness example took Josephus away to a life of piety in the 50s, but not to an αἵρεσις as such. In fact, Josephus does nothing to disguise the fact that there were many varieties of thought and practice in Judaism, and Bannus was a teacher with disciples who adopted a particular lifestyle. But the Bannites are not classified as one of the three αἱρέσεις at all. Far from simplifying, Josephus has created a curious division between entities that are classified as real choices, αἱρέσεις, and entities that are not.

After being with Bannus, in the wilderness, Josephus then states that 'I returned to the city' (*Life* 12). Josephus, in preparing to enter public life, felt bound to choose one of the three αἱρέσεις to follow. Josephus appears to indicate that if a man such as himself chose to opt out and go and live in the wilderness, then he would not follow an αἵρεσις as such, because he would no longer be engaging in a school of law, a society, that had an impact on public life in terms of authority and potency. An αἵρεσις had an authoritative position within the judicial framework, while Bannus did not. The Essenes are then not a category of people who had opted out of normal society, because they are not classified by Josephus as being like Bannites. They are a choice.

---

[10] John is defined as a Nazirite (Luke 1:15), though he is described as 'neither eating bread nor drinking wine' (Luke 7:33–4, cf. Matt. 11: 18–19; see Joan E. Taylor, *The Immerser: John the Baptist Within Second Temple Judaism* (Grand Rapids: Eerdmans, 1997), 32–4, which is more than the asceticism of Nazirites. In the account of John's birth in Luke, reference is clearly made to the births of Samson and Samuel (Judges 13: 2–25; 1 Sam. 1: 1–2: 11, cf. Mishnah, *Naz.* 9: 5), two prophets who were also lifelong Nazirites. The Nazirite vow of holiness (Num 6: 1–21) involved not cutting (also not combing) the hair, abstinence from all grape products, and avoidance of corpses and graves in order to avoid corpse-impurity; see Stuart D. Chepey, *Nazirites in Late Second Temple Judaism: A Survey of Ancient Jewish Writings, the New Testament, Archaeological Evidence, and other Writings from Late Antiquity* (Leiden: Brill, 2005). Given the importance of maintaining such purity, a Nazirite appears to have undertaken cleansing for the removal of corpse-impurity before beginning the vow and had to repeat that if ever a corpse was touched, an occurrence which rendered prior days of the vow invalid (Mishnah, *Naz.* 7: 2–3). Such people were then separated from the rest under a special vow, in the case of a lifelong vow, though Jews in general could undertake such a vow for a period of anything over 30 days. The Nazirites, if under lifelong vows, would have been a distinctive group undertaking special piety, but they are never classified as a sect, and such a lifestyle indicates individual rather than corporate identity.

The association of the three αἱρέσεις with the potential to assume public office and act in law courts is also found in *Ant.* 20: 199. The younger Ananus, new in the office of High Priest, 'followed the school of the Sadducees, who are more savage concerning judgements than all the other Jews'. In this instance— judging James—Sadducees had an opportunity to exercise their power, but in *Ant.* 18: 17 it is stated that when they assumed rule, they still had to do 'what the Pharisee says', because of the Pharisees' influence over the masses, as we have seen. The Sadducees are identified by Josephus as a small number of men (androcentrism being a given) who were situated in the most influential echelons of society (*Ant.* 13: 297–8; 18: 17), wielding judicial power, but their more severe legal interpretations were usually ameliorated by the Pharisees in practice.

That the Pharisees' role at the heart of Judaean legal authority is not overly stressed by Josephus might well result from Josephus' problematic relationship with this society. As Steve Mason has also pointed out, several Pharisees, including Simon son of Gamaliel, tried to remove him from office in Galilee (*Life* 191–8), and the Pharisees were, according to Josephus, largely responsible for the collapse of the Hasmonean dynasty (*War* 1: 110–14; *Ant.* 13: 288–98), to which he traced his family.[11] His repeated stress on how influential they were over the masses (e.g. *Ant.* 13: 400) is no compliment from an aristocrat; as Mason notes, he mentions the Pharisees to 'express annoyance at their influence and tactics'.[12] His acceptance of Pharisaic rulings in his public life, despite his preferring the Essenes, seems a kind of acceptance of the inevitable, because they were so much in control. However, as Douglas Finkbeiner has pointed out, following Mason's noting of similarities of expression, Josephus in *Against Apion* configures the entire Judaean nation as an idealized monolithic entity, as being 'Essene' in character: they are his primary paradigm for what it means to be Jewish.[13]

The question of whether Josephus was a Pharisee or not is nevertheless a tricky one. Given that he followed Pharisee rulings (while in his heart preferring the Essenes), he would have sided with them in terms of praxis and interpretation. The trouble is that we do not know the boundary markers in

[11] See Steve Mason, *Flavius Josephus on the Pharisees: A Compositional-Critical Study* (Leiden: Brill, 1991), 325–53, id. 'Narratives,' in Neusner and Chilton (eds), *Quest*, 34–8.

[12] Mason, 'Narratives,' 38.

[13] Douglas Finkbeiner, 'The Essenes according to Josephus: Exploring the Contribution of Josephus' Portrait of the Essenes to his Larger Literary Agenda,' unpublished University of Pennsylvania Ph.D. dissertation (2010), 200–20, noting *Apion* 1: 43, 2: 146, 170, 178–81, 192, 199, 220, 215–18, 232–5, 276–83, 291, 293–4. I am very grateful to Doug Finkbeiner for sending me a copy of his work. See also the analysis of *Apion* 2: 146 and 2: 293–4 in Mason, 'The Essenes of Josephus' *Judean War*,' 259, also Gunnar Haaland, 'What Difference does Philosophy Make? The Three Schools as a Rhetorical Device in Josephus,' in Zuleika Rogers (ed.), *Making History: Josephus and Historical Method* (Leiden: Brill, 2007), 262–88, at 281, n.64, though Haaland looks to Philo for influence.

terms of membership. Was there an outer and inner circle? We find this kind of problem with the Gospel of Mark 2: 18, where 'the Pharisees' are named initially in the first part of the sentence, and subsequently 'the disciples of the Pharisees' are referred to. Technically Josephus might well have been 'a disciple of the Pharisees', without classifying himself as a Pharisee fully, but the fact that it was four Pharisees (not Sadducees or Essenes) who came to question him in Galilee (Life 191) might well suggest that they were concerned precisely because he was considered one of their own.

Finally, even though in his early life there were traditionally only three societies—Pharisees, Sadducees, and Essenes (*War* 2: 119; *Ant.* 18: 10; *Life* 10)—Josephus adds the later followers of Judas the 'Galilean' (the leader of the revolt in 6 CE), whom he calls a 'sophist', σοφιστής (*War* 2: 118), and teacher (*War* 2: 433), 'of a society of his own not like the others' (*War* 2: 118; cf. *Ant.* 18: 8–10). This new group could be said by Josephus to constitute a αἵρεσις because—given when Josephus is writing—this 'fourth philosophy' (*Ant.* 18: 9, 23–5) did indeed assume legal authority in Jerusalem, at the time of the Judaean Revolt, much to Josephus' disapproval. As Josephus writes, while the society—most likely known as 'Galileans' from the epithet of their founder Judas (*War* 2: 115; 433; *Ant.* 18: 23; 20: 102; Acts 5: 37)—was established in the time of Archelaus, 'it began to sicken the nation after Gessius Florus . . . provoked it to rebel against the Romans' (*Ant.* 18: 25), Florus being governor from 64 to 66 CE. The 'teacher' Menahem (*War* 2: 445), who took over besieging the Jerusalem praetorium (in 66), was a son or grandson of Judas (*War* 2: 433), as was Eleazar, son of Jairus, commander of Masada (*War* 7: 433),[14] but actually Josephus lumps all the revolutionary factions of Jerusalem (*War* 7: 262–70) together under the aegis of this 'philosophy': those who followed the anti-Roman legal interpretation of the Galilean Judas. For him it was a poisonous way of thinking which underpinned all the warring revolutionary governments. It is important to note too that the revolutionary factions themselves are not individual αἱρέσεις by Josephus' definition.

The over-arching society of radical theocrasists then actually belongs to the period of the Revolt, the language of αἵρεσις being retrojected to the time of Judas the Galilean himself, as David Rhoads has pointed out, as part of a simplifying theory of causation.[15]

There is then the question of whether Josephus means to imply that the societies are largely sub-classes of the body of priests, whom he defines as the holders of positions in public life. Josephus writes that there were 18,000–20,000 priests and Levites (*Apion* 2: 108), of which 1,500 received a tithe to

---

[14] See Martin Goodman, *Rome and Jerusalem: The Clash of Ancient Civilizations* (New York: Alfred A. Knopf, 2007), 383–96; David M. Rhoads, *Israel in Revolution 6–74* CE: *A Political History Based on the Writings of Josephus* (Philadelphia: Fortress, 1979), 54.

[15] Rhoads, *Revolution*, 57.

administer public affairs (*Apion* 1: 188). The High Priest governs 'with his associates' (*Apion* 2: 194); it is the body of priests who deal with the law (*Ant.* 4: 304), try cases, and punish wrongdoers (*Apion* 2: 165). The nation is ruled by priests (*Ant.* 14: 41), but clearly some expert non-priestly Pharisees could also be among the authorities sent on a deputation (*Life* 196–8).[16] Despite the actual jurisprudential rule of Israel being in the hands of the High Priest and his chief priestly associates (*Apion* 2: 185–6; cf. *Life* 190), the three schools of law appear also to be involved in decisions that affect the Temple and public offices, with the Pharisees generally winning out.

Josephus' various presentations of priestly authority and the importance of the αἱρέσεις are resolved by seeing priests as a significant part of all three legal schools.

The three schools would then be represented in the bulk of those 1,500 priests who are involved in a public life of administration. The public serving priests would follow the regulations of an αἵρεσις, as Josephus appears to think is necessary for someone in his priestly position, and receive a tithe as a salary. Those who are not priests within the αἵρεσις would not have received a tithe to maintain their income and therefore would have had to earn their livelihood in diverse other ways, as would priests not involved in public life. This model then allows for there to be different administrative bodies: assemblies for individual αἱρέσεις in which those reflecting and interpreting the law discuss and arrive at conclusions, and courts administered by priests from different αἱρέσεις with sundry others who may not have adopted an affiliation.

To conclude, Josephus is quite technical in his definition of αἱρέσεις, and does not use the term in the loose way of Philo to refer to varieties of thought. In Josephus' writings there are many groups with variant ideas, but these are not defined as being αἱρέσεις. None of the diverse men Josephus describes as being hailed as 'prophets' or leaders (e.g. *War* 2: 258–63; *Ant.* 20: 167–72), like Theudas (*Ant.* 20: 97–8), John the Immerser (*Ant.* 18: 116–19), or even James, Jesus' brother (*Ant.* 20: 200–201), are identified as founding αἱρέσεις.

Josephus defines *only* three choices or societies with authority in Judaean politics and law—the Pharisees, Sadducees, and Essenes—in the pre-Revolt period. He does not include the followers of his esteemed Bannus or any other messianic or prophetic group as constituting a αἵρεσις because—unlike the 'Galilean' revolutionaries of 66–70 who became the 'fourth philosophy'—they never actually held any legal authority to govern their or anyone else's conduct. Other varieties of Judaean thought and practice would have had to follow the decisions of one of the three societies that authoritatively defined Mosaic law and its application in the courts. This tallies with what we have already seen in Philo, that the Essenes were 'autonomous': they could define

---

[16] E. P. Sanders, *Judaism: Practice and Belief 63 BCE–66 CE* (London: SCM Press 1992), 170–1.

and live according to their own interpretation of Mosaic law. Their interpretation of the law would, however, have been valid for all of Israel, if Israel would accept it. One would expect their interpretations then to have had a pan-Israel approach.

In rabbinic Judaism there were many possible theological and practical points of view outside what was deemed acceptable, all 24 categories of the *minim* according to Rabbi Yohanan (j.Sanh. 10:6, 29c), but these do not represent groups that can be compared with the legal societies of pre-70 Judaea.[17] Even when Josephus forces the fourth philosophy out of the zealous Pharisees tending towards insurgency, they do still follow Pharisaic judgements, γνῶμαι (*Ant.* 18: 23). After all, it is the Pharisees who 'are considered the most accurate interpreters of the law' by the populace and therefore hold the position of the leading society (*War* 2: 162; *Ant.* 18: 17; cf. *Life* 191).

THE NAME OF THE ESSENES

Unlike Philo, Josephus refers to the Essenes without explaining their name, and—to complicate the picture—he gives us two variants. Josephus uses the same term as Philo, Ἐσσαῖοι, at some points (*Ant.* 13: 311; 15: 371; 17: 346; *War* 1: 78; 2: 113, 167; 3: 11) and otherwise Ἐσσηνοί (*Ant.* 13: 171–72, 298; 15: 372; 18: 18–22; *War* 2: 119, 158, 160; 5:145; *Life* 10–12). The latter variant might possibly derive from knowledge of the same word being used as a designation of the priests of Artemis of Ephesus, who had to observe strict rules of purity for a year.[18] Alternatively, it may be significant that the High Priest's breastplate—which was thought to be imbued with oracular powers of prediction—was called by Josephus an ἐσσήν (*Ant.* 3: 163, 166, 170–1, 185, 216–18).[19] There is no very great difference between the two forms of names, as Mason has persuasively argued, and one cannot use the names as a reason to assume different etymologies: it is simply a case of two Greek choices, in

---

[17] As I have argued elsewhere, John the Baptist may well have been close to the Pharisees; he need not be considered independent of their legal tradition; see Taylor, *Immerser*, 155–211.

[18] See Pausanias, *Descr. Graec.* 8: 13: 1, British Museum inscription 578c7; Ἀρχαιολογικόν Δελτίον 7: 258 and the discussion by John Kampen, 'A Reconsideration of the Name "Essene" in Greco-Jewish Literature in Light of Recent Perceptions,' *HUCA* 57 (1986): 61–81 = id. *The Hasideans and the Origin of Pharisaism: A Study in 1 and 2 Maccabees* (SBL Septuagint and Cognate Studies Series 24; Atlanta: Scholars Press, 1988), Chapter 4, and id. 'The Cult of Artemis and the Essenes in Syro-Palestine,' *DSD* 10 (2003): 205–20. For further discussion on the name of the Essenes see Joseph B. Lightfoot, 'On Some Points Connected with the Essenes,' in id. *The Epistles of St. Paul iii. The First Roman Captivity. 2. The Epistle to the Colossians, 3. Epistle to Philemon* (Macmillan: London, 1875), 114–79, at 116–17.

[19] Finkbeiner, 'Essenes,' 165.

rendering an Aramaic or Hebrew word, employed for stylistic reasons.[20] These two forms may simply reflect the fact that the Essenes were known in the Greek-speaking world by two different Greek renderings of their Aramaic/ Hebrew designation. Rather than opt for one above the other (as Philo, with Ἐσσαῖοι), Josephus uses both. In particular, given the Roman context, the form *Esseni* is the only form evidenced in Latin, which would mean that in Latin-influenced circles the corresponding Greek rendering of Ἐσσηνοί was more common.

Josephus' main descriptions of the Essenes are found in *War* 2: 119–61 and *Ant.* 18: 18–22, but the Essenes appear as players in religio-political events at various points in the two histories, and we need to examine these separately. The underlying presupposition of this exercise is that the Essenes have a narrative identity, or character, within the works of Josephus. This results from the Essenes as an actual historical entity, but is also the result of Josephus' rhetorical interests. The source of Josephus' information on the Essenes would have been partly from personal knowledge and instruction (given *Life* 10–12), but also from written material such as the extensive history written by the pro-Herod scholar Nicolaus of Damascus, apparently frequent-ly used by Josephus, though his work has largely perished.[21] While Josephus reworked his material thoroughly, to cohere with his own style and themes, to make his own composition,[22] resonances of Nicolaus may yet be retained in terms of focus and language.

In terms of the broad aspects of rhetoric of relevance here, both *War* and *Antiquities* display Josephus' own particular understandings of Judaean history to a non-Jewish audience in Rome, who needed to be convinced of the positive aspects. This is not to say that Josephus' works present a combined narrative as a unified block, without any internal contradictions, but rather that his work flows more or less along an overarching defined route of intention, as an apologetic history, alert to Roman negative stereotypes. The *apologia* itself is most clearly evidenced in *Against Apion*,[23] but the

---

[20] Mason, 'What Josephus Says about Essenes in his Judean War,' in Stephen G. Wilson and Michel Desjardins (eds), *Text and Artifact in the Religions of Mediterranean Antiquity: Essays in Honour of Peter Richardson* (Waterloo, Ontario: Wilfrid Laurier University Press, 2000), 434–67, at 441, 446–7.

[21] Schürer, with Vermes, Millar, and Black, i, 28–32; Ben Zion Wacholder, 'Josephus and Nicolaus of Damascus,' in Louis Feldman and G. Hatas (eds), *Josephus, the Bible and History* (Leiden: Brill, 1989), 147–72; Daniel R. Schwartz, 'Josephus and Nicolaus on the Pharisees,' *JSJ* 14 (1983): 157–71. Menahem Stern, *Greek and Latin Authors on Jews and Judaism* (Winona Lake: Eisenbrauns, 1974), i. 227–60.

[22] Steve Mason, 'Josephus and the Authorship of War 2: 119–61 (on the Essenes),' *JSJ* 25 (1994): 207–21; id. 'What Josephus Says'; id. 'Excursus I: The Essenes of Josephus' War,' in id. with Honora Chapman, *Flavius Josephus: Translation and Commentary*, Vol. 1b: *Judean War 2* (Leiden: Brill, 2008).

[23] Stern, *Greek and Latin Authors*, i, 389–416.

philosopher Apion was by no means alone. He was joined with Chaeremon, an Alexandrian Stoic philosopher who taught Nero.[24] At the time Josephus was writing, the memory of the Roman victory procession after the quashing of the Judaean revolt was fresh, the Arch of Titus was being built in Rome commemorating Judaean defeat, along with the sacking of Temple treasures. Judea (and thus Jews) was portrayed as a humiliated (raped?) woman sitting on the ground at the feet of a victorious (mighty and virile) Roman soldier on the *Judaea Capta* coins issued for 25 years by Vespasian, Titus, and Domitian: a numismatic image of Judaea advertizing effeminate weakness.[25] As Davina Lopez notes, in these coins:

> Roman forces have defeated and feminized (i.e. placed in the subordinate 'female' role) the people of Judea. Such feminization articulates a position of lowliness and humiliation in a Roman-defined, male-dominated hierarchy. The nation's collective femininity is not only humiliating, but contributes to the definition and reinforcement of Roman masculinity. The soldier appears as a 'real' man.[26]

As Lopez also notes, in some *Judaea Capta* coins the soldier stands positioned with a giant phallic *parazonium* sticking up from his groin. We approach the texts of Josephus with this powerful numismatic propaganda firmly in view.

THE JUDAEAN WAR (c.76 CE)

Josephus himself notes that there were representations of the Judaean war against Rome that aimed 'to portray the Romans as great, and yet they continually deprecate and disparage the actions of the Judaeans. But I do not see that those who conquer the weak (οἱ μικροὺς) are great' (*War* 1: 7–8). The point is, then, that the Judaeans were anything but weak: they were strong. The Essenes are presented as superlative Judaeans, with this in mind.[27]

This point has been well presented in both Steve Mason's commentary on *War* 2, and in the recent doctoral work of Douglas Finkbeiner,[28] who has

---

[24] Stern, *Greek and Latin Authors*, i. 417–21; Pieter van der Horst, *Chaeremon: Egyptian Priest and Stoic Philosopher* (Leiden: Brill, 1987); Taylor, *Jewish Women Philosophers*, 44–6.

[25] Finkbeiner, 'Essenes,' 70, 130–1. Jews were defined by Seneca as 'an accursed race' (*De Superstitione*, in Augustine, *The City of God* 6: 11) and also by Quintilian: 'a race which is a curse to others' (*Institutio Oratoria* 3.7.21).

[26] Davina C. Lopez, 'Before Your Very Eyes: Roman Imperial Ideology, Gender Constructs and Paul's Inter-Nationalism,' in Todd Penner and Caroline Vander Stichele (eds), *Mapping Gender in Ancient Religious Discourses* (Leiden, Brill, 2007), 115–62, at 123.

[27] Note here that the translation 'Judaean' is used given the connection with the concern to liberate the land of Judea from Roman control.

[28] See above, n. 13.

provided an excellent discussion of Josephus' Essenes within the context of his narrative world and his overarching literary agenda. Finkbeiner concludes that Josephus' portrait of the Essenes furthers his wider apologetic purposes, by a portrayal of the Essenes as an ideal community of Judaean philosophers, to be contrasted with the Judaean rebels. Given these two preceding analyses, and in the interests of some brevity, the following review will not dissect every aspect of Josephus' portrayal, but concentrate on a concise review of the overall presentation, with a concentration only on particular points of interest or debate.

War 1: 78–80 (cf. *Ant.* 13: 310–13): Judas

The Essenes are first mentioned by Josephus in *War* as existing in the reign of the Hasmonean priest-king Aristobulus I (105–4 BCE), at which time an old man named Judas is described: Ἐσσαῖος ἦν γένος οὐκ ἔστιν ὅτε πταίσας ἢ ψευσθεὶς ἐν τοῖς προαπαγγέλμασιν: 'He was an Essene, it is a type [that] never is tripped or falsified in the[ir] predictions' (*War* 1: 78). The interplay between the past (of Judas) and present (of Essenes now) of the verb 'to be' in this sentence is interesting, implying in Josephus' own time there *are* Essenes who are never wrong in foretelling the future. This Essene, Judas, predicted the death of Antigonus, Aristobulus' younger brother (*War* 1: 78–80; cf. *Ant.* 13: 310–14). It is stated that Judas was with 'not a few' (= many) students of this predictive art when he saw Antigonus passing through the Temple [court] (*War* 1: 78; cf. *Ant.* 13: 311). This is important because Josephus situates an Essene master teaching publicly in the Temple, assuming some Essene presence in this institution. He indicates that prediction (prophecy) was an Essene skill that was communicated to students. Such true prophecy was something that Josephus himself highly valued, and there is an implicit allusion here to himself, given that his life was spared on account of his amazing and timely prediction of Vespasian's ascent to imperial power (*War* 3: 399–408, cf. Suetonius, *Vespasian* 5). In the narrative of *War*, Judas is shocked to see Antigonus in the Temple and announces that he was mistaken in his prophecy that he would die since he was supposed to have died in Straton's Tower, the city so-called—later renamed Caesarea—being six hundred stadia distant: since it was the fourth hour, he could not now get there the same day from Jerusalem. However, shortly afterwards Antigonus was indeed killed in an underground location (in Jerusalem) called (colloquially) 'Straton's Tower' (*War* 1: 80), murdered by his brother's bodyguards.

There is no description of what an Essene is here. Josephus, in *War*, had begun with a brief synopsis of Judaean history from the time of Antiochus Epiphanes and the building of a rival temple in Egypt, through to the rise of the Hasmoneans and the expansion of Judaea under their leadership. Then he describes the rivalry between Aristobulus and Antigonus, but nothing at all has been said of different schools of Judaean law. What has been introduced, however, is the 'gift of prophecy', by reference to John Hyrcanus who foresaw prophetically that his two eldest sons would not succeed in holding control of government (*War* 1: 68–9).

Judas, the master of predictive arts, appears as a curious successor to John Hyrcanus, therefore, in having the capacity to predict the future. Yet he stands apart from the Hasmonean dynasty and their rivalries. The designation Ἐσσαῖος appears without any qualification or description, as if Josephus relied on his readers to understand what was meant from their general knowledge. That he could do this may be because the descriptions by Philo, written nearly 40 years earlier, had already introduced the Essenes to the Graeco-Roman world. There were also other accounts of the Essenes in circulation, as we shall see in regard to the evidence of Pliny and Dio.

The portrayal of Judas here as a master of predictive arts is an important paradigm that runs throughout the presentation of Essenes in *War*, and one that Josephus assumes will cause 'wonder' among his readers, as Gray has pointed out.[29] But his readers are supposed to be prepared for his own wonder. Josephus would himself interpret a dream of Vespasian (that he would become emperor) (*War* 3: 351–4; 399–408). This would be the turning point of his entire life, since when Vespasian became emperor Josephus was honoured. Given this, as he was writing *War*, Josephus would have needed to plant early on in the narrative some indications of the importance of successful dream interpretation. Like John Hyrcanus, he would be 'inspired' too in his predictive ability (*War* 3: 353).[30] Essenes, where they occur, are then an important cipher: as masters of prediction and paragons of virtue they point to the excellence not only of Jewish wisdom, but to the achievement of Josephus himself.

War 2: 112–3 (cf. *Ant.* 17: 345–8): Simon

In *War* 2: 112–3 (and *Ant.* 17: 345–8) the son of Herod, Archelaus (who ruled 4 BCE to 6 CE), also encounters an Essene master of prediction. Archelaus is warned of his impending misfortune by Simon the Ἐσσαῖος, who correctly interprets Archelaus' dream—in which he sees nine fully grown heads of corn

---

[29] For an exploration, see Rebecca Gray, *Prophetic Figures in Late Second Temple Jewish Palestine: The Evidence from Josephus* (Oxford: OUP, 1993), 80–111, for Judas see 92–5: Josephus 'introduces the account . . . by remarking that the reader may well be "astonished" (θαυμάζω: *War* 1: 78; *Ant.* 3: 311) by the story he is about to tell', p.94. Gray notes also the use of the term μάντις for Judas, Simon, and other Essenes. This may best be translated as 'master predictor' rather than 'prophet' or 'diviner'.

[30] See Gray, *Prophetic Figures*, 52–69.

eaten by oxen—as indicating the years of Archelaus' rule, meaning he was soon to be deposed. His success in this is contrasted with the uselessness of other masters of prediction and 'Chaldeans'. This indicates that Josephus considered the Essenes adept at dream interpretation as a means of predicting the future, on the precedent of Joseph (Genesis 41, cf. *Ant.* 2: 75–86).[31] As Gray points out, there is no reference to scriptural interpretation as a means of predicting the future, but dreams are a resource for independent analysis.[32] Simon explains the dream (*War* 2: 113) better than the other experts Archelaus can call upon at court. Five days after Simon predicted the end of Archelaus' rule, and his death, he was called by Rome to trial.

From this characterization of brilliant Essene masters of prediction, and specifically Simon's expertise with dream interpretation, Josephus continues to reflect on dreams, and notes then the dream of Glaphyra, the daughter of another Archelaus (the King of Cappadocia), first wife of Herod's executed son Alexander. Glaphyra, who had married Archelaus, died two days after a dream in which she saw her first husband decry the marriage (*War* 2: 114–16), though Essene interpretation was not needed to understand this nightmare. The point of this story is to underscore the importance of dreams, which in turn endorses Simon's skills and points ahead to Josephus' own brilliance.

War 2: 119–61: Essenes in Detail

When the Essenes are described in detail in *War* 2: 119–61 they have therefore already been introduced in the narrative of *War* as astonishing experts in the art of prediction, in terms of Judas' foretelling of the death of Antigonus (*War* 1: 78–80) and Simon's prediction of the end of Archelaus' reign (*War* 2: 112–13). When the word Ἐσσαῖος had been first mentioned in *War*, regarding Judas, it was simply given without any explanation, as we saw, but it rapidly becomes linked with the esoteric wisdom of predictive arts. After this, Josephus gathers historical data relating to the years 6–9 CE: Archelaus' part of Judaea became a Roman province, governed by the 'procurator' Coponius. Judas the Galilean led a revolt, refusing to pay taxes to the Romans; and, as we have seen, Josephus describes him as 'a sophist of his own choice (ἰδίας αἱρέσεως) not resembling the others'. In the next breath Josephus indicates what Judas does not resemble—the legal societies of the Essenes, Pharisees, and Sadducees—before returning to the end of Archelaus' rule in *War* 2: 167. It is

---

[31] See Frederic Cryer, *Divination in Ancient Israel and its Near Eastern Environment: A Socio-Historical Investigation* (JSOT Suppl. Series 142. Sheffield: JSOT/Sheffield Academic Press, 1994), 157–9, 267–72; Ann Jeffers, *Magic and Divination in Ancient Palestine and Syria* (Leiden: Brill, 1992), 125–43.

[32] Gray, *Prophetic Figures*, 104.

this spurious legal school (in Josephus' opinion), that would hold legal authority during the Revolt, that triggers his exposition of the contrasting schools that are the legitimate exponents of Judaism and, among them, it is the Essenes who are the most worthy as the best examples to illustrate the whole.

As noted above, the term αἵρεσις is used here of the Galileans with a view to what will happen in due course, when the teaching of Judas would become a Jerusalem legal school proper during the Revolt. Josephus himself probably would have referred to it as a αἵρεσις during this time, because it did have legal authority. In the same way that he has just used the term 'procurator' for Coponius, when he was officially, in 6 CE, a prefect, as we know from the Pilate inscription found in Caesarea,[33] so also here with the term αἵρεσις. At the beginning of the first century the group around Judas the Galilean would have been no more a αἵρεσις than the group around Bannus. This language belongs to the later era of the Revolt. But the use of the term prompts Josephus to explain what he means by αἱρέσεις, and it is clear that in the era in question there were legitimately only three: the Pharisees, the Sadducees, and the Essenes. Given he has mentioned Simon, and given Josephus' great esteem for the Essenes (*Life* 10–12), it is no wonder they are mentioned first and in much detail.

As Mason has shown in his commentary on *War* 2, the Essenes (Ἐσσηνοί) of 119–61 appear after a broad description of the inadequacies and errors of Herod's heirs (2: 1–118) and the Essenes provide a strong moral contrast, with emphases and characteristics designed to highlight what Josephus has just discussed.[34] The Essenes here are introduced as seeming to practice great 'worthiness', a word that implies austerity (σεμνότητα; 119). They 'are called' (καλοῦνται) Essenes (Ἐσσηνοί; 119)—though we are given no explanation why—and they love each other (φιλάλληλοι; 120). How very different from the example of the Herodian dynasty, indeed. As Mason demonstrates, Josephus presents the Essenes as examples of Judaean virtue, self-control, and 'manliness' at a time Romans doubted Judaeans had such 'Roman' qualities given their revolt and defeat, and for this reason, also, the language Josephus uses is redolent of an austere martial order.[35]

This lengthy section may indicate Josephus had access to a discussion of the Essenes by the pro-Herod Nicolaus of Damascus, who may well have made a point of identifying them as very admirable given their prediction of Herod's accession (see below). The similarities and slight differences between *War* 2: 118–61 and Hippolytus, *Refutatio omnium haeresium* 9: 18–29, have led some scholars to propose that Josephus' descriptions of the Essenes here may

---

[33] See Joan E. Taylor, 'Pontius Pilate and the Imperial Cult in Roman Judaea,' *NTS* 52 (2006): 555–82, at 564–75.

[34] Mason, *War* 2, 84–5.

[35] Mason, *War* 2, 85–7.

not have derived from his own observations but rather from a Hellenistic Jewish source or sources.[36]

If the text is sound, there is some possible grammatical indication that literary sourcing has led to an awkward join: after introducing the three societies as elsewhere with: 'Three types [of societies] expound philosophy *among the Judaeans*' (παρὰ Ἰουδαίοις; *War* 2: 119), Josephus then repeats himself: 'They are called Essenes, being a category of *Judaeans* (Ἰουδιαῖοι μὲν γένος ὄντες) . . .' The repetition of 'Judaeans' is odd, and perhaps is indicative of some cutting and pasting from Nicolaus of Damascus.

At any rate, Josephus states in *War* 2: 119:

> Three forms [of societies] expound philosophy among Judaeans: [the first] of the [three] are Pharisee choosers (αἱρετισταί), [the second] of them the Sadducees and the third—which really appears to practice most worthiness/austerity—are called Essenes, being a category of Judaeans showing mutual love even more than the others.

Thus, while Josephus lists the legal schools in terms of their influence on the religio-political machinations of the nation, with the Pharisees first, Josephus chooses to put the last first as indicative of the most worthy example of Judaean legal societies, to illustrate not just how woefully un-Judaean the Herodian dynasty was but also to show how different Judas the Galilean and his legal school were from the rest, given what everyone knew of what happened in the Revolt.

Thus Josephus describes the Essenes. Space here does not permit a detailed exposition of every aspect of Josephus' long account. Much of the description may be understood within the context of general virtue and manliness understood within the ancient world.[37] The language and context has been explored in great detail in Steve Mason's rich commentary, and, as noted above, discussion here will focus on main features and characteristics of the Essenes as Josephus describes them, with a concern with controversies and misinterpretations. At this point, it is not my purpose to reflect on any possible points of similarity or difference between the Essenes as described by Josephus and the communities evidenced by the Dead Sea Scrolls. It is of concern here simply to understand Josephus and his portrayal.[38]

To begin with, we are given an extraordinary example of Essene self-control, governed by a tight structure of μέν . . . δέ clauses 'on the one

---

[36] See below, pp. 104–7.

[37] Steve Mason, 'Essenes and Lurking Spartans in Josephus' *Judean War*: From Story to History,' in Zuleika Rodgers (ed.), *Making History. Joseph and Historical Method* (Leiden: Brill, 2007), 219–61.

[38] The following section develops parts of what I have explored already in 'Philo of Alexandria on the Essenes: A Case Study on the Use of Classical Sources in Discussions of the Qumran-Essene Hypothesis,' *SPA* (2007): 1–28.

hand . . . on the other', that may be translated with 'and' or 'yet' in the second clause. *War* 2: 120 reads:

> These [Essenes] turn away from the pleasures as an evil, and undertake the virtue of self-control and not to submit to the passions; so [choosing] a disregard of marriage among themselves and selecting the still pliable children of others, they lead [them] towards the hereditary lessons and mould [them] to their customs: not abolishing marriage and the succession [coming] from it, yet guarding against the laxity of women and being persuaded that none [is able] to keep faith with one man.[39]

We are told that the Essenes reject 'the pleasures as an evil' (τὰς . . . ἡδονὰς ὡς κακίαν), and consider self-control (ἐγκράτεια) and not to submit to the passions as a special virtue (120). The immediate example of a pleasure so rejected—introduced by a consequential καὶ ('even', 'so') may be ἔρως, erotic love,[40] so that the Essene can resist sex (marriage), but the focus rapidly becomes the issue of the consequences of marriage: children. The focus is then not about sex but about progeny.

In Thackeray's Loeb edition, *War* 2: 120 reads: 'Marriage they disdain, but they adopt other men's children, while yet pliable and docile, and regard them as kin and mould them in accordance with their own principles.'[41] The choice here of the word 'adopt' is a problem, since it presents a scenario whereby Essenes adopt children in substitution for having any of their own.[42] But Josephus does not state this. The adjective συγγενεῖς is one implying something innate, inborn, but also related by kinship,[43] and, in association with τὰ μαθήματα, indicates a quality of the lessons: the teaching is something relating to Judaeans as a people. I translate it here as 'hereditary' in that these innate principles are usually passed down through families, but here through the

---

[39] οὗτοι τὰς μὲν ἡδονὰς ὡς κακίαν ἀποστρέφονται, τὴν δὲ ἐγκράτειαν καὶ τὸ μὴ τοῖς πάθεσιν ὑποπίπτειν ἀρετὴν ὑπολαμβάνουσιν. καὶ γάμου μὲν παρ' αὐτοῖς ὑπεροψία, τοὺς δ' ἀλλοτρίους παῖδας ἐκλαμβάνοντες ἁπαλοὺς ἔτι πρὸς τὰ μαθήματα συγγενεῖς ἡγοῦνται καὶ τοῖς ἤθεσιν αὐτῶν ἐν τυποῦσι, τὸν μέν γάμον καὶ τὴν ἐξ αὐτοῦ διαδοχὴν οὐκ ἀναιροῦντες, τὰς δὲ τῶν γυναικῶν ἀσελγείας φυλαττόμενοι καὶ μηδεμίαν τηρεῖν πεπεισμένοι τὴν πρὸς ἕνα πίστιν

[40] See discussion in Todd S. Beall, *Josephus' Description of the Essenes Illustrated by the Dead Sea Scrolls* (Cambridge: CUP, 1988), 111–12.

[41] Thackeray, *Josephus II*, 369. Mason, *War* 2, 99, retains this translation but rightly questions how it could possibly be true, given that Josephus indicates he enters the training of the school as a young man, not as a child.

[42] Thackeray's highly influential mistranslation is an example of what happens when there is a pre-existing notion that the Essenes lived a separated, monastic life and must have been very different from other Jews; this being the dominant characterization of the Essenes within scholarship of the nineteenth and twentieth centuries, as explored in Chapter 1. If the strict template of an Essene 'monastery' is removed, then translation itself is liberated so that we can more clearly read what Josephus actually states.

[43] LSJ 1659–60.

giving of tuition by those outside physical families. This illustrates a mode of special generosity and selflessness on the part of the teachers.

The Essenes' interest in the unrelated children 'of others' means that they reject taking pleasure in their own physical offspring or their physical succession. It is not about the rejection of sexual pleasure. In place of any of their own children they choose out or select (ἐκλαμβάνοντες) other people's children, but they do not abolish marriage and having children. The language reflects the closeness of the teacher–student relationship in antiquity, since students, having been accepted for instruction, could co-habit with a teacher and serve his needs.[44]

In the fatherly teaching of people that are not their own offspring, the Essenes exhibit the very quality of love Josephus has just referred to (Ἰουδαῖοι ... γένος ὄντες, φιλάλληλοι). Such is the lovingness of the Essenes and their resistance to pleasure that they overlook having their own children and select[45] other people's in which to instil the ancestral laws, providing their own legal teaching as other fathers would provide it for their own sons. Moreover, Josephus does not actually indicate that there are any small children under the age of 14 involved here: the discussion is about physical progeny, not about children of tender years. When Josephus later describes the mode of entry into Essene communities, it is clear they 'choose out' the children of others at the age they are ready to embrace an extremely hard discipline, and Josephus himself does not sample this until he is a young man on the cusp of a public career (*Life* 11): he is one of these 'children of others' then, given teaching by a fatherly Essene, at an age he can take it.

Furthermore, any natural pride fathers may have in their own offspring is removed by the assertion that women cannot be trusted to keep faith with one man: a man's children may not in fact be his own. The word ἀσελγείας is actually much broader than one that focuses on the danger of adultery (μοιχεία) or sexual misconduct (πορνεία). It can encompass wanton violence, for example, or plain insolence, in its range of meanings.[46] Women are the opposite of being self-controlled. They are prone to be loose and careless; the verb ἀσελγαίνω indicates various forms of unrestrained behaviour.[47] A man's concern with trusting his children are his own explains the law's strict adultery laws (*Ant.* 3: 276). But even with these in place, why should a man invest his love and tuition in the children of women who are by nature untrustworthy?

---

[44] In a Q saying, 'the sons of the Pharisees' appear to be students of the Pharisees (Matt. 12: 27; Luke 11: 19); see Joachim Jeremias, *Jerusalem in the Time of Jesus*, 3rd ed. (London: SCM Press, 1969), 177; Taylor, *Immerser*, 102–3.

[45] In Whiston's translation (*War* 2: 8: 2), he correctly uses the words 'choose out'; see William Whiston, *The Works of Flavius Josephus*, ed. by D. S. Margoliouth (London: Ward, Lock and Co., 1906), 597.

[46] LSJ 255.

[47] For comparable comments in Josephus, see Mason, 'What Josephus Says,' 434–5.

The conclusion is that in teaching the pliable children of others, the Essenes are exhibiting a selfless fatherly concern not bound to any reliance on a physical succession: they are better fathers without women or their own children. The image becomes more masculine, more resilient, and without egotism: with singularly-focused *virtus*, they remove wanton women from the picture.

Josephus might have told us that all Essenes never marry, but the language twists around the issue peculiarly. Instead, these Essenes 'are not abolishing marriage and the succession [coming] from it', but they proceed by choosing[48] 'a disregard of marriage among themselves'. The noun ὑπεροψία, I translate as a 'disregard' to avoid too pejorative a sense here, though this noun can be translated as 'disdain', since 'disregarding' something can mean a rejection. The verb which informs this word, ὑπεροράω, has a sense of looking beyond or above something, as if the Essenes are looking to higher things, and marriage is beneath them.[49] For Josephus, the Essene practice of teaching the children of others, rather than their own progeny, is 'higher' than that of the general normal practice. At this stage, we should not be concerned that of course other teachers than Essenes also accepted children of others and that a common designation for a teacher was 'Father':[50] we are concerned with Josephus' rhetoric here.

Josephus' language-carefully avoids absolutist implications: it is not a condition of being an Essene that a man should never have married, but rather marriage is somehow beneath the Essenes' high principles, as they are characterized here by Josephus, because they are not concerned about physical progeny. An ideal Essene is detached from physicality in this way.

The exhortation to men to exhibit self-control, in line with concepts of 'manly virtue' (*virtus* or ἀνδρεία), was well known in the wider Mediterranean world,[51] and found in a range of post-exilic Jewish literature (e.g. Sirach 18: 30; Prov 16: 32).[52] It would have been understood by anyone who recognized that manly virtue (courage, bravery) was not what women could normally achieve. As Mason has explored, Josephus sets up the Essenes as paradigms of perfect Judaean men in terms of their exceptional lifestyle, which manifests the kind of exemplary *andreia* one might associate with the Spartans of old,

---

[48] ἐκλαμβάνοντες is the verb that governs both parts of this μέν ... δέ phrasing.

[49] LSJ 1867. Note also the curious 'among themselves', παρ᾽ αὐτοῖς, which anticipates the affirmation of marriage for others.

[50] Jastrow, 1–2.

[51] Michel Foucault, *The History of Sexuality 3: Care of the Self* (trans. by Robert Hurley; New York: Random House, 1988) 39–68; Michael L. Satlow, '"Try to Be a Man": The Rabbinic Construction of Masculinity,' *HTR* 89 (1996): 19–40 at 21–2.

[52] Satlow, 'Try to Be a Man,' 22–4; Stephen D. Moore and Janice Capel Anderson, 'Taking it Like a Man: Masculinity in 4 Maccabees,' *JBL* 117 (1998): 249–73; Maxine Grossman, 'Affective Masculinity: The Gender of the Patriarchs in *Jubilees*,' *Henoch* 31 (2009): 91–7.

who are the closest parallel in the Greek world Josephus adduces for Judaeans as a whole (*Apion* 2: 225–35).[53] Roman ideal manly virtue, enshrined in the concept of *virtus*, has been explored in detail by Myles McDonald, and it clearly underpins Josephus' presentation for a Roman audience. Toughness, discipline, military orderliness, propriety, courage, resistance to passion, self-control, frugality, restraint, austerity, weightiness, and resilience are the essential components.[54] The Essenes of *War* 2 are so manly they do not even live with women (like men in army training). Josephus, like Philo, configures Essene identity as only applying to men: the androcentrism is a given.

Yet Josephus then insists that marriage is accepted, quite emphatically, since the Essenes are 'not abolishing (οὐκ ἀναιροῦντες) marriage and the succession [coming] from it' (*War* 2: 121). That Essenes, according to Josephus, do not in fact take away marriage and resulting offspring completely is a very important concession. After all, male Jews throughout the Roman world did usually marry, in accordance with the commandments of Genesis 1–2: it was a fundamental *mitzvah* that men were obligated to multiply (cf. Philo, *Praem.* 108–9; *Det.* 147–48; *Spec.* 3: 32–4; m.Yeb. 6: 6). In extolling the Essenes, Josephus is very careful to insist that marriage and the procreation of children are of course accepted by them, for an Israel in which they are themselves intrinsically included as being representative. It is simply that the celibate Essenes Josephus defines as his most excellent exemplars of Israel's legal choices, defined as a αἵρεσις, do not live normally as married men within a family situation, teaching their own children, and rather they do not focus on marriage for the production of the legitimate children to which they will direct their attention. An Essene is that manly and strong.

It is when this initial section in *War* 2 is read with what comes later in the passage regarding 'married Essenes' (*War* 2:160–1) that the emphasis on reproduction becomes underscored. Josephus concedes early in the passage that actual Essenes do not do away with marriage in any extremist way, but his focus will not be on those who marry until the end because it would muddy the waters of his rhetoric. He chooses the celibate group for his paradigm, as Philo had done, a paradigm that we shall see with Pliny had become an example of 'wonder' in the ancient world. One can visualize the attitude to marriage Josephus appears to present as the peak of a pyramid of virtue.

To what extent might this represent historical actuality? This concept is similar to the attitude of the early male disciples of Jesus of Nazareth. In the Gospel of Matthew, Jesus himself advises that whoever can be a 'eunuch' for the Kingdom of Heaven should do so (Matt. 19: 10–12), but celibacy is not a

---

[53] See Mason, 'Essenes and Lurking Spartans'.

[54] Myles A. McDonald, *Roman Manliness: Virtus and the Roman Republic* (Cambridge: CUP, 2006) notes *inter alia* that Roman *virtus* lacked any connection with sexual prowess or sexual function at all (168–9).

requirement for discipleship. As Paul also indicated, the celibate state is superior: 'it is good for a man not to touch a woman' (1 Cor. 7: 1) and 'I wish that all people were indeed as I am myself' (1 Cor. 7: 7). Paul states that both men and women who are not married are concerned about the things of the Lord, but the married are concerned about the things of the world, that is, how they might please their partners (1 Cor. 7: 32–5), and their interests are divided; but Paul concedes it is acceptable to be both married and sexually active within marriage (1 Cor. 7: 2–5), since to the unmarried and widows he can affirm that while 'it is good for them if they remain also like me . . . if they do not have self-control, let them marry' (1 Cor. 7: 9). In other words, Paul—the former Pharisee—is here adopting a position that Josephus associates with the Essenes. A superior self-controlled state entails rejecting a sexually active marriage.[55] In the church, as Mark Kuefler has explored, the male celibate would come to be construed as the ultimate in manliness,[56] as in Josephus' description in *War* 2.

However, the church did not separate out married and celibate people into different communities: celibates and non-celibates appear to have eaten together. Nothing in early Christian literature indicates this was an issue in table-fellowship. The celibates of the church are not an elite as such, but their lifestyle might be configured (by Paul) as better.

In *War* 2: 160–1, where this topic is continued, Josephus' middle concentric ring becomes clearer:

> Yet there is also another order (τάγμα) of Essenes, thinking in the same way as the others in lifestyle, customs and ruling, but differing in the opinion concerning marriage. For it would be to cut off (ἀποκόπτειν)[57] a major part of life, the succession, their not being married, and further, if everyone thought the same, it would be to abandon the entire category (γένος).[58]

Here the μέν . . . δέ form is now more opposing, requiring 'but' in the second clause. This differing opinion (δόξα) then concerns the 'disregard of marriage among themselves'. In defining it as 'opinion' the choice of celibacy or marriage becomes a *non-essential* feature of the Essenes, not one that is fundamental to their identity. An Essene could have one opinion or another about marriage, which—as at the beginning of the piece—focuses entirely on

---

[55] See Stefan Heid, *Celibacy in the Early Church: The Beginnings of a Discipline of Obligatory Continence for Clerics in East and West* (San Francisco: Ignatius Press, 2000).

[56] Matthew Kuefler, *The Manly Eunuch: Masculinity, Gender Ambiguity, and Christian Ideology in Late Antiquity* (Chicago: University of Chicago Press, 2001), esp. 170–7.

[57] The word directly correlates with a term for eunuchs, as ἀποκεκομμένος in the LXX Deut. 23: 1, cf. Gal. 5:12. LSJ 203.

[58] Ἔστιν δὲ καὶ ἕτερον Ἐσσηνῶν τάγμα, δίαιταν μὲν καὶ ἔθη καὶ νόμιμα τοῖς ἄλλοις ὁμοφρονοῦν, διεστὼς δὲ τῇ κατὰ γάμον δόξῃ μέγιστον γὰρ ἀποκόπτειν οἴονται τοῦ βίου μέρος, τὴν διαδοχήν, τοὺς μὴ γαμοῦντας, μᾶλλον δέ, εἰ πάντες τὸ αὐτὸ φρονήσειαν, ἐκλιπεῖν ἂν τὸ γένος τάχιστα.

the production of children: the διαδόχη (the succession, cf. *War* 2: 121). As stated at the outset, the celibate Essenes do not abolish marriage and the succession in principle, but Josephus' initial paradigm of Essenes focuses on those who pass it over for an apparently higher goal. The opinion of those Essenes against this practice is because of the importance of maintaining the γένος, a word used at the start of the passage not to refer to Jews as a whole but to the Essenes only as a category who promote a particular interpretation of law (*War* 2: 119). The continuation of the teaching of the rulings within the succession—the boys of the family—is prioritized over and above generously teaching the children of others. One senses here the tremendous power of family for education in the ancient world.

Josephus creates ideal models of marriage elsewhere in his work. Shani Tzoref points out that an absolute model followed by qualification is found in *Ant.* 4: 246–9: the Hebrews must marry free virgins born of good parents, but then Josephus immediately notes marriage to a non-virgin. Likewise, Josephus states in *Apion* 1: 35 and *Ant.* 3: 276 that priests were not permitted to marry a captive woman; in *Life* 414 he, a priest, marries a captive woman.[59]

The model of the celibate Essene is then followed by the model of the marrying Essene, which concludes the passage. But, given that for Josephus 'manly' self-control, rejection of the pleasures, and eschewing of anything womanly forms a chief paradigm governing his portrayal of the Essenes, he emphasizes that these marrying Essenes still eschew pleasure and think of sex in purely utilitarian terms, in *War* 2: 161 insisting:

> However, [only] after testing the women for three years, when they have purified three times for proof of being able to bear children, do they lead [them] away (= marry them).[60]

I use the word 'lead away' for ἄγονται here, since it relates to what Philo has stated also; in this case it encompasses getting married, authority, sexual activity, and cohabitation, away from the girl's parental home. Josephus then stresses that 'they do not consort with the pregnant ones, indicating that the reason to marry is not because of pleasure, but for children'.[61]

This may sound very austere in itself, yet this is what Josephus claims all Jewish men do, as is made clear in *Apion* 2: 199: 'the law only recognizes sex that is according to nature, that is with women, and this only if it is intended to

---

[59] Shani Tzoref, 'Realism, Nominalism, Subjectivism, and Gynephobia: Qumran Texts and Josephus on the Faithlessness of Women,' paper read at the International Society of Biblical Literature Conference, London, 4th–6th July 2011. I am grateful to Shani Tzoref for sharing this with me.

[60] δοκιμάζοντες μέντοι τριετίᾳ τὰς γαμετάς, ἐπειδὰν τρὶς καθαρθῶσιν εἰς πεῖραν τοῦ δύνασθαι τίκτειν, οὕτως ἄγονται.

[61] Mason has argued that Josephus reflects his own ideas in the ideal behaviour of his married Essenes and this is not authentically representative of Essenes; see: 'What Josephus Says,' 435.

be for the sake of [producing] children' (μῖξιν μόνην οἶδεν ὁ νόμος τὴν κατὰ φύσιν τὴν πρὸς γυναῖκα, καὶ ταύτην εἰ μέλλοι τέκνων ἕνεκα γίνεσθαι).[62] In *Ant.* 4: 260, he defines that parents cohabit 'not for the sake of pleasure . . . but in order that they may have children to care for them in their old age and so by them should have what they require'.[63] He then implies that this is an understanding that would have been accepted by all the legal schools: sex is for procreation and practical considerations. There is no legal school that condones sex as permissible for pleasure. In other words, Josephus tells us in *War* that marrying Essenes follow the strict guidelines on what he thinks is agreed by all Jews regarding sex.[64]

Such an attitude is not that of later rabbinic Judaism. There were rabbis like Rabbi Eliezer, who apparently had sex with his wife only 'as if being forced to by a demon' (b.Ned. 20a), who believed it was only for procreation, but this was qualified in numerous ways, as Daniel Boyarin has explored.[65] The rabbis thought that sex was even appropriate in the last trimester of pregnancy, at a time when it would be good for mother, baby, and birth (b.Niddah 31a). For the rabbis, sex within marriage was essentially a good thing in itself, and marriage can be justified even if it does not produce children, as can contraception.[66] One wonders if, in *Apion*, Josephus presents an Essene understanding as normative for all Jews when there was in fact a more nuanced discussion taking place. For example, Philo believed that marriage itself was justified even if no children resulted, on the basis of the high value he placed on love and companionship (*Spec. Leg.* 3: 34–36, cf. *Spec. Leg.* 1: 138; *Quaest. Gen.* 1: 26),[67] which presumably indicated that he accepted that sex could happen with little or no hope of producing children. But perhaps Josephus' favouring of austere

---

[62] As a further parallel, in the Loeb edition Thackeray translates *Apion* 2: 202 as indicating that no man should have intercourse with a pregnant woman, though John Barclay, *Flavius Josephus: Against Apion: Translation and Commentary* (*Josephus* 10; Leiden: Brill, 2006), 286, argues it should be understood in relation to touching a miscarried or aborted fetus, in that it would cause corpse impurity.

[63] I am grateful to Shani Tzoref for this reference and her comments on a draft of this chapter.

[64] Mason, on the other hand, suggests that Josephus may have invented the marriage-endorsing type of Essenes, 'What Josephus Says,' 447–50; *War* 2: 130. However, it would have been surprising for Josephus to invent something that complicates his description without adding anything beneficial to his rhetoric on the Essenes. Rather, the rhetorical minimization of the married Essenes—despite an acknowledgment of their existence—would reflect Josephus' recognition that the simple male celibate model of Essenes did not adequately reflect the actuality of the Essenes he had surely encountered. Details such as the exact type of wrap the women wore in the purification bath (*War* 2: 161) could hardly be expected in a fantasy.

[65] Daniel Boyarin, *Carnal Israel: Reading Sex in Talmudic Culture* (Berkeley: University of California Press, 1993), 46–57.

[66] See Rabbi Simeon ben Yohai, *Song Rabbah*, 1.31, and widowers can remarry even women shown to be infertile (b. Yeb. 61b); see Boyarin, *Carnal Israel*, 53–6. Boyarin himself suggests an earlier Palestinian discourse on sexuality that was more ascetic than the rabbinic.

[67] David Winston, 'Philo and the Rabbis on Sex and the Body,' *Poetics Today* 19 (1998): 41–62, at 53–4.

Essene legal rulings as being representative of what all Jews should do is not such a surprise given how he presents the Essenes consistently in his writings as the best of all the legal schools in being so manly.

If sex is only allowable strictly for procreation, and this is the (only?) purpose of marriage, it does leave open the possibility that Josephus imagined that married Essenes might join a community of celibate men after their wives were past the age of childbearing. However, we are not told by Josephus the ages of the two orders, nor are we told how many are in one or the other, nor are we told that all the Essenes who spurn marriage and teach students have always been celibate and unmarried. Josephus simply does not give the information that would create a holistic picture. He only states that the marriage-accepting group are 'thinking in the same way to the others in lifestyle, customs and law' (*War* 2: 160). If this is so, everything he has just said about the first group's lifestyle (δίαιτα) applies to the married men too.

In this case, given what Josephus states about the untrustworthiness of women and the issue of purity regarding entrance grades (*War* 2: 150), it seems quite likely that he imagines that the celibate Essenes could not have been comfortable about the sexually active married Essenes and would have looked down on them in terms of the hierarchy of purity, so that they did not share meals with them. That the issue of women's trustworthiness is expressly configured in terms of *purity* follows from what appears in *War* 2: 161, that they have the same baths as men, but wear different (more modest) clothing. The purity standards of Essene wives were clearly critical for married male Essenes. Furthermore, since the baths are configured as being designed to prepare people for the eating of a pure meal (see below), then it would follow that Essene wives also ate a pure meal.

What Josephus does by the structure of his description is to establish the marriage-eschewing Essenes as the prototype that is associated with fundamental Essene characteristics, with the other group a kind of inferior alternative. He focuses on the unusual (celibate males) as the standard model for his manly Judaeans. Taken independently, nowhere does Josephus in *War* state anything explicitly in terms of which Essene order is in fact the larger one numerically, or that the celibate Essenes are superior. However, in putting the celibates first, Josephus identifies the marriage-eschewing order as a kind of standard. The reason why Josephus marginalizes the married Essenes is simple: they muddy the rhetorical picture. Given that the focus was on manliness, it was the marriage-eschewing Essenes who were the most manly, in that they exhibited the highest degree of self-control. However, Josephus' own opinion was that the rejection of marriage, in pursuit of such extreme manliness (that of the Spartans), was not quite right. In *Apion* 2: 273 he asks, 'How were the Lacedaemonians not likely to observe the law of avoiding contact with outsiders and the eschewing of marriage, or the Eleans and Thebans the unnatural and licentious mixing with males?' Celibacy and homosexuality are linked together here as being un-Judaean; the 'correct' form of Judaean sexuality is indeed that of the married Essenes: sex within marriage, and only engaged in for procreation. It is a type of asceticism, but that of the Lacedae-monians is one step 'higher' in respect to *virtus* as configured for a Graeco-Roman audience. Josephus then modifies the normative Judaean/Essene here to focus on the celibates primarily, even though for him personally this was not his ideal.

In Philo's presentation in *Hypothetica* there was not the same concern with *virtus*, and Philo did not focus on the untrustworthiness of women so much as the distraction of married life. As we saw, Philo appears to indicate that marriage is something for younger men, and the men he considers as exem-plary are elderly and beyond the impulses of passion. In the same way that Philo's presentation of Essenes who have moved on from cohabitation does not deal with the issue of the women and children who have been left behind when men join celibate Essene communities, so here, there are 'hidden' women and children who remain in the shadows of the rhetoric.

After setting the template in *War* 2: 119–21, Josephus marches on through a survey of features that characterize this exemplary legal choice, with the first block being *War* 2: 122–7. The Essenes despise wealth and have a community of goods in which all share equally, with a fund for the aged and sick (122). They consider oil a disgrace (κηλῖδα δ' ὑπολαμβάνουσι τοὖλαιον), and will rub it off if they get it on their skin, 'because they hold it in esteem to be dry (unoiled) and to dress in white' (τὸ γὰρ αὐχμεῖν ἐν καλῷ τίθενται, λευχειμονεῖν τε διαπαντός) (123). They elect by a show of hands (χειροτονητοὶ) the over-seers (ἐπιμεληταί) for their communities, determining their duties collectively (123). They settle in large numbers in 'every town', rather than dwelling in one city exclusively (124), and welcome all other Essenes, from different places, in their houses, so they carry no possessions (or food) when travelling except weapons against robbers (124–5). Every city (where they dwell) has one person dealing with hospitality to strangers, including providing clothing and necessities (126). They are like children under a hard discipline, and do not change their clothes or shoes until they are worn out (126). They share things (127).[68]

As we have seen with Philo, the sharing of goods is a common philosophical 'good'.[69] Philo mentions that there is a communal fund designed to pay for treatments (buying expensive medicines?) and that the junior members of the communities look after the elders (*Prob.* 87; *Hypoth.* 11: 13). Josephus' carrying of weapons (*War* 2: 124–5) is important to note, and acts as

---

[68] For detailed commentary on this see Mason, *War* 2, 100–5.

[69] See above and also Brian Capper, 'The Palestinian Cultural Context of Earliest Christian Community of Goods,' from Richard J. Bauckham (ed.), *The Book of Acts in its Palestinian Setting* (Grand Rapids, Eerdmans, 1995), 323–56.

corrective to the notion derived from a superficial reading of Philo (*Prob.* 78) that the Essenes were pacifists; this is simply not indicated in our sources. Josephus' evidence of Essene weaponry is not contradictory to Philo, but indicates only a misreading of Philo. The Essenes travel light, but are armed.

The mention of avoiding oil is not presented as being to do with purity,[70] as Beall has suggested, but rather Josephus focuses on the Essenes wanting a dry (unoiled) skin. Lubricating oil is indicative of softness and care, or a vestige of personal pampering that was a common form of self-care (Matt. 6: 17). It connects with the portrayal of manly, tough Essenes eschewing all softness, as Mason has pointed out.[71] Their avoidance of oil is linked with the avoidance of colour in clothing, indicating a rejection of sensory pleasure in regard to their appearance, when being oiled was a usual part of ancient grooming and body-maintenance. They are to look plain, untended, and rough, and not soft in any way. The dry (unoiled) skin and uncoloured clothing links with the fact that they do not change their clothing or shoes until these are worn out. If Josephus had wished to indicate that the Essenes avoided oil for purity, or advertized their purity by means of white dress, then he probably would have said it here, but this is not his emphasis in this section; the concern is to promote the image of roughness, self-denial, discipline, and 'manliness'.

Election of officers by the group tells us something of their democratic processes within the society, but we are not told anything about the pool from which the officers might be drawn; we do not know here whether they are priests, for example. While the levels of Essene membership are determined without any reference to whether someone is levitical or not, the officials would be drawn from only those who are full members (the top of the four categories). Within this group of full members, Josephus tells us nothing about sub-divisions. While Mason assumes the election is 'not according to caste',[72] this is not actually said by Josephus; he says nothing either way at this point. It may or may not have been the case that the candidates for positions were levitical. Later on, it is stated explicitly that a priest gives a blessing over food (*War* 2: 131), but there is no indication that this priest is elected to do this. However, in *Ant.* 18: 22 this is an elected position.

Josephus interrupts this general survey of Essene features to give an account of their daily routine. They get up before sunrise, say ancient prayers directed towards the rising sun, and then go to their work (*War* 2: 128). They assemble and wash their bodies in cold water every day at the fifth hour (around 11 a.m.), wearing simple linen cloths, and then congregate in a private room

---

[70] The translation of κηλίς, 'stain', 'disgrace', as 'defilement' by Thackeray is misleading; oil on the skin is clearly indicated as a 'blot', not a welcome substance, but this is not to say it was necessarily impure, *contra* Kenneth Atkinson and Jodi Magness, 'Josephus's Essenes and the Qumran Community', *JBL* 129 (2010): 336–40.

[71] Mason, 'Essenes of Josephus' Judean War', 267–8; id. *War* 2, 101–2.

[72] See Mason, *War* 2, 103, for parallels.

where no one 'heterodox' can come in, thereafter going to the dining room as if it is a holy place (129), where, after they have sat down, a (male) baker gives them bread and a cook gives them each only one plate of food (130). A priest says a blessing, after which they eat (131) and another prayer is said at the end of the meal, praising God as the giver of life (131). They then put away their cloths as if they are sacred and go back to work (131). Later they eat in the same way, along with any guests (132), and here they are very quiet in their house, speaking in turn, making outsiders (τοῖς ἔξωθεν) feel there is some great mystery (133).[73] This last comment is remarkable, since it reads as if Josephus—or his source— has in fact been a guest in observing an evening meal; the language expresses being an outsider, and awe. It also indicates that the Essenes accepted people classified as 'outsiders' as part of their community (see 137).

These mealtimes of the Essenes are described to indicate how antithetical they are to usual mealtimes, where chatting would be expected. The meals are orderly, dignified, quiet, and focused. Only one plate of food is served, indicating no sensuous wish for food, with individual dishes allowing for careful equality of servings.[74] In many ways this parallels a similar description by Philo of the mealtimes of the Therapeutae (*Contempl.* 65–82).

The passage then continues as if picking up from *War* 2: 127, which deals with personal sharing of items. Josephus notes that 'in all other matters nothing is done without overseers instructing', except that there are two other things for individual choice: aiding the needy and compassion to the destitute, but they are not allowed to give aid to relatives without permission from the overseers (134).

In stating this, Josephus indicates that the Essenes are not entirely self-servicing and neglectful of outsiders, since two matters left to individual discretion are defined as ἐπικουρία and ἔλεος, aid and compassion (*War* 2: 134). In other words, the Essenes are permitted 'to help the worthy when asked . . . and to provide sustenance to the needy'. These must be outside the society, since those within the society are cared for communally. They are asked to provide ἐπικουρία, 'aid', a word which is broad in meaning. This aid or assistance was a matter they themselves could individually decide upon, though in terms of limits Josephus states that, when giving to relatives, they needed express permission from the ἐπίτροποι, the 'guardians', or 'overseers', perhaps to avoid family exploitation and the draining of communal resources. One wonders, though, whether here the hidden women and children are alluded to.

Josephus mentions that the Essenes avoid swearing oaths, but speak the truth always (*War* 2: 135). This is not inconsistent with what is stated a little later concerning great oaths sworn upon entry to the order (139), since it

---

[73] For detailed commentary see Mason, *War* 2, 105–8.

[74] See Atkinson and Magness, *Josephus's Essenes*, 332; Beall, *Josephus' Description of the Essenes*, 59.

concerns swearing the truth by appeal to God, rather than an entry oath of a true assent.

Josephus then writes (*War* 2: 136):

> They have an extraordinary enthusiasm concerning the works of the ancients, especially selecting those for the benefit of soul and body; thus with these they search out roots, remedies and properties of stones for treatment of diseases.

The 'stones' referred to here would indicate minerals: rocks ground up and used with plants (Theophrastus, *De Lapidus* 3: 5, 41: 1; 48: 1).[75] The Essenes are clearly concerned with medicines. Their aid then may be connected with this activity.

The interest in healing is also specifically alluded to a few lines on in Josephus' account, when he mentions the importance of not divulging the 'names of the angels' (*War* 2: 142).[76] In Jubilees 10: 10–17, Noah is given special knowledge by angels: 'And the healing of all their illnesses together with their seductions were told Noah so that he might heal by means of the herbs of the earth. And Noah wrote everything in a book just as we taught him according to every kind of healing.' In Jubilees, medical knowledge is passed to Noah's son Shem (cf. b.Baba Bathra 16). Here demonic agency is suggested as the cause of illness and the knowledge of medicinal cures is given to the chosen few (Jub. 48: 10). A 'Book of Shem, the son of Noah' was cited by 'Asaph the Jew', a Byzantine Jewish physician, which contained the story of the angel Raphael ('God heals') instructing Noah's family on drugs to take from the trees, plants, and roots of the earth.[77]

In the Book of Enoch, it is said that the *rephaim*/'watchers' (or angels)— under the control of Azazel—taught humanity a secret use of root cuttings and plants (7: 1; 8: 3, 'eternal secrets which are in heaven' 9: 6) and the angel Raphael expels them, and heals the earth (10). Raphael is set over all the diseases and wounds of humanity in the Parables of Enoch (40: 9). Knowledge of the names of angels provides people with exorcistic and healing powers. To this evidence, we can add also the Testament of Solomon, since here demons control humanity 'because people do not know the names of the angels who rule over us' (*Test. Sol.* 5: 4–5). The comment by Josephus concerning how strongly the Essenes guarded the names of the angels then relates to the Essene practices of healing, and fits well with what we know of healing practice in Second Temple Judaism.[78]

---

[75] See Mason, *War* 2, 110.

[76] Samuel S. Kottek, 'The Essenes and Medicine,' *Clio Medica* 18 (1983), 81–99, at 83; id. *Medicine and Hygiene in the Works of Flavius Josephus* (Leiden: Brill, 1994).

[77] Kottek, 'Essenes and Medicine', 84.

[78] Samuel Kottek notes that it was not only the names of angels that could be used to effect cures: a physician (אסי) in Sepphoris used the name of God (j.Yom. 3: 7 [40d]).

After this, Josephus describes the situation of those who want to live the Essene lifestyle. For one year new entrants conceptually remain 'outside' (ἔξω) the society, while appearing to be included by embracing the same lifestyle (δίαιτα). A new entrant is given a cloth to use for purification (before eating a meal), a small mattock for digging a hole for defecating (cf. *War* 2: 148–9 for the procedure), and white clothing for general wear (137). After this time, after proof of self-control, he proceeds nearer the lifestyle and partakes in the purification of purer water, without participating in the συμβιώσεις, a word which means 'companionships' literally, but in context appears to indicate the meals. He has another two years of proving himself worthy before he is admitted into the 'throng' (εἰς τὸν ὅμιλον) (138) and—after swearing oaths (139)—he is allowed to touch the common food.[79]

The admission of people to the society on merit in *War* 2: 137–8 correlates with Philo, *Prob.* 76–7 and *Hypoth.* 11: 2. There are then in Josephus three years with three different levels before someone can become a full member of the society, pure enough to be allowed to eat the common food. Combined with what has been noted above about 'outsiders' at meals, this seems to mean that those embarking on the path towards full membership can observe the full members at their mealtimes, while still remaining 'outside' this group. They are nevertheless engaged in following the Essene lifestyle, despite not being pure enough to participate in these meals with full members. They had 'observer' status, while they would need to eat separately.

The oaths of commitment are that a new entrant will observe piety to God, justice to people, and never wrong anyone; he will hate the unrighteous and struggle with the righteous (*War* 2: 139); he will keep faith with all, especially the ruling authorities, because no ruler is in power except by God's will (140). He swears that if ever he should rule he will not abuse his authority or show superiority in clothing or in any way (140). An Essene vows at entry that on taking public office he will not be superior in his manner. He will be truthful, expose liars, not gain from his position, and will stay true to the society (*War* 2: 140–1). He will always love truth and expose liars. He will not steal or gain (from his position). He will keep nothing secret from the other members of the society, or give away their secrets to outsiders, even if tortured to death (141). He swears also to pass on the dogmas as he received them, not to steal, to preserve the books of the society and the names of the angels/messengers (142). If anyone has sinned badly he is expelled from the society, though that person—bound by oaths and practices—can starve since he, 'grass-eating', cannot eat normal food, so such a person is often taken back in the end (143–4). In legal judgements they are very just and careful, since in their

---

[79] Mason, *War* 2, 111–13.

decisions they do not pass a sentence in a court of fewer than 100 men, and the decision reached is unchangeable (145).[80]

All of this is extremely important. In terms of what Josephus states concerning the Essenes as a whole, it may be noted that he indicates they had actual juridical authority at the heart of public life. Josephus states that the Essenes had their own court to decide verdicts, even a sentence of death for blasphemy (*War* 2: 143–5), the implication possibly being that they did not accept the authority of the High Priest's court. Such a statement parallels Philo's mention of the Essenes being autonomous in law (*Prob.* 91). As for the main High Priestly court, Martin Goodman has persuasively argued that the council was effectively 'an extension of the High Priest'[81] (see *War* 1: 208–11) and could be variable in composition. Here Josephus presents a court that stands in an independent position; but it does not indicate a sectarian court separate from Jerusalem life.[82]

In taking up public office, an Essene will not abuse his authority or show superiority in clothing or in any way; he will always love truth and expose liars; he will not steal or gain (from his position). In terms of Essene loyalty to rulers, Josephus writes that a new member must swear 'to keep faith/loyalty forever with all, especially with those exercising power (τοῖς κρατοῦσιν), for no one is able to rule (ἄρχειν) but by authority of God' (*War* 2: 140). That Josephus does not mean to refer to the leaders of the αἵρεσις here is clear from what follows, when, quite separately, Josephus writes that they hold it to be good/beautiful 'to obey the elders' (*War* 2: 146). However, this loyalty to rulers may be hyperbole, since the Essenes in Josephus are not averse to predicting the downfall of particularly bad royal rulers: as we saw in *War* 2: 112–13 (= *Ant.* 17: 345–8), the ethnarch Archelaus is warned of his impending doom by Simon the Essene. Destiny seems to be the underlying paradigm here: if God is in charge of all things, then even bad rulers are placed in their positions by God; this does not mean the rulers are good, and this does not stop the Essenes criticizing such rulers or predicting their downfall.

Josephus goes on to state that the Essenes (in their court) will pass judgement of death on anyone who blasphemes against the name of 'the lawgiver', ὁ νομοθέτης, meaning Moses, whom they rank second after God in awe (*War* 2: 145).[83] This relates back to the mention of the Essene court that enabled

---

[80] Mason, *War* 2, 113–16.

[81] Martin Goodman, *The Ruling Class of Judaea: The Origins of the Jewish Revolt against Rome A. D. 66–70* (Cambridge: CUP, 1987), 115 and see 111–12.

[82] *Contra* Beall, *Josephus' Description of the Essenes*, 91–2.

[83] See Beall, *Josephus' Description of the Essenes*, 92–4, *contra* André Dupont-Sommer, *The Essene Writings from Qumran*, trans. by Geza Vermes of *Les Écrits esséniens découverts près de la Mer Morte* (Oxford: Blackwell, 1961), 31, 358, who thinks this refers to the Teacher of Righteousness mentioned in Qumran literature. Thackeray translates this as 'their lawgiver', inserting a personal pronoun where there is none; Whiston had rendered this likewise as 'their legislator'

them to decree a death sentence for such blasphemy (*War* 2: 142). That Josephus uses the term 'the lawgiver' rather than 'our lawgiver' does not mean that there is a separate teacher for Essenes apart from Moses.[84] Moses is the lawgiver for all Jews (Mal. 4: 4; Deut. 11:13), 'an instrument for the Divine voice' (*Ant.* 4: 329). The term νομοθέτης was known as an epithet for Moses in the Graeco-Roman world,[85] and was used by Josephus for Moses: 'hearing Moses the lawgiver was hearing God' (*Ant.* 3:93, cf. *Ant.* 1: 18, 20, 22 et al.). In *War* 2: 152, Josephus describes how the Romans tried to make the Essenes 'blaspheme the lawgiver or eat unpermitted food'.[86]

Josephus continues by affirming the Essenes' obedience. They will always obey their 'elders' and the majority (opinion), so that if there are ten sitting together, one will not talk if nine want silence (146). They will not spit 'into middles'[87] (in front) or to the right (147).

Kenneth Atkinson and Jodi Magness note that spitting was prohibited in the precincts of the Temple (m.Ber. 9: 5; t.Ber. 6: 19) as it was in temples in general (Epictetus, *Diss.* 4: 11: 32),[88] but Josephus does not indicate a total ban on spitting, or connect it with purity, but rather this is a rejection of spitting in a certain way in a context he has established of 'ten sitting together' (δέκα γοῦν συγκαθεζομένων), where one will not speak if nine desire silence, respecting majority opinion, 'and they guard against spitting into middles or on the right side'. This would also then follow on as something concerned with care for the majority.[89] As Thackeray noted,[90] the Jerusalem Talmud contains a similar ban which allows spitting to the left or behind while wearing *tefillin*, that is, while praying, but not spitting in front or to the right (j.Ber. 3: 5, 6d). In Josephus, if the 'ten sitting together' indicates a quorum (*minyan*) of men assembled for

---

but added the mention of Moses in brackets. In Hippolytus, *Haer.* 9: 25 in the phrasing: τιμῶσι δὲ τὸν νομοθέτην μετὰ τὸν θεὸν, 'they honour the lawgiver after God', Moses is being clearly indicated by reference to what appears in *Haer.* 9: 17, where Moses teaches the law. This indicates that Hippolytus understood there was no separate teacher indicated here.

[84] A notion well refuted by Mason, *War* 2, 116.

[85] John G. Gager, *Moses in Greco-Roman Paganism* (New York: Abingdon Press, 1972), 27; John Lierman, *The New Testament Moses: Christian Perception of Moses and Israel in the Setting of Jewish Religion* (Tubingen: Mohr Siebeck, 2004); Wayne Meeks, *The Prophet King: Moses Traditions and Johannine Christology* (NT Suppl. 14; Leiden: Brill, 1967); Louis H. Feldman, 'Parallel Lives of Two Lawgivers: Josephus' Moses and Plutarch's Lycurgus', in Jonathan Edmundson, Steve Mason, and James Rives (eds), *Flavius Josephus and Flavian Rome* (Oxford: OUP, 2005), 209–43; Louis H. Feldman, 'Josephus' Portrait of Moses', *JQR* 82 (1992): 285–328; id. 'Josephus' Portrait of Moses, Part Two', *JQR* 83 (1992): 7–50; id. 'Josephus' Portrait of Moses, Part Three', *JQR* 83 (1993): 301–30.

[86] See also Philo, *Hypoth.* 11: 1.

[87] See Mason, *War* 2, 117.

[88] In my view the full stop placed in Niese's edition between these two clauses is not quite right, and should be a comma.

[89] The suggestions by Mason, *War* 2: 117, that the Essenes refuse to spit on their bellies for health or fortune does not follow the rhetoric here.

[90] Thackeray, *Josephus*, 379, and see Atkinson and Magness, *Josephus's Essenes*, 328.

Scripture reading and prayer (m.Meg. 4: 3; b.Meg. 23b, cf. Lev. 22:32; Num. 16: 21), then complete silence existed until an appropriate time for the readings or prayers to be uttered. The following statement regarding the strictness of refraining from work on Sabbath days (cf. Exod. 35: 3; Jer. 17: 21–7) likewise provides an overall impression of small assemblies, especially on the Sabbath, with each connected observation (sitting in silence, not spitting badly, not working at all in any way) linked by καί, 'and'.

The word συγκαθεζομένων, 'sitting together', harks back to the use of the word καθισάντων, 'sitting', in *War* 2: 130, in association with the pure meals, but meals are not the only time ten men may sit together. A context of mealtimes regarding the spitting injunction would in fact create an absurd situation in which a man is allowed to spit towards someone seated at the table on his left but not onto the table. The 'ten sitting' model of *War* 2: 146–7, combined with the spitting direction rule, indicates there was in a group of ten men sufficient space on the left and behind the person to spit, but spitting ahead would mean spitting 'into middles' of people. Early synagogues in fact generally have an arrangement in which stone seating was created around a central open space (see Plate 1). The plural εἰς μέσους, 'into middles', combined with the singular τὸ δεξιὸν μέρος would indicate this collective open space in the centre, hence the plural is relative to the fact that there are many individuals around it, while the reference to the right was relative to the individual, so the singular was used. The concern remains the acceptability of spitting in regard to members of the group. With such a ruling, it is a lesson to us about the different world this text comes from, a world where spitting etiquette is critical. Importantly, it implies a synagogue space.

Josephus then states that on seventh days the Essenes are stricter than all Jews in refraining from work. They prepare all food the day before to avoid lighting a fire, do not pick up any object, or even defecate (147). He then indicates that going to the toilet for them required 'selecting more deserted places' (τοὺς ἐρημοτέρους τόπους ἐκλεγόμενοι) where they go with a mattock (σκαλίς) or small axe (ἀξινίδιον),[91] and they dig a hole a foot deep. Then, 'with a cloak hiding [them] around (περικαλύψαντες θοιμάτιον)', they pass motions μή τὰς αὐγὰς ὑβρίζοιεν, 'without offending the rays of God' (148–9).

Viewed from a Jewish perspective, this simply shows particular care in being obedient to Deut. 23: 13–15, where the Israelites at war are instructed to go to an allocated portion/place (יָד)[92] outside the camp in order to dig a hole with a stick.[93] The fastidiousness of the Essenes in regard to toileting indicates that they always took care to leave the many towns in which

---

[91] See K. D. White, *Agricultural Implements of the Roman World* (Cambridge: CUP, 2010), 60–8.

[92] See Jastrow, 563, sense 3. LXX τόπος.

[93] LXX πάσσαλος, a wooden stick or peg.

Josephus describes them living (*War* 2: 124)[94] in order to go to special latrines outside. While Albert Baumgarten reads Josephus as indicating the Essenes squatted where there was open ground, in an ad hoc fashion,[95] the description does not state this. That the cloaks are described as protecting a view from God above would indicate that Josephus imagined a roofless zone, but with fencing that would have otherwise protected them from view; there is no mention of the cloak preventing a view by other people from ground level. The curious situation is that while normally a person might well cloak themselves for modesty where others might see them, the Essenes—in their latrines—wrap themselves in cloaks to protect themselves from *God's* gaze alone.

The mention that Essenes needed to wash, as if defiled or polluted (μεμιασμένοις), after passing a motion would likely mean that Josephus thought there were washing facilities proximate: not necessarily entire *miqvaot* but sufficient water for their requirements. Josephus then indicates toilet areas that have been selected, marked, fenced (but not roofed or entirely roofed), and adjacent to water: properly defined installations in a land where the agricultural use of the landscape was intense and immediately outside a town there were not many uncultivated wild places. The deep holes dug within these areas meant there was no open sewer or pit to attract flies, rendering them particularly clean in a hot climate where flies are everywhere. These are the best toilet facilities imaginable, as befitting the purest and best Judaean legal school.

This description by Josephus serves the purpose of indicating that the Essene demands of purity outstrip any concern with personal comfort. Their restrictions on the Sabbath, that no one should work by walking out of the town to the toilet grounds, would have led to particular personal discomfort and endurance.

Josephus has God seeing human behaviour, with rays from above, as believed of the rays of the sun-god Apollo. In describing God as Apollo, one can note just how much Josephus has a Roman audience in mind, for whom such language would be understandable,[96] but this does not mean the Essenes equated God with Apollo.

---

[94] Mason, *War* 2, 119.

[95] Albert I. Baumgarten, 'The Temple Scroll, Toilet Practices and the Essenes', *Jewish History* 10 (1996): 9–20; Jodi Magness, *The Archaeology of Qumran and the Dead Sea Scrolls* (Grand Rapids: Eerdmans, 2002), 105–13; Joe E. Zias, James D. Tabor, and Stephanie Harter-Laiheugue, 'Toilets at Qumran, the Essenes, and the Scrolls: New Anthropological Data and Old Theories', *RQ* 22 (2006): 631–40, the latter disputed by Ian Werrett, 'A Scroll in One Hand and a Mattock in the Other: Latrines, Essenes, and Khirbet Qumran', *RQ* 23 (2008): 475–89. For toilet habits in Judaea at this time see Jodi Magness, *Stone and Dung, Oil and Spit* (Grand Rapids: Eerdmans, 2011), 130–44.

[96] See the examples in Mason, *War* 2, 119, and his observation that Philo uses similar terminology: *Fug.* 136; *Mut.* 6; *Somn.* 1: 72, 116, 239; *Praem.* 25; *Mos.* 1: 66.

Rather, the biblical prescription the Essenes followed concludes with the assertion:

> For the LORD goes about the inside of your camp to guard you and put your enemies at your mercy. Your camp must therefore be a holy place. The LORD must not see anything indecent there or he will leave you. (Deut. 23: 15)

This indicates that an anthropomorphized God is watching for unseemly actions within an encampment, including defecation. In keeping this commandment, and being ultra-modest and clean in terms of the toilet habits, the Essenes were ensuring the favour of God.

Josephus then notes that the Essenes are divided 'into four parts' (εἰς μοίρας τέσσαρας) from junior to senior, the junior imparting impurity to a senior (150). The focus is then on a growing degree of purity that separates out each level. This needs to be read with *War* 2: 137–8, as it seems this is all it actually refers to. There are three grades connected with the three years of the entrance process with gathering degrees of purity, until someone becomes a full member.

After this we learn that the Essenes 'have longevity, as most of them live over a hundred years' (*War* 2:151). This should alert us to other hyperbolic elements of Josephus' description, such as the situation of extreme toileting (that takes no account of illness or infirmity), but his point also demonstrates a key theme. In this case, Josephus' apparent creation of a feature of Essene identity—they all live past a hundred years—reflects a notion that longevity accompanies a healthy and good lifestyle, an endorsement found also in Lucian's *Macrobioi* as applying to many philosophers and orators as a result of careful diet and exercise (*Macr.* 6; see esp. 18–19, 23). Josephus moves in the same sort of world of exotic commonplaces, and it all fits with his emphasis of diet and exercise producing good health (as also Noah in *Ant.* 1: 104–6 or Daniel in *Ant.* 10: 190–2). That lifestyle affected health was well known in antiquity.[97] In *War* 2 Josephus focuses not only on the philosophical excellence of the legal school but also on the Essenes' simple and regular lifestyle, replete with much bathing for purity. A simple life with numerous purifications was both a spiritual and a material prophylactic.

The Essenes, according to Josephus, do not care about danger or death, so that even when the Romans tortured them to make them blaspheme their lawgiver or eat some forbidden thing, they died unyielding (*War* 2: 152–3). They release their souls at death as if expecting them back again. They believe that the body is destructible but the soul is not, and once released from materiality it will go to an 'abode beyond the sea' which is much like 'the

---

[97] See Fred Rosner, 'Pharmacology and Dietetics in the Bible and Talmud', in Irene Jacob (ed.), *The Healing Past: Pharmaceuticals in the Biblical and Rabbinic World* (Brill: Leiden, 1993), 1–26 at p.6.

Isles of the Blessed' (156), but evil people's souls will go to never-ending punishment (156); in this he refers to the punishments of Sisyphus, Tantalus, Ixion, and Tityus (2: 156, cf. Homer, *Odyssey* 11). The Essenes, however, look for a reward after death (157).

This statement on Essene beliefs about the afterlife has been much debated, the key question being whether Josephus' comment indicates that the Essenes rejected belief in the bodily resurrection of the dead by means of an anthropological dualism in which matter and spirit are contrasted. Casey Elledge's careful examination has shown that Josephus does not discuss the resurrection of the dead in the other seven places where it might occur,[98] ambiguously in regard to the Pharisees, since he says the souls of the good migrate into a 'different body' (*War* 2: 163), which concurs better with Pythagoraean concepts of the transmigration of the soul.[99] In addition, Elledge notes that Josephus was cognizant of Graeco-Roman mythological concepts of the afterlife and used them elsewhere (*Ant.* 1: 73; *Apion* 2: 161–2), and in passages where he might refer to the typically Judaean concepts he 'has translated these underlying beliefs into a Hellenistic philosophical synthesis that has obscured their original forms'.[100] The reference to the Essenes dying as if they expected to receive their souls back again (*War* 2: 153) can be paralleled with *War* 3: 374, where there is mention of the return of souls to 'undefiled bodies': this might be the closest Josephus gets to hinting at some form of resurrection that was not so much about resurrection of a physical body but transformation of that body into a spiritual entity (see 1 Cor. 15: 44).[101]

Josephus then notes that some of the Essenes claim to foretell the future, after being instructed in the sacred books, diverse purifications, and sayings of the prophets, and they rarely fail in predictions (159). This relates back to the point at which they have been introduced, in *War*, following on from Simon's prediction of Archelaus' downfall, ensuring we are reminded of it. What is interesting here is the means by which predictions are made. The ordering is slightly odd, with the purifications placed in between what is essentially reading of the law and the Prophets. However, by placing purifications centrally Josephus makes these essential to the predictive arts.

As we have seen, Josephus then adds at the end that there is another order of Essenes who do marry for procreation, and who are otherwise exactly the same as the others. They have wives who have three years of probation (like the men) and who show also that they have had three purifications (following

---

[98] Casey D. Elledge, *Life after Death in Early Judaism: The Evidence of Josephus* (WUNT ii/208; Tübingen: Mohr Siebeck, 2006), 94–5. These instances are *Apion* 2: 218–19; *War* 1: 648–50; 3: 372–6; 6: 46–9; 7: 343–57; *Ant.* 1: 229–31 and 17: 354.

[99] Ibid. 50–1, 60–1.

[100] Ibid. 98, and see p.100 where there is discussion of the widespread knowledge of the *decensus ad inferos* myth.

[101] As suggested by Mason, *Flavius Josephus on the Pharisees*, 169–70.

menstrual periods) to demonstrate fertility. These wives on probation are then in the same position as the men who wish to join the order, with additional issues attached to their fertility. Since sex is only justified for the procreation of children, infertile wives would lead to accusations of having sex for pleasure. They, like the men, appear to ascend in purity across levels. The women wear a linen wrap in the bath—while the men wear a loincloth (2: 160–1). All this reads as an afterthought by Josephus, even though he has signalled this 'secondary' class of Essenes at the beginning of his description, and I have therefore considered them above.

As a final observation on this passage, the clothing of the Essenes referred to at various points is interesting to note. As discussed above, the reference to wearing white clothing is linked with having dry, unoiled skin, and is indicated as a resistance to sensory pleasure (*War* 2: 123). In *War* 2: 137 a new entrant to the society is given a cloth wrap (περίζωμα) and 'white clothing' (λευκήν ἐσθῆτα) as part of his equipment. The Essenes work (in white clothing) until the fifth hour and then assemble in one place, where they 'gird their loins with linen cloths' (λινοῖς) and 'bathe their bodies in cold water' (129). Josephus does not say they put on any new outer clothing, and so it appears that they go off directly to a pure meal resiliently wearing these (uncomfortably wet) linen wraps. After this pure meal, 'they lay aside the clothing like holy vestments' and again return to work (131), though obviously they must have changed back into their ordinary clothing. Later on, when Josephus acknowledges the order of Essenes that marry, he notes that in the bath 'the women wrap garments around [themselves]' (ἀμπεχομέναις ἐνδύματα) as the men wear a cloth wrap (περίζωμα) (*War* 2: 161), in order to preserve their modesty. Josephus also indicates in *War* 2: 148 that the Essenes wore cloaks (ἱμάτια). Clothing would not be replaced until it was threadbare (*War* 2: 126).

Nothing in Josephus' description indicates that the wearing of white clothing indicates anything but austerity and lack of sensory interest (in colour), but elsewhere in Josephus white clothing is the attire for people going to the Temple. According to Josephus, when David heard that Bathsheba's child had died he changed from black to white (festive) clothing (*Ant.* 7: 156), and Solomon also wears white for the Temple (*Ant.* 8: 146). After Archelaus has mourned for his father, Herod, he also changes into white clothing and goes to the Temple (*War* 2: 1). White clothing does not in Josephus equate with linen garments worn by priests: in *Ant.* 2: 327 the people of Jerusalem wear white to come to the Temple and the priests wear the linen garments prescribed by law.[102] It is wrong to think that white indicates linen as if a particular kind of material has the sole monopoly on the colour. The linen cloths worn by the Essenes are the wraps they wear in the baths and during their pure meals, not

---

[102] Sanders, *Judaism*, 97.

their everyday white clothing.[103] E. P. Sanders initially assumed that the Essenes were wearing priestly attire,[104] but later revised his view, arguing against this proposal.[105] But white was universally the colour of purity, cleanliness, freshness, and holiness,[106] and a reference to the white clothing of the Essenes would have ticked numerous boxes for Josephus' Graeco-Roman audience. This dress worn beyond the Temple in everyday life would have advertised their high aims, distinctiveness, and identity to the world at large.

War 2: 567; 3: 11, 19

As we move on chronologically, within the narrative of *War*, a certain 'John the Essene' ('Ιωάννης ὁ Εσσαῖος) is noted as a revolutionary commander of the toparchy of Lydda, Joppa, and Emmaus in the Judaean Revolt, *c.*67 CE (*War* 2: 567), and he is identified as one of the leaders of the attack on Ascalon, where he was killed in battle (*War* 3: 11, 19). The two other people mentioned with John here are 'Niger the Peraean' (the man from Peraea, *War* 2: 520; 3: 11–28; 4: 359–63), and 'the Babylonian Silas' (*War* 2: 520; 3: 11–19), with all of these indicated to be strong and wise (*War* 3: 11).

Mason, following Schalit, has questioned whether the reference here is to John as an Essene, suggesting instead that he is a man from Essa, namely Gerasa, since this city is called 'Essa' in some of the manuscripts of *Ant.* 13: 393 (for Gerasa in *War* 1: 104).[107] However, since the city of Gerasa is found nowhere else with this name it is probably a manuscript copyist's error. John's fellow generals are indeed named in accordance with their region of origin outside the heartland of Judaea, but, given the use of the term 'Εσσαῖος elsewhere in *War* as 'Essene', it seems consistent to read it this way here. Judaeans were often identified by their specific distinctive features, not only by region (e.g. *War* 2: 566–7) and the definition of a person by means of an affiliation with one of the three schools of law is appropriate, as in the case of Pollion the Pharisee (*Ant.* 15: 3, 370) as Finkbeiner has pointed out.[108]

---

[103] However, Jodi Magness believes that 'Josephus' testimony indicates that . . . sectarian [Essene] men wore only linen garments', *Archaeology of Qumran*, 196, which she associates with priestly attire and purity (200–2).

[104] E. P. Sanders, *Jewish Law from Jesus to the Mishnah: Five Studies* (London: SCM Press, 1990), 37.

[105] Sanders, *Judaism*, 96–9.

[106] See Mason, *War* 2, 4.

[107] Mason, 'What Josephus Says', 428–9; A. Schalit (ed.), *Namenwörterbuch zu Flavius Josephus* (Leiden: Brill, 1968), 46.

[108] Finkbeiner, 'Essenes', 120–1.

As noted above, Philo does not indicate that the Essenes were pacifists, and Josephus describes the Essenes as carrying weapons when they travel (*War* 2: 125) and being tortured by the Romans (2: 159). Overall, they are not detached observers that would have had nothing to do with leadership in the Judaean revolt. Given that Josephus does indicate they take up public office, there is no reason to find mention of John the Essene, a revolutionary leader, in any way anomalous. As Finkbeiner also points out, Josephus differentiates between the erroneous rebels who hijacked the movement of opposition to the Romans and the initial military opposition appointed by the aristocracy, under Ananus II, at the beginning of the revolt, at which time he himself was appointed as a military leader; Niger was in fact murdered by the rebels for his association with Ananus (*War* 4: 314–25). Finkbeiner concludes that 'John's brief appearance seems consistent with Josephus' rhetorical portrait of ideal Jews'.[109]

War 5: 145: the Essene Gate

Lastly but significantly, in *War*, when Josephus discusses Titus setting up encampments around Jerusalem, and he describes the city, a place in Jerusalem is noted by Josephus as being called 'the Gate of the Essenes' (*War* 5: 145). It is defined as being in part of the wall of Jerusalem, which begins at the Hippicus Tower (with remains in the present citadel) and it then proceeded southwards, 'continuing through the place called Bethso to the gate of the Essenes' before it went along the southern side of Jerusalem eastwards to the Pool of Siloam. Some scholars identify this as a gate that led to Mount Zion, at the south-western angle of the First Wall, and argue for the presence of an Essene Quarter there.[110] Yigael Yadin argued that 'Bethso' indicated Hebrew *Beth Tso'a*, 'place of sewers', and there were Essene latrines outside the gate.[111]

---

[109] Finkbeiner, 'Essenes', 123.

[110] Bargil Pixner, 'An Essene Quarter on Mount Zion', in *Studia Hierosolymitana in onore di P. Bellarmino Bagatti* (Jerusalem: Franciscan Printing Press, 1986), 245–87, id. 'The History of the 'Essene Gate' Area, *ZDPV* 105 (1976): 96–104; id. 'Jerusalem's Essene Gateway: Where the Community Lived in Jesus's Time', *BAR* 23/3 (1997): 23–31, 64–6; Bargil Pixner, D. Chen, and S. Margalit, 'The "Gate of the Essenes" Re-Excavated', *ZDPV* 105 (1989): 85–95; Rainer Reisner, 'Josephus' Gate of the Essenes' in Modern Discussion', *ZDPV* 105 (1989): 105–9; Brian J. Capper, 'Essene Community Houses and Jesus' Early Community', in James H. Charlesworth (ed.), *Jesus and Archaeology* (Grand Rapids, Eerdmans, 2006), 472–502.

[111] Yigael Yadin, 'The Gate of the Essenes and the Temple Scroll', in Yigael Yadin (ed.), *Jerusalem Revealed: Archaeology in the Holy City 1968–1974* (Jerusalem: Israel Exploration Society, 1976), 90–1, relating this to 11Q19 46: 13–16, where it is specified that latrines should be made outside the city to the north-east, but these have permanent holes, and thus do not cohere with the Essene latrines as described in *War* 2: 148.

This suggestion seems to account for the gate's name, given what Josephus states in *War* 2: 148–9.[112]

Shimon Gibson, however, identifies this south-western gate as Byzantine, and argues that the remains of the Essene Gate are located midway along the present western city wall (see Plate 2), south of the Citadel.[113] It consisted of an inner (Hasmonean) and outer (Herodian) fortification wall with separate gates. There is an open area in between them measuring 30 by 11 metres, flanked by two towers, with a monumental flight of steps leading down the slope towards the west. Accepting Yadin's suggestion of the meaning of 'Bethso', Gibson identifies the sewers as huge tunnels south of the present Citadel running under the wall towards the western valley. An intriguing aspect of Gibson's identification is that this gate afforded access to the Herodian palace compound. Gibson proposes therefore that the Essenes may have established themselves outside the gate in a tent encampment.

Gibson suggests this with a basic model of the Essenes as living 'in separate communes' for the sake of purity and, while Gibson accepts Stegemann's proposal that the Essenes could be the Herodians of the Gospels (Mark 3: 6; 12: 13; Matt. 22: 16), he believes that Essenes could not have come and gone through this gate since it 'led directly into the property of the palace of Herod the Great (and the later Praetorium), with its extensive gardens and military barracks. Neither Herod nor the Roman governors would have allowed the constant movement of Essenes within the privacy of their grounds'.[114] However, this supposition that Herod would not have allowed the Essenes entry may not be correct, given what Philo states in terms of gifts and honours from the 'great kings' of the Herodian dynasty. We will revisit this issue in Chapter 4 below.

If the Essenes were actually provided with access to the Herodian palace complex, then they could have gone from there to the Temple via the priestly sector of Jerusalem, located in the present Armenian quarter.[115] It seems reasonable to think that the Essenes exited from this gate to the latrines associated with Bethso.

---

[112] Geza Vermes and Martin Goodman (eds), *The Essenes according to the Classical Sources* (Sheffield: JSOT Press, 1989), 48–9.

[113] Shimon Gibson, 'Suggested Identifications for "Bethso" and the "Gate of the Essenes" in the Light of Magen Broshi's Excavations on Mount Zion', in Joseph Patrich and David Amit (eds), *New Studies in the Archaeology of Jerusalem and its Region. Collected Papers* (Jerusalem: Israel Antiquities Authority, 2007), 25–33; abbreviated in id. *The Final Days of Jesus: The Archaeological Evidence* (New York: HarperOne, 2009), 96–102.

[114] Gibson, *Last Days*, 100–1.

[115] Harmut Stegeman, *The Library of Qumran: On the Essenes, Qumran, John the Baptist and Jesus* (Grand Rapids: Eerdmans, 1998), 160–1, 267.

ANTIQUITIES OF THE JEWS (c.93–94 CE)

Antiquities was completed about twenty years after *War*, c.93–94 CE,[116] and, while it has the same apologetic purpose, it is a far more complex and substantial work, being a retelling of the entire span of Jewish history, from Adam to the present time. Parts of *War* are repeated, sometimes with corrections and modifications. The Essenes appear occasionally, largely in regard to predictions.

Ant. 13: 171–3: Destiny

Essenes appear first in relation to the Hasmonean king Jonathan Maccabeus (ruled 152–143/2 BCE), who sought independence from Seleucid control and who was attacked by the armies of the Seleucid king Demetrius II. Unlike in *War*, Josephus introduces the Essenes properly, and writes that 'at this time there were three societies (αἱρέσεις) of the Judaeans', naming them as Pharisees, Sadducees, and Essenes (Ἐσσηνοί). He then sums up their respective positions in regard to free will and destiny. The Pharisees say some but not all things were the work of Destiny (εἱμαρμένης ἔργον), the Sadducees remove Destiny and assert that human beings have free will (*Ant.* 13: 173, cf. *Ant.* 18: 18), but: 'The category (γένος)[117] of the Essenes declare Destiny the mistress of everything, and nothing happens to human beings that is not by her vote (*Ant.* 13: 172).'

In writing this Josephus appeals to Greek concepts of Destiny, anthropomorphising and exaggerating Jewish theology, in which there is clearly a debate regarding degrees of determinism but probably not the absolutist extremes that Josephus ascribes to either the Sadducees or the Essenes. As Jonathan Klawans has explored, one might see in Second Temple Judaism different types of a broadly conceived 'compatibilism' (that free will and determinism are compatible ideas)—given the biblical concept of Divine election and prophecy itself—but it is the Pharisees who are the true compatibilists, with the Essenes moving towards the determinist and the Sadducees the libertarian, without either in fact being as extremist as Josephus indicates.[118] The tripartite division Josephus provides here is very much like that of Cicero, *De Fato* 39–43, where Cicero provides the two extremes of determinism and free will before indicating the moderating Stoic position of

---

[116] See Mason, *Life*, xiv–xix.

[117] LSJ 344, sense V: 'sort, type, class', here applies to the αἵρεσις.

[118] Klawans also notes in fact that ultimately there are two forms of compatibilism Josephus ascribes to the Pharisees; see Jonathan Klawans, 'Josephus on Fate, Free Will and Ancient Jewish Types of Compatibilism', *Numen* 56 (2009): 44–90.

Chrysippus, but the actual debate within Judaism, writes Klawans, 'focused rather (just as Josephus . . . would have us believe) on the narrower question of whether one's individual actions are freely chosen or fore-ordained'.[119]

This alerts us immediately to Josephus' language, which bends Judaism to Hellenistic philosophical argument, in presenting Destiny in Stoic terms, in absolute ways.[120] Klawans concludes that 'it might be better for modern historians of ancient Judaism to embrace Josephus's tripartite typology as an example of good pedagogy, which can as a matter of course require both simplification and the use of clear, but imprecise, analogies'.[121]

Josephus here appears to lay the foundation of what he would say later, in terms of the expertise of the Essenes as prophets; one can only really foretell the future if one believes that the future is in some way already fixed, at least in important aspects, as Josephus recognized himself in his own claims to prophetic insight. Josephus rejects the position espoused by the Sadducees in rejecting the libertarian opinion of the Epicureans in *Ant.* 10: 277–80, and sees Destiny as the directing force throughout the history of the Judaean people. As Klawans points out, Josephus' personal belief was that Destiny was fixed, yet it allowed human impulsion.[122] Josephus writes: 'and we call her Destiny as there is nothing that is not coming to pass through her' (*Ant.* 16: 397), yet responsibility for actions must be attributed to ourselves since this 'has already been expounded as wisdom (ἤδη πεφιλοσόφηται) before us (πρὸ ὑμῶν) indeed in the law (καὶ τῷ νόμῳ)'.[123] This does not really perfectly match what he states about the Pharisaic view of Destiny in *Ant.* 13: 172,[124] since that position allows for more randomness than Josephus permits ('some but not all things the work of Destiny'), and more closely corresponds with the position of the Essenes here, who must indeed have accepted a caveat; after all, the law does indeed attribute individual choice and responsibility to human beings. A Judaean position of predestination cannot then be wholly determinist when the law defines individual responsibility so eloquently. The picture is muddled further by Josephus indicating that in fact Pharisees can also predict the future on the basis of Scripture (*Ant.* 14: 172–6; 15: 3–4; 17: 41–5).

[119] Klawans, 'Josephus on Fate', 62.
[120] See George Foot Moore, 'Fate and Free Will in the Jewish Philosophies according to Josephus', *HTR* 22 (1929): 371–89.
[121] Klawans, 'Josephus on Fate', 85.
[122] Ibid. 80; Mason, *Flavius Josephus on the Pharisees*, 140–2.
[123] The translation of Ralph Marcus here, 'as has been philosophically discussed before our time in the law', does not seem quite right. The law defines the correct position.
[124] To complicate the picture, Josephus provides an alternative understanding of Pharisaic opinion in *Ant.* 18: 13 that does indeed cohere more closely with what he states in *Ant.* 16: 397. This tends to confirm that we cannot take Josephus' statements on face value, and thus we might rather expect of the historical Essenes 'more determinism' than 'total determinism' in relation to the Pharisees.

In terms of his chronological referencing in the appearance of the Essenes in the narrative relating to Jonathan Maccabeus, in the middle of the second century BCE, Josephus' identification of Judaean religion being divided into three choices at this point may be a significant pointer in terms of the history of the Essenes,[125] though there is some discomfort about their apparent absence from the books of the Maccabees. Many have suggested that they are to be historically located within the category of the 'Ḥasidim', where both the origins of the Pharisees and the Essenes are found.[126] Joseph Sievers has argued that the passage concerning the three schools in Josephus' account of *Ant.* 13 is drawn heavily from 1 Maccabees, and pasted over what was a letter to Areus of Sparta found in 1 Macc. 12: 19–23, since the passage in question, before and after the description, paraphrases 1 Macc. 12:18 and 12: 24.[127] Nevertheless, it must have been considered an appropriate paste; that is, Josephus believed that the societies were in existence already in the middle of the second century BCE.

Nowhere in Josephus' narrative is there a suggestion that the legal schools actually arose just at this time, during the Maccabean revolt; the schools simply enter the historical narrative as fully formed entities. In fact, Josephus states that the practices of the Essenes were 'from ancient times', ἐκ παλαιοῦ (*Ant.* 18: 20), long before the time of the Hasmoneans. This coheres with what Philo states in *Hypoth.* 11: 1, that Moses himself trained throngs of his pupils for the life of κοινωνία· Both Philo and Josephus believed that the origins of the Essenes were very ancient. This may then reflect what the Essenes said of themselves, that they were genuinely following the ancient traditions. This is quite striking in an era of innovation, when the Hasmonean line laid exclusive claim to the High Priesthood.

Josephus himself then could not have assumed Essene origins lay among the 'Hasidaeans', or Ḥasidim, of Maccabean times. As we saw, Philo may attest to a belief that the name of the Essenes is associated with a cognate Aramaic word, in which case the Ḥasidim as a category would be considered ancient. However, Josephus indicates nothing of this; no such link is even slightly alluded to. In paraphrasing 1 Macc. 2: 42, where there is mention of the assembly (συναγωγή) of the Ḥasidim fighting on the side of Mattathias, Josephus refers only to a 'great army'; this term is understood in the light of Psalm 149 (קְהַל חֲסִידִים) as indicating those of Israel who fervently

---

[125] See Albert I. Baumgarten, *The Flourishing of Jewish Sects in the Maccabean Era: An Interpretation* (Journal for the Study of Judaism Supplement Series 55; Leiden: Brill, 1997), 20–1, noting corroboration from m.Abot 1 and Abbot deRabbi Nathan 5).

[126] See Philip R. Davies, 'Hasidim in the Maccabean Period', in id. *Sects and Scrolls: Essays on Qumran and Related Topics* (South Florida Studies in the History of Judaism 134; Atlanta: Scholars Press, 1996), 5–22.

[127] Joseph Sievers, 'Josephus, First Maccabees, Sparta, the Three Hairesis—and Cicero', *JSJ* 32 (2001): 224–51.

celebrate God, trusting that he will take vengeance on the nations. The so-called *Ḥasidim* who trusted Alcimus in 1 Macc. 7: 13, only to be killed, are identified by Josephus as just 'some of the people'.[128]

The term as found in 2 Macc. 14: 6 is probably the most telling in terms of the specific use of the designation in Hasmonean times (post 124 BCE, the latest date indicated), since it shows that supporters of Judas overall are 'called *Ḥasidim*'. Josephus would then have understood that this generalized term should be applied here as a positive endorsement of these supporters who behaved piously and zealously, in order to preserve Judaism against extreme persecution.[129] But the Essenes, given that he assumes they existed from ancient times, would have been already formed at this point, in Josephus' opinion, and thus there is no simple equation made between the supporters of Judas Maccabeus (*Ḥasidim*) and the Essenes.

More curious though is why any description of the three legal schools' positions on Destiny appear at this point in the narrative of *Antiquities*. However, Josephus sees God as directing history, with Destiny as an inescapable force, revealed by prophecy (*Ant.* 8: 418–19; 10: 277–80). This passage is an excuse to note implicitly that his own view is clearly not Sadducean, though he admits such an Epicurean position does exist in Judaism. As Finkbeiner has argued, the aside is a nod in the direction of philosophical schools of the Graeco-Roman world, with which his readers were familiar: the Epicurean and Stoic positions on Destiny are ascribed to the Sadducees and Pharisees; the deterministic notions Cicero ascribed to Democritus, Heraclitus, Empedocles, and Aristotle (Cicero, *De Fato* 4: 5–7) are ascribed to the Essenes.[130]

Ant. 13: 310–13: Judas

In *Antiquities*, since readers have already been told of the Essenes' belief in Destiny (*Ant.* 13: 171–3), they are here well prepared for a practical example of how a sense of Destiny is linked to an interest in predictive arts that would

---

[128] See also Daniel Schwartz, 'Hasidim in 1 Maccabees 2: 42', *Scripta Classica Israelica* 13 (1994): 7–18, who sees no *Ḥasidim* here.

[129] Nevertheless, historically, there may well have been support from the Essenes for the Maccabean uprising against Antiochus Epiphanes, which did not in fact translate into continuing support for the resulting Hasmonean dynasty of priest-kings. There is some reason to suppose that there could have been this scenario, given literature like Jubilees or the Animal Apocalypse of 1 Enoch 85–91, in which Maccabean victories against the Syrians are acclaimed; see James VanderKam, *Textual and Historical Studies in the Book of Jubilees* (Missoula, Montana: Scholars Press, 1977) 230–58; James VanderKam, *Enoch and the Growth of an Apocalyptic Tradition* (Catholic Biblical Association of America: Washington, DC, 1984), 161–3; John J. Collins, *The Apocalyptic Imagination: An Introduction to Jewish Apocalyptic Literature*, 2nd ed. (Grand Rapids: Eerdmans, 1998), 77–9.

[130] Finkbeiner, 'Essenes', 141–6.

enable a knowledge of what is determined to happen. Josephus replicates much of what he has written already in *War* 1: 78–80.[131] Judas the Essene (᾿Εσσηνός) had never been known to speak falsely in his predictions, which connects with what Josephus has said of true prophets (Elijah, *Ant.* 8: 417–19; Isaiah *Ant.* 9: 276, 10: 35; Ezekiel and Jeremiah, *Ant.* 10: 141–2; Daniel, *Ant.* 10: 269).[132] Judas' role as a teacher of prediction is more explicitly stated here than in *War*, with his companions (in the Temple) being with him 'on account of his teaching, in order to predict the future' (*Ant.* 13: 311). Judas' prediction to Antigonus becomes part of a sequence of remarkable Essene masters of predictive arts, yet they have no friends among the Hasmoneans. We are told in *Antiquities* that John Hyrcanus supported the legal school of the Sadducees (*Ant.* 13: 298). In fact, it comes as somewhat ironic that Hyrcanus is described as being supportive of the Sadducees given their position on Destiny, as Josephus describes it, but the Essenes remain detached.

Ant. 15: 368–71: Menahem

While in *War* we have only Judas and Simon mentioned as brilliant masters of the predictive arts, in *Antiquities* there is the most striking prediction by an Essene master, named Menahem, and it is related to the young Herod. In *Ant.* 15: 368–71 Josephus recounts how Herod the Great insisted on an oath of loyalty from his discontented subjects, but 'those among us called ᾿Εσσαῖοι' were excluded from this, because of Menahem. Like Philo, Josephus indicates that people in general 'called' the ᾿Εσσαῖοι by this name (*Ant.* 13: 371), but he does not give a meaning for it. He then defines the Essenes as living the same way of life as revealed to the Greeks by Pythagoras, though one cannot extrapolate from this that Josephus thought that the Essenes were entirely identical to Pythagoraeans[133] any more than one can extrapolate that the Pharisees really were Stoics on the basis of Josephus' comments in *Life* 12. The term 'a Pythagoraean way of life' was understood not to mean living a life exactly identical to that of the Pythagoraeans, but rather to mean that such practitioners followed a careful attention to religious ritual and dietary restrictions, among other prescriptions of lifestyle.[134]

---

[131] See above, pp. 60–1.

[132] See Finkbeiner, 'Essenes', 146–50.

[133] Pythagoras himself was said to have sacrificed a hecatomb after discovering his theorem of the right-angled triangle, see Diogenes Laertius, *Vitae* 8: 12, though Laertius goes on to report the common view that Pythagoras eschewed the eating of meat; see also Athenaeus, *Deip.* 10, cf. Cicero, *De Natura Deorum* 3.36. Importantly, Josephus considered the influence to have gone from Jews to Pythagoreans, not the other way around; see *Apion* 1: 165, 2: 168.

[134] Walter Burkert, *Lore and Science in Ancient Pythagoreanism*, trans. E. Minar Jr (Cambridge, MA: Harvard University, 1972), 177, though see Justin Taylor, *Pythagoreans and Essenes*.

Josephus then states (*Ant.* 15: 372–9; 17: 345–8) that Herod honoured the Ἐσσηνοί (note the change of the Greek form of the name, despite the equivalence) and had an opinion of them greater than one would expect of mere mortals because of an Essene named Manaemos (Menahem) who had knowledge of the future (cf. *War* 2: 159). The story is then told that Menahem, seeing Herod as a boy on his way to tuition with a teacher (in Jerusalem, probably in the Temple), addressed Herod as 'King of the Judaeans', and when the boy protested Menahem spanked him 'with his hand on his buttocks', stating: 'You will rule, for God has deemed you worthy.' Therefore, from that time, Herod 'continued to honour all the Essenes'. The spank was apparently designed to make Herod remember the changes wrought by Fortune (= God). The feud between Aristobulus and Hyrcanus II, and the eviction of Aristobulus from rule as priest-king in 63 BCE, is described from the perspective of a supporter of Hyrcanus II in Josephus' narrative of both *War* 1: 120–58 and *Ant.* 13: 405–14: 79. Antipater, Herod's Idumaean father, was on the side of Hyrcanus II, and arranged a refuge for him within the domains of Aretas, the Nabataean kingdom (*War* 1: 124), sending a huge army to Judaea which initially defeated Aristobulus, only to find Scaurus—Pompey's general—in support. Antipater and Hyrcanus then transferred their allegiance to the Romans, with stunning consequences. Pompey besieged Jerusalem and won, establishing Hyrcanus II as ruler. The prediction of Menahem, as told by Josephus, was when Herod was a boy, and took place some time just after these events had taken place, but before Herod was, in 47 BCE—apparently at the age of 15—appointed as governor of Galilee (*Ant.* 14: 58).

But the Essene prediction was not exactly an endorsement of Herod as deserving to rule Israel as a virtuous monarch chosen by God. Menahem predicted that Herod would not love justice, or show piety to God or decency to the citizens, these being matters which would not be forgotten by God at the end of Herod's life. It is truly a bizarre prophecy, that God himself would destine an unrighteous man to rule Israel, and he would be punished for his deeds; in the narrative Herod is clearly bothered by the ambiguity of this. When he becomes king of Judaea, Herod sends for Menahem and asks him about the duration of his rule (*Ant.* 13: 377–8). Initially the Essene prophet is silent, but eventually he states that there could be twenty or thirty years and he would put no limit to the end of the appointed time. It is at this point, given the astute reply, that Herod then shows him respect and gives all Essenes

Structural Parallels (Collection de la Revue des Études Juives 32; Louvain: Peeters, 2004) for some substantive correlations and, regarding ascertaining the worthiness of new entrants and subsequent status, Philip S. Alexander, 'Physiognomy, Initiation, and Rank in the Qumran Community', in Hubert Cancik, Hermann Lichtenberger, et al. (eds), *Geschichte—Tradition—Reflexion: Festschrift für Martin Hengel zum 70. Geburtstag: Band I: Judentum* (Tübingen: Mohr Siebeck, 1996), 385–94. The question is possibly a more general one about cultural influence.

'honour', though Josephus notes that this may well seem παράδοξα, 'paradoxical' or 'unbelievably strange' (*Ant.* 15: 379) given Herod's character, in contrast to the virtue of the Essenes. It seems, indeed, perverse that the pure and pious Essenes would herald Herod as the destined king of Judaea.

The basis for Menahem's remarkable prediction that Herod would become king is passed over without much explanation, and the astonishing prophecy that a man who was not of the house of David, and not even a descendant of Israel (his father was Idumaean and mother Nabataean), would become the king of the Judaeans and thereby replace the established Hasmonean priest-kings is not given its full due as absolutely extraordinary. It is no wonder that Herod made much of it, but both its basis and its impact are ignored in Josephus' account. This is an important passage, springing from a famous historical event, but its further ramifications and explanation we will reserve for Chapter 6. For now the focus will remain on the way that Josephus characterizes the Essenes in his narrative. Up to this point, the focus is very strongly on their religio-political visibility at the heart of Jerusalem, with predictive skills born of their firm emphasis on Destiny.

The 'honour' received by the Essenes from Herod is the exemption from a vow of loyalty imposed on his subjects. This relates to what has already been discussed in regard to Philo's account in *Hypoth.* 11: 18, where Philo identifies the Essenes as being 'magnified' by the (Herodian) kings.[135] The reception of royal favours did not necessarily mark the Essenes out as the chosen legal school of these rulers: but rather they appear as people who were rewarded for their endorsement of Herod's right to rule, by divine determination.

Ant. 17: 345–8: Simon

As in *War* 2: 112–13, Archelaus is warned of misfortune by Simon the Ἐσσαῖος, who correctly interprets Archelaus' dream (*Ant.* 17: 345–8). The number of years of Archelaus' rule is changed to ten, to accurately reflect what Josephus now understood in terms of chronology (*Ant.* 17: 342; *Life* 5). It seems curious in relation to what has gone before, that on the one hand an Essene master can predict Herod's ascendancy, but another should predict the downfall of his son, but Archelaus is introduced in *Antiquities* as an unmitigated disaster (*Ant.* 17: 339–44). The Essene is classed in a group of 'masters of prediction', μάντεις, that Archelaus sends for.

As in *War*, the description of Simon's prediction by means of dream interpretation is followed by the description of the dream of Glaphyra, Archelaus' wife, to indicate the importance of dreams in terms of determining

---

[135] See above, pp. 45–6.

what might happen. In *Ant.* 17: 354 Josephus comments on these two in-
cidents regarding the importance of dreams, acknowledging that some may
think his reports are incredible. His language is defensive, as if some have
criticized him for including such material. To one who is sceptical, 'let him
indeed profit by his own obstruction, but let him not hinder the one that
would side with virtue'. The telling of these stories is because of their virtuous
lessons. Josephus anticipates reader response: 'both the response about the
immortality of the soul and [the response about] the forethoughts of God
embracing human affairs' (τοῦ τε ἀμφι τὰς ψυχὰς ἀθανασίας ἐμφεροῦς καὶ τοῦ
θεῖον προμηθεία τὰ ἀνθρώπεια περιειληφότος). The latter point seems to be
concerned with Destiny, that God thought out events on earth beforehand: the
position Josephus has ascribed to the Essenes. The former point, about the
immortality of the soul, relates to the fact that Glaphyra's dream, in which her
first husband Alexander speaks to her, truly indicates that Alexander's soul
continues. A dream is therefore a window into a deep heavenly reality. Both
Archelaus and Glaphyra are sinners, who are warned by dreams that are sent
to reveal the truth: Archelaus needs a godly interpreter to make it clear, and
Glaphyra dies having recognized what is right. These stories are therefore
lessons in virtue.

Josephus himself counts as one who can interpret dreams in order to reveal
the truth of the present and the future, as we have seen, and in *Antiquities*
he notes the significance of these at various points in his narrative, particularly in regard to Joseph (*Ant.* 2: 11–16, 63–86) and Daniel (*Ant.* 10: 237–9).
Their esoteric wisdom was one requiring education: Joseph was trained in
Egypt (*Ant.* 2: 39) and Daniel in Babylon (*Ant.* 10: 186–9, 194). As Rebecca
Gray has pointed out, esoteric 'wisdom', 'understanding', and 'intelligence'
are repeatedly identified by Josephus as necessary for the interpretation of
dreams.[136] The Essene Simon is one with such wisdom who can be called
upon by the Herodian ruler.

The oxen of Archelaus' dream are seen in terms of their function as
ploughers of the field. They are the years of misery (they are sad from hard
work) that eat up the wheat, and 'the earth, having been ploughed by their
labour, cannot remain in that [condition] . . . for in the course of one [year]
the harvest arrives' (*Ant.* 13: 347). The ploughing of the oxen, and their
subsequent eating of the grain, indicate the years of misery that have produced
a harvest that is then consumed by misery. Van Henten has suggested that the
harvest is the Roman takeover, though perhaps it is rather the consequence of
the consumption.[137]

---

[136] Gray, *Prophetic Figures*, 27, 66–78. *Ant.* 2: 63, 65, 76, 80, 87, 91.

[137] Jan W. van Henten, 'The Two Dreams at the End of Book 17 of Josephus' Antiquities', in
J. U. Kalms and F. Siegert (eds), *Internationales Josephus-Kolloquium Dortmund 2002* (Münsteraner Judaistische Studien 14; Münster: Lit, 2003), 78–93, at 90–1.

On the Essenes: *Ant.* 18: 18–22

In *Ant.* 18: 18–22, there is a much briefer treatment of the Essenes. Since it has some considerable overlaps with Philo's account in his *Hypothetica*, and also with *De Vita Contemplativa*, it has been suggested that Philo and Josephus used a common source,[138] though it seems more straightforward to think that Josephus was simply quarrying Philo, who wrote over fifty years earlier, without simple replication, even if one may note immediately that Josephus uses the term Ἐσσηνοι rather than Philo's Ἐσσαῖοι. Given that many of Philo's writings have been lost, and he could be quite repetitive, there may well have been a simple summary of the Essenes that Josephus used from Philo as a quick tool. It should also be noted that the text of *Antiquities* is much more fraught with textual problems than that of *War* 2, given the poor state of the manuscripts.

The literary context at the start of *Antiquities* 18 means that the foregoing mention of Simon the Essene and his prediction of Archelaus' downfall is fresh in readers' minds. Book 18 begins with the arrival of Cyrenius, after Archelaus' departure, and the census for taxation, and so then laments the rebellion led by Judas and Saddouk, a Pharisee. There then follows a great denunciation of what these men stood for and did, resulting in the destruction of the Temple. They 'roused up a fourth philosophy imported (ἐπείσακτον) among us, and this, abounding with passionate supporters, filled up our government with clamours' (*Ant.* 18: 9), an 'infection' that spread among the young (*Ant.* 18: 10). Up until this point, the Judaeans had three philosophies 'from the many ancient ages of the ancestors' (ἐκ τοῦ πάνυ ἀρχαίου τῶν πατρίων) (*Ant.* 18: 11). These ancient and legitimate philosophies (the legal schools) are then set out to contrast with the misguided heterodox followers of Judas and Saddouk: Pharisees first (*Ant.* 18: 12–15), Sadducees second (*Ant.* 18: 16–17), and Essenes third (*Ant.* 18: 18–22). After these true philosophies are defined, the 'fourth philosophy' is described, as a kind of madness (*Ant.* 18: 23–5), so that the descent towards civil war and revolt is signalled.[139]

Josephus states that the Essenes ascribe everything to God (18), regard the soul as immortal, and so strive for the reward (πρόσοδον) of righteousness (18). They send votive offerings to the Temple, but employ different

---

[138] See Morton Smith, 'The Description of the Essenes in Josephus and the Philosophumena', *HUCA* 29 (1958): 273–313, at 278–9 and Randal A. Argall, 'A Hellenistic Jewish Source on the Essenes in Philo, Every Good Man Is Free 75–91 and Josephus, Antiquities 18.18–22', in Randal A. Argall, Beverly A. Bow, and Rodney A. Werline (eds), *For a Later Generation: The Transformation of Tradition in Israel, Early Judaism and Early Christianity* (Harrisburg, PA: Trinity Press International, 2000), 13–24. Given that Philo wrote about Essenes in a missing treatise preceding *De Vita Contemplativa* (see *Contempl.* 1), Josephus' source may have been this, for all we know.

[139] Note that in Whiston's translation (470–2) the word 'sect' repeatedly occurs, where it is not found in the Greek text.

purifications, so separate themselves from the common precincts and perform their sacrifices by themselves (19). They work in agricultural labour (19, cf. Philo, *Hypoth.* 11: 8), adopted their practices in ancient times (20), hold possessions in common equally (20, cf. *Hypoth.* 11: 4), are more than 4,000 in number (20, cf. *Hypoth.* 11: 1), do not bring wives into the communal possessions, because it would be a source of conflict (21, *Hypoth.* 11: 14), or own slaves because this practice adds to injustice (21, cf. *Hypoth.* 11: 4), but do all services themselves (21, cf. *Hypoth.* 11: 5-6). They elect by show of hands the good men, namely priests, who receive the wages and as much as the earth produces both for making bread and other food (22, cf. *Hypoth.* 11: 10). They are like 'the founders' among the Dacians (22).[140]

The reference to leaving everything in the hands of God (*Ant.* 18: 18) correlates with what Josephus has stated about the Essenes in *Ant.* 13: 171-2.[141] The understanding of the soul (ψύχη) being immortal, in connection with drawing near to righteousness (with a view to reward), ties this statement with what is said in *War* 2: 154-8.

Importantly, in the most likely reading of *Antiquities* 18: 19, Josephus states that 'while sending votive offerings (ἀναθήματα στέλλοντες) to the Temple, they [the Essenes] perform sacrifices with very different[142] purifications (θυσίας ἐπιτελοῦσιν διαφορότητι ἁγνειῶν), which they hold as a legal interpretation (ἃς νομίζοιεν), and because of this they perform the sacrifices by themselves, keeping away (εἰργόμενοι)[143] from the common precincts (τοῦ κοινοῦ τεμενίσματος).' A variant has led to some scholars doubting this reading. The earliest extant manuscript of *Antiquities* 18 (A, the Codex bibl. Ambrosianae F 128 at Milan) is from the eleventh century, but this is one of a family of manuscripts that Niese (1885) considers less reliable than what is available for chapters 1–15. Because of this, attention has focused on the epitome (E) used for the *Chronicon* of Zonaras (twelfth cent.) and the Latin version made by order of Cassiodorus in the fifth to sixth centuries, in which it is stated slightly nonsensically that Essenes 'do not sacrifice' with very different

---

[140] The final section (22) is fraught with textual difficulties, and the version given here reflects the Greek codices without amendment from the epitome; Louis H. Feldman, *Josephus: Jewish Antiquities XVIII–XX* (Loeb Classical Library; Cambridge, MA: Harvard University Press, 1965), 18–21, accepts many textual modifications and translates accordingly, minimizing the role of priests in the community.

[141] See above, p. 88.

[142] Note the comparative intensification which can be read as superlative 'most different'.

[143] Feldman, *Antiquities XVIII–XX*, 17, translates the word εἰργόμενοι as 'excluded', which means reading a passive rather than the perfectly appropriate middle form. There appears no reason to read a passive, *contra* Albert I. Baumgarten, 'Josephus on Essene Sacrifice', *JJS* 45 (1994): 169–83, when this would mean that the Essenes were excluded by others on account of their particular concern with purity, when fastidiousness with purity would mean that the Essenes themselves must surely have wanted to keep away from those who did not share their customs for fear of being rendered impure.

purifications (18: 19)[144] However, all Greek manuscripts indicate that they do so.[145] It is hard to read even in the Latin version that the Essenes do not sacrifice at all, and in fact it would be absolutely perverse to credit that the priestly Josephus' eulogy of the Essenes as the optimum Jewish philosophy would contain any suggestion that they either rejected the Temple or refused to sacrifice as part of his commendation of the group. As Beall has concluded from his examination of this passage, 'both Josephus and Qumran literature present a picture of a group that did offer sacrifices, though with a greater concern for ritual purity in the process'.[146] What we have here is an indication of the Essenes' stress on the greatest standard of purity within the Temple, and rigorous separation from non-priestly areas (the common precincts). Josephus seems to indicate that, even within the priestly area, Essene priests demanded additional purity regulations to govern their sacrifices, in a separated zone. They are thus high achievers, but with an underlying concern for the greatest possible standards within the Temple, which they esteem enormously.

Josephus' comment on their avoidance of common precincts may also assume an Essene purity-enhanced zone delineated in Solomon's portico or elsewhere since, as we have seen, the Essenes are conspicuous by their presence in the Temple at certain points of Josephus' narrative (*War* 1: 78–80; 2: 562–7; *Ant*. 13: 311–13).[147] The sending of special gifts to the Temple indicates that, for Josephus, they wished to honour it (and had the money to do so in terms of sending votive gifts). The Essenes kept away from the common precincts, τοῦ κοινοῦ τεμενίσματος, not because of any problem with the Temple but because of the 'commonness' there. One could not normally enter the holiest parts of the Temple without going through the common precincts of the Court of the Gentiles and the Court of the Israelites (Azarah), unless you were a priest. The main point is that the Essenes had particular practices of purification/purity (ἁγνεία) that entailed some kind of separation from others. Given that Josephus had already indicated in *War* 2: 150 that a senior Essene could be rendered impure from contact with a junior Essene, and most likely women could not be trusted in regard to purity (*War* 2: 121),

---

[144] See Feldman, *Antiquities XVIII–XX*, 16–17.

[145] Greek manuscripts of Josephus do not have οὐκ here, despite the Latin version and epitome. For discussion, see Beall, *Josephus' Description of the Essenes*, 115, 164; Gabriele Boccaccini, *Beyond the Essene Hypothesis: The Parting of the Ways between Qumran and Enochic Judaism* (Grand Rapids: Eerdmans, 1998), 183, n. 21.

[146] Beall, *Josephus' Description of the Essenes*, 119. See also Kenneth A. Matthews, 'John, Jesus and the Essenes: Trouble at the Temple', *Criswell Theological Review* 3 (1988): 101–26 at 105–14; Joseph M. Baumgarten, 'Sacrifice and Worship among the Jewish Sectarians of the Dead Sea (Qumran) Scrolls', *HTR* 46 (1953): 141–59, repr. in id. *Studies in Qumran Law* (Leiden: Brill, 1977), 39–56; id. 'The Essenes and the Temple: A Reappraisal', in id. *Studies in Qumran Law* (Leiden: Brill, 1977), 59–62.

[147] As noted by Matthew Black, *The Scrolls and Christian Origins: Studies in the Jewish Background of the New Testament* (London: T. Nelson, 1961), 40.

any contact with non-Essenes (let alone Gentiles) would clearly have been considered very polluting. Essene fastidiousness is here endorsed, not Essene alienation from the centre of Jewish life.

The Gate of the Essenes may be relevant here. Given the importance of purity to the Essenes, Josephus seems to imply that movement itself within the city of Jerusalem—or any other city—could not have been easy, particularly at entrance gates which were places where crowds could be crushed together. Given Herod's favouring of the Essenes, on the basis of Menahem's prediction, he may have allowed the Essenes to use the gate to facilitate their movement in and out of the holy city, a gate that could be particularly guarded by his soldiers since it led in to part of his own huge palace compound. The way through from this compound to the Temple is unclear, but it would most likely have gone through the wealthy priestly sector and over 'Wilson's Arch', as it has been called: a bridge that linked this sector with the Temple. This would have meant the Essenes could have avoided the main public entries to the south of the Temple. This bridge led directly to the back of the Sanctuary (see Map 1).

Josephus continues then: 'βέλτιστοι δὲ ἄλλως [ὅι] ἄνδρες τὸν τρόπον καὶ τὸ πᾶν πονεῖν ἐπὶ γεωργίᾳ τετραμμένοι: 'Otherwise, best are [the] men who have directed their way and all to work hard in agriculture' (*Ant.* 18: 19). The word ἄλλως 'otherwise' can be interpreted as a mild negative in regard to what has just preceded. This is understandable in regard to the Essenes having a separate zone within the Sanctuary for sacrifice and rejection of the common precincts—which would ordinarily be the place where all Jews could go and Josephus himself would not have eschewed this area. The little word ἄλλως could not possibly follow a statement by Josephus that his paragon of Judaean excellence, the Essenes, fundamentally rejected the Temple sacrifice system that lay at the heart of Judaean worship; nothing in Josephus indicates that any Jew could reject the Temple cult. In the statement that follows the Essenes' special concern with purity, it is as if Josephus is announcing a truism, and he characterizes all good Jews as doing precisely this at the end of *Against Apion*: what could be better than 'to attend to crafts and agriculture' (*Apion* 2: 294)?[148]

Josephus therefore tries to balance a possible negative concerning the Essenes' extreme Temple practices by emphasizing they are best via an ideal of simple labour in agricultural cultivation: on the one hand they may seem snooty, but he balances this by making them work in physical labour. Hyperbole aside, Josephus did not think all Essenes everywhere were farmers and had no other occupations. He sees Essenes as earning money (*Ant.* 18: 22), and in *War* 2: 129 he had mentioned τέχναι—crafts, artisanal

---

[148] Plutarch (*Cato the Elder* 2: 1; 3: 1–4) defines agriculture as the ideal Roman pursuit.

skills—in which the Essenes were proficient. In *War*, he cannot have imagined the Essenes living within 'every city' (*War* 2: 124) as farmers, and when Josephus writes of individual Essenes in his historical narratives they are teacher-prophets (*War* 1: 78; 2: 113; *Ant.* 13: 311–13; 15: 370–9; 17: 346–8). In *War* 2: 140, as we have seen, he notes their humility and honesty in public office. In *Antiquities* the picture of Essene labour on the land is created as a remedy to Essene hyper-scrupulousness in terms of the Temple. Far from the Essenes rejecting the Temple, Josephus provides us with an image of Essenes who take more care with it than any other Jews.

Josephus goes on in *Ant.* 18: 20 to stress how much the Essenes deserve admiration for their virtue, stressing that their practice comes from ancient times (ἐκ παλαιοῦ). Their communality of possessions is stressed. As we have seen, this was a philosophical ideal. The pooling of possessions was advocated by Plato for the guardians of the city (*Rep.* 416d, 5: 462c) and was practised by Pythagoraeans (Iamblichus, *De Pyth. Vita* 167–9), who could be male and female. The model of their associations shows considerable indebtedness to the model of the guardians of Plato's *Republic*: these civic leaders are also philosophers who eschew wealth, live communally and eat together, and have no personal property, yet they are also an elite.

That there are 'more than 4000' Essenes (*Ant.* 18: 20) agrees with Philo (*Prob.* 75, more than *Hypoth.* 11: 1 where the emphasis is simply on how many Essenes there were). Josephus notes comparatively that there are 'over 6000' Pharisees (*Ant.* 17: 42) and 'a few' Sadducees (*Ant.* 18: 17). The Essenes are the second largest legal school as well as being the most admirable, in his view.

In *Ant.* 18: 21 Josephus describes women not being included among communal male Essene groups in terms very similar to Philo. He curiously writes that they 'do not bring wives into their [shared] possessions (κτῆσιν)' (*Ant.* 18: 21), because of the discord (στάσις) this may produce. In Philo's *Hypothetica*, the verb κτάομαι is used in preference to the noun: the Essenes do not continue to possess (ὑπομένει κτήσασθαι) private items (*Hypoth.* 11: 4); Philo discusses women later on, and at length, as a qualification, but there is a clear overlap in language and theme. That women are essentially 'property' is an important point to note. In antiquity, women and children were very commonly included in a man's possessions; for example, the proscription against coveting your neighbour's property in Deut. 5: 21 lists 'your neighbour's wife . . . house, field, or his manservant, his ox or his donkey or anything that belongs to your neighbour'. Josephus' comments seem to relate to the same problem with the 'community of wives' concept alluded to by Philo.[149]

However, in societies of the ancient world where communal living and sharing of possessions was practised, women could be classified outside the

---

[149] See above, p. 43.

category of male 'possessions', and be individual agents with their own belongings. The story of what happened to Ananias and Sapphira in Acts 5: 1–11 implies that as a married couple they were to surrender the sale of their (joint) property to the Christian community.[150] Often this did mean in reality a kind of 'openness' of possessions, so that it was not so much communal ownership but rather a willingness to give away or exchange anything.[151] In the practice of the Therapeutae, as described by Philo, men are defined as leaving their families, including wives and children (*Contempl.* 13, 18) in order to live a special celibate lifestyle, where they shared property, and essentially— despite their communal philosophical existence away from the household— most of their possessions and property had been left behind to these families (*Contempl.* 13–14).[152]

Josephus states that the Essenes 'live by themselves', not implying a location in the wilderness but rather that any wives and children are excluded. Never- theless, the apparent reading is that there were men who had wives among their 'possessions' already before choosing the celibate, communal lifestyle. But in this lifestyle they are the ones who do the menial tasks women would normally do, like preparing bread and other food (*Ant.* 18: 22). This may seem at first sight inconsistent with what Josephus wrote in *War* 2, but given that Josephus in *Antiquities* refers readers back to his fuller treatment there (*Ant.* 13: 171–2; 13: 298; 18: 18), it is unlikely that Josephus himself thought he was being inconsistent at all.

The election of officers relates to *War* 2: 123, 129, 134, and priests are in charge: while the election may be by vote of hands, the selection of the best candidates appears to have been drawn from a limited priestly pool: the 'good men' are 'priests': ἄνδρας ἀγαθούς, ἱερεῖς . . . This clarifies what has formerly been stated in *War* 2: Essenes replicate the role of priests in wider society within their own communities, so the priests are chosen for positions of administration.

The curious final comment on the question about the Dacians in *Ant.* 18: 22 has been particularly hard to fathom. The Essenes, states Josephus, 'live a manner of life in no way different, but as close as possible, to the Dacians called *Pleistoi*'. Where Josephus found such a titbit is anyone's guess, and it is

---

[150] See Justin Taylor, 'The Community of Goods among the First Christians and Among the Essenes', in David Goodblatt, Avital Pinnick, and Daniel R. Schwartz (eds), *Historical Perspec- tives: From the Hasmoneans to Bar Kokhba in Light of the Dead Sea Scrolls* (Leiden: Brill, 2001), 147–64, at 156–8.

[151] Justin Taylor, 'Community of Goods', 154. Taylor notes both forms of community of goods among the Christians and also the Essenes of Josephus.

[152] Philo was moralistic about a careless attitude to 'wealth' exhibited by certain renowned philosophers, and here specifically spells out how responsible these men were in terms of leaving their households to join a philosophical community (and though women were part of the community also, Philo tells us nothing about how they divested themselves of wealth).

often considered simply a copyist's blunder, with Dupont-Sommer suggesting the original was 'Sadduceans', and Feldman suggesting for *Pleistoi* (literally: 'Founders') the 'Ctistae'.[153] However, the manuscript reading has been very strongly defended by scholars who actually know the ancient literature on the Dacians,[154] who have suggested the word *Pleistoi* is a form of paronomasia, whereby a Greek form is given to a Barbarian word, signifying the devotees of a Thracian god called Pleistoros by Herodotus (*Hist.* 9: 119, cf. Demosthenes, *Or.* 37: 4). At any rate, since this makes good sense, it seems unnecessary to amend the text.

CONCLUSIONS

In terms of the reliability of Josephus' evidence, it does not seem unlikely that Josephus, investigating the three legal schools, participated in the first year of Essene probation in order to learn thoroughly about them (*Life* 10–12). As his description demonstrates, those at this level were 'outsiders' to those who were full members, yet the neophytes followed a lifestyle as part of the 'insider' four grades. If what he states in *Life* is true, then he himself would have had the opportunity to learn within the initial level, and would therefore not be entirely reliant on literary source information or hearsay, unlike our other ancient authors. Josephus investigated the Essenes at a time when he was a very young man, in the early 50s, when he was considering what legal school he should follow in public life, and ultimately rejected this school for his own course while yet admiring it very much. That he portrays its manly austerity by reference to the character of Roman *virtus* in some ways exonerates him: this degree of tough and self-denying masculinity was for him a little too much, as it would be for nearly every male reader of his description. Yet it is this lifestyle that points to the heart of the deep *virtus* of Judaism, as Josephus describes it.

Overall, it is important to note that Josephus does not consign the Essenes to the margins of Judaean life. They are, rather, an important and ancient (see *Ant.* 18: 20) school whose virtue is paramount. They are practitioners of predictive arts and, for this, they are—paradoxically—given special exemptions by the morally suspect King Herod (*Ant.* 15: 371–9), who honoured them more than one might expect 'mere mortals to be honoured'. Josephus

[153] André Dupont-Sommer, 'On a Passage of Josephus relating to the Essenes (Antiq. XVIII, 22)', *JSS* 1 (1956): 361–6; Feldman, *Antiquities XVIII–XX* (Loeb Classical Library; Cambridge, MA: Harvard University Press, 1965), 20–1, note a. The Ctistae were mentioned in Strabo, *Geogr.* 7: 3: 3 (quoting from Posidonius), as being a tribe who lived without wives.

[154] E. Lozovan and Safia F. Haddad, 'Dacia Sacra', *History of Religions* 7 (1968): 209–43, at 219–28; Jean Gagé, 'Du culte thrace de Pleistoros à la secte dace des "Pleistoi", à propos d'une dédicace épigraphique à Diana Plestrensis', *Noul Album Macedo-Roman* 1 (1959): 15–26.

also stresses that in terms of reputation they are deemed virtuous and seem to practise great worthiness (*War* 2: 119). People widely esteem them. Both public opinion and the Herodian rulers support them. This parallels directly what is found in Philo: that despite Judaean ruiers being impious and violent (Hasmoneans), the rulers of the past could not fault the Essenes (*Prob.* 89–91), and great kings (Herod and Archelaus) give them honour (*Hypoth.* 11: 18). In other words, they are presented by Josephus as being a kind of exemplary alternative in terms of religious authority, almost too perfect to be entirely human, shunning associations with the chief priests and the lax purity practices of the Temple, while astutely enjoying royal favours and protections and participating in certain roles of public life.

They are curiously priestly, adopting a style of life that seems to be modelled on the life of priests while on duty in the Temple, though their communities included non-priests also. Josephus mentions priests specifically among the Essenes in key positions, saying a blessing over their special meals (*War* 2: 131), and being elected for community positions (*Ant.* 18: 22, cf. *War* 2: 123). Even though there are non-priests among them, and voting was democratically done by a show of hands, it may be that priests compulsorily had to hold such important positions in their societies. As such, there is a composite mix of priests and non-priests who are engaged in legal exposition, advising those within the council around the High Priest (who are only priests, as a true hierarchy). However, the Essenes, it appears, avoided this council by their own choice, preferring a court of their own. That they were permitted to have this separate jurisdiction is plainly stated by Josephus. But this does not remove them from society; they could take command in battle as well as any other public figures. They did not reject the Temple.

The other familiar features of their private and celibate communal life within the many towns of Judaea provide us with a picture of their extreme toughness and high standards of purity, piety, and righteousness. However, Josephus interrupts this perfect picture to present a complication: some men of this school had wives who practised the same regimen of purification prior to mealtimes. He does not give a holistic presentation, enabling us to catch no more than a glimpse of these women, let alone children. Sex is simply done for procreation, and Josephus gives us no hint of family life. In fact, Josephus may have assumed that women and children would lead a highly separated existence. There is no reason to think that celibate and married Essene men lived separately: Josephus does not present a picture of men and women cohabiting, only men. Overall, much is unstated. Josephus' description creates many gaps it is all too easy to fill with assumptions.

Yet, the Essenes' expertise in scripture and healing, emphasis on purity, avoidance of soft oil, renunciation of private money, and their model welfare system, all need to be configured around a paradigm Josephus creates of the Essenes as central and favoured. They are paragons of virtue, of Judaean manliness, and the pinnacle of Judaean philosophical achievement. They, among all the schools, even have a physical structure named after them in the holy city: the Gate of the Essenes.

POST-SCRIPT TO JOSEPHUS

Josephus was used independently by two third-century authors: the Christian bishop Hippolytus of Rome and the neo-Platonist philosopher Porphyry.

HIPPOLYTUS

When Hippolytus of Rome wrote about the Ἐσσηνοί in a work known either as the *Philosophoumena* or *Refutatio omnium haeresium*, 'Against All Heresies' (c.230 CE),[155] he appears to have used Josephus' discussion from *War* 2: 119–61. It is an interesting choice. Hippolytus' focus was on denouncing a range of Christian heresies, after an initial chapter reviewing Greek philosophy, but in his writing there is a short section in which various Judaean groups are also included (*Haer.* 9: 13–28) in order to show how in both Greek philosophy and Judaism there was diversity, and one thing led to another. Christianity was no different from them in this regard. However, by the third century, in Christian circles, the understanding of what was meant by the term αἱρέσεις contained a meretricious undertone: deviant heresies.

As noted above, there have been propositions that Hippolytus did not use Josephus, but rather both Hippolytus and Josephus used another pre-Josephan source—or sources—independently.[156] Thanks to the refutations by Christoph Burchard, and also by Steve Mason and Tessa Rajak,[157] the view has

---

[155] Hippolytus of Rome, *Hippolytus, Refutatio omnium haerisium*, ed. M. Marcovich (Patrische Texte und Studien 25; Walter de Gruyter: Berlin and New York, 1986). The manuscript of *Philosophoumena* was discovered in the monastery of St. Athos in 1842 and originally thought to be the work of Origen.

[156] The proposition that Josephus and Hippolytus (*Haer.* 9.18–28) used the same source independently was argued by Morton Smith, 'Description of the Essenes', and Matthew Black, 'The Account of the Essenes in Hippolytus and Josephus', in William D. Davies and David Daube (eds), *The Background of the New Testament and its Eschatology* (Cambridge: CUP, 1956), 172–82. Multiple sources have been proposed by Roland Bergmeier, *Die Essener-Berichte des Flavius Josephus: Quellenstudien zu den Essenertexten im Werk des judischen Historiographen* (Kampen: Kok Pharos, 1993), 66–107.

[157] Christoph Burchard, 'Zur Nebenüberlieferung von Josephus Bericht über die Essener, *Bell.* 2, 119–61 bei Hippolyt, Porphyrius, Eusebius, Niketas Choniates und anderen', in Otto Betz, Klaus K. Haacker, and Martin Hengel (eds), *Josephus Studien: Untersuchungen zu Josephus dem antiken Judentum und dem Neuen Testament, Festschrift für Otto Michel* (Göttingen:

nevertheless prevailed that the text of Hippolytus does indeed use Josephus, with some additional material blended in. Some have suggested that the variants occur because Josephus was already reworked by a Christian author prior to Hippolytus,[158] and Albert I. Baumgarten has suggested that Hippolytus' source was a modified Josephus incorporating some pro-Pharisaic material.[159] Nevertheless, Hippolytus did not necessarily cut-and-paste with exact literary accuracy when he used sources he was not directly quoting from.[160]

At any rate, the most extensive additional passage in Hippolytus' work that might seem to indicate a distinct source is actually material on the Sicarii which seems to be mere extrapolation inserted into the basic source text of *War* 2: 150–3, the passage which mentions four levels of Essenes. In Hippolytus these four levels turn into four distinct fractured parts, all of which appear to be understood as indicating followers of Judas the Galilean. Thus Zealots and Sicarii are considered by Hippolytus to be types of *Essenes* (*Haer.* 9: 26), a stunning mistake that is hard to attribute to any first-century Judaean source but rather to later blunder, when the differences between Judaean groups were not so well understood. The insertion here simply furthers Hippolytus' goal of indicating the great fragmentation of Judaism.

Perhaps Hippolytus was drawing on an alternative manuscript of Josephus. Could the manuscript used by Hippolytus have had some textual or editorial variations that are not evidenced in the surviving texts on which Niese's standard version of Josephus' *War* is based? Since we are far from having any contemporary Josephus manuscripts with which to compare Hippolytus' text, there is no way of surmising how many variants there might have been in the textual tradition as manuscripts were copied and recopied. Might Hippolytus' version be explored more closely in case it may retain elements of Josephus' original writing that have not survived in the dominant textual

---

Vandenhoeck & Ruprecht, 1974), 77–96; id. 'Die Essener bei Hippolyt, REF. IX 18, 2–28, 2 und Josephus, Bell. 2, 119–61', *JSJ* 8 (1977), 1–41; Mason, 'Josephus and the Authorship of War 2'; id. 'What Josephus Says'; Tessa Rajak, 'Ciò che Flavio Giuseppe Vide: Josephus and the Essenes', in Fausto Parente and Joseph Sievers (eds), *Josephus and the History of the Greco-Roman Period. Essays in Memory of Morton Smith* (Leiden: Brill, 1994), 141–60; reprinted in ead. *The Jewish Dialogue with Greece and Rome. Studies in Cultural and Social Interaction* (Leiden: Brill, 2002), 219–40.

[158] Michael E. Hardwick, *Josephus as an Historical Source in Patristic Literature through Eusebius* (Atlanta: Scholars Press, 1989), 51–7; Solomon Zeitlin, 'The Account of the Essenes in Josephus and the Philosophoumena', *JQR* 29 (1958–59): 292–9, suggests the missing source is Hegesippus (cf. Eusebius, *Hist. Eccles.* 4: 22: 7). For a good argument for the intermediate source theory see also Finkbeiner, 'Essenes', 36–41, 264–9.

[159] Albert I. Baumgarten, 'Josephus and Hippolytus on the Pharisees', *HUCA* 55 (1984): 1–25.

[160] Catherine Osborne, *Rethinking Early Greek Philosophy: Hippolytus of Rome and the Presocratics* (London: Duckworth, 1987), 187–8, 213. Miroslav Marcovich, *Studies in Early Greco-Roman Religions and Gnosticism* (Leiden: Brill, 1988) argues that Josephus knew both a Christian redaction and an original copy of Josephus (144–54), since he considers that Hippolytus was more careful when quoting his sources.

tradition, as quotations of New Testament books in the early church fathers can shed light on developments in the textual developments in that corpus?

The variants could also indicate Hippolytus' or his predecessor's editorial hand in shaping Josephus in a particular way. While keeping to the same structure as Josephus for his topics, Hippolytus often uses different vocabulary and Greek syntax (9: 18–23, 26–7), interwoven with exact renderings (9: 23–5, 28). He may do this because in fact he does not claim to offer a quote of a piece of text from Josephus; it is just that it happens to be very close to what Josephus wrote. Hippolytus seems much more a plagiarist than a citer of Josephus; he never claims to be exactly quoting Josephus or using him as his source.

Even with paraphrasing, the issue of possible missing bits of Josephus may yet remain. Apart from the anomalous inclusion of the Sicarii as Essenes, the more significant additional or modifying elements in Hippolytus' paraphrasing of Josephus are as follows. The Essenes 'turn away from every act of desire, having an aversion against even hearing such things' (*Haer.* 9: 18, addition to *War* 2: 120), and they 'do not trust women in any way'. He condenses the mention of avoidance of oil, but adds that the Essenes consider it defiling to be anointed (*Haer.* 9: 19; *War* 2: 123). 'Modesty' replaces the image of a child under tuition (*Haer.* 9: 20; *War* 2: 126). During their dawn services they 'do not speak a word until they have praised God in a hymn', rather than pray towards the sun (*Haer.* 9: 21, modifying *War* 2: 128–9). Their linen wrap is to 'conceal their private parts' (*Haer.* 9: 21, addition to *War* 2. 129). At the end of the pure meal their linen cloths are put 'in a vestibule' (*Haer.* 9: 21, addition to *War* 2: 131). They 'abstain from all fury and anger, and all such, judging these things dangerous to humanity' (*Haer.* 9: 22, addition to *War* 2: 135). Regarding their expertise in the medicinal properties of plants and stones they have gained their knowledge from 'the law and prophets' rather than 'the ancient ones', and say 'that these things were not created in vain' (*Haer.* 9: 22, addition to *War* 2: 136). The Essenes swear not to injure anyone and 'will not hate a person who injures him, or is hostile to him, but pray for him, and that he will aid the righteous' as opposed to the Essenes hating the unrighteous (*Haer.* 9: 23, modifying *War* 2: 139). On the Sabbath 'some would not even rise from a couch' (*Haer.* 9: 25, addition to *War* 2: 147). 'Forbidden things' of *War* 2: 152 become 'things offered to idols' in *Haer.* 9: 26, and there is no mention of Essenes being tortured by the Romans. The doctrine of the immortality of both the body and the soul is asserted and the soul on death rests in a ventilated, light place until final judgement (*Haer.* 9: 27, modifying *War* 2: 154–5).

The final assertion ties the Essenes more closely to the doctrine of the Pharisees and also the Christians, when Josephus had referred to immortality of the soul only (*War* 2: 154–6). However, studies have shown how Hippolytus introduces resurrection of the body at other places where it is not attested in his sources.[161]

The belief in the resurrection of the body and final judgement seem highly Christianising, as also the assertion that Essenes will pray for those who injure or curse them, and abstain from anger, or even praise God with a hymn at the beginning of the day. There are also intensifications: that Essenes cannot even bear to hear of desirous acts, or will not get up from a couch on the Sabbath. Only a few small details, such as putting the purified cloths in a vestibule, serve no purpose in this rhetoric.

PORPHYRY

The variants of Hippolytus might seem more significant if we did not have Porphyry. The celebrated Neoplatonist philosopher Porphyry wrote about the Essenes positively in his pro-vegetarian work *On Abstinence from Killing Animals* (*De Abstinentia* 4: 11–13), around the year 263, in a text quoted by Eusebius, *Preparation for the Gospel* (*Praep. Evang.* 9: 3: 1–21.[162] Here Porphyry mentions descriptions of Essenes by Josephus in 'many of his writings', namely *War* 2, *Antiquities* 18 and 'in the second of the two books he wrote *To the Greeks*'. As regards the latter, no description of the Essenes is found in manuscripts of *Against Apion*, though this is a two-book work, and Josephus is not otherwise known to have written a work by the name 'To the Greeks'. In *Abstin.* 4: 11 Porphyry inserts a comment that the Essenes wish to avoid the lasciviousness of women, taken from Philo, *Hypoth.* 11: 14–17. Porphyry may then have wrongly ascribed Philo's *Apologia* (= *Hypothetica*) to Josephus, given that *Philo's* account of the Essenes (i.e. *Hypoth.* 11: 1–13) is in the second part of the work Eusebius refers to as 'Apologia on Behalf of the Jews' (*Praep. Evang.* 8: 10: 19). This title could have been referred to also as 'To the Greeks'.

At any rate, Porphyry gives a fairly accurate rendering of Josephus, *War* 2: 118–61[163] without any major interpolations from other writings, though there are small modifications of word order and language which may represent a slightly different manuscript version of Josephus. For example, the plural of *War* 2: 139 'great oaths' is singular in Porphyry: one great oath is sworn (*Abstin.* 4: 13). Notably, Porphyry writes that the food of the Essenes was

[161] See Elledge, *Life after Death*, 94–5 and see Jaap Mansfeld, 'Resurrection Added: The *interpretatio christiana* of a Stoic Doctrine', *VC* 37 (1983): 218–33.

[162] Porphyry, *Porphyrie de l'Abstinence*, Greek text and French trans. and ed. Michel Patillon and Alain P. Segonds (Paris: Société d'édition, Les Belles-Lettres, 1995).

[163] Burchard, 'Nebenüberlieferung von Josephus', 77–96; Patillon and Segonds, *Porphyrie*, 18–23; Finkbeiner, 'Essenes', 270–4.

'sacred and pure' (4: 12, addition to *War* 2: 131). Porphyry also misses pieces out, though the longest omission is *War* 2: 134–6, a segment that does not neatly follow 2: 133, so that in Porphyry the passage continues quite appropriately with 2: 137, and indeed sections 134–6 interrupt the flow of Josephus' presentation, so that one may wonder if the sequence we now have is entirely original. But Porphyry also links the abstention from defecating on the Sabbath, illustrating the Essenes' great power of endurance, with their endurance of torture by the Romans (4: 13, cf. *War* 2: 147, 152). The frugality and toughness of their regime, a theme dear to Porphyry (*Abstin.* 1: 45, 47; 4: 2),[164] gave them extraordinary strength.

In both Hippolytus and Porphyry there may be small snippets then that go back to ancient manuscripts and indeed these may tell us something about manuscripts' textual history and redaction, but more than anything they give us a sense of the reception history of Josephus' descriptions of the Essenes. The Essenes in Josephus could be remade to serve different purposes at different times and, with these purposes driving the work, writers can think they read words in Josephus that are not in fact there. If anything, both Hippolytus and Porphyry send us lessons across the centuries, as we struggle to read Josephus correctly. We will inevitably be time bound, and culture bound, but we need to be careful we are not misreading, for our own purposes, with presuppositions fixed so firmly we do not know what we are seeing.

---

[164] Patillon and Segonds, *Porphyrie*, xxxii.

4

The Herodians of the Gospel of Mark

In the Gospels, the Essenes are not specifically mentioned by name, a matter which—by implication—has tended to endorse the impression that they were removed and disengaged from the concerns of other Jews and the heart of public and religious life, so that the only really important religio-political players at the time of Jesus are the Pharisees and Sadducees. The glaring lacuna of the missing Essenes in the New Testament has removed them from centre field. It would be hard to construct a notion of Essene marginality on the basis of Philo or Josephus, yet they are missing in the New Testament and thus—given the dominant conceptual paradigms created by biblical literature—it seems obvious. Why would the Gospel-writers have avoided mentioning the Essenes if they were powerful players, deeply involved in public debate? If the Pharisees and Sadducees were concerned about Jesus' interpretations of the law and actions, surely the Essenes—if they played a public role—would also have been concerned? As we have seen, in Philo and Josephus the Essenes are presented as the most exemplary of all Jewish legal 'societies' in Judaea and a key paradigm for Judaism as a whole; in the New Testament they are absolutely nowhere.

In contrast, we have the duality of the Pharisees and Sadducees, linked together in the Gospel of Matthew (Matt. 3: 7; 16: 1, 6, 12; 21: 45; 23: 32–6), as a combined contingent, though we know these two schools disagreed with each other on certain matters, as evidenced in Josephus (*War* 2: 162–6; *Ant.* 13: 16–17; 172–3; 292–6; 18: 178) and also in the Acts of the Apostles (23: 6). Mark, the earliest extant Gospel, contains references to the Pharisees as Jesus' opposition from a point early in the narrative through to the story of events in Jerusalem (Mark 2: 16, 18, 24; 3: 6, 7: 1–3, 5; 8: 11, 15; 10: 2; 12: 13).[1] Matthew has additional Pharisees where they do not occur in Mark (Matt. 9: 11, cf. Mark 2: 16; Matt. 9: 34 and 12.24, cf. Mark 3.22), possibly interpolating them in the same way that Justin Martyr would add Pharisees to quotations

---

[1] For a review of the Pharisees in Mark see Martin Pickup, 'Matthew's and Mark's Pharisees,' in Jacob Neusner and Bruce Chilton (eds), *In Quest of the Historical Pharisees* (Waco, Texas: Baylor University Press, 2007), 67–112.

where they do not appear (*Dial.* 51: 2; 76: 7; 100: 3). Matthew contains more references to this group than any other gospel, including rigorous denunciations of apparent aspects of their behaviour (Matt. 23: 6, 13, 15, 23, 25, 26, 27, 29).[2]

In Luke-Acts the Pharisees are identified as the elite who enjoy public honour and esteem (Luke 7: 36; 11: 37, 43; 14: 1, 7–11, 12–14).[3] They are concerned with defining the correct interpretation of Torah, and function as teachers of the Law (Luke 5: 17, and see Gamaliel in Acts 5: 34; 23: 6, 9). In Acts, the Pharisees and Sadducees are each individually described in Josephus' terms as an αἵρεσις, a '[philosophical/legal] school' (Acts 5: 17; 15: 5; 26: 5, cf. Acts 23: 6–9).[4]

In the synoptic gospels and Acts, the Sadducees are more strongly linked to religious authority in Jerusalem, where they appear independently of Pharisees in Mark 12: 18–27 (Matt. 22: 23, 24/Luke 20: 27–40). They are portrayed as linked with the Temple hierarchy: in Acts 4: 1 priests come with the captain of the Temple 'and the Sadducees' to arrest Peter and John in the Temple, and in 5: 17 the High Priest acts with 'all his supporters from the school of the Sadducees' to arrest the apostles and put them in prison.

The Sadducees, however, do not occur in the Gospel of John, and the designation 'Pharisees' is linked with the hostile Ἰουδαῖοι, 'Judaeans', a term which often indicates the ruling class of the Judaean authorities, as von Wahlde has observed.[5] For example, 'Pharisees' are, at the very beginning of the gospel, defined essentially as 'priests and Levites' sent by the council in Jerusalem to John the Baptist (1: 19, 24). Nicodemus is both a Pharisee and a 'ruler of the Judaeans', ἄρχων τῶν Ἰουδαίων. In John 4: 1 Jesus leaves Judaea

---

[2] In Matt. 23: 2–7 Jesus' recommendation that his disciples do as the Pharisees 'speak'—given that they 'sit on the seat of Moses' but not what 'they do'—would indicate that his largely illiterate disciples need to listen to Torah as recited by the Pharisees, as synagogue readers and leaders, but not look to the Pharisees as a model of behaviour (including praxis based on their interpretation of the law), see Mark Allan Powell, '"Do and Keep What Moses Says" (Matthew 23.2–7),' *JBL* 114 (1995): 419–35.

[3] Amy-Jill Levine, 'Luke's Pharisees,' in Neusner and Chilton, *Quest*, 113–30, at 129. Steve Mason, 'Chief Priests, Sadducees, Pharisees and Sanhedrin in Acts,' in Richard Bauckham (ed.), *The Book of Acts in its Palestinian Setting* (Grand Rapids: Eerdmans, 1995), 115–77, rightly differentiates, in the Gospel of Luke and in Acts, between the kind of authority enjoyed by the Pharisees—who are influential over the common people—and the Sadducees—who are influential over the chief priests in Jerusalem. This is a significant differentiation that remains even when in Acts they are both portrayed as being in the High Priest's council.

[4] For the meaning of this term, see above, p. 49–57. See also Joan E. Taylor, 'The *Nazoraeans* as a "Sect" in "Sectarian Judaism"? A Reconsideration of the Current View via the Narrative of Acts and the Meaning of *Hairesis*,' in Sacha Stern (ed.), *Sects and Sectarianism in Jewish History* (Leiden: Brill, 2010), 87–118.

[5] Urban C. von Wahlde, 'The Johannine Jews: A Critical Survey,' *NTS* 28 (1982): 33–60. Von Wahlde noted that the term 'does not simply indicate nationality nor even regional differentiation (i.e. Judaean) but seems to refer to a certain class (or classes) of persons within Palestinian society', namely the religious authorities, aside from John 6: 41, 52. See also Raimo Hakola and Adele Reinhartz, 'John's Pharisees,' in Neusner and Chilton, *Quest*, 131–48.

when he knew that the 'Pharisees' had heard he was making and immersing more disciples than John, as if this action would incite them, as rulers, dangerously (cf. John 7: 1). The 'Pharisees' and 'the chief priests' send officers to seize Jesus (John 7: 32, 45). They are linked with 'rulers' in John 7: 47–8, and Nicodemus is identified as 'one of them' (7: 50). They are linked with 'scribes' in John 8: 3, and they define the legitimacy of a witness in John 8: 13, being referred to subsequently as Ἰουδαῖοι (8: 22). The Pharisees are those who can specify law in the case of the blind man (9: 15–16), and here appear to be equated again with the Ἰουδαῖοι (9: 18),[6] who have the power to put people out of the synagogue if they confess Jesus to be the Christ (9: 22, cf. 12: 42, 16: 2); in fact they do this to the cured blind man (9: 34–5), because they are 'blind' (9: 40). After the raising of Lazarus, the 'chief priests and the Pharisees' convene a council (11: 47–8) and 'the chief priests and the Pharisees' give orders that if anyone knows Jesus' whereabouts it should be reported to them. The 'chief priests' are concerned that so many people are believing in Jesus. They take counsel about putting Lazarus to death (12: 10), and, after Jesus' triumphal entry to Jerusalem, 'the Pharisees' (apparently within the same group of rulers) complain to each other that they are not making progress (12: 19). When Judas acts to betray Jesus, he comes with a cohort of troops sent from 'the chief priests and Pharisees' (18: 3), which comprise the Judaean court (7: 32, 45; 11: 47, 54), in turn equated with the category of the Ἰουδαῖοι (18: 2, 14). This heavy association of 'Pharisees' with the chief priests and the council advising the High Priest—a body of rulers with the power to exclude people from synagogues, pronounce authoritatively on matters of law, and send troops—has greatly influenced the traditional understanding of this school of law at the time of Jesus. It is enhanced further by the presentation of Matthew, which has the chief priests and Pharisees linked together in Matt. 21: 45 and 27: 62, with Pharisees plotting against Jesus at Matt. 22: 15, 34, 41 (cf. Gospel of Peter 8: 28).

This entire scenario appears to reflect a time when the Pharisees were—in a crisis situation—placed in a position of leadership along with the chief priests, as von Wahlde has explored. On three occasions in Josephus there is indeed the curious conjunction of the chief priests and Pharisees, at the period of the Jewish Revolt (66–70 CE).[7] The Pharisees' claim to authority in the

---

[6] De Jonge thinks there is a differentiation here between the 'Pharisees' who are divided about Jesus and the Ἰουδαῖοι who are utterly opposed to him: Henk Jan de Jonge, '"The Jews" in the Gospel of John,' in Reimund Bieringer, Didier Pollefeyt, and Frederique Vandecasteel-Vanneuville (eds), *Anti-Judaism and the Fourth Gospel* (Louisville, KY: Westminster John Knox Press, 2001), 121–40, at 133. It is true that the equation is not necessarily absolute, but the Pharisees can still overall be included within the wider category of those ruling authorities hostile to Jesus; see Peter J. Thomsen, '"Jews" in the Gospel of John as compared with the Palestinian Talmud, the Synoptics and some New Testament Apocrypha,' Bieringer, Pollefeyt and Vandecasteel-Vanneuville, *Anti-Judaism*, 176–221.

[7] Urban C. von Wahlde, 'The Relationships between Pharisees and Chief Priests: Some Observations on the Texts in Matthew, John and Josephus,' *NTS* 42 (1996): 506–22.

synagogues—as opposed to their loving the 'first seats' (see Matt. 23: 6–Luke 11: 43)—might be placed just at this time. For how long was their top position of authority maintained?

Justin Martyr, from Neapolis in Palestine, and writing in the middle of the second century, does note in passing that the 'Pharisees' are the 'chiefs of the synagogues' (*Dial.* 137: 2). But the evidence of the first-century Theodotus inscription is that ἀρχισυναγώγοι were priests, and among the many inscriptions from synagogues throughout the Roman world there is not a single mention of an ἀρχισυνάγωγος defined as a Φαρισαῖος.[8] Given the simple equation Justin makes, we could read this as indicating not that Pharisees were in charge of all Jewish synagogues in the second century, but rather that Justin equated synagogue leaders of his age with 'Pharisees' found in the gospels and thus made sense of the references to a group of an earlier time. This would mean that the texts needed to be 'translated' to his era, when synagogue leaders in general were opposing Christians.

Following the picture presented in the gospels, nevertheless, scholarly literature has focused on the Pharisees and Sadducees as being the prime parties, 'sects', in Second Temple Judaism, with the Pharisees—who engage with Jesus most often—generally considered to be the most important; only Jacob Neusner has suggested that their position was far more withdrawn and introverted than commonly assumed, on the basis of his analysis not of the Greek sources, but of rabbinic references to the *haberim*, with whom they are often equated.[9]

---

[8] *CIJ* i. 140.

[9] Jacob Neusner, *The Rabbinic Traditions about the Pharisees before 70*, 3 vols (Leiden: Brill, 1971), argued that the Pharisees withdrew from public life during the Herodian period. However, Steve Mason, *Flavius Josephus on the Pharisees: A Composition-Critical Study* (Studia Post-Biblica 29; Leiden: Brill, 1991) successfully argued against this notion, and pointed out that while the Pharisees were not authoritative, as were the later rabbis, they were nevertheless very influential, backed by popular support. The scholarly literature on the Pharisees is vast, but noteworthy is the work of Albert I. Baumgarten, *The Flourishing of Jewish Sects in the Maccabean Era: An Interpretation* (Journal for the Study of Judaism Supplement Series 55; Leiden: Brill, 1997), who focuses on the Pharisees as a reformist sect in the period from the second to first century BCE. Roland Deines has somewhat revived the argument of Ellis Rivkin, *The Hidden Revolution: The Pharisees' Search for the Kingdom Within* (Nashville: Abingdon, 1978), in seeing the Pharisees as encapsulating normative Judaism both pre- and post-70: Roland Deines, *Die Pharisäer. Ihr Verständnis als Spiegel der christlichen und jüdischen Forschung seit Wellhausen und Graetz.* I (WUNT 101; Tübingen: Mohr-Siebeck, 1997), 540–55, see also Martin Hengel and Roland Deines, 'E. P. Sanders' "Common Judaism", Jesus and the Pharisees,' *JTS* 46 (1995): 1–70, and Roland Deines, 'The Pharisees between "Judaisms" and "Common Judaism",' in D. A. Carson, P. T. O'Brien, and M. A. Seifrid (eds), *Justification and Variegated Nomism: Volume 1—The Complexities of Second Temple Judaism* (Tübingen/Grand Rapids; Mohr Siebeck/Baker Academic, 2001), 443–504, though this is not to present them as the ruling elite as such: in Josephus they are invited to participate in the court because of their popularity (*Ant.* 13: 288). In the presentation of E. P. Sanders, *Judaism: Practice and Belief 63 BCE–66CE* (London: SCM Press, 1992) and Anthony Saldarini, *Pharisees, Scribes and Sadducees in Palestinian Society* (Edinburgh: T & T Clark, 1989), 120–2, the Pharisees are an influential force, who did not have

The Sadducees, on the other hand, are often presented as a small, elite, and rather Hellenized group, linked to the rich and the priestly class, and not concerned with the common people (Josephus, *Ant.* 13: 298), though aspects of this picture have now been challenged by Martin Goodman.[10]

However, if we do not prioritize the New Testament and early Christian literature for our history of these groups, we might be asking different questions. Does the apparent absence of the Essenes from the gospels mean that the Essenes themselves were small or marginal, or are there other reasons why they are apparently absent? Are we simply not seeing them when they do appear, because they are named differently in Christian material?

Partly to explain the 'missing Essenes' in the gospels and Acts, some have suggested that John the Baptist and/or Jesus were themselves Essenes.[11] As noted above, this proposition is old, but it has been revived in various forms, often in popular literature, and has since the 1950s been fused with the notion that Jesus had some relationship with Qumran, or that Jesus is found covertly referred to in the Dead Sea Scrolls.[12] The association between Jesus and the Essenes does not stand up to much scrutiny, and is dependent on the creation of a model of the Essenes that is highly 'Christian' to begin with.

If we credit the polemic of the gospels with a historical basis, one alternative is to explain it in terms of Jesus' struggle to win the hearts and minds of the common people. If it is right that the Pharisees had the most influence over the ordinary population in the first century (see Josephus, *Ant.* 13: 288, 298; 18:

absolute power, with Saldarini classifying the Pharisees as belonging to the 'retainer class' who attempted to influence policy. Also supportive of seeing the Pharisees as a powerful scholarly class are Gedalyahu Alon, *Jews, Judaism and the Classical World: Studies in Jewish History in the Times of the Second Temple and the Talmud* (Jerusalem: Magness, 1977) and Daniel R. Schwartz, 'Josephus and Nicolaus on the Pharisees,' *JSJ* 14 (1983): 157–71. Hillel Newman, *Proximity to Power and Jewish Sectarian Groups of the Ancient Period: A Review of the Lifestyle, Values and Halakhah in the Pharisees, Sadducees, Essenes and Qumran* (Leiden: Brill, 2007) resists the term 'sect', preferring 'group', and defines the Pharisees as a 'regime-powered dissenting group', meaning they functioned at the centre of Judaean religious life.

[10] Martin Goodman, 'The Place of Sadducees in First-Century Judaism,' in id. *Judaism in the Roman World: Collected Essays* (Leiden: Brill, 2007), 123–36; but see James C. VanderKam, 'Who Were the Sadducees? The Sadducees of Jerusalem and Qumran,' in Isaiah M. Gafni, Aharon Oppenheimer, and Daniel R. Schwartz (eds), *The Jews in the Hellenistic-Roman World. Studies in Memory of Menahem Stern* (Jerusalem: Zalman Shazar Center and the Historical Society of Israel, 1996), 393–411; Günther Stemberger, 'The Sadducees: Their History and Doctrines,' in William Horbury, W. D. Davies, and John Sturdy (eds), *The Cambridge History of Judaism 3: The Early Roman Period* (Cambridge: CUP, 1999), 428–43; Gunther Baumback, 'The Sadducees in Josephus,' in Louis H. Feldman and Gohei Hata (eds), *Josephus, The Bible and History* (Leiden: Brill, 1988), 173–95.

[11] See above, p. 4 n. 7.

[12] Barbara Thiering, *Jesus and the Riddle of the Dead Sea Scrolls* (London: HarperCollins, 1992); Hugh Schonfield, *The Essene Odyssey: The Mystery of the True Teacher and the Essene Impact on the Shaping of Human Destiny* (Tisbury: Element Books, 1984); Robert Eisenman, *James the Brother of Jesus: The Key to Unlocking the Secrets of Christianity and the Dead Sea Scrolls* (New York: Penguin, 1998).

17) then Jesus as an ordinary person may well have been challenging those whom people esteemed most of all for scriptural guidance and legal interpretation, when the Sadducees and Essenes were not as popular and therefore not so threatening. Jesus had to ensure the legal school the people most respected was undermined.[13] In the Gospel of Matthew, Jesus defies the Pharisees' interpretations as being—essentially—not as God intended, but the result of (faulty) human rationalizing (Matt. 23: 2–3, cf. 15: 3).

But, more importantly, we have seen from Philo (*Prob.* 89–91) that the Essenes were autonomous, allowed to go about their lives subject to their own interpretation of Mosaic law. Josephus states that they had their own court or council with 100 men to decide verdicts (*War* 2: 145). If so, then they were not involved with the council presided over by the High Priest, since theirs was a separate jurisdiction appropriate to their school of legal interpretation. This in itself is consistent with what we have in Acts 23 when Paul goes before a council composed of Pharisees and Sadducees under the direction of the High Priest. The Essenes, given that they were not part of this court, would not have played a role in advising the High Priest about what should happen to Jesus, or Paul. That is, of course, to assume that such a court was always properly convened: in Mark's gospel Jesus is interrogated at the High Priest's residence, at the time of Passover, where 'all the chief priests and the elders and the scribes were assembled' (Mark 14: 53): a privately domestic night-time consultation. Since this could not have constituted a proper court of law, Luke turns night to day, to make the court sit correctly, yet it was a festival when, like a Sabbath, it could not be convened (Luke 22: 66; 23: 1, cf. m.Sanh. 4: 1; Philo, *Migr.* 16). Mark is probably clearer in implying it was not a proper trial, but simply an interrogation by the High Priest with witnesses accusing Jesus of various wrongdoings, since ultimately the judgement would be that of the Roman governor Pilate. But whatever way this 'non-trial' was configured, the nocturnal gathering under the High Priest would not have included Essenes, if they maintained a separate court.

The Essenes would not then have been considered by Christians in the category of those responsible for handing Jesus over to the Romans, since they were not part of the High Priest's council. If Josephus and Philo are right, the Essene jurisdiction seems to have only concerned people who were classified as part of their society, or accepted their authority. They were then a legal

---

[13] In addition, as I have argued elsewhere, John the Baptist may have had a special relationship with the Pharisees, a relationship evidenced in the Gospels by the practice of shared fasting, see Mark 2: 18–20. The Pharisees, on their part, may have seen Jesus as a disciple of John who should therefore behave as one in accordance with Pharisaic *halakha*; instead, against expectations, he challenged the Pharisees with his own radical interpretations of law. See Joan E. Taylor, *The Immerser: John the Baptist within Second Temple Judaism* (Grand Rapids: Eerdmans, 1997), 203–11.

anomaly, not under the authority of the High Priest, protected because of their special peculiar status vouchsafed by Herod the Great and his descendants.[14]

However, why assume that the Essenes were not engaged with synagogues? Since the council of the High Priest was a different matter to participation in synagogue leadership or public oversight, some positions of authority in synagogues could surely have been granted on the basis of the support of key individuals in any given city, town, or village. Where Essenes dwelt in large numbers, then their role in synagogue life could have been important, even if they maintained a certain separation for the sake of purity. Neither Philo nor Josephus insists on utter separation from synagogues or any forum of public life for their pre-eminent Jews. We simply assume it, on the basis that Essenes must have withdrawn from situations in which their purity could have been violated. But purity could be violated at any time; Josephus indicates that this was a possibility even within an Essene dwelling: if a junior member touches a senior it is considered polluting (*War* 2: 150). As Josephus has it, purification was necessary for Essenes prior to common meals, those dinners that are 'sacred and pure' (Porphyry, *Abstin.* 4: 12: 3), twice a day (*Ant.* 18: 19; *War* 2: 129); Philo too refers to continual purifications (*Prob.* 84). These are necessary because of the potential that one might have been rendered unclean.

Purity in Judaism is not envisaged as a permanent condition, and indeed it was impossible for anyone to maintain purity in all situations throughout one's whole life; the issue for an Essene was that purification was necessary not just for the Temple, but for common meals.

If there is no reason to suppose that Essenes always excluded themselves from the synagogues, and Christians met problems of acceptance in synagogues, then Essenes may well have encountered them as an opposing force in that environment.

From the High Priest's perspective, and the operations of his council, which was the one governing the law of the land, it may be true to say that the Essenes were marginal, but here we must beware of assuming that this indicated they were a small group of no significance in religio-political terms overall in the Second Temple period. The Sadducees, according to Josephus (*War* 2: 164–6; *Ant.* 18: 16–17), were by far the smallest of the three legal societies, but they were far from marginal because certain leading men of Judaea supported them, the leading men in this case being usually understood to be members of the chief priestly class. The Essenes were far more numerous than the Sadducees, and also more esteemed in terms of their high reputation

---

[14] As we shall see, this may be reflected in the language of Dio Chrysostom: they functioned as a kind of independent *polis* within Judaea (Synesius, *Dio* 3: 2), like the *poleis* of the Decapolis that clustered around the province, in an astonishingly complex world of legal systems sitting side by side.

for piety, yet they kept themselves somewhat detached. This 'detachment' is not quite the same as 'marginality'. As explored above, both Philo and Josephus indicate that they were separated by their own choosing, in adopting higher standards. We might then expect to find them somewhere in the life of Jesus, being particularly scrupulous about matters of the law and purity.

The question of whether there are missing Essenes in the gospels because of different naming is therefore important to consider. In the earliest gospel, the Gospel of Mark, there are references to the Ἡρῳδιανοί. Many theories have arisen to explain who they are,[15] with the most popular theory today being that the Herodians are simply supporters of Herod Antipas. The suggestion that they were actually Essenes, named differently, was made by the Romanian scholar Constantin Daniel, in 1966, and has been revived more recently by Hartmut Stegemann: both explain the name by reference to the endorsement of the Essenes by Herod the Great and his descendants and their acceptance of royal gifts.[16] As we have seen, both Philo and Josephus indicate this historical circumstance, and the Gate of the Essenes leading into the Herodian complex on the western side of Jerusalem would have reminded people of the Herodian favours continually. The association between the Essenes and the Herodian dynasty would have resulted in a popular 'slang': one person's respected Essene was another person's suspicious 'Herodian'.

The definition of the Herodians needs to be found internally within the Gospel of Mark, since they function as 'characters' within the narrative with a

---

[15] F. J. Foakes-Jackson and Kirsopp Lake, *The Beginnings of Christianity: Part 1, The Acts of the Apostles* (London: Macmillan, 1920), 119–20, believed the Herodians to be members of Herod Antipas' court or party, and this is the common view expressed today in most commentaries, though B. W. Bacon, 'Pharisees and Herodians in Mark,' *JBL* 39 (1920): 102–12 championed the identification of this group as indicating that Herod was the Messiah, a notion rejected by Elias J. Bickerman, 'Les Hérodiens,' *RB* 47 (1938): 184–97 reprinted in id. *Studies in Jewish and Christian History* (Leiden: Brill, 1976), 22–34. H. H. Rowley, 'The Herodians in the Gospels,' *JTS* 41 (1940): 14–27 considered them a group of pro-Herod aristocrats. W. J. Bennett, 'The Herodians of Mark's Gospel,' *NT* 17 (1975): 9–14, thought they were an invention by Mark designed to link the enemies of John (Herod Antipas and his house) with the enemies of Jesus. Ever since Graetz identified the Herodians of the Gospels with the Boethusians of rabbinic literature (Heinrich Graetz, *Geschichte der Juden: Von den ältesten Zeiten bis auf die Gegenwart. Aus den Quellen neu bearbeitet*, 11 vols (Leipzig: Leiner, 1853–75), iii. 2, 693), this view also at times surfaces, for example in Harold W. Hoehner, *Herod Antipas* (Cambridge: CUP, 1972), 10. For further bibliography see John P. Meier, 'The Historical Jesus and the Historical Herodians,' *JBL* 119 (2000): 740–6, n. 1. Meier follows the usual supposition that the reference is simply to 'a group of servants, officials, and other supporters around Herod Antipas,' 744.

[16] Constantin Daniel, 'Esséniens, zélotes et sicaires et leur mention par paronymie dans le N.T.,' *Numen* 13 (1966): 88–115; id. 'Les "Hérodiens" du Nouveau Testament sont-ils les Esséniens?' *RQ* 6 (1967): 31–53; id. 'Nouveaux arguments en faveur de l'identification des Hérodiens et des Esséniens,' *RQ* 27 (1970): 397–402; Hartmut Stegemann, *The Library of Qumran: On the Essenes, Qumran, John the Baptist and Jesus* (Grand Rapids: Eerdmans 1998), 267–8. Daniel's thesis was dismissed as mere conjecture by Willi Braun, 'Were New Testament Herodians Essenes? A Critique of an Hypothesis,' *RQ* 14 (1989): 75–88, but by using a very limited model of who the Essenes were, and assuming deep introversion on their part.

certain role and purpose. In order to clarify what the Herodians do within the Gospel of Mark it is necessary to contextualize them within the wider framework of Mark's determination of Jesus' opposition. In the following discussion the approach is then by means of narrative criticism, so that the Herodians are understood as protagonists within a story that has its own integrity.[17] This may enable us to be alert to fine nuances of their characterization.

Before progressing here, a few words are needed on the authorship and context of this gospel. While this is a vast and debated topic, it seems most likely that the Gospel of Mark was written at about the same time that Josephus was writing *War*. In terms of authorship, Papias of Hierapolis, near Ephesus, states of the testimony of an elder:

> This, too, the elder [John] said that Mark, who had been Peter's translator, carefully wrote down everything that he remembered of the words and actions of the Lord, but not in order. He had not heard the Lord or been one of his followers, but later, as I mentioned, he was one of Peter's [followers]. Peter used to modify his teachings to the situation, not making an orderly arrangement of the Lord's sayings, so that Mark was right in presenting certain things as he remembered them [being presented]. He had only one aim—to omit nothing that he had heard, and to make no mistake about it. (Eusebius, *Hist. Eccles.* 3: 39: 15)

In this story, Peter is understood not to have spoken fluent Greek, and he apparently needed someone like Mark to communicate to a Greek-speaking audience. Mark wrote down what he remembered, some time after Peter's death. The basic authenticity of this tradition has now been effectively defended, aided by careful literary analysis, by Richard Bauckham.[18] While it is popular to argue that this authorial attribution to Mark was a patristic concoction,[19] in favour of a clean slate that allows for a situation of the Marcan community in Syria or elsewhere,[20] John Donahue has also argued very persuasively for the authenticity of ancient tradition.[21] This Roman Mark is

---

[17] See John Donahue and Daniel J. Harrington, *The Gospel of Mark* (Sacra Pagina; Collegeville, MN: Liturgical Press, 2002), 20–2.

[18] Richard Bauckham, *Jesus and the Eyewitnesses: The Gospels as Eyewitness Testimony* (Grand Rapids: Eerdmans, 2006), 155–239.

[19] For an interesting though sceptical discussion of patristic literature see C. Clifton Black, *Mark: Images of an Apostolic Interpreter* (Columbia: University of South Carolina Press, 1994). Early traditions do not conflate the Roman Mark with the other person with this name, 'John Mark', who appears in the Acts of the Apostles in association with Paul: Marcus was a common praenomen.

[20] Joel Marcus, 'The Jewish War and the *Sitz im Leben* of Mark,' *JBL* (1992): 441–62 locates this gospel in Hellenistic cities of Palestine. Burton Mack, *A Myth of Innocence: Mark and Christian Origins* (Philadelphia: Fortress, 1988), locates the gospel in Syria in the 70s, as does Howard Clark Kee, *The Community of the New Age: Studies in Mark's Gospel* (Philadelphia: Westminster, 1977), but these contextualizations are highly hypothetical and disregard all tradition concerning the writer.

[21] John R. Donahue, 'Windows and Mirrors: The Setting of Mark's Gospel,' *CBQ* (1995): 1–26.

probably not 'John Mark' (Acts 12: 12, 25; 13: 5, 13; 15: 37), an associate of
Paul and a cousin of Paul's fellow-apostle Barnabas (Col. 4: 10, Philem. 24),
son of an important Jewish disciple of Jesus in Jerusalem named Mary (Acts
12: 12). The Roman Mark associated with Peter (as indicated in 1 Peter 5: 13)
was a different man.[22] Even though the Roman Mark must have originally
been from the Jewish community himself to know both Aramaic and Greek,
Jewish customs and Aramaic terms are explained, which indicates a concern
for a non-Jewish audience and perhaps a distancing from Jewish praxis (e.g.
Mark 5: 41; 7: 1–4, 11; 14: 12, 36; 15: 42), unless these come from a later
editorial hand. The numerous Latinisms make sense in a Roman context. But
while the tradition might appear to endorse veracity, and the authority of
Peter, Papias actually makes clear that the Gospel of Mark was not a simple
recording of Peter's words; it was based on Mark's *memory*.[23] The interpreter
Mark was presumably also able to include other useful material.[24] The issue of
the editorial hand and the cases where Matthew and Luke agree against Mark
has raised the question of whether our present Gospel of Mark is a redacted
form of an original *Ur-Markus*.[25] At any rate, if we accept what is stated by
Papias, in this gospel Judaean society is filtered then through different lenses:
firstly that of Peter, and then of Mark.

In the narrative of Mark 1: 21–2 Jesus enters a synagogue and begins to
teach as one having (prophetic) authority, 'not as the scribes'. Mark leaves us
without explanation of what this means, but at least indicates that the scribes
in question were teachers in the Capernaum synagogue. The scribes of
Capernaum are present at the healing of the paralysed man, and are bothered
by Jesus pronouncing that the sick man's sins were forgiven (2: 6). The next
time these 'scribes' appear they are more specifically defined as 'scribes of the

---

[22] See Eusebius (*Hist. Eccles.* 2: 24: 1), who writes that the evangelist Mark wrote down the
sermons of Peter before he left for Alexandria, though his dates are wildly wrong.

[23] A similar story is reflected by Clement of Alexandria, later in the second century, who said
that people in Rome urged Mark to write down what he remembered that Peter said (Eusebius,
Hist. Eccles. 6:14), though here Clement assumes Peter was still alive. Yet Papias' statement
implies that it was Peter's death that prompted his former translator to record as much as he
could. Peter was crucified upside down (Eusebius, *Hist. Eccles.* 3: 1) by the emperor Nero some
time after the fire of Rome in 64 CE, when Nero blamed Christians for in some way being the
cause. During the reign of Nero, Paul too was killed, by beheading (Eusebius, *Hist. Eccles.* 2: 25),
and the Christian cemeteries there were duly named after both Peter and Paul. During the
twelfth year of Nero's reign, war flared up in Judaea (66 CE), resulting in cataclysmic consequences for the Jewish people and the destruction of the Temple in Jerusalem by the Romans.
Mark 13: 14–23 (cf. 14: 58–9) indicates the destruction of the Temple and Mark 12: 9 refers to the
exile and killing of Jews after this event. This leads most commentators to place the Gospel of
Mark in the years 70–75, some twenty years after the letters of Paul.

[24] See Eusebius, *Hist. Eccles.* 3: 28 and 7: 25. The underlying Aramaic of Mark's Gospel has
been explored extensively by Maurice Casey, *Aramaic Sources for Mark's Gospel* (Cambridge:
CUP, 1998), without attributing this Aramaic stratum to Peter.

[25] See the discussion in E. P. Sanders, *The Tendencies of the Synoptic Tradition* (Cambridge:
CUP, 2006), 6–7, Appendix II, 292–3.

Pharisees' (Mark 2: 16, cf. Luke 5: 30), but then in Mark 2: 18–19 these have become both 'the Pharisees' and 'the disciples of the Pharisees', who fast along with the disciples of John the Baptist. In Mark 2: 24 the 'Pharisees' ask Jesus to explain why he is picking grain on the Sabbath. The loose terminology seems to group anyone who studies or teaches under the Pharisees with the Pharisees proper.

The Herodians then appear as people acting in consultation with the Pharisees, opposed to Jesus. That the Pharisees consult with the Herodians indicates that the latter are in some way similar, and they are both defined as having a wish 'to destroy him', $α\mathring{v}τ\grave{o}ν \mathring{a}πολέσωσιν$ (Mark 3: 6). Importantly, up until this point in the narrative, there has been no mention at all of the tetrarch Herod Antipas. The issues of conflict presented in the narrative are entirely about Jesus' practice of 'working' on the Sabbath (Mark 1: 21–8, 29–31; 2: 23–8) or reclining at table with 'sinners and tax-gatherers' (Mark 2: 15–16) or not fasting with the Pharisees and disciples of John (Mark 2: 18–22), and the opposition is from scribes and others who are concerned with the correct interpretation of the Law of Moses. The catalyst of the Pharisees' consultation with the Herodians is Jesus' action of healing a man with a withered hand on the Sabbath (3: 1–5), after which 'the Pharisees went out ($κα\grave{ι} \mathring{ε}ξελθόντες ο\mathring{ι}$ $Φαρισα\mathring{ι}οι$) [of the synagogue] and immediately were making counsel ($συμβούλιον \mathring{ε}δίδουν$) with the Herodians, against him, on how they would destroy him'. Strikingly, the Herodians themselves are not in the synagogue, but somewhere outside, since the Pharisees go out ($\mathring{ε}ξελθόντες$) to meet them. They are nevertheless soon engaged in the process of counsel about how they could remove Jesus because of a matter of legal interpretation of Mosaic law concerning the Sabbath.

To read this as indicating that the Pharisees are presented as discussing matters with people who are believed to have the ear of the tetrarch Herod Antipas,[26] would be to import a totally unknown character (Herod Antipas) into the narrative at this point, when we know nothing about him from the story itself. It would also require us to suppose that Herod's supporters or court officials were vitally interested in the issue of 'working' on the Sabbath, and other matters of religious law, when Herod Antipas himself is fundamentally characterized later on as anything but a pious practitioner of that law (see Mark 6: 18).

Having identified both the Pharisees and Herodians as religious authorities who interpret Sabbath laws against Jesus, Mark then reverts to the use of the word 'scribes', further defining them as being bolstered by 'scribes who came down from Jerusalem', who claim that Jesus is possessed by Beelzebub (Mark 3: 19). The initial fury at Jesus has meant Jerusalem authorities have been

---

[26] As Meier supposes, 'Historical Jesus,' 743, which is a common view, though Meier also doubts the historicity of these Marcan stories.

summoned. Mark then does not focus again on this opposition until he has presented a long survey of Jesus' healings and miracles, returning to the possible opposition only in 6: 14, when he introduces Herod Antipas for the first time: 'And King Herod heard of it.'

If Mark were presenting the Herodians as indeed connected with Herod Antipas' court, then we have the absurdity that the tetrarch himself does not hear of anything about Jesus until his interest is piqued by Jesus' amazing healings. Far from wanting to get rid of either Jesus or John because of legal infringements, Herod Antipas is presented in Mark as being wrong himself in terms of law, weak and confused, yet essentially accepting of John the Baptist's righteousness. In Mark, John's death is recounted as being caused by Herod Antipas (6: 14–29) despite the fact that Herod Antipas 'feared' or 'respected' him, and recognized that John was a 'righteous and holy man'. Mark 6: 20 reads: 'when he heard him he was very perplexed and [yet] he was hearing him gladly.' Herod Antipas kills John—regretfully and against his will—not because of 'Herodian' advice, but because he is tricked by his wife. He hears of Jesus' healings as a remarkable occurrence, and it is this that causes him to take an interest in him, for the first time.

The Herodians simply cannot be Herod's officials in Mark. In Mark 7: 1 the 'Pharisees and some of the scribes who had come from Jerusalem' form a deputation to query Jesus' interpretation of the law in regard to purity, specifically asking why Jesus' disciples do not 'walk according to the tradition of the elders' in regard to eating bread with impure hands. As has been much pointed out, here they appear to be asking Jesus 'why are you not a Pharisee?' The Pharisees then again argue with him, asking him for a sign from heaven (Mark 8: 11), at which point Jesus tells his disciples to 'watch out for the leaven of the Pharisees and the leaven of the Herodians' (Mark 8: 15), as if they are part of the same deputation. However, this reads better as a general statement classifying different groups together; they had not necessarily fired identical questions, but had interpretations of Torah (the 'leaven') that should not be accepted.

This reference to ʽΗρῳδιανοί in Mark 8: 15 is often passed over as a copyist's error, despite the fact that it appears in one of the oldest papyri of the Gospels: 𝔭45. The judgement that 𝔭45 is secondary because it may be influenced by Mark 3: 6 and 12: 23,[27] however, does not take into account the fact that Matthew clearly read in his source text that there was a group that could be equated with the Pharisees as having a teaching tradition: 'leaven'. The alteration of the word to ʽΗρῴδου, 'of Herod', in most later manuscripts, is understandable given that later copyists did not know who the Herodians were any more than did Luke (12: 1), who omits the problematic group here as

---

[27] Bruce Metzger, *A Textual Commentary on the Greek New Testament* (New York: United Bible Societies, 1994), 83.

elsewhere. In using Mark, Luke would have had no reason to omit a reference to Herod Antipas,[28] but very good reason to omit a reference he could not understand: the Gospel of Luke consistently drops the term 'Herodians' from the other passages where they are found in Mark. Recognizing the reading of p45 is then crucial for a correct understanding, since the characterization of the Herodians in Mark 8: 15 is very important for confirming that this group comprises those who teach a particular interpretation of law.

'Scribes' do not appear to be an entirely equivalent group to 'Pharisees' in Mark, but rather a larger body whose members could be Pharisees. In Mark 8: 31 Jesus makes a prediction concerning the identity of those who will condemn him to death: they are 'the elders and the chief priests and the scribes' ('the chief priests and the scribes' 10: 33), but this is not the same group as the 'Pharisees and Herodians' previously mentioned. Overall, 'scribes' are a broader category that can be attached to any legal authority, sometimes Pharisees, and sometimes the chief priestly group in Jerusalem. That 'scribes' can be either wrong or right to Mark is clear from the pericope in which a good 'scribe' asks about the great commandment (Mark 12: 28–34). They can simply read the Law: after the Transfiguration 'the scribes' are identified as saying that Elijah would come before the End (possibly just by reading out Malachi 4: 5 [Heb. 3: 23]),[29] and this is endorsed (Mark 9: 11). However, in Mark 9: 14 'scribes' are defined as arguing with disciples and appear to be not on the side of Jesus.

Where 'scribes' appear with 'chief priests and elders' in Jerusalem they are a different body to those scribes of village Galilee who are bothered by Jesus. Those who will be responsible for Jesus' death are identified by Mark as being only in Jerusalem, but given the deputation of Pharisees (and Herodians?) from this city already referred to, we may expect them to turn up there. From Mark 11: 27 the physical context of the story is the Temple, where various interlocutors question Jesus. The 'chief priests, scribes and elders' ask by what authority Jesus has the right to 'do these things' and are characterized—unlike Herod Antipas—as not believing in the authority of John the Baptist (Mark 11: 27–33). Jesus speaks the parable of the vine-growers against them, at which point they wish to 'seize' him (and clearly had the power to do so), but are afraid of the crowds (Mark 12: 12). Thus, it is no surprise then that 'they sent some of the Pharisees and Herodians to him in order to trap him in a statement'; the Pharisees and the Herodians are used as envoys by the chief priests, elders, and scribes. The question they ask is in regard to paying taxes to Rome (Mark 12: 13–14).

---

[28] Hoehner, *Herod Antipas*, notes how Luke is particularly concerned with the Tetrarch in his Gospel, 335, so it is strange he omits mention of the Herodians here if he read the term as indicating an association with the Tetrarch.

[29] See Powell, 'What Matthew Says,' 434.

'They'—the ruling Judaean authorities—in the narrative of Mark's Gospel then have the power to send 'Pharisees and Herodians' in order to ask Jesus a question in regard to legal interpretation, meaning that both groups were concerned with such interpretation. Herodians are not associated with Herod Antipas at all. The Pharisees and Herodians are linked together in probing Jesus about his interpretation of the law in regard to Roman interests. Importantly, Mark distinguishes the Herodians from the Sadducees: the Sadducees only appear in Mark 12: 18–27, asking about resurrection; ironic given that they say 'there is no resurrection' (12: 18). The Sadducees are not identified as being sent, but rather they come independently. The physical context remains the Temple, with discussion witnessed by a 'teacher of the law' whose reaction is positive (Mark 12: 28–34). The Temple context continues until Mark 13: 1–2, when Jesus leaves it, predicting its destruction.

The question of whether to identify the Herodians with Essenes in Mark 12 is both suggested and complicated by the narrative concerns of the gospel; clearly Mark believed that the ruling elite rustled up questioners from these two parties, the Pharisees and the Herodians, but Mark—or his source—need not have known very much about the historical 'Herodians', any more than he knew about the Pharisees. But that they did question Jesus in Galilee and Jerusalem and that Jesus identified them as being in error lies behind the presentation in the narrative. The author believed that in Jerusalem they were sent by the High Priest's council. However, the identification of the Essenes with the Herodians cannot hang on a question about whether any Essenes would actually have deigned to do the bidding of 'chief priests, elders and scribes' associated with the High Priest, or even co-operated with Pharisees. For all we know, in this case, they may well have wished to co-operate with the enquiry, if they already had concerns about Jesus from their investigations in Galilee.

As noted above, the Herodians do not appear to be mentioned in the High Priest's ad hoc council (14: 53–65; 15: 1). Those who question Jesus and hand him over to the Romans are 'the chief priests, the elders and the scribes' (Mark 12: 1, 10, 43, 53; 15: 1, 3, 10, 11, 31) who assemble in the High Priest's house. Neither the Pharisees nor the Herodians are identified as being part of this council, even though they have been sent by it to ask Jesus questions. This same council 'sent' also 'armed men with swords and clubs', one of whom is 'the servant of the High Priest' (14: 43–7), but these too are not members of the council, rather they are only those who do the council's bidding. The Pharisees and Herodians are then culpable for doing what is requested of them—in the Marcan narrative—and are represented as wanting to question Jesus in Galilee and 'destroy' him, but they are not in the end identified as making any decisions affecting Jesus being handed over to Pilate.

In summary, in the narrative of Mark we have three bodies of legal authorities identified who are concerned with the correct interpretation and

practice of the law: Pharisees, Herodians, and Sadducees. They are characterized negatively, as part of the opposition against Jesus. Nothing in this
characterization links them with Herod Antipas, but rather they act independently to investigate Jesus and also do the bidding of the High Priest's advisory
council in asking him questions. The narrative of Mark is based on historical
memory, and in this case this memory fits well with what we have in Josephus.
In Josephus we have three legal schools identified as being in authority during
this time period also: Pharisees, Essenes, and Sadducees, in order of numbers.
It seems then not unreasonable to assume that the Herodians of Mark are the
Essenes of Josephus and Philo, by another name.

We then turn to the use of the designation 'Herodians' in other gospels. We
have already seen how Luke avoids the term altogether. The Gospel of
Matthew, however, is generally quite faithful to Mark's use of 'Herodians',
though in Matthew 16: 6 'Herodians' are replaced by a reference to another
body: the Sadducees. The writer of Matthew could make this change because
he clearly understood the 'Herodians' in Mark to be a legal school or society
with authority, the Sadducees being an equivalent entity.[30] In Matthew 16: 12
it is specifically explained that 'leaven' indicates their teaching (16: 12), as
noted above. The multiplication of bread is a visual metaphor: Jesus'
teaching expands the bread like superlative leaven, providing food for
thousands. The statement reflects the positive image of leaven in Matthew
13: 33 (= Luke 13: 20–1) in which leaven functions as a means to show how the
Kingdom of God will expand. The 'leaven' or teaching of the Pharisees and
Herodians cannot enable the Kingdom of God to expand (cf. the image in b.
Ber. 17a). In Luke 12: 1, by contrast, Mark is not read accurately here; the
writer of Luke interprets 'leaven' only negatively, linking it with Jesus' denunciations of the Pharisees as hypocrites.

Unlike with the use of Mark 8: 15, the writer of Matthew does not change
the designation 'Herodians' to 'Sadducees' in the pericope about paying taxes
to 'Caesar' (Mark 12: 13–17), but slightly alters the language, so that 'the
Pharisees went and took counsel on how to entangle him in his speech and
they sent their disciples to him along with the Herodians' (Matt. 22: 15–16).
Here neither the Herodians nor the Pharisees are being sent directly by the
chief priestly council, and the Herodians seem to be sent by the Pharisees.

The evidence of the narrative of Mark then builds on the language of a
Judaean, and a historical memory that there was a legal school dubbed the
'Herodians' (negatively) who engaged with Jesus by questioning him. The
equation of this school with the Essenes relies on the fact that Josephus insists
that there were *only* three legal schools of legal interpretation prior to the rise
of the Fourth Philosophy. If this is historically true, it would be natural to

---

[30] See Bacon, 'Pharisees and Herodians,' 104. Luke omits them altogether (Luke 12: 1).

assume that the Herodians were the Essenes. However, there is another reason than this to make this equation, and it comes from the writings of Julius Africanus (early third century), as reflected in Eusebius.

As we have seen, in Josephus' account of *Ant.* 15: 368–71, the Essene master Menahem makes the prediction that Herod would become king, and yet not be righteous, but the basis for Menahem's announcement is passed over without much explanation. The actual prophecy itself is, however, explicitly defined in Eusebius, *Hist. Eccles.* 1: 6–7, on the basis of what is written by the chronographer Julius Africanus,[31] but here the basis of the prophecy is given without an explicit connection made with Menahem the Essene. We are provided with what reads as a type of *pesher* interpretation of Gen. 49:10. In the Masoretic text, this passage reads:

לא־יסור שבט מיהודה רמחקק מבין רגליו
עד כי־יבא שילה ולו יקהת עמים

> The sceptre [of office] will not depart from Judah, or the staff [of authority] from between his feet/loins, until tribute (?) [or Shiloh?] comes, and to him is the obedience of peoples.[32]

In the Septuagint, Gen. 49: 10 reads:

Οὐκ ἐκλείψει ἄρχων ἐξ Ἰούδα, καὶ ἡγούμενος ἐκ τῶν μηρῶν αὐτοῦ, ἕως ἐὰν ἔλθῃ τὰ ἀποκείμενα αὐτῷ· καὶ αὐτὸς προσδοκία ἐθνῶν.

> A ruler shall not fail from Judah, nor a leader from his loins, until reserved things come for him; and this man is the expectation of nations.[33]

In regard to this passage, Eusebius writes:

> At this time Herod became the first Gentile to become king of the nation of the Jews, fulfilling the words of Moses: 'A ruler shall not fail from Judah, nor a leader from his loins, until reserved things come for him; and this man is the expectation of nations'. There could be no fulfilment of the prophecy as long as they were free to live under rulers of their own race, starting with Moses himself . . . and after the return from Babylon they maintained in succession an aristocratic and oligarchic

---

[31] Martin Wallraff (ed.), *Iulius Africanus: Chronographiae. The Extant Fragments.* In collaboration with Umberto Roberto and Karl Pinggéra. *Die griechischen christlichen Schriftsteller der ersten Jahrhunderte*, NF 15, translated by W. Adler (Berlin-New York: Walter de Gruyter, 2007), 258–63.

[32] For a detailed analysis of this verse in context see Raymond de Hoop, *Genesis 49 in its Literary and Historical Context* (Leiden: Brill, 1999), 114–48, especially for the issues of שילה (pp. 122–4). Rabbinic and targumic interpretations read the word as indicative of the Messiah: a ruler over Judaea will not cease until the *Messiah* comes, with the corrupt text שילה read as שילו, Shiloh.

[33] de Hoop points out (p.122) that this reading of the LXX presumes a Hebrew text that reads for שילה the words שלה, a contraction of אשר לו, '[that] which is for him', a reading de Hoop notes as possibly validated by Ezek. 21: 32, though ultimately he remains unpersuaded of a simple solution.

constitution, with priests being in full authority. This lasted until the Roman commander Pompey arrived and laid siege to Jerusalem with superlative strength. He defiled the sacred precincts and went into the innermost sanctuary of the Temple. He removed the man who had continued the succession of his ancestors until that time as both king and high priest, named Aristobulus, as a prisoner to Rome, together with his children. He transferred the high priesthood to Hyrcanus (II), Aristobulus' brother, and made the whole nation of Judaea give tribute to Rome. (*Hist. Eccles.* 1: 6: 1–2, 4–6)

According to Eusebius, the interpretation of Genesis 49: 10 indicated the legitimacy and divine requirement of Herod's rule, even though he was—strictly speaking—a Gentile by birth. This account by Eusebius is not pro-Roman, let alone pro-Herod, but it presents a kind of fait accompli: because of the circumstances, the prophecy would now be fulfilled.

Eusebius states—from Africanus—that Herod was indeed a foreigner (*Hist. Eccles.* 1: 6: 3–5). He was not strictly speaking an Idumaean, but rather his father Antipater was the son of a Herod of Ascalon, a Gentile temple-servant of Apollo there, who was brought up in Idumaea after being taken prisoner. The notion that he was ordained to be the 'expectation of the Gentiles' is stressed.

It would be hard to credit that this prophecy derived from any other source than the Essene prophet identified in Josephus: Menahem. Two astounding biblical prophecies for one ascension to the throne by Herod the Great would be rather too many. The passage used by Menahem the Essene was therefore Genesis 49: 10 and it legitimated Herod's rule as necessary on the basis of scripture.

In other patristic literature, the same group of people responsible for making this prediction to Herod are duly called 'Herodians', but the Church Fathers missed the historical context of legitimising Herod's rule in a time of social upheaval and war, and thought instead that those who used Genesis 49: 10 were claiming that Herod was the expected *Messiah*. Thus, Ps.-Tertullian (*Adv. Omn. Haer.* 1: 1) mentions 'the Herodians who declared Herod to be the Messiah', while Jerome (*Adv. Lucifer* 23) likewise states that the *Herodiani* were people who assumed King Herod to be Christ (*Herodem regem suscepere pro Christo*). Epiphanius, in his description of the Herodians, appears to use Eusebius, though he blends this source with further Messianic supposition (*Pan.* 1: 20: 1–2): the Herodians who believed 'that Herod was Christ, thought that the Christ awaited in all scriptures of the Law and prophets was Herod himself, and were proud of Herod because they were deceived in him'.[34] If this were so, it would mean that the Herodians believed that someone not only not of the line of David, but someone not of the line of Judah, would be the

---

[34] Frank Williams (ed.), *The Panarion of Epiphanius of Salamis*, 2nd ed. (Leiden: Brill, 2009), 48.

Messiah. This is ridiculous, and the result of confusion in the minds of later Christian authors.[35]

These authors miss the obvious point that in Hebrew, the primary biblical meaning of the term *Meshiḥa*, 'anointed one' (*Christos* in Greek), is simply 'king' (1 Sam. 24: 7; Ps. 2: 2). Eusebius, from Julius Africanus, states nothing about Herod being considered the Messiah, but rather, because he was a Gentile, he was 'the expectation of the Gentiles' and 'with him the succession of Judaean rulers, from Moses, came to an end' (*Hist. Eccles.* 1: 6). Ultimately, Eusebius notes that this indicates that 'without question the advent of the Christ took place in his time . . . in accordance with the prophecy'. The end of the rule of kings of Judaean ethnicity therefore was the time when the Messiah would appear. If we place this conclusion together with Menahem's prediction as found in Josephus, then he would have prophesied that the Davidic Messiah would come on the heels of Herod, whose rule as a Gentile king was predicted by Genesis 49: 10 as necessary in God's plan. No wonder Herod—as King of the Judaeans—was particularly on edge. That the rebellions of Judas (*Ant.* 17: 271-2), Simon (*Ant.* 17: 273-6), and Athronges broke out on Herod's death (*Ant.* 17: 278-84) may be understood against a backdrop of intense Messianic expectation. Josephus' story that another Essene, Simon, predicted that the reign of Herod's son Archelaus would be short would likewise fit with this wider context of intense speculation that the Messiah would follow soon after Herod's rule (*War* 2: 112-13 and *Ant.* 17: 345-8).

Curiously, an interpretation of Genesis 49: 10 survives within the corpus of Qumran *pesharim*. 4Q252, or 4QCommGen A, column 5, fragment 6 reads:[36]

1 [לוא] יסור שליט משבט יהודה בהיות לישראל ממשל
2 [ולוא־י] כרת יושב כסא לדויד כי המחקק היא ברית המלכות
3 ואל[פי] ישראל המה הדגלים [ ] עד בוא משיח הצדק צמח
4 דויד כי לו ולזרעו נתנה ברית מלכות עמו עד דורות עולם אשר
5 שמר] [התורה עם אנשי היחד כי
6 [ ] [היא כנסת אנשי
7 [ ] [נתן

[35] The confusion seems to have resulted from the later interpretation of 'Shiloh' being indicative of the Messiah, for which see de Hoop, *Genesis 49*, 122-4, 129-30. On this interpretation, if Herod is identified with the word read as 'Shiloh', then he would be identified as the Messiah, but there are numerous other readings indicated by the textual history of the passage given the ambiguity of letters. Eusebius indicates this was not his reading of the passage.

[36] For text and discussion see Joseph L. Trafton, 'Commentary on Genesis (4Q252),' in James H. Charlesworth (ed.), *The Dead Sea Scrolls: Volume 6b: Pesharim, Other Commentaries, and Related Documents* (The Princeton Theological Seminary Dead Sea Scrolls Project; Louisville, KY: Westminster John Knox, 2002), 203-19; Daniel K. Falk, *Parabiblical Texts: Strategies for Extending the Scriptures Among the Dead Sea Scrolls* (London/New York: T & T Clark, 2007); George Brooke, 'The Thematic content of 4Q252,' *JQR* 85 (1994): 33-59.

My translation of this is as follows:

(1) [he] 'will not cease from the tribe of Judah' a ruler for Israel;

(2) [nor will] 'one sitting' on the seat of David be 'cut off', because the 'staff' is the covenant of kingship

(3) [. . . and thousands] of Israel are the 'feet/loins' 'until' the anointed of righteousness comes, the sprout of

(4) David, for to him and to his descendants has been given the covenant of kingship of his people for all everlasting generations, which

(5) has kept [ ] the Law with the people of the union (יחד), for

(6) [the 'obedience of the people]s' is the assembly of the people of

(7) [ ] he gave . . .

It seems necessary to supply a negative in line 1 in accordance with the Masoretic text, since this seems to be a quotation of Genesis 49: 10. There is also an implicit reference to Jeremiah 33: 17: לא־יכרת לדוד איש ישב על־כסא בית־ישראל: 'there shall not be cut off for/to David a man sitting upon the throne of the house of Israel', as George Brooke has noted.[37]

Brooke follows Allegro in his suggestion of אלפי 'thousands' at the start of the third line.[38] It is clear that the 'anointed of righteousness' stands as an interpretation for what reads as the word שילה in the usual MT of Genesis 49: 10,[39] so that there is a guarantee that there will be rulers from the tribe of Judah (= Judaeans) on the throne, the 'seat of David', *until* (עד) the arrival of the Messiah of Righteousness, who is the returned Davidic descendant, the 'sprout of David', who will sit on his rightful throne.[40] The *pesher* assumes an unbroken chain of rulers leading Israel from the 'loins' of the thousands of Israel. There is no equation between a non-Judaean ruler and the Messiah, and one could read the *pesher* as just a simple reassurance that there will always be Judaean rulers on the throne up to the time the Messiah comes. There might be an indication from the quoted words יסור 'will fail/cease' and יכרת 'will be cut off' that there may be a lapse, when the tribe of Judah is cut off from the throne of Israel, so then the Messiah of Righteousness would come to restore it, but if this is assumed, it is not spelt out. The Messiah is not only Judaean but more specifically Davidic and would sit on the throne for everlasting

---

[37] See also George Brooke, 'The Deuteronomic Character of 4Q252,' in John C. Reeves and John Kampen (eds), *Pursuing the Text: Studies in Honor of Ben Zion Wacholder on the Occasion of his Seventieth Birthday* (Sheffield: Sheffield Academic Press, 1994), 121–35, at 129.

[38] John M. Allegro, 'Further Messianic References in Qumran Literature,' *JBL* 75 (1956): 174–87, with illustrations.

[39] The interpretation of 'Shiloh' as indicating the expected eschatological Messiah is found also in the Targum Onkelos and Yerushalmi translations of this verse, and is therefore not exclusive to the writer of 4Q252.

[40] Though Schwartz has read this as referring to the departure from Judah of the monarchic line from the house of David, see Daniel Schwartz, 'The Messianic Departure from Judah (4Q Patriarchal Blessings),' *Theologische Zeitschrift* 37 (1981): 257–66.

generations in the interim period of Judaean kings. The reassurance of an unbroken sequence of these rulers seems more likely, which would mean historically this text is to be dated before the disruptions following the Roman invasion of 63 BCE.

Those responsible for the Dead Sea Scrolls clearly endorsed the concept of a Messiah who was from the Davidic line, even if it was long fallen, as we see in 4Q174 (4QFlorilegium): 10–13:

> 'I will establish the throne of his kingdom [forever. I will be] his father and he shall be my son' (2 Sam 7: 12-14). He is the Branch of David who shall arise with the Interpreter of the Law [to rule] in Zion [at the end] of time. As it is written, 'I will raise up the tent of David that is fallen' (Amos 9: 11), that is to say, the fallen tent of David is he who shall arise to save Israel.

Unfortunately, the exegesis of 4Q252 breaks off before the important final part of the passage is interpreted. We do not know who is equated with the 'obedience of the peoples', but it is an 'assembly of people of' some identity, and it would make sense if that assembly is that of the covenant, given the wide use of the word נכסה to indicate the congregation of Israel.[41]

The *pesher* of 4Q252 most probably does not give Menahem's interpretation. What it does do is indicate the type of interpretative tradition—the use of *pesharim*—from which prophecy could be made. From the evidence of Josephus and Eusebius (Julius Africanus), the latter using the LXX, the 'Herodians'—or rather those associated with Menahem the Essene—endorsed Herod's kingship, because it was necessary in terms of the prediction found in Genesis 49: 10, interpreted in a particular way. The later patristic notion that the Herodians viewed Herod himself as the Righteous Messiah, however, is most likely the result of confusion.

If it is historically correct that the Essenes legitimated Herod's rule by their prediction of a Gentile king ruling Judaea, as a kind of glitch, and that they received honours and gifts from Herod in return, then any High Priest—especially those appointed by the Herodian dynasty—had to accept them as a legitimate and honoured legal school protected by the king and his successors. The High Priest would have had to accept them even though the Essenes themselves rejected aspects of how the Temple was run as being insufficiently pure (see Josephus). Interestingly, High Priests chosen by Herod are not said to have come from the school of the Essenes. Herod appointed Hananel, a Babylonian (*Ant.* 15: 22, 40–1), and then Aristobolus III, the last Hasmonean (*Ant.* 15: 31–41; 20: 247–8), whom he drowned in his swimming pool (*Ant.* 20: 249). Hananel was then reinstated, followed by Jesus son of Phiabi, Boethus, Simon son of Boethus, Matthias son of Theophilus, Josephus son of Ellemus,

---

[41] Jastrow, 650.

and Joazar son of Boethus.[42] It may be noted that the High Priests of Herod are not explicitly associated with any schools, though there is a family dynasty of Boethus. Herod may have hoped to keep them firmly under his command, as impartial and unaffiliated; clearly he deposed them easily at will.

Lying behind the Marcan Herodians then we may distinguish the historical actuality that the Essenes could maintain power not through popularity with the common people, but by the endorsement of the Herodian dynasty, and so were dubbed 'Herodians' by the Pharisee-supporting general populace.

We turn then to the word itself: Ἡρῳδιανοί. What we do not have here is an Aramaicism, or even pure Greek. As Bickerman pointed out, the Latin *-ianus* (meaning 'belonging to') is added to the stem 'Herod', in the same way that it is added to 'Christ' to make Χριστιανοί,[43] when a proper Greek term used by Josephus for those associated with Herod is Ἡρωδεῖοι (*War* 1: 319), which seem to be members of Herod's family or retinue. Nevertheless, it is slightly dangerous to assume that Mark's language reflects correct Greek in a gospel written—according to Papias (Eusebius, *Hist. Eccles.* 3: 39: 15)—by someone in the Roman Christian community whose role was to translate Simon Peter's Aramaic.[44] Mark's Greek is not excellent, and, as noted above, contains a number of other striking Latinisms.[45]

In Aramaic or Mishnaic Hebrew, to express the sense of someone 'belonging to' a particular school or persuasion of a particular leader or teacher, one uses the idiomatic expression 'from the house of'. Therefore, those following Hillel are 'from the house of Hillel': שֶׁל בֵּית־הִלֵּל. In the Syriac versions of Mark, the Greek term Ἡρῳδιανοί is then translated back into correct Semitic idiom as 'people from the house of Herod', which would have been rendered עַם־בֵּית־הוֹרוֹדוֹס in Palestinian Aramaic. A Greek writer might have used the term Josephus employs, Ἡρωδεῖοι. However, in *Ant.* 14: 450, curiously, the Greek text here has an awkward rendering for what would have been this Aramaic expression: Josephus describes Galileans attacking people in Galilee, and 'they drowned those *thinking the things of Herod* in the lake': τοὺς τα Ἡρώδου φρονοῦντας ἐν τῇ λίμνῃ κατεπόντωσαν. These victims are Herod-supporters in a war. They 'think' like Herod in terms of their loyalty to him.

The plain meaning of Ἡρῳδιανοί is then simply a 'Herod-supporter', someone loyal to Herod. Such a term in Aramaic or Hebrew may have been in reasonably wide circulation, but the application of this expression to a

---

[42] Peter Richardson, *Herod: King of the Jews and Friend of the Romans* (New York: Continuum 1999), 243.

[43] Elias J. Bickerman, 'The Name of Christians,' *HTR* 42 (1949): 109–24.

[44] For which, among many studies, see the assessment of Bauckham, *Jesus and the Eyewitnesses*, 202–10.

[45] See the excellent study of the full extent of these in Adam Winn, *The Purpose of Mark's Gospel. An Early Christian Response to Roman Imperial Propaganda* (WUNT II, 245; Tübingen: Mohr Siebeck, 2008), 80–2.

group who might be compared with the Pharisees is another thing again: it is not a technical term, but a popular slur on a group of people who are actually defined by their actions and concerns in Mark's story as interpreters of the Law. If we equate these with the Essenes, then it is easy to suppose why they were popularly designated by this slur. Against the Essene view that it was necessary for Herod to be king of Judaea, despite being ethnically a Gentile, there may have been many others who gravely doubted a divine hand behind his rule.

The strange term as it exists in the Gospel of Mark is then probably Mark's own invention, as a Greek–Latin hybrid word. By the time that Mark was writing, the disciples of Jesus were themselves known as *Christianoi* (Acts 11: 26; 26: 28; 1 Pet. 4: 16)—a term used by the Romans themselves (Tacitus, *Annals* 15: 44: 3; Suetonius, 16: 1–2). Mark, with his Latinisms, would have thought of the *-ianus* ending as befitting the meaning of Herod-supporters in Judaea.[46] Since the pejorative branding of the Essenes was local to Judaea, understood only by those who were living in that region (comprising Galilee also), this designation would not have travelled well into the Diaspora. It would not have survived into future generations either, especially within churches largely comprised of non-Jews. Thus, as the Herodian dynasty itself disappeared, so too would a sarcastic Judaean designation of a legal school associated with endorsing their rule.

CONCLUSIONS

This survey of the evidence within Mark's narrative, relevant early Christian texts, and the Dead Sea Scrolls concludes that the 'Herodians' of the Gospel of Mark (found also in Matthew) are indeed to be identified as Essenes. The Essenes test Jesus in terms of his obedience to Jewish Law. The presentation of the 'Herodians' of patristic literature became slightly warped, but they are nevertheless correctly understood to be those who supported Herod's rule on the basis of a prophetic interpretation of Gen. 49: 10. This is most accurately indicated by Eusebius, enabling us to make a link between what he states and what Josephus recounts in regard to the Essene master Menahem. We have two separate pieces of a puzzle that can be placed together. The Pharisees, Herodians, and Sadducees of Mark's Gospel are then the Pharisees, Essenes, and Sadducees of Josephus.

---

[46] Meier, 'Historical Jesus,' 745–6.

5

Pliny

The Roman scholar Gaius Plinius Secundus (*c*.23–79 CE)[1] makes mention of the Essenes (*Esseni*) in his monumental and very influential work, the *Natural History*. Because of his status, and also because he was writing in the important western language of Latin, his comments on the Essenes have been very important. This is despite the fact that he showed little interest or enthusiasm for Jews or Judaism.

Pliny, born during the reign of Tiberius, came from a privileged background, had a distinguished career in the military and in provincial administration (as a procurator), and came to be honoured as a 'friend' of Vespasian, an official advisory status involving a salutation to the emperor every morning. He died in the eruption of Mount Vesuvius in August 79 CE when going to the aid of survivors. Pliny was a true Roman, basically Stoic in his philosophical ethos, moderate, traditional, and deeply concerned to understand the workings of the natural world. The *Natural History* was 'published' in 77 CE, very soon after Josephus' *War* and the Gospel of Mark, though Pliny would have been writing this great work, in 37 books, for many years prior to its release.[2] Pliny mentions the Essenes briefly in Book 5 of this work.

The Essenes are a passing curiosity. Since the passage on the Essenes is short, it can be translated and given in full (*Hist. Nat.* 5: 15 [73]).[3]

> On the west [of Lake Asphaltites] the Essenes flee away from the shores that are harmful, a people (*gens*) alone and in all the world strange (*mira*) above the rest, [being] without any woman, abdicating all sexual acts, without money, companioned by palms. Daily the swarm (*turba*) is renewed with equal multitudes, filled with huge numbers of those, wearied of life and the fluctuations of fortune, who keep to their ways of life. So through a thousand ages—incredible to say—it is an eternal people (*gens*), in which no one is born, so fecund is this dissatisfaction

---

[1] For which see John Healy, *Pliny the Elder on Science and Technology* (Oxford: OUP, 1999), 1–35.

[2] Ibid. 36–41.

[3] Charles Mayhoff, ed., *C. Plini Secundi, Naturalis Historiae* I (Stuttgart: B. G. Tübner, 1967), 392–3.

(or: repentance) of life in others. Below these (*infra hos*) was the town of En Gedi—second only to Jerusalem [= Jericho] in fertility and groves of palms, now another ash-heap—then Masada, a fortress on a rock, and this not far from Asphaltites.[4]

The rhetorical aspects of this description are immediately recognisable as being very different from those of Philo and Josephus, or the Essenes/Herodians in the Gospel of Mark. Like Mark, the presentation is negative. Pliny does not praise the Essenes, but rather characterizes them as an oddity. The swarm (*turba* is not a positive word) of strange (*mira*) people resort to a grim and solitary lifestyle because of their exhaustion with the world and general unhappiness.

This peculiar portrayal of the Essenes has been noted by classical scholars who have considered Pliny's *Natural History* as a whole. For example, Mary Beagon writes that Pliny's attitude to the Essenes is one of 'baffled fascination rather than approval' and states that he notes 'as *mira* the rejection of normal human reproduction in the community of the Essenes on the Dead Sea. They are a paradox of Nature, their numbers being supplemented only by other men's *vitae paenitentia*'.[5] Trevor Murphy comments that the example of the Essenes is drawn upon in order to 'revile asceticism, when luxury happens to confirm the moral universe of Roman power and asceticism threatens it'.[6] Here, by Asphaltites:

> The Essenes have removed themselves from all productive exchange...The encyclopaedia emphasizes the complete sterility of their society with a pun: 'so fruitful for them is others' distaste for life'...For the *Natural History*, the Essenes are not mystics who pursue some inner-directed goal; they are not Gymnosophists. Rather, their asceticism is directed outwards, a marker of their disgust for the life the rest of us lead. It is a token of their rejection of the world, their repentance of life.[7]

Murphy points out that Pliny juxtaposes his description of the Essenes with places associated with death: with the life-denying, river-swallowing lake itself, and with En Gedi and Jerusalem—two charred pyres—and Masada, notorious for the mass suicide of Eleazar's Sicarii (Josephus, *War* 7: 275–406). The portrayal of the ascetics is 'hostile', with the emphasis placed on their sterility and refusal of life itself.[8]

Despite their celibacy, the swarm of Essenes survive on an influx of men who are weary of life, living in a grim landscape where palm trees are the only

---

[4] The following discussion revises and expands part of my published article, 'On Pliny, the Essene Location and Kh. Qumran,' *DSD* 16 (2009): 129–49.

[5] Mary Beagon, *Roman Nature: The Thought of Pliny the Elder* (Oxford: OUP, 1992), 79.

[6] Trevor Murphy, *Pliny the Elder's Natural History: The Empire in the Encyclopaedia* (New York: OUP, 2004), 113.

[7] Ibid. 117.

[8] Ibid. 118.

signs of life. Like Philo, Pliny would imply that the men who become Essenes and live without any women (*sine ulla femina*) are reasonably mature, already having endured the fluctuations of fortune (Pliny, *Nat. Hist.* 5: 15 [73]). They are a wonder, in Roman eyes, in that, despite being men who have renounced sex, they keep on existing throughout the ages (from antiquity: 'a thousand ages') because there are so many dissatisfied people who join them. As with Philo and Josephus, Pliny presents a group of men who date from ancient times, and are in no way a recent phenomenon.

This characterization is essentially an exaggerated caricature, with only some very superficial correlations with Josephus and Philo. One may even call it a parody, when one considers everything we have from Philo, Josephus, and the Gospel of Mark. Pliny does not even describe Jews as a larger ethnic group from which the Essenes are drawn: in Judaea the Essenes are the defining human beings, not Jews. Or, perhaps, the Essenes are defining Jews, whose identity is as the people Pliny defines here. This parody is based on the following basic elements:

1. location beside the Dead Sea in the wilderness between En Gedi and Jericho, where there are palm trees
2. austere (life-denying) lifestyle that includes celibacy
3. large numbers, continually replaced by men who have grown weary of life
4. rejection of (personal) money
5. existing from ancient times.

Out of these bare bones the parody has been fleshed out, without any social or cultural context, in order to make the Essenes into an example of something paradoxical.

In terms of Pliny's source material, it is hard to see that he had access to the same body of evidence used by Josephus and Philo. As a non-Jew, Pliny must have been dependent purely on what he had heard or read about Essenes. It has been suggested by Stephen Goranson that Pliny's source on the Essenes is a lost geographical work by Marcus Vipsanius Agrippa (63–12 BCE),[9] though Nikos Kokkinos' recent insight that this particular section may come from another lost work, by C. Licinius Mucianus (legatus of Syria 67–69 CE), is very persuasive, since Mucianus made a compilation of observations regarding curiosities of the world (Pliny, *Nat. Hist.* 7: 4 [36]), a collection of *paradoxa* or *mirabilia* in which the wonders and paradoxes of Judaea's waters—the overall context of this description—would have been appropriate, as would the marvel of the ever-enduring, sex-eschewing Essenes.[10]

---

[9] Stephen Goranson, 'Posidonius, Strabo, and Marcus Vipsanius Agrippa as Sources on Essenes,' *JJS* 45 (1994): 295–8.

[10] Nikos Kokkinos, 'The City of "Mariamme": an Unknown Herodian Connection?' *Mediterraneo Antico* 5/2 (2002), 715–46, at 729–30; first identified by Alfred Klotz, *Quaestiones*

The literary genre of this passage is important for understanding its emphases and language, especially the language of hyperbole. The 'collection of wonders' was popular in antiquity, Iambulus' account of the 'children of the sun' (Diodorus Siculus, *Bibl. Hist.* 2: 55–60), written *c.*165–50 BCE, being one such example:[11] the 'children of the sun' were peaceful, happy people with forked tongues, bendable bones and amazing longevity who lived far away on a fabulous island. This type of utopian fantasy relies on the framework of a *voyage extraordinaire*,[12] so that the further away one went from civilization (the cities of the Greek world), the more bizarre things became (so Herodotus, *Hist.* 3: 116).[13] In the account used by Pliny, the remoteness and peculiarity of the Dead Sea created the image of a correspondingly strange people. They were both a wonder.

The context of this description of the Essenes is a passage that focuses on the remarkable water of the region, from the source of the Jordan in the north of Judaea to the termination of Judaea at the southern part of the Dead Sea. One could title the passage in which the description of the Essenes is found very simply: 'Judaea's Wonderful Water'. It is not a very scientific description, but is a fundamentally 'creative' piece. Pliny begins:

> The Jordan River rises from the spring of Paneas, which gives its name to Caesarea [Paneas], of which we will speak [later]. The river is pleasant, insofar as the situation of places permits. Twining and lingering, it shows itself as reluctant to the request of Asphaltites, a lake of a dismal nature, in which finally it is absorbed, and its praised waters lost, mixing with unhealthy ones.

This is not a cool, scientific description, but rather one that uses personification for the subject of the piece. In characterizing the water as reluctant to come to the party in Lake Asphaltites, Pliny has the water of the Jordan twisting and turning away, and—most especially—procrastinating in Lake Genesar. Pliny continues: *Ergo ubi prima convallium fuit occasio, in lacum se fundit, quem plures Genesaram vocant*, 'Therefore where the first convenience makes

Plinianae geographicae (Berlin: Weidmann, 1906), 160. Mucianus was legate of Syria at a critical time and wrote *c.*73–75 in Rome.

[11] For a discussion of Iambulus, see David Winston, 'Iambulus: A Literary Study in Greek Utopianism,' PhD thesis (Columbia University, New York, 1956), and his summary in 'Iambulus' *Islands of the Sun* and Hellenistic Literary Utopias,' *Science Fiction Studies* 3 (1976): 219–27. The date of Iambulus' work given here follows Winston, 'A Literary Study,' 38–58. See also John Ferguson, *Utopias of the Classical World* (London: Thames and Hudson, 1975), 124–9.

[12] Winston, 'Iambulus,' 61–8, finds precedents for Iambulus' *voyage extraordinaire* in Hecataeus of Abdera, Περὶ Ὑπερβορέων (*c.*330 BCE), whose exact location—also an island—was unknown, though they were 'beyond the North Wind' (Boreas), and also Euhemerus of Messana's Ἱερὰ Ἀναγραφῆς (*c.*300 BCE) about the Panchaean isles, somewhere in the Indian Ocean.

[13] See James S. Romm, *The Edges of the Earth in Ancient Thought: Geography, Exploration and Fiction* (Princeton: Princeton University Press, 1992). Lucian parodied the genre of telling fabulous tales about remote places in his 'A True Story', which was in fact a 'pack of lies' in the grand tradition of Ctesias, Iambulus, and Homer (*Ver. Hist.* 1: 3).

an occasion, it flows into a lake, which many call Genesar'. We are then given a note of the towns of this lake, which are 'pleasant', *amoenis*, as is the lake: *ab oriente Iuliade et Hippo, a meridie Tarichea, quo nomine aliqui et lacum appellant, ab occidente Tiberiade, aquis calidis salubri*, 'on the east Julias and Hippo, on the south Tarichea, by which name some call the lake, on the west Tiberias, with healthy hot springs'.[14] Pliny then has the river doing a reluctant loop, going down the east side, along the south, and then back up the west, before continuing southwards to the unhealthy water of Lake Asphaltites. The water remains the subject, with its pleasantness reflected in the towns, its alternative name coming from Tarichea. The healthy, hot springs at Tiberias mirror its own healthy quality.

In the same way, Pliny notes places around the strange water of Asphaltites:

> Asphaltites produces nothing except bitumen, hence its name. It receives no body of an animal; bulls and camels float. On account of this character nothing sinks in it. . . . Facing it in the east [corr. south] is Arabia of the Nomads. In the south [corr. east] is Machaerus, a Judaean citadel at one time second to Jerusalem. On the same side is the curative, healthy hot spring, Callirhoe, this name well-known because of the fame of its waters. On the west the Essenes flee all the way from the shores which are harmful . . . Below these was the town of En Gedi, second only to Jerusalem [corr. Jericho] in fertility and groves of palms, now another ash-heap. Then Masada, a fortress on a rock, and this not far from Asphaltites. And to here is Judaea.

Either this text is slightly corrupt or Pliny made mistakes using his source, requiring a number of *corrigenda*.[15] It seems that *ab oriente* and *a meridie* have been transposed, perhaps to replicate the reluctant turn of water around Genesar. Pliny writes that Arabia 'faces' or 'looks out at' the lake, which stresses its position beyond Judaea, but the specific sites he mentions are within Judaea. It was in Peraea, a part of Judaea, that Machaerus and Callirhoe lay (Ptolemy, *Geogr.* 5: 16; Josephus, *War* 1: 657–9): on the same side, close to

---

[14] Pliny's Tarichea is normally considered to be Magdala, north of Tiberias, but Nikos Kokkinos ('The Location of Tarichaea: North or South of Tiberias,' *PEQ* 142 [2010]: 7–23) has argued persuasively that it should indeed be placed in the south-western region of the lake shoreline. As Kokkinos shows, it would have been natural for the Romans to call the Sea of Galilee by the name Tarichea because C. Cassius Longinus had a victory there in 53 BCE (*Ant.* 14: 120; *War* 1: 180) and it was occupied by the forces of Vespasian and Titus in 67 CE, after which there was a great sea battle, won by the Romans (*War* 3: 445–542), who commemorated it in coinage. Later, the alternative name applied to this body of water was Lake of Tiberias, not Lake of Tarichea (see Eusebius, *Onom.* 74; 162). Likewise, Kokkinos argues for a more easterly location of Bethsaida than the current identification with et-Tell: Nikos Kokkinos, 'The Foundation of Bethsaida-Julias by Philip the Tetrarch,' *JJS* 59 (2008): 1–16.

[15] The vivid description offered by his nephew, Pliny the Younger (*Ep.* 3: 5: 7), does leave open the possibility of simple errors. Pliny the Younger writes how his uncle was prone to fall asleep at odd times, and would like to lie in the sun while a book was being read to him, taking notes from it. See Healy, *Pliny*, 24.

each other (see Map 2). Alternatively, it is possible the word *Iudaeae*, 'Judaean', has wandered in the text, and should be related to the direction, so that Machaerus is 'in the south of Judaea' (still within Peraea), with Arabia (further south than this citadel) facing the Dead Sea in the (south)east.[16]

At any rate, the general flow of water from north to south indicates the extent of Judaea itself as a region. Judaea is characterized as a 'wonder'—of a slightly bizarre kind—by having peculiar water, both healthful and harmful. The Dead Sea itself, described as toxic, is at the same time the locus of a paradoxical thing: a group of miserable men who are as dead sexually as the water nearby, but who remarkably manage to keep going through the centuries by acting as a magnet to a great crowd of miserable others, making up an enduring *gens*. The word *gens* may appropriately translate the Greek γένος of Philo and Josephus, but it is narrower than the better word *genus*. Pliny seems to have in mind more of an emphasis on the idea of a people or race rather than a 'category' of people. It is their race alone, as a kind of peculiar ethnic grouping, that is of interest in terms of the wonder.

The toxicity of the lake is avoided by the Essenes removing themselves sufficiently from its shores to allow survival, but this is not indicated as an ideal locality, a nice country villa in which one pursues philosophy.[17] The water apparently produced noxious fumes, so the further away from the shoreline one lived the better.[18] This belief is attested in Strabo, who has sooty smoke coming out of the lake and tarnishing metal (*Geogr.* 16: 2: 42).

As Murphy has observed, in Pliny the miserable lake itself becomes a metaphor for something key in the representation of the weird people Pliny describes. They are indeed like the date palms that grow beside them in the desert, a kind of oasis of humanity, existing where no one should exist, thriving when celibacy should mean they die out. The paradox is clear. Date palms are the image of a humanity that thrives in the dry desert, as the Essenes live a desert life without sex.

The most important information here that takes us beyond what we already know about the Essenes from Philo and Josephus is Pliny's placement of the

---

[16] See Kokkinos, 'Tarichaea,' 9, who argues for the appropriateness of Pliny's directions in looking east then west, and sees Machaerus as being indicated as the southerly point of Judaea in the east.

[17] The focus on avoiding harm means that this is not a simple Ciceronian retreat to the country to live a philosophical existence, as we find with the *Therapeutae*, see Joan E. Taylor, *Jewish Women Philosophers of First-Century Alexandria: Philo's 'Therapeutae' Re-considered* (Oxford: OUP, 2003), 75–81.

[18] This is a view that persisted until modern times; see Daniel the Abbot (1106–8), 27; 38, trans. William F. Ryan, in John Wilkinson, *Jerusalem Pilgrimage 1099–1185* (London: Hakluyt Society, 1988). In the fifteenth century, Father Felix Fabri was told that no one should visit the lake because the stench from the sea makes you vulnerable to infection, sickness, and death: Felix Fabri, *Evagatorium*, 236a.

Essenes to the west of the Dead Sea with both En Gedi and Masada 'below these'. What exactly does this mean in terms of locality?

In terms of the whole passage, so concerned with water, the flow goes *e fonte Paneade*, 'from the spring Paneas', *hactenus* 'to here' (Masada), the water being the length of Judaea itself. In the Dead Sea area the movement is a zigzag, looking first to the east, where the area is wrongly defined as Arabia of the Nomads rather than Peraea, then west.[19] The movement then goes south so that 'below' the Essenes there lies En Gedi (*infra hos Engada*) and '[below] from there Masada' (*inde Masada*).[20] The word *inde* carries on the trajectory established by *infra hos*: 'below them . . . from there. . . .' It is a directional movement of flowing water, not one of height. If *infra hos* is understood to mean a site below the Essenes in height, then *inde* would have to mean that Masada is even lower down, also in height, which it is not.

The water remains the subject, Asphaltites' nature being bizarre and un-pleasant, in contrast to the River Jordan, and yet—paradoxically—there are famous restorative springs beside it, the weirdly enduring Essenes, and 'below these', i.e. 'downstream from these' (in terms of the water), a town once considered second only to Jericho[21] in fertility, and a fortress on a rock not far away from the lake. As Laperrousaz carefully surveyed, Pliny uses the term *infra* as 'downstream' in six other instances (*Nat. Hist.* 3: 12 [109]; 4: 7 [26]; 5: 11 [60]; 6: 31–2 [133, 136, 146]) and probably also in two further cases (*Nat. Hist.* 6: 23 [73–4]).[22] It fits both with his usage and the subject of his description: water. Accordingly, it would be appropriate to consider the location of Pliny's Essenes as being somewhere north of En Gedi.[23]

---

[19] A little earlier Pliny had written that the area of Judaea was called 'Peraea near Arabia and Egypt'. Arabia of the Nomads was east of the Red Sea, not the Dead Sea.

[20] To look at En Gedi separately in relation to the Essenes without noting the continuation of the direction indicated by 'below them' would be to take certain words out of context. If the reference indicates that En Gedi is below 'the Essenes' in height, then logically Masada would be below also, but it towers to a great height.

[21] Correcting the text here from 'Jerusalem'. The city of Jerusalem appears earlier in the passage in a very similar phrase, *secunda quondam arx Iudaeae ab Hierosolymis*, and a slip would have been easy to make.

[22] E. M. Laperrousaz, '"Infra hos Engadda", notes à propos d'un article récent,' *RB* 69 (1962): 369–80, at 375.

[23] So Roland de Vaux, *Archaeology and the Dead Sea Scrolls* (The Schweich Lectures of the British Academy; Oxford: OUP, 1973), 133–7; Geza Vermes and Martin Goodman, eds, *The Essenes according to the Classical Sources* (JSOT Press: Sheffield, 1989), 3 n. 19; Menahem Stern, *Greek and Latin Authors on Jews and Judaism* (Winona Lake: Eisenbrauns, 1974), i, 480–1; John J. Collins, 'Essenes,' in David Noel Freedman (ed.), *Anchor Bible Dictionary* (New York: Double-day, 1992), ii, 619–26, at 620. For the argument that Pliny refers to the Essenes as being further inland or west of En Gedi, see Jean-Paul Audet, 'Qumrân et la notice de Pline sur les Esséniens,' *RB* 68 (1961): 346–87, also Robert A. Kraft, 'Pliny on Essenes, Pliny on Jews,' *DSD* 8 (2001): 255–61, esp. 258; Yizhar Hirschfeld, *Qumran in Context: Reassessing the Archaeological Evidence* (Peabody, MA: Hendrickson, 2004), 231–3. For a strong defence of the reading that has the Essenes north of En Gedi see Christian Burchard, 'Pline et les Esséniens: à propos d'un article récent,' *RB* 69 (1962): 533–69. The debate has been nuanced recently by the

There is a valid objection that we are in a lake rather than a river and so 'downstream' for *infra* just seems wrong, even with the framework of 'from here ... to here' that Pliny presents, from Paneas to Masada. For *infra* to be 'downstream' the water would need some kind of south-moving momentum, when everyone knows that the Dead Sea is a dead end. On the one hand, the description of the water in Pliny's Judaea provides it with a looping trajectory that is not really scientific, but designed to characterize it in a certain way, touching on the localities of Judaea as it wanders down the spine of the Jordan Valley. However, interestingly, there are ideas of the continuation of the Jordan's momentum in later sources. For example, in the description by Burchard of Mount Zion in 1283, he reports a Muslim belief that the Jordan 'both enters the sea and leaves the same, but shortly after leaving it is swallowed up in the earth'.[24] Richard Pococke noted: 'It is very extraordinary that no outlet of this lake has been discovered; but it is supposed that there must be some subterranean passage into the Mediterranean'[25] and '[i]t is a common opinion that the waters of that river [Jordan] pass through it without mixing with the water of the lake, and I thought I saw a stream of a different colour; and possibly, as it is rapid, it may run unmixed for some way.'[26] Pliny clearly understood that there was a mixing, but this does not imply a lack of motion, and in fact there is indeed a largely south-moving current in the Dead Sea, which probably explains the belief that there was some unseen exit for water at the southern end. The true explanation for this current was not found until David Neev and K. O. Emery demonstrated that the greater density of the southern basin pulled the water of the northern basin towards it, which, combined with the Corolis effect from the earth's rotation, created a strong flow south along the west coast and a weak north-flowing stream on the eastern side.[27]

Pliny is interested in defining Judaea's extent, and he snaps the account shut at the boundary of the land. He does not speculate on the continuation of the flow he seems to allude to. The important thing is that Pliny does not much

---

suggestion that, while Pliny may refer to Qumran, he is untrustworthy and inaccurate: Albert I. Baumgarten, 'Who Cares and Why Does it Matter? Qumran and the Essenes, Once Again!' *DSD* 11 (2004): 174–90, at 177–8. Magen Broshi has responded by questioning Baumgarten's scepticism, noting that 'there is no reason why Pliny's testimony should be rejected': 'Essenes at Qumran? A Rejoinder to Albert Baumgarten,' *DSD* 14 (2007): 25–33, at 29.

[24] See Burchard, *Descriptio Terrae Sanctae* in *Burchart of Mount Sion AD 1280* (London: Palestine Pilgrim Texts Society XII, 1896), 60.

[25] Richard Pococke, *A Description of the East and Some Other Countries*, ii (London: W. Bowyer, 1745), 35.

[26] Ibid. 36. See also Barbara Kreiger, *The Dead Sea: Myth, History and Politics*, 2nd ed. (Hanover, NH: Brandeis University Press/University Press of New England, 1997), 19–20.

[27] David Neev and K. O. Emery, *The Dead Sea: Depositional Processes and Environments of Evaporites*, State of Israel, Ministry of Development, Geological Survey Bulletin 41 (Jerusalem: Ministry of Development, 1967).

move away from water as his reference point in terms of placements, and *infra* when used of water carries the sense that one is to look beyond a point according to the flow. A water-based understanding of *infra* really does make the best sense in terms of the language and content of the whole passage.

While the reference to palm trees associated with the Essenes creates a counterpoint to the sterile water, they are located spatially in terms of the picture Pliny draws. Palm trees, at the point that Essenes are introduced, are associated with the area of Jericho (*Hiericuntem palmetis consitam*). Only after the introduction of the Essenes do we learn that En Gedi also has palm trees (*secundum ab Hierosolymis fertilitate palmetorumque nemoribus*, 'second to Jerusalem [corr. Jericho] in fertility and groves of palms'), so in the way Pliny presents these trees in his narrative the Essenes are companioned on the one side with the palm trees of Jericho and on the other with those of En Gedi, which creates an image of a wide region, not one small locality. The Essenes are like human palm trees, flourishing in the desert of no sex.[28]

The wide and arid expanse Pliny imagines is indicated by other words. As Burchard pointed out, Pliny used the word *litora*, 'shores', in plural, meaning a stretch of bays—not one shore, at one place. The reference is to 'un district essénien'.[29]

That Pliny is referring to a large area comes through also in the emphasis placed on how many Essenes there were. When he uses the word *turba*, 'swarm, crowd, multitude', he is clearly not imagining one tiny settlement. Moreover, a *gens* is not an appropriate word for the inhabitants of one single settlement, but, as noted, rather refers to a people, like a clan or race, who stretch over a country or province, as Burchard has also observed.[30] That there were so many Essenes yet no sexual reproduction within their *gens* was precisely why the Essenes were a peculiar wonder in a Graeco-Roman assemblage of remarkable things: *ita per saeculorum milia, incredibile dictu, gens aeterna est, in qua nemo nascitur*, 'In this manner, through thousands of ages—incredible to say—it is an enduring people, in which no one is born.' The comment *incredibile dictu* indicates the entire tone of this description. The large size of the population is one key factor in why this celibate *gens* is so incredible.

Given the rhetoric of the 'wonder', it is not surprising that we have in Pliny a parody founded on a small cluster of pieces of information. In terms of the hyperboles, Pliny presents the life-denying Essenes *only* next to a life-denying lake, and the pile of ashes that is En Gedi (like Jerusalem): associations that magnify the characteristic of their paradoxical existence through the ages. They are in a region lying slightly inland from poisonous shores. This description does not tell us anything about the extent of the Essenes' actual spread

---

[28] See also Burchard, 'Pline,' 567.   [29] Ibid. 543.   [30] Ibid. 541.

throughout Judaea (which we know about from Philo and Josephus), though their being by the Dead Sea, according to Pliny, is of course interesting. They are placed next to death because they live.

Pliny's testimony seems to indicate that there was a collection of basic pieces of information about the Essenes. This could partly have been drawn from Philo's spare presentation in the *Hypothetica*: they are a group of celibate older men living a renunciatory life. The Essenes' ascetic existence and communal pooling of possessions is summed up by Pliny concisely. Their attested celibacy is described as a life 'without women, abdicating all sexual acts'. The Essenes are numerous and ancient: likewise features we have already found in Philo. The only new piece of information is that they live by the Dead Sea, in between En Gedi and Jericho. The details used may individually all be true, but—because they are so few, without any real context, and are configured in a highly exaggerated manner—a false picture is created.

CONCLUSIONS

Pliny therefore warps the historical Essenes by means of a parody. The picture presented by Philo, Josephus, and the Gospel of Mark of an esteemed and honoured legal school or society at the heart of public life, deeply concerned with purity, scriptural interpretation, prediction, and healing, devoted to a life of community and piety, is lost. That the Essenes live anywhere but by the Dead Sea is of no interest. Pliny's Essenes are a strange and rather unappealing wonder. However, this picture cannot be used to isolate the historical Essenes from the rest of Judaism: for Pliny there is no other Judaism, only the Essenes, isolated not from Judaism but from life itself. The genre of *mirabilia* does not give us a firm foundation for historical construction, only a few highlighted features, used for a reason. The 'wonder' of the Essenes in Pliny is only that a group of celibate and poverty-embracing men could continue through the ages by the fact that new miserable men join in every generation. The normal prerequisites for fecundity—sex and wealth—are eschewed. They grow like palm trees in the arid wilderness. They are by no means people to praise in terms of their excellent philosophical existence. They are strange.

6

Dio Chrysostom, Synesius, and Julius Solinus

Pliny was not the only non-Jewish author to seize upon the Essenes. We have already seen how the Christian Hippolytus of Rome and the Neoplatonist Porphyry used Josephus' descriptions in their own work. This shows that Josephus' work was circulating in erudite circles and could be drawn upon in numerous ways. What else was in circulation is almost impossible to know, given that the large part of Graeco-Roman literature has been lost. The important thing to ascertain for this study is whether all these later writers were derivative of Philo, Josephus, and Pliny, or whether they had independent information about the Essenes deriving from other sources. If they did have any independent information, how is this being used in their material and how valuable is it from a historical perspective?

DIO CHRYSOSTOM

At around the same time as Josephus and Pliny, another writer employed the Essenes in one of his works: the prolific sophist Dio Chrysostom.[1] Dio was even in Rome at about the same time as both Josephus and Pliny. His death is usually given as around 115 to 120.[2] Part of a movement dubbed the 'Second

---

[1] This chapter modifies and updates what I have previously published as 'Dio Chrysostom and the Essene Landscape,' in Charlotte Hempel (ed.), *The Dead Sea Scrolls: Texts and Contexts* (Leiden: Brill, 2010), 467–86.

[2] See Simon Swain, 'Dio's Life and Works,' in Simon Swain (ed.), *Dio Chrysostom, Politics, Letters and Philosophy* (Oxford: OUP, 2000), 1–10 at 1, his dates being here 45–115, also *Dio Chrysostom*, ed. and trans. J. W. Cohoon, 5 vols (Loeb Classical Library; Cambridge, MA: Harvard University Press/William Heinemann, 1961), i, ix, where his dates are given as 40–120. For bibliography on Dio see B. F. Harris, 'Dio of Prusa: A Survey of Recent Work,' in *ANRW* II.33.5 (1991), 3853–81 and, for an assessment of his life and work, see also Paolo Desideri, 'Dione di Prusa fra hellenismo e romantà,' *ANRW* II.33.5 (1991), 3882–902. Major examinations of Dio's life are to be found in id. *Dione di Prusa: un intellectuale greco nell'impero romano*

Sophistic'—a group which included Lucian, Plutarch, Aristides, and Galen—the bare details of his life may be reconstructed from what is written by Philostratus (*Lives of the Sophists* 7/487–8) and in Dio's surviving speeches. Suffice to say, Cocceianus Dio[3] was, like Josephus, Philo, and Pliny, from a wealthy and influential family, in Dio's case from a Greek city, Prusa (modern Bursa), in the Roman province of Bithynia. Since the circumstances and environments of his life may have a bearing on how we assess Dio's comments on the Essenes, it is important to review these briefly, though his 'biography' is not without controversy.

Dio was the son of a certain Pasicrates who had spent beyond his means on the city, receiving high honours in return, only to die early and leave Dio with the job of paying the debts. The brilliant young Dio at this point was a sophist—a practitioner of smart eloquence and rhetoric—and, when he was in a position to, he travelled to Rome—as well as to Rhodes, Alexandria, and elsewhere[4]—with a repertoire of speeches, sometimes on trivial subjects (exemplified by his eulogies on a gnat, parrot, or hair). Under the Flavian dynasty (69–96 CE) so close to Pliny, when Josephus was writing his histories, it was not always an easy time to be a philosopher. Dio appears to have been a student of the Stoic Musonius Rufus (*c.*20–90 CE), and, in the reign of Domitian (81–96), Dio fled from Rome and avoided also his homeland. He then wandered, pennilessly, dressed in rags, doing manual labour when he could, in the region of the northern Black Sea and along the Danube River, until Domitian was assassinated and his exile ended. This ascetic turn was key to his value system. Nevertheless, he returned to his home, to normal life, and then headed an embassy back to Rome to express thanks. He was liked by the emperor Trajan. Secure, finally, Dio travelled to Alexandria and elsewhere in 102, then went back to Prusa, became a benefactor of the city, and, in the course of official business, in 111–112, met the imperial legate Pliny the Younger, nephew of Pliny the Elder.

It is on the basis of this official business in Bithynia that David Graf has suggested that Dio might have been introduced to Pliny the Younger's uncle and learnt about the Essenes,[5] though Dio's residence in Rome during the 70s and his various journeys must have given him a considerable knowledge of all kinds of literature, oral traditions, and reports, even Pliny's *Natural History* itself. Clearly, in his massive repertoire of discourses, of which only some 76 survive, Dio drew very widely. He was not a stolid scholar tied to repeating or

---

(Messina/Florence: G. D'Anna, 1978), and Christopher P. Jones, *The Roman World of Dio Chrysostom* (Cambridge, MA: Harvard University Press, 1978).

[3] Jones argues that this surname was not derived as an honour from the emperor Nerva but from some local Cocceianus, on the basis of inscriptions showing this name in the region; see Jones, *Dio*, 7.

[4] The Alexandria Oration is dated early by both Jones, *Dio*, 36 and Desideri, *Dione*, 68–70.

[5] David Graf, 'The Pagan Witness to the Essenes,' *BA* 40/3 (1977): 125–9, at p.129.

epitomizing sources; it is largely impossible to locate exactly where he found information or when he wrote his works, given the paucity of surviving material.

Dio's work which deals with the Essenes is itself gone. It is known only from a work about Dio written by Synesius of Cyrene, *Dio, sive de suo ipsius instituto*, in which Synesius takes Dio as a model of dedication to true philosophy.[6] Dio's evidence on the Essenes is not given as a quotation or an epitome, but is simply reported as Synesius remembered it. The question is then not only where Dio took his information from, but how precisely Synesius presents that information.

Therefore, we must consider the 'reporter', the man who provides us with Dio's comments on the Essenes. Synesius was a contemporary of Augustine of Hippo, being born around 373. He was probably dead prior to 415 CE when his teacher in Alexandria, the Neoplatonist philosopher Hypatia, was torn apart by a Christian lynch mob.[7] Like Augustine, Synesius was a philosopher who ended up as a bishop, though his devotion to Christian theology was clearly nothing like his fellow North African. His intellectual home was Alexandria, and his main period of productivity was during the ten years he travelled between Cyrene and Alexandria, before accepting the position of bishop of Ptolemais in Libya in 410. Synesius' essay on Dio comes from this period, in which he also composed a witty discourse, *In Praise of Baldness*, which replies to Dio's *In Praise of Hair*. His *Dio* is addressed to the unborn son he had seen in a dream, and provides a kind of guide to reading *Dio* as a basis for forming a sound philosophy, while critiquing Philostratus' presentation, which, he argues, does not sufficiently differentiate between Dio pre-exile and Dio post-: the young sophist and the mature philosopher. However, Dio's interest was clearly also to recommend Dio as a creditable philosopher—rather than a sophist—to all other philosophers with whom he communicated, who could consult Dio's works to check the veracity of how Synesius represents him. It is then extremely unlikely that Synesius would have misrepresented Dio's comments on the Essenes.

In terms of the immediate context of the arrival of the Essenes in the piece, Synesius criticizes Philostratus for mentioning Dio's *In Praise of a Parrot* and the *Euboean Discourse* (*Or.* 7) in the same breath (Philostratus, *Lives* 7/487),

---

[6] See J. G. Krabinger (ed.), Synesius, *S. Cyrenaei quae exstant opera omnia I: Orationes et homiliarum fragmenta* (Landshut: Thomann, 1850); Kurt Treu, *Synesios von Kyrene, ein Kommentar zu seinem 'Dion'* (Texte und Untersuchungen zur Geschichte der altchristlichen Literatur 71; Berlin: AkademieVerlag, 1958).

[7] See Bengt-Arne Roos, *Synesius of Cyrene: A Study in His Personality* (Lund: Lund University Press, 1991); Jay Bregman, *Synesius of Cyrene: Philosopher-Bishop* (Berkeley: University of California Press, 1982); H.-I. Marrou, 'Synesius of Cyrene and Alexandrian Neoplatonism,' in Arnaldo Momigliano (ed.), *The Conflict of Paganism and Christianity in the Fourth Century* (Oxford: OUP, 1963), 126–50.

when the former is sophistry and the latter clearly philosophy. The *Euboean Discourse* might have an obscure subject—not the rulers of the noble *On Kingship*—but it presents a model of a happy life (εὐδαίμονος βίου) in deflating someone puffed up by wealth, to show that true happiness is to be found elsewhere, and, in boosting the poor, by its focus on a simple Euboean hunter and his family. Synesius then continues:

Ἔτι καὶ τοὺς Ἐσσηνοὺς ἐπαινεῖ που, πόλιν ὅλην εὐδαίμονα τὴν παρὰ τὸ νεκρὸν ὕδωρ ἐν τῇ μεσογείᾳ τῆς Παλαιστίνης κειμένην παρ᾽ αὐτα που τὰ Σόδομα· ὁ γὰρ ἀνήρ ὅλως, ἐπειδή τοῦ φιλοσοφεῖν ἀπήρξατο καὶ εἰς τὸ νουθετεῖν ἀνθρώπους ἀπέκλινεν, οὐδένα λόγον ἄκαρπον ἐξενήνοχε·

Furthermore, he somewhere [else] praises the Essenes, an entirely happy *polis* beside the dead water in the interior of Palestine, lying somewhere near the [place of] Sodom itself. For the man, wholly, once he moved off to philosophy and turned to admonish humanity, produced no unfruitful work. (*Dio* 3: 2)[8]

It is immediately apparent that, unlike with the other works mentioned by Synesius, in this case he does not give a title to the discourse in which the reference to the Essenes is found. Mention of the Essenes is recalled by him as being 'somewhere', που. But Synesius knows his Dio, and expects that his unborn son—and other readers—will find the discourse in question in due course; there is simply no reason for him to represent it inaccurately in this reference. To what extent this indicates an entire discourse on the Essenes remains unknown, but the fact that Synesius refers to it additionally as being not an 'unfruitful work', λόγον ἄκαρπον (in contrast to *In Praise of a Parrot*), would mean it was more than a passing treatment.[9] The point here concerns obscure but worthy subject matter used by Dio for philosophy as opposed to sophistry, a work designed to 'admonish humanity' by showing an example of people worthy of praise who were clearly not the sophisticated citizens of Rome or any other major city. The emphasis for Synesius is on how uncommon and seemingly unworthy the Essenes are as a subject of philosophical discourse, like the hunter in Euboea, but they are not to be equated with the parrot of Dio's youthful sophistry. They might live in 'Timbuktu', but they are still a fitting subject for praise, because they have achieved true happiness—the philosopher's goal—just as the Euboean hunter has achieved, in Dio's words, 'happiness and the blessed life' (*Or.* 7: 65).

---

[8] Adam Kamesar, Review of *The Essenes According to the Classical Sources*, ed. Geza Vermes and Martin D. Goodman (Sheffield: JSOT Press, 1989), in *Journal of the American Oriental Society* 111 (1991): 134–5, is rightly suspicious of a translation that would render Greek εὐδαίμονα as 'prosperous' here; rather, it needs to be read in line with Stoic philosophy, see below. The accusative ὅλην is probably to be understood adverbially, as in the LXX *Song of Songs* 4: 7. The name Σόδομα is a plural form in the Septuagint and elsewhere, hence the plural αὐτα.

[9] Treu's notion that it was purely a passing mention is therefore unjustified (Treu, *Synesius*, 42).

So Synesius tells us that these two examples have been used to illustrate how a happy lifestyle does not depend on wealth or any outside circumstances. This is exceptionally significant in terms of Dio's themes. As Dio states explicitly in *Oration* 3: 1, happiness is not determined by possessions but 'by each by himself and by his own mind (διανοία)'. Happiness of this kind is the ultimate goal of life, in the Stoic philosophy of Epictetus. To account someone 'happy', as having well-being, is the greatest compliment a Stoic could give to another. Happiness does not result from excellence in some skill, as Dio reflects upon in his *Oration* 24, or 'Discourse on Happiness', but without knowledge of virtue and intelligence, everything one tries to do is of little worth, and will not lead to true happiness. This necessity of virtue and wisdom for happiness is found also in Dio's *Oration* 23: 'I believe that the wise man alone is fortunate and happy' (*Or.* 23: 9, cf. 12).

How far could Dio have managed to extract a notion of Essene happiness from Pliny (*Nat. Hist*: 5.15 [73])? It is simply not possible. As we have seen, in Pliny's *Natural History* the only really important feature about the Essenes—which is a wonder—is that they survive over the ages, despite their celibacy and austerity, by drawing on a reservoir of miserable people fleeing from the vicissitudes of life.

Therefore, even though it may be that Dio knew the *Natural History*, at least in part, Dio must have had more information than Pliny in order to create the Essenes as an example of the very opposite state, namely, of philosophical *eudaimonia*, or as people worthy of praise that could be used to admonish humanity. Pliny does not praise the Essenes; he sees them as *mira*, 'strange' (or a 'wonder'), in that they continue to exist throughout the ages despite no one being born into their *gens*. Their fecundity comes from people's dissatisfaction with life. They are an oddity to marvel at as peculiar, not to praise.

What then of the attestation that the Essenes lived by the Dead Sea? Is this perhaps derivative of Pliny? Linguistically, clearly not. Dio, according to Synesius, uses the designation 'the dead water in the interior of Palestine', τὸ νεκρὸν ὕδωρ ἐν τῇ μεσογείᾳ τῆς Παλαιστίνης, for what in Pliny is *lacus Asphaltites*. One would expect Greek λίμνη for Latin *lacus* (see Aristotle, *Meteorologia* 2: 3/359a; Diodorus Siculus, *Bibl. Hist.* 2: 48: 6; Strabo, *Geogr.* 16: 2: 34; Alexander of Aphrodisias, *In Arist. Meteor.* 2:359a). The term τὸ νεκρὸν ὕδωρ is unparalleled in any extant ancient literature (though of course it is close to ἡ νέκρα θάλασσα found in Pausanias, *Descr. Graec.* 5: 7: 5).

The closest parallel to this phrase is found buried in a Hebrew manuscript of the Middle Ages: the translation of Aristotle's *Meteorologia* made by Shmuel Ibn Tibbon in 1210, in which there is an additional piece not found in any manuscript of *Meteorologia* or commentary on it. The piece is found slightly differently in the 21 manuscripts of Ibn Tibbon's work, but most interesting here is the Budapest manuscript (B), from around 1500.

והוא הים המת הנקרא איגא מורתו בארץ הודו ובצד בית המקדש
והוא אשר יצא ממנו החימר בכל שנה שהוא משל יך אותו

This is the Dead Sea, called *Aiga Mortu*, in the land of Hodo, on the side of
the Temple, and from it asphalt comes out every year, thrown by the same
(2: 184–5).[10]

Ibn Tibbon's translation utilized a ninth-century manuscript of the Arabic
paraphrase of Aristotle's *Meteorology* by Ibn al-Bitriq as well as quotations
from a lost Arabic translation of Alexander of Aphrodisias' commentary
(*c.*200 CE) and a commentary by Ibn Rushd, but none of these have this
piece.[11] There is no way of determining where it comes from, but the name
Aiga Mortu seems to be a rendering of the Latin phrase *aqua mortua* 'dead
water'. This term then relates to what appears in Dio Chrysostom.

The term 'dead water' is not likely to be a name, since ὕδωρ is used in
antiquity only for the substance of water, and not as a designation for a body of
water. It is unlikely to be a term used by Synesius, whose language—given he
was saturated in the language of Christian Scripture—should have been
biblical: 'the Sea of Arabah' (Deut. 3: 17), 'the Salt Sea' (Gen. 14: 3; Deut. 3:
17; Josh. 15: 5), or even 'the Eastern Sea' (Ezek. 47: 18), but most probably the
usual appellation, 'the Dead Sea', as it is named in Eusebius' *Onomasticon* (12:
17–18; 16: 4; 22: 27–8; 42: 3) and frequently elsewhere, throughout the fourth
century through to modern times. Synesius seems to be overturning his
contemporary Christian terminology in order to represent the distinctive
usage of Dio, who—like Aristotle (*Met.* 2: 3/359a) or Tacitus (*Hist.* 5: 6–7)—
did not know the name of the lake. The whole phraseology, 'the dead water in
the interior of Palestine', serves to emphasize the remoteness of the Essenes,
and the rough physical circumstances of their existence: the dead water is
unnamed, a desolate place in a faraway land. In terms of Dio, he situates the
Essenes, just as he had situated the shepherd in Euboea, a long way from
Rome.

The use of the term 'Palestine' is likewise not found in Pliny's description. It
may be a modification by Synesius, since the Roman provincial name of the
area of wider Judaea was not officially changed to 'Palaestina' until the time of
Hadrian, after the Bar Kokhba revolt in 132–5. The southern part of Arabia—a
Province of Rome from 106 CE—was designated as Palaestina Salutaris only
after the provincial reforms of Diocletian in the late third century. However,
the use of the term 'Syria Palestine' as a geographical designation predates
Roman official nomenclature, as can be seen in the writings of Herodotus
(*Hist.* 1: 105; 2: 104, 106; 3: 91; 4: 39; 7: 89), who defined Syria Palestine as

---

[10] Resianne Fontaine (ed.), *Otot ha-shamayim: Samuel Ibn Tibbon's Hebrew version of
Aristotle's Meteorology: A Critical Edition* (Leiden: Brill, 1995), 98–101.
[11] Fontaine, *Otot*, ix–xi. xvi–xvii.

stretching from Phoenicia to Gaza (*Hist.* 3: 5; 7: 89). Numerous authors followed suit, including Philo of Alexandria, who defined the Essenes themselves as living in *Suria Palaistinē* (*Prob.* 75).[12] Even in a Latin context, when the official provincial name of the region was 'Judaea', Pomponius Mela defined that part of Syria called 'Palaestina' in geographical terms as being the region which touches on both Phoenicia and Arabia (*Chorografia* 1: 54). Relevantly, while he did not know the name of the lake, Aristotle, in *Meteorologica* 2: 3, defined it as lying 'in Palestine'. This then forms the closest parallel to what we have in Dio according to Synesius.[13]

Then there is a reference to Sodom, which is not found in Pliny. It was assumed by Christopher Jones that mention of Sodom had to come from Synesius, 'since Sodom is only likely to have been mentioned by one who lived in a largely Christian society'.[14] However, the association between Sodom and the Dead Sea was already made by Strabo (*Geog.* 16: 2: 44), who mistakenly called the lake 'Sirbonis', and by Tacitus (*Hist.* 5: 6–7), though Tacitus gave no name to either the lake or the cities that were destroyed there. Josephus and Tacitus link the burning of the towns, by lightning bolts, with ash-filled fruit, later dubbed 'Sodom's apples' (Josephus, *War* 4: 484; Tacitus, *Hist.* 5: 7). That the destruction of Sodom and Gomorra was something known in the Graeco-Roman world outside Jewish and Christian circles may also be suggested by a graffito from Pompeii reading 'Sodoma Gomora' (*CIL* IV, 4976) as well as by the (bizarre) love charm of *PGM* XXXVI, which includes mention of the angels of god descending and overthrowing 'the pentapolis of Sodom, and Gomorra, Adama, Sebouie and Segor'. Celsus compared the story of Sodom and Gomorra with the narrative of Phaethon (Origen, *Contra Celsum* 4: 21, cf. Plato, *Timaeus* 22d).[15] It may well be that the epic destruction of the cities of Sodom and Gomorra (Gen. 19: 1–29) had the same kind of mythic resonances as the submerging of Atlantis, and could be used by pagan authors otherwise quite uninterested in biblical history. Strabo even mentions Eratosthenes as having an opinion on the matter. We do not then need to assume that only the Christian Synesius could have added the mention of Sodom to Dio's discussion.

Overall, Dio is an important independent witness to the situation of Essenes next to the Dead Sea, a witness very frequently overlooked.[16]

---

[12] See David Jacobson, 'Palestine and Israel,' *BASOR* 313 (1999): 65–74.

[13] That the lake's name was not as well known as its features is shown also by Diodorus Siculus, *Bibl.* 2: 4 and Tacitus, *Hist.* 5: 6, neither of whom name it.

[14] Jones, *Dio*, 64. Jones also assumes Sodom was located south of the Dead Sea, which is not so; see below.

[15] John Granger Cook, *The Interpretation of the Old Testament in Greco-Roman Paganism* (Tübingen: Mohr Siebeck, 2004), 45–6, 48, 103–4.

[16] Though see Jean-Baptiste Humbert, 'The Chronology during the First Century BC: De Vaux and his Method: A Debate,' in Jean-Baptiste Humbert and Jan Gunneweg, *Khirbet Qumran et Ain Feshkha: études d'anthropologie, de physique et de chimie* (Qumran ii; Fribourg/Göttingen: Editions universitaires Fribourg Suisse/Vandenhoeck & Ruprecht, 2003), 425–38, at 427–8.

JULIUS SOLINUS

The reference in Synesius may not in fact be the only snippet of Dio Chrysostom on the Essenes. Later compilers could use all kinds of material available to them, but long lost to us, and it is interesting to look even further forward in time to consider where else something of Dio's treatise may be reflected.

It is at this point then that we must consider the material in the work of Julius Solinus, whose work *Collectanea* 35: 9–12 remains something of a mystery, and whose very dating can be highly debated, though there seems no substantial reason to doubt that the *Collectanea*, also called 'The Wonders of the World' (*De mirabilibus mundi*), should be placed in the third century, as Theodor Mommsen proposed.[17] This work circulated in an initial and revised edition, the latter often cited as 'Polyhistor', Solinus' authorship for the revision being generally accepted.[18]

Solinus used Pliny extensively and yet curiously parallels Dio by referring to the lake as being 'in the interior of' the country. He then uses the Plinian 'Judaea' rather than 'Palestine': *interiora Iudaeae* (cf. ἐν τῇ μεσογείᾳ τῆς Παλαιστίνης).[19] This description of the situation of the lake cannot be derivative of Pliny's identification of Judaea as being *supra Idumaeam et Samariam*, even if *supra* indicates a place further inland ('beyond'), because with Dio and Solinus the references are specifically to the Dead Sea and not to Judaea as a whole.

Solinus clearly has used Pliny in his work overall, but Solinus' description of the Essenes is not a simple replication of what is substantively in Pliny, but rather, as Christoph Burchard explored, we have here a separate unknown text embedded in Solinus' work.[20] Solinus writes:

Interiora Iudaeae occidentem quae contuentur Esseni tenent, qui praediti memorabili disciplina recesserunt a ritu gentium universarum, maiestatis ut reor providentia ad hunc morem destinati. nulla ibi femina: venere se penitus abdicaverunt. pecuniam nesciunt. palmis victitant. nemo ibi nascitur nec tamen deficit hominum multitudo. locus ipse addictus pudicitiae est: ad quem plurimi licet undique gentium properent, nullus admittitur, nisi quem castitatis fides et innocentiae

---

[17] The work is dedicated to 'Adventus', whom Mommsen identifies with a consul attested in 218, Oclatinius Adventus: Theodor Mommsen (ed.), *C. Iulii Solini Collectanea rerum memorabilium* (Berlin: Weidmann,1895), i–xx, and see N. B. Rankov, 'M. Oclatinius Adventus in Britain,' *Britannia* 18 (1987): 243–9.

[18] Hermann Walter, *Die 'Collectanea rerum memorabilium' des C. Julius Solinus. Ihre Entstehung und die Echtheit ihrer Zweitfassung* (Hermes.Einzelschriften, 22; Wiesbaden: F. Steiner, 1969).

[19] The translation here is on the basis of the text established in Mommsen, *Collectanea*, 154–6. There are no modern translations of Solinus.

[20] Christoph Burchard, 'Solin et les Esséniens. Remarques à propos d'un article negligée,' *RB* 74 (1967): 392–407.

meritum prosequatur: nam qui reus est vel levis culpae, quamvis summa ope adipisci ingressum velit, divinitus submovetur. ita per inmensum spatium saeculorum, incredibile dictu, aeterna gens est cessantibus puerperiis.

The interior of Judaea, west of what is noted [as Lake Asphaltitis], the Essenes hold, [men] who, possessed of a remarkable discipline, retreat from the universal observance of people, to this way of excellence supposedly destined by providence. There is no woman there; they have abdicated sexual desire itself utterly. They are ignorant of money. They live by means of palms. No one is born there and yet they are not deficient in [maintaining] a multitude of human beings. The place itself is dedicated to virtue, into which, although many of the people hasten from everywhere, none is admitted, unless he is accompanied by merit, with continence, trust and innocence. For whoever is guilty of even a small thing, however much he wants to advance, is removed by the divinity. So, through the immense space of the ages—incredible to say—it is an eternal people devoid of childbirth.

The relationship between Solinus and Pliny here may best be seen by considering the two works side by side, as shown in Table 1. Here one can see how Solinus uses Pliny freely, yet also modifies Pliny by inserting other material.[21] This material is italicized in the table in order to show it more clearly.

Solinus not only adds in this material from a separate source, but he uses it to tone down Pliny's negativity about the Essenes. He inserts positive comments and deletes the more hostile statements. For example, where Pliny calls the *gens* of the Essenes *mira*, in regard to their peculiarity, Solinus admires them for being 'possessed by a remarkable discipline', *praediti memorabili disciplina*, and he goes on to describe how this is manifested. He deletes mention of the incomers being weary of life and the fluctuations of fortune, but rather indicates that people are eagerly attracted to a lifestyle of virtue. He removes the negative word *turba*, 'swarm, crowd', and refers to *plurimi . . . gentium*, 'many of the people', instead. He deletes the snide comment at the end, that 'so fecund is this dissatisfaction of life in others'. Where did Solinus get this radically different image of the Essenes from?

In terms of Solinus' *Collectanea* as a whole,[22] Theodore Mommsen, who provided the critical edition of the little-known Solinus in 1895, noted that

---

[21] For Solinus' use of Pliny overall, see Mommsen, *Collectanea*, 238–4.

[22] For which, see Walter, 'Collectanea rerum memorabilium'; Ira David Hyksell, *A Study of the Latinity of Solinus* (Chicago: Chicago University Libraries, 1925). Peter Lebrecht Schmidt has argued that Solinus' dates should be pushed to the fourth century, since some manuscripts have Constantius rather than Adventus as the dedicatee, and in both language and ethical tone Schmidt sees Christian influence, 'Solinus Polyhistor in Wissenschaftsgeschichte und Geschichte,' *Philologus* 139 (1995): 23–35, a view endorsed also by Zweder von Martels, 'Between Tertullian and Vincentius Lirinensis: On the Concept Constantia Veritatis and other "Christian" Influences on Solinus,' in Alasdair A. MacDonald, Michael W. Twomey, and G. J. Reinink (eds), *Learned Antiquity: Scholarship and Society in the Near East* (Groningen Studies in Cultural Change 5; Leuven: Peeters, 2003), though in fact, the vague 'Christian' language all too frequently seems indebted to Cicero and other Stoics, see citations by Von Martels, 71–2.

Table 1: 'The Wonders of Judaea'[i]

Pliny the Elder, *Naturalis Historia* 5: 15: 70–2	C. Iulius Solinus, *Collectanea Rerum Memorabilium* 35: 1
70. supra Idumaeam et Samariam Iudaea longe lateque funditur. pars eius Syriae iuncta Galilaea vocatur, Arabiae vero et Aegypto proxima Peraea, asperis dispersa montibus et a ceteris Iudaeis Iordane amne discreta. reliqua Iudaea dividitur in toparchias decem quo dicemus ordine: Hiericuntem palmetis consitam, fontibus riguam, Emmaum, Lyddam, Iopicam, Acrabatenam, Gophaniticam, Thamniticam, Betholeptophenen, Orinen, in qua fuere Hierosolyma, longe clarissima urbium orientis, non Iudaeae modo, Herodium, cum oppido inlustri eiusdem nominis.	Iudaea inlustris est aquis, sed natura non eadem aquarum omnium. Iordanis amnis eximiae suavitatis, Paneade fonte dimissus, regiones praeterfluit amoenissimas;
71. Iordanes amnis oritur e fonte Paneade, qui cognomen dedit Caesareae, de qua dicemus. amnis amoenus et, quatenus locorum situs patitur, ambitiosus accolisque se praebens velut invitus Asphaltiten lacum dirum natura petit, a quo postremo ebibitur aquasque laudatas perdit, pestilentibus mixtas. ergo ubi prima convallium fuit occasio, in lacum se fundit, quem plures Genesarum vocant xvi longitudinis vi latitudinis, amoenis circumsaeptum oppidis, ab oriente Iuliade et Hippo, a meridie Tarichea, quo nomine aliqui et lacum appellant, ab occidente Tiberiade, aquis calidis salubri.	mox in Asphaltiten lacum mersus stagno corrumpitur. qui Asphaltites gignit bitumen, animal non habet, nihil in eo mergi potest; tauri etiam camelique inpune ibi fluitant. est et lacus Sara extentus passuum sedecim milibus, circumsaeptus urbibus plurimis et celebribus, ipse par optimis. sed lacus Tiberiadis omnibus anteponitur, salubris ingenuo aestu et ad sanitatem usu efficaci.
72. Asphaltites nihil praeter bitumen gignit, unde et nomen. nullum corpus animalium recipit, tauri camelique fluitant; inde fama nihil in eo mergi. longitudine excedit C p latitudine maxima LXXV implet, minima vi. prospicit eum ab oriente Arabia Nomadum, a meridie Machaerus, secunda quondam arx Iudaeae ab Hierosolymis. eodem latere est calidus fons medicae salubritatis Callirhoe, aquarum gloriam ipso nomine praeferens.	Iudaeae caput fuit Hierusolyma, sed excisa est. successit Hierichus: et haec desivit, Artaxerxis bello subacta. Callirrhoe Hierusolymis proxima, fons calore medico probatissimus et ex ipso aquarum praeconio sic vocatus.

Naturalis Historia 12: 54: 111–23

111. sed omnibus odoribus praefertur balsamum, uni terrarum Iudaeae concessum, quondam in duobus tantum hortis, utroque regio, altero iugerum viginti non amplius, altero pauciorum. ostendere arborum hanc urbi imperatores Vespasiani, clarumque dictu, a Pompeio Magno in triumpho arbores quoque duximus.

112. servit nunc haec ac tributa pendit cum sua gente, in totum alia natura quam nostri externique prodiderant. quippe viti similior est quam myrto. malleolis seri didicit nuper, vincta ut vitis, et inplet colles vinearum modo. quae sine adminiculis se ipsa sustinet, tondetur similiter fruticans; ac rastris[ii] nitescit properatque nasci, intra tertium annum fructifera. folium proximum tuberi, perpetua coma.

113. saeviere in eam Iudaei sicut in vitam quoque suam; contra defendere Romani, et dimicatum pro frutice est; seritque nunc eum fiscus, nec unquam fuit numerosior. proceritas intra bina cubita subsistit.

114. arbori tria genera: tenue et capillacea coma, quod vocatur eutheriston; alterum scabro aspectu, incurvum, fruticosum, odoratius; hoc trachy appellant, tertium eumeces, quia est reliquis procerius, levi cortice. huic secunda bonitas, novissima eutheristo.

115. semen eius vino proximum gustu, colore rufum, nec sine pingui. peius in grano quod levius atque viridius. ramus crassior quam myrto. inciditur vitro, lapide osseisve cultellis; ferro laedi vitalia odit, emoritur protinus, eodem amputari supervacua patiens. incidentis manus libratur artifici temperamento, ne quid ultra corticem violet.

116. sucus e plaga manat quem opobalsamum vocant, suavitatis eximiae. sed tenui gutta; ploratu lanis parva colligitur in cornua, ex iis novo fictili conditur,

in hac terra balsamum nascitur, quae silva intra terminos viginti iugerum usque ad victoriam nostram fuit: at cum Iudaea potiti sumus, ita luci illi propagati sunt, ut iam nobis latissimi colles sudent balsama. similes vitibus stirpes habent: malleolis digeruntur, rastris nitescunt, aqua guadent, amant amputari, tenacibus foliis sempiterno inumbrantur.

lignum caudicis attrectatum ferro sine mora moritur: ea propter aut vitro aut cultellulis osseis, sed in sola cortice artifici plaga vulneratur, e qua eximiae suavitatis gutta manat.

(*continued*)

Table 1: Continued

crassiori similis oleo et in musto candida; rufescit deinde simulque durescit e tralucido.

117. Alexandro Magno res ibi gerente toto die aestivo unam concham impleri iustum erat, omni vero fecundidate e maiore horto congios senos, e minore singulos, cum et duplo rependebatur argento, nunc etiam singularum arborum largior vena. ter omnibus percutitur aestatibus, postea deputatur.

118. et sarmenta quoque in merce sunt. DCCC HS amputatio ipsa surculusque veniere intra quintum devictae Iudaeae annum; xylobalsamum vocatur et coquitur in unguentis. pro suco ipso substituere officinae. corticis etiam ad medicamenta pretium est. praecipua autem gratia lacrimae, secunda semini, tertia cortici, minima ligno.

119. ex hoc buxosum optimum, quod et odoratissimum, e semine autem maximum et ponderosissimum, mordens gustu fervensque in ore. adulteratur Petraeo hyperico, quod coarguitur magnitudine, inanitate, longitudine, odoris ignavia, sapore piperis.

120. lacrimae probatio ut sit e pingui tenuis ac modice rufa et in fricando odorata. secundus candidi coloris, peior viridis crassusque, pessimus niger, quippe ut oleum senescit. ex omni incisura maxime probatur quod ante semen fluxit. et alias adulteratur seminis suco, vixque maleficium deprehenditur gustu amariore; esse enim debet lenis, non subacidus, odore tantum austerus.

121. vitiatur et oleo rosae, cypri, lentisci, balani, terebinthi, myrti, resina, galbano, cera Cypria, prout quaeque res fuit, nequissime autem cummi: quoniam arescit, in manu inversa et in aqua sidit, quae probatio eius gemina est.

122. debet et sincerum arescere, sed hoc cummi addita fragili crusta evenit. et gustu deprehenditur, carbone vero quod cera resinaque adulteratum est, nigriore flamma. nam melle mutatur statim in manu contrahit muscas.

123. praeterea sinceri densatur in tepida aqua gutta sidens ad ima vasa, adulterata olei modo innatat et, si metopio vitiata est, circulo candido post lacrimam secundum in pretiis locum poma obtinent, cortex tertium, ultimus honos ligno.

cingitur. summa est probatio ut lac coagulet, in veste maculas non faciat. nec manifestior alibi fraus, quippe milibus denarium sextarii, empti vendente fisco trecenis denariis, veneunt: in tantum expedit augere liquorem. xylobalsamo pretium in libras vi.

Naturalis Historia 5: 15: 73

73. ab occidente litora Esseni fugiunt usque qua nocent, gens sola et in toto orbe praeter ceteras mira, sine ulla femina, omni venere abdicata, sine pecunia, socia palmarum. in diem ex aequo convenarum turba renascitur, large frequentantibus quos vita fessos ad mores eorum fortuna fluctibus agit. ita per saeculorum milia-incredibile dictu-gens aeterna est, in qua nemo nascitur. tam fecunda illis aliorum vitae paenitenta est. infra hos Engada oppidum fuit, secundum ab Hierosolymis fertilitate palmetorumque nemoribus, nunc alterum bustum. inde Masada castellum in rupe, et ipsum haut procul Asphaltite. et hactenus Iudaea est.

Longo ab Hierusolymis recessu tristis sinus panditur, quem de caelo tactum testatur humus nigra et in cinerem soluta. ibi duo oppida. Sodomum nominatum alterum, alterum Gomorrum, apud quae pomum quod gignitur, habeat licet speciem maturitatis, mandi tamen non potest: nam fuliginem intrinsecus favillaciam ambitio tantum extimae cutis cohibet, quae vel levi pressa tactu fumum exhalat et fatiscit in vagum pulverem.

Interiora Iudaeae occidentem quae contuentur Esseni tenent, qui praediti memorabili disciplina recesserunt a ritu gentium universarum, maiestatis ut reor providentia ad hunc morem destinati. nulla ibi femina: venere se penitus abdicaverunt. pecuniam nesciunt. palmis vicitant. nemo ibi nascitur nec tamen deficit hominum multitudo. locus ipse addictus pudicitiae est: ad quem plurimi licet undique gentium properent, nullus admittitur, nisi quem castitatis fides et innocentiae meritum prosequatur: nam qui reus est vel levis culpae, quamvis summa ope adipisci ingressum velit, divinitus submovetur. ita per inmensum spatium saeculorum, incredibile dictu, aeterna gens est cessantibus puerperiis. Engada oppidum infra Essenos fuit, sed excisum est. verum inclitis nemoribus adhuc durat decus lucisque palmarum eminentissimus nihil vel de aevo vel de bello derogatum. Iudaeae terminus Massada castellum.

(*continued*)

Table 1: Continued

Pliny the Elder, *Natural History* 5: 15: 70–2	
70. Beyond Idumaea and Samaria Judaea extends far and wide. The part of it adjoining Syria is called Galilee, but [is called] Peraea near Arabia and Egypt, covered with rough mountains and separated from the rest by the River Jordan. The remainder of Judaea is divided into ten toparchies, which we state in order: Jericho—planted with palms, watered by springs—Emmaus, Lydda, Joppa, Acrabatene, Gophanitis, Thamnitis, Betholeptepha, Orine, in which was Jerusalem—long the most brilliant city of the East, not only of Judaea—[and] Herodium, with a famous town of the same name.	
71. The Jordan River rises from the spring of Paneas, which gives its name to Caesarea [Paneas], of which we will speak [later]. The river is pleasant, in so far as the situation of the places permit. Twining and lingering, it shows itself as reluctant to [accept] the request of Asphaltites, a lake of a dismal nature, in which finally it is absorbed, and its praised waters lost, mixing with unhealthy ones. Therefore, where first convenience provides an opportunity, it flows into a lake, which many call Gennesar, 16 miles long and 6 miles wide, surrounded by pleasant towns, on the east Julias and Hippo, on the south Tarichea, by which name some call the lake, [and] on the west Tiberias, with healthy hot springs.	*Judaea is famous for waters, but not all of the waters are of one nature. The Jordan River, one of exceptional sweetness, flows out of the spring of Paneas, runs by very pleasant regions.*
72. [Lake] Asphaltites produces nothing except bitumen, hence its name. It receives no body of an animal; bulls and camels float. On account of this character nothing sinks in it. In length it exceeds 100 miles, at its broadest it is 75 miles and at its smallest 6. Facing it in the east [corr. south] is Arabia of the Nomads, in the south [corr. east] Machaerus, a citadel at one time second to Jerusalem. On the same side is the curative, healthy hot spring, Callirhoe, this name well-known because of the fame of its waters.	Soon ruined in Asphaltites. Sinking in a stagnant pool which produces bitumen; it has no animal; nothing in it is able to sink; bulls and also camels float there without danger. There is also Lake Sara [= Gennesar] extending 16 miles long, surrounded by many celebrated cities, [each] itself with the best. But the [water of the] lake at Tiberias is preferable of all, *wholesome in mild taste and effective in maintaining health. The capital of Judaea was Jerusalem, but it is destroyed. Jericho succeeded it, but this no more, overcome in war by Artaxerxes. Callirhoe is proximate to Jerusalem, a spring very commended for the medicinal heat and itself is so called from the proclaimed fame of the waters.*

Natural History 12: 54: 111–23

But balsam is considered preferable to all other perfumes [and is] bestowed only on one land, Judaea. Once cultivated only in two gardens, both royal [estates], one no more than twenty *iugera*, and the other smaller. The emperors Vespasian [and Titus] exhibited the tree here in the city [of Rome], and let it be clearly said that from Pompey the Great on we have brought trees in triumphal processions.

In this land balsam is produced, an orchard that was not found beyond twenty *iugera* until our victory, but, after we possessed Judaea, those groves were propagated so that now very wide hills provide us with balsam. The shrubs have a similarity to [grape] vines. They are arranged in rows. They thrive by *rastrum*[ii] (work). They relish water. They like pruning. *They are always overshadowed by their tenacious foliage.*

112. Now here this tree serves tribute and is weighed out with its people (*gens*), [and has] an entirely other nature to that which our own as well as foreign writers have stated. In fact, it is more similar to a vine than to a myrtle. Nowadays it is trained to be planted in rows, tied as a vine, so it sustains its own weight without supports, and it covers hills in the form of vineyards. Having been [root-]clipped in similar manner with a *rastrum*[ii] it thrives and hastens to sprout, bearing fruit within three years. The leaf [is] nearly a tube, [and it is] an evergreen plant.

113. The Judaeans vented their rage on this [plant] just as [they did] on their own life, while, against [them], the Romans protected it; indeed, there have been battles before for fruit. Now the *fiscus* plants it, and it has never before been so plentiful; it stands in height within a couple of cubits.

114. There are three kinds of trees: a plant thin and hairy which is named *eutheriston*, another of rough appearance, drooping, bushy and fragrant; it is called *trachy*. The third is *eumeces*, because it remains tall; with a smooth, bark. This is the second in quality, the *eutheriston* [until] very recently.

115. The seed of this tastes like wine, a red colour, not without flavour. The less good kernels weigh lighter and are greenish. The branches are thicker than myrtle. Incisions [in the bark] are cut with glass, a stone, or knives made of bone. It hates its life to be injured with iron, it dies right away. All the same, it permits superfluous parts to be removed. The hand of the cutter is balanced by an artificial measure, to not violate [anything] beyond the bark. Touched with iron, the wood of the stem dies without hesitation, and so they are cleverly wounded only with glass or with bone knives by a cut in the bark, from which issues a sap of excellent pleasantness.

(continued)

Table 1: Continued

116. A juice runs from the wound, which is named as *opobalsamum*; [it is] of exceptional beauty [in scent], but it is drawn out weeping in drops, collected with wool [and put] in small horns. When it is taken from these to new earthen vessels; it is like a thick oil, and is white when fresh. It reddens and then likewise hardens and loses its transparency.

117. When Alexander the Great was there on his matter, it took a whole of one day in summer to fill a *concha*; the entire actual productivity of the larger garden being six *congii*, and of the smaller a single one; the price, too, with [its weight] doubled paid back in silver. Yet now a single tree [provides] a larger sale. Three times every summer it is pierced; afterwards it is pruned.

118. The cuttings also are in the markets: within five years of the conquest of Judaea, these cuttings and twigs were sold for eight hundred sesterces. These are called *xylobalsamum* (*officinae*) as a substitute for the sap. Even the bark is of value to factories (*officinae*), and is boiled for perfumes; this [product] used by medicine, but usually the tears are the most esteemed; secondly the seeds, thirdly the bark, and the wood least.

119. Of this, the type like boxwood is the best, [a kind] which is also most strongly perfumed. But [the best] of the seed is the largest and heaviest, [having] in the mouth a biting or spicy taste. It is adulterated with *hypericum* [seeds] from Petra, which is exposed [thus]: they are larger, emptier, and longer, lacking smell, and taste of pepper.

120. The proof of the tears is flavour, slimness, and red hue, and odoriferous when rubbed. The second [quality] is of white colour; the less good is green and coarse, and the black is the worst; as one expects with oil it goes stale. Of all the incisions, the best is proven [to be from] before the formation of the seed. And, sometimes, it is adulterated with seed juice, and the fraud is detected with difficulty [thus]: by a bitter taste, which ought to be delicate with no acidity, the perfume [alone] being very pungent.

121. It is spoilt also with the oil of roses, cypress, mastic, balanites, terebinth, myrtle, resin, galbanum, and Cyprian wax, whatever thing may do. But the

Second place they get in value after the sap-drop is the fruit, third the bark, last honour [goes to] the wood.

very worst of these is gum, since it is dry when emptied on the hand, and sits in water, which is double proof of this.

122. The genuine article avoids being dried up, but when it is mixed with gum a fragile crust forms and the taste goes away. Burnt on coal, to determine what kind of wax or resin it has been adulterated with, the flame is black. Also, when mixed with different honeys in the hand it will attract flies.

123. In addition, a drop of the authentic type, if placed in tepid water, will sit at the bottom of the vessel, the adulterated [with oil] will float like oil, and if it is spoilt with *metopion* a white circle surrounds it. The best test, however, is that milk curdles, and it makes no stain on cloth. There is no more attractive a fraud, obviously, when a sextarius sold by the *fiscus* at three hundred denarii sells [again] for a thousand, so vastly it profits to augment the liquid. The price of *xylobalsamum* is six denarii per pound.

Natural History 5: 15: 73

On the west the Essenes flee away from the shores that are harmful, a people alone and in all the world strange above the rest, without any woman, abdicating all sexual acts, without money, [a people] companioned by palms. Daily the swarm is renewed with equal multitudes, filled with huge numbers

Far from Jerusalem is spread out an isolated, sad shore, which was touched by the heavens, witnessed by black earth dissolving into cinders. In that place [are] two towns, one named Sodom, the other Gomorra, near which is an apple that is produced which, although it has the appearance of maturity, is nevertheless unable to be eaten, for inside the skin going around the outside it contains ashy black soot which at a lightly-pressed touch puffs out smoke and crumbles into loose powder.

The interior of Judaea, west of what is noted, the Essenes hold, [men] who, possessed of a remarkable discipline, retreat from the universal observance of people, to this way of excellence supposedly destined by providence. There is no woman there; they have abdicated sexual desire itself utterly. They are ignorant of money. They live by means of palms. No one is born there and yet

(continued)

Table 1: Continued

of those, wearied of life and the fluctuations of fortune, who keep to their ways of life.

So through a thousand ages—incredible to say—it is an eternal people, in which no one is born, so fecund is this dissatisfaction of life in others.

Below these was the town of En Gedi—second only to Jerusalem [= Jericho] in fertility and groves of palms, now another ash-heap—then Masada, a fortress on a rock, and this not far from Asphaltites. And to here is Judaea.

they are not deficient in [maintaining] a multitude of human beings. *The place itself is dedicated to virtue, none is admitted, unless he is accompanied by merit, with continence, trust and innocence. For whoever is guilty of even a small thing, however much he wants to advance, is removed by the divinity. So, through the immense space of the ages—incredible to say—it is an eternal people devoid of childbirth.*

En Gedi was a town below the Essenes, but it is destroyed. *Truly, the notable plantations still continue and the glory of the very eminent groves of palms in no respect is detracted either by time or by war.* The end of Judaea is the castle Masada.

---

[i] Latin text from: *C. Plini Secundi, Naturalis Historiae*, ed. Charles Mayhoff (Stuttgart: B. G. Tübner, 1967); Solinus (C. Iulius) *Collectanea rerum memorabilium*, ed. T. Mommsen (Berlin: Weidmann, 1895).

English translation by Joan Taylor. Solinus' additions to Pliny marked in italics in the English text only.

[ii] A *rastrum* was a kind of sharp-toothed mattock, and could be used for cutting roots; see K. D. White, *Agricultural Implements of the Roman World* (Cambridge: CUP, 2010), 52–6, 66–8.

Solinus generally used both Pliny and the geographer Pomponius Mela, though he tended to paraphrase, contract, or reorganize his sources.[23] Mommsen also suggested that Solinus used a *chronicle*—perhaps by Cornelius Bocchus—and possibly a kind of epitome of Pliny with additions made around the time of Hadrian. This theory of sources was developed further by Gaetano Columba, who suggested that the second-century compiler reached back to a possibly Greek first-century source, along with Pliny.[24] It is this possibility that a compiler used a Greek source that allows us to explore such Greek sources in terms of Solinus' information. The emphasis is on a lifestyle dedicated to philosophical excellence: a theme for Philo and Josephus too when writing on the Essenes. There are correlations with Josephus in terms of the note on Destiny (cf. *Ant.* 13: 171–2; 18: 18) and with Philo and Josephus regarding the admission of people to the group on merit (cf. *War* 2: 137–8; *Prob.* 76–7; *Hypoth.* 11: 2). However, there are no distinct verbal overlaps between anything written by Philo and Josephus and Solinus. In fact, there is one glaring difference: the removal of those guilty of even a small thing is the opposite of what Josephus says; he states that they are only removed for serious sins and sometimes brought back when they are near to starvation (*War* 2: 143–4). Furthermore, as Burchard has noted, Philo and Josephus describe Essenes in communities all over Judaea/Syria Palestine, while here there is a clear focus on one centre only.[25]

Are there further features of the description of Judaea as a whole that may also come from the mystery source? If we look at the beginning of the description, Solinus begins by stating: *Iudaea inlustris est aquis, sed natura non eadem aquarum omnium*—'Judaea is famous for waters, but not all of the waters are of one nature.' It is as if Solinus has taken the theme of Pliny, even though Pliny does not state this outright. As such, this cannot come from another place than Pliny, unless Solinus himself—or his source—is drawing on the very source Pliny used, which, we have seen, was most likely Mucianus' collection of wonders.[26]

However, this possibility is confused by Solinus' extraordinary mention of the vanquishing of Jericho: 'The capital of Judaea was Jerusalem, but it is destroyed. Jericho succeeded it, but this is no more, overcome in war by Artaxerxes.' This seems to date to the recent past at Solinus' own time of writing rather than any source. From 222 CE the aggressive expansion of Artaxerxes (Ardashir) 'threatened Syria', as Herodian (*Hist. Rom.* 6: 2: 1–2) states. Herodian alludes to Ardashir's attacks more generally: 'he took to the

---

[23] Mommsen *Iulii Solini*, xv–xxiv.

[24] Gaetano M. Columba, 'Le fonti di Giulio Solino,' in id. *Rassegna di antichità classica* 1 (1895), 7–32; 2 (1896), 105–16, reprinted in id. *Richerche storiche i. Geografia e Geografi del Mondo antico* (Palermo: Trimarchi, 1935).

[25] Burchard, 'Solin et les Esséniens,' 400–1.

[26] See above, p. 133.

field, pillaging and looting all the Roman provinces' (Herodian, *Hist. Rom.* 6: 2: 5). Artaxerxes wanted the Romans to leave 'all Syria' (Herodian, *Hist. Rom.* 6: 4: 5), which of course included Palestine. Artaxerxes was pushed back by the defensive campaign of Alexander Severus in 231–7 CE (Herodian, *Hist. Rom.* 6: 5: 1–6). Solinus himself must be inserting this as an item of well-known recent history—if not current affairs—into his account.

But what of this implication that Jerusalem was succeeded by Jericho as a capital after Jerusalem was destroyed? The Roman provincial capital of Judaea in the first century was Caesarea Maritima; Jericho was the capital of a large toparchy, through the Roman period, extending down to En Gedi (P.Yadin 16: 16), east of a completely renamed and redesigned Jerusalem (Aelia Capitolina, from the mid-second century). Solinus has clearly used Pliny, *Hist. Nat.* 5: 15 [71–3] in terms of the information about the destruction of Jerusalem, and also used Pliny in assuming that Jericho was then the capital, since Pliny lists Jericho at the top of his list of post-70 toparchies: 'Jericho—planted with palms, watered by springs—Emmaus, Lydda, Joppa, Acrabatene, Gophanitis, Thamnitis, Betholeptepha, Orine, in which was Jerusalem—long the most brilliant city of the East, not only of Judaea—Herodium, with a famous town of the same name.'[27] Here Solinus seems to have drawn out what was in Pliny's past tense in terms of Jerusalem (*in qua fuere Hierosolyma*), confirmed later on in the passage in relation to En Gedi, which was 'another' heap of ashes, and then inserted the very new information about Artaxerxes' destruction of Jericho, but it does not alter the impression that we are overall dealing with Pliny at this point with an 'update' from Solinus' own time. The issue of whether Jericho was indeed some kind of interim Judaean capital at any point is probably unsolvable.

The condensed description of the wonders of opobalsam found in Solinus' description appears in Pliny in another place altogether (Pliny, *Hist. Nat.* 12: 54 [111–15]). Solinus places it geographically, summarizing only the main features, and then there is a brief return to the account he begins with.

While it is tempting to suggest that Solinus was here indeed reaching back to a pre-Plinian source (Mucianus), given the marriage of passages found in two very different parts of Pliny's work, this tendency of Solinus to extrapolate, paraphrase, condense, and dance from one part of Pliny's *Natural History* to another is typical of the manner in which Solinus works. He was not 'citing' Pliny or any other writer but rather using his source material freely in his own creative work.

Yet the dance from Pliny to another source entirely is very clearly signalled in Solinus. The next section, on the Dead Sea, starts with a glaring anomaly. Having just mentioned Callirhoe as being near to Jerusalem, Solinus describes

---

[27] These are indeed post-70 Roman toparchies; see Benjamin Isaac, *The Near East under Roman Rule: Selected Papers* (Leiden: Brill, 1998), 166–8.

the lake itself as being far away (*Callirrhoe Hierusolymis proxima . . . Longo ab Hierusolymis recessu tristis sinus panditur*). Solinus then presents the story of Sodom and Gomorra, the barren lands, and the ashy fruit. Nothing of this is found in Pliny. Strikingly, it is not so much the mention of Sodom that is surprising in Solinus, given the attestations of the town in other classical literature, but Gomorra. Even Josephus does not give us this name. Otherwise, Solinus' description is somewhat similar to what we have in Tacitus and Josephus, though without any clear overlaps (*Collectanea* 35: 7–10).

Directly following on from this we have Solinus' Essenes, introduced by the words *interiora Iudaeae*: 'in the interior of Judaea'. In fact, it would be better to detach this from the reference to the Essenes here and place these words at the beginning of the previous paragraph, so that it is *interiora Iudaeae longo ab Hierusolymis* ('in the interior of Judaea, far from Jerusalem') where the Dead Sea itself lies. The total non-Plinian source summarized by Solinus would then be this:

> *Interiora Iudaeae longo ab Hierusolymis recessu tristis sinus panditur, quem de caelo tactum testatur humus nigra et in cinerem soluta. ibi duo oppida, Sodomum nominatum alterum, alterum Gomorrum, apud quae pomum quod gignitur, habeat licet speciem maturitatis, mandi tamen non potest: nam fuliginem intrinsecus favillaciam ambitio tantum extimae cutis cohibet, quae vel levi pressa tactu fumum exhalat et fatiscit in vagum pulverem.*
>
> *[Ibi urbem] Esseni tenent, qui praediti memorabili disciplina recesserunt a ritu gentium universarum, maiestatis ut reor providentia ad hunc morem destinati. locus ipse addictus pudicitiae est: ad quem plurimi licet undique gentium properent, nullus admittitur, nisi quem castitatis fides et innocentiae meritum prosequatur: nam qui reus est vel levis culpae, quamvis summa ope adipisci ingressum velit, divinitus submovetur.*

Far from Jerusalem in the interior of Judaea is spread out an isolated, sad shore, which was touched by the heavens, witnessed by black earth dissolving into cinders. In that place [were] two towns, Sodom named one, the other Gomorra, near which is an apple that is produced which, although it has the appearance of maturity, is nevertheless unable to be eaten, for inside the skin going around the outside it contains ashy black soot which at a lightly-pressed touch puffs out smoke and crumbles into loose powder.

[There] the Essenes hold [a city]. [They are those] who, possessed by a remarkable discipline, retreat from the universal observance of people, to this way of excellence supposedly destined by providence. The place itself is dedicated to virtue, into which none is admitted, unless he is accompanied by merit, with continence, trust and innocence. For whoever is guilty of even a small thing, however much he wants to advance, is removed by the divinity.

Curiously, despite Solinus' reputation for being interested only in wonders, Pliny's paradoxically enduring but strange Essenes fit the genre of *mirabilia* much better than the virtuous people we have here in Solinus' work. And where could such Stoic-sounding words as *providentia* and *divinitus* have come from? If we extract the inserts from Pliny, we are left with a passage that assumes a prior mention of Jerusalem, then jumps to a location far from this city in the interior of the country. It contains a presentation of the grim landscape of a certain unnamed lake, the fate of Sodom and Gomorra, and the ashy fruit, followed by a passage about the admirable Essenes. The Essenes *tenent*, 'hold', somewhere that would in this context most naturally be defined as a city (since it was cities that were indeed 'held'). Into this city no one could be admitted unless they were of merit. The Essenes have retreated from the vices of the ordinary world, and live in a place where they have a distinctive, disciplined lifestyle of virtue, strict entrance requirements, and a law supposedly ordained by the divinity, who will remove anyone who transgresses.

Does this source derive from Dio? It was Christoph Burchard who first tentatively suggested this possibility: 'Quoi qu'il en soit, il reste toujours la possibilité que notre passage remonte à Dion ou à sa source, sur laquelle nous ne savons rien.'[28] I would like here to endorse this proposal. One can easily see how a presentation of the virtuous Essenes in an austere location next to the place where towns were destroyed for their moral depravity could well be used to 'admonish humanity', as Synesius read from Dio.

Would Solinus' presumed second-century source have used Dio? It may be relevant that one of Dio's lost works was a *History of the Getae* or *Getica* (Philostratus, *Lives* 7/487), the Getae being Dacians, one of the Thracian tribes, people with whom he lived during his exile. Dio's *Getica* was widely known in antiquity.[29] This ethnographic work is exactly what would have been of interest to Solinus. More likely, the second-century compiler, also interested in such matters, found Dio useful in this regard; Solinus does himself have geographical interests in Thrace (*Coll.* 9, 13), and, as noted above, Josephus, *Ant.* 18: 22, states that the Essenes 'live a manner of life in no way different, but as close as possible, to the Dacians called *Pleistoi*'.[30] This extraordinary linkage of the Essenes and the Dacians has baffled scholars for a long time; the fact that Dio's (lost) work on the Dacians may have appeared just as Josephus was completing *Antiquities* is suggestive.[31]

There is no reason to think that Solinus himself read Greek, but the suggestion that the mystery second-century Latin compiler used Greek material is relevant. Alternatively, perhaps there were versions of Dio's writings

---

[28] Burchard, 'Solin et les Esséniens,' 401.

[29] See Arne Søby Christiansen, *Cassiodorus, Jordanes and the History of the Goths* (Copenhagen: Museum Tusculanum Press, 2002), 232–3.

[30] See E. Lozovan and Safia F. Haddad, 'Dacia Sacra,' *History of Religions* 7 (1968), 209–43, at 229.

[31] Lozovan and Haddad, 'Dacia Sacra,' 224, n. 68, state: 'It was about the same period in AD 95 that Dio Chrysostomus made his voyage to Olbia and penetrated the interior of the country to inquire about the Getae.' The exact dating of the initial journey and the issuing of Dio's work is in fact unknown. Josephus' *Antiquities* was finalized in the last year of Domitian (who was assassinated in 96 CE), see *Ant.* 10: 267.

circulating in Latin, even works quarried early on by his bilingual pupil Favorinus of Arelate (*c.*80–160).[32] Since so much of Dio's writing is lost— not to mention all of Favorinus' works, apart from two orations that might be his despite being attributed to Dio, a papyrus with part of his *De Exilio*, and fragments found in both Latin (in Aulus Gellius) and Greek (in Philostratus, Galen, Diogenes Laertius, Suidas)—we simply do not know what may have existed in antiquity, but Favorinus' attestations in both languages is significant as evidence for linguistic cross-overs. Moreover, Favorinus wrote a work named Παντοδαπή Ἱστορία, *Miscellaneous Investigation*, which seems to have included geographical, biographical, and anecdotal as well as historical information (Diogenes Laertius, *Lives* 3: 24; 8: 12, 47).[33] The bridge between Greek sophistry and Latin geography is not as long as one might think.[34]

It was Dio who—unlike Pliny—emphasized positive aspects of the Essenes. Dio complimented the Essenes as an 'entirely happy *polis*', πόλιν ὅλην εὐδαίμονα. The use of the word πόλις might at first seem a rather grand over-statement given what remains in terms of the archaeology in the region of the north-western Dead Sea, but it is important to remember that, for a Stoic-influenced sophist like Dio, the word *polis* did not necessarily carry the meaning of being a city made up of a large number of dwellings, with major public buildings or walls. Paolo Desideri's translation of Dio here as writing of 'a community of complete happiness' is one that expresses the community sense of the ideal Stoic *polis*.[35] The nature and proper rule of the *polis* are major themes in Dio's work, since he was more than anything a political philosopher closely concerned in the actual running of his own city, Prusa, and very much concerned with everyone else's, as his addresses to various cities of the Roman Empire make abundantly clear.[36] When Philostratus describes the essentials of Dio's work, he focuses on how Dio rebuked or praised cities (*Lives* 7/487). Thematically then, his description of the Essenes is placed at the service of his most important concern.

Here Dio continues the political interests of Zeno, who, in his *Politeia*, defined the ideal Stoic *polis* as a community consisting of virtuous people.[37] As

---

[32] Philostratus, *Lives* 8/489–91. E. Amato (ed.) and Y. Julien (trans.), *Favorine d'Arles, Œuvres I. Introduction général—Témoignages—Discours aux Corinthiens—Sur la Fortune* (Paris: Les Belles Lettres, 2005).

[33] Adelmo Barigazzi, *Favorino di Arelate, Opere. Introduzione, testo critico e commento* (Testi Greci e Latini con commento filologico 4; Firenze: le Monnier, 1966).

[34] It may be noted also that Solinus describes the Essenes as if they are presently living by the Dead Sea; there is no sense that they used to live there in ancient times. The original source then derives from a period roughly contemporary with the Essenes.

[35] Paolo Desideri, 'City and Country in Dio,' in Swain, *Dio Chrysostom*, 93–107 at 103, cf. 98; Humbert, 'Chronology,' 428.

[36] See Swain, 'Life and Works,' 3.

[37] Malcolm Schofield, *The Stoic Idea of the City* (Cambridge: CUP, 1991). See also Anton-Hermann Chroust, 'The Ideal Polity of the Early Stoics: Zeno's Republic,' *The Review of Politics* 27 (1965): 173–83.

Plutarch noted in *Alexander* 31, Zeno proposed that 'the happiness of the city not less than the happiness of the individual consists basically in the exercise of virtue'; only this makes the citizens 'free, self-sufficient and self-controlled'. It was Zeno who proposed that 'good persons are free' (Diogenes Laertius, *Lives* 7: 32), the tenet on which Philo would hang his description of the Essenes (*Quod omnis Probus liber sit*).[38] Architecture was positively discouraged; as Chroust has pointed out, Zeno's cities were to be 'simple unadorned dwelling places of contented people'.[39]

In the Dio passage in Solinus, the Essene lifestyle is 'dedicated to virtue' and one in which 'none is admitted, unless he is accompanied by merit, with continence, trust and innocence'. The Essenes, 'possessed by a remarkable discipline, retreat from the universal observance of people, to this way of excellence supposedly destined by providence'. Here Dio explores the Essene *politeia*, even giving information on who might be accepted and who rejected: 'For whoever is guilty of even a small thing, however much he wants to advance, is removed by the divinity.' This relates perfectly to Zeno's conceptualization of an ideal city, entirely composed of virtuous people, living under a strict law. According to Diogenes Laertius, all people who are not virtuous in Zeno's city are to be dubbed 'enemies, troublemakers, slaves and aliens', that is, people no longer accounted citizens, for 'only the good are to be citizens, friends, kindred and free' (Diogenes Laertius, *Lives* 7: 33). Dio's extant works do not contain such a utopian programme explicitly, but the ideal of what a city should be lies close to his heart. The god that ultimately should rule is Zeus, called *Polieus*, 'god of cities', as one of his honorary titles (*Or.* 1: 39; 12: 75, 77), and good kings should be as much like Zeus as possible (*Or.* 1: 41; 53: 11). The attributes of Zeus, the heavenly Father and King, are those of the upholder of law, peace-maker; he is the kindly god who shows 'goodness' (*Or.* 12: 77). Zeus, with providence (*pronoia*) and goodness of soul, rules and guides the universe under one law (*Or.* 1: 42) and—interestingly—Dio insists that the king who rejects goodness and behaves without justice will suffer the consequences of Phaethon (*Or.* 1: 46-7), burnt by a lightning bolt from Zeus (cf. *Or.* 12: 78), the very myth to which Sodom was compared by Celsus. The model city is one that reflects the rule of heaven by Zeus (*Or.* 36: 29-37).[40]

The rule of sound law is fundamental. Dio regarded a *polis* not so much as an urban environment, but as 'a group of people living under the rule of law in the same place' (*Or.* 36: 20, cf. 29).[41] This is true in terms of an ideal Stoic *polis*, though in real terms autonomy was a privilege and even Prusa did not have

---

[38] Philo knew enough Zeno to quote him in this essay (*Prob.* 53-7) and hailed him here as one who was 'uncommonly led by virtue'.

[39] Chroust, 'Ideal Polity,' 178.

[40] Simon Swain, *Hellenism and Empire: Language, Classicism, and Power in the Greek World AD 50-250* (Oxford: OUP, 1996), 195-200.

[41] Kamesar, Review of *The Essenes*, 135.

full powers to make its own laws.[42] That the ideal *polis* of the Essenes had such autonomy is implicit in Solinus and Dio, and coheres well with what we find in Philo when he writes of the Essenes as, quite precisely, αὐτονόμος (*Prob.* 91), 'self-governing' according to their own law (cf. *Somn.* 2: 100, 293; *Jos.* 136, 242). Likewise, as we have seen, Josephus presents the Essenes as having an independent jurisdiction: the Essenes had their own court made up of no less than one hundred men to decide verdicts, and they could even pass a sentence of death for blasphemy (*War* 2: 143–5).

Nevertheless, even with the presentation of the happy *polis* made of virtuous people adhering to their own (divinely ordained) law, Dio cannot have lost sight of the physical *polis* situated on the ground as well, since in Synesius it is also a defined place which can be said to be 'lying' (τήν . . . κειμένην) in a landscape. The Essenes are at once a conceptual *polis*, in terms of their virtuous state of happiness, and a physical entity that is given a location by the 'dead water in the interior of Palestine', proximate to the location which demonstrated the consequences of the opposite state.

Therefore, Dio's focus was not on the remarkable continuation of the Essene *gens*, despite their lack of procreation and personal money, as Pliny presented them, but the nature of their existence itself, the means by which they attained *eudaimonia*, happiness. Dio appears to have looked for praise-worthy examples of happiness where no one would expect it, whether among the poor hunters of Euboea he met in his wanderings in exile, or the Essenes living beside a dead lake, proximate to cities destroyed by the judgement of God: a story he encountered from hearsay or descriptions he read somewhere. His focus was on examples illustrative of the simple, virtuous, and self-sufficient life he greatly admired.[43]

CONCLUSIONS

Dio Chrysostom, a contemporary of Josephus and Pliny, is an independent source on the Essenes. His description is found briefly referred to in Synesius, and absorbed in part in the later synthetic work of Julius Solinus. There is little reason to doubt that Synesius is giving us an accurate report of the substance of Dio's description, from one of his lost discourses, probably from his *History of the Getae*, where it may have been a tangential passage. Some of Dio's description is also found in the non-Plinian section of Solinus' description of

[42] Jones, *Dio*, 5; id. *Greek City*, 135–6.
[43] See Frederick Brenk, *'With Unperfumed Voice': Studies in Plutarch, in Greek Literature, Religion and Philosophy and in the New Testament* (Potsdamer Altertumswissenschaftliche Beiträge 21; Stuttgart: Franz Steiner, 2007), 279–300.

Judaea: the Essenes and the story of Sodom and Gomorra. This material would have been filtered through a lost compiler of the second century.

Significantly, Dio does provide independent evidence to that of Pliny for the Essenes living beside the Dead Sea, close to Sodom, at a location in the landscape of Judaea. Given Dio was writing this at around the same time that Josephus was writing his *Antiquities*, he is not a late source to be discredited as derivative of Pliny, but is a first-century source that needs to be placed alongside Pliny and Josephus, even though we have other people's brief summaries of what he wrote rather than his actual words.

7

Christian and Jewish Writings from the Second to Fifth Centuries

We now turn then to the end of the first century and beyond in the area of Judaea, in order to consider whether anything reflective of the historical Essenes might be contained within writings from this time and place. But, as we enter the period post-Josephus, from the mid-90s CE, we enter a more obscure period of history in terms of the region, since there is no Josephus to record the Second Revolt,[1] which is one reason why it is easy enough to assume that the Judaean αἱρέσεις that existed before 70 CE just did not continue for very long.[2] However, as the old adage goes, absence of evidence is not in fact evidence of absence.

The first part of the second century is poorly informed by historical—literary—testimony, apart from the epitome of Dio Cassius and by quotations preserved by Eusebius. However, archaeological discoveries and methods have shed new light on this period. While much of the material culture from 70 to 135 CE was highly conservative, especially in terms of pottery, which shows very few distinctive features from that of the mid first century repertoire, more refined dating techniques have allowed a number of identifications of stone vessels and stepped pools (*miqva'ot*) continuing in use through the post-destruction period until 135 CE.[3] The decline in their use does not correlate

---

[1] As observed by Michael Avi-Yonah, *The Jews under Roman and Byzantine Rule: A Political History of Palestine from the Bar Kokhba War to the Arab Conquest* (Jerusalem: Magnes, 1984), 13. For significant evaluations of this period, see also Fergus Millar, *The Roman Near East: 31 BC to AD 337* (Cambridge, MA: Harvard University Press, 1993), 367–75; Gedalyahu Alon, *The Jews in their Land in the Talmudic Age (70–640 CE)* (Jerusalem: Magnes, 1980).

[2] See, *inter alia*, Michael Avi-Yonah, *A History of Israel of the Holy Land* (London: Macmillan, 1969), which indicates that the whole apparatus of state and religion dissolved and the rabbinic movement centred on Jamnia took its place; yet for a more complex picture see id. *The Jews under Roman and Byzantine Rule*, 1–33.

[3] See Stuart S. Miller, 'Stepped Pools, Stone Vessels and Other Identity Markers of "Complex Common Judaism",' *JSJ* 41 (2010): 214–43, at 225–42; David Amit and Yonatan Adler, 'The Observance of Ritual Purity after 70 CE: A Reevaluation of the Evidence in Light of Recent Archaeological Discoveries,' in Zeev Weiss, Oded Irshai, Jodi Magness, and Seth Schwartz (eds), *'Follow the Wise': Studies in Jewish History and Culture in Honor of Lee I. Levine* (The Jewish

to a decline in ritual purity practice, but simply a decline in Jewish population after the end of the Bar Kochba revolt. The evidence suggests there was a fervent desire by at least some Jews to maintain the traditions of ritual purity in places where they lived, including cleansing from corpse impurity, which required a continuing supply of red heifer ash,[4] meaning either that there was a reserve of this ash or that red heifers were in fact sacrificed by priests using a temporary tabernacle. Ritual baths close to the second/third-century necropolis of Beth Shearim indicate a concern to immerse, in addition, after contact with the dead.[5] Various cultic practices could still have continued in modified form: it is hard to imagine that the destruction of the actual buildings of the Temple must have required an immediate total cessation of a cult that had its conceptual origins in a movable 'tent' of meeting (Exodus 25–31; 35–40).

Papyrological evidence is also relatively rich thanks to the discoveries in the Judaean desert caves close to En Gedi,[6] finds that illuminate the period immediately before the Bar Kokhba revolt, as well as the figure of Bar Kokhba (rightly Bar Koziba) himself. From these and also from enlightening examinations of numismatic evidence,[7] it seems clear that Jews/Judaeans continued to live in the area of wider Judaea as before, under the direct rule of the Romans who occupied Jerusalem militarily, and that Jewish law continued to function.

How did the Essenes fare? In the turbulent years of 66–70 CE, the Essenes appear at first sight to have kept apart from being deeply embroiled in central power politics; and yet 'John the Essene' is mentioned by Josephus as a military leader (*War* 2: 567; 3: 11). Josephus tells us that Essenes captured during the war were tortured (*War* 2: 152–3), which provides him with an opportunity to admire their fortitude. The fact that they were captured and tortured by the Romans would indicate more than Roman sadism: some Essenes must have been identified as being opposed to their rule.

It is increasingly recognized that the destruction of the Temple in 70 CE did not mean that Judaea's elite class was utterly transformed overnight. The Herodian dynasty itself continued to the end of the first century, with Agrippa II holding power in post-70 Judaea (Photius, *Bibliotheca*, 33), and becoming Praetor (Dio Cassius, *Hist.* 66:15). Given this, the legal autonomy of the

---

theological Seminary of America and Hebrew University of Jerusalem; Winona Lake: Eisenbrauns, 2010), 121–43.

[4] Amit and Adler, 'Observance,' 123–4, citing in particular the study by Yaakov Sussman, 'Babylonian Sugiyot to the Orders Zera'im and Tohorot' (unpublished Ph.D dissertation, Hebrew University of Jerusalem, 1969), 310–13 (Heb.).

[5] Yonatan Adler, 'Ritual Baths adjacent to Tombs: An Analysis of the Archaeological Evidence in Light of the Halakhic Sources,' *JSJ* 40 (2009): 55–73.

[6] Hannah M. Cotton, W. E. H. Cockle, and Fergus G. B. Millar, 'The Papyrology of the Roman Near East: A Survey,' *JRS* 85 (1995): 214–35.

[7] See Leo Mildenberg, with Patricia Erhart Mottahedeh (ed.), *The Coinage of the Bar Kokhba War* (Typos: Monographien zur antiken Numismatik, 6; Aarau, Frankfurt am Main, Salzburg: Verlag Sauerländer, 1984).

Essenes—if they continued to be sponsored by the Herodian dynasty—would have been maintained. The Essenes, with their wide dispersal in Judaea, and their focus on community life, asceticism and purity, interpretation of Scripture, and medicine, were in some ways very well equipped to withstand the trauma of the revolt, and continue, as Joshua Ezra Burns has rightly observed.[8] They fit well into the picture that is now emerging of a purity-focused Jewish life post-Temple.

In terms of the continuing practice of Jewish law, the Sanhedrin is linked with a variety of different localities, one centre possibly being outside Jerusalem in Jamnia, under the leadership of Yoḥanan ben Zakkai (see m.Rosh ha-Shanah 4:1–3; b.Sanh. 32b). As Philip Alexander has explored, the priesthood seems to have maintained authority over most of the Jewish law of the land, since in m.Ket. 1: 5 mention of a 'court of priests' is significant, and this body is here differentiated from the 'Sages', who 'did not reprove them'.[9] That the Sages (חכמים, *Ḥakhamim*), those with whom the rabbis identify as their predecessors, had some authority as well in such a court is interesting, and so this would indicate a time after the hegemony of priests in the legal system was absolute, though the precise time to which this can be dated is hard to determine. It seems that the maintenance of religious law as the law of the land, as interpreted by the scribes of the legal schools (or societies), would not be curtailed until 135 CE and the deconstruction of Judaean national identity.

In Jerusalem itself, the former physical holy centre of the operations of the priesthood was indeed no more; the Temple and walls had been destroyed, and within the city the Roman Tenth Legion was in control, encamped in the west, the city population now clearly being ethnically and religiously mixed. Confiscated Judaean land was sold off (*War* 7: 216, cf. *Life* 76).[10] After 117 CE two Roman legions controlled the Jewish population: one stationed in Jerusalem (X Fretensis) and one in Galilee, in Kfar Otnai, known as 'Legio' (II Traiana Fortis).[11] But Judaea remained 'Judaea'. The name of the whole country (including Galilee, Idumaea, and Samaria) remained until after the Second Revolt, and it is a term that parallels the maintenance of the law of the Judaeans in this area, the function of the courts being most thoroughly

---

[8] See Joshua Ezra Burns, 'Essene Sectarianism and Social Differentiation in Judaea after 70 CE,' *HTR* 99 (2006): 247–74.

[9] Philip Alexander, 'What Happened to the Jewish Priesthood after 70?' in Zuleika Rodgers, with M. Daly-Denton and A. Fitzpatrick-McKinley (eds), *A Wandering Galilean: Essays in Honour of Sean Freyne* (Supplements to the Journal for the Study of Judaism; Leiden: Brill, 2009), 3–34, at 29–30.

[10] Benjamin Isaac, 'Judaea after 70,' in id. *The Near East under Roman Rule: Selected Papers* (Leiden: Brill, 1998), 112–21, originally published in *JJS* 35 (1984): 44–50.

[11] Benjamin Isaac and Isaac Roll, 'Judea in the Early years of Hadrian's Reign,' in Isaac, *Near East*, 182–97, originally published in *Latomus* 28 (1979): 54–66.

explored in the discussion by Shemuel Safrai and Mordecai Stern.[12] The papyrological evidence clearly indicates that there was a continuation of Jewish law to 135 CE in the Jewish area around the Dead Sea (in En Gedi and its environs), even with Roman provincial government from 106 CE. Moreover, Jewish courts could even exist outside Judaea, as a special dispensation, for example in Alexandria, where the Jewish *politeuma* included legal autonomy, with the function of Jewish courts vouchsafed by Augustus, as was explored long ago by Erwin Goodenough.[13] Jewish law was not theoretical but practical: a justice system, in a world in which justice systems were tied to ethnicity and citizenship.

As we know now, already, after Hadrian visited Judaea en route to Egypt in 129, he ordered work on a new temple to Jupiter Capitolinus on the Temple Mount in Jerusalem. With this, the revolt led by Bar Kokhba erupted. A new Judaean Temple administration was established with a man named Eleazar, evidenced only by coins, installed as High Priest.[14] The subsequent revolt lasted from 132 until it was quashed in 135 CE, with disastrous consequences, including a ban on Jews living in a large part of the former core homeland of Judaea centred on Jerusalem (Tertullian, *Adv. Jud.* 13; Justin Martyr, *Dial.* 16; *Apol.* 1: 77; Eusebius, *Hist. Eccles.* 4: 6).[15] Judaea was re-branded as 'Syria Palaestina'. The renovation of Jerusalem as the *colonia* Aelia Capitolina went ahead, and with it Roman colonial law here and in its territory. In the new administrative zones of former Judaea, the land was divided up into individual cities, with their own city jurisdictions devoid of Jewish law.

The question of what happened to the αἱρέσεις of Judaea after the destruction of the Temple, and more particularly after the Second Revolt, has not been solved, and may not be given the present paltry evidence, but there is no need to suggest that there was a sudden termination of all the four legal societies that Josephus describes in 70 CE. As long as Jewish law functioned as a practical justice system, these societies would have needed to take authoritative leadership.

[12] For the function of courts in Eretz-Israel see: Shemuel Safrai and Mordecai Stern (eds), *The Jewish People in the First Century: Historical Geography, Political History, Social, Cultural and Religious Life* (Compendia Rerum Iudaicarum ad Novum Testamentum; Assen: Van Gorcum, 1974), i: 377–419, and the examination of private law, 504–33. Jacobine G. Oudshoorn, *The Relationship between Roman and Local Law in the Babatha and Salome Komaise Archives: General Analysis and Three Case Studies on Law of Succession, Guardianship and Marriage* (Leiden: Brill, 2007).

[13] Erwin R. Goodenough, *The Jurisprudence of the Jewish Courts in Egypt: Legal Administration by the Jews under the Early Roman Empire as described by Philo Judaeus* (New Haven: Yale University Press, 1929).

[14] See Emil Schürer, with Geza Vermes, Fergus Millar, and Matthew Black (eds), *The History of the Jewish People in the Age of Jesus Christ*, revised edition, 3 vols (Edinburgh: T & T Clark, 1973–9), i: 544.

[15] See Joan Taylor, *Christians and the Holy Places: The Myth of Jewish-Christian Origins* (Oxford: OUP, 1993), 48–85 for a synthetic survey of religious/ethnic groupings within Roman Palestine.

Martin Goodman rightly points out that writers of the second century use the present tense for Judaean 'sects'.[16] As Goodman has also shown, Judaism did not suddenly become rabbinic; the rabbis who traced their origins to the sages of pre-70 Jerusalem struggled for leadership and triumphed later rather than earlier, with their base now in Galilee.[17]

If the operation of Judaean courts continued at least through to 135 CE, then a suggestion of a sudden disappearance of the αἱρέσεις is far too simplistic a model. Clearly the manner in which the Yoḥanan ben Zakkai stories are presented, to indicate that different schools are to be rejected in favour of one tradition represented by the Ḥakhamim (b.Men. 65a; b.Baba Bathra 115b; m.Yad. 4:5; t.Parah 3: 8), indicates by implication their continuance as threats to that unifying idea. The notion that a council was convened in Jamnia that would usher in a new age of rabbinic Judaism, end sectarianism, and determine the canon[18] is no longer considered very convincing.[19]

In the Mishnah, from the very end of the second century, there are mentions of schools of legal interpretation differentiated from the Ḥakhamim, and named as the בייתוסים, *Baytosim*, usually rendered in translation as Boethusians (m.Men.10: 3, m.Hag. 2: 4 cf. t.Yom. 1: 8), צדוקים, *Tseduqim*, rendered as 'Zadokites' or 'Sadducees' (m.Erub. 6: 2; m.Makk. 1: 6; m.Par. 3: 3, 7; m. Nidd. 4: 2; m.Yad. 4: 6–7), and פרושים, *Perushim*, 'separatists' or 'Pharisees' (m.Sot. 3: 4; m.Toh. 4: 12; m.Yad. 4: 6–8).

But are actual groups in any way adequately represented by these designations? In addition, if the Essenes could also be called Herodians by Jews in the first century, as evidenced by the Gospel of Mark, we need to be alert to the fact that different names might have been used for the same groups. That a group could be called by different names by different people, by insiders or by outsiders, or by different groups of outsiders, is a common feature in the history of religions. No one today would know that 'Quakers' and the 'Society of Friends' are the same without some knowledge of the group in question. It was noted above that Philo and Josephus indicate that the Essenes 'are called' Ἐσσαῖοι' (*Prob.* 75; *War* 2: 119), Philo indicating that it is a term of acclaim; it is not stated that the Essenes call themselves by this designation and nothing is said of people who do not call them by a positive name. If the Marcan 'Herodians' is a term for the 'Essenes' used by people who did not rate them

---

[16] Martin Goodman, 'Sadducees and Essenes after 70 CE,' in id. *Judaism in the Roman World* (Leiden: Brill, 2007), 153–62, at 154.

[17] Martin Goodman, *State and Society in Roman Galilee, AD 132–212* (Totowa, NJ: Rowman & Allanheld, 1983), 51, 104, 107, 177, 181.

[18] See Shaye Cohen, 'The Significance of Yavneh: Pharisees, Rabbis and the End of Jewish Sectarianism,' *HUCA* 55 (1984): 27–53.

[19] See the critique in Daniel Boyarin, *Border Lines: The Partition of Judaeo-Christianity* (Philadelphia: University of Pennsylvania, 2004), 151–201 and also Burns, 'Essene Sectarianism,' 256.

highly, then Josephus must surely have known that they were also called by a term of disdain by those who did not particularly respect their honours from the Herodian dynasty. As a parallel, while Samaritans call themselves שׁמרים, *Shamrim*, 'Guardians (of the Law)' or simply בני ישראל, in Greek *Ἰσραηλῖται* ('Israelites'),[20] Jews called them שׁומרונים, *Shomronim*, 'Samarians/Samaritans', or כותים, *Kuthim*, usually rendered 'Cuthaeans'.[21]

As another example, the Acts of the Apostles defines that those called *Χριστιανοί* in Greek (Acts 11: 26) were not called this in Aramaic or Hebrew, since in Acts 24: 5, the Jewish disciples of Jesus are called *Ναζωραῖοι*, usually rendered in English as 'Nazoraeans' or 'Nazarenes', following the designation of Jesus as *Ναζωραῖος*.[22] Therefore, not surprisingly, נוצרים, *Notsrim*, is the designation for Christians in the Babylonian Talmud (see b.Taan. 27b; b.A. Z. 6a and 7b; also, amended b.Git. 57a) on the basis of Jesus being called הנוצרי, *ha-Notsri*: b.A.Z. 17a; b.Sanh. 43a; b.Ber. 17b; b.Sota 47a; b.Sanh. 103a, 107a et al.; Tertullian, *Adv. Marc.* 4: 8). A Greek loan word approximating *Χριστιανοί* is never found in Mishnaic Hebrew. If we only knew the Greek term, and did not have the early attestation of the Hebrew designation in Acts or the writings of the Church Fathers who reacted against an apparent curse on Christians under this name (Jerome, *in Amos* 1: 1: 11–12; Ep. 112: 13, cf. Justin, *Dial.* 16, 93, 96, 113, 123, 133; Tertullian, *Adv. Marc.* 4: 8: 1), we would not necessarily identify any Christians in rabbinic material. The indicators are otherwise too obscure.

People of later times may have seen one group of the past as being two or even three, because of variant names either in oral circulation or in written sources, or put variant names into another category. If names for groups changed over time, or if two or three names were in circulation, then two or three groups could be created out of one. In addition, groups may have changed in terms of their ideology (as a parallel, a Quaker today is not going to espouse the same views as a Quaker of the nineteenth century, or dress in the same way, though there is consistency in terms of worship forms). We must therefore be aware of the possibility of schisms and developments, as well as multiple names for the same group.

---

[20] As evidenced by the Delos inscription found in 1979: Philippe Bruneau, 'Les Israélites de Délos et la juiverie délienne,' *Bulletin de Correspondance Hellénique* (1982), 465–504, at 469–74.

[21] See Reinhard Pummer, *The Samaritans in Flavius Josephus* (Texts and Studies in Ancient Judaism 129; Tübingen: Mohr Siebeck, 2009), 6.

[22] In Acts—as in the Gospels of Matthew, Luke, and John (Matt. 2: 23; 26: 71; Luke 18: 37: 24: 29 (probably); John 18: 5ff; 19: 19)—Jesus is called *Ναζωραῖος* (Acts 2: 22; 3: 6; 4: 10; 6: 14; 22: 8; 26: 9), and hence the *Ναζωραῖοι* are his disciples. For cognates see H. H. Schäder, '*Ναζαρηνός / Ναζωραῖος*,' in Gerhard Kittel (ed.), *Theological Dictionary of the New Testament* (Grand Rapids: Eerdmans, 1964–76), IV: 874–9. Mark Lidzbarski, *Mandäische Liturgien* (Berlin: Weidmann, 1920, repr. Hildesheim, Olms, 1971), xvi–xvii noted that the Mandaeans could call themselves *Naṣorayya*.

HEGESIPPUS

In his *Ecclesiastical History* 4: 22, Eusebius notes that Hegesippus, 'earlier' (than he), refers to the αἱρέσεις among the Jews, and he then quotes directly from Hegesippus' *Hupomnemata*, 'Memoirs', a history consisting of five books that is entirely lost apart from random quotes within Eusebius. Almost nothing is known of Hegesippus, except that he was perhaps ethnically Jewish (Eusebius, *Hist. Eccles.* 4: 22),[23] and that he adopted Christian beliefs and praxis, in due course writing down stories about what had happened in the church up until his own time, including a confused and embellished version of the death of Jesus' brother James (Eusebius, *Hist. Eccles.* 2: 23). However, his evidence is interesting in that it may reflect the stories being told within the church of the middle of the second century. The latest occurrence quoted by Eusebius from Hegesippus is in reference to the city founded in honour of Hadrian's lover Antinous (*Eccles. Hist.* 4: 8), after which Hegesippus himself settled in Rome during the bishopric of Eleutherus (*Eccles. Hist.* 4: 11). This city, Antinopolis or Antinoë, was built in Besa, Egypt, where Antinous was drowned in 130 CE (Dio Cassius, *Hist. Eccles.* 59: 11); thus Hegesippus would have written sometime after its construction, perhaps as early as the 150s. Eusebius writes (*Eccles. Hist.* 4: 22):[24]

> Ἔτι δ᾽ ὁ αὐτὸς καὶ τὰς πάλαι γεγενημένας παρὰ Ἰουδαίοις αἱρέσεις ἱστορὲ λέγων;
> ἦσαν δὲ γνῶμαι διάφοροι ἐν τῇ περιτομῇ ἐν υἱοῖς Ἰσραηλιτῶν κατὰ τῆς φυλῆς
> Ἰούδα καὶ τοῦ Χριστοῦ αὑαι; Ἐσσαῖοι Γαλιλαῖοι Ἡμεροβαπτισταὶ Μασβώθεοι
> Σαμαρεῖται Σαδδουκαῖοι Φαρισαῖοι

> Still the same [author] also gives an account of the schools that have come into existence long ago among the Jews: 'There were different judgements in respect to the circumcision, in respect to the children of Israelites, in regard to the tribe of Judah and [the tribe of] the Christ, as follows: Essenes, Galileans, Hemerobaptists, Masbotheans, Samaritans, Sadducees, Pharisees.'

This translation requires a little explanation, since many commentators hit the rocks of multivalent Greek prepositions and Hegesippus seems to write in an idiosyncratic way. The two prepositions ἐν in the second line are translated as 'in respect to' (or one could read 'in connection with')[25] to differentiate the meaning from the preposition παρά in the first line which seems to mean 'among'. The preposition κατά with the genitive case should be translated as

---

[23] But see the discussion in William Telfer, 'Was Hegesippus a Jew?' *HTR* 53 (1960): 143–53 and J. Stanley Jones, 'Hegesippus as a Source for the History of Jewish-Christianity,' in Simon-Claude Mimouni (ed.), *Le Judéo-christianisme dans tous ses états: actes du colloque de Jérusalem, 6–10 juillet 1998* (Paris: Cerf, 2001), 201–12.

[24] Edouard Schwartz (ed.), *Eusebius, Werke*, Vol. 2 *Die Kirchengeschichte* (GCS 9:1; Leipzig: J. C. Hinrichs, 1903), 61.

[25] LSJ 552: 7; BDAG, sense 8, p.329.

'in regard to',[26] in the French sense of *à propos*, following on from an initial identification of there being schools that had started long ago (παλαί) that had different judgements concerning certain matters. Hegesippus uses the aorist tense of the verb 'to be', ἦσαν, 'they were', indicating a time before his own. The word γνώμη is more than mere opinion or point of view, since it was a word that was often used for formal declarations of law and official proclamations.[27] In other words, the different judgements in respect to circumcision and in respect to 'the children of Israelites' (the text does not read 'the children of Israel') in its original context in Hegesippus may well have been concerned with legal judgements about who was included within Israel, and how circumcision counted in terms of the identification of male babies being part of Israel. In this regard, there were different judgements in regard to the children born of the tribe of Judah and the children born in 'the tribe of the Christ': τῆς φυλῆς is semantically implied.[28] Overall, the subjects appear to be concerned with *identity*, so that the final point would be concerning whether the children of the Christians were part of Israel.[29] Perhaps this bears some relationship to what we have in Acts 15 regarding the acceptance of Gentile Christians into the church, or even what we have in Romans, where Paul could claim that Gentile Christians were grafted onto the tree trunk of Israel (Rom. 11). Not everyone agreed.

Thus Eusebius defined a subject that Hegesippus himself must have written about in his lost work, but Eusebius is not interested in this topic, relevant to a bygone era. He has quoted this entire section of Hegesippus in order to list these different 'sects' or 'heresies', by his understanding, simply to emphasize that Jews themselves were not all of one mind. Hegesippus might have been then setting the stage for his own Christian understanding as opposed to the various decisions reached within Judaism, but we know little about his rhetoric. Eusebius quotes Hegesippus as writing of the 'seven schools' that they

---

[26] LSJ 883: 7; BDAG, sense 6, p.513. See also Geza Vermes and Martin Goodman (eds), *The Essenes according to the Classical Sources*. JSOT Press: Sheffield 1989), 61, who render it as 'about'. Variant understandings of prepositions in this passage have resulted in translations that do not necessarily make sense. Vermes and Goodman, for example, translate the prepositions ἐν either as 'in' or 'among' (as replicating παρά) thus: 'The same author further describes the sects which in earlier times existed among the Jews, as follows: "There were differing opinions in the circumcision among the children of Israel about the tribe of Judah and the Christ".' More strangely, in G. A. Williamson's translation, *Eusebius, The History of the Church from Christ to Constantine* (Harmondsworth: Penguin, 1962), 182: 'Hegesippus also names the sects that once existed among the Jews: "There were various groups in the Circumcision, among the Children of Israel, all hostile to the tribe of Judah and the Christ".'

[27] BDAG, sense 4, p.203.

[28] See Marcel Simon, *Les sectes juives d'après les témoinages patristiques*, Studia Patristica 1 (1957), 526–39. Simon then believed that the 'sects' were both Jewish and Christian.

[29] In using this language of the 'tribe', in fact, Hegesippus reflects the language of the Testimonium Flavianum as cited by Eusebius (*Hist. Eccles* 1: 11), language that is appropriate to how Jewish-Christians could have defined themselves.

were 'already described' (*Hist. Eccles.* 2: 23) in his work, but we do not have this section.

Who were these αἱρέσεις? That there are seven is an interesting key number. In the paragraph before (*Hist. Eccles.* 4: 22: 2), Hegesippus is quoted as stating that the 'virgin' church (in Jerusalem?) was corrupted when, after Simeon son of Clopas was appointed bishop in Jerusalem, a mysterious person named Thebuthis 'began to corrupt out of the [things of] the seven schools' ἄρχεται . . . ὑποφθείρειν ἀπὸ τῶν ἑπτὰ αἱρέσεων. We are at this point in the First Revolt. There was a priest named Jesus son of Thebutis mentioned by Josephus (*War* 6: 387), who was forced to hand over Temple treasure to the Romans. According to Hegesippus, Simeon son of Clopas succeeded Jesus' brother James, martyred in 62 CE, which means that the Christian Thebuthis may be dated sometime in the later 60s, during the Revolt. We learn in Eusebius that Simeon, son of Clopas (brother of Joseph) and Mary, was Jesus' cousin, who was martyred during the time of Trajan and the consular governorship of Atticus (*c.*106–7), at the age of 120, after being accused of being a descendant of David and a Christian by the αἱρέσεις (*Hist. Eccles.* 3: 32: 1–6, cf. 3: 19: 1). This all sounds like Hegesippus, who sets up the αἱρέσεις as being legal authorities with the power to interpret the law and accuse.

Reconstructing Hegesippus then in the arrangement of the *Hupomnemata* there was apparently a discussion about the 'seven schools', after which there was the story of the death of James, and problems of the Jerusalem church under Simeon son of Clopas, culminating in his death. That Hegesippus presents the schools as active during the reign of Trajan indicates that in his understanding they could be placed in the second century as well as in the later first.

This 'seven school' model of Judaism found its way into the fourth-century *Apostolic Constitutions* 6: 6–7 where the 'schools' are listed as: Sadducees, Pharisees, Basmotheans, Hemerobaptists, Ebionites, Essenes, and the followers of Simon [Magus] the Samaritan, the last one distinguished as being new.[30] As Stanley Isser has noted, '[e]ither there was no standard list to go with the tradition of "seven sects", or such a list was lost or corrupted early, and the various writers made up lists of their own. Some of the differences may be due to reflection of different periods'.[31]

Hegesippus' list of 'seven schools' was one he himself believed to be relevant in terms of Judaism's past, but how far back was this past? He applies it to the period just before the destruction of the Temple, but he is not at all reliable in

---

[30] See discussion in Stanley J. Isser, *The Dositheans: A Samaritan Sect in Late Antiquity* (Leiden: Brill, 1976), 11–13. In Justin Martyr's *Dialogue with Trypho* (*c.*180 CE), the Essenes are omitted and the seven schools are listed as: Sadducees, Genistae, Meristae, Galileans, Hellenians, Pharisees, and Baptists (Justin Martyr, *Dial.* 80: 4); see below.

[31] Isser, *Dositheans*, 13.

regard to this time, if Eusebius quotes him correctly. We can see this in his story of the death of James: Hegesippus identifies James as 'the Righteous', and identifies him as a Nazirite *High Priest* who eschewed oil and [warm?] baths.

In Josephus' account, James—who is not a priest—was killed *by* a Sadducean High Priest, Ananus ben Ananus (*Ant.* 20: 197–203), who himself was killed in due course, despite being highly esteemed (*War* 4: 318–24). Indeed just after he recounts the death of James, Josephus states: 'The High Priest Ananus every day advanced greatly in reputation' (*Ant.* 20: 205). Ananus was clearly thought of as something of a model of virtue, despite his action. Hegesippus' version of the death of James might actually confuse the two men,[32] the esteemed High Priest and the brother of Jesus. If he only purified himself in cold water, this was an ascetic practice found among the Essenes (in Josephus, *War* 2: 129) or in Bannus (*Life* 11),[33] and the avoidance of oil is something Josephus also associates with the Essenes as an indication of their austere hardness (*War* 2: 123). In this case, ordinary bathing seems also to be classified as something soft. If the characteristics of 'James' in Hegesippus are actually features that could be associated with Ananus, then they would give us a rounder picture of Sadducees' own methods of indicating extreme piety. But how confidently can we trust Hegesippus at all, given this monumental mix-up?

As explored above, Josephus indicates that there were only three legal schools (or societies) of Jerusalem, but these were forced to include a fourth at the time of the Revolt in 66 CE, since at this point a 'Fourth Philosophy' (*Ant.* 18: 9, 23) did hold judicial authority in Jerusalem and was able to make legal decisions. Was there further fracturing after 70 CE? Could it be that the 'seven schools' model of 'Israel' (inclusive of Samaritans) was appropriate in the land as a whole between 70 and 135, when claims to correct interpretation of Torah and authority in Jerusalem must still have been of great importance in the areas where Judaean and Samaritan law could still be in effect?

In Hegesippus' account the Essenes ('Εσσαῖοι) are listed first, with the Pharisees and Sadducees last. The 'Galileans' Hegesippus notes as an αἵρεσις would not mean 'Galileans' as a regional category, and would most simply equate to the followers of Judas, 'the Galilean' mentioned by Josephus, since 'the Galilean' was often his epithet (*War* 2: 433; *Ant.* 18: 23; 20: 102; Acts 5: 37). Josephus identifies this philosophy as 'infecting the nation' as a prelude to

---

[32] For discussion of this passage in relation to other passages in early Christian literature, see F. Stanley Jones, 'The Martyrdom of James in Hegesippus, Clement of Alexandria, Christian Apocrypha including Nag Hammadi, a Study of the Textual Relations,' SBL Seminar Papers (Atlanta: Scholars Press, 1990), 328–31; Charles C. Torrey, 'James the Just, and His Name "Oblias",' *JBL* (1944): 93–8.

[33] According to Josephus, a cold bath is required for some types of ritual impurity, see *Ant.* 3: 263.

the Revolt (*Ant.* 18: 25).[34] 'Galileans' are targeted by Pontius Pilate in Luke's Gospel (13: 1), a reference to a killing in Jerusalem (in the Temple?), though this is not normally understood to indicate followers of Judas.[35] There is also the curious record by Arrian of his master Epictetus saying, regarding fearlessness, 'And is it possible that anyone should be thus disposed towards these things from madness, and the Galileans from mere habit?' (Epictetus, *Moral Discourses* 4: 7: 2). While this is often read as being indicative of Christians, on the basis of Julian the Apostate's fourth-century designation for 'Christians' in his treatise 'Against the Galileans', the designation better relates in the latter first century and early second century to Judaean rebels, whose reputation for withstanding torture was renowned (Tacitus, *Hist.* 5: 5; Josephus, *Ant.* 18: 23–4; *War* 7: 417–19).[36] The existence of a group designated as 'Galileans' through to the middle of the second century may also be suggested by a letter from Bar Kokhba,[37] where Bar Kokhba threatens Yeshua ben Galgula regarding some action concerning 'the Galileans' collectively. The comment in m. Yad. 4: 8 regarding 'a Galilean *min*' best relates to someone who pronounced an interpretative position as a 'Galilean'; he is able to point the finger at the rival *Perushim*.[38] A *min*, after all, could be anyone holding an interpretative opinion with which the rabbis disagreed; one who did not accept rabbinic *halakha*.[39]

'Masbotheans' in Hegesippus' list of Judaean schools are a group mentioned immediately beforehand as a Christian sect,[40] and so this name here may be a copying error by Eusebius for the word Basmotheans, which appears in the later Apostolic Constitutions as a name for one of the Jewish 'seven schools', in this case one defined as denying providence. They also support

---

[34] Though Sean Freyne, 'The Galileans in the Light of Josephus' *Life*,' in id. *Galilee and Gospel: Collected Essays* (Tübingen: Mohr Siebeck, 2000), 27–44, rightly notes that the main use of the term 'Galilean' in Josephus' *Life* is geographical, with special focus on the rural population. Still, main use aside, it would be appropriate to think that 'Galileans' could be designated as a distinctive group on the basis of Judas the Galilean in the same way that 'Nazoraeans' could be designated as a special group on the basis of Jesus the Nazoraean, even when all people from Nazareth would also have been called this too.

[35] Matthew Black, 'The Patristic Accounts of Jewish Sects,' in id. *The Scrolls and Christian Origins* (Edinburgh: Nelson, 1962), 50, however, identifies the Galileans here as part of the movement.

[36] Shimon Appelbaum, 'The Zealots: The Case for Revaluation,' *JRS* 61 (1971): 155–70, at 169.

[37] Published in *DJD* 2, no. 43.

[38] Yaakov Sussman, 'The History of Halakha and the Dead Sea Scrolls: Preliminary Observations on Miqsat Ma'ase Ha-torah (4QMMT),' *Tarbiz* 59 (1990), 11–76, at 51 (Heb.).

[39] Philip S. Alexander, 'The Parting of the Ways from the Perspective of Rabbinic Judaism,' in James Dunn (ed.), *Jews and Christians: The Parting of the Ways, A.D. 70 to 135, The Second Durham-Tübingen Research Symposium on Earliest Christianity and Judaism, Durham, September, 1989* (Tübingen: Mohr Siebeck, 1989), 1–26, at 9–10.

[40] The Aramaic for 'dip, moisten' is (צבע in Pa'al (see Jastrow, 1259). A term such as מצבעין would mean 'dippers', indicating a local name.

the spontaneous motion of the world and do not accept the soul's immortality (*Apost. Const.* 6: 6). It is possible there is some link with the 'Boethusians'. Men from the house of Boethus are described at various times in Josephus' narrative as being an elite priestly family from which High Priests could be drawn, during the time of Herod the Great in particular,[41] of unknown affiliation. However, in rabbinic literature the Boethusians, ביתוסים, could be defined as having specific legal opinions, especially in regard to the calendar (m.Men. 10: 3; m. Hag. 2:4; t.Rosh ha-Shanah 1: 15; though see also t.Men. 13: 21; b.Pes. 57a, t. Yoma, 1: 8; b.Yoma 19b), and be associated with the *Tseduqim* (Abot deRabbi Nathan 5). A very strong chronological indicator for their belonging to the second century is provided by mention of a Boethusian in debate with Rabbi Akiba (b.Shab. 108a), Akiba being Bar Kokhba's ally and endorser (j.Taan. 4:8, 68d). Given this, if this designation does relate to such a society, it suggests that around the years 130–5 CE there were men who could look back at their families' chief priestly authority some sixty years earlier, and could espouse certain legal interpretations with authority.

The term Ἡμεροβαπτισταί—'daily immersers'—appears no earlier than the second century (see Justin, *Dial.* 80). The Hemerobaptists are defined as a Jewish sect by Epiphanius (*Pan.* 1:11: 1: 1–11: 2: 5), who notes that a Hemerobaptist maintains that human life is impossible unless 'he is daily immersed in water, being washed and purified from all guilt'. The Hemerobaptists may have traced their antecedents to people like Bannus, who is described as living in the wilderness, wearing and eating whatever was provided naturally, 'with many ablutions of cold water for purity both day and night' (Josephus, *Life* 12). Josephus differentiates Bannus from the Essenes, and, as we have seen, he is not defined as being part of any αἵρεσις. Eusebius in fact explicitly calls Bannus a Hemerobaptist (*Hist. Eccles.* 4: 22). In some ways, as a wilderness-dweller living on what nature provided, Bannus has more in common with John the Baptist.[42] In the *Apostolic Constitutions* 6: 5–6, the Hemerobaptists are defined as those who 'do not eat until they have washed, and do not use their beds, tables, dishes, cups and seats until they have purified them'. In Hegesippus' use of the Bannus group as a αἵρεσις we see a clearly different employment of the term itself, so that while Josephus specifically indicated that Bannus was not to be counted among the three αἱρέσεις, in Christian usage there was not the same differentiation: the 'choices', αἱρέσεις, are in terms of lifestyle and practice, but the connection with central legal authority has been lost.

Rabbinic literature mentions 'Morning Immersers' who purified their bodies every morning even if already pure, prior to morning prayers (b.Ber. 22a),

---

[41] See above, p. 128–9. It is possible the Boethusians had Essene links.
[42] See Joan E. Taylor, *The Immerser: John the Baptist within Second Temple Judaism* (Grand Rapids: Eerdmans, 1997), 34–5.

and this may refer to the same people.[43] So, for example, R. Simson of Sens states, 'The Morning Immersers said to the *Perushim*: "We charge you with wrong-doing in pronouncing the Name in the morning without having immersed," and then the *Perushim* said: "We charge you with wrong-doing in pronouncing the Name with a body impure inside"' (t.Yad. 2: 20).[44] Likewise, there were Jewish-Christian groups of the second to fourth centuries who followed a practice of early morning immersion: Peter and his disciples in the Pseudo-Clementine literature immerse every morning *on getting up*, and every evening before the evening meal (*Hom.* 8: 2; 9: 23; 10: 1, 26; 11: 1; *Rec.* 4: 3, 37; 5: 1, 36; 6: 1, cf. Epiphanius, *Pan.* 1:30: 2: 4–5).[45] Philo and Josephus note that the Essenes practise continual purification, twice a day before meals, with assemblies to purify their bodies at the fifth hour and also at the end of the day (*Prob.* 84; *Ant.* 18: 19; *War* 2: 129). However, since the fifth hour was from about 11 a. m. until noon, this indicates that they purified themselves twice a day ahead of a midday and before an evening meal, which is a different practice from purifying on waking (before morning prayers) and is also not a case of continually washing throughout the day. Josephus states they get up before sunrise and say ancient prayers directed to the rising sun, before going about their tasks (*War* 2: 128); but there is no suggestion here that they immerse prior to these prayers. Therefore, in t.Yad. 2: 20, the *Perushim* are doing the same thing as the Essenes, and are being challenged by people who immerse immediately after getting up, before prayers. The Essenes therefore cannot be equated with the Morning Immersers, but correlate with the *Perushim*.

The Clementine Homilies themselves trace the lustrations of Peter and his disciples to John the Baptist (*Hom.* 2: 23; *Rec.* 1:54).[46] There may—in the second to third centuries—have been various people who adopted practices of 'extreme purification' even if not related to each other or part of a cohesive group,[47] on the basis of the example of John, and possible disciples of his like Bannus. There is no reason to suggest an Essene connection, or even any

---

[43] As Burns, 'Essene Sectarianism,' has pointed out, this fastidious purity concern may also be indicated in t.Parah, as opposed to the redaction in m.Parah 3: 3 where the Sadducees are inserted, though Burns associates these people with the continuing presence of the Essenes.

[44] See Moshe S. Zuckermandel (ed.), *Tosefta nach den Erfurter und Wiener Handschriften mit Parallelstellen und Varianten*, repr. with new foreword by Saul Lieberman (Jerusalem: Bamberger & Vahrman,1937), 684.

[45] Joseph Thomas, 'Les Ebionites baptistes,' *Revue d'historie ecclesiastique* 30 (1934): 270–96.

[46] In the Pseudo-Clementines the practice of morning and evening immersion is differentiated from Christian baptism proper (e.g. *Hom.* 7: 5, 8, 12; 11: 35; 14: 1; 20: 23; *Rec.* 6: 15; 7: 38; 10: 72).

[47] Burns, 'Essene Sectarianism,' has suggested that within the category of *minim* within the Mishnah and Tosefta it may be possible to distinguish the historical Essenes at various points. Burns rightly reads the sources as indicating that the Essenes were widespread, living in numerous communities throughout Judaea, and would have been well known to other Jews. He notes, for example, the presence of *minim* who wear white in a list of *minim* who wear the

necessary 'movement'; a practice of extreme purification could have been adopted by both Jews and Jewish-Christians for special purity and piety, with one group possibly becoming the antecedents of the Mandaeans.[48]

That Samaritans are included in Hegesippus' list indicates that not all his 'schools' were even Jews, so that we are left with the impression then that we have 'seven schools' of *Israel*, as noted above, not just of Jews alone. This collection of names does not then necessarily add to our knowledge of schools within Second Temple Judaism prior to the destruction of the Temple, or destabilize Josephus' presentation. Rather, it may illustrate some splitting of the legal schools of the first century so that—with the inclusion of the Samaritans—Christians of the second century could identify a 'seven school' model of Israel. Nevertheless, there is the issue of whether a template of 'seven' was forced on the actual pattern of schools in existence at this time.

JUSTIN MARTYR

Somewhat different to Hegesippus is Justin Martyr, native of Neapolis in Palestine, who, in his *Dialogue with Trypho* 80: 3–4, reels off names of possible Jewish groups with misguided beliefs as an illustration that Judaism also had to deal with variant opinions in his own day, ultimately in order to demonstrate that there were indeed also in Christianity people who are not really Christians (in rejecting the Parousia, as if when you die you will go to heaven directly on death!); likewise, such Jews are not really admitted by Trypho to be Jews. For Justin, this list of seven is defined as erroneous rather than authoritative, and clearly his Jewish conversation partner Trypho would need to believe they were only 'called Jews and children of Abraham':

> τοὺς Σαδδουκαίους, ἢ τὰς ὁμοίας αἱρέσεις Γενιστῶν, καὶ Μεριστῶν, καὶ Γαλιλαίων, καὶ Ἑλληνιανῶν, καὶ Φαρισαίων, Βαπτιστῶν . . .

> the Sadducees, and the similar schools: Genistae, and Meristae, and Galileans, and Hellenians, and Pharisees, Baptizers . . .

Strikingly, the 'Sadducees' and 'Pharisees' are indicative of divergent points of view from those accepted as truly Jewish by Trypho. Justin, in passing, notes later on that the Pharisees are the 'chiefs of the synagogues' in *Dial.* 137: 2, which, as we have seen, relates to the Gospel of John, where the Pharisees can evict people from the synagogue (John 12: 42), and this may indicate Justin's

---

wrong things: they go barefoot, make round phylacteries, put them low on the forehead or in the palm of the hand, to the disapproval of the rabbis (m.Meg. 4: 8).

[48] For which, see the remarkable study by Jorunn Jacobson Buckley, *The Mandaeans: Ancient Texts and Modern People* (New York: OUP, 2002).

attempt to correlate the leaders of the synagogues in his own time with the gospel; it would therefore not be a reflection of actual historical identity and Pharisaic authority. But the list of seven erroneous schools (the term αἵρεσις now being used in a pejorative Christian sense) reflects a different notion about the actual identity of the 'Pharisees' as configured in his own time.[49]

Matthew Black has rightly noted that 'Justin believed himself to be describing Jewish heretics' and that '[t]he most extraordinary feature of the list [of Justin] ... is ... his inclusion of the Pharisees in a list of Minim or heretics'.[50] It is hard to imagine that Justin acquired such notions from anywhere other than Jewish teachers of his own day who had begun to distinguish the historical legacy of the so-called *Tseduqim* and *Perushim* as being different from that of those to whom he looked to for authority, perhaps already the *Ḥakhamim*, as Daniel Boyarin has pointed out.[51]

Justin here must have believed that the *Perushim* referred to negatively in his own time were indeed the 'Pharisees' he knew from the gospels. The *Tseduqim* identified by Trypho were likewise called the 'Sadducees'. But these may not be simple equations. The latter group could have been equated with different historical groups as time went on, thanks to the use of the word *tsadok*, 'righteous', in the designation.[52] For 'Galileans' Justin presumably means the same as Hegesippus: the Galileans who took their name from Judas, extremists who were active at the time of Bar Kokhba. The Genistae and Meristae are unknown, but μεριστής means 'divider' or 'arbitrator' (in terms of being able to divide or distinguish right and wrong) and was a term even used as a positive epithet of the god Sarapis.[53] The 'Hellenians' are unknown.[54] Strikingly, while 'Pharisees' appear in this list of those who are not part of Trypho's tradition of Judaism, the Essenes are not found. The 'Baptizers' appear without an 'and' to link them, but are more likely to be differentiated since this gives us seven groupings.

If it is right that the defining moment in the end of the legal schools occurred at the time Jewish law was no longer operational, post-135, the

---

[49] As noted by Black, 'Patristic Accounts,' 51. Black proposed that the words Φαρισαίων Βαπτιστῶν in Justin's list not be separated by an 'and' in translation, so that they be translated as 'baptizing Pharisees', but this suggestion has failed to convince.

[50] Black, 'Patristic Sects,' 49–50; Simon, *Sectes*, 530.

[51] Boyarin, *Border Lines*, 40–2, 241–2.

[52] Ephrem apparently linked the name with the followers of John the Baptist; see Black, 'Patristic Accounts,' 53. Black wonders if these were the Qumran sectarians, the 'Zadokites'.

[53] PGM 13: 638, for other instances see BDAG, 632. Though see Boyarin, *Border Lines*, 241 n. 22. On these see Simon, *Sectes*, 85–107; Simon suggested that Genistae should be related to the Greek word γενός and therefore equated to *minim*; see too the Aramaic explorations of Daniel Gershonson and Gilles Quispel, 'Meristae,' VC 12 (1958): 10–26.

[54] Boyarin is taken with the suggestion that this be corrected to Ἑλληλιανῶν, but this amendment does not give us an appropriate Greek term for Hillelites. This may instead be related to the word הַרְנָלָה, 'murmuring, rebellion,' Exod. Rabbah 25; see Jastrow, 354.

schools would have lost their reasons for existence. Eventually, rather than classifying people in terms of any defining name, the term *minim* would be employed loosely as a catch-all term for those who asserted a legal interpretation contrary to rabbinic *halakha*.[55]

Ultimately, we need to remember that these names provided by Hegesippus and Justin exist for the purposes of polemical discourse within Christian writings of the mid-second century, almost a hundred years after the destruction of the Temple. Additionally, there is in Christian writing usually a sense that the term αἱρέσεις refers to schools of *thought*,[56] with an emphasis on belief—so central to the Christian mind—and so all kinds of different Jewish opinions could be mustered under certain designations; Josephus' terminology was not that of Justin. Once there was no proper autonomous Judaean legislature or courts, the whole exercise of legal interpretation must have changed in character, becoming more theoretical in terms of the nation as a whole, and more personal, in applying to small areas where there could be control.

The evidence of Hegesippus and Justin regarding the 'seven schools' cannot be used as data that can be read backwards to the pre-70 circumstances, as did Joseph Thomas, who argued from the Church Fathers and Josephus that there was a widespread Baptist movement within Second Temple Judaism, out of step with a supposed 'mainstream' Judaism, encompassing the Essenes, the Hemerobaptists, and the followers of John the Baptist, among others.[57] Rather, the evidence of the lists of different Jewish 'schools' in the Church Fathers— slender as it is—can be used in discussions about what happened to the forms of αἱρέσεις within Second Temple Judaism, after the destruction of the Temple.

From Hegesippus it seems that the Essenes could still be defined as a group, as could the Galileans, Pharisees, and Sadducees, and also the Samaritans. Along with these, there were those who followed the ultra-purificatory practices of Bannus—the Hemerobaptists—and a society that we may wish to identify as Boethusians, though there may have been others also that could be identified as significant in certain areas, for all we know. Bar Kochba and his supporters may have been designated as one of these, at some point, even though we have no record of what they could have been called. Our evidence is

[55] See in particular Martin Goodman, 'The Function of Minim in Early Rabbinic Judaism,' in id. *Judaism in the Roman World: Collected Essays* (Leiden: Brill, 2007), 163–74; Naomi Janowitz, 'Rabbis and their Opponents: The construction of the "Min" in Rabbinic Anecdotes,' *Journal of Early Christian Studies* 6 (1998): 449–62, esp. 459–60.

[56] Boyarin, *Border Lines*, 404-1.

[57] Joseph Thomas, *Le Mouvement Baptiste en Palestine et Syrie* (Gembloux: Duculot, 1935), following Wilhelm Brandt, *Die Judischen Baptismen oder das religiose Waschen und Baden im Judentum mit Einschluss der Judenchristentums* (Giessen: Topelmann, 1910). See Black, 'Patristic Accounts,' 54–8; Taylor, *Immerser*, 29–32.

slight. We may not have seven legal schools, we may have fewer or more, and there is no way of knowing on the basis of present evidence. At any rate, the Essenes may have been one of those who exercised some influence until the quashing of the Bar Kokhba revolt. After this, with the terrible destruction and reconfiguration under Hadrian, such legal schools must clearly have begun to seem less and less easy to define, with their names attached to historical legacies rather than to vibrant and important groups of scholars.

EPIPHANIUS

Certain references of Epiphanius, even though late, are also relevant. According to Sozomen, *Historia Ecclesiastica* 6: 32, Epiphanius was born Jewish, in a village named Besanduka of the huge city territory of Eleutheropolis in Palestine (which included En Gedi and the shores of the Dead Sea), and, after his conversion to Christianity, he founded a monastery in this vicinity where he lived for 30 years. His provenance and the local polemics in which he was involved mean he is potentially an important source on religious groupings in fourth-century Palestine, though he derides opposing points of view with much ferocity. *Panarion* (*c.*375 CE), 'medicine box', is written as an antidote to those bitten by the snake of heresy.[58] Given his Jewish origins, and his provenance in a region with a large Jewish population, his reflections on Jewish groups cannot be swept away too hastily. However, his exaggerated style and loose use of sources mean that his material must be used with caution.

One candidate for possible hidden Essenes in Epiphanius comes with his mention of 'Iessaeans' in *Pan.* 1: 29: 1: 3–4; 1: 29: 4: 9–5: 7, identified as a Jewish-Christian sect deriving their name from 'Jesus' (rather than more correctly from Jesse), which—according to Epiphanius—means 'healer', 'physician', and 'saviour' (*Pan.* 1: 29: 4: 9). He then leaps to Philo's treatise *De Vita Contemplativa* to identify them—though his source is clearly Eusebius, who had presented the Therapeutae as Christians in his history (*Hist. Eccles.* 2: 17).[59] The Iessaeans are then the Therapeutae. Epiphanius' words do indicate knowledge of Aramaic, a language he may well have spoken as an inhabitant of southern Palestine: יְשַׁי (Jesse) is linked with Jesus יֵשׁוּעַ (Yeshu'), which is linked to 'healer', אָסָא, and this happens to be a possible underlying Aramaic term behind Greek Ἐσσαῖος, but Epiphanius instead

---

[58] For full translation see Frank Williams, *The Panarion of Epiphanius of Salamis, Book 1* (Leiden: Brill, 2009).

[59] See Simon Mimouni, 'Qui sont les Jesseens dans la notice 29 du Panarion d'Epiphane de Salamine?' *NT* 43 (2001): 264–99.

looks to Eusebius' θεραπευταί ('healers' in later Greek). At the heart of this is the identification of a group that could be called אסיין, *assayyin*, but the wider context of their placement is vague.

When Epiphanius discusses the Essenes specifically as a named group, he states that they were one of four schools of the Samaritans (*Pan.* 1: 1: 10–13; 1: 10: 1: 1), along with the Gorothenes, Sebueans, and Dositheans,[60] which might seem baffling, though he has at the heart of this definition a story concerning the disputes between Jews and Samaritans regarding times of festivals (*Pan.* 1: 11: 1: 1). Since Epiphanius knew Samaritans to be (in his day) champions of a different calendar, then it is possible that a recorded discussion in which Essenes dispute the operative Temple calendar could have led Epiphanius to put them in the Samaritan camp. As a general rule, it is the substantive characteristics of the groups Epiphanius mentions that are important rather than the wider categories in which they are placed.

Four Samaritan schools are matched by the division of Judaism into seven. Epiphanius is conscious of reflecting a past, and acknowledges that the Jewish schools are no longer in existence at the end of the fourth century when he is writing (*Pan.* 1: 19: 5: 7), but how far back this past goes he does not indicate. Epiphanius adopts the 'seven school' model that had already been established, and here includes much more interesting information that he has clearly derived from Jews of his own day, particularly in regard to identifying the *Perushim*, a name he defines correctly as meaning 'separated ones' (*Pan.* 1: 16: 1: 6). His 'seven schools' are: the Sadducees, Scribes, the Pharisees, the Hemerobaptists, the Ossaeans, Nasaraeans, and Herodians.

Of these seven schools the name of the Ossaeans is initially suggestive. Epiphanius places them on the other side of the Dead Sea within the regions of Nabataea and Peraea (*Pan.* 1: 19: 1: 1; 1: 19: 2: 2; cf. *Pan.* 1: 53: 1: 1). However, Epiphanius' source is a 'tradition' that the origins of the Elchasites were to be found among Jews living in regions east of the Dead Sea, with their name defined specifically as meaning 'strong people'. In other words, Epiphanius indicates that they called themselves עצומים, *Otsomim* (cf. Lam. Rab. 3: 4). According to Epiphanius they were corrupted at the end of the first century by Elchai (*Pan.* 1: 19: 2: 2), thereby being dubbed Elchasites and Sampsaeans. Perhaps originally the Elchasites derived from refugees on the eastern side of the Dead Sea who did indeed consider themselves strong for surviving.

As for Epiphanius' description of other 'schools', there is his mention of 'Herodians' believing that Herod the Great was the promised Messiah on the basis of Gen. 49: 10: 'There shall not fail a ruler in Judah until he come for

---

[60] The Dositheans were indeed a Samaritan school originating in the first century, following a leader known as Dusis in the Samaritan records; for an excellent exploration of this school see Isser, *Dositheans*.

whom it is prepared.' As discussed in Chapter 4, these are indeed the Essenes, hidden behind a tremendously obscure reference.[61]

How much else is valuable here? Epiphanius indicates that the Sadducees (*Pan.* 1: 14) are named by means of the Hebrew word צדק, providing some link with the term *Tseduqim* as found in rabbinic literature, though Epiphanius also links them with Dositheus, noting how close they are to Samaritans apart from worshipping in Jerusalem. Epiphanius' 'Scribes' appear to be built up from the reference to Jesus' criticizing ostentatious scribal attire in Matthew 23: 7; since 'scribes and Pharisees' are denounced by Jesus by separate designations, so the 'Scribes' become a separate sect in Epiphanius' list, but are linked especially to Rabbi Akiba (1: 15: 2: 1). These may simply be the *Hakhamim* of rabbinic literature. As noted above, in the references by Christian authors intent on presenting a 'seven school' model, it is not necessarily the case that differently named groups are in fact different groups, but rather they may be the same group named and described differently in different sources. Instead of taking these as instances of one entity considered from multiple perspectives, the entity itself has been multiplied.

Epiphanius then describes the 'Pharisees' (*Pan.* 1: 16) and makes the equation between the Pharisees of the New Testament and the Hebrew term *Perushim*, 'separated ones', by noting that they derive their name from Hebrew פרש, but these 'Pharisees = *Perushim*' as described by Epiphanius are not *substantively* at all the Pharisees as described by Josephus or in the New Testament. Epiphanius struggles to relate them to Matt. 23, but otherwise they appear very different, and—given Epiphanius' knowledge of the term *Perushim*—it seems he has some source on this group.

Epiphanius writes that these *Perushim* marked off ten, eight, or four years for celibacy, and, in order to avoid nocturnal emissions, they would sleep on 'benches only a span wide and stretch out on these at evening so that, if one went to sleep and fell on the floor, he could get up again for prayer. Others would gather pebbles and scatter them under their bedclothes, so that they would be pricked and not fall asleep, but be forced to keep themselves awake. Others would even use thorns as a mattress, for the same reason'.[62]

Epiphanius had already identified that the 'Scribes' could also mark out a period of celibacy, and this was why they had tassels on the four corners of a cloak, to give notice of what they had undertaken (*Pan.* 1: 15: 1: 7), so reference is made then to Pharisees' tassels as being the same as the Scribes', also presumably for the same reason (to indicate their celibacy), and their wearing of 'women's' (= long) cloaks, wide boots, and wide tongues on their sandals. There is then a comment about their fasting, from Matt. 23: 23 (Luke 18: 12, cf. Didache 8: 1), and insistence on their offering of first-fruits on the thirtieth and fiftieth days, along with sacrifices and prayers without fail. This situates these people in the time before 70.

---

[61] See above, pp. 124–9.
[62] Translation by Frank Williams, in Epiphanius, *Panarion*, 1: 42–3.

More importantly, Epiphanius (*Pan.* 1: 16: 2: 1) records that the 'Pharisees' 'acknowledged the resurrection of the dead and believed in angels and a [Holy] Spirit, but like the others they knew nothing of the Son of God. Moreover fate and astrology meant a great deal to them.' This then makes Epiphanius launch into a useful description of Jewish astrology: the art of making predictions through the alignment of the stars. He argues against this type of reliance on Fate and its indicators.[63]

Overall, Epiphanius' description of the 'Pharisees/*Perushim*' as following a lifestyle in which there is a commitment to very long periods of celibacy, an ascetic routine, dutiful sacrifice, fasting, and prayer, along with a belief in the resurrection, angels, over-arching Fate, and the importance of astrology, is actually more suggestive of Josephus' Essenes than Pharisees, unless Epiphanius is truly giving us an indication of ascetic Pharisees we have no idea about. According to Josephus, as we have seen, the Pharisees say some but not all things are the work of Destiny, and the Sadducees remove Destiny and assert that human beings have free will (*Ant.* 13: 171–3, cf. *Ant.* 18: 18), but: 'The category [of school] of the Essenes declare Destiny the mistress of everything, and nothing happens to human beings that is not by her vote' (*Ant.* 13: 172).[64] It is anyone's guess what Epiphanius' source might be, and we do not know how well he relates it. Nevertheless, the notion that a man could adopt celibacy for a period of time is actually an interesting one, and may provide a model for Essene celibacy that seems more in keeping with what we have noted in Philo.

Clearly, there are many elements missing in Epiphanius' description of 'Pharisees/*Perushim*' in terms of how Josephus describes the Essenes, particularly the focus on communality, and there is no mention of white attire, but celibacy and asceticism are strongly associated with them and with no other Judaean group apart from Christians. If so, this raises an important issue: if *Perushim* as a term used by Jews of Epiphanius' time could describe not first-century Pharisees at all (as Epiphanius thought) but rather indicate some memory of the ancient Essenes, are the *Perushim* found within rabbinic texts always historical Pharisees? Or could they be Essenes? As noted above, Justin too could identify 'Pharisees' as people that Trypho could accept as not part of his tradition.

RABBINIC LITERATURE

It is usually assumed that, just as there is apparently no mention of the Essenes in the New Testament, there is no mention at all of the Essenes in rabbinic

---

[63] Translation by Frank Williams, in Epiphanius, *Panarion*, 1: 43.
[64] See above, pp. 88–91.

literature, from the Mishnah, at the end of the second century, to the Palestinian and Babylonian Talmuds compiled during the fifth and sixth centuries. Rachael Elior has used the apparently resounding silence of the corpus to argue that Philo invented the Essenes as an ideal society, and Josephus was influenced by him in presenting the Essenes in the ways he did.[65] However, this notion that the rabbis never referred to the Essenes was not at all the opinion of Jewish scholars a century ago. As noted above, they worked with a completely different model of the Essenes to that presented by Christian scholars.[66] Kaufman Kohler, in his entry in the *Jewish Encyclopaedia*, suggested numerous places in the rabbinic corpus where the Essenes might be reflected, considering them essentially a 'branch of the Pharisees', but here he understood 'Pharisees' in accordance with the rabbinic presentations of the *Perushim*.[67]

Kohler accepted the view that the origins of the Essenes should be found within the חסידים '*H*̣*asidim*' (as mentioned in 1 Macc. 2: 42; 7: 13; 2 Macc. 14: 6),[68] and so looked widely for references within the rabbinic corpus, searching for people who exhibited exceptionally pious behaviour, and were accorded a variety of respectful names. Most interestingly, perhaps, Kohler noted a rather obscure body of people called צנועים, *tsenu'im* (Aramaic *tseni'in*), 'the chaste/decent ones',[69] who could be priests that had passed the prime of life and had embraced celibacy, in a kind of retirement; it was to this group of elite among the priesthood that the mysteries of the Holy Name and other divine lore were entrusted (b.Kidd. 71a; Eccles. Rabba 3: 11; j.Yoma 2:3, 39d, 3:3, 40a), which likewise coheres somewhat with Philo's presentation of the Essenes. Kohler wrote that Rabbi Simeon the Tsanua, 'while disregarding the Temple practise, shows a certain contempt for the high priest', and 'appears on all accounts to have been an Essene priest' (t.Kelim 1: 6). In addition, Kohler identified these with the חשאים, *hashsha'im*, 'secret ones', to whom were given secret scrolls concerning the Temple service (t.Yoma 2:7; j.Yoma 3:8, 41a). These people had a special chamber in the Temple where they put their charitable donations, while in every city they had a special secret chamber for their own charity box (t.Peah 4: 6, 16; t.Sheb. 2: 18, cf. m.Shek. 5: 6).[70] Along the same lines,

---

[65] Rachael Elior, *Memory and Oblivion: The Secret of the Dead Sea Scrolls* (Jerusalem: Van Leer Institute and Kibbutz haMeuchad, 2009) (Hebrew). She does not address the issue of why Philo would create a fantasy in order to present the Jewish religion as philosophically superlative, at a time of deep pagan hostility to Jews in Alexandria, given that opponents could simply state that he was dreaming, when they had a host of actual philosophical schools to use as examples. Only a real group would function as rhetorically persuasive.

[66] See Chapter 1, pp. 5–7.

[67] Kohler, 'Essenes,' 224.

[68] Though Josephus assumes the Essenes were already in existence by the time of the Maccabean revolt.

[69] See the definitions and references of Jastrow, 1290–2: צניעות צניע צנוע.

[70] Kaufman Kohler, 'Essenes,' *The Jewish Encyclopedia* (New York: Funk and Wagnalls, 1901–1906), 5: 224–32 at 225–6.

a serious challenge to the notion of Essene absence in the rabbinic corpus has now been presented by Joshua Ezra Burns, who finds the Essenes unnamed in a number of passages, by focusing on behaviour and characteristics rather than on designation.[71]

Such suggestions indicate the fruitful possibilities for further study. It is clearly not the case that the rabbis would have named Ἐσσαῖοι or Ἐσσηνοί as Josephus or Philo named them. Since Philo and Josephus do not indicate that the Essenes call themselves Ἐσσαῖοι as a self-reference, but rather that others call 'certain people among them by the name': λέγονταις τινες παρ αὐτοις ὄνομα Ἐσσαῖοι (*Prob.* 75, so also in Philo, *Hypoth.* 11: 1 they 'are called', καλοῦνται, Ἐσσαῖοι, cf. Josephus, *War* 2: 119) Ἐσσηνοί καλοῦνται), we do not know how the Essenes identified themselves. We do not know how many ways people referred to them, even if 'Herodians' was one such term. However, if the rabbis indicated them in a descriptive way, it is doubtful whether they are referred to specifically by any fixed designation. It was noted above that Philo may indeed have heard of the Ἐσσαῖοι being called ὅσιοι (*Prob.* 75, 91), when this was a translation of a conjectural Palestinian Aramaic word found in later Syriac as *ḥesayya* (pl.),[72] which is attested in singular as translating the word ὅσιος in the Syriac Peshitta (Acts 2: 27; 13: 35; Titus 1: 8).[73] This would then be equivalent to the Hebrew word *Ḥasidim*. But since *ḥasidim* can simply indicate 'pious people' generically, the difficulty then is how one can differentiate between when this may mean 'Essenes' and when this means something broader.

Another strong contender for an underlying Aramaic name remains the term for 'physician', אָסֵי, *'āsē*,[74] a proposition most lucidly defended in recent times by Geza Vermes.[75] Comparative Aramaic dialects support the identification of the word *'āsē* as a standard term for 'physician' or 'healer'; for example, the Hebrew word רֹפֵא, *rapha*, in Exod. 15:26 ('for I, the LORD, am your healer') is translated in the Peshitta (Syriac) as *'āsē*. Related words such as *āsūtha'* or *asyūtha'*, 'cure', *asyīna'*, 'physician', and the Aramaic verb *assī*, 'cure',[76] provide a broad range of Aramaic healing terms which all appear to relate to the name אָסֵי, *'āsē*.

However, if the Essenes were called 'healers', how can we distinguish an individual Essene from an ordinary healer? When it is said that Benjamin the אָסֵי was complaining about rabbis who did not 'permit the raven or forbid the dove' (b.Sanh. 99b), was he saying this as a physician or an Essene?

---

[71] Burns, 'Essene Sectarianism.'
[72] Robert Payne Smith, *A Compendious Syriac Dictionary* (Oxford: OUP, 1903), 150.
[73] Schürer, with Vermes, Millar and Black, *History* ii, 558–9.
[74] Jastrow, 93.
[75] Geza Vermes, 'The Etymology of "Essenes",' *RQ* 2 (1960): 427–43.
[76] Jastrow, 89, 93.

But we do not need to assume that the rabbis ever accepted definitions known from other sources. If *Perushim* could at times substantively be (somewhat mutated) Essenes, as indicated by the comparative data of Epiphanius, and possibly also Justin, so might the *Tseduqim*, in certain situations, for all we know. Yohanon ben Zakkai uses the term 'we' in differentiating himself from the *Perushim* in m.Yad. 4: 6, and yet, as Jack Lightstone has explored,[77] the opinions of the *Perushim* are those endorsed by the rabbis in the Mishnah and the Tosefta. Curiously, though, this comfortable endorsement does not follow through to all the later texts. Daniel Boyarin has pointed out that the *Perushim* can be associated with *minim*; while the 'Pharisees' of the New Testament, for example Gamaliel (e.g. Acts 5: 34), are just rabbis.[78]

Ellis Rivkin has noted that the term *perushim* (avoiding the capital letter) might just as well be 'separatists', and '[o]ne cannot use indiscriminately any and every text in which *perushim* occurs as though the term means "Pharisees"'.[79] However, Rivkin remained confident that where there was a clear debate between *Tseduqim* and *Perushim* the historical Pharisees were meant, resting on an assumption that the *Tseduqim* were at least accurately named (b.Yom. 19; b. Nid. 33b; t.Yom. 1: 8) and were Sadducees.[80]

One problem may be that the names of the groups attested in the extant manuscripts of rabbinic texts are not necessarily original. For example, when a Boethusian appears in t.Yoma 1: 8 a Sadducee appears in b.Yoma 19b; is this because a Boethusian was a Sadducee,[81] or is this simply a random switch, given that a Sadducee is better attested in the earlier literature and therefore more fitting? This illustrates a lack of interest in maintaining the integrity of historical groups. There are other instances: a High Priest pelted with citrons in m.Sukk. 4: 9 becomes a Sadducee High Priest in b.Sukk. 48b. Actually, it was Alexander Jannaeus (*Ant.* 13: 372–4), but was he a Sadducee? Günter Stemberger notes how the term can replace an original reference to *minim*, and therefore discounts these as useful for any analysis.[82] But changes of name could have occurred long before extant manuscripts provide testimony. Nevertheless, because of the language of the 'Zadokite document', found among the Scrolls corpus, with its emphasis on the Zadokite priesthood, as well as the material of the letter known as 4QMMT, the *Tseduqim* in rabbinic literature

---

[77] Jack Lightstone, 'The Pharisees and Sadducees in the Earliest Rabbinic Documents,' in Jacob Neusner and Bruce Chilton (eds), *In Quest of the Historical Pharisees* (Waco, Texas: Baylor University Press, 2007), 255–90.

[78] Boyarin, *Border Lines*, 42, 69.

[79] Ellis Rivkin, 'Who Were the Pharisees,' in Alan J. Avery Peck and Jacob Neusner (eds), *Judaism in Late Antiquity, Part 3* (Leiden: Brill, 2000), 1–30, at 6.

[80] Ibid. p.15.

[81] Safrai and Stern, *Jewish People*, 603–6.

[82] Günther Stemberger, 'The Sadducees: Their History and Doctrines,' in William Horbury, W. D. Davies, and John Sturdy (eds), *The Cambridge History of Judaism 3: The Early Roman Period* (Cambridge: CUP, 1999), 428–43; id. *Jewish Contemporaries*, 38–66.

have been linked with those responsible for the sectarian Dead Sea Scrolls, either as 'Zadokites' proper,[83] or indeed as Sadducees.[84]

While it has been common to equate the *haberim* and *Perushim* of rabbinic literature,[85] which takes us closer to the rabbis, the *haberim*, 'associates', are clearly under the authority of the Sages, the *Ḥakhamim*, who are the rabbis (m. Dem. 2: 3–5), but various *Perushim* make mysterious appearances that are difficult to contextualize, and do not have any obvious association with the *haberim*.

With Rivkin's observations in mind, what we find in the Mishnah is clearly a differentiation between different types of persons who could be called *perushim*, and here we need to employ a lower-case 'p', since these may not be designated as a 'society' as such but simply as a category of persons separated out. In m.Hag. 2: 7 it is stated that to the *perushim* the clothes of an *am ha-arets* (Person of the Land) have *midras* uncleanness, and so the passage goes through degrees of purity leading to ultimate purity. For those who eat the heave-offering, the clothes of *perushim* will impart impurity, for the priests eating the hallowed things, so the clothes of those who eat the heave-offering are impure, and to those who are concerned with sin-offering water, the clothes of the priests concerned with hallowed things impart impurity. The sequence is designed to emphasize the degrees of purity for priests within the Temple operations; the *perushim* here are clearly a starting point within those who are engaged in priestly functions within the Temple. The whole discussion is situated in a discussion about purity within the priesthood serving in the Temple and begins with m.Hag. 2:6: 'If someone [i.e. a priest] immersed himself . . .' with the intention of eating unconsecrated food, then he may not eat consecrated second tithe produce. If he immersed himself with the intention of eating the second tithe produce, he may not use that immersion as being fit for eating the heave-offering, and so on: the man who was immersed in order to eat the heave-offering was not fit to eat the hallowed-things-offering. Therefore, in terms of the development of the theme in m.Hag. 2: 6–7, those who are immediately 'below' those who eat the heave-offering are *priests* who have immersed in order to eat the second tithe. They are separated from the ordinary people, the *amme ha-aretz*, by virtue of their immersion in order to eat consecrated food with the Temple context. The word *perushim* is here then not a term that can be rendered by the word

[83] Joseph M. Baumgarten, 'The Pharisaic-Sadducean Controversies about Purity and the Qumran Text,' *JJS* 31 (1980): 157–70; Ben Zion Wacholder, *The Dawn of Qumran: The Sectarian Torah and the Teacher of Righteousness* (Cincinnati: Hebrew Union College Press, 1983), 141–3.

[84] Most importantly in Lawrence H. Schiffman, *Reclaiming the Dead Sea Scrolls: The History of Judaism, the Background of Christianity, and the Lost Library of Qumran* (Philadelphia: Jewish Publication Society, 1994).

[85] Schurer, with Vermes, Millar, Black, *History*, ii, 388–403.

'Pharisees', as Rivkin indeed concludes.[86] The *perushim* of this passage are not a legal school within Judaism, but—on the basis of behaviour—priests separated off by a higher purity, ready to serve in the Temple.

The same may be said of the instance of m.Toh. 4:12, '"A condition of doubt about common food"—this concerns the cleanness practised by the *perushim*'. Likewise, given the previous usage this would most likely mean priests who have separated themselves by immersion to administer various functions in the Temple. The priests would eat common food together during their Temple service. As Rivkin observed, here too we do not at all necessarily have historical Pharisees, unless their origins are firmly rooted in the priesthood.

In m.Sot. 3: 4 there is a saying of Rabbi Joshua: 'A stupid pious person, a clever sinner, a *perushah* woman and the punishments of the *perushim*—these wear out the world' (cf. b.Sot. 21b). Given the word plays of the first two subjects, who are opposites (stupid/clever versus pious person/sinner), the latter two subjects would also be opposites (woman separated [for punishment] versus punishments from the *perushim*). Here it seems the *perushim* are characterized by inflicting harsh punishments, *makkot*. In j.Sot. 3: 4, 19a the interpretation is that these *makkot perushim* are defined as people who advise those who inherit a father's property not to pay money to his widow: likewise harsh judgements, but the sense is different. The overall context of Sotah—concerning a suspected adulterous woman having to suffer the ordeal of bitter water—and woman's 'lustfulness', seems to indicate that the punishments here are in relation to this, in a Temple context where those who put the woman through the ordeal are priests (who are *perushim*, in accordance with the previous definition). The fact that the term *perushah* relates to a woman in this context indicates one such woman who has been separated out for the stated ordeal, but then immediately afterwards there is a criticism aimed at a group of people so-named, generically, the *perushim*. Rivkin's suspicion about the designation *perushim* may be borne out here also: are these not the priests separated out in order to perform a certain duty of punishment?

As Lightstone presents it, the most important evidence in the Mishnah in terms of historical Pharisees is clustered in m.Yad. 4: 6–8 and in the Tosefta in 1(2): 19–20, with *Tseduqim* and *Perushim* adopting rival legal positions. The rabbis decided in favour of the *Perushim* position, or more especially against the *Tseduqim* position. Lightstone notes that this debate shows 'simply the portrayal of Yohanan's rhetorical (as opposed to legal) prowess at besting the Sadducees in the latter's challenges of Pharisaic law'.[87] In short, all this may make this section of the Mishnah particularly old, and may confirm that the historical Pharisees could be designated *Perushim*, or at the least that the Sages were minded to agree with the *Perushim* as opposed to the *Tseduqim*. But what

---

[86] Contra Herbert Danby, *The Mishnah* (Oxford: OUP, 1933), 214.
[87] Lightstone, 'Sadducees and Pharisees,' 277.

we have in the Mishnah in terms of the wide usage of the term *Perushim* is the notion that others than the historical Pharisees could also be designated by it. And this is then ultimately what may allow us to query a simple *Perushim* = Pharisee equation in other places of the rabbinic corpus and allow that at times we may have a different group reflected, especially in later texts. This is not the place for a thorough analysis of all rabbinic evidence concerning the identity of the *Perushim*, but rather here I wish only to endorse this as a possibility, as one that ultimately explains the perspective of Justin and Epiphanius.

There is one place in the Mishnah where a specific Essene sage may be referred to: the famous Menahem, as described by Josephus, who predicted Herod the Great's rise to kingship. Kaufman Kohler identified him with the Menahem of the Mishnah, who was the predecessor of Shammai.[88] In m.Hag. 2: 2a this Menahem is described as being one of the pairs of sages who oversaw the legal assembly in first-century BCE Jerusalem, the partner of Hillel the Elder. Menahem 'went forth', to be replaced by Shammai. In b.Hag.16b Rabbi Rava states that 'Menahem went forth towards the service of the king, and there went forth with him eighty pairs of students dressed in silk', while in j. Hag. 2:2 (77d) their clothing is described as תירקי זהב, which is usually corrected to סירקי זהב, 'silken garments of gold': the word סירק is a Greek loan word, σηρικόν, meaning 'silken garment' (cf. b.Kidd. 31a).[89] This tradition has been read by Israel Knohl as referring to the Essene Menahem, who predicted the royal ascendency of Herod, according to Josephus (*Ant.* 15: 372–9), but with a reading of the Hebrew as indicating that the disciples were wearing shining armour, leading him to suppose wrongly that there was a militaristic (even Messianic) interest on the part of Menahem.[90] The Hebrew is, however, very unlikely to mean 'shining armour'; instead, there seems to be a disparagement of the disciples of Menahem for wearing extremely fine clothing. The wearing of lavish garments tallies with their portrayal as being in the service of the king, who seems to have absorbed them into his court. There is the implication that the king has donated this extremely luxurious clothing, since this fine apparel is clearly not typical of students, or sages, more of angels.

The name Menahem itself is not so striking, as it was quite common, but the association between a leading sage and 'the king' is interesting. As we have seen, Josephus presents the Essenes as being in a favoured position under Herod; they were treated by the king as if they were more than human: as if they were indeed angels (*Ant.* 15: 378–9). Here, in *Hagigah*, they are dressed as

---

[88] Kohler, 'Essenes,' 224.

[89] Jastrow, *Dictionary*, 988, 1667.

[90] Israel Knohl, *The Messiah before Jesus: The Suffering Servant of the Dead Sea Scrolls* (Berkeley: University of California Press, 2000), 53–60; see the critique by James C. VanderKam and Peter Flint, *The Meaning of the Dead Sea Scrolls* (London: T & T Clark, 2002), 270–2.

angels. There is no explanation in the Mishnah as to why these students should have received such garments.

Josephus' Menahem was active in Jerusalem—teaching students (in the Temple)—at the time the young Herod was himself studying. It has been noted above that the relationship between the Essenes and the Temple was not severed, but that they were permitted a special area of purity (*Ant.* 18: 19). The expression 'went forth' then may imply exactly that: a schism of the Temple court whereby Menahem—now under Herod's patronage—no longer continued to be involved in the main jurisprudential body of Jerusalem. The disparagement of Menahem's departure and association with King Herod, by means of a description of the luxurious clothing of his students, is a device meant to indicate Menahem's moral corruption, indicating a rupture between the Sages and Menahem, after which the Essenes no longer participated in the common court. This likewise corresponds to what we find in Josephus, where it is stated that the Essenes had a separate court (*War* 2: 145). Separation is then the paradigm that governs the presentation of Menahem in b.Hag. 16b; a separation that hinges on association with Herod.

Josephus himself presented a picture of the Essenes that was antithetical to a presentation of Essene moral corruption. He insists that the Essenes wore threadbare clothing and lived a strongly ascetic life. Notwithstanding this being a generally accurate portrayal, the story of the Mishnah may represent an extraordinary gift from Herod of fine, white clothing, recognizing the need for clothing in Essene communities. It would not have been an inappropriate gift, and it is to be remembered that Josephus' presentation of Menahem's prophecy indicates that Menahem was far from condoning Herod's behaviour. Josephus then becomes an Essene apologist at a time when even he could note that the school enjoyed royal favours. Yet, it is in the stories of rabbinic literature that we may get vignettes indicating the resentment against the Essenes from the other side: those who received gifts from Herod were by no means considered positively by everyone. The negative term 'Herodians' trailed after them. They left the council of sages, to become independent of that legal body, at a cost.

CONCLUSIONS

In summary, from this discussion it appears that there is reason to believe that the Essenes continued to exist in the second century in Judaea/Palestine. The Judaean legal societies may have split into sub-groups in the period from 70 to 135, but often groups were not properly distinguished by later authors. Christian authors viewing diverse Jewish interpretative groups tidied things up into a 'seven school' model, which may have had some relevance in terms of naming the memory or actuality of schools in later second-century Palestine, but the veracity of these lists is doubtful. The watershed for Judaean schools was much more likely to have been 135 than 70. After this, a growing rabbinic ascendency, region by region, would create a consensus that could differentiate between the norms of the Sages and diverse forms of *minuth*. By the fourth century, Epiphanius could reach widely and inaccurately in formulating his catalogue of heresies, with occasionally illuminating material included. Epiphanius knows the designation *Perushim*, and matches it with a negative appraisal that may describe the Essenes. He garbles a description of the 'Herodians' without understanding their identity. The issue is then whether *perushim* could at times designate Essenes in rabbinic literature. While this does seem possible, it appears that the term *perushim* can be used in different ways, indicating different types of separation in different contexts, given that designations of groups could change and be loose.

Whatever sects we may identify in the second century, it is important to avoid reading this evidence back to the pre-70 context, and to avoid a Christian definition of αἱρέσεις, so that the concept of a multiplicity of Jewish 'sects' is applied to a time for which there is no evidence for their existence. A growing multiplicity of Jewish 'schools of law' better belongs to a time of social turmoil following the destruction of the Temple, culminating in the Second Revolt.

8

Conclusions: The Essential Essenes

In this survey of the ancient literary material relating to the historical Essenes we have reviewed the way the Essenes are constructed rhetorically and also probed their actuality. If Philo and Josephus are prioritized, then we can see the Essenes as an elite school or society of law, living communally, working manually, keeping a high degree of ritual purity, focusing on the law and its interpretation, contributing to public life, and even leading the fight against Rome (under John the Essene) in the 60s. The Hasmoneans—who opposed them—were not able to lay a finger on them, and they were honoured and protected by the Herodian dynasty. This connection with the Herodian dynasty resulted in the popular designation of 'Herodians': the term used in the Gospel of Mark. By contrast, in Pliny the Essenes are a caricature, described for the sake of presenting a paradoxical wonder. As a result of Pliny, nevertheless, the parody has become the paradigm, and the Essenes have been seen as marginal rather than central.

Nevertheless, Pliny does note the Essene presence beside the Dead Sea, as does Dio Chrysostom, who praised the Essenes, probably in his lost work *Getica*. Their continued existence is attested into the second century, along with other Jewish legal schools, and it may be that in the complex rabbinic references to a variety of groups, including the *Perushim*, we may find allusions to the Essenes: in these cases they may be obscured behind different names, but they are by no means entirely absent. Supposed characteristics of the Essenes such as a rejection of the Temple, vegetarianism, extreme insularity, adoption of small children, or pacifism have no basis in the ancient texts and result from faulty readings.

If we are now to draw up a list of features of the historical Essenes, on the basis of the soundest elements of the sources surveyed, we would have to conclude that collectively they had the reputation of being the most pre-eminent of all Jews in the first century CE. The Essenes were an esteemed αἵρεσις, 'choice', for men of a certain education who could choose to belong to a legal society that relied on distinctive interpretations of the Mosaic law as providing ground rules for a lifestyle. They could be seen then, in Graeco-Roman terms, as a type of philosophical school, though this correlation needs to take into account the important difference between the philosophical schools of the ancient Mediterranean and Judaism: in Judaea these 'schools' worked within a justice system, under the ultimate authority of the High Priest. From the sources examined here it would appear that from the first part of the second century BCE to the civil war of 66 CE there were three of these 'schools' or 'societies' of Jewish law which had authority to establish rulings in courts and fix Temple procedures: the Pharisees, the Sadducees, and the Essenes. After this date a fourth 'school' was added, given the revolutionary government of Jerusalem.

Essenes were not thought of as new: they claimed a noble and ancient precedent, given the stress on their antiquity (Josephus, *Ant.* 18: 20; Pliny, *Nat. Hist.* 5: 15 [73]); their interpretation of scripture was said to be according to an ancient tradition (Philo, *Prob.* 82) and their communal life was thought to have been taught by Moses (Philo, *Hypoth.* 11: 1).

The Essenes were not a small group, but had a relatively large number of adherents in terms of their category, i.e. over 4,000 at any one time: 'many' or a 'throng' (Josephus, *Ant.* 18: 20; Philo, *Hypoth.* 11: 1; *Prob.* 75), 'multitudes' and 'huge numbers' (Pliny, *Hist. Nat.* 5: 15 [73]). There were large numbers in every town of Judaea/Syria Palestine (Josephus, *War* 2: 124; Philo, *Hypoth.* 11: 1; but cf. *Prob.* 75–6 where only villages are mentioned), and they were second numerically only to the Pharisees (about 6,000 men), outnumbering the Sadducees by far (Josephus, *War* 2: 119; *Ant.* 13: 171–2; 18: 18; *Life* 10–12). They had a reputation for avoiding polemical debate with the other societies, focusing instead on the practice of their own lifestyle (Philo, *Prob.* 88).

They were active in Jerusalem (Josephus, *Ant.* 13: 171–2; *Ant.* 15: 371–9), and in this city there was a 'Gate of the Essenes' (Josephus, *War* 5: 145), for their use, built into part of the Herodian palace complex, the name being retained even when circumstances did not allow for this, when the palace was used by the Roman prefects as a *praetorium*. They played an active role in teaching in the Temple (Josephus, *War* 1: 78–80; 2: 562–7; *Ant.* 13: 311–13; 18: 19). In addition, they had a presence in the Judaean sector of the Dead Sea coast, probably to the north of En Gedi (Pliny, *Nat. Hist.* 5: 15 [73]; Synesius, *Dio* 3: 2; Solinus, *Collectanea* 35: 9–12).

The Essenes could gain priestly public office, in which they were believed to have maintained humility and acted honestly (Josephus, *War* 2: 140). Nevertheless, such office aside, most of the Essenes maintained themselves by living a simple life of τέχναι—craftwork—and agriculture (Josephus, *War* 2: 129; *Ant.* 18: 19; Philo, *Prob.* 76; *Hypoth.* 11: 8–9). They lived with their colleagues communally (Philo, *Prob.* 85; Josephus, *Hypoth.* 11: 1, 5; *Ant.* 18: 21) rather than in family units.

In terms of their names, they were called, in positive terms, *Essaioi* or *Essenoi* (in Greek) (e.g. *War* 2: 119; *Prob.* 75; Synesius, *Dio* 3: 2), or *Esseni* (in Latin) (Pliny, *Nat. Hist.* 5: 15 [73]), but could also be dubbed 'Herodians' (Mark

3: 6; 8: 15; 12: 23; Matt. 16: 68), or perhaps also, later on, *Perushim*, given their separation for the sake of purity, though this term seems originally to have been employed cultically in terms of serving priests (m.Hag. 2: 6–7; m.Toh. 4: 12; m. Sot. 3: 4). For this reason *Perushim* were not considered to be identical with the Ḥakhamim, the sages (e.g. m.Yad. 4: 6, cf. Justin, *Dial.* 80: 3–4).

In terms of their participation in defining law, the Essene rulings were contained in a jurisdiction that enabled them to maintain their own court (Philo, *Prob.* 89–91), made up of no fewer than one hundred men, which even had the right to give judgements of death for blasphemy (Josephus, *War* 2: 145). They concerned themselves with correct interpretation of Sabbath law for all Jews (Mark 3: 6; 8: 15; 12: 23; Matt. 16: 68), and were not just inward-looking. Their ability to exercise self-government, and administer justice to all who called on their authority, enabled them to be considered a *polis* (Synesius, *Dio* 3: 2), in a world in which cities each had their own legal autonomy, perhaps functioning as Jewish courts functioned in Egypt, within the *politeuma* there, technically subsumed to the High Priest's authority, but in practice having a great degree of autonomy.

In terms of entry into the society of the Essenes, a young man (Josephus, *Life* 1–12) through to mature or elderly (Philo, *Prob.* 76–7; *Hypoth.* 11: 2), could join. A newcomer was not accepted without testing, and had to submit to a strict entry procedure, designed to prove merit (Solinus, *Collectanea* 35: 9–12), consisting of a year of probation followed by another two years, after which he had to swear many oaths (Josephus, *War* 2: 137–42). Many of the Essenes were quite elderly (Philo, *Hypoth.* 11: 3, 7), perhaps leading to a belief in Essene longevity (Josephus, *War* 2: 151). The first-year students were selected by senior teachers and held to be their 'relatives', their sons, since they were taught as fathers teach their own sons (Josephus, *War* 1: 78; 2: 120; *Ant.* 13: 311).

Once within the society, an Essene could be expelled in the case of wrong-doing (for a small thing only: Solinus, *Collectanea* 35: 9–12; for serious wrongdoing: Josephus, *War* 2: 143–4).

The Essenes were reputed to be celibate, some probably never marrying (Josephus, *War* 2: 120–1; Pliny, *Nat. Hist.* 5: 15 [73]), others having wives who were not included in the community when possessions were shared, since they believed wives living with them could cause problems for community living (Josephus, *Ant.* 18: 21; Philo, *Hypoth.* 11: 14–17), and purity (Josephus, *War* 2: 120–1). Those with wives did not live differently to those that were entirely celibate, but married in order to ensure they had physical offspring (Josephus, *War* 2: 160–1). Given this, we may suppose that their wives may then have lived in separate women's communities, also following Essene purity regulations. Women had their own entrance procedures to the Essene way of life, and required proof of fertility and also immersed prior to pure meals

(Josephus, *War* 2: 160–1). No Essenes cohabited with their wives, children, or extended families.

The Essenes had in their communities shared clothing and meals (Philo, *Prob.* 86, cf. 91; *Hypoth.* 11: 4–5, 10, 12; Josephus, *Ant.* 18: 20; *War* 2: 122, 129–32). Their clothing was plain white, devoid of colour (Josephus, *War* 2: 123), consisting very simply of a thick mantle for winter and a lighter one for summer (Philo, *Hypoth.* 11: 12), items kept in use until threadbare (Josephus, *War* 2: 127). They did not care about their appearance, and rejected the use of [perfumed] oil because looking rough was their goal, so they scraped off oil if it touched them (Josephus, *War* 2: 123).

They had a common fund into which wages for work went (Philo, *Prob.* 86) supervised by a treasurer who did all the buying (Philo, *Hypoth.* 11: 10). Out of this, all costs of medical treatment were paid for, with younger members looking after the older ones (Philo, *Prob.* 87; *Hypoth.* 11: 13). Such money-earning labour was concerned with artisanal crafts (Philo, *Prob.* 76) including agriculture, shepherding, cow-herding, animal husbandry, and bee-keeping (Philo, *Hypoth.* 11: 6–9; Josephus, *War* 2: 129; *Ant.* 18: 18). They were not interested in commerce, pleasure, or luxury, and rejected individual property-ownership or hoarding of money in favour of communal ownership (Philo, *Prob.* 76–8; *Hypoth.* 11: 4; Josephus, *War* 2: 120, 122). They exchanged personal things among themselves and shared (Josephus, *War* 2: 127), thus they had 'no money' in terms of individuals (Pliny, *Nat. Hist.* 5: 15 [73]).

Essene community leaders were overseers who were elected democratically by a show of hands (Josephus, *War* 2: 123, 129, 134), though it is not said whether the pool of these leaders had to come from the category of the priests. The prime role of priests in their society was maintained, since they were placed in key positions: preparing the meal as bakers and cooks, blessing the food, and leading prayers (Josephus, *Ant.* 18: 22; *War* 2: 129–33). Indeed, there was a somewhat 'priestly' understanding of their lifestyle, since—unlike the way some priestly service might only concern the Temple—their whole life was configured as a service to God (Philo, *Prob.* 75).

They rejected slavery as unjust (Philo, *Prob.* 79; Josephus, *Ant.* 18: 21), so at mealtimes they were not served by slaves (as in elite households), but rather by the priestly baker and cook (Josephus, *War* 2: 130).

They could travel easily, since incomers from other communities were welcomed and supplied with all their needs (Josephus, *War* 2: 124–5). They carried arms when travelling (Josephus, *War* 2: 125) and could fight in battle (see John the Essene, *War* 2: 567; *War* 3: 11, 19). Their life involved a strict daily routine of prayer, purifications, and meals (Josephus, *War* 2: 128–33). In this regimen they got up before sunrise and said ancient prayers directed to the east (the rising sun) and sang a hymn, before going about their tasks (Hippolytus, *Haer.* 9: 21).

They assembled to purify their bodies at the fifth hour (11 a. m.) and also at the end of the day, before dinner. In purifications they wore a linen loincloth, after which they went to a private room, which they treated as if it were a holy place, to eat a meal. They put their linen loincloths away afterwards in a vestibule as if they were priestly vestments (Josephus, *War* 2: 129–33, Hippolytus, *Haer.* 9: 21). These meals were considered to be 'sacred and pure' (Porphyry, *Abstin.* 4: 12: 3). Outside the communities, Essenes could die of starvation since they would not eat food that was not pure (Josephus, *War* 2: 144).

Despite all this communality, the rendering of assistance to those in need, and charity, was left up to individual discretion, but members of the society could not give to relatives without permission from the overseers (Josephus, *War* 2: 134).

The Essenes, like all Jews, rested on the sabbath and assembled in synagogues for reading scripture and teaching (Philo, *Prob.* 81–2). The sabbath was so important to them that they prepared food the day before to avoid kindling a fire, did not carry any objects, and avoided defecating, which they otherwise did by adopting the highest standards of cleanliness and modesty, digging a hole in their isolated toileting areas, using a small hatchet or axe, and covering their bodies (Josephus, *War* 2: 147).

The practice of continual purification was not necessarily just twice a day before meals (Philo, *Prob.* 84; Josephus, *Ant.* 18: 19; *War* 2: 129), since they thought that if a junior member touched a senior it would constitute defilement (Josephus, *War* 2: 150). This goes to show that they would have considered touching outsiders even more defiling. Not surprisingly, then, they avoided the common precincts of the Temple, because of their different (more fastidious) purifications, to avoid being defiled in the Temple precincts, after they had purified, and performed their sacrifices there by themselves in a special area of the Temple (Josephus, *Ant.* 18: 19). They also honoured the Temple by sending votive gifts (Josephus, *Ant.* 18: 19).

In public testimonies they avoided any swearing of oaths to insist they were telling the truth by appealing to God (Philo, *Prob.* 84; Josephus, *War* 2: 135), though they did swear oaths of affirmation in joining the order and vowed to be virtuous in many ways (Josephus, *War* 2: 139).

They accepted that all rulers were placed in power by God (Josephus, *War* 2: 140); in fact, they had such an emphasis on destiny that they thought that all events were determined by God (Josephus, *Ant.* 13: 171–3; *Ant.* 18: 18; Solinus, *Collectanea* 35: 9–12). With this belief, and with their exceptional ways, they excelled as masters of prediction, using dream interpretation, the interpretation of sacred books and sayings of the prophets, and various purifications (Josephus, *War* 2: 159), with noted masters being Judas (Josephus, *War* 1: 78–80; *Ant.* 13: 310–14), Simon (*War* 2: 112–13 and *Ant.* 17: 345–8), and Menahem (*Ant.* 15: 371–9).

Despite the Hasmoneans being the antithesis of the Essenes, they could not harm them (Philo, *Prob.* 89–91). In terms of Herod, given Menahem's prediction that he would rule—based on Genesis 49: 10 (Eusebius, *Hist. Eccles.* 1: 6)—he exempted them from an oath of loyalty and honoured them enormously (Philo, *Hypoth.* 11: 18; Josephus, *Ant.* 15: 371–9); indeed, in terms of reputation they were held to be virtuous and seemed to act with great worthiness (Josephus, *War* 2: 119). They also had a vow that if they were ever rulers themselves, they would be just and not show any superiority (Josephus, *War* 2: 140).

They had a great interest in ancient writings, looking for those that would profit soul and body (Josephus, *War* 2: 136). In terms of the soul, in their Scriptural interpretations they practised allegorical exegesis according to ancient tradition (Philo, *Prob.* 82; Josephus, *Ant.* 18: 11, 20). This was important because they believed in the immortality of the 'soul' (Josephus, *Ant.* 18: 18), and in subsequent rewards and punishments (Josephus, *War* 2: 154–7). As for the body, they very devotedly studied medicinal roots, remedies, and the properties of stones in order to treat diseases (Josephus, *War* 2: 136), since they believed that nothing was created in vain (Hippolytus, *Haer.* 9: 22).

This examination therefore constitutes a major revision of the basic conceptualization of the Essenes, their history, and their role in Second Temple Judaism, in removing them from the perimeters and putting them in the centre. It also asks questions about whether we should see Second Temple Judaism as a whole as 'sectarian'. At the very beginning, we considered the way that the Essenes have been presented in scholarship, finding in Christian research a tendency to alienate the Essenes from the rest of Judaism, so that they stood apart as a type of Judaism that prefigured Christianity: spiritual, ascetic, and monastic. This was possible in an ambiance that would see Judaism of the time of Jesus as lacking a spiritual dimension, as being far too caught up with matters of law and praxis. This image sprang particularly from Lutheran theology that distinguished Christianity, as a religion of faith and grace, from Judaism, as the religion of works.

It was noted that challenges to the concept of the marginality of the Essenes as a whole have come from the Groningen school, with the Essenes being roughly equivalent to what they call 'Enochic' Judaism, a type of Judaism arising in the third century BCE and constituting the main type of Judaism until the destruction of the Temple, though they tend to accept the marginality of those responsible for the Dead Sea Scrolls.[1] The Qumran Essenes themselves have been reconfigured by Harmut Stegemann who, on the basis of close readings of the Scrolls material, has envisaged the Essenes (identified as the

---

[1] Gabriele Boccacini, *Beyond the Essene Hypothesis: The Parting of the Ways between Qumran and Enochic Judaism* (Grand Rapids: Eerdmans, 1998); id. *Enoch and Qumran Origins: New Light on a Forgotten Connection* (Grand Rapids: Eerdmans, 2005).

authors) as being the main Jewish *yaḥad*, 'union', opposed to the Hasmoneans, a movement that continued with the support of Herod and his dynasty: the Qumran Essenes are simply one part of the whole.[2] In addition, in the recent work of Michael Stone, major questions are asked about the nature of Second Temple Judaism.[3] It is a far more robustly variegated phenomenon than previously assumed.

The Scrolls are not the subject of our investigation here. Rather, we have examined the surviving ancient written evidence for the Essenes that exists outside the Scrolls. We can nevertheless conclude that Stegemann's reading of the Scrolls—assuming that their authors are Essenes—matches our conclusions about the nature of this society quite well.

But can we assume that the authors of the Scrolls are Essenes? In order to answer this question, we must look at other ancient evidence. We must consider the Scrolls as physical artefacts found in caves on the western side of the Dead Sea. In order to contextualize them, we must concern ourselves with the history of a region, and the ways that the Hasmonean dynasty and Herod the Great developed it, in order to determine a historical chronology. We need to investigate the Dead Sea's remarkable products, particularly those that were valued for medicine. And so we turn to Part II of our enquiry.

---

[2] Harmut Stegeman, 'The Qumran Essenes—Local Members of the Main Jewish Union in Second Temple Times,' in Juan T. Barrera and Luis V. Montaner (eds), *The Madrid Qumran Congress. Proceedings of the International Congress on the Dead Sea Scrolls, Madrid, 18–21 March*, I (Leiden: Brill, 1992), 83–166; id. *The Library of Qumran: On the Essenes, Qumran, John the Baptist and Jesus* (Grand Rapids: Eerdmans, 1998).

[3] Michael Stone, *Ancient Judaism: New Visions and Views* (Grand Rapids: Eerdmans, 2011).

Part II

The Dead Sea, The Essenes, and the Scrolls

13

14

15

16

17

18

19

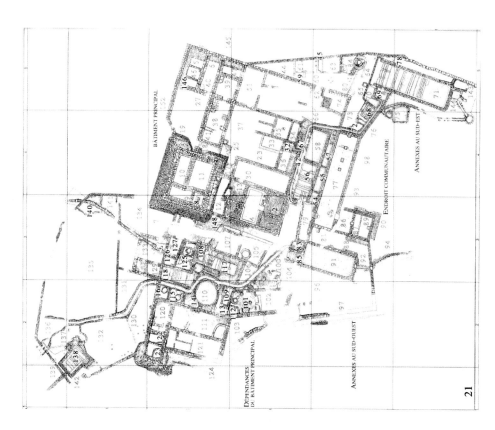

BÂTIMENT PRINCIPAL

DÉPENDANCES
DU BÂTIMENT PRINCIPAL

ANNEXES AU SUD-OUEST

ENDROIT COMMUNAUTAIRE

ANNEXES AU SUD-EST

21

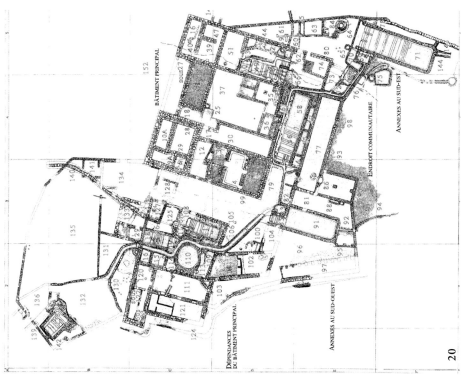

BÂTIMENT PRINCIPAL

DÉPENDANCES
DU BÂTIMENT PRINCIPAL

ANNEXES AU SUD-OUEST

ENDROIT COMMUNAUTAIRE

ANNEXES AU SUD-EST

20

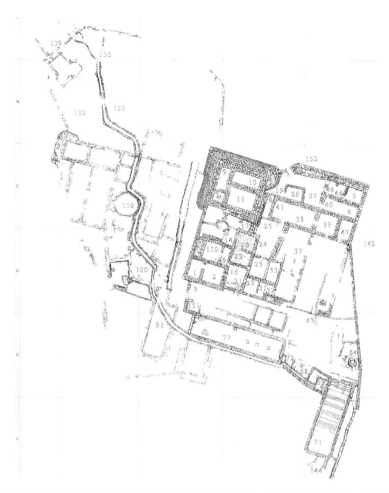

25

26

27

28

29

30

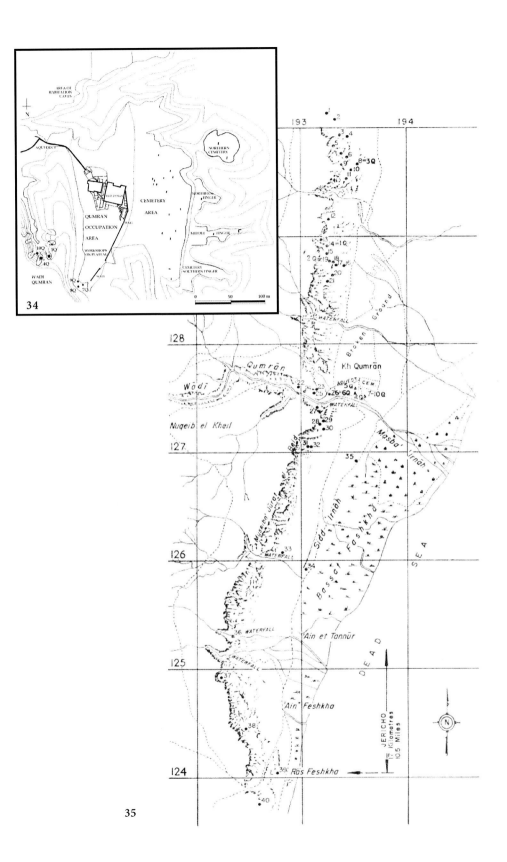

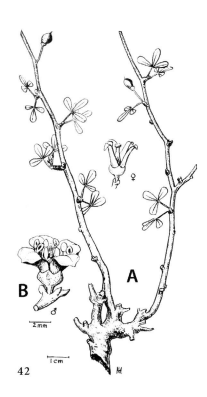

44A

44B

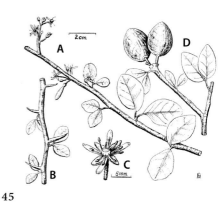

45

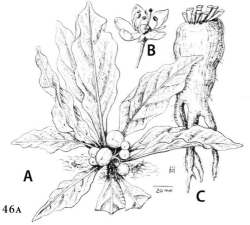

46A

46B

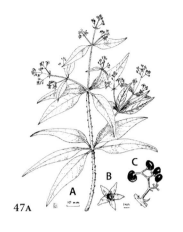

47A

48

47B

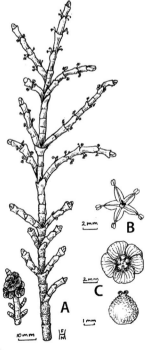

49A

49B

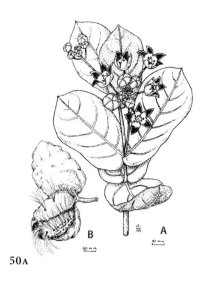

50A

50B

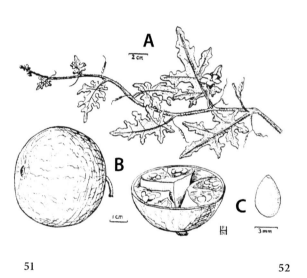

51

52

53

9

The History of the Dead Sea

The Dead Sea is 67 km long and—at its maximum—18 km wide. This is a small lake by global standards, yet it is one of the world's most remarkable places. The water of the Dead Sea contains a large amount of mineral salts (28–33 per cent potassium, natron, chlorine, with compounds of manganese, calcium, and bromide), a concentration about four to six times higher than the proportion of these in the Mediterranean Sea. The minerals can form encrustations, as if the rocks of the shoreline are covered in ice. It can even create white sculpturesque shapes that protrude from the surface. On hot days it is misty; the other side of the lake fades away in haze. Added to this, the lake is the lowest point on earth, 422 m. below sea level (and descending), and its air temperature is invariably several degrees hotter than that of the higher land around it. There is little rainfall, only 50 mm annually. It forms a natural geographical barrier, though in times past there was more activity on its waters than today. This is a great earthquake rift, and the two shores—west and east—are different. On the west, there is a wider stretch of flattish land close to the water than on the east, where often the sheer faces of towering sandstone mountains rise up dramatically from a slim roadway skirting the water's edge, too huge and imposing to capture successfully on camera.

On both sides wadis carve out channels for fresh rainwater to tumble into the lake, its origins high in the hills, which are in the east much higher than in the west. In these wadis and valleys, or close to springs, palm trees and other wild plants manage to grow, creating splashes of green on a cream and brown backdrop. The most remarkable of the valleys of the Dead Sea is the Wadi Mujib, known as the Arnon in antiquity, a continual torrent on the eastern side that lies directly opposite the natural oasis of En Gedi in the west. The springs of En Gedi and the torrent of the Wadi Mujib together create a watery halfway point on either side of the lake.

It is a curious phenomenon that, in the midst of much aridity, freshwater springs irrigate zones of extraordinary lushness. The desert sits side by side with regions of farming and fertility. The sweet waters bubbling up from the earth contrast with the acrid waters of the lake. It is no wonder that people throughout the ages have been struck by the paradoxes of this remarkable landscape.

The Dead Sea's peculiar nature as a mass of water too salty to sustain life was, from time immemorial, reflected upon by the people who lived in its region; and people have lived here for millennia. Far from being a place rejected as a site for habitation, the archaeology of the Dead Sea region indicates that there were settlements dating back to the fifth millennium BCE (at En Gedi, Nahal Arugot, and Teleilat al-Ghassoul). At Bab edh-Dhra, on the south-eastern end of the lake near the protruding Lisan (the 'tongue'), a town has been excavated dating to the Early Bronze age (3150–3000 BCE) with an adjacent huge cemetery of pit graves containing no fewer than 20,000 burials.[1] The town must have been supported by an industry associated with the locality; clearly, humans made use of resources of the lake very early on, farming in the rich alluvial plain east and south-east of the Lisan. Other Early Bronze age settlements are now known as existing further to the south at Numeira, Safi, Feifa, and Khanazir. The aetiological legends of the inhabitants of these settlements of the Dead Sea are long gone, but what we have are the possible residues of these in a legend of Genesis. So influential were they that we will need to reflect upon them at the outset. We will do so very briefly using a narrative-critical approach, with a focus on the 'character' of water.[2]

GENESIS

In Genesis, the area that we know as the Dead Sea was the site of a cataclysm affecting five cities. In Genesis 10: 19 we are told that the land of Canaan spread from west to east from Gerar near Gaza to 'Sodom, Gomorrah, Admah and Zeboim, near Lesha'. In addition, there was Bela or Zoar (see Gen. 14: 3), all located in the Valley of Siddim, where there were 'bitumen wells' (Gen. 14: 10). The story goes that Chedor-Laomer and his allies vanquished the kings of these cities (the kings of Sodom and Gomorra). Falling into the 'bitumen wells' as they retreat, their cities are taken. Lot, Abram's brother, is captured, but the victors then are themselves defeated by Abram, who rescues Lot and his household and possessions, and refuses to take war booty as payment (Gen. 14: 13–24).

---

[1] R. Thomas Schaub and Walter E. Rast, *Bab edh-Dhra': Excavations in the Cemetery Directed by Paul Lapp* (Winona Lake: Eisenbrauns, 1989); id. Bab edh-Dhra': Excavations at the Town Site (1975–1981) (Winona Lake, IN: Eisenbrauns, 2003).

[2] Robert Alter, *The Art of Biblical Narrative* (New York: Basic Books, 1981); Jan Fokkelman, *Reading Biblical Narrative: an Introductory Guide* (Louisville: Westminster John Knox, 1999).

It is clear from this account that the Valley of Siddim in which the cities lay was understood to have once been a plain (Gen. 13: 12; 19: 25), a flat valley between the hills of the east and the mountains of the west, filled with useful 'bitumen wells', as if bitumen could be found like oil at the bottom of a deep pit. Genesis 19: 24–9 goes on to tell us that this lucrative valley was incinerated after God hailed down fire and brimstone. Abraham saw 'smoke rising up from the ground, like smoke from a furnace' (Gen. 19: 28): the ground in which the bitumen was sealed beneath thus broke open. Only Zoar, where Lot fled, was spared destruction.

Essentially this is recognizable as an aetiological myth that accounts for the peculiarities of the environment. It was necessary to explain the geography: from the perfect template of the earth as made by God, there needed to be an explanation for the odd characteristics of the Dead Sea.

In this perfect creation, water is the primary substance (Gen. 1: 1–2), and the earth is formed after God separates out the waters: 'Let there be a barrier through the middle of the waters to divide the waters into two parts. And it was so. God made the barrier, and it divided the waters under the barrier from the waters above the barrier. God called the barrier "sky"' (Gen. 1: 6–7). The waters are then gathered into one place and called 'seas', dry land appears, 'and God saw that it was good' (Gen. 1: 10). God commands, 'Let the waters swarm with swarms of life forms . . . and God created great sea-creatures, and every life form that moves with which the waters swarmed after their kind . . . and God saw that it was good and God blessed them, saying, "Be fruitful and multiply, and fill the waters in the seas . . ."' (Gen. 1: 20–2). With this kind of basic template established of 'good' seas filled with aquatic creatures, the Dead Sea was a glaring anomaly.

The 'good' Valley of Siddim then became the 'bad' Salt Sea (Gen. 14: 3; Num. 34: 3, 12; Deut. 3: 17; Josh. 3: 16, 12: 3, 15: 5), also called the Sea of Arabah (Gen. 15: 2, 5; 18: 19; Deut. 3: 17; 4: 49; Josh. 3: 16; 2 Kings 14: 25) and the Eastern Sea (Joel 2: 20; Ezek. 47: 18; Zech. 14: 8), or just 'the sea' (2 Chron. 20: 2). The 'Sea of Arabah' is really a very poignant term: עֲרָבָה simply means 'desert', the assumption being it is an area of lifelessness, the very opposite of the seas created in Genesis 1. A paradox was built into its very name: 'the Desertified Sea'. It was 'bad' as a result of a cataclysm caused by the bad behaviour of the people of Sodom, in particular because of their request to rape Lot's guests (Gen. 13: 11; 19: 1–26).

Not all the aetiological components to account for the characteristics of the Dead Sea are explicitly stated in this narrative, but they are nevertheless implied. The River Jordan originally flowed throughout the 'valley of the Jordan', which was 'well watered everywhere . . . like the Garden of YHWH, like the land of Egypt coming into Zoar' (Gen. 13: 10). 'The land of Egypt coming into Zoar' is actually the continuation of the valley south around the oasis area of Zoar, on the road to Egypt, and indicates Judaean knowledge of this vicinity. It is one of the zones of lush fertility, paralleled in the north in the area of Jericho, where the land is fed by sweet aquifers and springs. The understanding appears to have been that the plain in between these two sites of Zoar and Jericho was once even lusher, like the Garden of Eden. The contrast between Jericho—as the 'city of palm trees' (Deut. 34: 3; Judges 1: 16, 3: 13; 2 Chron. 28: 15)—and the barren region of the salty lake was clearly an anomaly.

The Genesis legend indicates that the perfect creation of the Plain was inverted as a divine punishment for the social inversion of the customs of hospitality: the desire to rape (and murder) guests being the antithesis of divine will.[3] God therefore destroyed the towns and the fertile land all around them by hailing down fire and brimstone, and by the breaking up of the surface of the earth also. The water of the Jordan filled up the Plain, stopped up somehow in its southern part to create a great basin where the bitumen continued to be belched out from beneath, contaminating the waters and creating conditions where there was no life in this particular 'sea'. The judgement on the towns continues into the present of the narrative, the 'now', by revealing this odd circumstance at the bottom of the lake: where the towns were located, the ground still remains unstable, the bitumen once mined by their kings is now haemorrhaging into the water. This 'now' of the legend reflects two things: that there is a resource of valuable bitumen and that it is the prerogative of royal rulers to 'mine' it.

Likewise, the salt of the vicinity is introduced in the legend as a kind of curse. In fleeing Sodom, Lot's unnamed wife disobeys God by looking back at the destruction of the city, and is turned into a 'pillar of salt' (Gen. 19: 26).

In Genesis too there is another resource that would feature in descriptions of the region of the Dead Sea: balsam. This 'Balsam of Gilead' appears in Gen. 37: 25. The sons of the patriarch Israel, who have just thrown their brother Joseph down a pit, are approached by 'a caravan of Ishmaelites . . . coming from Gilead, with their camels bearing נכאת, צרי and לט, going towards Egypt'. All of these words indicate some types of resins, gums, or saps, but צרי is usually identified as the sap from *Commiphora gileadensis* (Linneaus),[4] an aromatic, medium-sized evergreen tree or shrub 2–5 m high, Pliny's opobalsam.

When Israel asks his sons to go to Egypt for food, once Joseph has risen to a great and powerful position, he tells them to take the 'best produce of the land', the very products the merchants that took Joseph to Egypt were trading,

---

[3] The crime of the inversion of hospitality has been much explored in recent studies; see Ronald Hendel, Chana Kronfeld, and Ilana Pardes, 'Gender and Sexuality,' in Ronald Hendel (ed.), *Reading Genesis: Ten Methods* (Cambridge: CUP, 2010), 71–91, at 77–9.

[4] Michael Zohary, *Plants of the Bible* (Cambridge: CUP, 1982); F. Nigel Hepper, *Planting a Bible Garden* (London: Lion Hudson, 2000), 84–5.

including the resins: נכאת, צרי and לט (Gen. 43: 11). The 'balsam in Gilead' mentioned in Jer. 8: 22, צרי בגלעד, is clearly indicated as having healing and pain-killing properties (cf. Jer. 51: 5) and is prized by the Egyptians (Jer. 46: 11). It is noted as an important trade item in Ezekiel 27: 17. However, the growing of balsam within Judaea itself is not evidenced in any biblical literature; it is consistently located as coming from Gilead. This long region of Moab (Deut. 1: 5; 32: 49) lay on the eastern side of the Jordan Valley and the Dead Sea, stretching from the River Yarmuk in the north to the Wadi Numeira and beyond, though where exactly it ended in the south seems variable.[5] The opobalsam plant requires high temperatures to thrive, and can only have been grown in the heat of the area adjacent to the lower Jordan Valley and Dead Sea. Not even En Gedi is said to be a place for growing balsam; En Gedi has palm trees (Wisdom of Solomon 24: 14) and henna (Song of Songs 1:14), but balsam is never mentioned.

In terms of the possible zones for the propagation of balsam in Gilead, there are even now only a few areas where the combination of intense heat, fertile soil, and fresh water exists: the region to the east of the lower Jordan River (north of the Dead Sea), the Wadi Zarqa Main, a small zone around Callirhoe, and the eastern part of the Lisan near Bab edh-Dhra, if Gilead stretched that far south.

GREEK AND ROMAN COMMENTATORS ON THE DEAD SEA: A CHRONOLOGICAL APPROACH

The fact that the Dead Sea was a place of mystery and paradox to western writers of antiquity, as well as a locality of valuable resources, has been explored in various syntheses of their writings, particularly by Jürgen Zangenberg.[6] In the present discussion, however, the known sources will be reviewed

---

[5] Eusebius, Joan Taylor (ed.), with Greville Freeman-Grenville (trans.), and Rupert Chapman, *The Onomasticon by Eusebius of Caesarea: Palestine in the Fourth Century A.D.* (Jerusalem: Carta, 2003), 132; Avraham Negev and Shimon Gibson (eds), *Archaeological Encyclopedia of the Holy Land* (New York/London: Continuum, 2001), 202.

[6] See Jürgen Zangenberg, 'Das Tote Meer in neutestamentlicher Zeit,' in E. A. Knauf, U. Hübner, and R. Wenning (eds), *Nach Petra und ins Königreich der Nabatäer: Festschrift Manfred Lindner* (Bonner Biblische Beoiträge 118; Bodenheim: Beltz Athenäum, 1998), 49–59; id. 'Opening Up our View: Khirbet Qumran in Regional Perspective,' in Douglas R. Edwards (ed.), *Religion and Society in Roman Palestine: Old Questions, New Approaches* (London/New York: Routledge, 2004), 170–87; id. 'Wildnis unter Palmen? Khirbet Qumran in regionalen Kontext des Toten Meers,' in Bernard Mayer (ed.), *Jericho und Qumran: Neues zum Umfeld der Bibel* (Regensburg: Friedrich Pustet, 2000), 129–63; id. 'Die hellenistisch-romische Zeit am Toten Meer,' in Jürgen Zangenberg (ed.), *Das Toten Meer: Kultur und Geschichte am Tiefsten Punkt der Erde* (Mainz: Philipp von Zabern Verlag, 2010), 39–52.

chronologically. In this arrangement, descriptions of the Dead Sea will be considered in order of the first known writer to describe features of the area in a particular way, not by means of the chronology of the extant accounts. In looking to the source texts, even if later quoted and redacted, this enables us to construct a history of the region on the basis of the literary material. In our survey of ancient sources on the Essenes, the rhetoric and purposes of the authors was of concern, since it was important to consider the way actuality and sources were shaped for particular reasons, despite the ultimate purpose of the exercise being to consider historical reality. In this chapter the concern is with the earliest source material since, historically, it is only by rightly assigning our evidence to specific time periods that we can learn of a progression of real developments in the Dead Sea region. The time periods of the sources are critical in establishing a chronological sequence, indicative of changing historical circumstances. The concern here is then with the primary material, though of course later authors invariably adapted and selected from it, employing it for their own reasons, and altering vocabulary. Nevertheless, their 'updating' tends not to mask the chronological indicators of their sources. In addition, archaeological material will be noted in connection with the sources surveyed, as will considerations of landscape.

Aristotle (384–322 BCE)

Outside biblical literature, the Dead Sea is first mentioned in the surviving texts from the ancient world in the writings of Aristotle, who states in *Meteorologica* 2: 3 (359a):[7]

> If it was as some people recount, [there] is a certain lake in Palestine, in which if anyone binds a man or beast and throws him into it he floats and does not sink beneath the water; . . . they say the lake is so bitter and salty that no fish live in it and that if you soak clothes in it and shake them it cleans them. All of the following facts support our hypothesis that there is some material of the earth in the water that makes it salty.

There is no prior written text referred to by Aristotle, but rather he is reporting what he has heard from certain people. This indicates that there was scientific discussion of the lake's bizarre properties already in the Greek world of the fourth century BCE, and these features would have attracted observers. The dominant feature of the lake of interest to Aristotle was its saltiness, a feature

---

[7] For Greek text see Aristotle, *Meteorologica*, H. D. P. Lee (ed.) (Loeb Classical Library; London/Cambridge, MA: Heinemann/Harvard University Press, 1952); Menahem Stern, *Greek and Latin Authors on Jews and Judaism*, 2 vols (Winona Lake: Eisenbrauns, 1974, 1980), I, 7.

of the earth that creates the lake's capacity to kill fish, support bodies, and cleanse clothing (salt being a natural cleansing agent). The popularity of Aristotle's *Meteorologica* and also the (largely lost) later commentaries on it, such as that by Alexander of Aphrodisias (200 CE),[8] ensured that the lake of Palestine became famous.

Hieronymous of Cardia (*c.*370–280 BCE), *apud* Diodorus Siculus

In the *Bibliotheca Historica* of Diodorus Siculus, dating to the first century BCE,[9] a source is used that enables him to describe the curious lake in two places very similarly: *Bibl.* 2: 48: 6–9 and 19: 98–100. In Book 19 the discussion of the lake, here called Lake Asphaltitis (19: 98: 1), appears in the context of the wars of Antigonus Monophthalmus (382–301 BCE), more particularly the campaign of his son Demetrius Poliorcetes against the Nabataeans in 311 BCE. The information Diodorus provides is cited as deriving from a source contemporary to the events, namely the *History* of Hieronymous of Cardia (19: 100: 1), a general in Demetrius' army who also wrote a chronicle of events.[10]

We learn that the 'great lake' produces asphalt in large quantities, from which the Nabataeans obtain significant revenue (2: 48: 6). The length of the lake is about 500 stadia and it is 60 stadia wide (rather too long and too narrow).[11] It has bitter, foul-smelling water, so that no fish or other sea creatures live in it. Great fresh-water rivers empty into it, but they do not alleviate the bad smell of the lake. From the middle of the lake, once a year, asphalt is released, between two and three plethra,[12] the smaller size being called a 'calf' and the larger a 'bull' (2: 48: 7). This asphalt floats on the surface, looking like an island. The people living up to many stadia from the lake know

---

[8] Richard Sorabji (ed.), *Aristotle Transformed: The Ancient Commentators and their Influence* (London: Duckworth, 1990); John Sellars, 'The Aristotelian Commentators: A Biographical Guide,' in Peter Adamson, Han Baltussen, and Martin Stone (eds), *Philosophy, Science and Exegesis in Greek, Arabic and Latin Commentaries (Bulletin of the Institute of Classical Studies,* supplementary volume 83.2; London: Institute of Classical Studies, 2004), 239–68; Alexander of Aphrodisias, *On Aristotle Meteorology* 4, trans. Eric Lewis (London, Ithaca, NY: Duckworth and Cornell University Press, 1996), and see Joseph Moraux, *Alexandre d'Aphrodise: exégète de la noetique d'Aristote* (Liège/Paris: Faculté des Lettres, 1942); E. Droz and R. W. Sharples, 'Alexander of Aphrodisias: Scholasticism and Innovation,' *ANRW* 36.2, 1176–243.

[9] Diodorus of Sicily, *Books II. 35–IV. 58,* C. H. Oldfather (ed. and trans.) (Diodorus II; Loeb Classical Library; Cambridge, MA: Harvard University Press, 1967); Diodorus of Sicily, *Books XIX. 66–110 and XX,* Russell M. Geer (ed. and trans.) (Diodorus X; Loeb Classical Library; Cambridge, MA: Harvard University Press, 1972).

[10] Stern, *Greek and Latin Authors* (Winona Lake: Eisenbrauns, 1974), i, 18–19.

[11] Using the standard of a stadium being 185 m this indicates the length was assessed as 92.5 km and width 11.1 km, or 57.5 and 7 miles respectively.

[12] The plethron is a unit of area measuring 30 x 30 metres (100 x 100 feet), 0.09 hectares, or 900 m^2, so the blocks are described as being a maximum of about 46 metres wide.

when such asphalt will be released twenty (or twenty-two) days in advance by the foul smell, borne by the wind, and silver, gold, and bronze is dulled. Once the asphalt has been released the metal returns to normal. However, because the environs of the lake are fiery and foul-smelling, the bodies of the inhabitants are prone to illness, and the people are short-lived (2: 48: 8). Nevertheless, the land grows palm trees, wherever there are rivers with good water or springs that can irrigate it (cf. *Bibl.* 19: 98). This observation by Hieronymous is quite true: we can see wild palms today around the lake (Plate 3).

Hieronymous (*apud* Diodorus) notes that there is here also a valley (αὐλῶν) where the so-called 'balsam' grows, from which they obtain a large revenue since it is found only in this region, and it is highly regarded as a medicine for physicians (2: 48: 9). While the word αὐλῶν might normally be thought to refer to the entire Jordan rift valley, the mention of one particular valley within the context of a discussion of the Dead Sea seems to indicate that its location is in one of the valleys stretching away from the lake, presumably one very well irrigated with natural springs. At any rate, this assembling of information about asphalt, opobalsam, and palms together indicates the main resources of the Dead Sea region that were of great interest to those who wished to command revenue. The location of the lake is described as lying in the middle of the (Persian) 'satrapy' of Idumaea.

While the quotation in 19: 98 repeats what is found in Book 2, the account in Book 19 continues with further details (19: 99: 1–3) of asphalt collection. When it has been ejected by the lake, 'those living around on both sides of the lake' (οἱ περιοικοῦντες ἐξ ἀμφοτέρων τῶν μερῶν τὴν λίμνην) carry it away like war booty, since they are hostile to each other. They sail off in reed rafts carrying three men, two of whom row with lashed-on oars, while the third has a bow and arrows to defend them (19: 99: 1). When they get to the asphalt they jump onto it and cut it with axes as if it were soft rock, loading these onto the raft (δέσμη). If this raft falls to pieces, a person will float even if he does not know how to swim (19: 99: 2), because the water supports heavy living bodies, but more solid ones like silver, gold, lead, and so on will sink but more slowly. The 'barbarians' here take the asphalt to Egypt to use for embalming, to be mixed with other aromatic substances (19: 99: 3).

When Demetrius returns to Antigonus, he is praised for 'examining the lake' (19: 100: 1), or more particularly for finding a good source of revenue for the kingdom, and Hieronymous himself is instructed to make boats ready in order to collect all the asphalt. However, the 'Arabs' (οἱ Ἄραβες) come in a throng of 6,000 men with bows and arrows, on reed rafts, and successfully attack Hieronymous' boats (19: 100: 2). The Macedonian command therefore fails to plunder the resources of the lake.

With this account of Hieronymous in circulation from the beginning of the third century BCE it is no wonder that 'the asphalt lake' became fascinating to writers of the Graeco-Roman world. It was both foul and fair, in that despite its smelly and unwholesome qualities there were three lucrative resources: the asphalt belched up by the lake itself, special palm trees, and the balsam that grew in a 'valley'. It was Hieronymous who seems to have provided the first mention in Graeco-Roman literature of the highly prized plant *Commiphora gileadensis*, here associated with the Nabataeans (Arabs) who now owned the areas that were once the southern parts of Gilead. The locus of the conflict reported by Hieronymous is very much on the eastern and southern sides of the lake, and no association is made between balsam and Judaea.

Theophrastus (372–288/7 BCE)

Theophrastus, Aristotle's student in the fourth century BCE, first describes the propagation of opobalsam in his work, *An Enquiry into Plants*.[13] He calls this bush simply 'balsam' or 'the balsam in Syria', τὸ ἐν Συρία βάλσαμον (9: 1: 2; 9: 1:6–7; 9: 4: 1–4), noting that it is cut to extract the resin in the hottest time of the year, on the rising of the 'Star' (Sirius, in July).[14] He continues:

> The balsam exists in the valley (αὐλῶν) which pertains to Syria [Palestine]. It is said that there are only two orchards, one of about four plethra,[15] and the other much smaller. The size of the tree is that of a large pomegranate (ῥόα) and it has very many branches. The leaf it has is like rue, but pale, being evergreen. The fruit is like the terebinth in size, shape and colour, very fragrant is this too, and more so the resin. The resin is collected from incisions, cut with iron claws, at [the time of] the Star, when there is the greatest heat, both in the trunks and the upper parts. The collection is done all the summer. The flow is not large, but in a day the workman can collect around a *concha* (shell). The fragrance disperses and is great, so that from a tiny part it is noticed far away. However, it does not come here unmixed, but the product is blended. For it gladly receives many blends, so that [the balsam] known in Greece is mostly mixed. The branches and the twigs are also fragrant, and on account of this it is pruned. (*Historia Plantarum* 9: 6: 1–2)

Theophrastus goes on to note that the trees are constantly watered, and the trees do not grow very tall, mainly because they are cut so much, so that they grow wider with many branches. The balsam does not grow wild, but only in these two cultivated orchards. From the larger orchard twelve vessels containing a *hemichous* (six Greek cups) is obtained, and from the other orchard only two vessels. However, the pure resin sells for twice its weight in silver, while

---

[13] For this see Theophrastus, *Enquiry into Plants*, Arthur Hort (ed. and trans.) (Theophrastus II; Loeb Classical Library; London: Putnam and Sons, 1916).

[14] See Stern, *Greek and Latin Authors*, i, 15–17.

[15] Four plethra (a plethron was 30 x 30 metres) indicates only an area of 60 x 60 m (0.36 ha), not that much larger than the blocks of asphalt identified by Diodorus (from Hieronymous) in the lake.

the mixed version sells according to its quality (9: 6: 3–4). This description seems to be designed to indicate just how extremely rare balsam is, which would have increased its mystique and value. Theophrastus' emphasis on the minute amount of balsam generated by these groves may owe more to the advertising pitch of Nabataean merchants who, in selling the valued substance, stressed its rarity. Theophrastus notes elsewhere that balsam is mixed with wine to create an astringent medicine (*De Odoribus* 32).

Theophrastus does not locate the propagation of the balsam next to the Dead Sea, or connect it with Judaea. In Theophastus, the reference to the αὐλῶν in Syria indicates the whole Jordan Valley down to the Red Sea (*Hist. Plant.* 2: 6: 5), a very large region, but his emphasis on heat would indicate the Dead Sea trough. He is reliant on information told to him ('it is said'), so a precise location is probably beyond the information he received. While it is common to associate the references of Theophrastus to groves of opobalsam in Jericho and En Gedi,[16] Theophrastus suggests no such locations. Nothing at all in our sources viewed in chronological order yet relates balsam to Judaea. As noted above, the presentation by Hieronymous of Cardia situates the opobalsam groves in association with the Nabataeans.

Theophrastus also mentions dates in the region, noting that wherever they grow in abundance the soil is salty, and notes the reliance on spring water rather than rain. In the valley that extends from Syria to the Red Sea, the date palms grow in the lowest part of it, producing dates that will keep (*Hist. Plant.* 2: 6: 2, 5, 8).[17]

Xenophilus (*fl. c.*250 CE) *apud* Antigonus of Carystus

In a passage quoted by Antigonus of Carystus, who died in 240 BCE, Xenophilus (about whom little is known) mentioned a lake 'near Joppa [where] not only every weight [is said] to float but also every third year [is said] to bring forth moist asphalt. When this happens, for those living inside three stadia [circumference] copper vessels [are said] to tarnish'. Antigonus wrote a collection of *mirabilia*, largely based on Callimachus.[18] That the Dead Sea has entered this genre of literature by the middle of the third century BCE is

---

[16] Emil Schürer, with Geza Vermes, Fergus Millar, and Matthew Black (eds), *The History of the Jewish People in the Age of Jesus Christ*, revised edition, 3 vols (Edinburgh: T & T Clark, 1973–9), i, 300; Katharina Galor, Jean-Baptiste Humbert, and Jürgen Zangenberg (eds), *Qumran, The Site of the Dead Sea Scrolls: Archaeological Interpretations and Debates* (Leiden: Brill, 2006), 241–8, esp. 242; F. Nigel Hepper and Joan E. Taylor, 'Date Palms and Opobalsam in the Madaba Mosaic Map,' *PEQ* 136 (2004): 35–44.

[17] Stern, *Greek and Latin Authors*, i, 13.

[18] In Alexander Giannini (ed.), *Paradoxographorum Graecorum Reliquae* (Milan: Istituto Editoriale Milano, 1965), 96, and see Stern, *Greek and Latin Authors*, i, 87–8.

important to recognize. From this point on it was a wonder and could accrue other marvellous features. The reference to the lake from a western perspective (from Joppa) indicates the importance of asphalt for traders (via the Seleucid port of Joppa) at this stage, which tallies with what Hieronymous noted of people on both sides of the lake seeking asphalt on the water.

Eratosthenes (276–205 BCE), *apud* Strabo

Eratosthenes, the chief librarian of the Alexandrian library and mathematician, wrote about the Dead Sea in his *Geographica* (second half of third century BCE), an account now lost.[19] He apparently discussed the Dead Sea's origins scientifically, proposing that it was once a bigger lake that was partly filled up by volcanic eruptions (Strabo, *Geog.* 6: 2: 44).[20] This contradicted the story of the destruction and engulfing of cities in Gen. 19. Strabo's preamble to what he specifically states as Eratosthenes' opinion would be a fitting discussion by Eratosthenes himself. Strabo writes that people believed the stories of the local inhabitants, that there were once thirteen (*sic*) cities where the lake was now, one being Sodom. By reason of earthquakes, eruptions of fire, and hot waters containing asphalt and sulphur, the lake burst its boundaries and some were swallowed up and others abandoned. Showing no real knowledge of what is stated in the narrative of Gen. 19: 24–9, Strabo states that 60 stadia from the central metropolis of Sodom everything remained unharmed, but within this range Sodom and its daughter towns were destroyed, and many were swallowed up with water, though some of the thirteen cities were just abandoned (*Geog.* 16: 2: 44). This account presents a picture of some cities engulfed by a smaller lake that expanded outwards in a kind of tsunami, with some remaining visible around the shoreline of the present lake. Strabo then notes Eratosthenes as disagreeing with this view (stating that it was a bigger lake filled up by eruptions). As noted above in the discussion of Dio, this destruction of Sodom and other cities was widely known by Greek and Roman authors, possibly then because it was mentioned by the influential Eratosthenes.

Strabo also gets from Eratosthenes a comment that Judaeans are 'farmers' (*Geogr.* 16: 4: 2) and thus may also derive from Eratosthenes that the shortest distance from Petra to Hierichus (Jericho) is three or four days, and to the

---

[19] Duane W. Roller (ed.), *Eratosthenes' Geography, fragments collected and translated, with commentary and additional material* (Princeton: Princeton University Press, 2010), 55, 135. Most of what we know of Eratosthenes' work is in Strabo, but he does not quote so much as paraphrase.

[20] Stern, *Greek and Latin Authors*, i, 88–9.

(φοινικῶνα) 'grove of palm trees' five days (*Geogr.* 16: 4: 21), though this would much better refer to Phoenicia (Φοινίκην).

Posidonius (135–51 BCE), apud Strabo

We then jump about two hundred years forward in time to the middle of the first century BCE for our next extant source. The Dead Sea was discussed at some length by philosopher and scientist Posidonius (135–51 BCE), but his work is, like that of Eratosthenes, known only from its use by later writers, such as Diodorus Siculus (*Bibl. Hist.* 2: 28; 19: 98); Strabo (*Geogr.* 6: 2); Pliny (*Nat. Hist.* 5: 15); Tacitus (*Hist.* 5: 6–7), and Pausanias (*Descr. Graec.* 5: 7: 50).[21]

Strabo, who completed his *Geography* just before his death (*c.*24 CE), considered the Dead Sea within the context of Judaea rather than Nabataea. As Stern notes, Strabo explicitly states that he used Posidonius in noting that the people who cut asphalt were 'sorcerers' who used incantations (*Geogr.* 16: 2: 43); this negative appraisal is consistent with the portrayal of Judaeans in very negative terms, as Josephus indicates regarding Posidonius in *Apion* 2: 79.[22] Strabo quarried much from Posidonius, but the maximum extent of his usage is difficult to determine, given that he also used Eratosthenes for his geography of Egypt and Syria. Did he find in Posidonius the erroneous information that Jerusalem is visible from the seaport of Joppa (*Geogr.* 16: 2: 28; 16: 2: 34), or that the ancestors of Judaeans were Egyptians (*Geogr.* 16: 2: 34–6)?[23]

What does seem to come from Posidonius—even without a specific attestation of the source—is a core of military history, when Strabo notes that Judaea was under the rule of tyrants, 'the first to declare himself king instead of priest being Alexander (Jannaeus), with Hyrcanus (II) and Alexander (*sic* = Aristobulus) being sons of his. When they (the sons) were disputing concerning the leadership, Pompey went and overthrew them, and destroyed their fortresses' (*Geogr.* 16: 2: 40). This summarizes a historical situation, recounting Pompey's actions in Judaea in 63–2 BCE: Posidonius was asked

---

[21] Posidonius, *Fragments I*, Ludwig Edelstein and I. G. Kidd (eds), rev. ed. (Cambridge: CUP, 2005); Posidonius, *Fragments II. The Commentary (i) Testimonia and Fragments 1–149*, I. G. Kidd (ed.), (Cambridge: CUP, 1988); Posidonius, *Fragments III. The Translation of the Fragments*, I. G. Kidd (ed. and trans.) (Cambridge: CUP, 1999).

[22] Stern, *Greek and Latin Authors*, i, 141–7. Posidonius, *Fragments I*, ed. Edelstein and Kidd, F.279.

[23] Edelstein and Kidd have therefore adopted a highly conservative approach in their collection of fragments, and see the comments by Kidd, Posidonius, *Fragments III*, 354. Nevertheless, Felix Jacoby, *Fragmente der Griechischen Historiker* (CD Rom; Leiden: Brill, 1994) includes Strabo, *Geogr.* 16: 2: 34–45 as Posidonius (No. 169), F70.

by Pompey to write this history.[24] In fact, Strabo states that he had this history in hand: τήν ἱστορίαν ... περὶ αὐτόν for the writing of his *Geography* (11: 1, cf. 3: 5: 7–8).[25] Thus, most likely, Strabo provides the substance of Posidonius' account of the taking of Jerusalem, and then Pompey's journey towards Jericho and other Hasmonean fortresses named Threx and Taurus, situated on the passes leading to Jericho, and others such as Alexandrion, Hyrcania, and Machaerus. Despite completing his final edition of the *Geographica* in 23 CE,[26] nothing much in Strabo's account of Judaea indicates a situation post-Pompey. As Stern notes, Gaza is uninhabited, when it was restored by the Romans after the downfall of the Hasmoneans, and Strato's Tower is not renamed Caesarea.[27] Therefore, Strabo is employing the information of Posidonius without an update.

Posidonius' history of Pompey, as used by Strabo, includes an important description of the region of Jericho we can then situate as an eyewitness account from 63–2 BCE. Jericho is described as being in a plain 100 stadia (18.5 km) in length, surrounded by mountainous lands. Posidonius identifies that there is a palace, palm grove, and balsam orchard, and here the date palm grows, along with other kinds of cultivated fruit-bearing trees, with numerous dwellings (*Geogr.* 16: 2: 41). The palace referred to, given the context of his description concerns the arrival of Pompey, is the Hasmonean palace of Jericho, located close to the Wadi Qelt, which he notes had gardens stretching northwards and eastwards, involving complex irrigation systems.[28]

Indeed, what is now known of the archaeology of this palace confirms well Posidonius' description of Hasmonean circumstances. The palace was on a hill, now called Tulul Abu el-`Alayiq, affording a view over Jericho. The first palace is usually dated to the reign of John Hyrcanus (134–104 BCE), a building that was improved by Alexander Jannaeus, who added a swimming pool and made renovations that fortified the enclosure (built *c.*90–75 BCE). Not just one but at least two further palaces were built proximate to the first.[29] Posidonius provides us with a glimpse of this Hasmonean world.

---

[24] Florus, *Rom. Hist* (Epitome), 1: 41: 8. Florus, *Epitome of Roman History*, E. S. Forster (ed. and trans.) (Loeb Classical Library; London: Putnam and Sons, 1929).

[25] Kidd, Posidonius, *Fragments II*, 331–3, see too Clare Franklin, 'To what extent did Posidonius and Theophanes record Pompeian ideology?' in 'Romanization?' *Digressus, The Internet Journal for the Classical World*, *Digressus Supplement* 1 (2003): 99–110, at 102–4: www.digressus.org.

[26] Daniela Dueck, *Strabo of Amasia: A Greek Man of Letters in Augustan Rome* (London/New York: Routledge, 2000), 145–53.

[27] Stern, *Greek and Latin Authors*, i, 263.

[28] Ehud Netzer, *The Palaces of the Hasmoneans and Herod the Great* (Jerusalem: Yad ben Zvi Press, 2001), 1–29; id. *Hasmonean and Herodian Palaces at Jericho* (Jerusalem: Israel Exploration Society, 2001), i; Katharina Galor, 'Winterpaläste in Jericho,' in Zangenberg (ed.), *Das Toten Meer*, 53–62, and also David Stacey, 'Was there a Synagogue in Hasmonean Jericho?' article on the *Bible and Interpretation* site, http://www.bibleinterp.com/articles/Hasmonean_Jericho.shtml

[29] Netzer, *Hasmonean and Herodian Palaces*, 28–39.

Jericho is described as a well-inhabited and fertile area of special trees, like the caryotic palm, as well as other fruit trees (*Geogr.* 16: 2: 41–2). Interestingly, the description of the opobalsam here does not owe anything substantively to the language of Theophrastus. The balsam is noted as being a shrub, like cytisus (broom) or terminthus (terebinth), with a spicy flavour. People make incisions in the bark and capture the juice in vessels, the liquid being white until it solidifies. It is said to be wonderful for curing headaches and bad eyesight, while the wood of the balsam is used as a spice. Because of this, and because it is produced nowhere else, it is very costly.

It is therefore here, with Posidonius, that we get the first identification of the opobalsam as being propagated in Judaea, rather than in Gilead (Nabataea), and it is entirely within the confines of the Hasmonean royal property where there is also the special palm grove.

From this description of Hasmonean Jericho, Posidonius passes on to the Dead Sea (*Geogr.* 16: 2: 42). At this point Strabo wrongly calls this 'Lake Sirbonis', a lake in fact in Egypt, here perhaps misreading Latin 'Lacus Salinis'. He notes that 'some people say' it is over 1,000 stadia (185 km) in circumference, giving its length as 200 stadia (37 km), and stating that it is deep to the shore. To what extent Strabo is weaving in Eratosthenes at this point of Posidonius' text is hard to determine. The lake is then described as having heavy water and anyone who walks into it past his navel is raised up afloat. It is full of asphalt, which rises to the surface irregularly from its midst, and bubbles up at the same time as if the water were boiling. The water of the lake is convex, like a hill, and from it a kind of invisible soot comes up which tarnishes copper, silver, and gold, but when this happens the people around the lake know that the asphalt is beginning to rise, and they prepare to collect this using reed rafts. There seems to be some use of Diodorus or Hieronymous here, complicating the picture.

The account continues to indicate that the asphalt is liquefied by heat within the lake and is blown up to the surface and spreads out, after which it solidifies in the cold water, so that it needs to be cut and chopped. People reach the floating pieces on rafts and then chop it up, carrying off as much as possible. As noted above, Strabo then writes here explicitly that 'according to Posidonius the people are sorcerers and pretend to recite incantations, and also use urine and other ill-smelling liquids' (*Geogr.* 16: 2: 43) which they pour over the asphalt, apparently to soften it. Posidonius' name is provided here because this is opinion rather than information. Strabo notes again that there is a fire in the middle of the lake and that the bubbling up of the asphalt is irregular. He comments too on the fiery aspect of the area, and that 'near Moasada' there are rugged rocks that are scorched, as well as fissures, ashy soil, and smelly pitch. Masada was, like Jericho, first fortified by the Hasmoneans, probably by

Alexander Jannaeus (*c*.83–76 BCE),[30] and thus would have been known as a Judaean fortress by Posidonius, given Pompey's interest in Hasmonean defences.

In none of Strabo's sources was there anything that noted the presence of the paradoxical Essenes being present in the Hasmonean era in this vicinity. Apart from the appearance of local people who are characterized very negatively as using forms of sorcery to cut the asphalt, the resources of the Dead Sea region—balsam, date palms, and asphalt—are all associated with Hasmonean hegemony in the area. The Talmud also would remember the importance of what may be opobalsam (*afarsemon*) to the royal rulers of Judaea (b.Ker. 5b; j.Sotah 8: 22).[31]

The literary evidence of Posidonius, as integrated into Strabo's survey, can be related to the contemporaneous archaeological remains in the area beyond Jericho as well and what we know of wider history.[32] The Hasmoneans utilized the mountains for strongholds that were positioned in close proximity to one another, from Alexandrium in the north, to Doq (Dagon), located on Mount Qarantal, along with Strabo's 'Taurus' (Nuseib el- 'Uweishira?), Jericho, Cypros (perhaps Strabo's 'Threx', at Tel Aqaba), Hyrcania, founded by John Hyrcanus, further inland to the west (Plate 4), Machaerus in the mountains east of the Dead Sea, and some encampment on Masada to the south (Plate 5).

In addition, archaeology indicates that there was a range of small fortified settlements and anchorages built very close to the Dead Sea, positioned along a route from Jericho to En Gedi, at places where there were natural springs or pre-existing water systems in old Iron Age ruins (from the seventh to sixth centuries BCE) that could be utilized for reconstruction. Eleven km south-east from Jericho there was the nearby anchorage at Rujm el Bahr (Plate 6), by the spring of Ain ej-Jahir.[33] 12 km from Jericho due south was Kh. Qumran

---

[30] Cf. Josephus, *Ant.* 15: 185, *War* 7: 171, 285. See Ariyeh Kasher, *Jews, Idumaeans and Ancient Arabs: Relations of the Jews in Eretz-Israel with the Nations of the Frontier and the Desert during the Hellenistic and Roman Eras (332 BCE–70 CE)* (Tübingen: Mohr Siebeck, 1988), 88; Netzer, *Hasmonean and Herodian Palaces*, 79–81. No clearly definable Hasmonean structures have been found at Masada, and the Hasmonean contribution might have been to create cisterns for an encampment.

[31] See Yizhar Hirschfeld, *Qumran in Context: Reassessing the Archaeological Evidence* (Peabody, MA: Hendrickson, 2004), 58. The term *afarsemon*, however, became associated with the persimmon. The legend in b.Ker. 5b is that after King Josiah hid the holy oil of Moses, the oil of *afarsemon* was used in its place to anoint kings. The balsam sap is not actually an oil. This is an archaizing legend that might yet have some value.

[32] Yizhar Hirschfeld, 'The Archaeology of the Dead Sea Valley in the Late Hellenistic and Early Roman Periods,' *Geological Society of America Special Papers* 401 (2006): 215–29; id. *Qumran in Context*, 11–14, 211–30.

[33] Heinrich Schult, 'Zwei Häfen aus römischer Zeit am Toten Meer: Rujum el-bahr und elbeled (ez-Zara),' *ZDPV* 82 (1966): 139–48; Pesach Bar-Adon, 'Excavations in the Judaean Desert,' *Atiqot* 9 (1989) (Hebrew): 3–14; Hirschfeld, 'Archaeology of the Dead Sea Valley,' 221–2.

(using an Iron Age water cistern complex).[34] Just over 7 km further south was Kh. Mazin (Qasr el-Yahoud) (Plate 7) at the exit of the Kidron stream where there was once a spring, now dried up, a settlement, and an anchorage.[35] At the spring of Ain el-Ghuweir (Enot Qaneh) there was another small Hasmonean site,[36] and at the spring Ain et-Turaba (Enot Samar) a fortified settlement known as Qasr et-Turabeh likewise dates to the Hasmonean era, some 8 km south from Kh. Mazin (see Map 2 for locations).[37] Yizhar Hirschfeld notes the many Hasmonean coins found in the vicinity of Kh. Mazin dating to the time of Alexander Jannaeus, with an anchor motif: he suggests this relates to his development of shipping on the Dead Sea and associated anchorages,[38] the archaeological evidence for such shipping being explored by Gideon Hadas.[39]

Another 16 km further south there was a port at En Gedi, referred to in a Bar Kokhba letter (Letter 49), but it is no longer visible, even though anchors have been found in its vicinity. At Tel Goren there, amid the ruins of the Iron Age city, the Hasmoneans likewise established a fortress overlooking agricultural terrace systems, which remain all around to the east and north of Tel Goren to this day, though now they are dried out and barren, with only ancient potsherds testifying to their antiquity (Plate 8).[40] The archaeological evidence thus indicates that from Jericho to En Gedi there were constructions

---

[34] Hirschfeld, *Qumran in Context*, 59–87; Joan E. Taylor and Shimon Gibson, 'Qumran in the Iron Age in Comparison with the Hasmonean to Early Roman Periods: A Cross-Temporal Study,' Sidnie White Crawford (ed.), *Qumran Archaeology*, forthcoming.

[35] Bar Adon, 'Excavations,' 18–29; Howard E. Stutchbury and George R. Nicholl, 'Khirbet Mazin,' *Annual of the Department of Antiquities of Jordan* 6/7 (1962/3): 96–103; Hirschfeld, *Qumran in Context*, 215, 218–19.

[36] Bar Adon, 'Excavations,' 33–40.

[37] Hirschfeld, *Qumran in Context*, 212.

[38] Ibid. This bronze coin type with an anchor on one side and a sun-wheel on the other has also been examined by Dan Barag, 'Alexander Jannaeus—Priest and King,' in Aren M. Maeir, Jodi Magness, and Lawrence Schiffman (eds), *'Go Out and Study the Land' (Judges 18: 2): Archaeological, Historical and Textual Studies in Honor of Hanan Eshel* (Leiden: Brill, 2011), 1–5. This coin type includes one that is dated to the 25th year of his reign, in 78 BCE.

[39] Gideon Hadas, 'Dead Sea Sailing Routes during the Herodian Period,' *BAIAS* 26 (2008): 31–6. Three stone anchors from the Roman period and two wooden anchors dating to the late Iron Age and the early Roman period have been found near Gedi, id. 'Stone Anchors from the Dead Sea,' *Atiqot* 21 (1992): 55–7; id, 'A Stone Anchor from the Dead Sea,' *International Journal of Nautical Archaeology* 22 (1993): 89–90; id. 'Where was the Harbour of En Gedi Situated?' *IEJ* 43 (1993): 45–9; Gideon Hadas, Nili Lifschitz, and Georges Bonani, 'Two Ancient Wooden Anchors from Ein Gedi, on the Dead Sea, Israel,' *International Journal of Nautical Archaeology* 34 (2005): 307–15. Josephus mentions ships on the Dead Sea (*War* 4: 7, 439, 475–81).

[40] Benjamin Mazar, 'En-Gedi,' in Ephraim Stern (ed.), *New Encyclopedia of Archaeological Excavations in the Holy Land* (Jerusalem: Israel Exploration Society/Carta, 1993), 399–405, at 403–4. I am grateful to Shimon Gibson, with whom I visited En Gedi, for alerting me to the significance of the ancient terraces and the surface pottery dating. Excavation of these terraces for ancient seeds would be very valuable in determining what crops were grown here.

to be dated most likely to the time of Alexander Jannaeus, which connected Jericho and En Gedi.[41]

The conquests of Jonathan Maccabeus (160–142 BCE) had led to the inclusion of the land east of the Jordan River, in Gilead, south to the town of Tyrus. Under John Hyrcanus (134–104 BCE) the area further south of this, down to the Arnon halfway along the Dead Sea, as well as all of Idumaea beyond Masada, would be included in Judaea, and during the conquest of Alexander Jannaeus (103–76 BCE) former Nabataean territory to the south and south-east of the Dead Sea, including Zoara, would be added as well, so that all the Dead Sea resources where opobalsam had formerly grown came to be under the control of the Hasmonean dynasty.[42] It is at this point, strikingly, that what had once been the 'Balsam (Balm) of Gilead' was henceforth the balsam of Judaea. This extraordinary Hasmonean activity then relates well to Posidonius' description, as found in Strabo, and archaeology. The Hasmoneans were clearly active in the Dead Sea area, for both military and economic reasons. Posidonius gives us a glimpse of the Dead Sea in the first part of the first century BCE, from a Roman perspective.

Diodorus Siculus, *fl. c.*60–30 BCE

The descriptions of the Dead Sea in Diodorus' *Bibliotheca Historica* (2: 48: 6–9 and 19: 98–9) have been discussed above in regard to Hieronymous of Cardia, since Diodorus' accounts appear to have been lifted from this much earlier work. As noted above, the historical situation described, relating to the campaign of Demetrius Poliorcetes, relates to the third century BCE, not to the time of Diodorus.[43]

Pompeius Trogus, *c.*20–18 BCE, *apud* Justinus

It should be noted that, despite Strabo's error of nomenclature, the lake was already known as the 'Dead Sea', from the later first century BCE when Pompeius Trogus—according to the epitome of Justinus (*c.*200 CE)—testifies

---

[41] For the connectivity of the road here, first established in the Iron Age, see Joan E. Taylor and Shimon Gibson, 'Qumran Connected: The Paths and Passes of the North-Western Dead Sea,' in Jorg Frey and Carsten Claussen (eds), *Qumran und Archäologie—wechselseitige Perspektiven* (Tübingen: Mohr Siebeck, 2011), 1–51. For the dating, see Netzer, *Hasmonean and Herodian Palaces*, 78.

[42] For a concise summary of these advances, see Norman Gottwald, *The Hebrew Bible: A Socio-Literary Introduction* (Philadelphia: Fortress, 1985), 439–56, and especially the map on p.407.

[43] Stern, *Greek and Latin Authors*, i, 167–92.

that it 'is called' (*dicitur*) by that name: *Mortuum Mare* (Justinus, *Epitome* 36: 3: 6).[44] This may have become generally known, however, only after the time of Posidonius.

Like Posidonius, Pompeius Trogus reflects a Hasmonean environment. In his *Philippic History* (36), as we have it summarized by Justinus, Trogus tried to explain the intricacies of Hellenistic politics and warfare in the mid-second century BCE, beginning when Demetrius II became ruler of Syria in 145 BCE. Trogus tackled the complex situation in which Demetrius II lost out to the machinations of Diodotus Trypho, who ostensibly wished to install Antiochus IV, the son of Alexander Balas, on the Syrian throne, only to seize it for himself, killing Antiochus IV shortly thereafter (*c*.143–2 BCE). After Demetrius II was held captive by the Parthians, his brother Antiochus V Sidetes then fought against him. Demetrius II was backed by the Hasmoneans (partly because, in fact, Trypho had killed Jonathan Maccabeus, see 1 Macc. 11: 14–43; Josephus, *Ant.* 13: 187–212; Strabo, *Geogr.* 16: 2: 8), and thus the Hasmoneans enter the history of the Romans, who are invited in to help.

According to the epitome, Pompeius Trogus introduced the Judaeans as fiercely independent fighters, originating ethnically from Damascus (apparently an interpretation of the 'Haran' of Abraham; 36: 2: 1–3). Trogus went through something of the story of Joseph in Egypt, presenting him as an expert in magic and dream interpretation, with Moses as his son, likewise a magician, who was expelled with all his people from Egypt, thereafter returning to Damascus. From Moses, Trogus passed to 'Aruas' (Aaron), his 'son', whom he defined as both priest and king, and noted 'and always after it was a custom among the Judaeans that they have the same [rulers] for kings and [high] priests . . . in which religion and justice mixed to cultivate incredible power'.[45] This, in reality, only refers to the Hasmonean innovation of priest-kings. At this point Pompeius Trogus was writing as if in the present, but was in fact describing the Hasmonean dynasty rather than the ruler of his own time, Herod the Great (37–4 BCE).

From this mention of Hasmonean power Trogus then turned to opobalsam, which generated the huge wealth of these rulers, since it was produced only in containment. That the rulers could claim *vectigalia* (taxes, payments to

---

[44] Since we do not have the original of Pompeius Trogus' work there are the difficulties of ascertaining what is the original phraseology of Trogus and what is contributed by the epitomiser, but substantive points are usually chosen and rendered accurately in epitomes since anyone could have compared them with the extant originals. For careful work distinguishing the language of Trogus and Justinus see John Yardley, *Justin and Pompeius Trogus: A Study in the Language of Justin's Epitome of Trogus* (Toronto: University of Toronto Press, 2003); Stern, *Greek and Latin Authors*, i, 332–43.

[45] *semperque exinde hic mos apud Iudaeos fuit, ut eosdem reges et sacerdotes haberent, quorum iustitia religioni permixta incredibile quantum coaluere*, reading the final word as *colere*. See *Epitome of the Phillippic History of Pompeius Trogus*, J. C. Yardley (ed. and trans.), with introduction and notes by R. Develin (Atlanta, GA: Scholars Press, 1994).

the state; 36: 3: 1) indicates that the growing of this crop was not entirely in royal hands, and could be farmed out, but that any transactions on this product were subject to duties.

According to Justinus, Trogus provided a description indicating that the region of balsam propagation was now distinctively found in the Hasmonean cultivation of Jericho:

> for there is a valley, encircled with continual ridge of hills, like a wall, in the form of a [military] camp, the space being about two hundred *iugera*,[46] and called by the name of Aricus (Jericho) in which there is a wood, distinctive for fertility and pleasantness, since it is divided into palm and opobalsam. The trees of opobalsam have a similar form to pitch-pine trees (*Pinus silvestris*), except that they are lower in height, and are cultivated in the manner of vines. In a certain time of the year they exude the balsam. But not less the place is admired for the quality of sunshine which is abundant, indeed the sun being strongest in this region in all the world, so there is a certain natural warmth in the air perpetually even in the shade. In this region is a wide lake, which, from its size and the immobility of its water is called the Dead Sea (*Mortuum Mare*); for it is neither moved by the winds—resistant to turns by the bitumen, with which all its water is inundated— nor does it allow the sailing of ships, for all things devoid of life sink to the depths; and it will not support any matter unless it is smeared with alum.

The valley here is defined as being 23 square kilometres, and it is within this region that the groves of opobalsam and palm are planted, though the size and number of these groves is not given. There is no reason to assume that Trogus had in mind the two groves mentioned by Theophrastus, which—as we have seen—are not linked with Jericho but could be located anywhere in the Jordan rift valley, according to this description.

In the same place is the Dead Sea. Interesting is the note regarding shipping, which does not necessarily indicate a total absence of regular sailing vessels but only that all craft had to have alum (alumen, cf. Pliny, *Nat. Hist.* 35: 52 [183–5]) smeared on their hulls in order for them to survive. Trogus then returned to his political and military history, in noting the positive Roman intervention in Judaean affairs (cf. 1 Macc. 14: 20–4).

For both Posidonius (as found in Strabo) and Trogus (as found in Justinus), what is most interesting in terms of the land of Judaea as a whole are its great resources in the region of the Dead Sea. The palms, balsam, and asphalt of Judaea make the place rich. While their original words have not survived, the portrayal has, and they give us a sense of Hasmonean expansion and economic energy. The question of whether Trogus in fact used Posidonius for his description is unclear on the basis of the epitome, but they cover similar ground, and give us together an important presentation of the region relating

---

[46] An 'iugera' was a rectangular area of land equivalent to 0.26 hectares (73 x 37 m); therefore, 200 iugera is 52 hectares.

to the latter part of the second and the early first centuries BCE, a presentation in which Hasmonean royal hegemony is strongly stressed, with a testimony to their economic exploitation of the Dead Sea area.

Strabo (64 BCE–26 CE)

The *Geographica* has already been considered as primarily utilizing Eratosthenes and Posidonius.[47] Elsewhere Strabo states in broad terms the geographical situation of Syria, noting that the Jordan River waters a fertile region which 'produces also balsam' (*Geogr.* 16: 2: 16). The main passage discussed above occurs in *Geogr.* 16: 2: 40–6.

Strabo has a comment at the end of his section on the Dead Sea that is not from Posidonius. Strabo notes 'Pompey ... appointed Herod to the priesthood' (*Geogr.* 16: 2: 46), meaning to refer to the appointment of Antipater as governor. Strabo continues by noting that his descendant Herod received the title of 'king' from Antony, confirmed by Augustus Caesar, and records Herod's execution of his sons and the exile of one in Gaul. This snippet most likely does not come from an alternative source to that of Posidonius, but simply from common knowledge in Augustus' court. The quip by Augustus, 'I would rather be Herod's pig than his son,' is preserved in Ambrosius Macrobius, *Saturnalia* 2: 4: 11. Overall, Strabo does not seem to have other sources for the Dead Sea than Posidonius and Eratosthenes (*Geogr.* 16: 2: 44).

Strabo also comments as an aside on the 'shrewd practices of the Judaeans ... in the case of the palm tree—particularly the caryotic palm—and the balsam' in not allowing it to be grown in many places, to increase its price (*Geogr.* 17: 1: 15), a comment that relates back to what he has stated regarding the Hasmoneans on the basis of Posidonius.[48] The Hasmoneans were clever businessmen.

Philo of Alexandria (*c.*30 BCE–45 CE)

Philo does not in his extant works mention the Dead Sea explicitly, but he does describe both the aetiological myth of Genesis and also the continuing situation of the area of the destruction of the five cities of the plain, in *De Abrahamo* 138–141.[49] As Philo tells the story, the vegetation of the plain was burnt up with fire rained down from the sky, as was the woodland of the

---

[47] Strabo, *The Geography of Strabo*, Horace Leonard Jones (ed. and trans.), 8 vols (Loeb Classical Library; London/New York: Heinemann/G. P. Putnam's Sons, 1917–32).

[48] Stern, *Greek and Latin Authors*, i, 313–14.

[49] Philo of Alexandria, F. H. Colson (ed. and trans.) (Philo VI; Loeb Classical Library; London/Cambridge, MA: Heinemann/Harvard University Press, 1959).

mountains around it, so that the land would not be able to bear fruit or grow vegetation (140). Then Philo writes: 'and until now it burns, for the thunderbolt fire never is quenched or controlled or is smoked out [to its end]. The clearest testimony is visible, for the memorial of the disastrous suffering is the smoke always issuing forth and the sulphur they mine' (141). Philo then indicates a belief that the mistiness of the lake is caused by smoke, and that the sulphur is a by-product of the ancient cataclysm. He goes on to mention one surviving city and land around it, by which he must mean Zoara and its oasis, a city that is 'much populated' and the land very fertile (141). Philo's principal information of interest here is the testimony to sulphur being mined. This is the first mention of this in the historical record, and indicates an industry that continues to the present (see Plate 9).

Josephus (37–*c*.100 CE)

Josephus provides the fullest data for a historical framework that allows us to see the expansion of the Hasmoneans into the Dead Sea region, particularly during the reign of Alexander Jannaeus (103–76 BCE). Already firmly established on the north-western side of the Dead Sea, Josephus tells the story of Alexander Jannaeus' expansion of Judaean territory into the regions of Moab and Gilead (*War* 1: 89, 104–6; 113, 374; *Ant.* 13: 393–4, cf. b.Kidd. 66a), leading to direct war with Nabataea in 93–90 BCE, some surrender of territory (*Ant.* 13: 382), and also its reclamation at the end of Alexander Jannaeus' reign, probably after internal conflicts were settled around 83 BCE (*Ant.* 13: 397; 14: 18).[50] This led to a short period in which there was the enclosure of the whole of the Dead Sea as Judaean territory, creating a Hasmonean monopoly of all Dead Sea resources.

Josephus assumes that the readers have some knowledge of the immense value of these resources, for example when he mentions the date palm grove and precious medicinal balsam of Jericho (*War* 1: 138, 361; *Ant.* 4: 100; 14: 54; 15: 96, 106, 132; 17: 340). He indicates an intermixture of balsam and date palm groves when he writes that Cleopatra of Egypt appropriated from Herod the Great 'the palm grove of Jericho where the balsam grows' (*War* 1: 361; *Ant.* 15: 96), in 34 BCE.

Josephus' main description of the Dead Sea and its resources in fact comes quite late in his narrative, with his account of Vespasian's attack on Jericho in 68 CE, in which it sits as an aside (*War* 4: 451–85). The inhabitants of Jericho are described as fleeing to the hill country around Jerusalem, while those who remained behind were put to death by the Romans. Josephus describes Jericho

---

[50] See Kasher, *Jews, Idumaeans and Ancient Arabs*, 88–105.

as lying in a plain next to a bare, uninhabited mountain range running north to Scythopolis and south to the extremity of Lake Asphaltitis. On the other side of the Jordan is another range beginning at Julias in the north and ending at Somora, bordering Petra, in the south, a range that includes 'Sideroun' 'the Iron Mountain', so-called, which stretches into Moab (implying the mining of iron); perhaps then lying along the Dead Sea. Within these two mountain ranges is what Josephus calls 'the Great Plain', the *Aulon* (the Jordan Valley), from the Sea of Galilee to Lake Asphaltitis, 'salty and barren' (*War* 4: 452–8).

Josephus notes the palm trees on both sides of the River Jordan and explains how extremely fertile the region of Jericho is because of the perennial spring (Ain es-Sultan) which irrigates a tract of land 70 by 20 stadia where date palms grow, 'palms of many varieties and with different flavours and medicinal properties' (*War* 4: 468), from which date honey is made, not inferior to bee honey, and there are plenty of bees here too (469). There is also the precious opobalsam, the cypress, and the myrobalan. So rich was this area in fertility, combined with the warm air and the rich water, that Josephus calls it 'divine', the inhabitants relying so much on the climate that they wear linen all year round (469–70). The importance of the medicinal plants of the Jericho region may be noted here. For the first time the date palms themselves are identified as medicinal, as is the opobalsam, and thus Josephus' mention of other plants in the Jericho area such as the cypress and myrobalan (= *Balanitis aegyptiaca*) is suggestive of their medicinal use as well. The 'divine' nature of the place appears associated not with scenery but with the healing power of plants.

Josephus then goes on to the adjacent lake (*War* 4: 476). By contrast with this region of healthful fertility, Lake Asphaltitis is bitter and unproductive, but its buoyancy is famous. Josephus tells a story that when the emperor Vespasian came to this lake (in 68 CE) to put down the Jewish Revolt, he ordered that certain people who were unable to swim should have their hands tied behind them and be thrown into the deep water, to test the buoyancy (477), clearly with Aristotle in mind. Josephus passes over this horror without comment, noting only that they floated, and then goes on to describe the colour of the lake, which apparently changed three times every day.

Regarding the asphalt of the lake, Josephus notes that the lumps float on the surface like decapitated bulls, and includes a story that asphalt sticks to boats and is only unglued by menstrual blood (*War* 4: 480). He then mentions the uses of asphalt in medicines, as well as for caulking boats. This reference to the use of asphalt in medicines is striking (cf. Dioscorides, *De Materia Medica* 1: 73: 1), and complements Josephus' mention of opobalsam and other medicinal plants in the area of Jericho, creating an implication of the Dead Sea being a zone of extreme interest for anyone concerned with the healing properties of plants and minerals.

Josephus also mentions the therapeutic waters of Callirhoe, where Herod went for healing (*War* 1: 656–9, cf. *Ant.* 17: 171–3). Herod 'crossed the Jordan to take the warm baths at Callirhoe, the waters debouching into Lake Asphaltitis, and because of their sweetness they are also a drink' (Plate 10). Archaeological investigations have shown that this site was extensively developed by Herod, as archaeological excavation has shown: Herod built a large villa and developed the harbour.[51]

While Josephus indicates then the reasons why Alexander Jannaeus would have wished to control this area, Josephus' explicit focus on the Dead Sea resources more often concerns a post-Hasmonean scenario, beginning with Cleopatra's gigantic gift from Herod in 34 BCE. Thereafter, Herod's association with the Dead Sea region is strongly indicated in the writings of Josephus, various activities of the king taking place in the palace-fortresses he either founded or developed, in the north: Jericho (as mentioned above) and Phasaelis;[52] in the north-east Betharamptha,[53] and more remotely Heshbon.[54] On the east Callirhoe, Machaerus, and eastern Herodium;[55] on the west Hyrcania and Masada.[56]

---

[51] Christa Clamer, 'The Hot Springs of Kallirrhoe and Baarou,' in Michele Piccirillo and Eugenio Alliata (eds), The Madaba Map Centenary 1897–1997. Travelling through the Byzantine Umayyad Period, Proceedings of the International Conference Held in Amman, 7–9 April 1997 (Collectio Maior 40; Jerusalem: Studium Biblicum Franciscanum, 1999), 221–5, and see also ead. Fouilles archéologiques de `Aïn ez-Zâra/Callirhoé, villegiature herodienne (Beirut: Institut Français d'archéologie du Proche-Orient, 1997); ead. 'Paradies am Meeresrand,' in Zangenberg (ed.), Das Tote Meer, 113–24; August Strobel, 'Zur Ortslage von Kallirhoe,' ZDPV 82 (1966): 149–62; August Strobel and Christa Clamer, 'Excavations at ez-Zara,' Annual of the Department of Antiquities of Jordan 30 (1986): 381–4; Strobel, August, and Wimmer, Stefan, Kallirrhoë (`En ez-Zara): Drittes Grabungskampagne des Deutschen Evangelischen Instituts für Altertumswissenschaft des Heiligen Landes und Exkursionen in Süd-Peräa (Wiesbaden: Harrassowitz, 2003).

[52] Phasaelis has natural springs which Herod organized for irrigation, promoting agriculture (Ant. 16: 145); see Ehud Netzer, The Architecture of Herod, the Great Builder (Tübingen: Mohr Siebeck, 2006), 226.

[53] Betharamptha (Tell er-Rama [Ant. 17: 277]) was a palace estate destroyed after Herod's death (War 2: 59), and rebuilt by Herod Antipas, who named the town Livias or Julias in honour of the empress (Ant. 18: 27); Netzer, Architecture of Herod, 226–7.

[54] Heshbon was founded by Alexander Jannaeus (Ant. 13: 397) and developed by Herod (Ant. 15: 294); see Netzer, Architecture of Herod, 227.

[55] This eastern Herodium is often overlooked, but has been addressed in the work of Strobel and Wimmer, Kallirrhoë, 96–104, where it is identified as Qasr er-Riyashi, a complex of three sites looking over the Wadi Mujib on both sides. See also the website http://www.datasync.com/~rsf1/Herodium.htm, put up by R. S. Fritzius, summarizing Jerry Vardman's unpublished exploration, 'The Lost Fortress of Herodium beyond the Jordan Rediscovered' (30 July 1981). Vardman identified a site named er-Raya, 8 km south-east of Machaerus. Achim Lichtenberger, Die Baupolitik Herodes des Grossen (Wiesbaden: Harrassowitz, 1999), 113–15, follows the suggestions by August Strobel. Given that all these sites date to the time of Herod (according to surface pottery), the question seems to be whether the eastern 'Herodium' was in reality a cluster of fortresses, including er-Raya. As noted in Negev and Gibson, Encyclopedia, 418, the Bedouin names er-Riyashi and er-Riyadshi have a curious resonance with the name 'Herodes', as also er-Raya.

[56] For these and other Herodian buildings, see Duane Roller, The Building Program of Herod the Great (Berkeley: University of California Press, 1998); Lichtenberger, Baupolitik; Netzer, Architecture of Herod.

An interest in healing resources continues at the end of *War* when Josephus returns to the Dead Sea in his narrative of the progress of Lucius Bassus, who arrived in Judaea in 71 CE to mop up Judaean resistance (*War* 7: 163–89). Bassus first takes eastern Herodium, and then sets his sights on nearby Machaerus, the fortress-palace (Josephus calls a 'city'). Josephus describes the circumstances of Machaerus accurately, noting the height of the hill and the depth of the valleys all around (Plate 11), and telling his readers that it was Alexander Jannaeus, 'King of the Judaeans', who built the fortress there (173). Demolished by Gabinius in his war on Aristobulus (57 BCE), it was rebuilt by Herod, who constructed walls, towers, a palace, and many water reservoirs (7: 174–6), a description that correlates with the evidence from archaeological excavations here.[57] While the invincibility of Machaerus is appropriate to the subject, Josephus also mentions giant 'rue' (7: 178–9), a reference that has been rightly noted by John Allegro as striking.[58] Josephus writes:

> There once grew in the palace grounds a rue ($\pi\acute{\eta}\gamma\alpha\mu\text{o}\nu$), worthy of wonder for its size, for it was no smaller than a fig tree in height or width. The report was that it lasted from the times of Herod, and may have remained later, but was cut down by the Judaeans who took over the place.

Josephus mentions a 'report' ($\lambda\acute{o}\gamma\text{o}\varsigma$), and this report is very current, since it refers to the Judaean rebels who have cut down the rue. This destruction of the plant is strange, and the implication seems to be that it had some association with Herod. But this is interesting also: Herod, according to Josephus, was a planter and tender of a medicinal garden of massive rue. This rue appears not to have been indigenous to the region, since it was specially cultivated by Herod.

Josephus' 'report' of the landscape of the Dead Sea and Jericho is a curious insert into a military history. Rather than a description of the economic

---

[57] Virgilio Corbo, 'La fortezza di Macheronte: Rapporto preliminare della prima campagna di scavo: 8 settembre–28 ottobre 1978,' *Liber Annuus* 28 (1978): 217–38; id. 'La reggia-fortezza erodiana. Rapporto preliminare alla seconda campagna di scavo: 3 settembre–20 ottobre 1979,' *Liber Annuus* 29 (1979): 315–26; id. 'La fortezza di Macheronte (Al-Mishnaqa). Rapporto preliminare alla terza campagna di scavo: 8 settembre–11 octobre 1980,' *Liber Annuus* 30 (1980): 365–76; Virgilio Corbo and Stannislao Loffreda, 'Nuove scoperte alla fortezza di Macheronte. Rapporto preliminare alla quarta campagna di scavo: 7 settembre–10 ottobre 1981,' *Liber Annuus* 31 (1981): 257–86; Michele Piccirillo, 'Le monete della fortezza di Macheronte (El-Mishnaqa),' *Liber Annuus* 30 (1981): 403–14; August Strobel, 'Das römische Belagerungswerk um Macharus. Topographische Untersuchungen,' *ZDPV* 90 (1974): 128–84.

[58] 'Josephus' digression to speak of a particular Rue plant in a topographical account of the Machaerus fortress as it bore on a vital Roman campaign in Transjordan, is strange, to say the least.... [T]he introduction by this author of plant physiology and folk-lore into an otherwise non-botanical discussion usually implies some hidden reference to a matter which he is reluctant to bring fully into the open', John Allegro, *The Sacred Mushroom and the Cross* (London: Hodder and Stoughton, 1970), 92. This sound observation exists in an otherwise extremely imaginative work.

resources of the Dead Sea region, or its paradoxical characteristics, its main topic was medicinal plants. For example, from Machaerus Josephus goes on to describe a valley to the north where a plant grows called 'baaras', apparently a type of mandrake (*War* 7: 178–89). This valley is clearly the Wadi Zarqa Main: an arresting canyon with high cliff faces with various types of hot and cold waterfalls and springs. According to Josephus, these waters are also tasted (they can be sweet or bitter). For him, these waters are themselves 'medicinal' (παιώνιον).

Interestingly, Josephus' account confuses the effect of the sun in the valley at dusk with the colour of the baaras, which he says has 'a colour like flame and sends out a ray like lightning towards the evening' (180). There is an extraordinary effect of the setting sun in the Wadi Zarqa Main: the sun shoots a picturesque ray of light through the majestic rocky opening to the west as it descends (behind Bethlehem and western Herodium, at certain times of the year); it is a natural phenomenon that appears as magical today as it must have seemed to those of long ago, and is hard to capture on camera (Plate 12). The rest of Josephus' description about the harvesting of the plant repeats a myth about mandrake (Theophrastus, *Hist. Plant.* 9: 8: 8), one of the most prized medicines of antiquity.

Josephus also states that sulphur and alum are mined beside the lake (189), again substances known to be important in medicine (Dioscorides, *De Materia Medica* 5: 123). Given that Josephus overall does not continually mention the medicinal properties of plants and other resources at every turn throughout his *Judaean War*,[59] the curious clustering of medical resources around the Dead Sea suggests that his recent report was one that focused on the region as a locus for yielding these, and he inserted this data to provide interesting contextual information about the locality to flesh out the main Roman conquest narrative. The interest in medicinal plants, waters, and substances of the Dead Sea area does not continue in Josephus' account in *War* 7 when Josephus returns to Bassus' conquest of Machaerus and the hunting of refugees in the forest of Jarden. Here the Roman conquest source—devoid of medicinal concerns—appears to have been utilized, and returned to again in the account of the campaign by Silva, who succeeded Bassus, in regard to the taking of Masada (*War* 7: 252–404). If the former 'medicinal interest' source were part of this conquest source, we would expect some mention of the plants that grew in En Gedi, near Masada, particularly opobalsam, but En Gedi is overlooked here as a medicinal location just when one might expect it, because the

---

[59] However, this is not to say that Josephus is completely uninterested in medicine. Incidentally, his works contain numerous details of the work of ancient physicians, healing practices, exorcisms, and medicine; see Max Neuburger, *Die Medizin in Flavius Josephus* (Bad Reichenhall: Buchkunst, 1919); Samuel S. Kottek, *Medicine and Hygiene in the Works of Flavius Josephus* (Leiden: Brill, 1994).

chronicle is now clearly a military history. Josephus otherwise mentions En Gedi in *Ant.* 9: 7 as being a place where the best kind of palm tree and opobalsam is growing; it is Josephus who, for the first time in the chronological sequence of ancient sources, indicates that En Gedi had an opobalsam plantation, and this is post-Hasmonean.

In terms of what else Josephus tells us about the Dead Sea, the account of Josephus in *War* 7 is the most important one from antiquity in regard to Masada and the south-western (Judaean) Dead Sea vicinity at the time of the siege, lasting until 73 CE. Before this, when Josephus describes the revolutionary fighters who take over Masada, they attack and raid En Gedi, where they apparently put to death men, women, and children and carry off spoils: Josephus gives the number of deaths as being over seven hundred people. This seems to assume that the fighters saw the people living in the town after 68 CE as being their enemies (Josephus, *War* 4: 402–3). Mention of the Feast of Unleavened Bread, on which the massacre occurs, indicates that the En Gedi people were Jews. There seems no reason for the Masada fighters to act with such terrible ferocity against fellow Jews unless those people were considered to be in league with the Romans. This indicates a scenario in which Jews continued to live on the western shores of the Dead Sea post-68, with the understanding that they were loyal to Rome.

Importantly, Josephus also describes the location of Sodom. As noted above in terms of Dio's reference to Sodom,[60] Greek and Roman writers knew about the destruction of this city (Strabo, *Geog.* 16: 2: 44; Tacitus, *Hist.* 5: 6–7; Julius Solinus, *Coll.* 35: 8, cf. Gen. 19: 1–29). Josephus links the burning of the towns, by lightning bolts, with ash-filled fruit, later dubbed 'Sodom's apples' (*Ant.* 1: 169; *War* 4: 484) as would Tacitus (*Hist.* 5: 7). It is anyone's guess how early this association was made; the fruit is usually identified as *Calotropis procera*, and is found around the Dead Sea today.[61] This further note of a medicinal plant in Josephus' discussion adds another item to his list. Josephus' interest in medicinal resources around the Dead Sea relates suggestively to a source known to Roman medical writers, evidenced in the writings of Cornelius Celsus in the first half of the first century CE, referred to mysteriously, only as 'Judeus': 'the Judaean'.[62]

Josephus has Lot possessing the Jordan plain and river (Gen. 13: 10–12) 'not far from the city of the Sodomites' (*Ant.* 1: 169), the ashes of which he claims to have seen (*War* 4: 483), which would mean it was in the north. In his description in *War* 4: 453–4, as we saw, Josephus writes of two mountain

---

[60] See above, p. 147.

[61] John Granger Cook, *The Interpretation of the Old Testament in Greco-Roman Paganism* (Tübingen: Mohr Siebeck, 2004), 45–6, 48, 103–4.

[62] Stern, *Greek and Latin Authors*, i, 368–9. Celsus, *De medicina*, Latin text and Eng. trans. by W. G. Spencer, 3 vols (Loeb Classical Library; London/Cambridge, MA: Heinemann/Harvard University Press, 1935–8).

ranges facing each other: in the east was the range beginning at Julias (north-east of the Sea of Galilee), extending all the way to Petra, and in the west was a range that went northwards to Scythopolis 'and southwards to the region of the Sodomites and those [parts] the other side of the [lake] of Asphaltites': κατὰ δὲ τὸ μεσημβρινὸν μέχρι τῆς Σοδομιτῶν χώρας καὶ τῶν περάτων τῆς Ἀσφαλτίτιδος, the 'other side' here apparently indicating the south, which is differentiated from the region of the Sodomites that the range passes through. The 'region of the Sodomites' is the barren land stretching along the western (Judaean) side of the Dead Sea, an area which is 'both uneven and uninhabited because of the sterility' (*War* 4: 453).

Josephus later notes that the lake itself stretched in its dimensions to Zoara of Arabia (*War* 4: 482); Zoara, though in fact fertile and inhabited, was one of the five cities, as Philo recognizes (*Abr.* 141). It is this city with its surrounding fertile fields (Plate 13) that is located south of the lake, not Sodom, at all.[63] For Josephus, it is in a wide area around the Dead Sea that 'the vestiges of *five* cities are still to be seen' (*War* 4: 483–4).[64] In other words, Josephus differentiates between the specific ruins of the city of Sodom, located apparently near the Jordan river and plain, and 'the region of the Sodomites': the extensive, barren area lying west of the Dead Sea, in which the ruins of the five condemned cities were apparently visible.[65] Here he ignores the fertile anomaly of En Gedi and other occupied sites beside potable water.

Josephus also claimed to have seen the pillar of salt into which Lot's wife was turned as they fled Sodom (*Ant.* 1: 203, cf. Gen. 19: 26),[66] but he gives no indication where this was located. In later times there were two locations for this monument, one in the north and one in the south. For the northern pillar, in the eighth-century account of Epiphanius the Monk (*Civ. Sanct.* 32), it is

---

[63] In *War* 4: 482 the subject proximate to Sodom is the lake, not Zoara, which is only a point to which it stretches. γειτνιᾷ δ' ἡ [χώρα] Σοδομῖτις αὐτῇ [λίμνη] : 'Bordering on this the [land of] Sodomites . . .' (*War* 4: 483). Thackeray read the Greek here as the cities of the plain were all lying adjacent to Zoara, perhaps thinking of Jebel Usdum, which in modern times has become known as 'Mount Sodom', though he notes that '[m]any older authorities located the cities of the plain to the *north* of the Dead Sea'; see H. St. J. Thackeray (ed.), *Josephus III* (Loeb Classical Library; Cambridge, MA/London: Harvard University Press/Heinemann, 1968), 143 note e.

[64] There were numerous ruined settlements around the north-western Dead Sea at the time of Josephus, these were not ancient Bronze Age sites but rather ruins of Iron Age settlements destroyed by the Babylonians in 586 BCE. Only a few of these were reconstituted by the Hasmoneans.

[65] Stern thought that Josephus was not consistent, and that Strabo located Sodom to the south of the Dead Sea (*Geogr.* 16: 2: 44), see Stern, *Greek and Latin Authors*, i, 539–40. But Strabo's evidence does not do this, and is not exactly the most reliable on which to base a localization, given he does not have the right number of destroyed cities or the correct name of the lake in question.

[66] John Wilkinson, *Egeria's Travels* (Warminster: Aris and Phillips, 1981), 219, notes that it is a commonplace in early Christian tradition from the late first and second centuries that this pillar may be seen (Clement of Rome, *Ep. Cor.* 11: 4; Irenaeus, *Haer.* 4: 31: 3).

two miles south of the cave of John the Baptist, a Byzantine site located in the lower reaches of the Jordan River.[67] The corresponding location of Sodom in the north evidenced by Josephus also has a continuing legacy. At the end of the fourth century, the Spanish nun Egeria (*Itin.* 12: 5–6), looked out to 'the whole country of the Sodomites' as lying to the left (south) of her lookout on Mount Nebo, which likewise reflects a notion that it is a broad area of land bordering the north-western part of the lake. She noted that while Segor remains (here meaning a wrongly identified site close to Mount Nebo),[68] 'all that is left of the other [cities] is heaps of ruins, because they were burned to ashes'.[69] Egeria was pointed towards 'the place where Lot's wife had her memorial', but this 'was not the actual pillar, but only the place where it had once been' because 'the pillar has been submerged by the Dead Sea; at any rate, we did not see it, and I cannot pretend that we did'. The Bishop of 'Segor' informed Egeria that it was a long time since the pillar had been visible; it used to stand near the sixth milestone [one encountered] out of Segor (Egeria, *Itin.* 12: 6–7), on the road to Livias; so then being near present-day Suweima.[70] This corresponds with the placement of the monument by Epiphanius the Monk.

By comparison also, the sixth-century Piacenza Pilgrim (*Itin.* 15/169) writes that going westwards[71] from Jericho (i.e. leaving Jericho on the west and then travelling south) 'you encounter the ashes of Sodom and Gomorra, which are on your left'. The monk Adomnan (*Loc. Sanct.* 2: 17: 7; cf. Bede, *Loc. Sanct.* 11: 1), on the basis of Arculf's journey of *c.*670–5 CE, measures the sea as 580 stadia from the north 'to Zoar of Arabia' (correctly identified) in the south and 150 stadia across it 'to the region of Sodom', meaning either the eastern or western shore, and—given Josephus and the Piacenza Pilgrim—it is clearly the western.[72]

---

[67] The Piacenza Pilgrim scoffs at the suggestion that Lot's wife was being reduced in size by animals licking her (Piacenza Pilgrim, *Itin.* 15/169–70, cf. Benjamin of Tudela 37). Theodosius (*Top.* 20) notes that 'when the moon waxes she grows, and when it wanes she shrinks'.

[68] The place where Moses died is Ras el-Siyagha on Mount Nebo (Egeria, *Itin.* 12: 1; Theodosius, *Top.* 19/145; John Rufus, *Vita Per. Iber.* 85–9), the Arabic name deriving from this wrong placement; a Byzantine town was located close by at el-Makhayyat, see Joan E. Taylor, 'The Dead Sea in Western Travellers' Accounts from the Byzantine to the Modern Period,' *Strata* 27 (2009): 9–29, at 11–12, and ead. 'Aus dem Westen ans Tote Meer: Frühe Reisende und Entdecker,' in Zangenberg, *Das Tote Meer*, 149–64, at 151.

[69] The Piacenza Pilgrim also notes the ruins of Segor here: 'From the Jordan it is eight miles to the place where Moses departed from this life, and a little further on is Segor. . . . and we saw too the tomb of Absalom' (*Itin.* 10/166). The tomb of Absalom is also mentioned in the Copper Scroll (3Q15 10: 12–13). See Taylor, 'Dead Sea in Western Travellers' Accounts,' 12.

[70] Zoara was usually in the Byzantine period rightly situated south of the lake, as shown in the Madaba mosaic map. The Byzantine evidence appears to indicate that there were two rival locations for the pillar: one visible from the lookout on Mount Nebo, and another between Zoara/Segor on the way to Bennamareim (Eusebius, *Onom.* 138: 20–1).

[71] The term can mean anything from north-west to south-west, here clearly south-south-west.

[72] See Theodosius, *Top.* 20, *Gesta Francorum Expugnantium* 15; *Descriptio locorum* 25; *Second Guide* 127/9). Eusebius placed the cities close to Lasan (*Onom.* 150 cf. 60, 120), perhaps al-Lisan, the tongue which juts into the lake from its south-eastern side.

This location of the ruins of Sodom—and indeed the associated pillar of Lot's wife—in a north-western area, close to the Jordan Valley, is something then to bear in mind in regard to Dio's mention of Essenes located in a city not far from Sodom.

There is one final point to note in regard to what Josephus states in regard to the Dead Sea, and it provides an important watershed in terms of the developments in this area. In the year 35 BCE it seems that Queen Alexandra still lived in the Hasmonean palace in Jericho, along with her son Aristobulus, but Herod had power enough to ensure the young man was drowned in the swimming pool (*Ant.* 15: 50–6; *War* 1: 437). Herod had then to answer to an accusation of murder from Cleopatra of Egypt, and appear before Mark Antony, in Laodicea. Antony mollified Cleopatra by giving her 'Jericho', the Jordan Valley, and the bitumen rights to the Dead Sea (*Ant.* 15: 96), so that Herod had to lease back this land, paying her 200 talents per year (*War* 1: 362; *Ant.* 15: 96, 106–7, 132).[73] This financially unfortunate situation continued until Antony and Cleopatra's downfall in September 31 BCE, when Herod's Dead Sea holdings were returned to him.

Pliny *c.*23 BCE–79 CE

Pliny's material on Judaea has been examined above, since he embeds his caricature of Essenes within it (*Nat. Hist.* 5: 15 [70–73]). It is in Pliny and his contemporary Dio that we find Essenes situated in connection with the well-known features of the area, and their appearance seems more interesting now that we can see the various elements of the portrayal of the Dead Sea region developing over time (see Table 1). Pliny's source material for the 'wonders of Judaean waters' was most probably, as argued above, the book prepared by Licinius Mucianus (*fl.* 73–5 CE).

Elsewhere Pliny mentions Lake Asphaltitis as producing bitumen, and notes that nothing can sink in it (*Nat. Hist.* 2: 106 [226]). In accordance with the arrangement of his work, he discusses this bitumen in Book 7, and describes it occurring in a Judaean lake which is called 'Asphaltites'. At certain times of the year it floats on the surface. It sticks to everything, and cannot be cut except by a thread soaked in poisonous fluid (7: 15 [65], cf. 28: 23 [80], 35: 51 [178]). Callirhoe (*Hist. Nat.* 5: 15 [72]) appears in this account as a famous site but unfortunately is not mentioned elsewhere in Pliny's work.[74]

---

[73] Peter Richardson, *Herod: King of the Jews and Friend of the Romans* (New York: Continuum 1999), 166–7.

[74] See Josephus, *War* 1: 657–9; *Ant.* 17: 169–76; Ptolemy, *Geogr.* 5: 15: 6; Iulius Solinus, *Collectanea Rerum Memorabilium* 35: 1; Martianus Capella, *De Nuptiis Philologiae et Mercurii* (*Satyricon*) 6: 679.

Pliny's discussion of opobalsam (*Nat. Hist.* 12: 54 [111–15]) stresses the importance of this economic resource to the Romans who took over the area in 68 CE. As with the source that concerns the waters of Judaea, which is best attributed to Mucianus, this part also is firmly situated in the time immediately following the Roman conquest of the area, and would therefore appropriately derive from Mucianus also. The element of 'wonder' is clear here. This is possibly used by Julius Solinus (*Coll.* 35: 1–5), who included balsam where Pliny cuts and pastes it to a different part of his work (see Table 1). Given Pliny's arrangement in accordance with certain subjects, it would make sense that Pliny lifted it out of Mucianus and placed it elsewhere in terms of his ordering of things, so that he could discuss opobalsam in terms of its properties. In this description Pliny seems to have also inserted details from other sources of information, in order to make the account more comprehensive and scientific, particularly referencing Theophrastus; it is therefore impossible to lift out Mucianus from Pliny in this part of the *Natural History*.

Pliny notes that one of the lands vouchsafed for balsam is Judaea, where it was 'once (*quondam*) cultivated only in two gardens, both royal [estates], one of 20 iugera and the other smaller' (*Nat. Hist.* 12: 54 [111–13]),[75] but now this was not the case, for 'nowadays' or 'recently' (*nuper*) it had been taught to grow in rows, like a vine. It 'covers hills' and has 'never been more plentiful' (*Nat. Hist.* 12: 54 [112–14]). In this case, the historic circumstance of *Judaean* balsam is assigned to two orchards that may be identified (given what Josephus states) as Jericho and En Gedi, but this circumstance relates to the past. It also relates to perhaps a Latin version of Theophrastus that Pliny appears to be referring to at various points, interpreted as relating to Judaean cultivation. The 'now' of the text indicates wider cultivation than former times. Pliny emphasizes that the capturing of the economic resource of opobalsam was especially significant to the Romans. Opobalsam plants formed part of the victory procession in Rome: 'The emperors Vespasian [and Titus] exhibited the tree here in the city [of Rome] . . .' states Pliny, and 'this tree serves tribute and is weighed out with its people (*gens*)' (*Hist. Nat.* 12: 54 [111–12]). This is a striking image of the opobalsam being on sale in Rome along with Jewish slaves.

When the Romans swept into this region in 68 CE, the Jews tried to destroy the balsam plants, so that the Romans would not enjoy the profit from them. Pliny writes:

[75] Perhaps thinking of only the Hasmonean plantations of opobalsam in Jericho and En Gedi (cf. *War* 1: 361; *War* 4: 469; *Ant.* 15: 96; *Ant.* 9: 7). Note that Pliny has no interest or awareness of opobalsam plantations in Nabataea.

> The Judaeans vented their rage on this [plant] just as [they did] on their own life, while, against [them], the Romans protected it; indeed, there have been battles before for fruit. (114).

The reference to venting their rage on their own life is interesting given that the fall of Masada, with its mass suicide of Jewish fighters, occurred in 73 CE, just when Pliny was writing. It was now cultivated by the Roman *fiscus* (the personal treasury of the Roman emperors). According to Pliny, within five years after the Roman conquest of Judaea (dated from 70 CE), the sale of Judaean balsam trimmings alone—regardless of the actual sap—apparently brought in 800,000 sesterces to the Roman treasury (*Nat. Hist.* 12: 54 [118]). The importance of the balsam cultivation as an economic resource from this area is confirmed by a document from Masada, post-73 CE, which mentions *xylobalsamum* (Inv. no. 1039–122/1), wooden trimmings,[76] probably re-sourced from nearby En Gedi.

This much may come from Mucianus, but Pliny weaves in another source that is much more concerned with the botanical nature of opobalsam and how one can test for the genuine article given the numerous mixes and false versions. In terms of its botanical character, Pliny states that it is not at all like a myrtle (*myrtus*), the bush to which it had been compared in the version of Theophrastus that Pliny knew, though Theophrastus had compared the tree to a large ῥόα, which would be better translated as a pomegranate (*Punica Granatum*), as above. Pliny states that it is more like a vine but stands no more than three feet high, with thicker branches (112, 114, 115). An unsupported balsam bush is root-clipped, with a *rastrum* (a kind of hatchet), which makes it sprout and fruit within three years. Pliny writes that there were three varieties of opobalsam, and here Pliny transliterates Greek, possibly indicating here a Greek source text: i. *eutheriston* (εὐθέριστον), 'easy-to-gather', with thin, hairy foliage; ii. *trachy* (τραχύ), 'rough', with a rugged, curving bushy appearance and a stronger scent; and iii. *eumeces* (εὐμέκης), 'tall', with a smooth bark. In order of quality, the τραχύ was considered the best, then εὐμέκης, and, finally, εὐθέριστον (Pliny, *Nat. Hist.* 12: 54 [114]).

That Pliny mentions tasting balsam seeds (115) would indicate their use as a medicine to be ingested, though initially Pliny introduces the balsam as a perfume (111). To gather the sap, incisions are made in the bark with a piece of glass or stone, or with bone knives, not with iron, though pruning can be done with iron tools. This sap is called 'opobalsam' and is collected by tufts of wool in small horns, thereafter poured into a new pottery vessel for storage. It is sweet (implying also it is ingested) and is thick and white, but later hardens and turns red (115–16). Pliny then mentions that in the time of Alexander the

---

[76] Hannah M. Cotton, 'The Date of the Fall of Masada: The Evidence of the Masada Papyri,' *Zeitschrift für Papyrologie und Epigraphik* 78 (1989): 157–62, at 161.

Great (fourth century BCE) a whole day's work would go into filling a single 'shell' (*concham*), here again referring to Theophrastus, but he goes on to state that the whole produce of the larger of the two gardens was once only six shells, and the smaller garden filled one shell, when today one tree alone produces more than that, bled of its sap three times in summer (117). This comparison of present abundance with the past seems to indicate Pliny had an account that expanded on Theophrastus, and included the appearance of Alexander, but this is clearly part of an advertising pitch of the first century with no credible origin in historical actuality. The 'once small, now large' paradigm increases the sense of Roman success.

Pliny follows Theophrastus—or the expanded version of Theophrastus—by exploring mixtures and the issue of authenticity. Lower grades of the sap could be produced from the branches, fruit, or seeds of the plant, for example by boiling the twigs in water and by various mixings with other substances (Pliny, *Nat. Hist.* 12: 54 [118–23]), this inferior opobalsam alone being lucrative, and boiled down for perfumes. In terms of value the sap is most prized, the seed second in value, and the wood third (118). Wood is clearly ingested, as Pliny comments on its taste (119), and he then gives various methods of testing whether the opobalsam is genuine and mixed with other substances (120–3).

Elsewhere, Pliny also discusses the Judaean palm trees at great length (*Nat. Hist.* 13: 6–9 [26–49]), situating the Judaean varieties in a general discussion of all kinds of others. The caryotic date palm is identified in the region of Archelais, Phasaelis, and Livias (the Jericho region),[77] grown for food and the juice that is made into a powerful wine, though all the types of date palms mentioned (Caryotic, Nicolaitan, Patetic) seem to be growing here, and Pliny notes that Judaeans call a certain type by the name Chydaeus (46), all of which are good for keeping (49).

As we saw, in Pliny's description of the Dead Sea, the focus is on Judaean water and its peculiarities, from the source of the Jordan to its end at the south of Lake Asphaltites. Judaea's length is the extent of the flow of the River Jordan, which continues through to the end of the Dead Sea. The people are essentially defined by means of this water also, with the peculiar Essenes, situated next to the peculiarly lifeless Dead Sea and vibrant palm trees of Jericho and En Gedi. It is in Pliny that we have the Essenes first referred to in this locality, and thus in terms of historical chronology this locates them quite firmly in the period *c.*68–75 CE, since the circumstances Pliny presents of the Dead Sea area, both in terms of the named sites (En Gedi, Jerusalem, Jericho, Machaerus, and Masada) and also the post-68 cultivation of opobalsam, places us within a narrow range of dates, reflecting most likely the observations of Mucianus.

---

[77] For the extension of date palm plantings from Jericho to Archelais and Phasaelis see Josephus, *Ant.* 18: 31.

Dio Chrysostom (*c.*93 CE), *apud* Synesius

The mention of the Dead Sea by Dio Chrysostom has already been discussed in Part I, where its relationship to what later appears in Julius Solinus was explored. We have examined how, like Pliny, Dio refers to the Essenes close to Sodom, which—as we have seen from Josephus—is a site best located in the north-western part of the Dead Sea area. Dio does not use the sites of Pliny in terms of his placement, but rather the ruins of an ancient city destroyed for its disobedience to divine will. It just so happens that this was thought to have been somewhere just south of Jericho, in the north-western part of the Dead Sea. This area is the same Essene region Pliny defines. We can observe here, though, that in the historical circumstances of both Pliny and Dio the Hasmoneans are long gone.

Tacitus (*c.*105 CE)

The Roman historian Tacitus, writing his monumental *History* (5: 6–7),[78] mentions the palm groves and balsam. The palm groves are high and elegant, and the balsam is a shrub, its branches pierced with a piece of stone or pottery, since iron makes it shrink. This reference may indicate he has read Pliny. He notes that the balsam sap is used by physicians. Tacitus also employs the motif of the water, which starts from the Libanus range and runs through two lakes before being lost in a third. This third one is huge in circumference and creates illness in those who live close to it by its awful smell. It is unmoved by wind and has no fish or water fowl. It causes people to float. At a certain point of every year it tosses up asphalt, which is made to float by pouring vinegar upon it. Old stories have it that it shrinks from cloth which is soaked in menstrual blood, but actually 'those who know the country' say that the bitumen floats on the water in great lumps and is drawn in to the shore where it is dried by evaporation in the sun, after which it is cut into pieces with axes and wedges.

Tacitus also refers to the destruction of the ancient cities here, without mentioning any names. He reflects the biblical narrative in stating there was once a fertile plain that was struck by lightning and destroyed, so that the soil even today has lost its fertility. Anything planted goes rotten and black. Tacitus himself states it is more likely that the soil and air are infected by the exhalations of the lake. By implication, he refers to the fruit filled with an 'ashy' interior reputed to have come into existence as being the result of this cataclysm (*Calotropis procera*).

[78] Tacitus *Cornelii Taciti Historiarum Libri*, C. D. Fisher (ed.) (Oxford: OUP, 1911); Tacitus, *The Histories, Books 4–5*, Clifford H. Moore (ed. and trans.) (Loeb Classical Library: Cambridge, MA: Harvard University Press 1970).

Pausanias (*fl. c.*155–80 CE)

Pausanias' geographical work on Greece relied on numerous sources no longer extant. In an aside, he mentions 'the Dead Sea' (Pausanias, *Descriptio Graecae* 5: 7: 4–5)[79] as an example of peculiar water. As we saw, there is the descriptive term 'dead water' used by Dio, but it is not a name for the lake. Pausanias states that in the Dead Sea 'living creatures float in it naturally without swimming; dying creatures sink to the bottom. Hence the lake is barren of fish; their danger stares them in the face, and they flee back to the water which is their native element'. This representation of fish struggling to swim back up the Jordan River is shown in the sixth-century Madaba mosaic map (Plate 43), though in fact both living and dying creatures float in these waters. He also mentions palm trees in Palestine that always yield a delicious fruit (*Descr. Graec.* 9: 19: 8). Here, as elsewhere, we have a sense of the influence of the *mirabilia*.

Claudius Ptolemy (*fl. c.*140–65 CE)

Claudius Ptolemy's *Geographica* provided a great compendium of knowledge in terms of the placements of cities and lands in the ancient world, information that would form the basis of medieval cartography, resulting in a standard Ptolemaic map of Asia, including Palestine. The information about Judaea appears in Book 5, where *pars Asphatitem lacum* are mentioned as well as the main cities. In the region east of the Jordan, there are sites that are not all easy to determine: Cosmas, Libias, Callirhoe, Gazorus, Epicaeros (Ptolemy, *Geogr.* 5: 15: 6).[80] The sequence should be north to south. Only Livias and Callirhoe can be identified easily by reference to other ancient authors. Cosmas is probably Esbus (Heshbon) and Gazorus seems to indicate Zoara, which could also be rendered Zoora (Eusebius, *Onom.* 42). The main town at the southern part of the Dead Sea was Zoara, and it would be most likely that the term 'Gazorus' indicates this city, being a contraction of what in Aramaic (Nabataean) would have been *Ganneth-Zoara*, 'the gardens of Zoara'. Epicaeros is then somewhere further south.

---

[79] Pausanias, *Description of Greece*, W. H. S. Jones and H. A. Omerod (eds and trans.) (Loeb Classical Library; Cambridge, MA: Harvard University Press, 1918).

[80] Alfred Stückelberger and Gerd Graßhoff (eds), *Klaudios Ptolemaios: Handbuch der Geographie, Griechisch-Deutsch*, 2 vols (Basel: Schwabe Verlag, 2006); Claudius Ptolemaeus, *Geographica Universalis, vetus et nova complectens* (Basel: Henricum Petrum, 1540) and Edward Luther Stevenson (ed.), *The Geography by Claudius Ptolemy, Greek geographer of the 2nd century A.D.* (New York: Dover, 1932, repr. 1991).

Later Authors

As we have seen already from Julius Solinus, Graeco-Roman writers continued to draw on bodies of information about the Dead Sea. Interest in the Dead Sea developed further with Christian authors, who testify from the fourth century onwards to its observed features—mixed with the traditions they knew. Pilgrimage to sites such as Lot's Cave, in the south-east, brought Christian tourists to this environment. One can see in later sources much use of earlier texts, such as in that of Martianus Capella, *De Nuptiis Philologiae et Mercurii (Satyricon)* 6: 679 (*c*.400 CE):

> Beyond Idumaea and Samaria Judaea extends far and wide. The part of it adjoining Syria is called Galilee, divided from the rest of it by the River Jordan, which river rises from the spring of Paneas [. . .] a high place of Judaea second to Jerusalem, on which side is the spring of Callirhoe. On the west [are] the Essenes who live without copulation and all sexual desires. A good deal interior from this place is Masada fortress, at which Judaea ends.[81]

Here, for example, the summarized source is clearly Pliny. The later travellers are important for preserving traditions and snippets of sources now lost to us, as we have explored above in relation to the placement of Sodom, but space here does not permit a thorough survey of all of these.[82]

CONCLUSION AND EXCURSUS: THE DEAD SEA FROM THE HASMONEANS TO BAR KOKHBA

This survey has shown that the writers of Greece and Rome were interested only in particular aspects of the lake and its surroundings (the lucrative resources of asphalt, date palms, balsam, the myth of destroyed cities, the contrast between fertility and sterility). The evidence they present, arranged chronologically, and with reference to archaeology, nevertheless provides an indication of the historical changes in the region that would affect settlement and ownership.

Most striking is the indication of Hasmonean expansion and economic exploitation, with a transfer of Nabataean balsam (the balsam of Gilead) into

---

[81] supra Idumaeam et Samariam Iudaea longe lateque funditur. pars eius Syriae iuncta Galilaea vocatur, a ceteris eius partibus Iordane amne discreta, qui fluvius oritur de fonte Paneade [. . .] secunda elatio Iudaeae ab Hierosolymis, in quo latere est fons Callirhoe. ab occidente Esseni, qui sine concubitu et cunctis cupiditatibus vivunt. hinc aliquanto interius Masada castellum, in quo Iudaeae finis est. See James Willis (ed.), Martianus Capella, *De Nuptiis Philologiae et Mercurii* (BSG; Berlin: Teubner, 1983), 241.

[82] See Taylor, 'Western Travellers'; ead. 'Aus dem Westen ans Tote Meer.'

Judaean royal control; from the Hasmoneans onwards it is known as the balsam of Judaea, grown only in the royal estates, most probably in Jericho and En Gedi. This impression from the literary sources is complemented by the archaeological evidence of Hasmonean fortified settlements along the western coast between Jericho and En Gedi, settlements which create a chain that lies along a supply route, alternative to sea travel, most likely dating to the reign of Alexander Jannaeus (103–76 BCE). For shipping there was an anchorage at Rujm el-Bahr, not far from Jericho, which would have connected with the harbour of En Gedi and other anchorages. The settlements along the western side of the Dead Sea, established in the Hasmonean era, are then fortified installations which served the purposes of defence and the harnessing of local resources.

The relatively small and highly lucrative amounts of balsam that would have been shipped on to markets apparently never required a highly developed settlement area or road system here, but the hegemony of the Hasmoneans in this region is visible in the archaeological record. The establishment of the grand fortresses of Hyrcania, Machaerus, and Masada at this time likewise created—along with Jericho—a constellation of four major strongholds located roughly north, south, west, and east of the Dead Sea, with medium-sized named forts close to Jericho (Alexandrium, north-west of Jericho; Doq; Cypros) and minor fortified settlements between Jericho and En Gedi.[83]

The lucrative resources of the Dead Sea, and all the fortresses, of course passed to Herod when he became 'King of the Judaeans', and he began some building work in Jericho[84] and Masada,[85] though there was a problematic blip in his enjoyment of the area when Mark Antony gave it to Cleopatra in 34 BCE, and he had to lease it back until their demise at Actium in 31 BCE, which meant these were restored to Herod by Augustus (*War* 1: 386–96; *Ant.* 15: 187–201).[86] Afterwards, Herod appears to have claimed the region with a vengeance. Herod developed the old Hasmonean strongholds (Alexandrium, Doq, Cypros, Taurus),[87] and expanded the palace-fortresses with extensive

---

[83] Netzer, *Architecture of Herod*, 202–3.

[84] Netzer, *Hasmonean and Herodian Palaces*, 40–2. This first building was not part of the main Hasmonean palace complex but south of the Wadi Qelt, occupied by Herod while Queen Salome Alexandra was still in residence in the palace.

[85] Netzer, *Hasmonean and Herodian Palaces*, 79–87; id. *Architecture of Herod*, 204–12.

[86] The year 31 BCE was also the date of an earthquake recorded by Josephus (*Ant.* 15: 121–2), affecting armies, people, and herds of cattle around Kanatha and Dion, east of the Jordan Valley, though it may have been quite localized and far less significant than has been supposed, see Iaakov Karcz, 'Implications of Some Early Jewish Sources for Estimates of Earthquake Hazard in the Holy Land,' *Annals of Geophysics* 47 (2004): 759–88, at 774–8.

[87] Netzer, *Architecture of Herod*, 204–12; id.*Hasmonean and Herodian Palaces*, 68–75; Yoram Tsafrir and Yitzhak Magen, 'The Desert Fortresses of Judaea in the Second Temple Period,' *The Jerusalem Cathedra* 2 (1982): 120–45.

water systems, at Jericho,[88] Machaerus,[89] and Masada.[90] Everywhere in the region, the archaeological evidence of Herod's building on Hasmonean structures is found. As is well known, Herod was an enthusiastic builder,[91] and when it came to the Dead Sea region he did not only focus on the old Hasmonean sites, but created new smaller ones out of rudimentary beginnings, at Betharamptha, or the eastern fortress of Herodium, developing the healing centre of Callirhoe,[92] along with a pharmacological site at En Boqeq,[93] and gardens—apparently—at Ain Feshkha.[94] These latter two new sites would have been created as valuable royal estates, as defined in Samuel Rocca's study.[95] Significantly, as Rocca states, such '[r]oyal lands were also given, temporarily or permanently, as gifts to certain individuals and groups. Herod gave lands as gifts, to people such as Ptolemy, to urban settlements that he founded on his own land, and to military colonists'.[96] At this point we may recall Herod honouring the Essenes (Philo, *Hypoth.* 11: 18; Josephus, *War* 2: 135).

One further piece of evidence for Herod's hold on the Dead Sea might be relevant. As we saw in the discussion concerning Dio Chrysostom, in the Hebrew translation of Aristotle's *Meteorologia* made by Shmuel Ibn Tibbon in 1210 there is in the Budapest manuscript of 1500 an additional piece not found in any other manuscript of *Meteorologia* or commentary on it: 'This is the Dead Sea, called *Aiga Mortu*, in the land of Hodo, and on the side of the Temple, and from it asphalt comes out every year, thrown by the same' (2: 184–5).[97] This addition appears to indicate the absorption into the Hebrew

---

[88] As noted above, he filled over the former palace at Jericho and built a hippodrome at Tel es-Samarat, 1.5 km north of the palaces (Netzer, *Hasmonean and Herodian Palaces*, 43–67).

[89] See above for the archaeological excavations at Machaerus, and Netzer, *Hasmonean and Herodian Palaces*, 75–6; id. *Architecture of Herod*, 213–17.

[90] See in particular Samuel Rocca, *Herod's Judaea* (Tübingen: Mohr Siebeck, 2008), 171–5. The first Herodian construction phase at Masada is actually dated before the watershed of 31 BCE, dating from 35 BCE, followed by another phase from 30 BCE, but the main building time was that of 20–4 BCE, see Ehud Netzer, *Masada III, Buildings, Stratigraphy and Architecture* (Jerusalem: Israel Exploration Society, 1991); Netzer, *Hasmonean and Herodian Palaces*, 79–97; id. *Architecture of Herod*, 17–41. Gideon Forster, *Masada V, The Yigael Yadin Excavations 1963–1965, Final Reports, Art and Architecture* (Jerusalem: Israel Exploration Society, 1996), 209–13.

[91] See in particular Richardson, *Herod*, 175–216; Lichtenberger, *Baupolitik*; Roller, *Building Program*; Netzer, *Architecture of Herod*.

[92] See above, n. 51.

[93] A small part of this structure, the tower, may be originally Hasmonean. Moshe Fischer, Mordecai Gichon, and Oren Tal, *'En Boqeq: Excavations in an Oasis on the Dead Sea: Volume II, The Officina: An Early Roman Building on the Dead Sea Shore* (Mainz: Verlag Philipp von Zabern, 2000).

[94] Hirschfeld, *Qumran in Context*, 183–210.

[95] Rocca, *Herod's Judaea*, 213–14.

[96] Ibid. 215, see Josephus, *Ant.* 17: 289, *War* 2: 69.

[97] Resianne Fontaine (ed.), *Otot ha-shamayim: Samuel Ibn Tibbon's Hebrew version of Aristotle's Meteorology: A Critical Edition* (Leiden: Brill, 1995), 99–101. Fontaine notes that there is a variant of 'Gor' for 'Goz'.

text of an original editorial comment by a Jewish or Christian author (given the use of the term 'the Temple'), but there is no way of determining exactly how early this textual comment could have been made. While it was noted above that the term *Aiga Mortu* appears to be a rendering of the Latin phrase *aqua mortua*, another interesting feature is the corrupted word הדוד, which is followed by an unnecessary *waw*, 'and', at the beginning of the following word.[98] Given that in Hebrew Herod's name is found as הורדוס (b.Baba Bathra 3b; 4a; b.Taan. 23a), it is possible that the textual peculiarities result from a corruption of his name, so that we would read 'the land of Herodos'. The Dead Sea, that was once so much the preserve of the Hasmoneans, passed into Herod's hands, and he developed it enormously, surpassing the architectural brilliance of his predecessors at every turn.

Both the testimony of Josephus and the archaeology of the Dead Sea area testifies to Herod's land holdings in this vicinity, from his accession in 37 CE, but even more so after 31 CE (and the end of Cleopatra's rule) when he was free to develop his property.

Most important too is what the extant literary evidence from antiquity has not told us. The discovery of numerous letters and documents from the Bar Kokhba period, along with the caves where Bar Kokhba rebels hid themselves during the revolt of the years 132–5 CE, indicate that the southern Dead Sea was an area with a significant Jewish population until this time.[99] The documents found in the Judaean desert caves testify to the fact that Jews continued to live here past the quashing of the First Revolt, and siege of Masada in 73 CE. Not all Jews were rebels, and these people survived and prospered. Jews were clearly living on the western and eastern sides of the Dead Sea from the time of the conquests of Alexander Jannaeus (*c*.83 BCE). These unrecorded persons and settlements that we find in the Judaean desert documents alert us to the very selective material we find in our extant classical sources, with their overwhelming emphasis on what matters to those in power: largely economic resources, military conquests, and impressive building construction.

The documents that name a number of places in the southern part of the Dead Sea raise issues in terms of what existed in terms of comparable settlements in the north. En Gedi is described as the 'village of lord Caesar' (P. Yadin 11, cf. P. Hever 13), which is defined as being within Jericho's

---

[98] Note also that in the main manuscript tradition (L) used for Fontaine's edition of Ibn Tibbon reads: והוא הים הנקרא ים המת בארץ הגוז, 'And this is the sea that is called the Dead Sea in the land of Guz,' Fontaine, *Otot*, 98–101. At this point we may remember that Ptolemy indicates there was a major site south of Callirhoe called 'Gazorus'. 'Guz' then would be a late contraction of the place name.

[99] See for a thorough review of this evidence, Lawrence Schiffman, 'On the Edge of the Diaspora: Jews in the Dead Sea Region in the First Two Centuries CE,' in Aren M. Maeir, Jodi Magness, and Lawrence Schiffman (eds), *'Go Out and Study the Land' (Judges 18: 2): Archaeological, Historical and Textual Studies in Honor of Hanan Eshel* (Leiden: Brill, 2011), 175–95.

borders (P. Yadin 16). Zoara is a town we know (P. Yadin 5 a, 14, 15, 17, 18, 19, 20, 21, 22, 25, 26, 27). But there are other places mentioned in these texts that have not been identified for sure, for example Mazraa (P. Yadin 20), and the composite village or small town named Mahoza or Mahoz Eglatain (P. Yadin 3, 5, 7, 12–27, 37), which was also the port of Zoara, associated with a 'moschantic estate of our Lord Emperor' (P. Yadin 16).[100] There is a place named Kfar Baryu, where there is a press (P. Ḥever 8a), also Tzuk (Mur 8 ar), Siwaya, and Kislon (Mur 19 ar), and Harmona (Mur 28 ar).[101] Perhaps some of these should be identified with ruins we have around the Dead Sea, or in the Lisan's fertile zone (Plate 14). The industry of date cultivation is clearly extremely important in these texts, and possession of date groves or the products deriving from them is a legal issue that the documents attest.[102]

These texts, combined with the relics of those who hid in caves along the western side of the Dead Sea, tell us a great deal.[103] What is clear from the evidence of both skeletal remains and artefacts is that the Roman assault on the Jewish population of the Dead Sea was so severe and comprehensive that no one came to retrieve precious legal documents, or bury the dead. Up until this date, the Bar Kokhba documents indicate that towns, villages, and ports where Jews lived were busy with industry and activity. Afterwards there is an eerie silence, and the archaeological record testifies to little Jewish presence until the Byzantine era, in En Gedi. This picture coheres with what we have already determined in Part I of this study, that the crucial date for what can only be described as genocide, and the devastation of Jews and Judaism within central Judaea, was 135 CE and not, as usually assumed, 70 CE, despite the siege of Jerusalem and the Temple's destruction.

We now turn back to the evidence of Essenes living beside the Dead Sea with this wider appreciation of the history of the environment, both as it was represented in classical literature and also as it appears from the archaeology of the region.

---

[100] Hannah Cotton and Jonas C. Greenfield, 'Babatha's "Patria": Maḥoza, Maḥoz Eglatain and Zo`ar,' *ZPE* 107 (1995): 126–34. See for these texts: Naphtali Lewis (ed.), *The Documents from the Bar Kochba Period in the Cave of Letters: Greek Papyri* (Jerusalem: Israel Exploration Society, 1989); Hannah M. Cotton and Ada Yardeni, *Aramaic, Hebrew and Greek Documentary Texts from the Naḥal Ḥever and Other Sites, with an Appendix Containing Alleged Qumran Texts, the Seiyal Collection*, ii (DJD 27; Oxford: OUP, 1997); Pierre Benoit, J. T. Milik, and Roland de Vaux, *Les Grottes de Murabba`at* (2 vols; DJD 2; Oxford: OUP, 1960).

[101] Schiffman, 'On the Edge,' 186.

[102] For example, P. Yadin, 21–2, 23–4, discussed in Jacobine G. Oudshoorn, *The Relationship between Roman and Local Law in the Babatha and Salome Komaise Archives: General Analysis and Three Case Studies on the Law of Succession, Guardianship and Marriage* (Leiden: Brill, 2007), 169–71.

[103] Hanan Eshel and David Amit, *Refuge Caves of the Bar Kochba Revolt*, i (Jerusalem: Israel Exploration Society, 1998) (Heb.); Hanan Eshel and Roi Porat, *Refuge Caves of the Bar Kochba Revolt*, ii (Jerusalem: Israel Exploration Society, 2009) (Heb.).

10

Essenes beside the Dead Sea: Qumran

The site of Qumran, located in the north-western region of the Dead Sea, on a plateau, proximate to a natural pass through to the higher level of the Judaean wilderness and yet close to the original edge of the lake (Plates 16, 17), was excavated in the 1950s shortly after the first discoveries of the Dead Sea Scrolls in caves nearby. The excavations were undertaken by the Palestine Archaeological Museum, the Department of Antiquities of Jordan, and the École Biblique et Archéologique Française de Jérusalem, headed by Fr. Roland de Vaux of the École Biblique and preliminary reports were published, along with a book synthesizing some of the material from the site.[1] De Vaux's excavations are still being published in a series under the direction of Jean-Baptiste Humbert at the École Biblique: a series that will culminate in final reports, the first publications being of photographs, plans, and de Vaux's field notes, and a scientific volume.[2] De Vaux assumed that the site was occupied by Essenes.

---

[1] Preliminary reports: Roland de Vaux, 'Fouille au Khirbet Qumran,' *RB* 60 (1953): 83–106; id. 'Exploration de la Région de Qumran,' *RB* 60 (1953): 540–61; id. 'Fouilles au Khirbet Qumrân,' *RB* 61 (1954): 206–36; id. 'Fouilles de Khirbet Qumrân,' *RB* 63 (1956): 533–77; id. 'Fouilles de Feshkha,' *RB* 66 (1959): 225–55. De Vaux synthesized results in *L'archéologie et les Manuscrits de la Mer Morte* (London: British Academy, 1961), which was then expanded in an English version: *Archaeology and the Dead Sea Scrolls* (London/Oxford: British Academy/OUP, 1973), henceforth cited as *ADSS*. In addition, for this excavation, there is the work by Ernest-Marie Laperrousaz, *Qoumran, l'etablissement essénien des bords de la Mer Morte, histoire et archéologie du site* (Paris: Picard, 1976), and see also his articles, 'Problèmes d'histoire et d'archéologie Qoumraniennes: a propos d'un souhait de précisions,' *RQ* 10 (1980): 269–91; id. 'Brèves remarques archéologiques concernant la chronologie des occupations esséniennes de Qoumran,' *RQ* 12 (1966): 199–212. New photographs of the progress of the dig have also come to light, see Bart Wagemakers and Joan E. Taylor, 'New Photographs of the Qumran Excavations from 1954 and Interpretations of L.77 and L.86,' *PEQ* 143 (2011): 134–56.

[2] Jean-Baptiste Humbert and Alain Chambon, *Fouilles de Khirbet Qumrân et de Ain Feshka I: Album de photographies. Répertoire du fonds photographiques. Synthèse des notes de chantier du Père Roland de Vaux* (Novum Testamentum et Orbis Antiquus, Series Archaeologica 1; Fribourg: Editions universitaires, 1994); Jean-Baptiste Humbert and Jan Gunneweg, *Khirbet Qumran and `Ain Feshkha II: Études d'anthropologie, de physique et de chimie* (Gottingen: Vandenhoeck & Ruprecht; Fribourg: Editions universitaires, 2003).

The placement of Essenes here was made on the basis of literary attestation, particularly Pliny (*Hist. Nat.* 5: 15 [73]) who—as we have seen—notes: *ab occidente litora esseni fugiunt usque qua nocent, gens sola ... socia palmarum*, 'in the west [of the Dead Sea] the Essenes flee away from the shores that are harmful, a people alone ... companioned by palms'; *infra hos engada oppidum fuit ... inde masada*, 'below these was the town of Engedi ... then Masada'. As argued earlier, those who read Pliny as situating En Gedi 'below' the Essenes in terms of a movement to the south are most likely correct. Pliny followed the direction of a supposed flow of water, from the source of the Jordan in the north, to the borders of Judaea at the southern side of the Dead Sea, where it was believed until recent times there was a subterranean exit to the lake. He also envisaged a region, not just one tiny site, where a large population lived.[3]

The testimony to Essenes in the north-western part of the Dead Sea does not begin and end with Pliny. We have also explored how the association between Essenes and the Dead Sea was also made independently by Dio Chrysostom (*c.*90 CE), in a discourse mentioned by Synesius (*c.*400 CE): πόλιν ὅλην εὐδαίμονα τὴν παρὰ τὸ νεκρὸν ὕδωρ ἐν τῇ μεσογείᾳ τῆς Παλαιστίνης κειμένην παρ' αὐτά που τὰ Σόδομα. Essenes have 'an entirely happy city by the dead water in the interior of Palestine, [a city] lying somewhere near Sodom itself' (Synesius, *Dio* 3: 2). As we saw, the positive use of Essenes as an example of philosophical excellence, the mention of Sodom, and the peculiar term τὸ νεκρὸν ὕδωρ means it is unlikely that Dio derived his information from the parody of Pliny. Solinus (*fl.* 250 CE), in his *Collectanea* 35: 1–12, reflects Pliny and also another source, which may (through a compiler) be Dio, since here too there is mention of Sodom as well as Gomorra (*ibi duo oppida, Sodomum nominatum alterum, alterum Gomorrum*: 'in that place [are] two towns, the one named Sodom, the other Gomorra'). The curious lake is described as being 'in the interior of Judaea': *interiora Iudaeae*, paralleling Dio's ἐν τῇ μεσογείᾳ τῆς παλαιστίνης.[4] We have now explored in the last chapter the placement of Sodom according to Josephus, paralleled in other texts, and located the ruins he identified with Sodom on the north-western side of the Dead Sea, not far from Jericho. Why then do Essenes not appear associated with the Dead Sea in Philo and Josephus? If they knew of Essenes beside the Dead Sea it is perhaps a strange omission in their accounts.

Philo wrote in *Prob.* 76 that Essenes chose to live 'in villages' (κωμηδόν) rather than cities, which may mean he knew of Essenes living far from Jerusalem,

---

[3] See above, p. 139.

[4] C. Iulii Solini, *Collectanea Rerum Memorabilium*, ed. Th. Mommsen (Berlin: Weidmann, 1895), 155. To some extent this could reflect Pliny's identification of Judaea as being *supra Idumaeam et Samariam*, if *supra* indicates a place further inland, 'beyond', though with Dio and Solinus the references are specifically to the Dead Sea and not to Judaea as a whole.

even as far away as the Dead Sea. But if Philo knew of any specific association between Essenes and the lake, there is a very powerful reason for him to have avoided noting it in his writing: the Dead Sea was considered a noxious locality because of its air.[5] As we have seen, there was an idea that fumes came out of the lake (Diodorus Siculus, *Bibl. Hist.* 2: 48: 8, cf. Strabo, *Geogr.* 16: 2: 42). To deal with this problem in terms of the survival of the peculiar *gens sola*, Pliny himself concedes that the Essenes 'flee all the way from the shores which are harmful' (*Hist. Nat.* 5: 15 [73]). Philo was conscious of the need to breathe good air (*Gig.* 10) and Philo praises the Therapeutae's chosen locality because of its health-giving breezes from both the Mediterranean Sea and Lake Mareotis (*Contempl.* 22–3). While Philo is content to characterize his Essenes as living healthily away from city life in *Probus*, he does not situate them in any place exactly. If he ever did situate some Essenes by the Dead Sea in any writing now lost, Philo would have had to insist, as Pliny did, that they were a fair distance away from the shores, so as not to imply that they lacked good judgement in any way concerning air. It would have been less complicated for him if he just omitted to mention any locality here. They were, at any rate, found in many places of Judaea.

For Josephus, as noted above, it seems that the locus of Essenes is invariably Jerusalem, though he was content to spread them out populously throughout Judaea, as did Philo in the *Hypothetica*, which of course includes the north-western hinterland of the Dead Sea and indeed Peraea on the other side of the lake, in its wider reach. Josephus may not have mentioned them specifically in this locality simply because he had no reason to do so in terms of his narrative; there would have been numerous other places Essenes lived in Judaea that have gone unmentioned also. In the case of Josephus and Philo, no explicit mention of Essenes by the Dead Sea does not mean no Essenes could have lived by the Dead Sea, since they are found all over Judaea, and we have two independent witnesses that locate them here.

So we turn to archaeology. Yizhak Magen and Yuval Peleg, who have excavated at Qumran during recent years, have placed such literary testimony on one side and rejected—on archaeological grounds—any association be-tween Essenes and the site.[6] It is sometimes assumed today that it is

---

[5] This is a view that persisted until modern times, see Daniel the Abbot (1106–8), 27; 38, trans. William F. Ryan, in John Wilkinson, *Jerusalem Pilgrimage 1099–1185* (London: Hakluyt Society, 1988). In the fifteenth century Father Felix Fabri was told that no one should visit the lake because the stench from the sea makes you vulnerable to infection, sickness, and death: Felix Fabri, *Evagatorium in Terrae Sanctae, Arabiae et Egypti peregrinationem*, ii (ed. C. D. Hassler; Stuttgart: Stuttgard.-Literarischerverein, 1843), 236a.

[6] Yizhak Magen and Yuval Peleg, 'Back to Qumran: Ten Years of Excavation and Research, 1993–2004,' in Katharina Galor, Jean-Baptiste Humbert, and Jürgen Zangenberg (eds), *Qumran, the Site of the Dead Sea Scrolls: Archaeological Interpretations and Debates* (Leiden: Brill, 2006), 55–113; Yizhak Magen and Yuval Peleg, *The Qumran Excavations 1993–2004: Preliminary Report* (Judea and Samaria Publications 6; Jerusalem: Israel Antiquities Authority, 2007).

methodologically dubious to begin with literary evidence and then interpret material remains. However, archaeology proceeds with this method continually, since it is a perfectly appropriate circumstance to look to texts in order to interpret material remains. The previous chapter showed how the various archaeological sites around the Dead Sea cohere well with the evidence of the Hasmonean expansion and Herodian building boom that we can determine in historical literature. No one would suggest that Masada should have been excavated and interpreted without recourse to Josephus. Likewise, to interpret Qumran without recourse to the texts that bear upon the part of the Dead Sea in which Qumran is situated is methodologically flawed. The literary material provides a historical template which can then be critiqued by archaeology, but cannot be completely ignored.

If we look at the literary evidence, as surveyed in the previous chapter, and the related archaeological evidence found in the Dead Sea region for Hasmonean and Herodian building projects, it would *prima facie* be most natural to assume that the arrival of Essenes in the region had something to do with Herod. As with the Gate of the Essenes in Jerusalem, so beside the Dead Sea: Essenes appear to have been accommodated in a Herodian zone. Their name 'Herodians' in the New Testament indicates how part of the population of Judaea—far from esteeming them and calling them by a positive name—linked them with a despised ruler. Thus, given that they are described as being located in a region otherwise under Herod's sway in the latter part of the first century BCE, then we might surmise that the gifts given by Herod to Essenes included a tract of land between En Gedi and Jericho, close to the ruins of Sodom (which Josephus places near Jericho in the northern part of the Dead Sea). From other sources it is clear that this means they were sandwiched in between two zones of lucrative opobalsam and date cultivation held entirely in royal hands.

If we are to associate Essene occupation beside the Dead Sea with the rise of Herod, on the basis of literary texts analysed closely, then it would be reasonable to suggest as a working hypothesis, to be tested against the material record, that Essenes did not occupy sites such as Qumran prior to 37 BCE, when Herod came to power. There is surely no place for them while the region was ruled by the Hasmoneans, if we accept both the Hasmonean concerns to exploit the region economically and the impression we have gained that the Hasmoneans and the Essenes were not at all friendly. The dating of Pliny's probable source text, Licinius Mucianus (73–5 CE), is important, as this would mean that Essenes are indicated as existing just after the destruction of En Gedi, which is indeed described as a pile of ashes as a result of the Roman conquest. Their presence here is associated with the immediate aftermath of the quashing of the Judaean revolt, at least from 68 CE. There is in fact no reason to date the appearance of Essenes in the region much earlier, on the basis of the literary evidence alone. The arrival of Essenes in the area would therefore be some time between the end of the Hasmonean dynasty and the testimony of Pliny and Dio.

Therefore, we need to look to Herod's honouring of the Essenes. This is not to say that Essenes were in any way supportive of Herod the Great in terms of his policy and behaviour, but only that we need to imagine that they accepted this gift of land and property. We turn to the archaeology with this hypothesis in mind, with propositions about the chronology of Qumran as a primary concern.

THE LEGACY OF SCHOLARSHIP

Before going on, however, the history of scholarship needs to be briefly considered once more. Given the dominant paradigm of Essenes being a small, marginalized sect of Jews out of step with mainstream Judaism—a portrayal established largely in the nineteenth century by Protestant scholars whose view of Judaism was very narrow (as explored in Chapter 1)—the popular image of the Essenes in the north-western Dead Sea area has been one of a tiny monastic, alternative, and ascetic sect. Pliny's caricature has become the defining paradigm, and one which we need to dispense with altogether, on the basis of what was discussed in Part I.

With the image of a small sect at the margins of Judaism, the location of Essenes beside the Dead Sea suggested to scholars an isolated group of ascetics, similar to Christian ascetics of a later time. Despite the fact that Pliny was used as the primary source on the Essenes, his reference to large numbers—and the absence of all other Jews—was somewhat overlooked: Essenes were seen as eking out their solitary existence without contact with other Jews.

Added to this, there was the complication that En Gedi, which lay 'below' the Essenes, according to Pliny, was identified incorrectly.[7] It was in fact located not far from where Sodom had been identified by Josephus.[8] Eusebius (*Onomasticon* 68: 11; 86: 16; 96: 9) had said that 'Engadda . . . lies to the west of the Dead Sea', but this was interpreted as north-west. We see this in the map by William Holler, included in the King James Version of the Bible in the middle of the seventeenth century (Plate 18). It was not until the 1830s, when the visitor Edward Robinson successfully publicized Ulrich Seetzen's identification of En Gedi as being the spring still called *Ain Jiddi* in Arabic, that scholars identified En Gedi correctly, in its present location.[9] This then led Lieutenant

---

[7] See discussion in Joan E. Taylor, 'On Pliny, the Essene Location and Kh. Qumran,' *DSD* 16 (2009): 1–21.

[8] See discussion in Joan E. Taylor, 'The Dead Sea in Western Travellers' Accounts from the Byzantine to the Modern Period,' *Strata* 27 (2009): 9–29.

[9] Edward Robinson, 'A Brief Report of Travels in Palestine and the Adjacent Regions in 1839 undertaken for the Illustration of Biblical Geography,' in *The American Biblical Repository* (New York: Gould, Newman and Saxton, 1838), II, 418; Edward Robinson and Eli Smith, *Biblical Researches in Palestine* (Boston: Crocker and Brewster, 1856), 506–9, cf. Ulrich Jasper Seetzen,

Lynch, exploring the Dead Sea by US naval ship, to suppose that the solitary and ascetic Essenes lived in small caves literally above En Gedi.[10]

Lynch was no classical scholar, but, by the middle of the twentieth century, this association between the cliffs above and north of the spring of En Gedi and the supposedly small enclave of Essenes was much supported, especially in French scholarship, thanks to the influence of Félix-Marie Abel, who championed the close En Gedi association made by Lynch.[11] In this visualization of Essenes in the rocky crags above En Gedi, they were minimized into a miniscule group of cave-dwellers, like some kind of Christian anchorite community, befitting a conceptualization of Essenes being a quasi-Pythagoraean 'monastery' that had rejected the Temple and all things normatively Pharisaic (= Rabbinic), living a mystical existence in a way that prefigured Christian ascetics. This was to reduce Essenes even further than Pliny's paradigm.

There were nevertheless others in the nineteenth century who read Pliny more correctly and disagreed with too miniscule a location for Essenes. As Christian D. Ginsburg wrote in his essay on Essenes: 'the majority of them settled on the north-west shore of the Dead Sea'.[12] William Hepworth Dixon, who visited the area, stated in 1866 that the 'chief seats of this sect [of the Essenes] were pitched on the western shores of the Dead Sea, about the present Ras el Feshka and along the slopes of the wilderness by Mar Saba and Ain Jidy. Some of them dwelt in the villages below Bethlehem. One of the gates of Jerusalem bore their name ...' and when he gets to Ain Feshkha he identifies it as 'a saline spring in the ancient territories of the Essenes.'[13] Thus when Claude Conder came with the Palestine Exploration Fund survey team to make the first detailed maps of this region from 1872–5, he noted, regarding the Judaean wilderness north-west of the Dead Sea:

> From a very early period this horrible wilderness appears to have had an attraction for ascetics, who sought a retreat from the busy world of their fellow men, and who sought to please God by torturing their bodies he had given them. Thus the Essenes, the Jewish sect whose habits and tenets resembled so closely those of the first Christians, retired into this wilderness and lived in caves.

Reisen durch Syrien, Palästina, Phönicien, die Transjordan-Länder, Arabia Petraea, und Unter-Aegypten, 4 vols, ed. and comm. Fr. Kruse (Berlin: G. Reimer, 1854), ii, 226–7.

[10] William F. Lynch, *Narrative of the United States' Expedition to the River Jordan and the Dead Sea*, 7th ed. (Philadelphia: Lea and Blanchard, 1850), 294.

[11] Félix-Marie Abel, *Géographie de la Palestine*, ii (Paris: Librarie Lecoffre, 1938), 316–17.

[12] Christian D. Ginsburg, *The Essenes: Their History and Doctrines; The Kabbalah: Its Doctrines, Development and Literature* (reprint of *The Essenes: Their History and Doctrines* [London: Longman and Green, 1864]; London: Routledge and Paul, 1955), 26.

[13] William Hepworth Dixon, *The Holy Land*, I, 2nd ed. (London: Chapman and Hall, 1866), 279–80, 284–5.

Christian hermits, from the earliest period, were also numerous in all the country between Jerusalem and Jericho...[14]

These two different understandings of the zones of Essenes (one above En Gedi and one encompassing a large region on the north-western shore of the Dead Sea) existed from the middle of the nineteenth century to the middle of the twentieth.

THE DEAD SEA SCROLLS AND QUMRAN

When, then, in this area of the western coast of the Dead Sea, the first Scrolls were discovered in 1947, close to the ruins known as Kh. Qumran, the identification of their being Essene seemed plausible on the basis of locality from the point of view of those who saw Essenes living in a wide region. The site of Qumran had long been known, but it was not thought to come from the time of the first centuries BCE–CE.[15]

Qumran was dated either to a much earlier or to a later period than the Essenes. As with En Gedi, the ruins suffered from erroneous identification. It seems clear from the accounts of travellers that in the later Middle Ages the ruins of Qumran were identified with biblical Zoara/Segor which, along with En Gedi, was erroneously placed along the north-western part of the lake shore, while another city of the Plain, Seboim, was identified with the largely submerged ruins of Rujm el-Bahr (Plate 19 *cf.* 6).[16] As time went by this identification of Qumran as Segor was itself forgotten. When Félicien de Saulcy visited the Dead Sea in 1851 he proposed that Qumran was to be seen as another biblical city: Gomorra.[17] Despite a widespread scepticism about this identification, no one placed Qumran within the Second Temple Period, when Essenes lived in the area, and—when not making wild conjectures about biblical cities—travellers identified the site as a Roman or later fortress, as suggested by C. W. M. Van der Velde in 1856: 'The ruins called Ghomran are those of a small fortress which has been built to guard the pass above; and around it, on the E. and S., a few cottages have stood, which probably afforded

---

[14] Claude R. Conder, *Tent Work in Palestine*, ii (London: Richard Bentley and Sons, 1878), 301.

[15] Lena Cansdale has noted correctly that 'before the discovery of the Dead Sea Scrolls in 1947, no connection had been made between the sect of the Essenes and the ruined, ancient settlement of Qumran,' *Qumran and the Essenes: A Re-Evaluation of the Evidence* (Tübingen: J. C. B. Mohr, 1997), 19, though she misses the reason why.

[16] For discussion see Taylor, 'Western Travellers,' 20.

[17] For a summary of the reports by explorers who visited the area in the nineteenth century see Joan E. Taylor, 'Khirbet Qumran in the Nineteenth Century and the Name of the Site,' *PEQ* 134/2 (2002): 144–64.

shelter to the soldiers, the whole having been surrounded by a wall for defense.'[18] This was a perfectly valid interpretation of the ruins of Period III at Qumran (see below), which had been left to weather the centuries after the site was abandoned.[19] It was believed that there was no synchronicity between the ruins and Essenes: that is the reason it was not identified as an Essene site, despite the fact that it lay in what was identified as an Essene area in the Second Temple Period.

It was then inevitable and entirely sensible that when the site of Qumran was excavated and understood to date not from the Roman period but from the time of the Second Temple, the question of whether it was in some way associated with Essenes would be raised. With the classical sources at hand, Roland de Vaux quite rightly noted that peculiarities of the site—large rooms suitable for communal eating, sizeable pools that would fit the requirements of ritual purification baths, a cemetery with largely adult male skeletons, and so on—seemed to match an Essene identification.[20] In the course of his excavations, he defined the period in which the structures of Qumran developed these distinctive features as Period Ib (Plate 20), and determined that there was a preceding Hasmonean phase he called Period Ia; de Vaux dated Ia to the time of Qumran's resettlement in the late second century BCE.[21]

Overall, as Jodi Magness points out, on the basis of the evidence de Vaux provides for Period Ia as a whole, '[d]e Vaux found no coins associated with Period Ia, and there were only a few potsherds which he could not distinguish in type from those of Period Ib'.[22] This led her to assign most of the apparently Period Ia developments to Period Ib, agreeing with de Vaux that this phase began in the first part of the first century, with various points of development. However, this makes the period of initial Essene occupation correspond to the time of the Hasmoneans.

We have seen that the Hasmoneans from Alexander Jannaeus onwards had a particular hold on the region of the northern Dead Sea, and if Essenes placed themselves in this vicinity they would have been adapting a site that lay in a sequence of Hasmonean fortified settlements from Jericho to En Gedi. The establishment and occupation of the Qumran settlement in the Hasmonean era must be seen in line with the string of other Hasmonean fortified settlements and anchorages that run between these two cities, which were

---

[18] C. W. M. Van der Velde, *Memoir to Accompany the Map of the Holy Land* (Gotha: Justus Perthes, 1856), 257.

[19] See Joan E. Taylor, 'Kh. Qumran in Period III,' in Galor, Humbert, and Zangenberg, *Qumran*, 133–46.

[20] De Vaux, *ADSS*, 126–38.

[21] The date 150 is sometimes given; see Philip R. Davies, *Qumran* (Cities of the Biblical World; Cambridge: Lutterworth Press, 1982), 54.

[22] Jodi Magness, *The Archaeology of Qumran and the Dead Sea Scrolls* (Grand Rapids: Eerdmans, 2002), 64.

developed in association with the Hasmonean conquest to the south and the economic exploitation of the resources of the Dead Sea. The Hasmoneans, as we have seen, created a chain of forts and fortified settlements that protected the eastern border, all the way from Alexandrium in the north to Masada in the south, with Machaerus on the other side of the lake, and fortified docks at Rujm el-Bahr and Kh. Mazin, Qumran's location as a lookout at the foot of a pass being critical for its development. These were probably manned by mercenaries working for the royal house. Magen and Peleg have well explored, by reference to Josephus, the Hasmonean historical context of the archaeology, in their assigning of the development of Qumran at the earliest to a time late in the reign of John Hyrcanus (after the conquest of Samaria and Idumaea was completed in 104 BCE) and most likely in the later reign of Alexander Jannaeus (*c*.90–75 BCE).[23] The establishment of Qumran would indeed then be later than the date proposed by de Vaux for Period Ia, a date also endorsed by Yizhar Hirschfeld in his presentation of a more developed Hasmonean villa.[24] Nothing actually dates the establishment and occupation of Hasmonean Qumran before the reign of Alexander Jannaeus.

Importantly, on archaeological evidence alone, Jean-Baptiste Humbert has also rejected de Vaux's sequence of phases, and configured a new series of stages of development ranging from an initial Hasmonean square enclosure through to an expanded form with complex water systems and industrial units.[25] In this sequence, the building of the initial Hasmonean villa is dated to the time of Alexander Jannaeus (Level 2, Phase A). Humbert has determined that the major expansion of the site took place only after the time that Jericho was assigned to Cleopatra (34 BCE): his Level 3, Phase A, somewhat punctuated by an earthquake (31 BCE), with subsequent rapid expansion in a phase he calls Level 3, Phase B, from 30 BCE onwards. Humbert's archaeological chronology would fit with the historical scenario indicated by our survey of the literary sources.

There was, in this scenario, an initial Hasmonean phase, but not one that is either as early or as rudimentary as de Vaux's Period Ia. Following it, there was the expanded settlement of Qumran, de Vaux's Period Ib. This would then be dated at the very earliest from Herod's accession, in 37 BCE, but more particularly from his return to rule the area, after Cleopatra, from 31 BCE onwards. It is at this point the buildings reach their 'definitive form', as de

---

[23] Magen and Peleg, 'Qumran Excavations,' 27–32.

[24] Hirschfeld, *Qumran in Context*, 59.

[25] Jean-Baptiste Humbert, 'Reconsideration of the Archaeological Interpretation,' and 'Arguments en faveur d'une résidence pré-Essénienne,' Jean-Baptiste Humbert and Jan Gunneweg, *Khirbet Qumran et Ain Feshkha: études d'anthropologie, de physique et de chimie* (Qumran ii; Fribourg/Göttingen: Editions universitaires Fribourg Suisse/Vandenhoeck & Ruprecht, 2003), 419–44, 467–82. Hirschfeld begins his stratum III in 37 BCE, *Qumran in Context*, 87.

Vaux said.[26] Period Ib was followed by a period of abandonment, a phase evidenced most clearly by a spread of silt in locus 132, overlying ash, which de Vaux connected with the earthquake of 31 BCE followed by fire; after this a new phase began: Period II (Plate 21). However, Magness has rightly critiqued de Vaux's long abandonment scenario, and extended Period Ib to approximately 4 BCE, which is interestingly the date of Herod the Great's death.

In terms of Qumran's features in Period Ib and II, there was a 'tower', which was accessed only from the second floor, the first (or ground) floor being for storage, with high windows only (Plate 22).[27] It could be disconnected from the rest of the buildings, since it was surrounded by open spaces (loci 12 and 18) and the only way of getting into it would have been from a wooden balcony extending over two small courtyards (loci 12 and 13). It seems very likely that this part of the complex was built to withstand attack, as de Vaux surmised, since the lower walls are also thickened at the base and very robust, though it is not correct to call it a 'tower' as such. It did not loom above any other part of the building complex, since much of this complex was two-storied (seen in loci 1, 2, and 30, and probably to be considered as a possibility elsewhere also). The building complex is not as a whole built defensively, as a fortress.

The tower was at the corner of the eastern block of buildings, and in the west another block of buildings clustered around what de Vaux determined was a Hasmonean cistern complex, though its origins were in the Iron Age. Overall, the water system was expanded further, possibly indicating not only that a great deal of water was needed for the larger population, but that this population was particularly concerned with ritual purity. An immersion pool (*miqveh*, locus 138) was built near an open doorway near where a new aqueduct entered the complex, and another (locus 68) in the southern part of the site (Plate 23). It should probably be noted that not all the cisterns would have been full of water. The water travelled from the north along the aqueduct and filled the round cistern and adjacent Iron Age II rectangular cisterns first (loci 117 and 118),[28] and then went on to fill the south-west cistern (locus 91). The size of this cistern indicates that the builders expected it to be fairly full, but not always. Cisterns that are expected to hold at times small amounts of water are built with many steps leading down to a shallow depression, as in the case of cisterns 117 and 118. As one travels along the new aqueduct, the cisterns are built with more steps (cf. loci 56 and 71). The south-east cistern (locus 71) may not have been much more than half-full very often. It would have been useful to have this water very close to a potters' workshop located in the south-eastern corner of the main buildings (Plate 25),

---

[26] De Vaux, *ADSS*, 5.

[27] Ibid. 6–7.

[28] For the dating of this cistern complex as Iron Age, see Joan E. Taylor and Shimon Gibson, 'Qumran in the Iron Age,' in Sidnie White Crawford (ed.), *Qumran* (forthcoming).

however, even if it was the last cistern to fill. The water system is designed so that no water should go to waste.

The pottery workshop was necessary for whatever product was being stored in the pots produced here, which presumably continued to be marketed. It would have been useful to manufacture pottery containers for whatever else was being processed at the site, and the presence of a date press, and an industrial complex on the western side of Qumran, indicates that there was much more going on here than pottery manufacture.

This area indicating manufacturing interests has led to a variety of researchers doubting the so-called 'Qumran-Essene' hypothesis, as they adopt a very narrow concept of the Essenes, prioritizing Pliny's caricature, so that any money, industry, women, commerce, or connectivity apparently is good cause to undermine this theory. For example, Alan Crown and Lena Cansdale have suggested that Qumran was a commercial *entrepôt* located on a significant trade route, with the settlement serving as a fort designed to guard an important pass or villa,[29] though recent study has shown that the roads are in fact a legacy of Iron Age settlements in the region—with Qumran existing also as an Iron Age site—and were maintained but not developed by the Hasmoneans and later occupants.[30] Norman Golb argued Qumran was a secular fortress.[31] Robert R. Cargill sees this only in the second century BCE, with the site changing to a sectarian settlement later on.[32] According to Yizhar Hirschfeld, following the suggestions of Pauline Donceel-Voûte,[33] Qumran was in the Hasmonean and Herodian periods a fortified manor house that functioned in connection with the lucrative opobalsam trade, being connected by roads to En Gedi and Jericho, as well as to Hyrcania and Jerusalem.[34] Yizhak Magen

---

[29] Alan D. Crown and Lena Cansdale, 'Qumran: Was it an Essene Settlement?' *Biblical Archaeology Review* 20 (1994): 24–35, 73–4, 76–8; Cansdale, *Qumran and the Essenes, passim.*

[30] As demonstrated in the study by Joan E. Taylor and Shimon Gibson, 'Qumran Connected: The Paths and Passes of the North-western Dead Sea,' in Jorg Frey and Carsten Claussen (eds), *Qumran und Archäologie—wechselseitige Perspektiven* (Tübingen: Mohr Siebeck, 2011), 1–51.

[31] Norman Golb, *Who Wrote the Dead Sea Scrolls? The Search for the Secret of Qumran* (New York: Scribner, 1995).

[32] Robert R. Cargill, 'The Fortress at Qumran: A History of Interpretation,' http://www.bibleinterp.com/articles/qumfort.shtml, and id. *Qumran through (Real) Time: A Virtual Reconstruction of Qumran and the Dead Sea Scrolls* (Bible in Technology 1; Piscataway, NJ: Gorgias Press, 2009); id. 'The Qumran Digital Model: An Argument for Archaeological Reconstruction in Virtual Reality and Response to Jodi Magness,' *Near Eastern Archaeology* 72/1 (2009): 28–47.

[33] Pauline Donceel-Voûte, 'Les ruines de Qumrân réinterprétées,' *Archéologia* 298 (1994): 24–35; ead. 'Traces of Fragrance along the Dead Sea,' *Res Orientales* 11 (1998): 93–124.

[34] Yizhar Hirschfeld, 'Early Roman Manor Houses in Judea and the Site of Khirbet Qumran,' *Journal of Near Eastern Studies* 57 (1998): 161–89; id. 'The Architectural Context of Qumran,' in Lawrence H. Schiffman, Emanuel Tov, and James C. VanderKam (eds), *The Dead Sea Scrolls: Fifty Years after Their Discovery. Proceedings of the Jerusalem Congress, July 20–25, 1997* (Jerusalem: Israel Exploration Society in cooperation with the Shrine of the Book, Israel Museum, 2000), 673–83; id. 'Qumran in the Second Temple Period. Reassessing the Archaeological Evidence,' *Liber Annuus* 52 (2002): 247–96; id. *Qumran in Context: Reassessing the*

and Yuval Peleg have suggested that Qumran was a Hasmonean fort then developed in the Herodian period into a pottery-manufacturing centre, for economic reasons.[35] However, both Jodi Magness[36] and Hanan Eshel[37] have continued to defend many of de Vaux's most significant conclusions, and have stressed the site's key identification as an Essene community centre. In fact, a settlement devoted to a variety of artisanal crafts is exactly what we would expect on the basis of the literature on Essenes, who are described as engaging in these (Philo, *Prob.* 76), with their work also including agriculture, shep-herding, cow-herding, animal husbandry, and bee-keeping (Philo, *Hypoth.* 11: 6–9; Josephus, *War* 2: 129; *Ant.* 18: 18). Even an area of the site, the 'tower', fortified for defence is no problem for an Essene hypothesis, since Essenes are not actually characterized as being pacifists, as we have noted. The notion that any fortification or indication of weaponry found at the site must nullify the Qumran-Essene hypothesis is based on a false understanding of who the Essenes were.

Moreover, a definition of the site as a 'villa', 'manor house', 'fort', and so on assumes that there is a standard by which it can be judged. In Samuel Rocca's study, the categories of fortification (fortresses) are very carefully analysed, as 'forts', 'fortlets', 'towers',[38] and Rocca inclines to the view that fortlets precede agricultural functions, which then become associated with a site with strategic importance, which complicates the classification of 'fortified manors/estates'. In addition, Rocca notes that numerous great Herodian 'fortresses' had adja-cent villages (e.g. Machaerus, Herodium, et al.) and palace complexes, and could include agricultural elements, bathhouses, etc. (Masada, Machaerus, Hyrcania, et al.), so a classification of a 'fortress' as being essentially one thing avoids addressing these royal hybrid types. In fact, rather than assuming a sequential mode of 'fortlet', to which agriculture is attached, the hybrid

---

Archaeological Evidence (Peabody, MA: Hendrickson Publishers, 2004); id. 'Qumran in the Second Temple Period: A Reassessment,' in Galor, Humbert, and Zangenberg, *Qumran*, 223–39.

[35] Magen and Peleg, 'Back to Qumran'; id. *Qumran Excavations.*

[36] Jodi Magness, 'What Was Qumran? Not a Country Villa,' *BAR* 22 (1996): 40–7, 72–3; ead. 'The Chronology of Qumran, Ein Feshkha, and Ein El-Ghuweir,' in Zdzislaw Jan Kapera (ed.), *Mogilany 1995: Papers on the Dead Sea Scrolls Offered in Memory of Aleksy Klawek* (Kraków: Enigma Press, 1998), 55–76; ead. 'Two Notes on the Archaeology of Qumran,' *BASOR* 312 (1998): 37–44; ead. 'Qumran Archaeology: Past Perspectives and Future Prospects,' in *The Dead Sea Scrolls after Fifty Years: A Comprehensive Assessment,* ed. Peter W. Flint and James C. VanderKam, 2 vols (Leiden: Brill, 1998–9), 1: 47–77; ead. 'A Reassessment of the Excavations of Qumran,' in Schiffman, Tov, and VanderKam, *Dead Sea Scrolls* (Jerusalem: Israel Exploration Society in cooperation with the Shrine of the Book, Israel Museum, 2000), 708–19; ead. *Archaeology of Qumran*; ead. *Debating Qumran: Collected Essays on its Archaeology* (Interdisci-plinary Studies in Ancient Culture and Religion 4; Dudley, MA: Peeters, 2004).

[37] Hanan Eshel, *Qumran: Scrolls, Caves, History* (Jerusalem: Carta, 2009).

[38] Samuel Rocca, *Herod's Judaea* (Tubingen: Mohr Siebeck, 2008) has a lengthy discussion of fortifications (pp. 153–88) and see also pp. 213–40, considering structures such as manors/villas within a broader discussion of the division of land in Herodian times.

nature of Hasmonean and Herodian sites is important to bear in mind, whether these are large or small. Like the Iron Age sites that preceded the Hasmonean developments, these enclosures are 'fortified'—with a concern for defence and strategic locations—while yet also having other functions in order to maintain a certain economic sustainability.

Classifying Qumran's structures by means of a typology, at any stage of its development, founders when the problem is that there is a wider discussion about how to classify various structures of the Hasmonaean and Herodian period in terms of primary/secondary functions. It is not a case that archaeologists agree about form/function issues. Classifying the Hasmonean sites along the western Dead Sea as 'fortified settlements', in the present discussion, is a term used in order to embrace the Hasmonean structures of the north-western Dead Sea coast by reference to a reasonably cohesive type, without assuming that these are indicative of a ruling elite actually living within them, as 'villa' or 'manor house' implies. In fact, life along the Dead Sea shores would have been hard, owing to the extreme heat of this region, and not a choice place for any of the elite, at any time, unless there were healing springs to draw them temporarily (as at Callirhoe or the Wadi Zarqa Main) or oases.

Qumran, as a Hasmonean fortified settlement, is one of a type. It does appear to have had the 'tower' built by the Hasmoneans, and this is a fairly standard part of this kind of roughly square structure, as Hirschfeld has shown.[39] That this type of square building including a fortified corner is the form of the Hasmonean construction at Qumran has been argued by Humbert,[40] Hirschfeld,[41] and Magen and Peleg.[42]

However, the important thing to stress is that Qumran did not stay in its Hasmonean form, and changed to something much less symmetrical, with an extremely expanded water system and a variety of manufacturing industries. This non-symmetrical phase, including manufacturing industries, is distinctive, and would rightly take place from 34 BCE initially, and then with vigour after 30 CE, according to Humbert. It is this that would match our hypothesis in terms of the arrival of Essenes. The problem for archaeology is that Essenes may have lived at Qumran even if there is not a single incontestable archaeological indicator of their presence, just as Christians lived throughout the Roman Empire in the first two centuries—as we find in numerous literary sources—but there is almost nothing in the archaeological record to prove their existence before the third century CE. Archaeology can at times greatly help solving historical problems and it may illuminate the past in myriad ways,

---

[39] See above, and see also Yizhar Hirschfeld, 'Fortified Manor Houses of the Ruling Class in the Herodian Kingdom of Judaea,' in Nikos Kokkinos (ed.), *The World of the Herods* (Stuttgart: Franz Steiner Verlag, 2007), 197–226.

[40] Humbert, 'Chronology,' 433.

[41] Hirschfeld, *Qumran in Context*, 59–87, and see reconstruction in his Plate 21.

[42] Magen and Peleg, 'Qumran Excavations,' 28–32. They include stables in the north-west.

but it also has its limits in terms of the hard evidence it can provide to prove any given historical hypothesis one way or another.

Pliny and Dio's evidence does not require a strictly minimalist either/or situation of only one archaeological site being Essene within this broad region; potentially any site in the north-western Dead Sea vicinity might have been occupied by Essenes in the Second Temple period, if we credit Pliny and Dio with any validity at all. For all we know, given what Josephus and Philo state, Essenes could have lived in Jericho, without leaving any obviously distinctive archaeological record, just as they lived in Jerusalem, or any other Judaean city. One does not look for Sadducee or Pharisee archaeology; and it is strange that scholars have had to justify seeing Essenes as occupying Qumran on purely archaeological grounds, as if the archaeology of the Essenes *has* to be fundamentally distinctive. This supposition itself relies on an underlying assumption that Essenes were in some way out of step with 'mainstream' Judaism.

This demand for an archaeological answer to the question of Essene occupation seems to misapply current methodology in archaeological practice. The problem in past decades of the discipline has been that literary evidence has dictated the kinds of questions asked, so that material culture can be considered 'illustrative' to a model of the past dictated by texts. If one wishes to ask different questions of the past—especially those springing from social science theory (regarding class, gender, groups, family, economics, funerary practices, and so on)—literary evidence does not necessarily answer these questions properly, since it derives generally from elite circles with assumed knowledge, rhetorical concerns, social bias, and so on—hence the detachment of literature and archaeology proposed in order to free up archaeology from text-bound discourse.[43] One can recover the past more holistically, in a more egalitarian way, by looking at aspects of the past that texts do not address. Archaeology can respond independently to new questions from social science for which texts may provide only cursory and skewed answers. The point is that archaeologists can ask *different questions*, reading against the grain of texts, destabilizing their hegemony. However, if there is a classical text answering a basic question of population identity, relevant to a particular site, then to look solely at archaeology as if the text does not exist is an intellectual exercise that needs to be acknowledged as such, but it is not in fact a better or purer method for establishing historical actuality. The critical integration of texts and archaeology is a sounder method of procedure; this is not to claim that texts as they stand are entirely historical, since the method is necessary

---

[43] See David B. Small (ed.), *Methods in the Mediterranean: Historians and Archaeologists' Views on the Use of Texts and Archaeology* (Leiden: Brill, 1995) and id. 'The Tyranny of the Text: Lost Social Strategies in Current Historical Period Archaeology in the Classical Mediterranean,' in Pedro Paulo A. Funari, Martin Hall, and Siân Jones (eds), *Historical Archaeology: Back from the Edge* (London: Routledge, 1999), 122–35.

even when narratives are legendary or fictional.[44] It requires a double expertise in literary analysis and archaeology.

The 'scoffers' of the Qumran-Essene theory can set a kind of impossible standard before the site of Qumran is credited as having an Essene population at some point in time. In ancient history, we cannot look to archaeology for clear proof of every literary attestation, or we would have precious little history at all. Ultimately—as historians are forced to do very frequently—we need to rely on sound textual evidence even when archaeology provides inconclusive data, or no data at all, in order to make any propositions about the past. Historical study does not result in absolutes, merely plausible suggestions and probabilities that may or may not be corroborated. Ancient history is not an exact science that can necessarily provide a great many sure, provable results. It proceeds by means of argument.

Perhaps the best archaeology can do in this case is to establish that certain sites such as Qumran and Ain Feshkha were Jewish, with additional features very appropriate to Essene occupation. However, these are not religious/cultic sites, and it is surely questionable whether industrial or agricultural settlements of any kind anywhere provide any firm indicators of the ethnicity or religious affiliation of the inhabitants. A date-press in an area attested as being Jewish by literary sources, and near to archaeological sites of synagogues or *miqvaot* (and so on), can be assumed to have probably been operated by Jews even if nothing else indicates this, when exactly the same date-press in Zoara would be understood as a Nabataean installation; likewise an agricultural or technical installation in an area attested as being occupied by Essene Jews might well have been operated by them even without a single artefactual indicator. It is not even as if we have in Herod's fortresses inscriptions to identify his ownership or developments. It is simply reasonable to associate them with what is written in Josephus.

Given this, the onus cannot be on archaeologists to prove a distinctively Essene archaeology as such. We have seen how easily this can come unstuck in the case of the Qumran cemetery, which at one time was thought to indicate quite clearly a particularly Essene form of burial (as if even burial had to be out of step with 'mainstream Judaism'),[45] so that other similar burials in Judaea could be identified as Essene,[46] until it was realized that Nabataeans could also bury their dead in this way, given that on the Nabataean side of the lake at Kh.

---

[44] See for example the discussion in Anthony J. Frendo, *Pre-Exilic Israel, the Hebrew Bible, and Archaeology: Integrating Text and Artefact* (New York: T & T Clark, 2011).

[45] E.g. see Emile Puech, 'The Necropolises of Khirbet Qumran and Ain el-Ghuweir and the Essene Belief in Afterlife,' *BASOR* 312 (1998): 21–36.

[46] Boaz Zissu, '"Qumran Type" Graves in Jerusalem: Archaeological Evidence of an Essene Community,' *DSD* 5 (1998): 158–71, trans. of id. 'Field Graves at Beit Zafafa: Archaeological Evidence for the Essene Community,' in Avraham Faust (ed.), *New Studies on Jerusalem* (Ramat Gan: Bar Ilan University, 1996) 32–40 (Heb.).

Qazone—near Bab edh-Dhra—there is a vast Nabataean cemetery (first to fourth centuries) with identical types of loculus-pit graves,[47] and it might actually simply be a method of burial appropriate for people too poor to afford rock-cut tombs: a type of burial therefore *appropriate* to the ascetic Essenes while not necessarily being *distinctive* to them alone.[48]

If we are to search the literature to define actual artefacts that might indicate the presence of Essenes, we find very little, apart from baths suitable for immersion prior to their meals, and Qumran has these. One might look for further evidence of a strong degree of concern with ritual purity, but this kind of analysis can only be done by comparative discussion with other sites. There is mention of white clothing, but textiles are found rarely in archaeological excavations; only one piece of carbonized textile has been found in the buildings of Qumran (in locus 96).[49] Josephus mentions the Essene hatchet (σκαλίς or ἀξινάδιον), used in their meticulous toileting (*War* 2: 148). But we then have to ask how Essenes used this implement: from the discussion above,[50] one would assume that it was not continually carried, but left in the toilet area, and identified there as personal to the user. The archaeological excavations of Qumran have brought to light such small axes.[51] The problem is that these tools do not necessarily have a single use.

With such concerns in mind, interesting results have recently been drawn by the careful study undertaken by Dennis Mizzi, in an Oxford doctoral thesis under Martin Goodman.[52] Mizzi's aim was to examine archaeological material at Qumran in order to determine whether on the basis of looking at this body of evidence alone it may be concluded that the site was at any time a sectarian settlement. Mizzi examined the stratigraphy/chronology, architecture, economic activity, pottery, glass, stone vessels, small finds, metal objects, and coins: including unpublished Qumran materials made available to him by courtesy of Jean-Baptiste Humbert at the École Biblique in Jerusalem. Importantly, he situated the material within the context of other excavated sites in the region. The conclusions Mizzi has reached are that while the site of

---

[47] Konstantinos Politis, 'Khirbet Qazone,' *American Journal of Archaeology* 102.3 (1998): 596–7; id. 'Rescue Excavations in the Nabataean Cemetery at Khirbat Qazone 1996–1997,' *Annual of the Department of Antiquities of Jordan* 42 (1998): 611–14; id. 'Khirbet Qazone: une nécropole nabatéene à la mer Morte,' *Le Monde de la Bible*, 121 (September–October 1999): 95; id. 'The Nabataean Cemetery at Khirbet Qazone,' *Near Eastern Archaeology*, 62: 2 (1999): 128; id. 'Chirbet Qazone. Ein nabataischer Friedhof am Toten Meer,' *Welt und Umwelt der Bibel* 16 (2000): 76.

[48] As I have argued in Joan E. Taylor, 'The Cemeteries of Khirbet Qumran and Women's Presence at the Site,' *DSD* 6 (1999): 285–323 at 312–13.

[49] Mirielle Bélis, 'The Workshops at 'Ein Feshkha: A New Hypothesis,' in Galor, Humbert, and Zangenberg, *Qumran*, 253–62.

[50] See p. 80–2.

[51] For example, KhQ 367, 421, 462, 2128.

[52] Dennis Mizzi, *The Archaeology of Khirbet Qumran: A Comparative Approach*, D.Phil. thesis (Oxford), forthcoming, published by Brill.

Qumran conforms to other sites in many respects, there are features of Qumran that remain distinctive. While usually the argument in favour of a stronger concern with ritual purity than other Jews is thought to be indicated by the numerous pools suitable for use as *miqvaot* (immersion pools), Mizzi has noted other material. He has argued that while there is no evidence that there was a large number of people living at the site of Qumran, there is in Period II a large amount of broken pottery, noting stockpiles, discards, and deposition of whole cooking pots. Rejecting the framework of a pottery workshop, he ties this in with an interest in ritual purity, since 'once pottery acquired ritual impurity it could not be cleansed, and thus it had to be discarded'.[53] There are also more stone kraters (for water) than is usual at comparable sites (e.g. there are none at ez-Zara and Machaerus). These are not luxury items but were used for ritual purity (so Gospel of John 2: 6). Additionally, there is a large number of stone stoppers/lids, designed to protect storage jars from ritual impurity, as well as perforated stone disks, the use of which is unknown.

Mizzi himself defined three main periods that seem appropriate as a broad category: 1. post-68 (Period III)—for which he wisely gives no definite end date; 2. pre-68 (Period II)—which means effectively 31 BCE to 68 CE; 3. pre-31 (Period I)—prior to an earthquake of 31 BCE.

Mizzi's Period I is then essentially the Hasmonean fortified villa, like others in the region; Period II encompasses the developments of the Herodian period; and Period III the state of the site after Vespasian's invasion, in which he has proven that the same repertoire of objects continues without great change. He classifies Qumran throughout as a kind of fortified farmstead ('villa' is technically correct, but can imply a grander structure than is the case here). However, as we have seen, most likely the initial expansion of the Hasmonean structure took place prior to the earthquake. Moreover, both Humbert and Magness validate a short period of abandonment *c*.10–4 BCE with a new phase beginning subsequently *c*.4 BCE–1 CE (Humbert's Level 3, Phase C; Magness' Period II).

Given the literary evidence, and the characteristics of the site of Qumran in the period following 34 BCE, there seems no good reason to doubt that Essenes lived here, as the literary sources attest. An image of a regional Essene locality in which Qumran was one of many Essene settlements would mean also that Yizhar Hirschfeld might be right about some possible temporary Essene presence behind and above En Gedi, even though the latter structures he identifies are not hermits' retreats but seasonal huts for agricultural work,[54]

---

[53] Lev. 11: 33–4; Mizzi, 'Qumran,' 137.

[54] Hirschfeld, *Qumran in Context*, 233–40; id. 'A Community of Hermits above En Gedi,' *Cathedra* 96 (2000), 8–40 (Heb.); id. 'A Settlement of Hermits above En Gedi,' *Tel Aviv* 27 (2000), 103–55. Hirschfeld notes that this area was sparsely occupied, containing twenty-eight small cells. David Amit and Jodi Magness, 'Not a Settlement of Hermits or Essenes: A Response

since once the dichotomizing tendencies of the debate are removed then one can read both Pliny and Dio as accommodating numerous Essene sites within the general area, sites used not for anchoritic contemplation but for productive work. In fact, Hirschfeld himself ended his entire archaeological reassessment of Qumran by noting not only his own discovery of small huts behind En Gedi as being suitable for Essenes, in accordance with a reading of Pliny that focused on height, but also by noting that Pesach Bar Adon's surveys showing that similar sites were found in *sixteen* locations at the foot of the cliffs or on the natural terrace that runs between En Gedi and Kh. Mazin.[55] He then stated that '[a]nalysis of Pliny's testimony supports the assumption that the site above En-Gedi and similar sites were part of a general phenomenon of ascetic colonies *along the western shore of the Dead Sea* in the Second Temple Period [italics mine]'.[56]

If it is correct that there was an Essene 'region', a zone that could be classified by Dio as a 'city', then Qumran is clearly not the only site between En Gedi and Jericho that may have had Essene occupation, though it would indeed fit as a place appropriate as their main centre within this locality. In terms of timing for their arrival here, as we have seen, if we are to situate the evidence of Essenes being beside the Dead Sea in the northern part of the lake, in view of the wider literature on the region from antiquity, this would have taken place under the patronage of Herod, which would fit with Qumran's chronology: the expansion of the site, with numerous pools and manufacturing development, took place with the arrival of Essenes *c.* 34 BCE. This is a 'best fit' method; it is not a method that demands definitive proof of the existence of Essenes.

As for the latest date for Essene occupation of this area, Pliny and Dio independently attest the presence of Essenes after the destruction of the Temple, a point that Pliny indicates by reference to the destruction of En Gedi. Given that it is unnecessary—and even quite wrong—to suggest that all Essenes were completely annihilated in 68 CE and could no longer have existed in Judaea, given the evidence we have considered above about the continuation of Jewish legal societies into the second century, there is no reason to assume that they ceased to exist in this region of the Dead Sea immediately after the arrival of Vespasian's troops. They may well have continued with reduced numbers, under the watchful eye of the Romans and their local auxiliary troops. I have argued elsewhere that from 68 to at least the mid-90s of the first century Qumran was most likely occupied by Jewish soldiers serving as auxiliaries, and including a

---

to Y. Hirschfeld, "A Settlement of Hermits above 'En Gedi",' *Tel Aviv* 27 (2000): 273–85, have pointed out the seasonal, agricultural character of these structures.

[55] Pesach Bar Adon, 'Another Settlement of the Judean Desert Sect at En el-Ghuweir on the Shores of the Dead Sea,' *BASOR* 227 (1977): 1–26; id. 'Excavations in the Judean Desert,' *Atiqot* 9 (1989): 1–88 (Hebrew).

[56] Hirschfeld, *Qumran in Context*, 240.

percentage of women. These used the site in Period III of the settlement, since the Roman legions worked as a fighting force as single entities, securing sites by means of auxiliaries and others loyal to Rome (Josephus, *War* 4: 442). The militarized population of Qumran under the hegemony of the Romans in the area would have been similar to that of the Hasmonean period; in Period III the manufacturing elements of the site disappear, and it is reduced to a form much more like it had been at the start, with a roughly square enclosure, this time surrounded by trenches and with room partitions.[57] Yet, there is continuity in terms of artefacts; Mizzi has supported this by demonstrating the continuity of diverse artefacts between Periods II and III at Qumran as indicating the same culture of inhabitants, not an alien group of Roman soldiers, and a far more extensive period of occupation than de Vaux supposed (Plate 26).[58] Even with this site being partly destroyed and requisitioned for an auxiliary Roman military purpose, both for its strategic location and its role in a balsam route, we may yet have Jews. In addition, it is unclear from the archaeological record whether the auxiliary troops stayed at Qumran for long: if the site did continue for decades, it may have reverted to habitation by its previous occupants.

In other words, Essenes may well have managed to continue to live in settlements in the area of the north-western Dead Sea for many decades, perhaps even restoring themselves in Period III Qumran, given its continuing existence. The latest proven dates of coins that coincide with occupation were found together in an upturned bowl in a lower room of the tower: five from the Second Revolt from locus 29 (KhQ490–93, 495), one denarius of Vespasian (69–79 CE; KhQ 486), and—most tellingly—three denarii from the time of Trajan (98–117 CE; KhQ 487–9).[59] In fact, there is absolutely no reason why Period III could not have continued into the second century. De Vaux created an idea of long abandonment prior to 135 CE by attributing a single wall built in a cistern (to create a sheltered living space) to Bar Kokhba rebels: this wall divides cistern 58 and is built on collapse from Period III along with a layer of natural deposit that could only have built up over a long time,[60] but it would be much better to attribute this wall to the rebuilding work of a Byzantine hand. There is otherwise absolutely nothing to associate it with Bar Kokhba. The Byzantine era of the Dead Sea is overlooked here, when there are coins from the fourth century including two from the reign of Theodosius (379–95) in loci 34 and 152 and six other coins of the fourth century in loci 7, 68, 88, 91, 96, and 119.[61] This is quite a large assemblage of fourth-century coins and would indicate that people used the Period III ruins for transient settlement.

---

[57] Joan E. Taylor, 'Qumran in Period III,' *passim*.
[58] Mizzi, 'Qumran,' *passim*.
[59] See de Vaux, with Rohrhirsch and Hofmeir, *Ausgrabungen*, 127–8.
[60] De Vaux, *ADSS*, 45.
[61] De Vaux, with Rohrhirsch and Hofmeir, *Ausgrabungen*, 127–8.

There are other Byzantine coins found in loci 42 and 76 from the fifth to sixth centuries.

We should bear in mind that caves in the vicinity were also inhabited at certain times by Byzantine anchorites. A cave situated above 'Ain Turaba and near 'Ain el-Ghuweir was occupied in the Byzantine period.[62] De Vaux noted Byzantine sherds in cave no. 23, which is located just above Qumran near the aqueduct route.[63] At Kh. Mazin (Khirbet el-Yahoud), 3 km south of Ras Feshkha, there is evidence of Byzantine settlement. Anchorites lived all over this region in the wilderness (cf. Egeria, *Itin.* 10: 9) and numerous lauras and monasteries were established.[64] At Ain Feshkha, to the south of Qumran, a Byzantine renovation was built in the southern enclosure: locus 20.[65] It was made into a dwelling of some kind: the walls were repaired with blocks, the threshold was raised, the inside walls were faced with a coating of pebbles dug up from the pavement of Period II, and an earth floor was prepared. Pottery sherds from this level are Byzantine. A Byzantine lamp and juglet were found in a layer of silt against the north wall of the enclosure. In his work *The Spiritual Meadow* (*Pratum Spirituale*), written *c.*600, John Moschus refers to a gardener who grew vegetables in a garden right beside the Dead Sea for the anchorite community of Mardes (or Marda), which was located on the hill of Khirbet Mird, ancient Hyrcania. Moschus wrote:

> There is a mountain by the Dead Sea called Mardes and it is very high. There are anchorites living in that mountain. They have a garden about six miles away from where they live, near the edge of the Sea, almost on its banks. One of the anchorites is stationed there to tend the garden.[66]

A Byzantine mile was approximately 1,485 m and Ain Feshkha is located 9 km away from Kh. Mird (Hyrcania), which could be understood as a distance of about 6 Byzantine miles. John Moschus refers to other sites along the Dead Sea and anchorites who 'grazed' there, such as Abba Sophronios 'the grazer', who 'grazed around the Dead Sea. For seventy years he went naked, eating wild plants and nothing else whatsoever'.[67] An elder named Cyriacos from the

---

[62] Ian Blake, 'Chronique archeologique,' *RB* 73 (1966): 566.

[63] *DJD* III, 23.

[64] See Yizhar Hirschfeld, *The Judean Desert Monasteries in the Byzantine Period* (New Haven: Yale University Press, 1992); John Binns, *Ascetics and Ambassadors of Christ: The Monasteries of Palestine 314–631* (Oxford: OUP, 1994), esp. 100–1.

[65] De Vaux, *ADSS*, 72, 74; id. 'Fouilles de Feshkha,' (1959), 225–55, at 253–4, Pl. VII.

[66] Chap. 167. Translation by John Wortley from John Moschus, *Pratum Spirituale* PG 87, col. 3026 in *The Spiritual Meadow of John Moschus* (Kalamazoo, MI: Cistercian Publications, 1992), 137. Mardes was a laura founded in 425 at Hyrcania. The monastery of Castellion was established there by St. Sabas, *c.*492; see Derwas A. Chitty, *The Desert a City: an Introduction to the Study of Egyptian and Palestinian Monasticism* (Oxford: Blackwell, 1966), 108–11.

[67] *Spiritual Meadow*, Chap. 159, Wortley, *Spiritual Meadow*, 131, cf. Abba Gregory Chap. 139 (p.113).

laura of Mar Saba went down to an unidentified place named Coutila: 'He stayed for a little while [there] beside the Dead Sea; then he started back to his cell'.[68] The route from Mar Saba along the Wadi en-Nar takes you south of Ras Feshkha, to Kh. Mazin, but Cyriacos could have gone anywhere along the north-western Dead Sea shore. Whatever anchorites dwelt at Qumran, it is unlikely that they left much in the archaeological record, but in taking shelter in ruins or caves, the anchorites should always be borne in mind as a disturbance factor when considering material here. People living and visiting the monasteries of the Judaean desert and lower Jordan Valley also greatly expanded the path system, to ensure connection between localities that were at first remote and in unknown territory for those that went there.[69]

This point about Byzantine activity is laboured here simply because in ignoring the Byzantine period in regard to the wall of cistern 58, and wrongly attributing it to the middle of the second century (Bar Kokhba rebels), the end of Period III was pushed back in time by de Vaux, so that the entirety of Period III was squashed into a few years between 68 and 73. Period III itself could have continued into the second decade of the second century and even been reasonably intact at the time of the Bar Kokhba rebels. We do not need to assume, on the basis of what we have considered in Part I, that Essenes ceased to exist in this region after the end of Period II. This notion of a destruction that finished the settlement of Qumran in 68 CE, with only a handful of Romans occupying the site briefly in Period III, is a false one.[70] The site was reduced in size, fortified, and lacked industry, but it continued to be occupied. The definitive end for the eastern side of the site appears to have been at the time of an earthquake that created two significant north–south rifts: major fissures which damaged the aqueduct system and cistern 48 irreparably, meaning that the site became uninhabitable, though some transient use could still have been made of parts of the surviving buildings.[71] This damage was assumed by de Vaux to have occurred at the time of the earthquake of 31 BCE, but since many elements essential in Period III (e.g. cistern 48) were damaged and never repaired, it seems that this earthquake terminated Period III settlement.

---

[68] Chap. 53 (p.42).

[69] Hirschfeld, *Judaean Desert Monasteries*, 206–12.

[70] Mladen Popović questions whether the site was attacked in 68, and has also rightly wondered why the Romans destroyed this small site: 'Roman Book Destruction in Qumran Cave 4 and the Roman Destruction of Khirbet Qumran Revisited,' in Jörg Frey, Carsten Claussen, and Nadine Kessler (eds), *Qumran und Archäologie—Texte und Kontexte* (Tübingen: Mohr Siebeck, 2011), 239–91.

[71] See Magen and Peleg, *Qumran Excavations*, 8, 59, though they suggest a much later earthquake was responsible for the damage at the site. The zigzagging fissures are indicated clearly in Humbert, 'Reconsideration,' 436, 443, Plate 10. The water channel was cut off from basins 68, 69, 70, 71, and 72. One fissure ran along to the west of the main building, and one ran along its eastern side.

There was a very strong earthquake recorded in extant literature, and confirmed by archaeological evidence from Caesarea to Petra, around 113–5 CE, in the reign of Trajan, with an estimated measurement of 7.4 on the Richter scale, which may be the one also felt in Antioch (Dio Cassius, *Hist.* 68).[72] With this, we can provide a conclusive end date for Qumran's occupation. In short, without here embarking on too detailed an archaeological discussion, and taking into account diverse propositions, the observations of de Vaux in terms of sequencing, but not exactly forms and dating, can be respected, thus: Period Ia (Hasmonean fortified settlement) *c.*80–*c.*37 BCE; Period Ib (Herodian/Essene settlement) *c.*37 BCE–*c.*4 BCE; Period II (Essene settlement) *c.*1 CE–68 CE; Period III (temporary Roman auxiliary post followed by re-instated Essene settlement) 68–115 CE.

AIN FESHKHA

Mention of Byzantine renovations at Ain Feshkha and the garden for Mardes then brings us to this site. The earliest Essene chronology is not, I think, most clearly evidenced at Qumran, since this is complicated by the Hasmonean phase and the problem of determining the precise time of redevelopments and Essene settlement, but rather the chronology is revealed in the neighbouring linked settlement of Ain Feshkha (Einot Tsukim), 2.5 km to the south (plate 27). The buildings here are clearly constructed for the first time in the period of Herod's hegemony. At Ain Feshkha, to this day, there is a great amount of sweet and drinkable water in natural pools,[73] formed by springs which support plant and aquatic life (Plate 28). In contrast to Qumran, this is a beautiful, mellow zone. The spring-fed pools would have comprised large natural *miqvaot* for the purposes of purification, the best type of purification water (m.Miq. 1: 9), far better than the artificially filled pools of Qumran. A large stone vessel used for storing pure water was found in Ain Feshkha, a striking discovery given the rarity of this type of vessel; in no other small sites apart

---

[72] See Kenneth W. Russell, 'The Earthquake Chronology of Palestine and Northwest Arabia from the Second through the Mid-Eighth Century AD,' *BASOR* 260 (1985): 37–59, at 40–1. This corrects the dating of 130 found in David H. Kallner-Amiran, 'A Revised Earthquake-Catalogue of Palestine,' *IEJ* 1 (1950–1): 223–46, at 225; Claudia Migowski, Amotz Agnon, Revital Bookman, Jorg F. W. Negendank, and Mordechai Stein, 'Recurrence pattern of Holocene Earthquakes along the Dead Sea transform revealed by Varve-counting and Radiocarbon Dating of Lacustrine Sediments,' *Earth and Planetary Science Letters* 222 (2004): 301–14; E. G. Reinhardt, B. N Goodman, J. Boyce, G. Lopez, P. Van Hengstum, W. J. Rink, Y. Mart, and A. Raban, 'The Tsunami of 13 December AD 115 and the Destruction of Herod the Great's Harbor at Caesarea Maritima, Israel,' *Geology* 34/12 (2006): 1061–4.

[73] I have personally drunk this water and found it good.

from Qumran have such vessels been found, and otherwise only in Jerusalem priestly mansions.[74]

Close to the Ain Feshkha pools was, and still is, a surrounding oasis, crossed by both natural and artificial channels, providing many possibilities for growing plants. The oasis today supports tall reeds, tamarisks, and oleanders, among many other trees and shrubs. In antiquity, similar sweet-water springs existed at Ain et-Tannur/Tanourih and Ain Ghazal, irrigating a fertile area between Ain Feshkha and the Wadi Qumran.

The ruins of Ain Feshkha were excavated in 1956 and 1958 by de Vaux,[75] and again in 2001 by Yizhar Hirschfeld.[76] They have determined that there was a main structure (18 × 24 m) that was constructed in the time of Herod, comprising a courtyard with a rectangular building on three sides, with exterior walls 1m thick (Plate 29). While de Vaux suggested an earlier construction date, Hirschfeld has opted for a date of construction late in Herod's reign, though his discovery of a coin hoard dated to the time of Antigonus (40–37 BCE), buried just under the threshold of the main building, would seem to date it much earlier.[77] However, Hirschfeld's understanding of the site as being essentially one period, with internal and external modifications, seems appropriate on the basis of the evidence. Two ground floor rooms were added, in the west, with an upper storey and a balcony. North of this were installations that may have been used for opobalsam processing,[78] according to Hirschfeld, though other possibilities are a date wine press,[79] fish farming,[80] or indigo manufacture.[81] Water was clearly fed to a reservoir next to this installation from a now extinct spring north of the site (Plate 30). In between the installations and the reservoir channel was a paved area, also to the southeast. South of the building was an animal pen (34 × 34 m) with a stable running along the northern side. Therefore, this was also a site of manufacture, industry, and animal husbandry, with living quarters.[82]

A wall running north from the settlement of Ain Feshkha leads towards Qumran, which would suggest the extension of an estate enclosure. The pottery forms are virtually identical to those found at Qumran during the same period of occupation, but large cylindrical jars have not been discovered here. While

---

[74] Mizzi, 'Qumran,' 202–6; Hirschfeld, *Qumran in Context*, 195, 199.

[75] De Vaux, *ADSS*, 60–84; id. 'Fouilles de Khirbet Qumrân,' (1956): 532–77; 'Fouilles de Feshkha,' (1959): 225–55; Humbert and Chambon, *Fouilles*, 353–67.

[76] Yizhar Hirschfeld, 'Excavations at 'Ein Feshkha, 2001: Final Report,' *IEJ* 54 (2004): 35–54; id. *Qumran in Context*, 183–209; Gabriella Bijovsky, 'A Hoard of Coins of Mattathias Antigonus from 'Ein Feshkha,' *IEJ* 54 (2004): 75–6.

[77] Hirschfeld, *Qumran in Context*, 189.

[78] Ibid. 201–8.

[79] Ehud Netzer, 'Did any Perfume Industry Exist at 'Ein Feshkha?' *IEJ* 55 (2005): 97–100.

[80] Frederick E. Zeuner, 'Notes on Qumran,' *PEQ* 92 (1960): 27–36.

[81] Mirelle Bélis, 'Workshops at 'Ein Feshkha.'

[82] Joan E. Taylor, 'Ain Feshkha,' *Encyclopaedia Judaica*, 2nd ed., Volume 6, 255–6.

Magness has doubted de Vaux's determination of the association between Qumran and Ain Feshkha, this has been vigorously defended by Hirschfeld. This association can only be circumstantially argued, without the presence of a continuous long wall between the two localities, but the evidence for a connection seems extremely probable. For example, while a great many animal bones are found at Qumran, an animal pen has only been found at Ain Feshkha; Qumran is not a good grazing area except in winter and early spring in the plateau to the north of the site, whereas on the Ain Feshkha plain animals could graze all year near spring sites. Shears found at Qumran (KhQ 2401) clearly indicate that wool was shorn at Qumran, but there are no animal pens. Both Qumran and Ain Feshkha were involved in date production and processing, given their installations, and a plantation could easily have spread between the two sites, irrigated by attested and also extinct springs. A landscape archaeology approach in which plantation/field systems are considered as well as architectural structures makes it almost incontestable that Ain Feshkha is the southern side of a farmed estate and Qumran the northern side, as both the excavators de Vaux and Hirschfeld have suggested. Hirschfeld has noted that identical *opus sectile* floor tiles, made of local grey bitumous limestone, were in Ain Feshkha and Qumran.[83] Fish live in the Ain Feshkha pools, even more in past times than now, and fish could have been farmed in pools here; but fish-hooks and net weights were found in de Vaux's excavations at Qumran,[84] and a net-weight also at Magen and Peleg's excavations,[85] meaning that there was possibly some seasonal fish-farming at Qumran, but it is hard to imagine this as taking place without a connection with Ain Feshkha as a main base.

Moreover, as a living space, the water of Ain Feshkha is potable throughout the year; the water of Qumran could not have been acceptable for drinking for very long, or through the summer. The drinking water itself was more likely sourced from the local spring of Ain Ghazal, near a cluster of Iron Age remains on the plain. The pools at Qumran were filled by the winter flash flooding of the Wadi Qumran and rainwater run-off filling an aqueduct leading up from the settlement towards the hills, the latter being invariably muddy, and necessarily it gathered a large amount of silt. This silt residue was used for pottery, as Magen and Peleg have explored.[86] As David Stacey has

[83] Hirschfeld, *Qumran in Context*, 195, 200–1.

[84] Mizzi, 'Qumran,' 231, 243; the fish-hooks are items KhQ264 (locus 18) and 603 (locus 34), net-weights KhQ 2625 (locus 144) with attached iron rings, which are the same as iron rings found elsewhere at the site (illustrated in Chambon's drawings, in Mizzi's figures 6: 16–18, 24), KhQ 485, 705, 2130, 2146, 2441.

[85] Magen and Peleg, 'Back to Qumran,' 233.

[86] Magen and Peleg, 'Qumran,' 32–42, for a discussion of the water supply and its associated spin-off for pottery manufacture.

noted, Qumran must have been a locus of seasonal activity,[87] manned only by guards during the hottest months of the year, when life here would have been almost intolerable. With the actual drinking water for Qumran below the site, on the plain, this again links the two sites closer together.

The establishment of Ain Feshkha would parallel the development of Machaerus by Herod, and the Herodian development of Callirhoe across the water. Yet it was not a site used by Herod: it shows no evidence of being a palace, and had no defensive function. It was unnecessary as a road station, since there was Kh. Mazin to the south and Qumran to the north, and the distance between these sites is only 7 km: an easy journey. The Hasmoneans had spaced out their fortified settlements appropriately.

The chronology of Ain Feshkha is more clearly dated at the end of its existence than it is at the beginning. The Herodian complex at Ain Feshkha was partly destroyed by fire after the Romans took control of this region in 68 CE, like Qumran, but occupation continued after this at least on the north side of the main building in the time period corresponding to Period III at Qumran. As for the latest date, a coin of Domitian from Antioch (81–96 CE; locus 16) and a coin hoard of seventeen coins of Agrippa II, dating from 78–95 CE, were found. But also here, there were coins from the Second Revolt, from locus 16 at the site: three Judaean Second Revolt coins and Roman coins of Aelia Capitolina (AF 137, 140, 141, 226); giving the *terminus post quem* for the abandonment of the settlement as sometime before or during 135 CE. Nothing about Ain Feshkha was military at this time. Given that Qumran's water system appears to have been damaged in the earthquake of *c.*115 CE, it is possible that the remaining inhabitants simply consolidated themselves at Ain Feshkha, until the absolute annihilation by the Romans in 135 CE.

Ain Feshkha bears some similarity to another Herodian enclosure, established at En Boqeq at the southern end of the Dead Sea, beyond Masada. This site was excavated by Mordecai Gichon and Moshe Fischer from 1968 to 1980 with a careful recognition of its landscape situation and environment as well as its function. The rectangular building of En Boqeq lies on the edge of a cultivated area served by an aqueduct, pool, and irrigation system fed from the pure spring water of Nahal Boqeq, flowing from En Boqeq, and another system with a long aqueduct from En Noith, a spring high on the hill, flowing down to a water tower and then to irrigation of terraces on the northern side of the river (Plate 31).[88] The earliest phase of construction was determined to be at the time of Herod the Great (Stratum III, second half of the first century BCE to the beginning of the first century CE). This building was then developed in

---

[87] David Stacey, 'Seasonal Industries at Qumran,' *BAIAS* 26 (2008): 7–30; id. 'Some Archaeological Observations on the Aqueducts of Qumran,' 14/2 (2007): 222–43.

[88] See Moshe Fischer, Mordecai Gichon, and Oren Tal, *En Boqeq: Excavations in an Oasis on the Dead Sea* (Mainz: Philipp von Zabern, 2000), xxiv–xxvi.

the first century (Stratum II) into the form of an *officina* (workshop) and finally occupied in the era of the Bar Kokhba war (Stratum I, *c*.132–5). As such, this parallels what we have determined would be appropriate for the development of Ain Feshkha and Qumran (following the latter's Hasmonean phase). This structure also had a square tower, on the south-western side, which was the first structure to be built.[89]

Not surprisingly, ceramic forms of En Boqeq are very similar to Qumran, Ain Feshkha, Rujm el-Bahr, Ain ez-Zara, Machaerus, En Gedi, Ain el-Ghuweir, and Jericho, and include some stone vessels (indicating Jewish occupancy).[90] It is also noted that pottery types from Stratum 1, the time of the latest settlement in the Bar Kokhba era, 'continue the 1st century CE tradition of pottery manufacture in the region'.[91]

The chronology of settlement at En Boqeq and its pottery typology is interesting, given its clear occupation continuing through to the Bar Kokhba era. This provides similar chronological parameters to those of En Gedi, even with Roman sacking and burning (Pliny, *Nat Hist.* 5: 15 [73]) and control of En Gedi after 68 CE, with the presence of the Thracian cohort there.[92] As noted, the rebel raids from Masada to En Gedi assumes that they saw En Gedi Jews between 68 and 73 CE as being their enemies (Josephus, *War.* 4: 402–5). As we have seen in the previous chapter, the Bar Kokhba texts clearly indicate that Jews did not cease to exist around the Dead Sea during the period after the Roman quashing of resistance at Masada: this was not the last stand of all Jews, but only the last stand of a particular rebel group. The definitive end to most Jewish settlements was 135 CE.

The occupation of En Boqeq needs to be seen within a larger picture of significant Jewish occupation of the southern Dead Sea area. The Bar Kokhba period letters and documents found in the Judaean desert caves clearly indicate a thriving Jewish presence on both sides of the southern Dead Sea, and in Zoara, through to 135 CE. If Jews existed there, and elsewhere, then we have no reason to assume Essenes could not have existed there and elsewhere also. If we connect the references of Pliny and Dio with what we have explored in terms of second to fourth-century literary sources, and consider the wider survival of Essenes, along with other schools of Second Temple Judaism, through to 135 CE, then a more holistic picture presents itself. Ain Feshkha may well have been a small outpost that continued on, into the early decades of the second century.

---

[89] See the model illustrated in 1.66.
[90] Fischer, Gichon, and Tal, *En Boqeq*, 29–72.
[91] Ibid. 43.
[92] P.Yadin 11: 1–7 from the Cave of Letters refers to En Gedi as a 'village of the lord Caesar' with camps and a camp headquarters, and refers to Magonius Valens, a centurian of the Cohors I Miliaria Thracum.

CONCLUSIONS: ESSENES BESIDE THE DEAD SEA

Our examination of evidence then suggests that Essenes occupied the north-western region of the Dead Sea. When we approach the archaeology of Qumran, it may be better to consider *how* it may illuminate Essenes, rather than whether it illuminates Essenes at all. Archaeology may challenge us not to make assumptions from our texts, and correct our readings, but the association of Essenes and this locality for some period of history seems sound.

In the light of what we have concluded in Part I of this study, however, the site of Qumran cannot have been in any way an Essene headquarters; it was a small Essene outpost, as was Ain Feshkha, with a reach to the landscape all around, but it was only a local centre. The true centre was undoubtedly Jerusalem. If Josephus and Philo are to be believed, there could have been hundreds of small Essene communities all over Judaea, in isolated settlements like this, or else embedded in towns and villages. The curiosity of this legal school of the Essenes was that while they focused on the correct interpretation of the law they also committed themselves to a lifestyle of communal living and physical labour. Industries and agricultural work were as much the preserve of Essenes as Torah study.

What attraction might this desolate place have had? We noted that the Dead Sea was a vicinity in which Herod had numerous holdings, and could then have been understood as being Herod's land. Herod, in becoming king, inherited various Hasmonean properties in the area, which included lucrative opobalsam plantations and palm groves at Jericho and En Gedi, with major fortresses at Machaerus, Masada, and inland, to the west of Qumran, at Hyrcania. He could gift this territory to anyone as a kind of leased possession. This network of royal holdings created a strong character to the region of the Dead Sea as being a place controlled by Herod and his successors.

It was noted also in the previous chapter how Herod fostered a giant medicinal rue in Machaerus, and developed the healing centre of Callirhoe.[93] Archaeology indicates that he created a pharmacological site at En Boqeq, and the verdant gardens at Ain Feshkha would fit with his general style of such developments of the region. As Samuel Rocca noted, however, Herod also gave gifts of parts of his royal estates.[94] Given that Philo and Josephus attest to special gifts given to Essenes by Herod, in return for Menahem's prediction of his kingship, there would be some explanation as to why they could be located in such a 'Herodian' geographical zone. Among the gifts, then, there was the former Hasmonean enclosure of Qumran, built along a local route from En Gedi to Jericho at the mouth of a pass, stretching through to the adjacent oasis of Ain Feshkha, and other sites useful to those with a particular ambition.

---

[93] See above, p. 226–7.
[94] Rocca, *Herod's Judaea*, 215, see Josephus *Ant.* 17: 289, *War* 2: 69.

But why did they want this area of land? There are two solutions to this puzzle that require no absolute spurning of the Temple and Jerusalem, and no inherent marginalization, and we will explore them now. In the first place there is the significance of the archaeological evidence of the Dead Sea Scrolls in the caves around Qumran. In the second place, Josephus' mention of the Essenes' concern with healing may be recalled here (Josephus, *War* 2: 136).[95] The curious interest of Herod in developing the resources of the Dead Sea— reflected in Josephus' source ('Judeus'?) that concentrated on the Dead Sea's medicinal plants, water, and other substances—creates a significant link to Essenes.

[95] John Allegro, *The Sacred Mushroom and the Cross* (London: Hodder and Stoughton, 1970), 55.

11

The Dead Sea Scrolls

If Qumran is situated appropriately in an Essene area of the north-western Dead Sea, then indeed so are the Dead Sea Scrolls. But the reasons why they came to be located in caves here are still debated. The most popular hypothesis to account for their presence is the 'quick hiding scenario', whereby a library at the site was hidden away ahead of the Roman invasion (in 68 CE). This theory was first suggested by Ibrahim Sowmy, the brother of Father Butros Sowmy of St. Mark's Monastery in Jerusalem, to John Trever, when the Isaiah scroll was taken to the American Schools of Oriental Research in 1948,[1] and has been commonly held ever since.[2]

However, the first scholar to consider the matter, Eleazer Sukenik, who had engaged with scroll dealers soon after the discoveries in Cave 1, had a different idea about why the scrolls were in caves. He wrote in his diary on 25th November 1947: 'A Hebrew book has been discovered in a jar. He [antiquities dealer Kando] showed me a fragment written on parchment. *Genizah!*'[3]

THE *GENIZAH* THEORY

A *genizah* is, strictly speaking, a temporary store for certain old, damaged, or otherwise unusable (sometimes heterodox) Jewish manuscripts, the most

---

[1] John C. Trever, *The Untold Story of Qumran* (Westwood, NJ: F. H. Revell, 1965), 25.

[2] I would like to thank Michael Stone, Jodi Magness, Geza Vermes, Jean-Baptiste Humbert, Dennis Mizzi, Daniel Stökl Ben Ezra, and Sidnie White Crawford for their comments on drafts of this Chapter, and also Shimon Gibson for visiting Qumran with me and discussing many aspects of the site. I would like to thank also the respondents and others at the Qumran session of the SBL in New Orleans, 23rd November 2009. This chapter was first published in Aren M. Maeir, Jodi Magness, and Lawrence H. Schiffman (eds), *'Go Out and Study the Land' (Judges 18: 2): Archaeological, Historical and Textual Studies in Honor of Hanan Eshel* (Leiden: Brill, 2011), 269–315, and is here modified and updated.

[3] Eleazer Sukenik, *The Dead Sea Scrolls of the Hebrew University* (Jerusalem: Magnes, 1955), 17. Sukenik published two volumes in Hebrew titled *Megilot Genuzot mitokh Genizah Kedumah shenimtse'ah beMidbar Yehudah* [Hidden Scrolls from the Genizah Found in the Judaean Desert], 2 vols (Jerusalem: Bialik Institute, 1948/1949).

famous 'genizah' discovery being the collection partly discovered in a hidden upper room in the Ben Ezra Synagogue in Fustat, Cairo. However, this name, applied to what has been found in Cairo, is slightly misleading, because a fair part of the Cairo *genizah* has actually come from the cemetery.[4] The final resting place for manuscripts in a *genizah* is indeed the cemetery, at which point they are not actually part of a *genizah* but rather *buried*. By 1947, the Cairo *genizah*—most of which was taken by Solomon Schechter to Cambridge—had yielded sensational manuscript finds, including parts of the Hebrew book of Ben Sira—a work previously only known in Greek—as well as two versions of the mysterious Zadokite work that we now know as the Damascus Document. Sukenik was clearly thinking of this.

As more manuscripts came to light, Sukenik held strongly to his initial belief that what was found in the caves by the Dead Sea was a vast *genizah*, 'instituted by the sect of the Essenes' which were associated with the western Dead Sea region in ancient sources such as Pliny, *Hist. Nat.* 5: 15 [73].[5] Unfortunately, Sukenik published only preliminary work on the scrolls. He died in 1953 and his voice was lost from subsequent debate. The *genizah* theory has had some supporters over the decades, for example Henri del Medico,[6] though del Medico argued for no connection between the scrolls in the caves and the site of Qumran, and G. R. Driver, who came to believe that the scrolls were hidden after the First Revolt, when heterodox literature was put away.[7] This linking of the *genizah* proposition with those who disassociate Qumran and the Essenes from the scrolls has not helped Sukenik's identification, and he himself died before the archaeological investigations of the site had progressed very far.

Furthermore, Roland de Vaux—the excavator of Qumran and the caves—was doubtful that this was a *genizah*. He wrote already in 1949, of Cave 1Q: 'on a supposé que c'était une "geniza", un endroit où les livres hors d'usage étaient relégués au cours des temps; mais ces rouleaux d'âge différent soigneusement

---

[4] Solomon Schechter and Elkan N. Adler, 'Genizah,' in *Jewish Encyclopaedia* (ed. Isidore Singer; New York: Funk & Wagnalls, 1901–6), vol. 4, 612–13. Adler was told in 1888 that most of the manuscripts—called *shemot* because of the name of God—were buried in the Jewish cemetery of Basatin and 'not the least important part of the Taylor-Schechter collection has come from the graveyard'.

[5] Sukenik, *Dead Sea Scrolls*, 29. See also Synesius, *Dio* 3: 2 and Solinus, *Collectanea* 35: 1–12.

[6] Henri del Medico, 'L'État des manuscrits de Qumran I,' *Vetus Testamentum* 7 (1957): 127–38; id. *L'Énigme des manuscrits de la Mer Morte* (Paris: Plon, 1957), 23–31.

[7] Godfrey R. Driver, *The Judaean Scrolls: The Problem and a Solution* (Oxford: Blackwell, 1965), 386–91; id. 'Myths of Qumran,' *The Annual of Leeds University Oriental Society* 6 (1966–8): 23–48 at p.28. He modified his opinion from initial rejection of the *genizah* hypothesis, namely, 'it was not attached to any synagogue and manuscripts stored in it would have been at the mercy of every curious searcher who could find a way into it, e.g. wandering shepherds or fugitives from justice, and the manuscripts found in it, though not new, are obviously in a state not of advanced decay but of very fair preservation,' *The Hebrew Scrolls from the Neighbourhood of Jericho and the Dead Sea* (London: OUP, 1951), 49–50. At this point he believed in the quick hiding scenario.

rangés dans des jarres d'une même époque ne sont pas pièces mises au rebut, ce sont des archives ou une bibliothèque, cachées dans un moment critique.'[8]

However, de Vaux's main issue was with the argument of Henri del Medico, who disassociated the scrolls from the site of Qumran: this theory is summed up by de Vaux as 'the manuscript caves were *genizot*, places where manuscripts of unknown provenance, and without any connection with the occupation of Khirbet Qumran, were discarded',[9] a view that for de Vaux could be 'definitely excluded'. Then de Vaux considers other arguments. He presents the hypothesis that 'these caves may have been used as *genizot* for the community of Qumran itself', but dismisses this also: 'If this hypothesis were true, the documents in the caves would be texts rejected by the community, and could not be used to determine its ways of thinking and living.' This makes it 'an unlikely hypothesis' to de Vaux. The problem here is that de Vaux assumes that a *genizah only* contains rejected, heterodox literature rather than also containing old, important, and sacred literature.

De Vaux then states that we may accept 'that the community had a *genizah* . . . but what we cannot admit is that it had eleven *genizot*' each cave separate. The state of the manuscripts is the same throughout, having the same kind of material (parchment), and the same works occur in different caves, so that none of the caves is a *genizah*, and all the works derive from the community and were accepted by it. Again we return to de Vaux's notion of what a *genizah* is: rejected, heterodox works, or a storeroom of scraps, collected over time. He shows no knowledge of understanding that in Judaism manuscripts beyond use are ultimately to be buried, and that the Cairo *genizah* (so-called) partly came from the cemetery.

Interestingly, the *genizah* theory was dismissed by Norman Golb. Golb writes that in mentions of scrolls discovered in previous centuries, no one comments that these scrolls were damaged, an *argumentum ex silentio* which is supposed to prove that they were in perfectly good condition, which makes the *genizah* theory 'implausible'.[10] Golb prefers the quick hiding scenario, but suggests it was Jerusalem libraries that were hidden, with others suggesting it was the Temple library.[11] Nevertheless, the *genizah* theory remains one that scholars note in passing as a possibility. For example, George Brooke has

---

[8] 'It has been supposed that this was a "*genizah*", a place to which books beyond use were relegated in the course of time, but these scrolls of different age, carefully packed in the jars in the same period, are not scrapped pieces; these are archives and a library, hidden in a critical moment,' Roland de Vaux, 'Post-Scriptum: La Cachette des Manuscrits Hébreux,' *RB* 56 (1949): 234–7, at 236.

[9] De Vaux, *ADSS*, 103.

[10] Norman Golb, *Who Wrote the Dead Sea Scrolls?* (New York: Simon and Schuster, 1995), 274.

[11] K. H. Rengstorf, *Hirbet Qumran und die Bibliothek vom Toten Meer* (W. Stuttgart: Kohlhammer, 1960); id. [Eng. ed.] *Hirbet Qumran and the Problem of the Dead Sea Caves* (Leiden: Brill, 1963).

suggested that Cave 1Q might have been a *genizah*.[12] David Stacey has stated: '[M]ost of the pottery found in caves together with scrolls dates to the time of Herod or later yet some of the scrolls are dated to the second or early first centuries BCE. Thus it seems very likely that some were *"geniza"* deposits.'[13] Stephen Pfann has also suggested that Caves 4Qa, 4Qb, and 5Q comprise Essene *genizot*, but here, like de Vaux, there is the issue of how exactly a *genizah* is defined. For Pfann, a *genizah* is represented—on the basis of the manuscripts of Masada and the Cairo *genizah*—as 'typically composite, often mixing manuscripts from various sources, including both libraries and archives'.[14] Apart from the scrolls of Deuteronomy and Ezekiel found under the synagogue floor, the Masada manuscript finds are not from a Jewish *genizah* but from cupboards in the casemate walls, where *Romans* threw not only Jewish texts but their own materials.[15]

Importantly, already in 1961 Matthew Black observed that some of the scrolls had been embalmed and carefully buried. Black suggested that this burial took place not quickly, during the ravages of war, but when the community was at the point of dying out, and was done with an intention to preserve the books as long as possible in an inaccessible place, as reflected in the Testament of Moses 1:16–18.[16] We will review the evidence for the scrolls being buried here, leading to a more similar but more complex solution.

QUMRAN AND THE CAVES

With de Vaux, we can reject del Medico *inter alia* and affirm the close connection between the scroll caves and the site of Qumran. In the first place, there are in the natural caves close to Qumran (1Q–3Q, 6Q, 11Q) the cylindrical jars and their distinctive jar covers (Plate 32), a subject that has been very well explored by Jodi Magness.[17] Similar forms of these hole-mouthed jars (KhQ groups 2 and 3) have

---

[12] George Brooke, *Qumran and the Jewish Jesus: Reading the New Testament in the Light of the Scrolls* (Cambridge: Grove Books, 2005), 68.

[13] David Stacey, 'Seasonal Industries at Qumran,' *BAIAS* 26 (2008): 7–30, at p.24.

[14] Stephen Pfann, 'Reassessing the Judean Desert Caves: Libraries, Archives, Genizas and Hiding Places,' *BAIAS* 25 (2007): 147–70.

[15] Emanuel Tov, *Hebrew Bible, Greek Bible, and Qumran: Collected Essays* (Tübingen: Mohr Siebeck, 2008), 172–4; Hannah M. Cotton and Joseph Geiger, *Masada II: The Yigael Yadin Excavations 1963–1965 Final Reports/the Latin and Greek Documents* (Washington DC: Biblical Archaeology Society, 1989).

[16] Matthew Black, The Scrolls and Christian Origins (NewYork: Scribners, 1961), 12.

[17] Jodi Magness, *The Archaeology of Qumran and the Dead Sea Scrolls* (Grand Rapids: Eerdmans, 2002), 79–89, ead. 'Why Scroll Jars?' in Douglas R. Edwards (ed.), *Religion and Society in Roman Palestine* (London/New York: Routledge, 1994), 146–61.

appeared occasionally in other places near the Dead Sea: in Jericho (Jr group 2), En Gedi, and at Masada (M. group 2) in contexts dating to the reign of Herod the Great and the first century CE,[18] though there are no parallels *exactly* identical to the classic cylindrical jar form found in the caves; only Qumran has these.[19] These jars were manufactured at Qumran, since 'wasters' were found in the Qumran dumps.[20] Dennis Mizzi's recent comprehensive examination of parallels explores the lack of precision in referring to Qumran jar types, which can be ovoid or cylindrical, and notes that the Jericho and Masada forms are 'close relatives' rather than exact parallels.[21] The concentration of *exactly the same* matching types of cylindrical jars in the buildings of Qumran and the caves nearby is very striking, indicating a firm connection between the caves and this site.[22]

In addition, the artificial caves that cut into the marl cliffs at the southern edge of the Qumran plateau (4Q–5Q, 7Q–10Q, see Plate 33) are within the site. They are not to be considered as something separate from the archaeology of Qumran but rather an intrinsic part of that archaeology, if 'Qumran' is defined not only as buildings but as all the occupation areas, which include: (1) industrial and processing areas of the buildings and plateau inside a walled-off zone; (2) a cultivation region—probably comprised of palm trees—north of the site, a region edged by retaining walls indicating irrigation and fertilization;[23] and (3) artificially created habitation caves to the north, also cut into the soft marl.[24] The marl caves are part of the occupation area of Qumran, separated and distinguished from the cemetery by a long wall (see Plate 34). This 'landscape archaeology' approach expands the total definition of the settlement of Qumran and means that the scrolls of 4Q–5Q, 7Q–10Q cannot be detached from it.

We therefore have a strong linkage of the natural Caves 1Q–3Q, 6Q, and 11Q with the site of Qumran by the exact correlation of the hole-mouthed jars

---

[18] See Rachel Bar-Nathan, 'Qumran and the Hasmonaean and Herodian Winter Palaces of Jericho: The Implication of the Pottery Finds on the Interpretation of the Settlement at Qumran,' in Katharina Galor, Jean-Baptiste Humbert, and Jürgen Zangenberg (eds), *Qumran, the Site of the Dead Sea Scrolls: Archaeological Interpretations and Debates* (Leiden: Brill, 2006), 264–77. I thank Gideon Hadas for information on the recent discoveries at En Gedi, and see http://www.planetnana.co.il/ghadas/season5.mht.

[19] DJD III, 12–13, and see, for many important comments on this material, Magness, 'Qumran, the Site of the Dead Sea Scrolls: A Review Article,' in *RQ* 22/4 (2006): 642–64, esp. at 662–3.

[20] Bar-Nathan, 'Qumran and Hasmonaean Winter Palaces,' 275.

[21] Dennis Mizzi, *The Archaeology of Khirbet Qumran: A Comparative Approach*, D.Phil. thesis (Oxford, forthcoming Brill), 120–4.

[22] For a full list of these jars found at the site, see Gregory L. Doudna, 'The Legacy of an Error in Archaeological Interpretation: The Dating of the Qumran Cave Scroll Deposits,' in Galor, Humbert, and Zangenberg, *Qumran*, 147–57, 155–7.

[23] Shimon Gibson, pers. comm.

[24] Magen Broshi and Hanan Eshel, 'Residential Caves at Qumran,' *DSD* 6 (1999): 285–323.

in which scrolls were deposited in these caves with those found at the site. We also have a strong linkage of the artificial marl Caves 4Q–5Q, and 7Q–10Q since they lie within the occupation area of the Qumran settlement.

THE CONNECTION BETWEEN JARS AND SCROLLS

While it is impossible to assert that all jars were necessarily used for scrolls within caves, on the basis of present evidence, the connection between jars and manuscripts in the natural cave group 1Q–3Q, 6Q, and 11Q is important to stress. Scrolls were found by Bedouin in an intact jar—or jars—in both Caves 1Q and 11Q. In Cave 1Q one decomposed scroll was still inside its linen wrapper, stuck to the broken neck of a jar (see the photograph in DJD I, Pl. I: 8–10); this is physical evidence found by archaeologists, showing that scrolls, wrapped in linen, were placed in jars. One should not see the jars, linen, and scrolls as independent items that happened to be placed side by side. Their separation was the result of disturbance and decay. Many caves in the area were ransacked and contents removed, from antiquity to modern times, or were damaged by collapse; the jars had been smashed and their contents subjected to decomposition and attack.[25]

When de Vaux excavated Cave 1Q and the rubbish thrown outside the cave by the original treasure-hunters, there were originally some 50 jars. Cave 1Q had in fact been collapsing for centuries; there was around 50 cm of fill and rocky debris. Copious animal droppings—in parts 15 cm thick—indicated that the cave had been used by wild animals for a long time, particularly by rats, well-known for omnivorous habits. Linen was found *underneath* this

---

[25] See the results of the caves survey in Maurice Baillet, Józef T. Milik, and Roland de Vaux, *Les 'Petites Grottes' de Qumran*, DJD III (Oxford: OUP, 1962), 13–15, 18–24, and also Joseph Patrich, 'Khirbet Qumran in Light of New Archaeological Explorations in the Qumran Caves,' in Michael O. Wise, Norman Golb, John J. Collins, and Dennis G. Pardee (eds), *Methods of Investigation of the Dead Sea Scrolls and the Khirbet Qumran Site: Present Realities and Future Prospects* ANYAS 722 (New York: New York Academy of Sciences, 1994), 73–95, and Lior Wexler (ed.), *Surveys and Excavations of Caves in the Northern Judean Desert (CNJD)—1993*, 2 vols (*Atiqot* 41; Jerusalem: Israel Exploration Society, 2002). Note that the numeration given by de Vaux to the scroll caves has a letter 'Q', so that Cave 1Q = survey Cave 14 (in the cave survey), 2Q = Cave 19, 3Q = Cave 8, and 6Q = Cave 26. Patrich's survey labelled caves differently to de Vaux; his 'Cave 13' and 'Cave 24' are not the same as de Vaux's, while his 'FQ37' is de Vaux's 'Cave 37' but is identified in a different place. Many caves were used by Judaean refugees in the First and Second Revolts; see Hanan Eshel, 'On the Ongoing Research of the Refuge Caves in the Judean Desert,' in Hanan Eshel and Roi Porat (eds), *Refuge Caves of the Bar Kokhba Revolt*, 2 vols (Jerusalem: Israel Exploration Society), ii, 1–9 (Heb.). This is a very important topic in terms of regional cave use, and it is possible there may be occasional overlaps, with caves being initially used for scroll storage and subsequently, shortly afterwards, used as refuge caves, which would confuse the archaeological picture.

layer of droppings, indicating the antiquity of the jar breakage and exposure of contents. Small remains of surviving scrolls—from 72 rolls—and linen were nevertheless found in the fill, largely that which was thrown outside the cave by the looters.[26] These fragments showed damage by white ants, who—like rats—had fed on leather.[27] The ancient disturbance led to fusions of scrolls compacted together, so that there were bundles of diverse fragments melded into one.[28]

In Cave 2Q (= survey Cave 19), along with thirty-three manuscript fragments, were two whole cylindrical jars and one jar cover, with pieces of six further jars smashed anciently. In Cave 3Q (= survey Cave 8), which had partly collapsed in antiquity, there was a large quantity of broken cylindrical jars and jar covers. De Vaux identified thirty-five different jars in all and over twenty lids. There were fragments of fourteen manuscripts, but, like Cave 1Q, rats had been the principal occupants of this cave; de Vaux noted in Cave 3Q 'nids de rats contenant des morceaux de tissus, quelques bouts de cuir et un fragment inscrit'. This long cave also contained, under fill, numerous pieces of linen and strips of leather used to bind up the scrolls, which indicates that many scrolls had once been there. In Cave 6Q (= survey Cave 26), where thirty-one manuscript fragments were found, there was one jar, but there may have been more that had been taken away, for all we know, since it too was disturbed. The Bedouin apparently took cylindrical jars from Cave 1Q and used these as water containers: anyone entering any of the caves may have taken jars as well. In Cave 11Q, discovered and partially emptied by the Bedouin in 1956, there was a large cylindrical jar in which the Temple Scroll and other manuscripts were found, subsequently placed in Kando's shop in Jerusalem, and also two jar covers, as well as linen scroll wrappers and other items.[29] It should be noted that in the front part of the cave there were some other items, including a small hatchet (perhaps tellingly), a chisel or file, a knife, a little pottery including a small jug (contemporaneous to periods of Qumran occupation, first century BCE to first century CE), bits of linen and basketry, pieces of rope, and 'un cigare durci et noirci', a hardened and blackened scroll

---

[26] G. Lankester Harding, 'The Dead Sea Scrolls,' *PEQ* (1949): 112–16, at 113. For scroll counts see Emanuel Tov, *The Texts from the Judaean Desert. Indices and an Introduction to* The Discoveries in the Judaean Desert *Series* (DJD XXXIX; Oxford: OUP, 2002). I am grateful to Sidnie White Crawford for this reference.

[27] Harding, 'Dead Sea Scrolls,' 114.

[28] Ibid. 114–15. Though the bundling is itself curious, see below.

[29] Roland de Vaux, 'Fouille de Khirbet Qumrân,' *RB* 63 (1956): 532–77, at 573–7; id. *ADSS*, 51. See also the items shown at http://www.schoyencollection.com/dsscrolls.htm#5095_1 from the Shøyen collection: the linen wrapper for the Temple Scroll and palm stylus. The large jar from Cave 11Q is apparently still in 'Kando's shop' in Jerusalem. Additional linen pieces from 11Q were found in the innermost crevice during Joseph Patrich's excavation; see Patrich, 'Qumran Caves,' 90. See too Farah Mébarki and Emile Puech, *Les manuscrits de la Mer Morte* (Rodez: Rouergue, 2002), 31.

that had clearly been very tightly wound in order for de Vaux to see it as a 'cigar'. Here de Vaux does not mention bitumen or leather strips. This small collection of artefacts led de Vaux to identify that Cave 11Q was 'habitée', meaning occupied or lived in, though he did not explicitly specify how brief that was: the nature of the deposit clearly indicates an exceedingly brief habitation, appropriate to a campsite; there is no hearth, cooking pot, floor levelling, or anything indicative of use beyond a few days.[30] Those depositing the scrolls in jars in the cave presumably used the front part for temporary shelter, since it would have taken a long time to reach this cave from Qumran.

When caves were surveyed in 1952 (see plan, Plate 35), the same kinds of jars were found in twenty-two of them and in eleven there were also lids. In disturbed caves, linen alone, preserved by fill and associated with jars, invariably indicates missing scrolls, since linen was used for the wrapping of scrolls or for stoppers and for no other purpose. For example, William Reed noted that in the rubble of Cave-Shelter 12 there was a jar still containing the linen scroll-wrappers, and there was a palm-fibre mat which once perhaps covered the jars, which were placed in an artificial stone recess.[31] In the survey Cave 29, which had no scroll fragments, there were elements of a dozen broken cylindrical jars, and seventeen jar covers, seven of which were piled up neatly. Given an attested correlation of scrolls, linen, leather strips, and jars, one does not need every component in a disturbed or partly collapsed cave with broken jars to recognize the synthesis, even when much material has been eaten, taken, or decayed, since we have a very simple equation to remember: scrolls/linen + rats = animal droppings. Organic material is only occasionally preserved, thanks to it being under fill.

Cave 29 seems quite clearly to be the cave referred to by Patriarch Timotheus of Seleucia (Baghdad), *c.*726–819 CE, who states in a letter (*c.*800) to Sergius, Metropolitan of Elam, that Hebrew manuscripts—including 200 copies of Psalms—were found in a cave somewhere in the region of Jericho, when a hunter, following his dog, slipped into a hole, and found a little chamber in the

---

[30] *Contra* Florentino García Martínez, 'Cave 11 in Context,' in *The Dead Sea Scrolls: Texts and Context* (ed. Charlotte Hempel; Leiden: Brill, 2010), 199–209, who reads de Vaux's words as indicating permanent long-term habitation, though this is not indicated at all by de Vaux himself. In noting that the cave was '*plus habitée*' ('Fouille,' 534) de Vaux was commenting on a small amount of broken pottery from three different periods: the Chalcolithic, the Iron Age, as well as the items from the period of Qumran. Cave 11Q was clearly a useful shelter (for shepherds, or people using it as a hideout), in previous periods, until Qumran inhabitants placed jars within it and briefly encamped. See also: Daniel Stökl Ben Ezra, 'Further Reflections on Caves 1 and 11: A Response to Florentino García Martinez,' in Hempel, *Dead Sea Scrolls*, 211–20, who rightly states that 'it is difficult to imagine . . . a prolonged period' of habitation, as '[c]ave 11 is quite far from the [Qumran] site (almost 2 km. as the crow flies) and does not have water . . . storage, cooking and eating vessels.'

[31] William Reed, 'The Qumran Caves Expedition of March 1952,' *BASOR* 135 (1954): 8–13, at p.13; DJD III, 8.

interior of the rock with many books inside.[32] The hunter reported the find to Jews in Jerusalem, who came into the area, and took away books of the Old Testament and others composed in Hebrew.[33] The description precisely matches the fact that Cave 29 is indeed a high, inner chamber, 3 m in diameter, accessed by a tunnel 2 m long.[34] In other words, this too was a scroll cave.

Such archaeological evidence is supplemented by further important literary attestation: jars and scrolls go together very strikingly in an account of a discovery in the third century CE. According to Eusebius, the famous scholar Origen, who wrote his *Hexapla* between the years 228 and 254, noted that he had the use of a (Greek) version of Psalms that was found 'in a *pithos* (ἐν πίθῳ) near Jericho at the time of Antoninus the son of Severus' (Caracalla, 211–27; Eusebius, *Hist. Eccles.* 6: 16: 3), a *pithos* being a storage jar. The finding of the manuscripts in πίθοι (plural) is reported by Pseudo-Athanasius in his *Synopsis* and also by Epiphanius, who writes of the discovery being 'in the seventh year of Antoninus, son of Severus' (217 CE). Both Pseudo-Athanasius and Epiphanius specify that the *pithoi* contained 'manuscripts of the Septuagint, as well as other Hebrew and Greek writings' (Epiphanius, *De Mens. et Pond.* 17–18; *PG* 43, cols. 265–8; Pseudo-Athanasius, *Synopsis PG* 28: col. 432).

No scrolls in jars were found in the artificial marl caves. But de Vaux did not differentiate the form of these from the natural caves, even though these are located in a compact area connected to the site of Qumran, they are clearly visible, and they were never sealed: their entrances were blocked by the collapse of the friable marl, not deliberately. There were ovoid storage jar fragments and lids in Caves 7Q and 8Q, along with pottery such as cooking pots, bowls, goblets, and lamps, indicating human occupation.[35] De Vaux noted that in Cave 5Q there were a number of manuscript fragments but only one single jar piece, which may be intrusive. In Cave 4Q there were very few ceramic items of any kind, but hundreds of small manuscript fragments. Given this, de Vaux concluded that a simple correlation between jars and manuscripts in caves as a whole was not then assured. He proposed that some cave jars might additionally have been for provisions,[36] an idea explored by

---

[32] Otto Eissfeldt, 'Der gegenwärtige Stand der Erforschung der in Palästina . . . Handschriften,' *Theologische Literaturzeitung* 74 (1949): cols. 595–600.

[33] There is also the report from the tenth-century Qaraite Yakub al-Qiriqisani who indicates a belief that there existed *magariyya*, 'cave-dwellers' responsible for manuscripts found in a cave, but there is no indication where these manuscripts were found; see Lena Cansdale, *Qumran and the Essenes: A Re-Evaluation of the Evidence* (Tübingen: J.C.B. Mohr [Paul Siebeck], 1997), 84; Norman Golb, 'Who were the Magariya?' *Journal of the American Oriental Society* 80 (1960): 347–59.

[34] Roland de Vaux, 'Exploration de la Région de Qumrân,' *RB* 60 (1953), 540–61, at 560. Hartmut Stegemann has suggested that Cave 3Q, where the Copper Scroll was discovered, might be a contender. Hartmut Stegemann, *The Library of Qumran: On the Essenes, Qumran, John the Baptist and Jesus* (Grand Rapids: Eerdmans, 1998), 68–9.

[35] DJD III, 26–31; DJD VI, 9–20; de Vaux, *ADSS*, 52–3.

[36] DJD III, 34–5.

Jodi Magness, who suggests that cave goods could have been especially pure.[37]

However, it is important to differentiate the typology of the natural caves from the artificial caves.[38] The open character of the artificial caves is very different from the natural fissures that are Caves 1Q–3Q, 6Q, and 11Q. The cluster 4Q–5Q and 10Q on one side (Plate 36) and 7Q–9Q on the other are located in a compact area, in marl recesses which are not accessible to animals, only accessible to humans via slim pathways, steps, and—probably—rope ladders. They were not sealed, and they show signs of human occupation. They were created for a particular purpose and can be distinguished from the natural caves further from the site. A typological approach may then help us to clarify the functions inherent in these forms.

THE NATURAL CAVES

If we take the natural caves as a typological category in themselves, what can be said about the nature of the scroll deposits within jars? One striking thing to note is that Lankester Harding and de Vaux were able to find among the many pieces of linen used to wrap up scrolls and seal the jars in Cave 1Q that some of this linen had been impregnated with bitumen. The Bedouin who first discovered the cave also indicated that bitumen had been used as a preservative for the scrolls. According to the story given by Edmund Wilson, when the shepherd Muhammad ed-Dhib and his companion Ahmed Mohammed (see Plate 37) opened the lids of the jars they found in Cave 1Q, a bad smell came out, and they saw inside big black oblong lumps. They took these out of the cave, and saw that there was something wrapped up inside the linen that had then been coated with black pitch. They later described the scrolls as being 'wrapped up like mummies'.[39] The manuscripts are described as 'some very dirty rolls, several wrapped in dirty cloth with a black substance on them'.[40] De Vaux noted that the linen was sometimes impregnated with wax, pitch, or asphalt: 'Ils sont souvent imprégnés de cire, de poix ou d'asphalte.'[41] Slightly confusingly, however, the leather of the scrolls decomposed to a black substance, which was originally thought by Lankester Harding also to be pitch directly stuck onto a manuscript.[42]

---

[37] See Magness, *Archaeology of Qumran*; ead. 'Why Scroll Jars?'

[38] I am grateful to Sidnie White Crawford for sharing a paper with me in which she has independently argued the same thing: 'Who Hid the Qumran Scrolls in the Caves?'

[39] Edmund Wilson, *The Scrolls from the Dead Sea* (London: W. H. Allen, 1955), 9, see also Trever, *The Untold Story*, 25.

[40] Driver, *Hebrew Scrolls* (London: OUP, 1951), 7.

[41] De Vaux, 'Post-Scriptum,' 235. Harding identified this as 'wax': 'Dead Sea Scrolls,' 114.

[42] Harding, 'Dead Sea Scrolls,' 114, corrected in DJD I: 7, 39.

There are numerous examples of linen clear of bitumen, and the wrappers immediately around the scrolls do not appear to be this bitumen-impregnated type. Only bitumen-free examples of linen were sent for analysis to Grace Crowfoot. However, clumps of asphalt within the linen are clearly visible on Mirielle Bélis' photographs of uncleaned textiles in boxes in the Rockefeller stores in Jerusalem, two of which are reproduced here (Plates 38 and 39).[43] Such examples appear to be jar stoppers rather than scroll wrappers. This material has never been analysed in order to ascertain its precise composition.

Bélis did not focus on these examples, but does note that, '[l]es indices recueillis montraient donc bien que les responsables du dépôt avaient mis en application une méthode destinée à protéger les manuscrits des agressions du temps et des parasites'.[44] She defines the following process: (1) the texts were wound up into a tight cylinder; (2) they were fixed by a strip of leather (dozens having been found in the caves); (3) the scrolls were wrapped in different types of prepared linen; (4) they were placed in jars with this linen.[45] This tight rolling, wrapping, binding, and jar-placement together was designed for preservation, and it is to be noted that a recent study has shown that the scroll wrappers were made of the best quality white linen.[46]

In her examination of the cylindrical jar forms, Jodi Magness has pointed out how the round bowl-shaped lids that capped the tops of these jars are significant. The lids 'completely covered the mouths of the jars, fitting snugly over the neck and on the shoulder. Any moisture (rain, dew, bird and bat droppings, etc.) that happened to fall on the cylindrical jars covered with these lids would have rolled off, down the sides of the jars and on to the ground. In other words, the bowl-shaped lids were designed to prevent moisture from entering the jars'.[47] The jar lids, however—unlike clay, lime, or stone stoppers—are not a seal, and are easy to remove.[48]

---

[43] I am grateful to Jean-Baptiste Humbert for supplying me with these photos. Mirielle Bélis, 'Des Textiles: Catalogues et Commentaires *Khirbet Qumrân et 'Ain Feshkha II: Études d'anthropologie,'* in Jean-Baptiste Humbert and Jan Gunneweg (eds), *Khirbet Qumrân et 'Ain Feshkha II: Études d'anthropologie, de physique et de chemie* (Novum Testamentum et Orbis Antiquus, Series Archaeologica 3; Academic Press, Éditions Saint-Paul, Fribourg, Suisse/Vandenhoeck & Ruprecht, Göttingen, 2003), 207–76, Pl. II, 4–6, described at 224–5. See also: ead. 'Les manuscrits de Qumrân: Comment se sont-ils conservés?' *L'Archéo-thema: Revue d'archéologie et d'histoire* 2 (May–June 2009): 41–5.

[44] Bélis, 'Les manuscrits de Qumrân,' 42.

[45] Ibid. 42–4.

[46] Analysis of about two hundred linen scroll wrappers have indicated that this fine linen was bleached white, possibly indicating re-used Essene clothing, see Orit Shamir and Naama Sukenik, 'Qumran Textiles and the Garments of Qumran's Inhabitants,' *DSD* 18 (2011): 206–25. But this 'priestly' cloth could equally be used because of the holiness of works wrapped up in it.

[47] Magness, 'Why Scroll Jars?' 154–5.

[48] Bar-Nathan, 'Qumran,' 277: 'its lid is very easy to remove and, therefore, is not suitable for storing food . . . the cover (bowl-lid) is easy to remove and not intended to keep products sealed.' Five ordinary jar stoppers have been found associated with dates and a storage jar in Patrich's Cave 13; see Patrich, 'Qumran Caves,' 91.

The question remains whether the bitumen-impregnated linen was sometimes part of the stopping of the jars rather than only wrapped around the scrolls, or both. A parallel for bitumen-impregnated linen as a casing around a scroll has in fact been found in Egypt and exists in the papyrological collection of the University of Pennsylvania.[49] Nevertheless, the protective jar lids and the bitumen-impregnated linen together give us the impression that those who placed scrolls in jars in caves were very much concerned with long-term preservation.

Bitumen was known in antiquity for its preservative function: bitumen from the Dead Sea was sold to the Egyptians for embalming.[50] There was therefore a trade route leading from the lake to Egypt across the Judaean wilderness to the western part of Palestine.[51] Because of this bitumen industry, as we have seen, the sea was known as Lake Asphaltites (Josephus, *War* 4: 476–85, Pliny, *Nat. Hist.* 5:15 [72]). The deposit of the scrolls right next to the 'Bitumen Lake' is perhaps not entirely coincidental, in that this allowed the people of Qumran to have ready access to material they needed for the careful processes involved in sealing scrolls within jars.

In addition, to bury manuscripts in cloth impregnated with bitumen could not have happened quickly, since bitumen requires a long time to be processed in order to be usable. Popularly it was thought that bitumen was initially softened by urine (e.g. Strabo, *Geogr.* 16: 2: 43) and menstrual blood (see Josephus, *War.* 4: 478), though Tacitus (*Hist.* 5: 6) said that the tale that bitumen would shrink from blood, particularly menstrual blood, was one of several old stories not confirmed by those who knew the country, and that bitumen was cut like wood with any implement sharp enough. But then it had to be melted and applied to the linen. Unlike the asphalt used on today's roads, the 'glance pitch' type of bitumen found today around the Dead Sea (Plate 40) has a relatively high melting point of 135 degrees Celsius. Attested Bedouin practice was to boil lumps in olive oil over a fire, though in antiquity animal fat

---

[49] I am very grateful to Robert Kraft for bringing this to my attention at the Qumran Session at the SBL Annual Meeting in New Orleans, November 2009, and for sending me links to pictures and the catalogue of the University of Pennsylvania. Item 38-28-45 is a scroll of 'papyrus/bitumen', actually with a casing of bitumen-impregnated linen in which the scroll was held; see http://ccat.sas.upenn.edu/rak/ppenn/museum/cartonnage/38-28-45-DSCF4560.jpg. Another papyrus has the bitumen and linen attached: 29-86-498; see http://ccat.sas.upenn.edu/rak/ppenn/museum/cartonnage/29-86-498-both.jpg and see 29-87-560, which is a piece of bitumen cartonage from Dra Abu el Naga. http://ccat.sas.upenn.edu/rak/ppenn/museum/old-egypt/29-87-560-DSCF4571.jpg. In Egyptian antiquity scrolls could be buried within the bitumen-impregnated linen casing of mummies, as with the Ebers Papyrus, found between the knees of a mummy in Thebes. The practice of scroll preservation would then have been known from Egyptian precedents.

[50] Diodorus Siculus, *Bibl. Hist.* 19: 99: 3; Galen, *Simpl. Med.* 9: 2: 10; Josephus, *War* 4: 481. Ze'ev Safrai, *The Economy of Roman Palestine* (London: Routledge, 1994), 187–8; Philip C. Hammond, 'The Nabataean Bitumen Industry at the Dead Sea,' *BA* 22 (1959): 40–8.

[51] Menahem Har-El, 'The Route of Salt, Sugar and Balsam Caravans in the Judaean Desert,' *GeoJournal* 2/6 (1978): 549–56.

could have also been used.[52] Only scientific analysis of the bitumen-impregnated linen would provide some clue as to how this was processed. Clearly, it would have been wrapped around the scroll or placed in the jar opening while the bitumen was still warm, and then the bitumen would have hardened as it cooled. If we think about the time and care required for the preparation of the impregnated linen wrapping, and the nature of the scrolls being 'buried' in jars in remote and hard-to-access caves, this does not fit well with a quick hiding scenario for the temporary storage of a nearby library with the expectation that the manuscripts might soon be retrieved.[53]

The bitumen-impregnated linen wrapping—where used—is consistent with a mentality that sought to preserve scrolls in a kind of special burial. It seems clear that the burial of scrolls was organized by those who lived at the site of Qumran. They used jars made at the site. They wrapped up the scrolls tightly in linen, rolled further linen around them, tied them up with leather strips, (sometimes?) sealed them with linen impregnated with bitumen, packed them into jars with scraps of linen, and closed the top of the jars with bowls and bitumen-impregnated linen to protect them. They then carefully placed the jars in awkward, natural caves, generally sealing the entries to these caves when they had finished.

Even without bitumen, the notion of preservation of documents as a motivation for placing them in jars is biblically attested. In Jer. 32: 14: 'And I charge Baruch before them saying, thus says the Lord of Hosts the God of Israel, take these documents, this deed of purchase and put them in a clay vessel that they may last for many days.' Jeremiah, of course, is not concerned to tell us what might have been involved in the preparation of a document placed in a jar. Importantly, in the Testament of Moses 1: 16–18, Moses instructs Joshua to order the Scriptures, 'embalm [them] with cedar oil [*chedriabis*], and place [them] in earthenware jars', but whether cedar oil was used on the Dead Sea scroll manuscripts may be impossible to determine chemically.[54]

---

[52] Aref Abu-Rabia, *A Bedouin Century: Education and Development among the Negev Tribes in the 20th Century* (New York: Berghahn Books, 2001), 57. James L. Kelso and Alfred R. Powell, 'Glance Pitch from Tell Beit Mirsim,' *BASOR* 95 (1944): 14–18 at 17. If animal fat was used, this might explain why animal parts were boiled in pots at Qumran, since fat rises to the surface and is scooped off. Bitumen adheres to a scroll jar in the Shøyen collection MS 1655/1.

[53] The quick hiding scenario of one date, 68 CE, has also been questioned on other grounds recently by Daniel Stökl Ben Ezra, 'Old Caves and Young Caves: A Statistical Re-evaluation of a Qumran Consensus,' *DSD* 14 (2007): 313–33, who notes that the average palaeographical dates of manuscripts in caves 1Q and 4Q are earlier than caves 2Q, 3Q, 5Q, 6Q, and 11Q. A similar differentiation between older and younger caves has been made by Pfann, 'Reassessing the Judean Desert Caves,' but Pfann differentiates the earlier group on the basis of *yaḥad* terminology as 1Q, 4Q, 5Q, 6Q, and the later 'Zealot' group as 2Q, 3Q, 11Q, and Masada texts.

[54] I am grateful to Michael Stone for discussing this with me, and for his paper, 'The Cedar in Jewish Antiquity,' read at the Talmudic Archaeology Conference, University College London, 22–4 June 2009. Stone noted that Romans used cedar or citron oil to prolong the longevity of manuscripts (Pliny, *Nat. Hist.* 13: 27 [84–7]; Horace, *Ars. Poet.* 331), since this oil or resin had strong anti-fungal and anti-bacterial agents. He has been interested in exploring whether cedar

With the additional procedures involved in placing the scrolls in jars in caves, we get the strong impression that this was a time-consuming process designed to ensure that the manuscripts lasted a very long time indeed. If those who buried the scrolls were applying techniques from mummification procedures in Egypt, there could have been other applications than cedar oil in terms of the scrolls themselves prior to their interment in jars. For example, recent studies of embalming substances in research led by Richard Evershed of Bristol University have shown that bodies were first treated with natron (a natural salt mixture), and then coated in fat, either from plant oils or the fat from cattle, sheep, and goats, followed by conifer, cedar, or *Pistacia* resin, balsam, and beeswax. The bitumen associated with mummies was not generally employed for the preservation of the bodies, but for the outer sealing and linen wrapping.[55] If this were the case also with the Dead Sea Scrolls manuscripts, then we may expect to find in their chemistry indicators of Dead Sea salts (similar to natron), other minerals, grease or oil, and beeswax. The latter issue is complicated by the fact that many scrolls were treated with wax after their discovery.

Evidence for local treatment of the scrolls has indeed been discovered in chemical tests. Analyses on the Temple Scroll, led by Giuseppe Pappalardo and done in the National Laboratories of the South, Italy, have indicated that there was a ratio of chlorine to bromide indicative of the high salt content of Dead Sea water, which was thought to prove that the scroll was originally manufactured at Qumran.[56] In fact, it seems more likely to show that the scroll was treated with Dead Sea salts prior to its arrival in the cave. This same kind of Dead Sea signature found in the scraped-off ink from a manuscript[57] likewise would indicate the salts of a pre-burial treatment. Further study of manuscripts that are too early to have come from Qumran (i.e. manuscripts clearly dating to before 37 BCE) would confirm that this signature is the result of treatment prior to the burial of the manuscripts, not provenance.

In addition, recent excavations of the Qumran plateau have uncovered bitumen deposits.[58] Associated with these was a medium-sized sealed storage

---

oil was used on the scrolls, but there may not be sufficient residue of a distinctive chemical signature in order to verify this hypothesis.

[55] Stephen A. Buckley and Richard P. Evershed, 'Organic Chemistry of Embalming Agents in Pharaonic and Graeco-Roman mummies,' *Nature* 413 (2001): 837–41; Stephen A. Buckley, Katherine A. Clark, and Richard P. Evershed, 'Complex Organic Chemical Balms of Pharaonic Animal Mummies,' *Nature* 431 (2004): 294–9.

[56] As reported in Science 329 no. 5989 (16 July 2010): 261; Ira Rabin also reported on the high ratio of bromides in her paper 'Archaeometry of the Dead Sea Scrolls,' in the ISBL Qumran session, London, July 2011.

[57] Ira Rabin, Oliver Hahn, Timo Wolff, Admir Masic, and Gisela Weinberg, 'On the Origin of the Ink of the Thanksgiving Scroll (1QHodayotᵃ),' *DSD* 16 (2009): 97–106.

[58] Randall Price, 'New Discoveries at Qumran,' *World of the Bible News and Views* 6/3 (2004) (online edition); id. 'Qumran Plateau,' *Hadashot Arkheologiyot: Excavations and Surveys in Israel* 117 (2005) (online edition).

jar which held contents which were initially thought to indicate the presence of tartrate, from grape wine,[59] but has now been found to contain gypsum (calcium sulphate). This was a common preservative, especially when mixed with salt.[60] It is found naturally in high concentration as a chemical precipitate from the salty water of the Dead Sea, which could also have been mixed with a preservative.[61]

The use of grease in mummy preservation is particularly interesting given the large number of animal bones found at the site of Qumran, buried deep in the ground in intact or broken pots. These bones indicate that edible and non-edible parts of sheep and goats were boiled for their gelatine and fat. As any cook knows, this releases the fat to the top of the pot, which can be scraped off on cooling.[62]

GENIZAH AND CEMETERY

As noted above, it is important to distinguish a *genizah* and a scroll cemetery, even though the popular designation of the 'Cairo *genizah*' blends the two together, and it seems this composite collection was in Sukenik's mind. The word *genizah* is related to the verb גנז, 'separate off, set aside, reserve, hide',[63] and, strictly speaking, can refer to a store for coins or treasure, or can be a temporary store designed for old or damaged sacred documents, heterodox, or rejected works, and other documents containing the name of God.

From the Torah's exhortation to destroy idolatry, there was a ramification: one should not destroy the name of God (see Deut 12: 3–4): 'You shall completely destroy all the places where the nations you dispossess serve their gods . . . and you shall obliterate their name from that place. You shall not act like this toward YHWH your God.' If you do not act like this toward YHWH, then, conversely, the name of God could not be destroyed. Religious

---

[59] Salvador Butí, Nati Salvadó, Nuria Lope, Emilia Papiol, Elena Heras, and Jan Gunneweg, 'Determination of Wine Residues in Qumran Amphora-35,' in Jan Gunneweg, Charles Greenblatt, and Annemie Adriaans (eds), *Bio- and Material Cultures at Qumran* (Papers from a COST Action G8 working group held in Israel on 22–3 May 2005; Fraunhofer IRB, Stuttgart, 2006), 71–80.

[60] Kaare Rasmussen, Jan Gunneweg, Johannes van der Plicht, Irena Kralj Cigic, Andrew D. Bond, Bo Svensmark, Marta Balla, Matija Strilic, and Greg Doudna, 'On the Age and Content of Jar-35—A Sealed and Intact Storage Jar found on the Southern Plateau of Qumran,' *Archaeometry* 53/4 (2011): 791–808; Martin Levey, 'Gypsum, Salt and Soda in Ancient Mesopotamian chemical Technology,' in *Isis* 49 (1958): 336–42.

[61] Amitai Katz, Avraham Starinsky, Nurit Taitel-Goldman, and Michael Beyth, 'Solubilities of Gypsum and Halite in the Dead Sea and in Its Mixtures with Seawater,' *Limnology and Oceanography* 26/4 (July 1981): 709–16.

[62] Magen and Peleg, *Qumran Excavations*, 42–9, cf. De Vaux, *ADSS*, 71–5; Hirschfeld, 'Qumran in Context,' 208. See n. 52, also, for the use of fat in melting bitumen.

[63] Jastrow, 258.

texts containing the name of God can become *pesul*, unusable, due to old age or illegibility. In this case they are called *shemot* on account of having the name (*shem*) of God; like an old American flag, however, they cannot just be thrown away, and in the case of Jewish manuscripts containing the name of God they are initially stored and eventually buried. In m.Shab. 9: 6 there is a reference to prohibiting, on the Sabbath, the taking out of 'worn-out sacred books or their worn-out covers that have been stored away in order to reserve them (לגנזן)'. Books that should not be read, like the pseudonymous heterodox text *The Book of Remedies*, ascribed to Solomon, might be 'reserved' as well (b.Pes. 56a, 62, cf. b.Shab. 13b, 30b, 115a). The languages of these writings could be Hebrew, Greek, and others (b.Shab. 115a). But the temporariness of a *genizah* is important to remember. The final destination for *shemot* was the grave. In the Babylonian Talmud, we find a comment that a *sefer*, 'book, scroll', that is worn-out is buried beside a scholar (b.Meg. 26b, cf. Moed Katan 25a, Baba Kamma 17a). It is no longer then in a *genizah*. It is buried.

Curiously, worn-out scroll wrappers may be used for making shrouds for corpses that do not have people to bury them (b.Meg. 26b). This was noted by Grace Crowfoot in her important study of the linen from Cave 1Q. She observed also that many of the linen cloths from this cave showed signs of wear and tear, and several had repairs; she found only two instances of linen cloths whose fringe ends were not frayed by use, i.e. it was clear to her that these were old, worn-out scroll wrappers. Crowfoot in fact was the one to suggest explicitly that scrolls and wrappers were buried and 'it is important to remember that burial in caves was the custom of the country, and so this concealment may only be the equivalent of the correct cemetery burial of the contents of a *Genizah*'.[64] In other words, Grace Crowfoot was the first to propose the hypothesis that I reiterate here, basing herself on the evidence of the linen.

As for the Dead Sea manuscripts themselves, they tend to be worn. The Genesis Apocryphon—neatly rolled up in one scroll—had been purposely cut.[65] 1Q34 (1QFestival Prayers), 1Q71 (Dan. 1: 10–17), and 1Q72 (Dan. 3: 22–8) were bundled together.[66] No one could argue that the scrolls exist overall in a pristine state, even in the case of relatively complete scrolls. It may be possible that the Temple Scroll was buried in good condition, and its current poor state is due to the vicissitudes of time.[67] But here it is to be

---

[64] DJD I, 25.

[65] I am grateful to Daniel Machiela for pointing this out to me at the SBL Qumran session at New Orleans, 25 November 2009, and see Daniel A. Machiela, *The Dead Sea Genesis Apocryphon: A New Text and Translation with Introduction and Special Treatment of Columns 13–17* (Studies on the Texts of the Desert of Judah, 79; Leiden: Brill, 2009).

[66] John Trever, 'Completion of the Publication of Some Fragments from Qumran Cave 1,' *RQ* 5/18 (1965): 323–44 at 330–4.

[67] I am grateful to Florentino García Martínez for his assessment of the 'beautiful' original condition of the Temple Scroll at the SBL Conference in New Orleans, November 2009.

remembered that books that were perceived as either heterodox or obsolete could also find their way into a *genizah* and into a burial. Scrolls from Caves 11Q and 3Q can be later palaeographically, with pottery also coming from the mid to late first century. The linen from the wrapping in 11Q was unusual: bleached white with distinctive indigo stripes.[68] However, if these caves include certain scrolls deemed no longer appropriate for use on account of somewhat variant ideas—considered within the context of the *yaḥad* ideology—then we would have a straightforward reason for the burial of a manuscript—the Temple Scroll—in good condition (if this could be proven), prior to 68 CE[69]

In the case of the Cairo *genizah* collection, it clearly contained a vast array of different texts, including entirely secular pieces—by no means only sacred scriptures. It is difficult to assume a criterion of selection. Likewise, we cannot know what led scrolls to be buried in the case of Qumran, but a simplistic criterion of 'only old scrolls' would be too narrow. If a text had been superseded by a new edition, would they keep the older one? If a text led to interpretative innovations that were problematic, did they assign it to burial? What were their policies in sustaining active library holdings? In terms of a biblical or other sacred manuscript, how damaged did it have to be before it was deemed too worn? If one column was no longer readable, did that mean it should be replaced, or did it need to be quite tattered around the edges? Could there have been an accident or destruction in the first century which resulted in damage to a number of recently made scrolls? We simply do not know. One cannot even say that any given manuscript was in too good condition for burial—or the opposite—without knowing anything about the criteria of assessment, or the original state of the entire manuscript.

The practice of burying old manuscripts in Jewish cemeteries continues today, and is accompanied by ritual, but the idea that burial of manuscripts is in some way intended to make these last is not found in current practices. Nevertheless, it would fit with a mentality of a certain particularly fastidious group that, in order not to seem negligent so that the name of God might perish by one's carelessness, steps would be taken to preserve it.

In regard to the burial of manuscripts in caves, there is a remarkable parallel not within the realms of Judaism, but within Islam. In the region of Quetta, Pakistan, the Chilton Mountains host a number of passageways designed to hold old Quranic texts, which are shrouded in cloth sacks as is customary for

---

[68] Pfann, 'Reassessing the Judean Desert Caves,' 159–61. For the linen, see Bélis, 'Textiles,' 236, Pl. III: 1–7. Pfann's theory is that the deposits in both 3Q and 11Q were made by Zealots of the 2nd century CE.

[69] However, the Temple Scroll is actually significantly damaged in its first fourteen columns. Given significant damage over the centuries, see Johann Maier, *The Temple Scroll* (Sheffield: JSOT Press; 1985), 1; so how sure can we be of the original state of leather and writing?

the dead. This area is called popularly 'The Mountain of the Quranic Light', and is a place of pilgrimage and prayer.[70]

A close chronological parallel to the practice of placing scrolls in jars comes from Egypt, and is found for example in Deir el-Medineh,[71] and from Egypt too is the parallel for burying manuscripts in jars in mountain caves or rocky overhangs. The Nag Hammadi codices, found in 1945, comprising thirteen Gnostic codices, were buried under a rock overhang (associated with tombs) by Coptic monks. These were placed in a jar, which was closed with a bowl-shaped lid, and sealed with bitumen.[72] In 1952 a later library of biblical, apocryphal, and other manuscripts of the Pachomian Order was found close to the Nile in this region. The Dishna papers or Bodmer Papyri, found 12 km from Nag Hammadi, were in a jar. In none of these instances do we appear to have burial of manuscripts coinciding with a rapid hiding scenario. In fact, two of the texts from Nag Hammadi specifically refer to books being stored for preservation until the end of time in a mountain: The Gospel of the Egyptians 68: 10–69: 5 and Allogenes 68: 6–20.[73]

Early Christian manuscripts have also been found buried with corpses in tombs in Egypt. The Gospel of Peter was found in a monk's tomb in the necropolis of Akhmim, in 1886–7, and the Gospel of Judas—found with letters of Paul and other manuscripts—was found in a tomb in al-Minya, within a limestone box, in 1978. In these cases, as well, the manuscripts seem to be buried in anticipation of their surviving for the future eschatological age, in accordance with Christian belief (not for use in the afterlife, as in previous Egyptian practice).

---

[70] Matthew Battles, *Library: An Unquiet History* (New York: W. W. Norton, 2003), 192–3.

[71] Minna Lönnqvist and Kenneth Lönnqvist, 'Parallels to Be Seen: Deir el-Medina Jars Containing Manuscripts,' in Armin Lange, Emanuel Tov, and Matthias Weigold (eds), *The Dead Sea Scrolls in Context: Integrating the Dead Sea Scrolls in the Study of Ancient Texts, Languages, and Cultures: An International Conference Organized by the University of Vienna and the Hebrew University of Jerusalem*, Vienna, 11–14 February 2008, 2 vols (Leiden: Brill, 2011), ii, 471–87.

[72] The jar itself was smashed and not recovered, but the bowl lid remains in the Coptic Museum, Cairo. James Robinson noted, after examining this: 'The diameter at the outer edge is 23.3–24.0 cm, with a diameter inside the bowl of 18.2–18.7 cm, adequate to close a mouth large enough to admit the codices, whose broadest leaves, in Codex VII, measure up to 17.5 cm. There are a few black tarlike stains about 2.0 cm from the outer edge on the under side of the rim, perhaps vestiges of a bitumen used to seal the bowl into the jar. Thus, the jar probably could not be opened readily to investigate its contents, which would explain why it was broken by its discoverers. This would also explain the excellent state of preservation of a number of the codices...' James M. Robinson, 'The Discovery of the Nag Hammadi Codices,' *BA* 42/4 (1979): 206–24, at 213–14.

[73] James M. Robinson (ed.), *The Nag Hammadi Library in English* (rev. ed. San Francisco: Harper One, 1988), 21–2.

BURIAL OF SCROLLS IN THE CEMETERY

Importantly, there is a possibility that some scrolls were buried not in the natural limestone caves in the hills behind Qumran, but in the cemetery itself. In 1856 Henry Poole visited Qumran, and had one of the graves of the cemetery opened. Poole noted the measurements carefully (6 ft long and 3 ft wide, 4 ft 10 ins deep) and its design ('it was built up on all four sides with rough stones and square corners'). But, in this grave there was apparently no loculus for a human body, and—mysteriously—as Poole recorded: 'there were no osseous remains traceable.'[74] Henry Poole had excavated an empty tomb.

Poole was not the only one to dig in the cemetery to find no skeletal material. In 1951 de Vaux excavated a curious stone circle, located in the middle of the east–west transversal path in the cemetery, recorded in the plan made by Clermont-Ganneau in 1873.[75] At the southern end there was a small wall of two rows of stones. At the northern end, the walls had crumbled into the pit, which was only about 75 cm deep. At the bottom, he found only stones and an earth surface.[76] Then Solomon Steckoll excavated eleven graves, but the first one contained no skeletal material.[77] Steckoll realized there was a peculiarity in the cemetery. He writes:

> However, not the least of the problems which remained to be unravelled, is the presence of what appear to be graves on the surface, carefully marked with stones, albeit smaller stones than those found in the main cemetery as markers on the tombs, in that area lying between the cemetery proper and the building of the Community. There are a number of these, all falling within a distance which is less than fifty cubits from the building.

Steckoll notes that in the Mishnah (Baba Bathra 2: 9; cf. b.Baba Bathra 25a) there is a strict prohibition against anyone burying corpses within 50 cubits (Steckoll estimates 22.352 m) of a town. Steckoll's first grave, containing no corpse, was within the 50-cubit range of the building. At a loss for any explanation, Steckoll identified the graves within this zone as halting places where a funeral party would stop and say prayers (m.Baba Bathra 6: 7).[78]

---

[74] Henry Poole, 'Report of a Journey in Palestine,' *Journal of the Royal Geographical Society* 26 (1856): 55–70, at 69.

[75] Charles Clermont-Ganneau, 'The Jerusalem Researches III,' *PEFQSt* (1874): 80–4 at p.81, see Joan E. Taylor, 'Khirbet Qumran in the Nineteenth Century and the Name of the Site,' *PEQ* 134 (2002): 144–64, Fig. 10.

[76] Jean-Baptist Humbert and Alan Chambon, *Fouilles de Khirbet Qumrân et de Ain Feshka I: Album de photographies. Répertoire du fonds photographiques. Synthèse des notes de chantier du Père Roland de Vaux* (Novum Testamentum et Orbis Antiquus, Series Archaeologica 1; Fribourg: Editions universitaires, 1994), I, 346, and see photo 453, Fig. XXXIII.

[77] Solomon Steckoll, 'Preliminary Excavation Report in the Qumran Cemetery,' *RQ* 23 (1968) 323–52, at 327–8.

[78] Ibid. 328. Note that the graves of this area have now been completely obliterated on the surface as a result of tourism and bulldozing outside the wall area.

But in the examination of the Qumran cemetery made by remote sensing published by Hanan Eshel et al. in *Dead Sea Discoveries* in 2002, a total of twenty-eight graves—like the one Steckoll excavated—were identified within about 22 m of the buildings, up to a distance of only 10 m from the buildings, though these are no longer visible on the surface.[79] These were clustered close to the eastern (cemetery) entrance. If these cavities had been used for corpses, then this would mean that the people who occupied the buildings were less scrupulous about purity than the rabbis who set down the Mishnah. However, if these graves were used for manuscripts or other items, then the proximity of such burials to the buildings would not be a problem for purity. In fact, the nearest attested corpse-yielding grave is about 40 m away from the buildings, meaning the Qumran people may well have had a stricter notion of the distance between burials of human corpses and habitations than became normative in rabbinic Judaism, though only proper examination of the cemetery could provide confirmation of this.

The evidence for 'empty graves' outside the range of 22 m from the buildings and workshop areas—within the main cemeteries—is also apparent. In the excavations conducted by Yitzhak Magen and Yuval Peleg from 1993 to 2004, a total of nine graves were excavated at the southern end of the regimented rows. Four out of the nine were empty, with no bones. Four contained bones of adults (from 25 to 60 years old), and one had a wooden coffin. In two of the graves without bones, fourteen jars sealed with lids came to light, with some kind of residue identified as date honey by initial tests, the jars themselves being dated to the first century BCE.[80] Magen and Peleg suggest that the burial of these pots indicates that they were contaminated with corpse impurity (Num. 19: 11–16, cf. Lev. 11: 33–4), requiring special treatment. Whatever the interpretation, this evidence indicates that the occupants of Qumran were burying materials other than bodies in the cemetery.

In all the cases of empty tombs, something was buried in the cemetery that had totally decomposed, as flesh and much of the coffin wood in the graves also had decomposed. The conditions of preservation in the soil of the Qumran cemetery are not the same as in the caves. Hydrochemical analysis has revealed that the briny subterranean aquifer was much higher than today and—as Olav Röhrer-Ertl states—'the cemetery, and the esplanade, were exposed to infusions of salty and bitter aquifer water over a long period of time'.[81] This would not have

[79] Hanan Eshel, Magen Broshi, Richard A. Freund, and Brian Schultz, 'New Data on the Cemetery East of Khirbet Qumran,' *DSD* 9 (2002): 135–65, at 142, and Figure 2.

[80] Yitzhak Magen and Yuval Peleg, *The Qumran Excavations 1993–2004: Preliminary Report* (Jerusalem: Israel Antiquities Authority, Judaea and Samaria Publications 6, 2007), 45–6; id. 'Back to Qumran: Ten Years of Excavation and Research, 1992–2004,' in Galor, Humbert, and Zangenberg, *Qumran*, 55–113, at 98.

[81] Olav Röhrer-Ertl, 'Facts and Results Based on Skeletal Remains from Qumran Found in the Collectio Kurth: A Study in Methodology,' in Galor, Humbert, and Zangenberg, *Qumran*, 181–93.

enabled many organic materials to survive. In the cemetery, some coffin wood was found (for example in T18), but mostly it is either very decomposed into brown powder or worm-eaten (T17, T19).[82] Excavation may yet tell whether any 'empty tombs' have fragments remaining of what was buried inside them. The rabbis defined various items, other than human corpses, that should be buried (b.Tem. 33b–34a); books were only one such item.

Sacred manuscripts continue to be buried to this day. Therefore, it seems possible that manuscripts were buried in the Qumran cemetery. If so, why would some manuscripts go into jars and be topped with covers, in remote, sealed caves, while others might go into the graveyard? Perhaps some sorting took place, so that only *shemot*—especially biblical manuscripts—were placed in jars in preservation-burials, and other texts not worth preserving were placed in the cemetery. Only further investigation and testing of soil samples could tell us more.

THE MARL CAVES—A *GENIZAH*?

We then return to the Caves 4Q–5Q, 7Q–10Q. If the natural caves comprise not a *genizah* but the final resting place of buried manuscripts, might the very different artificially created marl caves have been the temporary store? As noted above, they are part of the habitation region of the Qumran settlement, which was separated from the cemetery area by a long wall. They are ventilated and open, and include a more diverse range of pottery than any natural caves. Typologically, they cannot therefore be considered a burial area, but Cave 4Q contained in the fill small fragments of over five hundred manuscripts, Cave 5Q had fifteen, Cave 7Q nineteen (largely found on the entrance stairway), and Cave 8Q five—with about one hundred leather strips used for binding scrolls—while Cave 9Q had only one papyrus fragment and Cave 10Q an inscribed ostracon. There were hole-mouthed jars and lids found in Caves 7Q and 8Q, though these caves were partly collapsed and much of the contents would have been lost. As Hanan Eshel and Magen Broshi have proven, the artificial marl terrace caves where scroll fragments were discovered are paralleled by other artificial marl terrace caves north of the site in which evidence of human occupation from the Second Temple period has been found. Caves 4Q–5Q and 7Q–10Q were at least in part inhabited as residential zones and/or workshops, with other likely inhabited caves located nearby, in caves that have now collapsed.[83] Curiously, Cave 5Q also contained large animal bones.

[82] Humbert and Chambon, *Fouilles*, 349.

[83] Magen Broshi and Hanan Eshel, 'Three Seasons of Excavations at Qumran,' *JRA* 17 (2004): 321–32, at 325; Broshi and Eshel, 'Residential Caves.' The northern caves were also used in Period III, since numerous nails from Roman sandals have been found along the pathways; see

Were these hiding places? Could the people of Qumran have quickly hidden manuscripts here? In fact, the marl terrace caves are not good hiding places, since they are easily visible from both the plateau and from below. They were not noticed by archaeologists only because their entrances had collapsed over time. However, it is possible that the occupants of Qumran managed to save some of their manuscripts from out of the buildings, just ahead of the Roman burning of the buildings in 68 CE, by quickly taking them and throwing them into the marl caves.[84] In this case, the only rapid hiding scenario at Qumran would have been here, and very much an immediate—panic-stricken—activity, with the Roman army proximate.

There may have been shelves in Cave 4Qa that were then taken out in Period III, since there are holes in the walls of the cave which may have been used to support rough shelving. At any rate, the manuscripts were scattered on the cave floor at some point and no remnants of shelves have been found. Hannah Cotton and Erik Larson are not convinced of the common assumption that the scrolls were torn up in antiquity, which would account for their poor state.[85] Rather the supposed 'tears' are due to 'natural processes of deterioration' found also in such texts as 1QM, 1QH^a, 11QPs^a, and 11QTemple. In the case of the manuscript 4Q365, often wrongly used to illustrate tearing, the breaks are along 'natural creases or "fault lines" in the manuscript skin that developed as it lay in the cave'.[86] This identification of the disordered state and natural decomposition of the manuscripts lying on the floor of the cave was already noted by Frank Moore Cross.[87] In other words, all we really know about the manuscripts of the artificial caves is that they were simply lying there on the floor, left to weather the centuries, just like the adjacent site of Qumran. Over time, they disintegrated. They were not processed for preservation. They were not left in a neat state.

The separation of the scrolls from the buildings of Qumran in Cave 4Q may also indicate the mentality of a *genizah*, prior to the burial of the *shemot*, the texts potentially containing the name of God. It was important to separate them out in some way, even when there were only a few of these items; in Masada, copies of Deuteronomy and Ezekiel were found under the floor of the synagogue, but in general, in ancient synagogues *genizot* within the building are small stores for coins, in the form of a depression in the floor near the

---

Broshi and Eshel, 'Residential Caves,' Pl. 2, 4, and Joan E. Taylor, 'Kh. Qumran in Period III,' in Galor, Humbert, and Zangenberg, *Qumran*, 133–46, at 140–1.

[84] I am grateful to Sidnie White Crawford for this suggestion.

[85] De Vaux, *Archaeology*, 100, n. 3.

[86] Hannah Cotton and Erik Larson, '4Q460/4Q350 and Tampering with Qumran Texts in Antiquity,' in Shalom M. Paul, Robert A. Kraft, Eva Ben-David, Lawrence H. Schiffman, and Weston W. Fields (eds), *Emanuel: Studies in Hebrew Bible, Septuagint, and Dead Sea Scrolls in Honor of Emanuel Tov* (Leiden: Brill, 2003), 113–25, at 124.

[87] Frank Moore Cross, *The Ancient Library of Qumran*, rev. ed. (New York: Anchor, 1961), 27, n. 32.

Torah shrine, or in a cavity of some kind, as we see in the synagogues of Nabratein, Gush Halav, Kazrin, Hammath Tiberias, and Beth Alpha.[88]

Because they contain the name of God, *shemot* are not normal artefacts. In rabbinic literature, holy books render the hands unclean, though 'Sadducees' took the opposite line (m.Yad. 4: 5–6): presumably, to them, scripture was ultra-pure, even transferring holiness. There is no clue within the scrolls as to how this was ruled on for those who wrote these texts, but absence of discussion about scripture defiling the hands, when purity in general is so important, tends to indicate a 'Sadducee' approach.[89] Whatever the case, such concepts are dynamic and reflective of the fact that the sacred was to be treated in a special way. The very holiness of the divine name on the manuscripts caused impurity of the hands as a result of this intrinsic quality: the manuscripts are themselves actually pure and sacred for their having the name of God on them, and should be stored in pure space, which would be appropriate also for pure food and drink. At any rate, a separate store for such items is exactly what a *genizah* is. A separate store for manuscripts that are destined to be buried might well be what we would expect within the occupation zone.

However, the collection of scrolls in Cave 4Q, and associated artificial caves, cannot have been designed for long-term burial. Some corroborating evidence that this area of the site was linked to scroll processing for preservation-burial comes from the curious evidence of many pieces of fine leather straps and tongues for binding scrolls in Cave 8Q, as well as remains of fabric and thread.[90] Only 7Q and 8Q contained jars and lids, though much of the contents of these damaged caves have been lost when they collapsed into the Wadi Qumran.

If this processing took place close to cave cluster 7Q–9Q then manuscripts would have been taken up from the marl terrace caves, treated with preservatives, and then wrapped with linen and warm pliable bitumen (in a mixture), before being placed in jars and carried off for burial to a cave further away. If so, the

---

[88] Rachel Hachlili, *Ancient Jewish Art and Archaeology in the Land of Israel* (Leiden: Brill, 1984), 192–3.

[89] Shamma Friedman sees the rabbis as altering a concept that involved transfer of sanctity from the holy scriptures to the hands: 'The Holy Scriptures Defile the Hands—the Transformation of a Biblical Concept in Rabbinic Theology,' in Marc Brettler and Michael Fishbane (eds), *Minḥah le Naḥum: Biblical and Other Studies Presented to Nahum M. Sarna in Honour of his 70th Birthday* (Sheffield: Sheffield Academic Press, 1993), 117–32, and see Jodi Magness, 'Scrolls and Hand Impurity,' in Hempel, *Dead Sea Scrolls*, 89–97: '[A]lthough scroll wrappers are found at Qumran, sectarian legislation provides no indication that they considered scroll containers, straps, and wrappers as defiling, in contrast to the rabbis' (p.96). For other discussions of the issues here see Martin D. Goodman, 'Sacred Scripture and "Defiling the Hands",' *Journal of Theological Studies* 41 (1990): 99–107, esp. p.102; Chaim Milikowsky, 'Reflections on Hand-Washing, Hand-Purity and Holy Scripture in Rabbinic Literature,' in M. J. H. M. Poorthuis and J. Schwartz (eds), *Purity and Holiness: the Heritage of Leviticus* (Leiden: Brill, 2000), 154–9; Timothy M. Lim, 'The Defilement of the Hands as a Principle Determining the Holiness of Scriptures,' *Journal of Theological Studies* 61 (2010): 501–15.

[90] DJD III, 31.

processing area would have been close to these caves on the plateau itself. The recent excavations by Randall Price have brought to light bitumen deposits precisely in this vicinity, above Caves 7Q to 9Q.[91] That bitumen was not melted inside the buildings is no wonder. Bubbling bitumen and fires would have had to be carefully managed, and the fumes would have been pungent. It would have been much more practical to work with this material on the site of Qumran than in the caves.

A store of even large numbers of manuscripts in Cave 4Q would have been intended as temporary. It was not a repository that was built up over time; Cave 4Q was not a final destination. A *genizah* was not supposed to be that. The manuscripts remain in this cave simply because their processing was interrupted.

THE DATING OF THE SCROLLS DEPOSITS

Seeing the natural caves as repositories of buried manuscripts enables more flexibility in terms of when scrolls were placed in these localities. Various theories have been presented in recent years about the dating of the scrolls deposits. Greg Doudna has argued strongly against the quick hiding scenario of 68 CE on the basis of the archaeological repertoire of the scrolls caves and site, with jars mostly corresponding to Period Ib at Qumran.[92] Rachel Bar-Nathan locates these jars to the post-31 BCE phase of Period Ib and the first century.[93] Both Daniel Stökl Ben Ezra and Jodi Magness have also pointed out that the cylindrical jar forms of the caves, both ovoid jars which appeared before 31 BCE and cylindrical jars and wheel-made lamps which date to the first century BCE or CE, would mean that the jars were deposited over the entire course of the sectarian phase of Qumran's history.[94]

Stökl Ben Ezra has also noted, on the basis of palaeographical assessment, that Caves 1Q and 4Q contain proportionately more archaic and Hasmonean style manuscripts than 2Q–3Q, 5Q, 6Q, and 11Q. This works against 4Q only being a *genizah* (slowly accumulating manuscripts) he thinks, because the age distribution is not congruent with supposedly later caves, also assessed

---

[91] Randall Price, 'New Discoveries,' id. 'Qumran Plateau': '*The Western Square* was on a direct line with Cave IV on the opposite, facing plateau. A probe drilled in 1996 meant to locate and identify subsurface anomalies discerned on the seismic survey at a depth of 16 m, which is the approximate elevation of the entrance to Cave IV.... Our initial excavation from surface to a depth of 1.5 m revealed sparse potsherds and a single jar handle in topsoil, a shaped stone, probably a grinding stone, in a pebble fill just below topsoil, isolated bitumen deposits that might have been used as fossil fuel and several bone fragments in a sandy layer below the pebble fill.'

[92] Doudna, 'Legacy of an Error.'

[93] Bar-Nathan, 'Qumran,' 263–77.

[94] Stökl Ben Ezra, 'Old Caves,' 331; Magness, *Archaeology*, 85–7.

palaeographically (2Q–3Q, 5Q, 6Q, and 11Q).[95] However, the palaeographic dates can only be an approximation that needs to be balanced with archaeological data.[96] In fact, the radiocarbon dating of date pits probably from Cave 9Q in the marl terrace caves yielded a result of 1–130 CE, with high 95 per cent probability, which would fit either Period II or III at Qumran.[97] Whatever, there cannot be a neat chronological range for manuscripts either in a *genizah* or in a cemetery, because some popular manuscripts might have been recent but still well-used and worn. A collection of very old manuscripts in a particular *genizah* does not mean that the collection time necessarily pre-dated burials of some newer manuscripts; the newer manuscripts may have been damaged by accidents or else barely used but deemed heterodox. New and old manuscripts could be mixed at a particular burial time.

It is at this point, however, we need to consider the implications of what we have explored in the previous chapter, that from the historical sources it would appear that the Essene occupation of the north-western Dead Sea did not begin until after 37 BCE, and that the Essenes occupied the area past the partial destruction of the site of Qumran in 68 CE, in Ain Feshkha to the Second Revolt. In this case, the burial of manuscripts could have continued up until the Second Revolt, not only until 68 CE. As such, this makes the general palaeographical dating of the scrolls considerably earlier than the latest possible date for the occupation of the area of Qumran by Essenes, meaning that many scrolls may have been old.

THE SCROLLS CORPUS

The proposal that we are dealing with a collection having homogeneity needs to be affirmed. The identification of the same scribe writing a number of different scrolls in 1Q, 2Q, 3Q, 4Q, 6Q, and 11Q indicates the connectedness of the corpus

---

[95] Stökl Ben Ezra, 'Old Caves,' 329, n. 62. However, he suggests it may have been used as a *genizah* in Period II; see id. 'Further Reflections,' 212.

[96] See Doudna's critique of palaeographical dating in 'Legacy,' 152–3. Palaeographic dating can rely on circular argumentation and assume short ranges in dates for styles that may result from individuality. It does not take into account archaizing tendencies or the styles of old scribes that persist even when younger scribes might write differently. There is an insufficient 'control' group against which palaeographical dates can be tested. For an important challenge to dating see Stökl Ben Ezra, 'Further Reflections,' 217–20, suggesting manuscripts dated to the first century CE may in fact be older.

[97] Johannes van der Plicht, Kaare L. Rasmussen, Jens Glastrup, Joan E. Taylor, and Gregory Doudna, 'Radiocarbon Datings of Material from the Qumran Excavation,' in Humbert and Gunneweg, *Khirbet Qumrân*, 193–6; Tom Higham, Joan E. Taylor, and Dennis Green, 'New Radiocarbon Determinations from Khirbet Qumran from the University of Waikato Laboratories,' in Humbert and Gunneweg, *Khirbet Qumrân*, 197–200; Joan E. Taylor and Greg Doudna, 'Archaeological Synthesis of the New Radiocarbon Datings from Qumran,' in Humbert and Gunneweg, *Khirbet Qumrân*, 201–5.

of the caves, both artificial and natural. This scribe's handwriting is dated by Yardeni to the end of the first century BCE or possibly the beginning of the first century CE.[98] If the proposition of scrolls preservation-burial is correct, then these scrolls would have been placed in the natural caves 1Q, 2Q, 3Q, 6Q, and 11Q after some time, after they had aged, though Greg Doudna's critique of palaeographical dating is important,[99] since precision is far from sure.

More interesting perhaps is the fact that within the scrolls corpus historical references are clustered in the Hasmonean era,[100] but the scrolls preservation-burials continue through to the destruction of the site of Qumran by the Romans in 68 CE (at least). Given that the site of Qumran was probably not occupied by Essenes until after 37 CE, there is a remarkable absence of *pesharim* relevant to the Herodian and Roman contexts, which we might expect from people with an active and vibrant interpretative tradition. If the scrolls are generally (not necessarily) old, then this historical association of the *pesharim*—which may not have been relevant to the primary concerns of the groups in question in the first century CE (through to the beginning of the second century CE)—makes sense. Other manuscripts of the Dead Sea scrolls corpus are clearly much older than the time period of the occupation of Qumran, for example the Isaiah scroll (IQSaª) which is dated to the third century BCE. This raises the issue of the time-span of the burial of scrolls. If we do not have a rapid hiding scenario, then for how long were scrolls being placed in jars in caves? The solution can only come from precision of pottery dating and the assessment of the final occupation of Qumran. On current evidence, this would suggest a date in the reign of Herod as the *terminus a quo* (37 BCE), continuing at least to the destruction of 68 CE, but probably beyond, since many pottery forms continued in use through to 135 CE. It is only after the absolute devastation of 135 CE that no Jews were to be found in this vicinity; post-68 CE Jewish occupation continued in various places in this part of Judaea and on the north-western shore of the Dead Sea, as we have seen. The watershed here, as for all of Judaism, is the end of the disastrous Bar Kokhba revolt.

THE SIZE OF THE BURIAL COLLECTION

As noted above, we do not have the full corpus of manuscripts that were buried in the natural caves, and we do not know how many more manuscripts originally existed in the artificial caves. These caves were disturbed. However,

---

[98] Ada Yardeni, 'A Note on a Qumran Scribe,' in Meir Lubetski (ed.); *New Seals and Inscriptions, Hebrew, Idumean and Cuneiform* (Sheffield: Sheffield Phoenix Press, 2007), 287–98.

[99] Doudna, 'Legacy,' 152–3.

[100] Hanan Eshel, *The Dead Sea Scrolls and the Hasmonean State* (Grand Rapids: Eerdmans, 2008).

the potential size of the original burials is crucial for any historical reconstruction. All our conclusions about what was in the caves in terms of the manuscript repertoire are based on randomly surviving items. It is now determined that there is evidence of around eight hundred manuscripts, and around six hundred and sixty different texts. This is its minimum extent, with over four hundred texts coming from Cave 4Q. In terms of archaeology, apart from when there are unusual cataclysmic circumstances like the sealing of Pompeii in 79, it is not the case that excavation reveals an entire corpus of whatever existed at a particular time, in any particular place.

The maximum extent of the scrolls corpus remains unclear, but there were definitely more scrolls than we currently have positive evidence for. As noted above, from the very earliest excavations of Cave 1Q by de Vaux and Lankester Harding, it was clear that materials had been disturbed in antiquity.[101]

Other caves could have been re-used. Cave 3Q was a large cave, but the inner chamber had collapsed, leaving only a cavity 3 m by 2 m, prolonged by a straight ascending gallery.[102] Cave 3Q once clearly contained manuscripts, but these were taken away long ago, with only fragments indicating their existence. It seems that after they were initially deposited, the entrance was sealed shut, as in the case of other manuscript caves.[103] Then, at some stage, there was an earthquake, which resulted in the collapse of large sections of the cave. Importantly, Joseph Patrich reports that this collapse occurred *before* the pots were smashed. Patrich's team moved stones and boulders to check if any sherds were located under these, and found none, so he concluded that the cave was visited in antiquity only after this earthquake. However, when the explorers of 1952 found Cave 3Q, the way into the cave was sealed shut with blocks of stone, though potsherds that had fallen from the entrance gave a clue to the archaeological team that they should break through this sealing to enter the cave. That they found sherds outside and *under* the entrance blocks indicates that the way into the cave was sealed up after the earthquake and also after the destruction of the pottery jars, following a second deposit of something in the cave. As noted above, the most likely earthquake that would have caused the north–south fissures in the site of Qumran occurred *c*.115 CE. We can conclude that some time after this earthquake, which perhaps opened the mouth, the cave was entered and manuscripts were taken out.

The second sealing of the cave is one of the most interesting issues for the dating of the Copper Scroll, since on the basis of archaeology it could have

---

[101] DJD III, 14. De Vaux was initially able to identify the pottery—jars and bowls—as coming from the end of the Hellenistic period, to the second century BCE to the beginning of the first century CE; Roland de Vaux, 'Post-Scriptum,' 234.

[102] Roland de Vaux, 'Exploration,' 555, 557; DJD III (1962), 7–8, 201, cf. Reed, 'Qumran Caves Expedition,' 7–8, 201.

[103] 'Its mouth had been blocked and the Bedouin did not know of its existence,' de Vaux, *ADSS*, 95; id. 'Exploration,' 555.

been placed there prior to a purposely done second sealing following the earthquake: the two rolls of the Copper Scroll were isolated into a kind of niche, not under the cave collapse. It is hard to imagine that anyone would have sealed the cave for a second time when only pottery, potsherds, and tiny manuscript fragments remained in it: a second sealing implies a second deposit. Strangely, an early newspaper report tantalizingly states that the Copper Scroll was found with Bar Kokhba coins,[104] but this has never been mentioned again. At any rate, the evidence of Cave 3Q would suggest that the Copper Scroll was deposited at the very end of the Second Temple Period, in the era of Bar Kokhba, when the region was the locus of rebels and refugees.

Cave 4Q was also disturbed in antiquity, and may have contained more manuscripts. The manuscript fragments of Cave 4Q on the original floor of the cave were coated with marl sediment which had built up and solidified over a long time. But long before this the manuscripts were used as scrap paper, as has been argued by Hannah Cotton and Erik Larson, who note that 4Q460, Frag. 9/ 4Q350 on one side has a Hebrew text and the other side a cereal list written in Greek, with second-century features.[105] This would indicate that someone checking off cereals in storage used a Hebrew scroll to jot down what was there: 'After the list was written and the items were checked off, it was apparently of no further use and was allowed to remain on the floor of the cave together with hundreds of other texts that were not reused.' This is a rather astonishing statement. If the Greek is correctly dated to the second century, then the Romans who quashed the Bar Kokhba rebels—perhaps encamping on the plateau and in the ruins—may have used the cave for storing cereals, since no Jew would write a cereal list on the back of a Hebrew text containing the tetragrammaton.[106] This means that Romans found the manuscripts lying in Cave 4Q in 135 CE. Any number of manuscripts lying in the artificial caves may have been used as scrap, or else just kicked out of the cave entrance. However, this interpretation is not necessarily correct, owing to the very obscure nature of 4Q350, since there are another twenty Qumran opisthographs with different compositions on the verso and recto.[107]

---

[104] Report in the *New York Times*, Tuesday, 1 April 1952, less than two weeks after the discovery. This article was based on the report by the Religious News Service from Jerusalem, 31 March 1952 and appeared on p.13, col. 6; see Judah Lefkovits, 'The Copper Scroll-3Q15: A New Reading, Translation and Commentary,' New York University Ph.D., 3. De Vaux was not present at the time the Copper Scroll was found. The team was led by Henri de Contenson of the École Biblique, and included William L. Reed. However, later, de Vaux ('Exploration,' 553) indicated that no coins were found in any of the caves.

[105] It is a so-called opisthograph in that the writing on the *recto* and *verso* are independent.

[106] Cotton and Larson, '4Q460/4Q350,' 122.

[107] Mladen Popović 'Roman Book Destruction in Qumran Cave 4 and the Roman Destruction of Khirbet Qumran Revisited,' in Jörg Frey, Carsten Claussen, and Nadine Kessler (eds), *Qumran und Archäologie—Texte und Kontexte* (Tübingen: Mohr Siebeck, 2011), 239–91, at 241–9.

How many other unreported scroll discoveries and interferences might there have been? As noted, the discoveries mentioned in extant literary sources indicate at least two occasions when there were scrolls found and taken away. But these are instances that just happen to be recorded and survived for posterity within the written record. As we have seen, the archaeology of the caves has indicated that most of the caves in the hills to the west of Qumran were disturbed in antiquity, or suffered damage from collapse, as evidenced by broken, strewn pottery.[108]

As also noted in the previous chapter, there is evidence of Byzantine anchorites living in various places around Qumran and Ain Feshkha, as well as within the sites themselves. The probability of cave disturbance and manuscript discovery in the Byzantine period is great. At the end of the Byzantine period in the region, with the Persian invasion of 614, Arab invasion of 640, and severe raids from Bedouin through the Ayyubid period, the number of anchorites and monasteries decreased. In due course the region came to be under the control of Bedouin, who grazed herds in the wadis, and used caves for shelters. But prior to this time, for hundreds of years, the region was used by people who would have had an exceptional interest in biblical manuscripts, especially if they were in Greek. This needs to be born in mind as we assess what remains.

In terms of the disturbance of caves west of Qumran, we simply do not know how many scrolls were taken away long ago, or left to perish. If it was a common practice to open them *in situ* to see whether they were worth taking, then pieces might well have fallen at this time and been eaten by rats; others may have had some use in monasteries which themselves suffered destruction from raids during early Islamic times. It is a sad but obvious feature of history and archaeology that most of the artefacts from former times, bar a minute fraction, have gone.

All this indicates that the total number of scrolls buried in caves around the site of Qumran in antiquity was anything *above* the present count of 800 manuscripts, to a maximum that is anyone's guess. If 200 manuscripts of Psalms alone could be uncovered at the time of Patriarch Timothy, that surely represents a grand figure designed to show just how many manuscripts were discovered. There would have been, at one time, thousands of scrolls buried by the Dead Sea. This in itself makes a rapid hiding scenario logistically rather difficult, but it also points to the size of the originating collection.

What library would have been large enough to account for our evidence? One might think of a city library. The Pergamum libraries had apparently 200,000 volumes, at the time of Antony (Plutarch, *Antony* 58). The largest library of the ancient world had far more than double this figure. Callimachus'

---

[108] DJD III, 3–41, and see above.

Pinakes, listing the works of the libraries of Alexandria, apparently indicate that there were 530,000 scrolls.[109] Was there anything comparable in Judaea?

One may think of a library associated with the Temple. However, the model of a single library is possibly wrong. The originating holding would make sense as being broadly Essene, given their interests in ancient writings, as attested by Josephus (*War* 2: 136). The argument has been well made by numerous scholars and remains the most plausible solution for understanding many features of the scrolls.[110] As Hanan Eshel has explored, the scrolls themselves—particularly the *pesharim*, CD, and 4QMMT—indicate that it was not the collection of people who were normally in charge of the Temple, but rather of people who had a problematic relationship with many of the Hasmonean line (i.e. the Temple authorities), who saw themselves in some way as the true Israel who had been alienated from rightful rule.[111] It would therefore be very strained to identify the originating holding as the Temple library of the Hasmonean era, the time period in which most texts belong; it would much better be classified as belonging to a major school of Judaism who insisted on having their own legal autonomy, with a court apart from that convened by the High Priest, as both Philo and Josephus define the Essenes as having (Philo, *Prob.* 89–91; Josephus, *War* 2: 145).

Surely the vastness of the scroll preservation-burials (which indicates a correspondingly vast originating holding) can only be explained by thinking broadly of the entire Essene legal school or society, over a long period, not narrowly in terms of one single library hidden at one single point in time.[112] One important parallel here is the Mountain of Quranic Light in Pakistan, where sacred texts are brought for burial from thousands of different Muslim communities in the region. Our evidence from Josephus and Philo is clear that the Essenes lived in numerous communities throughout Judaea. They comprised over four thousand members (Philo, *Prob.* 75; Josephus, *Ant.* 18:20); Philo uses the word ὅμιλος, 'crowd' or 'throng' (*Prob.* 91), to describe their numbers, as also μυρίους, or 'multitudes' (*Hypoth.* 11:1): 'they dwell in *many*

---

[109] Nina Collins, *The Library in Alexandria and the Bible in Greek* (Leiden: Brill, 2000), 100, citing the Plautine Scholium of Johannes Tzetzes.

[110] Geza Vermes, *The Dead Sea Scrolls in English* (4th edition, Harmondsworth: Penguin, 1995), 20–40; James VanderKam, *The Dead Sea Scrolls Today*, rev. ed. (Grand Rapids: Eerdmans, 2010), 97–126, *inter alia*, and see Kenneth Atkinson and Jodi Magness, 'Josephus's Essenes and the Qumran Community,' *JBL* 129 (2010): 317–42.

[111] See Eshel, *Dead Sea Scrolls and the Hasmonean State*.

[112] Note that the identification of the connectedness of scrolls buried in the caves on the basis of the appearance of a single scribal hand (see Yardeni, 'A Note on a Qumran Scribe') does not necessarily imply one single library. Rather, while a scribe's work might have been associated with a library or single patron, it could also be dispersed into different libraries or private collections. What this scribal hand indicates is a remarkable link between the origin and final resting place of scrolls; the intermediate period remains open to different models, but the evidence must imply that the scribe was working for people who would ultimately gather together his manuscripts, i.e. that there was group cohesion in regard to manuscripts.

cities of Judaea, and *many* villages, and in great and much-populated throngs'
(*Hypoth.* 11:1, cf. 11:5). They live in large groups 'in every town' (Josephus,
War 2: 124), and also move around visiting each other (*War* 2: 125), with a
sense of common fellowship. In every single one of the Essene communities
there had to be some kind of library, since the Essenes are characterized as
being especially concerned with their scriptures: they display 'an extraordinary
interest in the writings of the ancients' (Josephus, *War* 2: 136, cf. *War* 2: 159;
Ant. 13: 311); they study the laws of their fathers—which they see as divine—at
all times 'but particularly on the Sabbath day' (Philo, *Prob.* 80–81). With over
four thousand Essenes living all over Judaea, there would have been hundreds
of small libraries.[113] In other words, only by thinking 'outside the box' in order
to see the large collective can we account for this particular: a corpus that
exhibits considerable diversity—for example in different versions of the *Serekh*
and Damascus texts—as well as strong bonds of unity. This is then not one
library, as such, though scriptures for all Essene communities might well have
been manufactured in one production centre; this is a collection from many
communities. In the social upheavals, destructions, and crises of the first
century BCE and through to the second century CE, especially in the time of
civil war and revolt, we may have numerous reasons why these many communities were left with old, redundant, or damaged scrolls they wished to
remove. But, whatever the case, in the Dead Sea scrolls, preserved and buried
with such care near to Qumran, we have physical evidence for the extraordinary devotion of the Essenes to their scriptures and their tendency to go to
extreme lengths to vouchsafe strict obedience to the law, in avoiding the
charge of any negligence whatsoever in preserving the name of God.

In addition, the library may have accommodated other scrolls which were
rejected for being heterodox in terms of their texts. In the Jerusalem Talmud
(j.Taan 4: 2, 20b, cf. Sifre Deut. 356; Abot deRabbi Nathan 19: 19) there is a
story of scrolls of Deuteronomy being examined in the Temple courtyard
against master scrolls that contain accepted readings. The examiners either
accepted or 'retired', ביטלו[114] three scrolls that were reviewed.[115] What
happened to the rejected scrolls? Given that the Essenes had a more central
place in Judaism than has been supposed, and that they continued to be active
in the Temple, would they have ensured that important scrolls with rejected

---

[113] If we take ten men (not including families) as constituting an average population of an
Essene community, we would have nearly four hundred small libraries required to facilitate their
group readings, see 1QS 6: 6. 'And where there are ten, they will not lack a man among them who
will study the law continually day and night . . .' This statement itself indicates just how many
scrolls may have been required overall.

[114] Or 'cancelled', 'rendered void'. See Jastrow, *Dictionary*, 157–8.

[115] Shemaryahu Talmon, 'Three Scrolls they found in the Temple Court,' in Jehoshua
M. Grintz and Jack Liver (eds), *Sefer Segal: M. H. Segel Festschrift* (Jerusalem: Kiryat Sefer,
1964), 25–37.

readings were nevertheless buried appropriately? This would raise further questions about the texts of scripture at Qumran that are beyond the scope of the present discussion.

For our present purposes, the conclusions are that Essenes lived at Qumran with a view to finding localities in which ancient manuscripts either containing the name of God or otherwise having significant value could be buried and preserved in perpetuity. The reason for Essenes to live in this location was not because they searched for asceticism in the desert, or sought solitude, but rather they came here in order to bury scrolls. The Dead Sea Scrolls are the small remnants of a huge cache of scroll burials. The scrolls and Qumran are not separated from one another archaeologically; the scrolls are found within the site of Qumran, interpreted in terms of a compound, and adjacent to it. The scrolls then need to be understood archaeologically as a kind of 'industry' of the settlement: it was, in part, a scroll burial centre. The Essenes used the resources of the Dead Sea (the mineral salts for their preservative function, and the bitumen for sealing) to create fitting burials for scriptures, to ensure that they could not be accused of negligence in preserving the name of God. In addition, it would seem possible that some manuscripts were copied, prior to their burial, to ensure that valuable texts were not lost. Cylindrical jars made for the purpose of burying the scrolls were manufactured at Qumran, from local and imported clay.

As such, Qumran was a scroll burial centre in which the occupants fulfilled the commandment of Moses, as stated in the Testament of Moses 1:16–18. Here, Moses instructs Joshua, in Amman, east of the Jordan River:

> Receive, then, this writing to recall the protection of the books that I hand over to you, which you must order, and embalm with cedar oil, and place in earthenware jars in the location which He made from the beginning of the creation of the world, so that his Name may be called upon until the Day of Repentance, in respect to which the Lord will look at them (the books) in the fulfilment of the End of Days.[116]

This text indicates a designated area determined from the beginning, to last until the end. This leads us then to further questions, and the world of ancient healing.

---

[116] My translation of the Latin text of A. M. Ceriani, '*Fragmenta Assumptionis Mosis,*' in *Fragmenta Latina Evangelii: S. Lucae, Parvae Genesis et Assumptionis Mosis, Baruch, Threni et Epistolae Jeremiae Versionis Syriacae Pauli Telensis* (Monumenta sacra et profana 1; Milano: Typis et impensis Bibliothecae Ambrosianae, 1861), 55–64.

12

'Roots, Remedies and Properties of Stones': Dead Sea Healing

The Dead Sea, as we have seen, was identified by ancient authors as a place of valuable resources—particularly balsam and bitumen—as well as a locus of paradoxes. It could have noxious fumes, but also healing hot waters. It was both arid and lush. It had no life in it and yet there was life around it.[1]

How isolated was it? There were sulphur mines and rafts going out to fetch in lumps of floating asphalt. There was salt extraction, royal visits to various palace-fortresses and healing spas, and there were those who searched for medicinal plants. Ships plied its waters.[2] Qumran's connectivity by sea seems clear even without a surviving anchorage. In En Gedi attested harbour installations have been washed away by the rising and falling sea levels. Simple slipways are even harder to detect, but they existed in various places: Callirhoe, Rujm el-Bahr, Khirbet Mazin, En Gedi, and Mahoza, to name a few. As we have seen, a Herodian villa, harbour complex, and spa were located nearby at Callirhoe, a short sail away on the other side of the lake, and local paths connected Qumran to Jericho, Rujm el-Bahr, Ain Feshkha, Kh. Mazin, and further afield to En Gedi.[3] This was a zone much occupied by Herod and his successors; there were palace-fortresses around it, from Masada in the south-west, Hyrcania in the west, Jericho in the north, Machaerus in the north-east, and Herodium in the east.

---

[1] In fact, there is life inside it: modern studies have confirmed the presence of Dead Sea biota; see Arie Nissenbaum, 'Life in a Dead Sea—Fables, Allegories and Scientific Search,' *Bioscience* 29/3 (1979): 153–7.

[2] Josephus mentions ships on the Dead Sea (*War* 4: 7, 439, 475–81), and for reed boats see Strabo, *Geogr.* 16: 2: 42; Diodorus Siculus, *Bibl. Hist.* 19: 99, 100; a ship with cargo is depicted on the sixth-century Madaba mosaic map, see Pl. 15.

[3] See the extensive study by Joan E. Taylor and Shimon Gibson, 'Qumran Connected: The Paths and Passes of the North-western Dead Sea,' in Jörg Frey, Carsten Claussen, and Nadine Kessler (eds), *Qumran und Archäologie—Texte und Kontexte* (Tübingen: Mohr Siebeck, 2011), 163–209.

There is one possible additional industry of Qumran that contextualizes the site within the Dead Sea region and correlates with what is stated about the interests of the Essenes: the processing of pharmacological products.

Such a hypothesis is not new. It was suggested long ago by John Allegro. Mention of John Allegro does not, overall, inspire confidence. In 1970 this expert on the Dead Sea Scrolls wrote one of the strangest books ever published on the subject of religion and pharmacology. Allegro's book, *The Sacred Mushroom and the Cross*, presented the thesis that the religious traditions of the Ancient Near East—including Christianity—were elaborate disguises of a fertility cult that used a hallucinogenic fungus, *Amanita muscaria*.[4] In 1979 he presented his ideas again in a more muted fashion in his book *The Dead Sea Scrolls and the Christian Myth*,[5] and later in a 30-minute CBS documentary, 'Healers of the Dead Sea' (1985).

Since Allegro, the subject of pharmacology and the Dead Sea Scrolls has seemed somewhat tainted. However, as he pursued his thesis regarding the mushroom, Allegro *en passant* nevertheless explored some important points. For example, he thought that the Essenes believed that they inherited hidden lore of healing that was transmitted over time when the Fallen Angels first came to earth (as attested in 1 Enoch).[6] In his book *The Dead Sea Scrolls and the Christian Myth*, Allegro noted that one reason for the Essenes to live in the barren land next to the Dead Sea might be related to an interpretation of a key prophecy of Ezekiel: a 'man whose appearance was like the appearance of bronze, with a line of flax and a measuring stick in his hand' (Ezek. 40: 3), shows the seer the Temple, and this man in 47: 1–12 shows too a river flowing out of the Temple to the Dead Sea. For Allegro, this appeared to relate to the region of Qumran.[7]

Allegro thought that the Aramaic name for 'Essenes' meant 'healers'.[8] He noted then in 1 Enoch the importance of the Watchers (Gen. 6: 1–6), who transmitted to humanity skills such as 'the cutting of roots and acquaintance with healing' (1 Enoch 7: 1–3), a secret knowledge passed down to Noah and Jacob (Jubilees 19: 27–8; 45: 16).[9] He then suggested that the rebellious angels were thought to be confined to fiery regions of hell (1 Enoch 67: 5–10), and the hot healing waters of the Dead Sea area might have been thought to have some

[4] John Allegro, *The Sacred Mushroom and the Cross* (London: Hodder and Stoughton, 1970), 55.

[5] John Allegro, *The Dead Sea Scrolls and the Christian Myth* (Newton Abbott: Westbridge Books, 1979).

[6] This is available for viewing on YouTube at http://www.youtube.com/watch?v=6KF1r0rH0ow and http://johnallegro.org/john-m-allegro-healers-of-the-dead-sea-post-1985/1986/01/

[7] See Allegro, *Dead Sea Scrolls*, 50.

[8] Ibid. 55.

[9] Ibid. 63–6.

association with them, noting Josephus' comments on Callirhoe, where Herod went to be healed (*War* 1: 657–9; *Ant.* 17: 171–3).[10]

Allegro was alert to the traditions concerning King Solomon, traditions that involved astrology, angelology, demonology, and pharmacological lore. Allegro identified instances within the Dead Sea Scroll fragments where this was reflected, emphasizing the link between healing and piety. Not only did he observe the curiosity of Josephus mentioning giant rue that grew at Machaerus, he also noted Josephus' comments about mandrake. Allegro also noted the medicinal importance of bitumen from the Dead Sea, which he thought could be mixed with acacia (*Acacia raddiana*), a regional tree.[11] In Ain Feshkha, stated Allegro, the Essenes grew healing herbs.[12] Furthermore, Allegro noted texts from the Dead Sea Scrolls that seemed to have associations with healing, particularly a text once called 4QTherapeia.[13]

Partly because such observations are buried in a melange of wild speculation and fantasy, the study of healing and medicine in the Dead Sea Scrolls has not had the attention it deserves, though from time to time in archaeological examinations of the site of Qumran and its environs, mention is made of possible medicinal products.[14]

In this final chapter we will examine anew questions relating to this topic, following on from suggestions first made by Allegro, and integrating numerous studies that have taken place over the past forty years, so that we can better understand the significance of the Dead Sea region in terms of the various medicinal products known in antiquity which the Essenes, with their attested interest in pharmacology, must have known.

JOSEPHUS

In order to be clear about what Josephus states in regard to Essene interest in pharmacology, we will look again at the passage in *War* 2: 136:

σπουδάζουσι δ' ἐκτόπως περὶ τὰ τῶν παλαιῶν συντάγματα, μάλιστα τὰ πρὸς ὠφέλειαν ψυχῆς καὶ σώματος ἐκλέγοντες· ἔνθεν αὐτοῖς πρὸς θεραπείαν παθῶν ῥίζαι τε ἀλεξητήριοι καὶ λίθων ἰδιότητες ἀνερευνῶνται·

They have an extraordinary enthusiasm concerning the works of the ancients, especially selecting those for the benefit of soul and body; thus with these they search out roots, remedies and properties of stones for treatment of diseases.

---

[10] See Allegro, *Dead Sea Scrolls*, 50.

[11] Allegro, *Sacred Mushroom*, 91–3; cf. id. *Dead Sea Scrolls*, 124.

[12] According to Allegro's narrative in 'Healers of the Dead Sea' film.

[13] Allegro, *Dead Sea Scrolls*, Appendix A, 235–40.

[14] Zohar Amar, 'The Ash and the Red Material from Qumran,' *DSD* 5 (1998), 1–15, at 14.

The enthusiasm for the works of the ancients we have already considered in terms of the focus on conserving texts. This comment by Josephus indicates a great passion for the Essenes in this study (σπουδάζουσι δ' ἐκτόπως). It is not simply a diligent interest, but something that urges them on to haste: the verb σπουδάζω means 'to hasten'. They are frantic about searching the works of the ancients to discover facets of texts that benefit the soul and body. While what benefitted the soul would presumably then refer to the vast corpus of the Dead Sea Scrolls, the works that were read for an interest in the body would not necessarily have had the same fortunate fate, since these would have been more practical in application. Perhaps all that is left of these is the brown powder in the Qumran cemetery.

That the Essenes were concerned with benefit to the body (σῶμα) warns us that we are not in the ascetic world of Byzantine Christendom, in which the body is diminished in importance. Here, there is a concern that the body should be benefitted. The texts of interest, of course, could be anything: there is no limit on what may be useful for soul and body, though there is an indication that these texts are from ancient days. The roots, remedies, and properties of stones would indicate a corpus of pharmacological lore. Given the types of healing methods known in first-century Judaism, it would also have included angelology, works on exorcism, astro-pharmacology, and methods of caring for the sick (cf. *War* 2: 122; *Prob.* 87; *Hypoth.* 11: 13).

It is easy to understand the theological underpinning of this healing interest, as Josephus describes it. To follow the way of righteousness—in all that it entails—is to undertake the practice of what we may term preventative medicine, since God is continually defined as a healer and a maintainer of health (or else as a destroyer of health) in the biblical tradition: as God states in Deut. 32: 39: 'I kill and I make alive; I wound and I heal' (cf. Job 5: 17–18).[15] Larry Hogan's study of healing in Second Temple Judaism indicates the importance of Exodus 15: 26: 'If you listen carefully to the voice of the LORD your God and do what he sees as right, and if you pay attention to his commandments and keep all his laws, I shall never inflict upon you any of the diseases that I inflicted upon the Egyptians, for I, the LORD your God, am your healer.'[16] It is almost too obvious to state that, in biblical texts, Divine

---

[15] See studies by Howard Clark Kee, 'Medicine and Healing,' in *The Anchor Bible Dictionary* 4 (New York: Doubleday, 1992), 659–64; Bernard Palmer (ed.), *Medicine and the Bible* (Exeter: Paternoster Press, 1986); David L. Freeman and Judith Z. Abrams, *Illness and Health in the Jewish Tradition: Writings from the Bible to Today* (Philadelphia: Jewish Publication Society, 1999); Julius Preuss, *Biblical and Talmudic Medicine*, trans. by Fred Rosner of *Biblisch-talmudische Medizin* (Berlin: S. Karger, 1911, repr. Jerusalem: Ktav, 1970), (New York: Sanhedrin Press, 1978); Fred Rosner, *Medicine in the Bible and the Talmud* (Jerusalem: Ktav, 1995).

[16] Larry Hogan, *Healing in the Second Temple Period* (Göttingen: Vandenhoeck, 1992), 3. See also Exod. 23: 25–6; Deut. 7: 13–15; 28: 1–68; 30: 15–20. For other explorations of healing in Ancient Israel and in Second Temple Judaism see the works cited in H. Friedenwald, 'The Bibliography of Ancient Hebrew Medicine,' *Bulletin of the Medical Library Association* 23/3 (1935): 124–57; Irena and Walter Jacob (eds), *The Healing Past—Pharmaceuticals in the Biblical*

chastening often takes the form of plague and sickness, and healing is a release from these (cf. Num. 12: 9–13; Deut. 28: 15; 1 Kings 14: 1–18; Ps. 38: 3–9, *inter alia*). The very many studies of Jesus as healer, and healing in the early Church, have consistently pointed out how healings were a kind of restoration of a right relationship between the cured person (devoid of demons, sin, impurity) and God.[17] It is then not surprising that, for a group that was striving for particular righteousness, matters concerning righteousness/purity (preventative) and medicine (curative) were very important, as two sides of the same coin, as both Menahem Brayer[18] and Samuel S. Kottek[19] have explored in regard to both the Essenes and the Scrolls.

It was certainly not a case of trusting everything to God without actively doing anything. The priest in Israel was supposed to have expertise in distinguishing certain key health issues. As Nigel Allan has pointed out, of 613 Mosaic commandments, 213 'are related to health and matters of hygiene'.[20] While in the earliest Hebrew sources the role of the physician in God's healing was either negative or ambiguous, by the second century BCE it was believed that God heals by means of physicians (Sirach 38: 1) and medicines, since God himself has created medicines on the earth (Sirach 38: 4, 12–14).[21] In Sirach the physician is esteemed.

---

and Rabbinic World (Leiden: Brill, 1993); Samuel S. Kottek, 'Hygiene and Healing among the Jews in the Post-Biblical Period: A Partial Reconstruction,' and 'Selected Elements of Talmudic Medical Terminology with Special Reference to Graeco-Latin Influences,' *ANRW* (1996), 2.37.3, 2843–65 and 2912–32; Samuel S. Kottek and H. F. J. Horstmanshoff (eds), *From Athens to Jerusalem: Medicine in Hellenized Jewish Lore and in early Christian Literature* (Rotterdam: Erasmus, 2000); Stephen T. Newmyer, 'Talmudic Medicine and Graeco-Roman Science. Crosscurrents and Resistance,' *ANRW* (1996), 2.37.3, 2895–911; M. Waserman and Samuel S. Kottek, *Health and Disease in the Holy Land: Studies in the History and Sociology of Medicine from Ancient Times to the Present* (New York: Edwin Mellen, 1996); Ed Wisen, *And You shall Surely Heal: The Albert Einstein College of Medicine Synagogue Compendium of Torah and Medicine* (Jerusalem: Ktav, 2009).

[17] The literature on this subject is exceedingly vast, but see for recent and significant studies: Howard Clark Kee, *Medicine, Miracle and Magic in the New Testament* (Cambridge: CUP, 1986); Steven L. Davies, *Jesus the Healer: Possession, Trance and the Origins of Christianity* (London: SCM, 1995); Harold Remus, *Jesus as Healer* (Cambridge: CUP, 1997); Graham H. Twelftree, *Jesus the Exorcist: A Contribution to the Study of the Historical Jesus* (Tübingen: J. C. B. Mohr/ Paul Siebeck, 1993); Todd Klutz, *The Exorcism Stories in Luke–Acts: A Sociostylistic Reading* (Society for New Testament Studies Monograph Series 129; Cambridge: CUP, 2004).

[18] Menahem M. Brayer, 'Medical, Hygienic and Psychological Aspects of the Dead Sea Scrolls,' *Harofe Haivri: The Hebrew Medical Journal* 37 (1964): 1, 9–118 (Heb.); 298–85 (Eng.); 2: 125–35 (Heb.), 272–61 (Eng.); 38 (1965) 1: 156–69 (Heb.), 254–48 (Eng.); id. 'Psychosomatics, Hermetic Medicine and Dream Interpretation in the Qumran Literature,' *JQR* 60 (1969): 112–27; 213–30.

[19] Samuel S. Kottek, 'The Essenes and Medicine,' *Clio Medica* 18 (1983): 81–99; id. *Medicine and Hygiene in the Works of Flavius Josephus* (Leiden: Brill, 1994); id. 'Hygiene and Healing.'

[20] Nigel Allan, 'The Physician in Ancient Israel: His Status and Function,' *Medical History* 45 (2001): 377–94, at 378.

[21] Ibid. 388–92.

EZEKIEL

Given all this, Allegro's identification of the importance of Ezekiel 47: 1–12 is interesting. In the vision described in this passage, a river of pure, fresh water flows eastwards from the Temple, apparently flowing through the Kidron Valley along its established path through the wilderness (Plate 41) to the exit of the wadi where Kh. Mazin stood (though for some reason Allegro imagined a direct route that split the Mount of Olives in two); this does not actually link the Temple to Qumran, but it does link it to the north-western Dead Sea coast, via this stream. But while the fresh water that flows along the Kidron presently does nothing to the saltiness of the Dead Sea, the huge river of pure water that flows out along this route in the vision of Ezekiel effects a transformation.

The heavenly man revealing this to Ezekiel says:

(8) These waters go out toward the eastern region and go down into the desert, then they go toward the [Salt] sea, into the sea of stagnant waters,[22] and the waters will be healed (ונרפאו). (9) And it will happen that every living being that swarms everywhere the rivers come will live. And there will be very many fish, for these waters go there and [the waters] will be healed (ירפאו), so everything will live where the river goes. (10) And it will happen that fishers will stand beside it, from En Gedi to En Egallaim, there will be a place for the spreading of nets. Their fish will be of (diverse) kinds, like the fish of the Great Sea, very many. (11) But its swamps and marshes will not be healed (ולא ירפאו); they will be given to salt. (12) And beside the river on its banks, this side and that side, there will grow every tree for food. Their leaves will not wither and their fruit will not fail. They will bear every month, because their water flows from the Sanctuary. And their fruit will be for food and their leaves for healing (לתרופה).

Allegro does not develop much discussion of this striking passage, though he notes its similarity to what is stated also in Zech. 14:3, Isaiah 61: 3, and 1 Enoch 26: 3. In fact, Ezekiel's text indicates a kind of undoing of the curse of Sodom and Gomorra, and an inversion of the present circumstances of the Dead Sea, by using the verb 'heal', רָפָא, repeatedly.[23] In each case, in the Syriac Peshitta, the (Aramaic) term 'āsē is used. If the Essenes are called 'healers', then, and had an outpost beside the Dead Sea, this passage is remarkable.

While in the present age the lake itself is life-destroying and salty, though the marshes around the edges—fed by sweet water aquifers—can hold fish and life, in this vision of Ezekiel 47 the situation will be reversed. The water of the lake is 'healed' by the pure water of the Sanctuary river, but the marshes are

---

[22] For the translation 'sea of stagnant waters', see Daniel Block, *The Book of Ezekiel, Chapters 25–48* (Grand Rapids: Eerdmans, 1998), 693–4.

[23] The word תרופה is a *hapax legomenon* within the biblical corpus. It could mean 'medicine'; see Jastrow, 1697.

not only not healed, but inverted from being fresh to salty, as if the current peculiarity of freshness needs a reversal to return the situation to its pristine state, as in first creation. As one needs just a little salt in one's food, so a little salt lies at the edges of the 'healed' lake.

The span of territory healed by the pure water is designated as being from En Gedi to En Egallaim: this range between two sites would appear to indicate the traditional region of Judaea bordering the Dead Sea. While Allegro quite arbitrarily identified En Egallaim with Ain Feshkha, in fact En Egallaim (עֵין עֶגְלַיִם: LXX Ἐναγαλλείμ) best relates to Beth Hoglah (Josh. 15: 6; 18: 19, 21), also called Beth Agla (Deir Hajla),[24] since there is a spring here, which is named Ain Hajla even in the present day. 'Agla' would continue the name of 'Egallaim', and would constitute the farthest northern settlement of the desert area affected by the curse of the Dead Sea, within Judaea.[25]

That the purpose of the vegetation that grows here in Ezekiel 47 would be for healing is indeed something worthy of note. In identifying En Egallaim with Ain Feshkha, Allegro believed that they grew their healing herbs there, as a kind of 'answer' to the prophecy.

THE DEAD SEA AND ANCIENT HEALING

Apart from Allegro's observations, the exploration of the Dead Sea as a site for pharmacological resources has been explored in detail by the excavators of En Boqeq,[26] and subsequently reviewed in articles by Glora Moss.[27] The Dead Sea, reviled for its odour, vapours, and grim landscape, was in antiquity paradoxically renowned as having plants and minerals in and around it that were used for medicines and healing resources. The great physician Galen

---

[24] Eusebius identifies Beth Agla three miles from Jericho and two miles from the Jordan River (*Onom.* 8: 17–20). It was a site developed, identified as Jacob's mourning place, Halon Atad (Gen 50: 10 and 11), in the Byzantine period as a monastery that is recorded on the Madaba mosaic map, surrounded by palm trees, and continues as such in its Medieval form today.

[25] A suggestion of a site on the east of the Dead Sea has no foundation, contra Block, *Ezekiel*, 695.

[26] Mordecai Gichon, *'En Boqeq I, Ausgrabungen in einer Oase am Toten Meer: Band I: Geographie und geschichte der Oase. Das spätrömisch-byzantinische Kastell* (Mainz: Philipp von Zabern, 1993), 15–36; Moshe Fischer, Mordecai Gichon, and Oren Tal, *'En Boqeq: Excavations in an Oasis on the Dead Sea: Volume II* (Mainz: Philipp von Zabern, 2000), 94–102.

[27] Gloria A. Moss, 'Religion and Medicine: The Case of Qumran,' *Faith and Freedom* 51, no. 146 (1998): 44–61; 'Historical Perspectives on Health Medicine 2000 Years Ago: The Case of Qumran and other Biblical Sites,' *The Journal of the Royal Society for the Promotion of Health* 120 (2000): 255–61, and in the popular magazine, *The Fortean Times* 131 (March 2000): 'Qumran Coverup,' 40–4. Moss builds sometimes on Allegro (using also his Ezekiel theory, in 'Case of Qumran,' 58–9), but she has also explored the wider healing context of the Dead Sea, like Gichon. Moss believes that Qumran was a medical centre.

visited this region sometime prior to 166 (*Simpl. Med.* 4: 19–20).[28] The curative properties of the region's date honey and wine, opobalsam, mandrake, madder, bitumen, sulphur, alum (*stupteria*), salt, and soap are mentioned in many classical, Byzantine, Arabic, and Medieval sources.

The Jericho area in particular, adjacent to the Dead Sea, was exempted from the salty and dry conditions that stymied growth on the lake shores, and was watered from the highly- esteemed spring at Ain es-Sultan that, according to Josephus, irrigated an area 70 stadia long and 20 wide (*War* 4: 467, 471–4). This was where date palms and opobalsam grew abundantly (*War* 4: 468–70, Bede, *Loc. Sanct.* 9: 3/313), though these crops could be found elsewhere around the lake and its environs where there was good, fresh water, such as at En Gedi and Zoara. We can now review the medicinal qualities of the crops mentioned in our sources here.

BALSAM (PLATE 42)

As we saw earlier, the Balm of Gilead or, later, Judaean balsam, *Amyris gileadensis*, or *Commiphora gileadensis*, produced a sap (opobalsumum) that was one of the rarest and most valued medicines of the ancient world (Theophrastus, *Hist. Plant.* 9: 6: 1–4; 9: 7: 3; Dioscorides, *Mat. Med.* 1: 19: 1; Strabo, *Geogr.* 16: 2: 41; Pliny, *Historia Naturalis* 12: 111–23, Diodorus Siculus, *Bibl. Hist.* 2: 48: 9; Pompeius Trogus, *Epitome* 36: 3: 1–4; Tacitus, *Hist.* 5: 6: 1; Galen, *De Antidotis* 1: 1–12). Bede, writing in the eighth century but using earlier sources, noted that in the Jericho plain, 'there are a wonderful variety of gardens, many types of palms and a huge quantity of bees, and there grows the opobalsam' (Bede, *Loc. Sanct.* 9).

Pliny describes it as the most valuable unguent of all, being an anticoagulant, very effective in treating snake venom, eye and ear ailments, shortness of breath, headache, spasms, and so on, though—he warned—it must be used sparingly (Pliny, *Nat. Hist.* 23: 47 [92]). Dioscorides (*Mat. Med.* 1: 18) notes its effectiveness against poisons, epilepsy, faintness, and dizziness. Strabo (*Geogr.* 16: 2: 41) mentions its reputation for curing headaches, incipient cataracts, and dimness of sight.[29]

---

[28] Vivian Nutton, 'The Chronology of Galen's Early Career,' *The Classical Quarterly* 23 (1973): 158–71, at 169; Joseph Walsh, 'Galen Visits the Dead Sea and the Copper Mines of Cyprus (166 ad),' *Geographical Club of Philadelphia Bulletin* 25 (1924): 92–110. See also Galen, *De Symptomatum Causis* 3: 7.

[29] See Efraim Lev and Zohar Amar, *Practical Materia Medica of the Medieval Eastern Mediterranean according to the Cairo Genizah* (Leiden: Brill, 2008), 349–52 for its uses in the medical texts of the Cairo Genizah. I mention here and in the following notes the Cairo Genizah texts as a repository of Judaic knowledge about medicines, in which the writings of both classical

Josephus associates balsam with Jericho (*War* 1: 138, 361; *Ant.* 4: 100; 14: 54; 15: 96) and En Gedi (*Ant.* 9: 7). As we have seen, there is no evidence of the 'Balsam of Gilead' having been cultivated in Judaea prior to the Hasmoneans, though Josephus records the myth ('they say') that some opobalsam root came from the Queen of Sheba as a gift to Solomon (*Ant.* 8: 174). The association with Solomon we will consider below.

In Judaea the cultivation of balsam remained a royal Hasmonean monopoly, passed on to Herod and his successors (though also held briefly by Cleopatra), until it was eventually directly controlled by the Roman administration after 70 CE.[30] Galen notes the superiority of En Gedi balsam: it had a name 'Engaddine', and was 'superior in quality to the [balsam] that grows in other parts of Palestine' (*De Antidotis* 1: 4). Incidentally, in noting 'other parts of Palestine', this proves Pliny's point about its wider propagation than in former times at the end of the first century CE and into the second. As Fischer, Gichon, and Tal point out, the passage of b.Shab. 26a refers to balsam plantations of Rabbi Judah ha-Nasi near Scythopolis, while those of the Roman emperor were located at En Gedi.[31] The plant was represented in various parts of the cultivated region of the lower Jordan valley in the sixth-century Madaba mosaic map (Plate 43).[32]

Pliny describes three different types of balsam and different parts of the shrub, with different uses. The seed (which was made into a wine-like substance of a red colour and greasy consistency), the bark, and wood were also

and Arabic scholars were preserved, among a great mass of unsourced documents (given that, so far, 1,360 fragments of medical books have been identified in the Taylor–Schechter collection). In their monumental study, Lev and Amar provide documentation of the correspondence between the medical lore of the texts and relevant classical, rabbinic, Arabic, and Jewish Byzantine to Medieval sources. For general discussions about the importance of opobalsam in the region and its uses see: Zohar Amar, 'The Balsam Wood in the Temple Incense,' *Tehumin* 17 (1997): 473–9 (Heb.); H. Cotton and W. Eck, 'Ein Staatsmonopol und seiner Folgen: Plinius, *Naturalis Historia* 12,123 und der Preis für Balsam,' *Rheinisches Museum für Philologie* 140 (1997): 153–6; Y. Feliks, 'The History of Balsamon Cultivation in the Land of Israel,' in Shimon Dar and Zev Safrai (eds), *The Village in Ancient Israel* (Tel Aviv: ERETZ—Geographic Research and Publications Project for the Advancement of Knowledge of Eretz-Israel, 1997), 275–96 (Heb.); F. Nigel Hepper and Joan E. Taylor, 'Date Palms and Opobalsam in the Madaba Mosaic Map,' *PEQ* 136 (2004): 35–44; Joseph Patrich and Benny Arubas, 'A Juglet containing Balsam Oil (?) from a Cave near Qumran,' *IEJ* 39 (1989): 43–59, also publ. in *Eretz Israel* 20 (Yadin volume) (1989): 321–9 (Hebrew); Joseph Patrich, 'Agricultural Development in Antiquity: Improvements in the Cultivation and Production of Balsam,' in Katharina Galor, Jean-Baptiste Humbert, and Jürgen Zangenberg (eds), *Qumran, the Site of the Dead Sea Scrolls: Archaeological Interpretations and Debates* (Leiden: Brill 2006), 241–8, and see also Fischer, Gichon, and Tal, '*En Boqeq*, 120–3; Moss, 'Historical Perspectives,' 259.

[30] This means that it is unlikely that Essenes cultivated opobalsam. As with other plants growing locally, the Essenes would have had to buy the product, or else glean it from the edges of cultivations: gleaners of opobalsam 'from En Gedi to Livias' are mentioned in b.Shab. 26a. However, it may be they were also given gifts of balsam from Herod and his successors.

[31] Fischer, Gichon, and Tal, '*En Boqeq*, 95.

[32] Taylor and Hepper, 'Date Palms and Opobalsam,' *passim*.

used in medicines, but the sap was most valued (Pliny, *Nat. Hist.* 12: 54 [118–19]). It was also used for perfuming tombs.

As in earlier times, in the Byzantine period too opobalsam is attested as being grown in the regions around Jericho (Bede, *Loc. Sanct.* 9: 3/313), and En Gedi (Eusebius, *Onom.* 86: 18; Jerome, *Loc.* 87; 19; *Letter 108 to Eustochium*, 11.5, here 'vines'),[33] as well as around Zoara.[34] Additionally, in the Byzantine period, there is a curse in the floor of the En Gedi synagogue (fifth century) on anyone who reveals 'the secret of the town', which may possibly refer to specific information about some aspect of opobalsam propagation and processing.

However, sometime before the twelfth-century *Descriptio locorum* these opobalsam trees had gone, the En Gedi orchard transferred to Matariya, outside Cairo.[35] In an eighteenth-century study, *An Essay on the Virtues of the Balm of Gilead*, John Cartwright notes that balsam plants originally grew only in the Valley of Jericho 'but since that part of the world has been subject to the Turks, they have transplanted them into various places', for example to the balsam garden of Mecca, guarded by high walls and soldiers, and in the gardens of Grand Cairo, where the plants were also guarded by janissaries (which he illustrates).[36]

Interestingly, excavation of the Herodian garden at Jericho has not revealed any evidence of it growing there, though it is surmised that it may have been propagated in pots. The main area of balsam growing would have been somewhat further away from the palace complex.[37]

DATE PALMS (PLATES 44A AND 44B)

Date palm trees (*Phoenix dactylifera*) were associated with Judaea as a whole (Pliny, *Nat. Hist.* 13: 6 [26], 13: 9 [44], cf. Theophrastus, *Hist. Plant.* 2: 6: 2–8), though in fact they were particularly found in the Jericho area (Deut. 34: 3, Judges 1: 16; *War* 4: 469–71; Pliny, *Nat. Hist.* 5: 15 [73] *corr.*; 13: 9 [44]), also

[33] Though see Patrich, 'Agricultural Development,' 244, n. 40, citing all the theories explaining the 'secret' of En Gedi.

[34] Eusebius, at the beginning of the fourth century, writes of opobalsam and date-palms growing in Zoara, at the southernmost point of the Dead Sea (*Onom.* 42: 1–5) as well as in Engaddi (*Onom.* 86: 16–19).

[35] See Marcus Milright, 'The Balsam of Matariyya: An Exploration of a Medieval Panacea,' *Bulletin of the School of Oriental and African Studies* 66 (2003): 193–209; Eugene Hoade, *Western Pilgrims* (Jerusalem: Franciscan Printing Press, 1952), 30.

[36] John Cartwright, *An Essay Upon the Virtues of Balm of Gilead* (London: G. Kearsly, 1760), 15–21.

[37] Kathryn L. Gleason, 'Garden Excavations at the Herodian Winter Palace in Jericho, 1985–7,' *BAIAS* 7 (1986–7): 21–39, at 31.

in En Gedi (Sirach 24: 13–14; Pliny, *Nat. Hist.* 5: 15 [73]; Eusebius, *Onom.* 86: 18), including around Archelais, Phasaelis, and Livias (Pliny, *Nat. Hist.* 13: 9 [44]). In the region of the Dead Sea, 'the land is good for the growing of palms, wherever it happens to be traversed by rivers with usable water or to be supplied with springs that can irrigate it' (Diodorus Siculus, *Bibl. Hist.* 2: 48: 9). In the sixth-century Madaba mosaic map date palms are shown around Livias, Jericho, Bethagla, Archelais, Callirhoe, and Zoara.[38] They are attested in the area of Mahoza—a town of the eastern Lisan—in the Babatha correspondence.[39] So strong was the association between famous date palms and the Judaean people that it became their symbol on *Judaea capta* coins issued by Rome to commemorate the quashing of the revolt in 70 CE.[40]

Pliny notes a variety of medicinal uses of dates, for example as a cure for spitting blood, and—when dried—as good nourishment to an ailing body, with date-stones being used as an ingredient in eye-salves (Pliny, *Nat. Hist.* 23: 51 [97]).[41] According to Josephus, dates came in different varieties with diverse flavours and healing properties (*War* 4: 468), famously the caryotic palm (Strabo, *Geogr.* 17: 1: 15, cf. Galen, *Aliment. Fac.* 2: 26: 2). Livias was famous for the Nicolaitan date palm (Theodosius, *Top.* 19/145). The Cairo Genizah texts have prescriptions using dates, and it appears in two lists of *materia medica* here.[42] Dates and their by-products, especially date honey, remained an important medicinal product until modern times. Pliny in particular associates date palms with Essene habitations (*Nat. Hist.* 5: 15 [73]), which—given his interests in medicines—may be significant;[43] Solinus wrote that the Essenes 'lived off palm trees', *palmis victitant* (*Collectanea* 35: 9). It should be noted in terms of those who may wish to detach Pliny's description of the Essenes from the Dead Sea that palm trees are a feature of this low-lying region beside the Dead Sea and not a feature of the Judaean hinterland.

The ancient types of date palm trees are not replicated today. However, in 2005 a team of researchers led by Dr Sarah Sallon, with Elaine Solowey, of the Hadassa Hospital Natural Medicine Research Center, managed to germinate a 2,000-year old date pit found at Masada.[44]

---

[38] Hepper and Taylor, 'Date Palms and Opobalsam' *passim*; Magen Broshi, 'Date Beer and Date Wine in Antiquity,' *PEQ* 139 (2007): 55–9

[39] For further see Fischer, Gichon, and Tal, *'En Boqeq*, 123–4.

[40] See Stephen Fine, 'On the Development of a Symbol: The Date Palm in Roman Palestine,' *JSP* 4 (1989): 105–18, which has an extensive bibliography.

[41] Moss, 'Case of Qumran,' 53; ead. 'Historical Perspectives,' 258–9.

[42] Lev and Amar, *Cairo Genizah*, 397–8.

[43] This is also interesting given the popularity of the *Judaea Capta* coins.

[44] Sarah Sallon, Elaine Solowey, Yuval Cohen, Raia Korchinsky, Markus Egli, Ivan Wood-hatch, Orit Simchoni, and Mordechai Kislev, 'Germination, Genetics, and Growth of an Ancient Date Seed,' *Science* 320/5882 (13 June 2008): 1464.

OTHER TREES OF THE JERICHO REGION

The Piacenza Pilgrim (*Itin.* 9/165; 14/169) mentions along with date palms in the lower Jordan Valley various other fruit-bearing trees: olive groves, citrons, and grape vines (see also Adomnan, *Loc. Sanct.* 13: 5; Bede, *Loc. Sanct.* 9: 3/ 314; Theoderic 37/30). In Jericho there was also the cypress and the myrobalan (*War* 4: 469) so, as Josephus says, it is a 'sacred' place, where the rarest and most beautiful plants are produced. All these plants had medicinal uses, even grape wine, which was used as a menstruum (for mixing in medicines to make a draught), especially when it was mixed with honey, though it could be used on its own for a variety of medical conditions.[45] Pliny discusses the medicinal uses of wines at length (*Nat. Hist.* 23: 19–26 [31–53], and also vinegar 27–8 [54–9]). *Omphacium*, made with grapes just beginning to form, was good for ulcerations, quinsy, spitting blood, discharge from the ears, and dysentery, while *enanthe* was an unguent made from wild vines, considered astringent, diuretic, and a cure for headache, dysentery, sores, and maladies of the stomach and liver (*Nat. Hist.* 23: 4–5, 19, 22 [7–9, 31–2, 37–40]).

Pliny notes various uses also of the myrobalan, the cherry plum (*Terminalia sp.*), as medicinal (*Nat. Hist.* 12: 46–7 [100–103]; 23: 52 [98]): it was made into an unguent and has fruit which, mixed with astringent wine, helps diarrhoea, menstruation, and healing of wounds. It is mentioned in early Islamic medical sources, while different kinds of myrobalan appear in twenty-one lists of *materia medica* in the Cairo Genizah.[46]

Citrons (*Citrus medica*)—the Hebrew *ethrog*—were considered to be an antidote to poisons and a gargle (Pliny, *Nat. Hist.* 23: 56 [105]). Dioscorides (*Mat. Med.* 1: 164) lists it as a cure for stomach problems, and it appears also in the Cairo Genizah medical texts.[47] There are other trees growing in the area that are well known as having medicinal uses, such as *Balanites aegyptiaca* (Plate 45), Egyptian balsam (Gen. 43: 11). Theophrastus (*Hist. Plant.* 4: 2: 2–6) notes that the oil of the berry from this plant was used in medicine and perfume.[48]

RUE

The giant rue grown by Herod in Machaerus was a medicinal plant, a well-known fact that must have been simply assumed as common knowledge by

[45] Salvatore P. Lucia, *A History of Wine as Therapy* (Philadelphia: Lippicott, 1963); P. A. Norrie, 'A History of Wine as Medicine,' in Merton Sandler and Roger Pinder (eds), *Wine: A Scientific Exploration* (Boca Raton, Florida: CRC Press, 2003).

[46] Lev and Amar, *Cairo Genizah*, 218–21.

[47] Ibid. 147–8.

[48] Michael Zohary, *Flora Palaestina*, with Naomi Feinbrun-Dothan, 3 vols (Jerusalem: Israel Academy of Sciences and Letters, 1966–79), ii, 258; Hepper and Taylor, 'Balsam.'

Josephus (*War* 7: 178).[49] Pliny identifies rue as one of the most important of all medicines, and lists eighty-four remedies derived from it (Pliny, *Natural History* 20: 51 [31–43]). Pliny states that painters and engravers eat rue with bread in order to preserve their eyesight. The Greek word Josephus uses, *peganon*, probably relates to wild rue, or *Peganum harmala*.[50] This plant grows around the Dead Sea. Its special cultivation inside Machaerus seems to be concerned with size: it was its unusual fostering to create a giant growth that was notable here.[51] Even though Josephus enthuses that it was as big as a fig tree near Machaerus, it most likely grew no higher than 50 cm. It is quite likely in fact that Josephus here mixed up something in his source ('Judeus'?), since Pliny states that rue was grown beneath fig trees in order to make it thrive (Pliny, *Natural History* 19: 45 [156]). This plant is recorded as important in medieval Arabic and Jewish medicine, and is found as a medicine in the Cairo Genizah.[52] The 'Syrian rue' was hugely esteemed in ancient medicine, and is valued to this day in herbal medicine. The seeds are used as an emmenagogue, diuretic, and emetic, containing the alkaloids harmin and harmalin.[53]

It is also the *Pegamon agoron* of Dioscorides (*Mat. Med.* 3: 52), used for dull eyesight. The significance of restoring eyesight as one of the uses of rue is very important within ancient Judaism, because the blind were not permitted in the Temple (2 Sam. 5:8) or allowed to be priests (Lev. 21: 16–24). Within the Dead Sea Scrolls communities, the blind were not permitted to be part of the 'Damascus' community because of the belief in the presence of angels there (CD 15: 15–19). In Qumran's Temple Scroll, the blind were not allowed in the holy city (11QTemple 45: 12–14; 4QMMT B 49–54). They could not participate in holy war (1QM 7: 4–5). This is one reason why the actions of the Messiah, in restoring sight to the blind (4Q521), were so important, as it restored a blind person to full participation within Israel. Likewise, in the New Testament, Jesus heals the blind a number of times (e.g. Mark 8: 22–8; 10: 46–52 and parr. Matt. 9: 27; John 9: 1–41), an action that is considered to be a messianic achievement.

---

[49] 'Josephus' digression to speak of a particular Rue plant in a topographical account of the Machaerus fortress as it bore on a vital Roman campaign in Transjordan, is strange, to say the least.... [T]he introduction by this author of plant physiology and folk-lore into an otherwise non-botanical discussion usually implies some hidden reference to a matter which he is reluctant to bring fully into the open', Allegro, *Sacred Mushroom*, 92.

[50] See Jacob and Jacob, *The Healing Past*, 100.

[51] See Dawud M. H. Al-Eisawi, *Field Guide to Wild Flowers of Jordan* (Amman: Jordan Press Foundation, 1998), 255–6.

[52] Lev and Amar, *Cairo Genizah*, 505–6.

[53] Michael Zohary, *Flora Palaestina*, ii, 245.

MANDRAKE (PLATES 46A AND 46B)

The rare and esteemed *baaras* or mandrake (the *duda'im* of Gen. 30: 14–16; Song of Songs 7: 14, cf. Jer. 24: 1 *dud*), *Atropa mandragora* (*officinalis*), or *Mandragora autumnalis* grew on the eastern shore of the Dead Sea (Josephus, *War* 7: 178–89), at a site accessible from Callirhoe, near the village of Baara (Eusebius, *Onom.* 44: 21–46: 2; Jerome, *Loc. Sanct.* 45: 25–47: 2), in what is now the valley of the Wadi Zarqa Main. This might have been a particular variety of the mandrake, only found in this valley, since a common form of mandrake is found in other regions. The ball-like fruit, left over after the plant has dried out, has a powerful fragrance.[54] Among its many uses, mandrake root was known as a powerful narcotic and cure for eye diseases, urinary infections, pains, nausea, anxiety, and insomnia, inducing a sleep so deep that it was employed in painful operations (Dioscorides, *Mat. Med.* 4: 75–6; Pliny, *Nat. Hist.* 25: 94 [147–50]; Celsus, *De Medicina* 3: 18: 12).[55] It is found in medical prescriptions of the Cairo Genizah and in Arab medicine.[56] So important was mandrake in ancient medicine that in the Vienna Dioscorides, *De Materia Medica* manuscript of the early sixth century CE, Dioscorides (dressed in white) gestures towards this plant, held up by a woman with the word $EYPE\Sigma I\Sigma$ ('discovery', with an epsilon for eta) written above her.[57] It appears in a group of terracotta amulets (eulogia) dated to the sixth century CE, now in the British Museum, where the curled, tubular root is depicted with the name 'Solomon'. As L. Y. Rahmani noted, in identifying the image as mandrake root, the notion that the root is human-shaped is not found in the earliest testimonies, and Dioscorides (*Mat. Med.* 4: 76) describes the mandrake root as being formed by two or three tubers 'wrapped within one another'.[58]

Mandrake root is also believed to be toxic and was supposedly harvested by pulling it up using dogs or a rod, in order to avoid direct contact with the potent roots (Theophrastus, *Hist. Plant.* 9: 8: 8; Pseudo-Apuleius, *Herbarius*

---

[54] Song of Songs 7: 13–14; Testament of Issachar 1: 3, 5, 7, and see Alexander Fleisher and Zhenia Fleischer, 'The Fragrance of Biblical Mandrake,' *Economic Botany* 48 (1994): 243–51.

[55] See Moss, 'Historical Perspectives,' 256–7.

[56] Lev and Amar, *Cairo Genizah*, 212–14.

[57] See the picture at: http://en.wikipedia.org/wiki/File:ViennaDioscoridesAuthorPortrait.jpg. V. A. Peduto, 'The Mandrake Root and the Viennese Dioscorides,' *Minerva Anestesiologica* 67/10 (2001): 751–66. Citations of the power of mandrake are extremely numerous, see for example: Macrobius, *Sat.* 7: 6: 7; Marcellus, *de Medicamentis* 8: 8: 12; Caelius Aurelianus, *Acutarum sive Celerum Passionum* 11: 4: 20; Quintus Serenus Sammonicus, *Liber Medicinalis* 54 v. 989; Suidas, *Lexicon* 136; Pseudo-Dioscorides, *De Herbis Fem.* 15; Isidore, *Etymol.* 17: 9: 30, and for further Alexander Fleischer and Zhenia Fleischer, 'The Fragrance of Biblical Mandrake,' *Economic Botany* 48 (1994): 243–51.

[58] L. Y. Rahmani, 'The Byzantine Solomon Eulogia Tokens in the British Museum,' *IEJ* 49 (1999): 92–104, at p.101.

131; Josephus, *War* 7: 182–4). Josephus considered the mandrake root effective in exorcisms, and tells the story of a certain Eleazar, who appears to use mandrake (it is hard to imagine what else) in a ring to render a man unconscious and exorcized in the presence of Vespasian (*Ant.* 8: 42–9).[59] Exorcism was of course one healing art in this period, classified by Josephus as τέχνη, 'craft' (*Ant.* 8: 45), but it would be too speculative to identify Eleazar as an Essene.[60]

MADDER (PLATES 47A AND 47B)

Madder (*Rubia tinctoria*) was another prized plant in this region. One species of *Rubia—Rubia danaensis—*is found only in one area south-east of the Dead Sea, now the Dana Nature Reserve. Pliny noted madder as a cure for jaundice, sciatica, and paralysis (the patient taking a bath in it), as well as a dye (*Nat. Hist.* 24: 56 [94]; 19: 17 [47]). The best evidence thus far that people of this region used this medicine comes from bones. When skeletons from the Qumran cemetery were excavated in the 1960s, physical anthropologists concluded that red staining on the bones was consistent with what would occur if large quantities of madder were ingested.[61]

Dioscorides (*Mat. Med.* 3: 160) lists its many uses, including its power to relieve skin diseases, cure partial paralysis, cleanse the liver, and reduce swelling of the liver.[62] Maimonides (*Aphorisms* 21: 69) rated this very highly as a drug.

BEES AND HONEY

The varieties of flowers in the Jordan Valley near Jericho created a very good environment for bees, which were 'abundant in this region' according to Josephus (*War* 4: 469), and it is important to note here that Philo specifically mentions 'managing swarms of bees' as an Essene activity (*Hypoth.* 11: 8), which would have required the Essenes to live in areas with a supply of

---

[59] Dennis C. Duling, 'The Eleazar Miracle and Solomon's Magical Wisdom in Flavius Josephus' *Antiquitates Judaicae* 8.42–49,' *HTR* 78 (1985): 1–25; Moss, 'Historical Perspectives,' 257.

[60] See Twelftree, *Jesus the Exorcist*, 13–52: 'Exorcism and Exorcists in First-Century Palestine.'

[61] S. H. Steckoll, Z. Goffer, H. Nathan, and N. Haas, 'Red Stained Human Bones from Qumran,' *Israel Journal of Medical Sciences* 7/11 (1971): 1219–23, and see also Moss, 'Historical Perspectives,' 258.

[62] Lev and Amar, *Cairo Genizah*, 441–3.

flowers.[63] Interestingly, the Bible does not mention beekeeping, but wild honey is noted (Judges 14:8; and possibly 1 Samuel 14: 25–9), most especially in regard to the diet of John the Baptist, who wandered in the region of the Jordan Valley (Mark 1: 6; Matt. 3: 4).[64] Hives were constructed by laying cylindrical jars on top of each other.[65]

Bee honey was more highly esteemed than date honey (Josephus, *War* 4: 468). It was highly valued in many kinds of healing, its mystique coming from the fact that it was a substance that never decomposed, so that it formed a component of numerous ointments (Dioscorides, *Mat. Med.* 2: 101).[66] Honey was much used in medicine, from ancient Egypt to modern times,[67] especially for eye problems. Managed honey was important, because unmanaged honey could cause poisoning, resulting from what the bees were feeding on, as Xenophon reported, when the retreating army in Persia ate some honey that caused a kind of intoxication, vomiting, and diarrhoea (*Anabasis* 4: 8: 20–1).[68]

PROPERTIES OF STONES

As for medicinal minerals, we have already noted how the Dead Sea produced the resource of asphalt/bitumen.[69] Trade in bitumen operated on both sides of the Dead Sea (Diodorus Siculus, *Bibl. Hist.* 19:99:1). The Piacenza Pilgrim (*Itin.* 10/166) also records that 'sulphur and pitch are collected' on the shore of the 'Salt Sea'. Bede (*Loc. Sanct.* 11/317) notes that bitumen is collected from the surface of the water by those going out in boats. Daniel the Abbot writes that the pitch rises to the surface and then 'lies on the shore in great quantity' (38). The medieval *Descriptio locorum* (31–2) describes the alum (alumen), tar, and bitumen being gathered.

Of these products, bitumen was very well known for its medicinal uses (Pliny, *Nat. Hist.* 35: 51 [178]): to cure coughs, dysentery, and loose bowels, among

---

[63] CD 12: 12 proscribes the eating of bee larvae, which seems to presume a situation in which someone actually had the opportunity to do so, i.e. this was addressed to someone working with bee-hives.

[64] James A. Kelhoffer, *The Diet of John the Baptist: 'Locusts and Wild Honey' in Synoptic and Patristic Interpretation* (Tübingen: J. C. B. Mohr/Paul Siebeck, 2005), 63–73.

[65] Eve Crane, *The World History of Bee-Keeping and Honey Hunting* (London: Routledge, 1999), 163–7, and see illustrations in Fig. 20.

[66] See Lev and Amar, *Cairo Genizah*, 185–7.

[67] Evidenced by the Ebers Papyrus and the Edwin Smith Surgical Papyrus, see Eve Crane, *A Book of Honey* (Oxford: OUP, 1980), 96, and for further, Anathea E. Portier-Young, 'Sweet Mercy Metropolis: Interpreting Aseneth's Honeycomb,' *JSP* 14 (2005): 153–7, nn. 17, 28–33. I am grateful to George Brooke for this reference.

[68] See the references in Kelhoffer, *The Diet of John the Baptist*, 65–7.

[69] See above, p. 285.

other things. It was also used as a substance in plasters, and mixed with vinegar to bring away coagulated blood. It was mixed with myrrh for malaria. The belief in the healing properties of bitumen continued into modern times, when Egyptian mummies were destroyed to extract it.[70] Josephus notes that bitumen is useful for healing bodies, 'for indeed it forms an ingredient in many medicines' (*War* 4: 481, noted also by Dioscorides, *Mat. Med* 1: 73; Galen, *Antidotis* 2: 10; *Simpl. Med.* 11: 2: 10).

Alum and sulphur, like bitumen, have numerous medicinal uses. Alum—*stupteria*—was recommended by Dioscorides for leprosy, infected gums, and disorders of the ear (*Mat. Med.* 5: 123).[71] Pliny notes sulphur as being particularly useful (*Nat. Hist.* 35: 50 [15]): for dispersing abscesses, for plasters, as a poultice, and a good cure for asthma, phlegm, scorpion stings, nits, and for fumigation. He notes also its benefits in hot mineral waters.

The salt of the lake should also be recognized as a healing resource. As Aristotle was the first to note, it was a renowned cleansing agent. Adomnan writes about the salt collection, noting that when the waves are churned up by a storm a great deal of salt is brought ashore. His source Arculf observed that the sun's heat dries it out, and he 'tested it in three ways', i.e. by sight, touch, and taste (Adomnan, *Loc. Sanct.* 2: 17: 2). The *Descriptio locorum* describes salt being taken from 'a mountain next to the Asphalt Lake . . . almost entirely made of crystal salt' (32). The tenth-century Muslim writer at-Tamimi wrote that a special type of salt was collected on the *north-western* shores of the Dead Sea.[72] Another type of salt called 'Andarani' was produced around the village of az-Zara, which is identified as Callirhoe.[73] So salt was not only quarried in the salt diapir now called 'Mount Sodom', on the south-western side of the Dead Sea. Bloch has suggested that the boats depicted on the Madaba mosaic map are carrying cargoes of salt, shown as different colours to illustrate the distinction between sea (red) and rock (grey) salt.[74] Pliny identifies salt as a cleansing agent and astringent (*Nat. Hist.* 31: 45 [98]). The medicinal uses of salt are described by Dioscorides (*Mat. Med.* 5: 126–30). Galen refers to Dead Sea salt 'sodomene' as a purgative and astringent (*Simpl. Med.* 4: 20: 60–75) and it appears in the Cairo Genizah medical corpus and Arabic medicine for treating teeth, for stomach and digestion problems, and as a purgative, among many

---

[70] Arie Nissenbaum, Jürgen Rullkötter, and Yoseph Yechielli, 'Are the Curative Properties of "Black Mud" from the Dead Sea due to the Presence of Bitumen (Asphalt) or Other Types of Organic Matter?' *Environmental Geochemistry and Health* 24 (2002): 327–35; Lev and Amar, *Cairo Genizah*, 343–5.

[71] See also Lev and Amar, *Cairo Genizah*, 99–100.

[72] At-Tamimi, *Al-Murshid* 36b–37a; 54b–55a.

[73] Zohar Amar, 'The Production of Salt and Sulphur from the Dead Sea Region in the Tenth Century According to at-Tamimi,' *PEQ* 130 (1998): 3–7.

[74] R. M. Bloch, 'Red Salt and Grey Salt,' *Mad`a* 6 (1962), 3–8, cf. J. Rosenson, 'What were the Ships sailing on the Dead Sea in the Map of Madaba carrying?' *Halamish* 3 (1986): 16–20; see Amar, 'Production of Salt,' 5.

other uses.[75] In addition, brine (salty water) is a well-known preservative, and was used as such in regard to very many substances, including mandrake, according to Pliny (*Nat. Hist.* 25: 94 [149]). Salt is also found in ancient Mesopotamian texts as a preservative, medicine, and ingredient of soap.[76]

HEALING WATERS

In addition to these medicinal products, south of Jericho around the Dead Sea itself, the region's thermal activity created hot mineral springs, as we have seen, most famously at Callirhoe and Baara,[77] in the Wadi Zarqa Main (Hammamat Ma'in), near Baalmeon (the village of Manyat Umm Hasan, Baaras[78]). These waters were not only used for therapeutic bathing but also drunk (Josephus, *War* 1: 657–9 cf. *Ant.* 17: 169–76). Pliny mentions Callirhoe as 'a warm spring, remarkable for its medicinal qualities' (*Hist. Nat.* 5: 15 [72], see also Solinus, *Collectanea* 35: 4; Ptolemy, *Geogr.* 5: 16).

The Piacenza Pilgrim (*Itin.* 10/166) and the pilgrim Theodosius (*Top.* 19/ 145; cf. John Rufus, *Vita Pet. Iber.* 89) note healing springs in the region of Livias, called 'the baths of Moses', where lepers go for cleansing in the evening, after lying in the Dead Sea itself (in the summer months). Here the term 'lepers' probably encompasses people with a range of different skin diseases, and it is noteworthy that soaking in the sea itself was considered effective, as it is today.[79] In the late Roman period there was the shoreline village of Bethasi-mouth (*Onom.* 48: 6–8), close to where the figure of Lot's wife was identified

---

[75] Lev and Amar, *Cairo Genizah*, 274–7.

[76] Martin Levey, 'Gypsum, Salt and Soda in Ancient Mesopotamian Chemical Technology,' *Isis* 49/3 (1958): 336–42.

[77] Christa Clamer, "Ain Ez-Zara Excavations 1986,' *Annual of the Department of Antiquities of Jordan* 33 (1989): 217–25; ead. *Fouilles archéologiques de 'Aïn ez-Zâra/Callirhoé, villégiature hérodienne* (Institut Français d'archéologie du Proche-Orient, Beirut, 1997); ead. 'The Hot Springs of Kallirrhoe and Baarou,' in Michele Piccirillo and Eugenio Alliata (eds), *The Madaba Map Centenary 1897–1997* (Jerusalem: Studium Biblicum Franciscanum, 1999), 221–5; August Strobel and Stefan Wimmer, *Kallirrhoë ('En ez-Zara): Drittes Grabungskampagne des Deutschen Evangelischen Instituts für Altertumswissenschaft des Heiligen Landes und Exkursionen in Süd-Peräa* (Wiesbaden: Harrassowitz, 2003); Estée Dvorjetski, 'The Medicinal Hot Springs of Kal-lirrhoe,' *Ariel* 110–11 (1995): 306–8 (Heb); Ulrich Hübner, 'Baaras und Zeus Beelbaaros,' *Biblische Zeitschrift* 39 (1995): 252–5.

[78] See Eusebius, *Onom.* 44: 21–3; 112: 17; R. Steven Notley and Ze'ev Safrai, *Eusebius' Onomasticon* (Leiden: Brill, 2005), 46, and also Peter the Iberian, 82. Both Callirhoe and Baaras appear on the Madaba mosaic map.

[79] Estée Dvorjetski has suggested that the ships shown in the Madaba mosaic map were actually carrying glass vessels containing healing liquids, possibly bottles of thermal waters from around the lake. Estée Dvorjetski, 'The Thermo-Mineral Springs and the Ships' Load in the Dead Sea According to the Madaba Map,' in G. Barkai and E. Schiler (eds), *Eretz-Israel in the Madaba Map* (Jerusalem: Ariel, 1996), 82–8 (Heb.).

appropriately at the northern end of the Dead Sea, to cohere with a northern placement of Sodom. At the Dead Sea those seeking healing would bathe during the day. The baths at the Springs of Moses in the valley north of Mount Nebo (Plate 48), which seems quite far away, but the connectivity between these and the Dead Sea in regard to healing practices means that we should consider them within the general locality.

Josephus notes that the Essenes' daily immersions were in 'cold water' (*War* 2: 129), so it is important to distinguish these curative warm springs from the kinds of pools used by Essenes on a daily basis for purification prior to meals. The natural cold springs in which Essenes may have immersed are found all around the Dead Sea, not only at Ain Feshkha. Immersion pools (*miqva`ot*) were not needed in Judaean settlements proximate to places where purifications could be done in natural bodies of water. As Kottek pointed out (as well as Allegro), the Essenes may have rejected the use of hot pools because of the association these had with the pleasures of the body and excess; in 1 Enoch there is reference to a valley where evil angels are imprisoned, where the waters 'serve for kings and the powerful and the exalted, and those that dwell on earth, for the healing of the body and the punishment of the spirit' (67: 8–13).[80]

The role soaking in waters of various kinds—balneology (hydrotherapy)—played in ancient medicine was immense, with Judaea having a wealth of healing spas.[81] These were not all natural bodies of water; certain baths in Jerusalem were used for healing as much as for purification. In the Gospel of John the Pool of Bethesda is identified as a place where sick people sought healing, particularly when the waters were turbulent (John 5: 1–9). Jesus heals a blind man by applying mud to his eyes and asking him to bathe in the Pool of Siloam (John 9: 1–7).

Cleansing the body and healing were closely related (cf. Jer. 2: 22), and thus it is noteworthy that there was the production of soap in the Dead Sea region. Zohar Amar has identified the installations and materials found by Vendyl Jones in the so-called 'Cave of the Column' as being connected with the production of soap from potassium-rich plants (from the family of *Chenopodiacae*), which grow wild in the vicinity, such as *Anabasis articulata*, jointed

[80] Kottek, 'Essenes,' 96–7, cf. Philo, *Hypoth.* 11: 11.

[81] Werner Heinz, 'Antike Balneologie in späthellenistischer und römischer Zeit, zur medizinischen Wirkung römischer Baäder,' in *ANRW* (1996), 2.37.3, 2411–32; Fikret K. Yegül, *Baths and Bathing in Classical Antiquity* (Cambridge, MA: MIT Press, 1992); Garrett G. Fagan, *Bathing in Public in the Roman World* (Ann Arbor: University of Michigan Press, 1999), 85–103; id. 'Bathing for Health with Celsus and Pliny the Elder,' *The Classical Quarterly* 56 (2006): 190–207; Estée Dvorjetski, *Leisure, Pleasure and Healing: Spa Culture and Medicine in Ancient Eastern Mediterranean* (Leiden: Brill, 2007); ead. 'Medicinal Hot Springs in Eretz-Israel and in the Decapolis during the Hellenistic, Roman and Byzantine Periods,' ARAM Periodical, 4, 1 & 2 (1992): 425–49; ead. 'Healing Waters: The Social World of Hot Springs in Roman Palestine,' *BAR* 30, 4 (2004): 16–27, and p.60; Moss, 'Case of Qumran,' 54; ead. 'Historical Perspectives,' 256, 258.

anabasis (Plates 49a and 49b).[82] Soap was also manufactured from the ash of the shrub *Atriplex halimus*, the orache, *maluach* in Hebrew (Job 30: 4), an edible salt-bush.[83] In ancient times, soap was used not so much on the body for cleansing to avoid personal body odour, but for healing, in association with hygiene practices, as we find in the Cairo Genizah and Arabic medicine.[84] The Greek goddess Hygeia was, after all, the deity of health and hygiene, the daughter of Asklepios.

Ironically, despite the Dead Sea having a great wealth of healing minerals and plants, and also spa waters, it is to be remembered that the vapours were considered noxious.[85] Pliny notes that 'on the west the Essenes flee all the way from the shores which are harmful' (*Nat. Hist.* 5: 15 [73]), a comment that indicates that the Essenes were conscious of the need to preserve their health given the supposed toxic fumes of the lake. They came here *despite* the danger.

TRADITIONAL PALESTINIAN AND BEDOUIN HEALING PRACTICES

When western explorers first came to the region of Palestine in the nineteenth century, they took with them an interest in drugs of the area that might be useful. In passing, mention of a variety of healing practices and medicines could be made.

The first of the modern travellers to leave an important record is Ulrich Seetzen, who travelled around the southern end of the Dead Sea in 1806. He noted that on the eastern shore salt is produced in lumps 'often a foot thick' in natural spots inundated by the sea in the rainy season.[86] Sodom's Apple he identified as a local plant he called 'aoeschaer': it produced a silky cotton used for lighting from a match-lock, which could also be used for cloth, and incisions could be made to release a kind of milk, recommended to barren women.[87] From this description he is clearly talking about *Calotropis procera* (Plates 50a

---

[82] Amar, 'Ash and the Red Material'; Zohary, *Flora Palaestina*, i, 177. http://www.flowersinisrael.com/Anabasisarticulata_page.htm.

[83] Zohary, *Flora Palaestina*, i, 145; http://www.flowersinisrael.com/Atriplexhalimus_page.htm.

[84] Lev and Amar, *Cairo Genizah*, 484–6.

[85] This is a view that persisted until modern times; see Daniel the Abbot (1106–8), 27–38, trans. William F. Ryan, in John Wilkinson, *Jerusalem Pilgrimage 1099–1185* (London: Hakluyt Society, 1988). In the fifteenth century, Father Felix Fabri was told that no one should visit the lake because the stench from the sea makes you vulnerable to infection, sickness, and death: Felix Fabri, *Evagatorium*, 236a.

[86] Ulrich Jasper Seetzen, *A Brief Account of the Countries Adjoining the Lake of Tiberias, the Jordan and the Dead Sea* (Bath: Meyler and Son, 1810), 43.

[87] Ibid. 45.

and 50b). Sulphur, according to Seetzen, was found in the ground south of the Dead Sea.

A short time later, John Lewis Burckhardt travelled in the region of the southern Dead Sea, arriving from Kerak. He mentioned a number of medicinal uses of local plants south of the Wadi Mujib (Arnon), including hot springs in Wadi Beni Hammad and the fertile eastern side of the Lisan. He noted the myth of 'Sodom's Apple', but Burckhardt does not equate this with the *Calotropis procera*, which he calls 'Asheyr'. He notes that the locals use the silky interior of the fruit for matches, and collect a juice by incising the thick branches, the white juice being sold to 'the druggists at Jerusalem, who are said to use it in medicine as a strong cathartic'.[88]

'Beyrouk honey' or 'Assal Beyrouk' is identified by Burckhardt as coming from a tree called the Gharrab, identified as something like an olive tree with leaves like a poplar but a little broader. The honey is described as forming on the leaves like dew and is collected from them or from the ground underneath. This is found in May and June, and is brownish or greyish, very sweet when fresh, but sour after two days.[89] This information links with Diodorus Siculus (*Bibl. Hist.* 19: 94: 10), sourcing Hieronymous, where there is a reference to 'much so-called wild honey from trees, which they use as a drink with water'. Pliny (*Nat. Hist.* 15: 7 [32]) also mentions such a tree and gives the name of the substance as *elaeomeli* from Greek ἐλαιόμελι ((ἔλαιον = oil, μέλι—honey), which is thicker than honey and thinner than resin, 'having a sweet flavour', and this is 'used by physicians'.[90] Dioscorides (*Mat. Med.* 1: 37) identifies the Elaiomeli tree of Syria, an olive type, as relieving dyspepsia, though this may refer to another plant. The sweet oil-honey may be nothing to do with a tree, but could be the result of certain insects leaving their waste products on the leaves of *Trabutina manniparat* and *Najacoccus serpentinus*: these solidify in a desert climate.[91] Alternatively, it is the spiky bush *Alhagi maurorum*, 'camel thorn', which does produce a kind of sweet secretion dubbed *Alhagi manna*; this plant is eaten by camels and used in traditional Palestinian medicine.[92] It also appears in the Cairo Genizah medical texts and rabbinic literature.[93]

The 'Arar' (Phoenician juniper, or *Juniper phoenice*) is mentioned also. This is a coniferous tree similar to a cypress. Burkhardt notes that the locals use it for a nutritious juice. It is mentioned also as having medicinal properties in Dioscorides (*Mat. Med.* 1: 103–5).[94] 'Talh', *Acacia raddiana*, much used as a wood for Temple furniture (see Exod. 26: 15; 27: 1, *inter alia*), is identified as

---

[88] John Lewis Burckhardt, *Travels in Syria and the Holy Land* (London: John Murray, 1822), 392.
[89] Ibid. 392–3.
[90] Kelhoffer, *Diet of John the Baptist*, 63–7.
[91] R. J. Forbes, *Studies in Ancient Technology* (Leiden: Brill, 1964), 100–1.
[92] Zohary, *Flora Palaestina*, ii, 112; http://www.flowersinisrael.com/Alhagigraecorum_page.htm
[93] Lev and Zohar, *Cairo Genizah*, 445–6.
[94] Ibid. 419.

producing a [medicinal] gum. This was used from very ancient times in Egypt, and was known as *akakia*: Dioscorides identifies it as a cure for diseases of the eyes and intestines, and mouth sores (*Mat. Med.* 1: 101).[95] Burkhardt also notes 'coloquintida' and 'Szadder' (Sidr) in the region. The former is a colocynth (*Citrullus colocynthis*; Plate 51), or bitter apple, which is a purgative (see Deut. 32: 32; 2 Kings 4: 39–40; Dioscorides, *Mat. Med.* 4: 178). It is part of the squash family and produces a round gourd the size of a tennis ball, filled with seeds that can be crushed to produce an oil. This is one of the oils that can be used for Sabbath candles (b.Shab. 24b). The latter plant mentioned by Burkhardt is the Christ-thorn *Ziziphus spina-christi*, or jujube (Plate 52).[96] The Byzantine Jewish physician Asaph mentions it strengthening the stomach, and it was renowned as having many medicinal uses.[97] Burkhardt mentions that bits of sulphur are found in the shallows of the lake and 'are used by the Arabs to cure diseases in their camels'. Burkhardt comments on the collection of asphalt, and the use of local 'stink-stone' in increasing the heat of camel dung fires.[98]

E. W. G. Masterman, in his study 'Hygiene and Disease in Palestine in Modern and Biblical Times', published in 1918, explored the correlation between medical practices of the Palestinians and ancient attestations.[99] The underlying presupposition of Masterman's study was that concepts of healing are very conservative, and therefore traditional ideas and methods common among the *fellahin* (settled populations) of Palestine are likely to have some relationship to what took place long ago. Masterman noted the prevalent notion of the (blue, jealous) evil eye, drawn by any form of pride or success, which invited in misfortune, including disease. To offset calamity, people wore amulets, which could include 'lumps of alum', thought to be irritating to 'the eye'.[100] Additionally, an amulet was worn called a *hajab*, which was a small metal or leather case containing an extract from the Quran or a charm, written by a *kateb* (scribe), with Jews having metal amulets in the shape of a hand, with Hebrew words. This modern practice is clearly a survival from ancient times, possibly also in *mezuzot* and *tefillin*, the oldest forms of which have been found in association with the scrolls in the caves close to Qumran.[101]

[95] Ibid. 325–6.

[96] For these botanical identifications I am very grateful to Nigel Hepper (letter 27 February 2007).

[97] Asaph 4: 38. Lev and Amar, *Cairo Genizah*, 381–2.

[98] Ibid. 394.

[99] E. W. G. Masterman, 'Hygiene and Disease in Palestine in Modern and Biblical Times,' 3 parts, *PEQ* 50 (1918): 13–20, 56–71, 112–19.

[100] Ibid. 113.

[101] Yigael Yadin, *Tefillin from Qumran (XQPhyl 1–4)* (Jerusalem: Israel Exploration Society, 1970); J. T. Milik, 'Tefillin, Mezuzot et Targums,' in DJD 6 (Oxford: OUP, 1977); Ruth Fagen, 'Phylacteries,' in David Noel Freedman (ed.), *Anchor Bible Dictionary* (New York: Doubleday, 1992); Lawrence H. Schiffman, 'Phylacteries and Mezuzot,' in Lawrence H. Schiffman and James

The reference to lumps of alum is interesting given its source in the Dead Sea. Masterman describes the practice of a healing woman (*rakweh*), who takes alum, salt, barley, and *meriamiyeh* (Sage, *Salvia triloba*), with olive leaves (or palm leaves from Palm Sunday processions, in the case of Christians), and burns them in an earthenware dish to release fumes, combining this practice with incantations that essentially 'bind' the evil eye.[102] Masterman notes in his day that 'Tetanus, epilepsy, and all forms of lunacy are ascribed to possession by evil spirits'.[103]

In addition, Masterman writes: 'Many springs and wells are credited with healing properties. Some, like *Ain es-Sultan* (Elisha's fountain) at Jericho, are beneficial to all diseases; some are useful for the cure of special diseases. Naturally, the hot springs at Tiberias and at el-Hammeh are much resorted to: that there is a supernatural influence believed to be present is shown by the fact that the name of God must not, so it is taught, be uttered while bathing.'[104]

The study of traditional medicine is still underway today. In the examination by Aref Abu-Rabia,[105] he makes the important point that in Bedouin society preventative and curative medicine were two sides of the same coin (whereas in modern western medicine the focus is far more on curative). Amulets are discussed in terms of the curative dimension, including amulets written by a *khatib* (scribe) with Quran texts folded in a triangle, wrapped in cloth or leather, and hung on the body. His observations cohere with Masterman's in terms of the protection against the evil eye, including the use of alum (*shabbeh*) in beads, and the use of alum by wise women in divination to determine the origin of the evil eye curse and its expulsion. Abu-Rabia confirms that plants of the Dead Sea region identified by western explorers are indeed medicinal among the Bedouin, as follows:

Citrullus colocynthis (Plate 51): inner part placed in a glass of water and drunk, for constipation, intestinal worms, and cleansing of the intestinal tract.

Mandragora officinalis (mandrake) (Plate 46): ripe fruit eaten following a woman's period, for barrenness; this is a holy plant and it is forbidden to damage it.

Artiplex halimus (*maluach*): leaves eaten as tonic, for diabetes.

VanderKam (eds), *Encyclopedia of the Dead Sea Scrolls* (Oxford/New York: OUP, 2000), and see discussion in Yehudah Cohn, 'Were Tefillin Phylacteries?' *JJS* 59 (2008): 55–79. Cohn identifies forty-five individual parchments slips of *tefillin/mezuzot* and about twenty-five *tefillin* cases (p.56).

[102] Masterman, 'Hygiene and Disease,'114.

[103] Ibid. 115.

[104] Ibid. 117

[105] In particular, see Aref Abu-Rabia, *Folk Medicine among the Bedouin Tribes in the Negev* (Sede Boqer: Social Studies Center, The Jacob Blaustein Institute for Desert Research, 1983), 15–20.

Calotropis procera (Sodom's apple) (Plate 50): leaves prepared as a drink, for stomach and intestinal pains; leaves and bark soaked and drunk, for malaria; cream prepared from leaves, for skin infections.

Ziziphus spina-christi (lote tree) (Plate 52): fruit eaten, for diarrhoea and barrenness; this is a holy tree and it is forbidden to damage it. Bedouin make pilgrimages to it, hang white cloth on it, read Quranic verses, and slaughter sheep and goats beside it.

Contemporary science has reached into the field of ethnopharmacology, with articles over the past decade now intensively exploring the Dead Sea area as a resource for various traditional medicines.[106] This only confirms that the area was and is a curious zone for a harvest of medicinal plants, as Josephus rightly noted. Some of the most important medicinal plants are fast disappearing from around the Dead Sea, for example *Moringa peregrina*, with an antibacterial agent in the leaves, which was once found in the south extensively.[107] Mining of potash and other minerals in the southern reaches of the lake has now greatly interfered with the natural flora here. The salt industry excavates Mount Sodom, and has converted much of the region south of the Lisan into an area of giant salt pans.

Today, too, there is a huge industry of healing around the Dead Sea. The high mineral content of the lake—with its intense concentrations of sulphur, potash, sodium, calcium, bromine, magnesium chloride, and some seventeen other substances—is renowned. Luxury hotels are found on both sides of the lake, furnishing Israel and Jordan with lucrative lures for tourists who come from all over the world to find relief from skin conditions, particularly psoriasis, in the waters and mud of the Dead Sea, as well as many visitors who come just to relax in a hot climate and bob about in the water. Soaps, oils, balms, creams, and other ointments are found for sale in hotel shops, and in traditional medicine stores all over Jordan, Palestine, and Israel. One can find Dead Sea sulphur included in these, advertised as anti-acne, antiseptic, and anti-fungal. It is today the minerals—imbuing the mud and the water—that are valued more highly than the plants that were once so well-known as coming from this part of the world. Both the quality of the sunlight and the

---

[106] Mohammad Hudaib, Mohammad Mohammad, Yasser Bustanji, Rabab Tayyem, Mohammed Yousef, Mustafa Abuirjeie, and Talal Aburjai, 'Ethnopharmacological Survey of Medicinal Plants in Jordan, Mujib Nature Reserve and Surrounding Area,' *Journal of Ethnopharmacology* 120/1 (2008): 63–71; Nidal A. Jaradat, 'Ethnopharmacological Survey of Natural Products in Palestine,' *An-Najah National University Journal of Research* 19 (2005): 13–67, where mud and soil are particularly noted. Oraib S. Nawash and Ahmad S. Al-Horani, 'The Most Important Medicinal Plants in Wadi Araba Desert in South West Jordan: A Review Article,' *Advances in Environmental Biology* 5/2 (2011): 418–25, which includes references and medicinal information for many species including *Balanites aegyptiaca*, *Citrullus colocynthis*, and *Ziziphus spina-christi*.

[107] Nawash and Al-Horani, 'Medicinal Plants,' 421.

air of the Dead Sea are now highly regarded, for the benefit of skin and lungs. There is also a simple enjoyment of stillness.

THE DEAD SEA SCROLLS AND HEALING ARTS

As we have noted, since pharmacological lore was written down on tracts that did not normally require conservation (i.e. they were not *shemot*), we should not expect them to be found within the corpus of the Dead Sea Scrolls. Nonetheless, within the scrolls corpus there are numerous fragments of texts that indicate that people were interested in healing arts: incantation formulae (4Q560; 5Q14), exorcistic works (e.g. 4Q510–11; 11Q11), and analyses of physiognomy (4Q186 = 4Q Zodiacal Physiognomy; 4Q534–6 The Birth of Noah; 4Q561 = 4Q Physiognomy ar).[108] It is not possible here to explore all the references to health and healing in the Scrolls, and preliminary remarks will need to suffice to illustrate that there is expertise in this regard evidenced in the texts. A major exploration of this topic is still to be done.

To begin with it can be noted that there was a fundamental belief that sicknesses were caused by demons, and people could therefore be cured by the expulsion of these evil forces.[109] In the Genesis Apocryphon Abraham cures Pharaoh by expelling a demon, and by the laying on of hands (1QapGen 20: 12–29).[110] The practice of laying hands on a person or handling them is otherwise attested only in roughly contemporaneous Christian material (e.g.

---

[108] Philip S. Alexander, 'Physiognomy, Initiation, and Rank in the Qumran Community,' in Hubert Cancik, Hermann Lichtenberger, et al. (eds), *Geschichte—Tradition—Reflexion: Fest-schrift fur Martin Hengel zum 70. Geburtstag: Band I: Judentum* (Tübingen: Mohr Siebeck, 1996), 385–94; Mladen Popović, *Reading the Human Body: Physiognomics and Astrology in the Dead Sea Scrolls and Hellenistic-Early Roman Period Judaism* (Leiden: Brill, 2007), cf. T. S. Barton, *Power and Knowledge: Astrology, Physiognomics and Medicine under the Roman Empire* (Ann Arbor: University of Michigan Press, 1994); Simon Swain (ed.), *Seeing the Face, Seeing the Soul: Polemon's Physiognomy from Classical Antiquity to Medieval Islam* (Oxford: OUP, 2007); Elizabeth C. Evans, 'Galen the Physician as a Physiognomist,' *Transactions and Proceedings of the American Philological Association* 76 (1945): 287–98.

[109] Ida Fröhlich, '"Invoke at Any Time": Apotropaic Texts and Belief in Demons in the Literature of the Qumran Community,' *Biblische Notizen* 137 (2008): 41–74; ead. 'Demons, Scribes, and Exorcists in Qumran,' in Kinga Dévényi and Tamás Iványi (eds), *Essays in Honour of Alexander Fodor on His Sixtieth Birthday* (The Arabist: Budapest Studies in Arabic 23; Budapest: Eötuös Loránd University Press, 2001), 73–81; Philip S. Alexander, 'The Demonology of the Dead Sea Scrolls,' in Peter W. Flint and James C. VanderKam (eds), *The Dead Sea Scrolls after Fifty Years: A Comprehensive Assessment* (Leiden: Brill, 1998–9), ii, 331–53; Herman Lichtenberger, 'Spirits and Demons in the Dead Sea Scrolls,' in James D. G. Dunn, Graham Stanton and Stephen C. Barton (eds), *The Holy Spirit and Christian Origins* (Grand Rapids: Eerdmans, 2004), 14–21.

[110] See Ida Fröhlich, 'Medicine and Magic in the Genesis Apocryphon. Ideas on Human Conception and its Hindrances,' *RQ* 25/98 (2011): 177–98, at 191–6.

Mark 1: 29–31, 41–2; 3: 10; Luke 4: 40–1). Likewise in the Prayer of Nabonidus the Babylonian king proclaims that 'an exorcist forgave my sins' (4Q242 [4QPrNab]: Frag. 1–3: 4), again relating to the practice of Jesus, as an exorcist, who forgives sins as part of his exorcistic work (e.g. Mark 2: 6–12).

Purification is linked with healing in 4Q514 (= 4QOrdᶜ). An individual is instructed: 'he shall bathe and launder on the [da]y of [his] healing', and then 'all those (who are) "impure of days" shall, on the day of their [he]aling, bathe and launder in water, and become pure' (Frg. 1, Col. 1, 6, 9).[111] It is unclear what these people are being healed from, but they can eat pure food immediately after they have become pure by bathing.

Specific medical or pharmacological terms have been suggested in only one text, originally called 4QTherapeia (4Q341). Allegro was particularly interested in this, reading it as designating a variety of medications. However, because of the difficulty in comprehending the meaning of this, the identification of it as a writing exercise is currently assumed.[112] Given what we have surmised in terms of the reasons for scrolls being conserved in jars in caves, it seems unlikely that a writing exercise would be included unless it was an end section of a scroll that was otherwise important. It would be possible to search the scrolls for specific mentions of plant lore, whether incidental or explicit, but this would require an initial careful determination of plant names as used at the time, which is a complex study in itself. For example, in 4Q386 Frag. 1: 2: 5, a fragment of a text of Pseudo-Ezekiel, there is a line that states 'and from the caper bush (נצפה) there will be no juice/wine (תרוש), nor will a *taziz* (תזיז) make any honey(דבש)'.[113] The more common word for caper-bush is צלף[114] and so נצפה may refer to a specific type here. Caper (*Capparis spinosa*) juice was not a general drink but a medication, the juice being made of the fruit for toothache, disorders of the liver and spleen, stomach ulcers, spasms, paralysis, and worms in the ears, among other things, according to Dioscorides (*Mat. Med.* 2: 204); the Talmud records the pharmacological produce of caper juice in vinegar (b.Shab. 110a).[115] Therefore, the mysterious word *taziz* (תזיז) may also

---

[111] Baillet, DJD 7, 295–8, Pl. LXXIV; Jacob Milgrom, 'Purification Rule (4Q514 = 4QOrdᶜ),' in James H. Charlesworth (ed.), *The Rule of the Community and Related Documents* (Louisville: J. C. B. Mohr/Paul Siebeck/Westminster John Knox Press, 1994), 177–9.

[112] See Philip S. Alexander, *Qumran Cave 4, Cryptic Texts*, DJD 26/1 (Oxford: OUP, 2000), 291–4. For the idea that it is a writing exercise, see Joseph Naveh, 'A Medical Document or a Writing Exercise? The So-Called 4QTherapeia,' *IEJ* 36 (1986): 52–5, contra Allegro, *Dead Sea Scrolls*, 235–40, pls. 16–17; James H. Charlesworth, *The Discovery of a Dead Sea Scroll (4QTherapeia): Its Importance in the History of Medicine and Jesus Research* (Lubbock: Texas Tech University Press, 1985); cf. id. 'A Misunderstood Recently Published Dead Sea Scroll (4Q341),' *Explorations* 2 (Philadelphia: American Institute for the Study of Religious Co-operation, 1987).

[113] Deborah Dimant (ed.), *Qumran Cave 4.XXI: Parabiblical Texts, Part 4: Pseudo-Prophetic Texts* (DJD 30; Oxford: OUP, 2001), 62, 64.

[114] Jastrow, 929.

[115] See also Asaph, Sepher ha-Refuot 4: 403; Lev and Amar, *Cairo Genizah*, 387–8.

refer to a bush or tree producing medicinal 'honey', as we have noted above. But there is still much work to be done to identify all such possible references.

A purification text 4Q512 refers to healing cleansing, as revealed by the words 'from the impure disease' (Frag. 34: 5: 5), 'his impure flux' (Frag. 10–11: 10: 1) and 'purification of his fl[lux]' (Frag. 7–9; 11: 2), which suggests that the relationship between purification and healing deserves further study. CD itself indicates the importance of a priestly declaration of purification from infirmity (CD 13: 5–7). The expertise required is quite remarkable. Copies of the Damascus Document found in Cave 4 contain a section defining priestly 'medical' examinations (4Q266 = 4QD[a] Frag. 9, col. 1, 7–11; 4Q272 = 4QD[g]; 4Q273 = 4QD[h]).[116] In 4Q266 the text concerns the observance of tumours and rashes that may be leprosy (requiring removal of the person), and it then continues to deal with ringworm, noting blood circulation in regard to healthy skin, after which it moves to gonorrhoea, as well as matters concerning women and childbirth.

In the Community Rule the 'sons of truth' enjoy 'healing', among other good things (1QS 4: 6), so that moral and physical weakness/illness are considered together (so also 11QPsAp[a] I: '[the sons of] his people have completed the cure').[117] CD 11: 9–10 (= 4Q271, frag. 3, col. 1, 5–6) contains a curious proscription that may be translated as: 'A man is not allowed to carry a leaflet (עלי) of (herbal) medicines (סממים) on the Sabbath.'[118]

At the end of the Psalms scroll from Cave 11 the list given includes 'four songs for charming the demon-possessed with music' (11Q5 27: 10). These have been identified by Emile Puech as the psalms written in 11Q11, prefaced with the subtitle 'for the stricken'.[119] The final one of these four (11Q11 6:3–14) is Psalm 91 (= 4Q88), a psalm included within the canonical corpus, though there are some differences in its form in Cave 11. It is a song of deliverance from illness and also prophylactic, in asserting God's protection from the harm caused by all forms of disease or danger, evoking angels to guard people from harm,[120] a text apparently quoted by Jesus—in reply to

---

[116] Joseph M. Baumgarten, 'The 4Q Zadokite Fragments on Skin Disease,' *JJS* 41 (1990): 153–65, at 157–8.

[117] James A. Sanders, 'A Liturgy for Healing the Stricken (11QPsAp[a]–11Q11),' in James H. Charlesworth and H. W. L. Rietz (eds), *The Dead Sea Scrolls: Hebrew, Aramaic and Greek Texts with English Translations Vol. 4A: Pseudepigraphic and Non-Masoretic Psalms and Prayers* (Tübingen/Louisville: J. C. B. Mohr/Paul Siebeck/Westminster John Knox Press, 1997), 216–33.

[118] Florentino García Martínez, *The Dead Sea Scrolls Translated: The Qumran Texts in English*, 2nd ed. (Leiden/Grand Rapids: Brill/Eerdmans, 1996), 42, has—interestingly— '[n]o-one should wear perfumes on the sabbath'.

[119] Emile Puech, 'Les psaumes davidiques du rituel d'exorcisme (11Q11),' in Daniel K. Falk (ed.), *Sapiential, Liturgical and Poetical Texts from Qumran* (Leiden: Brill, 2000), 160–81; J. P. M. van der Ploeg, 'Le Psaume XCI dans une recension de Qumran,' *RB* 72 (1965): 210–17; F. Garcia-Martinez, E. J. C. Tigchelaar, and A. S. van der Woude, *Qumran Cave 11.II (11Q2–18, 11Q20–31)* (DJD 23; Oxford: OUP, 1998), 181–205.

[120] I am grateful to Ida Frölich for sharing her paper on this text with me, provisionally entitled 'Healing with Psalms', publication forthcoming.

Satan—in Matt. 4: 6 (= Luke 4: 10–11). In the remaining three songs designed to define (visually) and charm demons, the aim seems to be to bind the demons, quarantining them so as to render them ineffective, by invoking also the name of Solomon (e.g. 11Q11 2: 2), with Raphael—the angel of healing—also mentioned (11Q11 5: 3).

Raphael was the arch-angel whose name carries within it a healing verb, רְפָא, and has a large part to play in the Book of Tobit, also found at Qumran in four Aramaic fragmentary texts and one in Hebrew (4Q196–4Q200). In the story of Tobit, Raphael heals him from blindness by getting his son to use the gall of a fish for anointing his eyes (Tobit 11). The gall of a *kuppu* fish was known as an eye salve in ancient Mesopotamia.[121] In 1 Enoch, important at Qumran (found in 13 Aramaic fragments in Cave 4 [4Q201–202, 204–212] and three tiny Hebrew fragments in Cave 1), Raphael sorts out the problematic Nephilim, and casts the demon Azazel into a cavern (1 Enoch 10: 47). The origin of 'medicine' is ambiguous, in that it is attributed to the Watchers (angels) who took human wives (Gen 6: 1–4), and taught them 'how to chop up roots and plants' (1 Enoch 7: 1; 8: 3).[122]

SOLOMON

Much of this evidence in the Dead Sea Scrolls can be contextualized within a body of literature now mostly lost: the scientific Solomonic corpus. Solomon's name continually pops up in incantations and as the source of knowledge, even regarding Judaean balsam (Josephus, *Ant.* 8: 178). This is not surprising. In Josephus *Ant.* 8: 42–6 Eleazar's (mandrake) ring is employed on the basis of the wisdom of Solomon; Solomon is said to have made botanical and zoological observations: 'he gained wisdom from all things and demonstrated the most advanced knowledge of their specific properties'. Likewise, in the Wisdom of Solomon 7: 15–22 Solomon prays to understand all things in the world including calendars, seasons, astronomy/astrology, the natures of animals, spirits and humans, and 'varieties of plants and the virtues of roots'. Solomon was thus considered the source of scientific knowledge in Second Temple Judaism. In other words, the name 'Solomon' was not so much a historical figure but a kind of cipher for the whole range of natural science, which, in this period, was beginning to become an essential part of wisdom known to certain

---

[121] Allan, 'Physician in Ancient Israel,' 384, n. 42.
[122] For which, see George Nickelsburg, *1 Enoch: A Commentary on the Book of 1 Enoch Chapters 1–36, 81–108* (Minneapolis: Fortress, 2001), esp. 182–99, 207–9; Siam Bhayro, *The Shemihazah and Asael Narrative of 1 Enoch 6–11: Introduction, Text, Translation and Commentary with reference to Ancient Near Eastern and Biblical Antecedents* (Münster: Ugarit-Verlag, 2005).

sages.[123] Thus it is increasingly noted how much of the sciences is found in Qumran literature, including cosmology (Jub. 2: 1–16), cosmography (1 Enoch 12: 36), and geography.[124]

The medical information was most likely contained in the so-called *Sefer ha-Refu'ot*, or 'Book of Remedies'.[125] In rabbinic literature this work of pharmacological knowledge attributed to Solomon was apparently hidden by King Hezekiah (b.Pes. 56a; b.Ber. 10b; Abot de Rabbi Nathan 2), as Kottek has pointed out.[126] The Solomonic tradition fused magic and science, and included demonology—and exorcism—as shown by the *Testament of Solomon* (in which Solomon addresses a range of different demons responsible for illnesses and other human problems).[127] In this text, we learn of a Solomon's ring that provided magical power over demons that bothered builders of the Temple.

The effectiveness of Solomon in routing demons is portrayed in numerous late Roman and Byzantine amulets depicting Solomon on horseback spearing a female demon.[128] A Book of Solomon is mentioned in the Gnostic text *On the Origin of the World*, and Origen, in his *Commentary on Matthew* (*in Matt.*

---

[123] Philip Alexander, 'Enoch and the Beginnings of Jewish Interest in Natural Science,' in Charlotte Hempel, Armin Lange, and Hermann Lichtenberger (eds), *The Wisdom Texts from Qumran and the Development of Sapiential Thought* (Leuven: Peeters/Leuven University Press, 2002), 223–43; George Brooke, 'Langues, sciences et techniques,' in Farah Mebarki and Emile Puech (eds), *Les manuscrits de la mer Morte* (Rodez: Rouergue, 2002), 142–8; Jonathan Ben-Dov, 'Scientific Writings in Aramaic and Hebrew at Qumran: Translation and Concealment,' in Katell Berthelot and Daniel Stökl Ben Ezra (eds), *Aramaica Qumranica: Proceedings of the Conference on the Aramaic Texts from Qumran in Aix-en-Provence, 30 June–2 July 2008* (Leiden: Brill, 2010), 379–402. Here definitions of 'science' are of course critical, but clearly it includes the study of astronomy, calendars, medicine, healing practices, meteorology, and observations of the physical world.

[124] So Fröhlich, 'Medicine and Magic,' 197. For geography see Philip S. Alexander, 'Notes on the "Imago Mundi" of the Book of Jubilees,' *JJS* 38 (1982): 197–213; Daniel A. Machiela, ' "Each to his own Inheritance": Geography as an Evaluative Tool in the Genesis Apocryphon,' *DSD* 15 (2008): 50–66; Esther Eshel, 'The *Imago Mundi* of the Genesis Apocryphon,' in L. R. LiDonnici and A. B. Liber (eds), *Heavenly Tablets: Interpretation, Identity and Tradition in Ancient Judaism* (Leiden: Brill, 2007), 111–31.

[125] See Rosner, *Medicine in the Bible*, 79–90; David Halperin, 'The Book of Remedies, the Canonization of the Solomonic Writings, and the Riddle of Pseudo-Eusebius,' *JQR* 72 (1982): 269–92; Arthur J. Silverstein, 'Censorship of Medical Works: Hezekiah and "The Book of Remedies",' *Dine Israel: An Annual of Jewish Law and Israel Family Law* 7 (1976): 151–7.

[126] Kottek, 'Essenes,' 84.

[127] Dennis C. Duling, 'Solomon, Exorcism and the Son of David,' *HTR* 68 (1975): 235–52; id. 'Testament of Solomon,' in James H. Charlesworth (ed.), *Old Testament Pseudepigrapha* (London: Darton, Longman and Todd, 1983), 944–56; id. 'The Legend of Solomon the Magician in Antiquity: Problem and Perspectives,' in *Proceedings: Eastern Great Lakes Biblical Society* 4 (1984): 1–23; id. 'Eleazar Miracle'; Pablo A. Torijano, *Solomon, the Esoteric King: From King to Magus, Development of a Tradition* (Leiden: Brill, 2002), 41–86, 192–224. In 11QPsAp[a] an exorcism takes place in the name of Solomon (see Torjano, *Solomon*, 43–52).

[128] Campbell Bonner, *Studies in Magical Amulets, Chiefly Graeco-Roman* (Ann Arbor: University of Michigan Press, 1950), 208–21; Torjano, *Solomon*, 130–8.

comm. ser. 33: 110) who writes of 'some books [of Solomon] taken from Hebrew'.[129]

Solomon's role as an arch-magician and healer has had a long history, and there is no way of determining how ancient the traditions are in his case. In terms of the Dead Sea Scrolls, books of Solomonic wisdom may either not have been found or survive in such minute forms among the scrolls corpus of over 15,000 fragments that they are not currently recognized. For example, a work known in six fragmentary copies (1Q26; 4Q415–18, 4Q423) begins with a cosmic framework and presents a student as giving a service, while several sections mention agricultural activity (references to ploughmen, baskets, barns, fruits of produce, trees, a garden, harvest), but little is known about the entire composition.

As Kottek has noted, the Book of Jubilees, mentioned above in relation to the importance of angels in the communication of healing knowledge, is one of the most attested works found in the Qumran caves, and contains various references to healing arts in Jubilees 10, in which Noah is taught knowledge by good angels to enable him to save humankind from further disasters, including knowledge of medicines (10: 17).[130] Two Qumran fragments—1Q19 and 1Q19bis (1QNoah)—specifically relate to the story of medical knowledge found in Jubilees 10. In the Aramaic text of 1 Enoch found at Qumran, 4Q Enoch[a] (4Q201) 4: 1–5 and 4QEnoch[b] (4Q202) 3: 1–5 have lists of the names of the angels who taught secret knowledge, providing a striking corroboration of the importance of the names of angels as indicated by Josephus, *War* 2: 142.[131]

This probably implies a usage of names of angels in incantations or mystical formulae for healing. One of the most mysterious things in the Dead Sea Scrolls corpus is the use of secret alphabets, rendering texts impossible to translate. Up until recently, such secret alphabets were found only in later incantations and magical formulae,[132] particularly on amulets and magic bowls of the fifth to sixth centuries, which could include angelic names as

---

[129] A rather tantalizing reference given that Origen used material found in a *pithos* near Jericho (see Eusebius, *Hist. Eccles.* 6: 16: 3). As we have seen, the find reported by Epiphanius and Ps.-Athanasius indicates that the πίθοι (plural) contained 'manuscripts of the Septuagint, as well as other Hebrew and Greek writings' (Epiphanius, *De Mens. et Pond.* 17–18; *PG* 43, cols. 265–8; Pseudo-Athanasius, *Synopsis PG* 28: col. 432).

[130] Kottek, 'Essenes,' 84.

[131] Michael Langlois, 'Shemihazah et compagnie(s). Onomastique des anges déchus dans les manuscrits araméens du Livre d'Hénoch,' in Katell Berthelot and Daniel Stökl Ben Ezra (eds), *Aramaica Qumranica. Proceedings of the conference on the Aramaic texts from Qumran in Aix-en-Provence, 30 June–2 July 2008* (Leiden: Brill, 2010), 145–80.

[132] Larry H. Schiffman and M. D. Swartz, *Hebrew and Aramaic Incantation Texts from the Cairo Genizah: Selected Texts from Taylor-Schechter Box K1* (Semitic Texts and Studies 1; Sheffield: JSOT Press, 1992). Philip S. Alexander, 'Incantations and Books of Magic,' in Emil Schürer, with Geza Vermes, Fergus Millar and Martin Goodman (eds), *The History of the Jewish People in the Age of Jesus Christ (175 B.C.E.–A.D. 135)* (Edinburgh: T & T Clark, 1986), iii/i, 342–79; and see Hans Dieter Betz (ed.), *The Greek Magical Papyri in Translation, including the Demotic Spells* (Chicago: The University of Chicago Press, 1986).

well as names and representations of malevolent demons.[133] This chronological gap meant that researchers were wary of assuming that the Qumran corpus may necessarily indicate something similar. However, contemporaneous use of such alphabets has been found in excavations on Mount Zion directed by Shimon Gibson and James Tabor, in 2009. Here fragments of a limestone cup from the first century CE were seen to have an inscription using cryptic alphabets. This bowl then would be related to other incantations designed for prophylactic or healing/exorcism.[134] The question arises though as to how many cryptic texts from the Dead Sea Scrolls corpus are also related to healing, given the association between such alphabets and incantations of various kinds.[135]

Nevertheless, we do not have texts which list roots, remedies, and properties of stones in a compendium of medicinal information that would definitively provide evidence of Essene interests as Josephus defines them. As such, it would be better to conclude that the scrolls themselves provide indications of healing interests and practices within Second Temple Judaism overall which would have been utilized by the Essenes (given they are situated within the world of Second Temple Judaism), but we cannot confine such knowledge to the Essenes alone. The 'science' of medicine in Judaea at this time seems to look both west and also east, in its combination of approaches, to the medical science of Mesopotamia, as Marc Geller has argued,[136] and also to Greek physiological philosophy.[137] It embraced astral science with all its ramifications, as Helen Jacobus has explored in her study of astrological lore at Qumran.[138] This was brought to bear on Judaea particularly during the Persian period—and seems to have left a lasting legacy. It is, after all, here that we have the fusion methods of divination, horoscopy, physiognomy, and astrology developed in terms of health and healing.[139]

---

[133] Joseph Naveh and Shaul Shaked, *Amulets and Magic Bowls* (Jerusalem: Magnes, 1985); id. *Magic, Spells and Formulae: Aramaic Incantations of Late Antiquity* (Jerusalem: Magnes, 1993), and see the Virtual Magic Bowl Archive at http://www.soton.ac.uk/vmba/index.html. About 400 of the 2000 published bowls have images depicting demons.

[134] Stephen Pfann, 'The Mount Zion Inscribed Stone Cup: Preliminary Observations,' *Bible and Interpretation*, http://www.bibleinterp.com.

[135] See Stephen Pfann, 'Cryptic Texts 249a–z, 250a–j and 313–313b,' in Stephen Pfann, Philip Alexander et al., *Qumran Cave 4 XXVI. Cryptic Texts and Miscellanea, Part 1* (DJD 36; Oxford: OUP, 2000), 515–701.

[136] As Mark J. Geller argued in his paper, 'Divination in Ancient Palestine: The View from Babylonia,' at the SOTS winter meeting, Fitzwilliam College Cambridge, 2009, and see his study, 'Look to the Stars: Babylonian Medicine and Magic, Astrology and Melthesis,' in *Max Planck Institute for the History of Science* 401 at http://www.mpiwg-berlin.mpg.de/en/resources/preprints.html

[137] Frohlich, 'Magic and Medicine,' 187–9.

[138] Helen Jacobus, '4Q318: A Jewish Zodiac Calendar at Qumran,' in Charlotte Hempel (ed.), *The Dead Sea Scrolls. Texts and Context* (STDJ 90; Leiden: Brill), 365–95, at 375–7.

[139] Francesca Rochberg, *The Heavenly Writing: Divination, Horoscopy, and Astronomy in Mesopotamian Culture* (Cambridge: CUP, 2009).

Just as astrology would play a large part in medieval medicine, we find it in this conceptual world. In Gen. 15: 5 God instructs Abraham to count the stars if he can, which was interpreted to indicate an astrological expertise.[140] Ps.-Eupolemus (Eusebius, *Praep. Evang.* 9: 17: 3; 9: 18: 1–2) has Abraham, pre-conversion, as an astronomer–astrologer, teaching this science to Phoenicians and Egyptians.[141] Josephus refers to [Ps.]Hecataeus as writing a book about Abraham in which he mentions that Abraham taught the Egyptians astronomy (*Ant.* 1: 159, 168). Jubilees 12: 16–21 has Abraham looking at the stars all night in order to divine weather forecasts.[142] But before Abraham took this up, this was a science apparently known to Enoch: Ps.-Eupolemus attributes this knowledge to Enoch, along with various other sciences, with Enoch equated with Atlas (see Eusebius, *Praep. Evang.* 9; 17: 2–9: 18: 2). Enoch is instructed in astrology by angels, a knowledge he then transmitted to Methuselah: 1 Enoch 72–82 contains a discussion of astronomical observations, and is usually considered to be the earliest of all the Enochic texts, with fragments of this found at Qumran: 4QEnastr^a (4Q208), 4QEnastr^b (4Q209), 4Q210=4 QEnastr^c (4Q210), and 4QEnastr^d (4Q211), including additional material with tables of moon phases, indicating that in the mid-first century BCE there was an Aramaic form of this work larger than the portions that have been preserved in Ethiopic Enoch.[143]

This illustrates in fact how wide the subject can be, since the science of pharmacology within ancient Judaism may be situated within a broader

[140] George W. E. Nickelsburg, 'Abraham the Convert,' in Michael E. Stone and Theodore A. Bergren (eds), *Biblical Figures Outside the Bible* (Harrisburg, PA, 1998), 151–75; James H. Charlesworth, 'Jewish Astrology in the Talmud, Pseudepigrapha, the Dead Sea Scrolls and Early Palestinian Synagogues,' *HTR* 70 (1977): 183–200.

[141] See Ben Zion Wacholder, *Eupolemus: A Study of Judaeo-Greek Literature* (New York: Hebrew Union College, 1974), 291, Appendix B, and also id. 'Pseudo-Eupolemus' Two Fragments on the Life of Abraham,' *HUCA* 34 (1963): 83–113. See also 'Pseudo-Eupolemus,' trans. Robert Doran, in Charlesworth, *Old Testament Pseudepigrapha*, ii, 873–82. Artapanus notes that Abraham taught the king of Egypt astrology, 'Artapanus,' trans. John J. Collins, in Charlesworth, *Old Testament Pseudepigrapha*, ii, 897.

[142] The identity of Abraham as an astrologer is noted also by early Christian authors: Ambrosiaster, *Questiones* 117: 5; the Ps. Clementine *Recognitions* 1: 32: 3–4, see Tim Hegedus, *Early Christianity and Ancient Astrology* (Frankfurt am Maim/New York: Peter Lang, 2007), 318–27.

[143] John Bergsma, 'The Relationship between Jubilees and the Early Enochic Books (Astronomical Book and Book of the Watchers),' in Gabriele Boccaccini and Giovanni Ibba, with the collaboration of Jason von Ehrenkrook, James Waddell, and Jason Zurawski (eds), *Enoch and the Mosaic Torah* (Grand Rapids: Eerdmans, 2009), in 36–51. The Cairo Genizah fragment of 3 Enoch indicates that this text had more astrology in it than the preserved text (see Charlesworth, *Old Testament Pseudepigrapha* i, 223–315), and also Peter Schäfer (ed.), *Geniza-Fragmente zur Hekhalot-Literatur* (TSAJ 16; Tübingen: Mohr Siebeck, 1984), 136–7; Daphna Arbel, 'Divine Secrets and Divination,' in April D. De Conick, *Paradise Now: Essays on Early Jewish and Christian Mysticism* (Atlanta: SBL, 2006), 355–79. Arbel notes how in Synopse §15 Enoch-Metatron is given a robe on which luminaries were set, and provides a translation of the Genizah text, p.371.

epistemological framework in which astrology, angelology, demonology, purity systems, and physiognomy were intertwined. The pharmacology evidenced may be defined as astro-angelological-pharmacology, which is essentially Mesopotamian in its cultural origins. It did not stop at the end of antiquity, but—since medicine is extremely conservative—it continued on to the medieval world.[144]

Knowledge of this beyond what is found in biblical literature, pseudepigrapha, and the Scrolls is patchy but nevertheless suggestive of a vibrant tradition of pharmacological lore. The source for Josephus' information about medicinal plants of the Dead Sea region will forever remain anonymous, as will the mysterious writer mentioned as 'Judeus', noted by Celsus (*De Medicina* 5: 19: 11; 5: 22: 4), since medical knowledge was not codified until the handbook prepared by Asaph in the sixth century CE.[145] But this handbook is extremely suggestive. Asaph knows and uses the great Greek medical writers Hippocrates, Dioscorides, and Galen, but also draws on an independent tradition. As Michael Stone has recently pointed out, the work begins with the words: 'This is the book of remedies which ancient sages copied from the book of Shem ben Noah, which was transmitted to Noah on Mount Lubar, one of the mountains of Ararat, after the flood.' Asaph then uses Jubilees 10, also attributed to Noah. Stone speculates that there were Books of Noah that dealt in part with medicine and demonology.[146] Given all this, it is clear we have the tip of the iceberg of a thriving medical world in ancient Judaism. It is quite likely that those with knowledge guarded this carefully, as esoteric wisdom, and avoided putting all of their vast range of scientific expertise in writing.

THE ARCHAEOLOGY OF QUMRAN AND PHARMACOLOGY

It is now known that the site of Qumran was used partly for the processing of date honey (or date wine), since a date press and sealed jars containing this substance have been found here.[147] This is very important, because date honey

---

[144] See too in Midrash Genesis Rabba 10: 6.

[145] Stephen Newmyer, 'Asaph the Jew and Greco-Roman Pharmaceuticals,' in Jacob and Jacob, *The Healing Past*, 107–20. The Hebrew text is published in Sussman Muntner, 'Asaph Harofe, Sefer Harefuoth (Asaph the Physician, Book of Remedies),' *Koroth* 3 (1965): 396–422 (Heb.).

[146] Michael Stone, *Ancient Judaism: New Visions and Views* (Grand Rapids: Eerdmans, 2011), 44–5.

[147] A large mound of date pits were found next to the date press installation of locus 75, see Yizhak Magen and Yuval Peleg, 'Back to Qumran: Ten Years of Excavation and Research, 1993–2004,' in Katharina Galor, Jean-Baptiste Humbert, and Jürgen Zangenberg (eds), *Qumran, the Site of the Dead Sea Scrolls: Archaeological Interpretations and Debates* (Leiden: Brill,

was a medicine (Josephus, *War* 4: 468–9), and dates themselves had medicinal value, as noted above. Date wine or date honey could have been manufactured wherever dates were grown. Both cultivated and wild date palm was found in Cave 24 in the caves survey.[148]

A Qumran-type juglet containing either date-stone oil or opobalsam (or both mixed together), found in a cave near Qumran, may be important as a clue to what was manufactured in the area, though it is impossible to know whether it came from Qumran specifically.[149]

Qumran had several workshops with basins that have not yet been identified in terms of their usage (e.g. locus 34, loci 51–3). Two other workshops included clusters of small jars (locus 4: KhQ48–71; locus 7: KhQ 96–7). The suggestion made by Donceel-Voûte, expanded on by Hirschfeld, that the processing of opobalsam may have occurred in these is possible (especially given we do not know how the substance was processed), but there may have been any number of other important products for which small jars were used. Not that many industries beyond that of pharmaceutical production required small jars, and the situation of Qumran in an area known for its medicinal products would suggest that the production of these local resources was a concern. Interestingly, Qumran has no large wine amphora: large receptacles commonly used for table wines.

While a full corpus of artefacts from Qumran is yet to be published, a thorough investigation of the pottery, glass, and metal objects (in storage at the École Biblique, Rockefeller Museum, and Israel Antiquities Authority in Jerusalem) in terms of the medicinal associations, is not yet possible. However, in recent studies of eighty-nine items of glassware from the 1951–8 excavations, there were eighteen ointment bottles, seven larger bottles, twenty-three goblets, three biconical receptacles and fourteen cups;[150] the number of ointment bottles is particularly interesting.

2006), 55–113, at 59–60, Fig. 3.6. Sealed jars buried in the cemetery contained a thick layer of polysaccharides, most likely indicating dehydrated date honey, see Stephen Pfann, 'A Table Prepared in the Wilderness; Pantries and Tables, Pure Food and Sacred Space at Qumran,' in Katharina Galor, Jean-Baptiste Humbert, and Jürgen Zangenberg (eds), *Qumran, the Site of the Dead Sea Scrolls: Archaeological Interpretations and Debates* (Leiden: Brill, 2006), 159–78, at p.177, and cf. Stephen Pfann, 'The Wine Press (and Miqveh) at Kh. Qumran (loc. 75 and 69),' *RB* 101 (1994): 212–14. A date press has also been identified at nearby Ain Feshkha: Ehud Netzer, 'Did any Perfume Industry Exist at `Ein Feshkha?' *IEJ* 55 (2005): 97–100.

[148] Nili Liphschitz and Georges Bonani, 'Wild and Cultivated Date Palm (Phoenix dactylifera) from Qumran Cave 24,' *Tel Aviv* 28 (2001): 305–9.

[149] Patrich and Arubas, 'Juglet,' and see discussion in Moss, 'Historical Perspectives,' 258–9.

[150] Helena Wouters et al., 'Antique Glass from Khirbet Qumran: Archaeological Context and Chemical Determination,' *Bulletin of the Institut Royal du Patrimonie Artistique, Brussels* 28 (2002): 9–40; ead. 'Archaeological Glass from Khirbet Qumran: An Analytical Approach,' in Jan Gunneweg, Charles Greenblatt, and Annemie Adriaans (eds), *Bio- and Material Cultures at Qumran* (Papers from a COST Action G8 working group held in Israel on 22–23 May 2005; Fraunhofer IRB, Stuttgart, 2006), 171–89. For the linkage of the ointment bottles with medicines

While the remains of animal bones buried with pots after use probably indicates an extreme fastidiousness about hygiene (as opposed to ritual purity alone), so that flies and wild animals are not attracted to the leftovers,[151] it is important to note again that remains show that the people who lived here were boiling animals rather than roasting them, when roasting would have been the normal way of cooking meat for a feast. As noted in the previous chapter, boiling sheep means that you can separate out the fat on the surface of the pot after cooling, which is significant given that sheep (or goose) fat was one of the base substances used in medicinal salves in antiquity (cf. b.Shab. 133b). A small livestock enclosure was excavated at the nearby site of Ain Feshkha,[152] and animals would have grazed in the Ain Feshkha plain south of Qumran.

A date-press (for date wine or date honey) excavated at Ain Feshkha is clearly indicative of one industry there,[153] while further south at Ain el-Ghuweir the appearance of juglets, storage jars, cooking pots, and many small flask fragments prompted Pesach Bar Adon to suggest that here there was the cultivation of 'medicinal and perfumery herbs and orchards'.[154]

Even further south still, in the south of the Dead Sea, there was the Herodian *officina* (workshop) at En Boqeq. As noted earlier, this is outside what we have suggested was the main Essene area beside the Dead Sea, an area defined as stretching between En Gedi and En Egallain (Beth Agla), and we cannot assume all medical manufacturing beside the Dead Sea was in the hands of the Essenes. The major locations of fertility and lucrative plantations of balsam (Jericho and En Gedi) remained in royal hands, and En Boqeq also. Nevertheless, it is very interesting to compare En Boqeq with Qumran and Ain Feshkha.

Like Qumran, the workshop of En Boqeq had numerous basins and ovens indicating processing of products, in the centre of an intensively irrigated region testifying to agriculture. The archaeologists Moshe Fischer and Morde-cai Gichon worked hard to determine precisely what these processes at the site might be, and arrived at the conclusion that it must be a place for the manufacture of pharmaceutical or cosmetic (perfume) products, utilizing the distinctive resources of the Dead Sea vicinity. This resulted from a thorough

see Moss, 'Historical Perspectives,' 259, though this is mainly founded on the association of the site with Donceel-Voûte's theories of balsam manufacture.

[151] Yizhak Magen, and Yuval Peleg, *The Qumran Excavations 1993–2004: Preliminary Report* (Judea and Samaria Publications 6; Jerusalem: Israel Antiquities Authority, 2007), 42–4. The importance of burying the bones deep in the ground within the settlement, to discourage wild animals from coming to the vicinity, is rightly noted.

[152] de Vaux, *ADSS*, 71–5; Yizhar Hirschfeld, *Qumran in Context: Reassessing the Archaeological Evidence* (Peabody, MA: Hendrickson, 2004), 208.

[153] Ehud Netzer, 'Did any Perfume Industry Exist at 'Ein Feshkha?' *IEJ* 55 (2005): 97–100.

[154] Pesach Bar Adon, 'Another Settlement of the Judaean Desert Sect at En el-Ghuweir on the Shores of the Dead Sea,' *BASOR* 227 (1977): 1–25, at 20. See also Moss, 'Historical Perspectives,' 259–60.

investigation using a variety of scientific techniques. They noted ash and bitumen deposits, and residues in pots, along with installations that indicated 'multiple heating, boiling and simmering processes that are the core of these industries'.[155] As they point out, the site is situated at the heart of an area famous for its medicinal plants and aromatics, and they note the products of the Dead Sea reviewed here: balsam, dates, bitumen. They observe also that perfumes themselves had healing properties, as Theophrastus' work *De Odoribus* (*On Odours*) 8 shows, titled as it is: 'The medicinal properties of certain perfumes'.[156] Animal fat was found in the chemical analysis of soil samples and animal bones were found within the building, including wool tufts in Room 6, perhaps indicating the extraction of lanolin from wool, used as an ointment, though tufts of wool were used to collect balsam (Pliny, *Hist. Nat.* 12: 54 [116]).[157]

As such, En Boqeq may be seen as an offshoot of En Gedi, the main oasis of lush vegetation. At En Gedi we find the Dead Sea's main centre for the growing of dates and balsam, and numerous other plants. Here, too, there would have been intensive balsam processing. We should remember though the relatively close proximity of the Herodian fortress of Masada, less than 10 km to the north of En Boqeq. While some food could be grown at Masada, Herod's settlement there stockpiled huge resources in the storerooms, indicating a concern to maintain provisions in the event of failure of crops grown there and siege. En Boqeq, with its irrigated terraces from the nearby springs, could provide a great range of fresh food, a few hours' journey away with pack animals. With Masada in the middle of En Boqeq and En Gedi, we do here seem to have a centre with two Herodian gardens proximate to this great fortress-palace. That Herod was interested in growing rue at Machaerus indicates his own concern with Dead Sea pharmacological products, as well as lucrative balsam, many of which would also have been highly sought-after commodities, of value commercially. We cannot therefore assume that every medicinal production centre of the Dead Sea area had something to do with Essenes, but only that it seems that they were permitted—as a gift from Herod—a small section of the Dead Sea coast to utilize as they saw fit, given that this region was a well-known locus of medicinal plants and minerals.

---

[155] Fischer, Gichon and Tal, *'En Boqeq*, 93.

[156] Ibid. 97.

[157] Pig bones were found outside the buildings, which would indicate the presence of Roman occupation of this site at some stage after 68 CE, since En Gedi came under the control of the Roman Cohors I Milliaria Thracum based in En Gedi after that date, though the excavators wonder if the pigs may have been used for their fat (Fischer, Gichon, and Tal, *'En Boqeq*, 141). Given the siege of Masada in 73 CE it would indeed be reasonable to suppose that Romans used the fertile field systems of En Boqeq as a resource to feed their army.

CONCLUSIONS

In conclusion, there were numerous pharmacological resources of the Dead Sea region, known widely in antiquity. Some medicinal lore about the benefits of these plants and minerals has been preserved through the centuries even to the present day. These resources of the Dead Sea would have been known also by members of a legal society that were particularly concerned to find 'roots, remedies and properties of stones' beneficial for healing. Under the patronage of Herod, who gave them gifts, the Essenes then sent a small group to establish themselves at Qumran and Ain Feshkha, to harness the local pharmacological resources next to the Dead Sea, working alongside those engaged with the processing and careful burial of scrolls. In working in pharmacology they were participating in the culture of medicine, within the wider field of science, understood to be the preserve of Solomon, to whom was attributed all knowledge and wisdom about the natural world, as well as secret knowledge of angels and demons, astrology, physiognomy, and other sciences helpful in preserving health and curing ailments.

Healing interests and procedures are indicated in a number of scrolls, their sectarian or non-sectarian identity being irrelevant in this case, since anything that had healing value would—if Josephus is right—have been searched by the Essenes for beneficial uses. Much of this material would not have been preserved in scroll burials in caves, and much of what was preserved has been lost.

The archaeology of Qumran provides evidence of medicinal products being manufactured at the site, particularly date honey and date wine. Small jars and glass receptacles would have been well suited to being containers for medicinal products. Pottery designed to contain such products was clearly manufactured on site. This is not to say that the production and mixing of medicines sourced from Dead Sea plants and minerals was the only significant industry of Qumran, but that it may well have formed one of several that provided a rationale for a settlement in this place (along with the work of scroll burials). Most importantly, it is an industry that coheres with an attested feature of Essene practice.

General Conclusions

For those who have reached the end of this book, the argument will hopefully seem plain. In our study we have considered the big picture of the context of the Dead Sea Scrolls within the world of Second Temple Judaism. This is important in order that the Scrolls can be properly situated as cultural artefacts within their own time. Because of current confusion about whether the Scrolls can be attributed to the Essenes, it seemed necessary at the start to ensure that the Essenes were defined accurately. In order to do his, all the ancient sources that referred to the Essenes were reviewed. From this close examination, it was possible to see that scholarship has been indebted to a certain biased precon- ception of Judaism, requiring the marginalisation of an esteemed and elite group. The Essenes were a legal society or school of Second Temple Judaism from long before the second century BCE to the second century CE, alienated from the Hasmonean dynasty but much honoured by Herod and his succes- sors. They were considered the most outstanding exemplars of Jewish piety, and were much valued for their expertise in the predictive arts.

They were not a small and isolated sect of ascetics, out of step with other Jews, but situated at the heart of Jewish life. They were influential and important, and they adopted higher standards of purity and law than was in practice in the Temple. Given these superior standards, they were permitted certain dispensations: a separate court than that convened by the High Priest, even though he remained ultimate arbiter of Jewish law, and a separate sacrificial area within the Temple precincts. Such dispensations in no way indicated a rejection of the Temple. Nothing requires us to see the Essenes as pacifists or vegetarians. Essenes were often not married (either by choice, by divorce, or widowhood), but if married this still required them to live in community with other men; there would have been then households of Essene wives, children, and others, but we are told nothing about them in our sources. Our sources channel our thinking in a particular way, but holistically they present a relatively consistent picture, even if at times this is a caricature, as with Pliny. The Essenes lived in many places, in community, eating a pure meal together and studying scripture, while engaging themselves in crafts and other forms of labour in order to be economically self-sufficient, sharing all things in common. They engaged in public life, and esteemed priests within their communities.

In the second part of this study the focus has been on the Dead Sea. A history of the Dead Sea was provided by reference to numerous sources, arranged chronologically. The evidence for Essenes as having a presence beside the Dead Sea is found in Pliny and Dio, two independent witnesses, and not contravened by any other literary source. The specific locus in both texts seems to indicate their occupation of the north-western side of the lake. If this is right, then it would fit easily with the evidence that Essenes were given special gifts and honours from Herod the Great. This area stretching from Jericho to En Gedi was developed as a royal holding by the Hasmoneans, mainly under Alexander Jannaeus in the first third of the first century BCE. When Herod the Great became King of the Jews in 37 BCE he inherited this lucrative zone and more, and developed palaces, forts, and smallholdings in the region in order to consolidate his power in this area and protect his resources, most especially bitumen and balsam.

The site of Qumran was first established by Alexander Jannaeus, utilizing an old Iron Age ruin, as one of a string of fortified settlements along the western side of the Dead Sea. However, from the time Herod came to power, or more probably from 34 BCE, a radical change to the Hasmonean square structure was made, consistent with new occupants creating industries not original to the site. It is suggested that Essenes came to Qumran at the same time that Ain Feshkha was founded, creating a linked zone. The zone was not a centre but an outpost. The Essenes were given this holding as a gift, or loan, and were able to use the area for the burial of scrolls, in order to preserve these texts in perpetuity after they had gone out of use.

The Scrolls are not at all to be detached from the site of Qumran, but exist in part within the precincts of the Qumran settlement, and activities on the southern end of the plateau should be seen alongside what is found in the artificial marl caves: the scrolls were considered and processed, by using preservatives and sealing methods, and wrapped in fine white linen. Qumran was therefore a scroll-burial centre, and probably functioned as such at least until the earthquake of *c.*115 CE destroyed most of the buildings and water system, even with some occupation of Qumran in Period III by Roman auxiliaries for a time, since the Essenes would have continued to live in Ain Feshkha. The final date for any Essene industry of scroll burial is 135 CE, when the severe quashing of the Bar Kokhba revolt absolutely removed Jews from this area and no Jews could return.

Along with the important operation of burying scrolls, the Essenes were also very likely to have been able to utilize the many medicinal resources of the Dead Sea area for the making of pharmacological products, growing plants at Ain Feshkha. The Dead Sea was renowned for its medicinal resources, and the prophecy of Ezekiel 47: 1–12 may well have pointed the Essenes to this area as a locus for their activity of furthering healing. The fact that at Qumran there was processing of medicinal date honey and wine would suggest that other types of pharmacological products were also made there as well.

The method employed in this study has integrated literature and archaeology, since it is a presupposition of this examination that literature, understood correctly, is crucial to a proper understanding of the archaeological material we have around the Dead Sea. However, archaeology itself can illuminate our texts, and in the case of understanding the relationship between the Scrolls and the site of Qumran it is *only* archaeology that tells us the real relationship, just as it was only archaeology that provided evidence of Jewish settlement in the southern Dead Sea after the First Revolt. Method does not, in the end, require an either–or approach, but method is invariably dictated by the types of questions we ask.

Much more could be said about the archaeology of Qumran and the Dead Sea Scrolls, and much more also could be done to explore possible references in the Scrolls to medicines and plants. This work, while seeking to solve intractable mysteries concerning the nature of the Dead Sea Scrolls and Qumran, is therefore offered as a small beginning for other lines of enquiry.

Bibliography

Principal Ancient Sources

Alexander of Aphrodisias, *On Aristotle Meteorology 4*. Eric Lewis (ed. and trans.) (London/Ithaca, NY: Duckworth and Cornell University Press, 1996).

Aristotle, *Meteorologica*, H. D. P. Lee (ed. and trans.) (Loeb Classical Library; London/ Cambridge, MA: Heinemann/Harvard University Press, 1952); Resianne Fontaine (ed.), *Otot ha-shamayim: Samuel Ibn Tibtibon's Hebrew version of Aristotle's Meteorology: A Critical Edition* (Leiden: Brill, 1995).

Asaph the Physician. S. Muntner, 'Asaph Harofe, Sefer Harefuoth (Asaph the Physician, Book of Remedies),' *Koroth* 3 (1965), 396–422 (Heb.).

Burchard, *Burchart of Mount Sion AD 1280* (London: Palestine Pilgrim Texts Society XII, 1896).

Celsus, *De medicina*, W. G. Spencer (ed. and trans.), 3 vols (Loeb Classical Library; London/Cambridge MA: Heinemann/Harvard University Press, 1935–8).

Daniel the Abbot, *Zhitie i knozhenie Danila rus'kyya zemli igumena 1106–1108*, ed. M. A. Venevitinov (Palestinskiy pravosloavnyy sbornik 3: 9; St. Petersburg, 1883–5).

Dead Sea Scrolls. Discoveries in the Judaean Desert (Oxford: OUP, 1955–2007);in particular, Florentino García Martínez, Eibert J. C. Tigchelaar, and A. S. van der Woude, *Qumran Cave 11.II (11Q2–18, 11Q20–31)* (DJD 23; Oxford: OUP, 1998); Stephen Pfann, Philip Alexander, et al. (eds), *Qumran Cave 4 XXVI. Cryptic Texts and Miscellanea, Part 1* (DJD 36; Oxford: OUP, 2000); Deborah Dimant (ed.), *Qumran Cave 4.XXI: Parabiblical Texts, Part 4: Pseudo-Prophetic Texts* (DJD 30; Oxford: OUP, 2001).

Dio Chrysostom. J. W. Cohoon (ed. and trans.), *Dio Chrysostom*, 5 vols (Loeb Classical Library; Cambridge, MA/London: Harvard University Press/William Heinemann, 1961).

Diodorus of Sicily, *Books II. 35-IV. 58*, C. H. Oldfather (ed. and trans.) (Loeb Classical Library; Cambridge, MA: Harvard University Press, 1967); Diodorus of Sicily, *Books XIX. 66–110 and XX*, Russell M. Geer (ed. and trans.) (Loeb Classical Library; Cambridge, MA: Harvard University Press, 1972); Diodorus Siculus (1956, 1968). *The Bibliotheca Historica of Diodorus Siculus*, trans. John Skelton, ed. F. M. Salter and H. L. R. Edwards, 2 vols (Oxford: OUP, 1968).

Dioscorides (Pedanius) of Anazarbus *De materia medica* (Medicorum graecorum opera quae exstant 25; Leipzig: C. Cnobloch, 1829); Dioscorides, *De materia medica*, Eng. trans. Lily Y. Beck (Hildesheim/New York: Olms-Weidmann, 2005).

Egeria, *Itinerarium*, ed. A. Franceschini and R. Weber (Corpus Christianorum Series Latina 175; Turnhout: Brepols, 1965); trans. John Wilkinson, *Egeria's Travels* (Warminster: Aris and Phillips, 1981).

Epiphanius of Salamis. K. Holl (ed.), Epiphanius *I. Ancoratus und Panarion Haer 1–33* (GCS 25; Leiden: Hinrichs, 1915); K. Holl and J. Dummer, *Panarion Haer. 34–64 9* (GCS; Berlin: Academie Verlag, 1980); id. Panarion Haer 65–80 (GCS; Berlin:

Academie Verlag, 1985); Epiphanius of Salamis, Frank Williams (ed. and trans.), *The Panarion of Epiphanius of Salamis, Book 1*, 2nd ed. (Leiden: Brill, 2009).

Eratosthenes. Duane W. Roller (ed. and trans.), *Eratosthenes' Geography*, fragments collected and transated, with commentary and additional material (Princeton: Princeton University Press, 2010).

Eusebius of Caesarea, *Historia Ecclesiastica*. Edouard Schwartz (ed.), *Eusebius, Werke*, Vol. 2 *Die Kirchengeschichte* (GCS 9:1; Leipzig: J. C. Hinrichs, 1903); Eusebius of Caesarea, *Onomasticon. Das Onomastikon der biblischen Ortsnamen,* ed. Erich Klostermann, with parallel work of Jerome, *De locis sanctis* (Hildesheim: Georg Olms Verlagsbuchhandlung, 1904; repr. 1966).

Fabri, Felix, *Evagatorium in Terrae Sanctae, Arabiae et Egypti peregrinationem*, ii C. D. Hassler (ed.) (Stuttgart: Stuttgard.-Literarischerverein, 1843).

Favorinus of Arles. E. Amato (ed.) and Julien, Y. (trans.), *Favorine d'Arles, Œuvres I. Introduction général—Témoignages—Discours aux Corinthiens—Sur la Fortune* (Paris: Les Belles Lettres, 2005); Adelmo Barigazzi (ed.), *Favorino di Arelate, Opere. Introduzione, testo critico e commento* (Testi Greci e Latini con commento filologico 4; Firenze: le Monnier, 1966).

Florus, *Epitome of Roman History*, E.S. Forster (ed. and. trans.) (Loeb Classical Library; London: Putnam and Sons, 1929).

Galen, *Galeni opera omnia*, ed. C. G. Kühn (Leipzig: C. Cnobloch, 1821–33; repr. Hildesheim, 1965).

Galen, *De facultatum naturalium substantia*, Greek text and Eng. trans. Arthur J. Brock (Loeb Classical Library; London: Heinemann, 1916).

Hippolytus of Rome, *Hippolytus, Refutatio omnium haerisium*, ed. M. Marcovich (Patrische Texte und Studien 25; Walter de Gruyter: Berlin and New York, 1986).

The Holy Bible (King James Version). *The Holy Bible Containing the Bookes of the Old & New Testament* (Cambridge: John Field, 1666).

Josephus. *Flavii Iosephi Opera*, Benedikt Niese (ed.), 7 vols (Berlin: Weidmanns, 1885–97); Whiston, William (trans.), *The Works of Flavius Josephus*, ed. by D. S. Margoliouth (London: Ward, Lock and Co., 1906); H. St. J. Thackeray, Ralph Marcus, and Allen Wikgren (ed. and trans.), *Josephus*, 14 vols (Loeb Classical Library; London/New York: Heinemann/G. P. Putnam's Sons, 1926–63); Louis H. Feldman, *Josephus: Jewish Antiquities* (Loeb Classical Library; Cambridge, MA: Harvard University Press, 1965).

Julius Africanus. Martin Wallraff (ed.), *Iulius Africanus: Chronographiae. The Extant Fragments*, with Umberto Roberto and Karl Pinggéra, trans. William Adler (*Die griechischen christlichen Schriftsteller der ersten Jahrhunderte*, NF 15, (Berlin/New York: Walter de Gruyter, 2007).

Justin Martyr, *Dialogue with Trypho*. Miroslav Markovich (ed.), *Iustini Martyris Dialogus cum Tryphone* (Patristische Texte und Studien 47, Berlin/New York: de Gruyter, 1997).

Martianus Capella. James Willis (ed.), Martianus Capella, *De Nuptiis Philologiae et Mercurii* (BSG; Berlin: Teubner, 1983).

The Mishnah. Philip Blackman (ed. and trans.), *Mishnayot: Pointed Hebrew Text, English Translation, Introduction, Notes, Supplement, Appendix, Addenda,*

Corrigenda, 2nd ed. (New York: Judaica Press, 1991); Herbert Danby (trans.), *The Mishnah* (Oxford: OUP, 1933).

The New Testament. Eberhard and Erwin Nestle, with Kurt Aland, Matthew Black, Carlo M. Martini, Bruce M. Metzger, and Allen Wikgren (eds), *Novum Testamentum Graece* (Stuttgart: Deutsche Bibelgesellschaft, 1979).

Pausanias, *Description of Greece*, W. H. S. Jones, and H. A. Omerod (eds and trans.) (Loeb Classical Library; Cambridge, MA: Harvard University Press, 1918); Leopold Cohn and Paul Wendland (eds), *Philonis Alexandrini opera quae supersunt* Editio maior, Vol VI, *Quod omnis probus liber sit. De vita contemplativa. De aeternitate mundi. In Flaccum. Legatio ad Gaium* (Berlin: George Reimer, 1915); F. H. Colson and G. H. Whitaker (eds and trans.), 10 vols (Loeb Classical Library; London/ Cambridge MA: Heinemann/Harvard University Press, 1929–62).

The Piacenza Pilgrim, *Antoninus Placentius: Itinerarium*, ed. H. B. Dewing and G. Downey (Loeb Classical Library; London/Cambridge, MA: Heinemann/Harvard University Press, 1961).

Pliny the Elder. Charles Mayhoff (ed.), *C. Plini Secundi, Naturalis Historiae* I (Stuttgart: B. G. Tübner, 1967); Pliny, *Historia naturalis*, H. Rackham (ed. and trans.), 10 vols (Loeb Classical Library; London/New York: Heinemann/ G. P. Putnam's Sons, 1938).

Pompeius Trogus. *Epitome of the Phillippic History of Pompeius Trogus*, J. C. Yardley (ed. and trans.), with introduction and notes by R. Develin (Atlanta, GA: Scholars Press, 1994).

Porphyry. Michel Patillon and Alain P. Segonds (eds and trans.), *Porphyrie de l'Abstinence* (Paris: Société d'édition, Les Belles-Lettres, 1995).

Posidonius. Felix Jacoby (ed.), *Fragmente der Griechischen Historiker* (CD Rom; Leiden: Brill, 1994). (No. 169); Posidonius. *Fragments I*, Ludwig Edelstein and I. G. Kidd (eds), rev. ed. (Cambridge: CUP, 2005); Posidonius, *Fragments II. The Commentary (i) Testimonia and Fragments 1–149*, I. G. Kidd (ed), (Cambridge: CUP, 1988); Posidonius, *Fragments III. The Translation of the Fragments*, I. G. Kidd (ed. and trans.) (Cambridge: CUP, 1999).

Claudius Ptolemy. Alfred Stückelberger and Gerd Graßhoff (eds), *Klaudios Ptolemaios: Handbuch der Geographie, Griechisch-Deutsch*, 2 vols (Basel: Schwabe Verlag, 2006); Claudius Ptolemaeus, *Geographica Universalis, vetus et nova complectens* (Basel: Henricum Petrum, 1540); Edward Luther Stevenson, (ed. and trans.), *The Geography by Claudius Ptolemy, Greek geographer of the 2nd century A.D.* (New York: Dover, 1932, repr. 1991).

Julius Solinus. Theodor Mommsen (ed.), *C. Iulii Solini Collectanea rerum memorabilium* (Berlin: Weidmann, 1895).

Strabo. *The Geography of Strabo*, Horace Leonard Jones (ed. and trans.), 8 vols (Loeb Classical Library; London/New York: Heinemann/G. P. Putnam's Sons, 1917–32).

Synesius. J. G. Krabinger (ed.), Synesius, *S. Cyrenaei quae exstant opera omnia I: Orationes et homiliarum fragmenta* (Landshut: Thomann, 1850); Kurt Treu (ed.), *Synesios von Kyrene, ein Kommentar zu seinem 'Dion'* (Texte und Untersuchungen zur Geschichte der altchristlichen Literatur 71; Berlin: AkademieVerlag, 1958).

Tacitus. *Cornelii Taciti Historiarum Libri*, C. D. Fisher (ed.) (Oxford: OUP, 1911); Tacitus, *The Histories, Books 4–5*, Clifford H. Moore (ed. and trans.) (Loeb Classical Library; Cambridge, MA: Harvard University Press, 1970).

Theophrastus, *Historia Plantarum. Enquiry into Plants,* Arthur Hort (ed. and trans.) (Theophrastus II; Loeb Classical Library; London: Putnam and Sons, 1916).

Tosephta. Moshe S. Zuckermandel, (ed.), *Tosefta nach den Erfurter und Wiener Handschriften mit Parallelstellen und Varianten,* repr. with new foreword by Saul Lieberman (Jerusalem: Bamberger & Vahrman, 1937).

Xenophilus. Alexander Giannini (ed.), *Paradoxographorum Graecorum Reliquae* (Milan: Istituto Editoriale Milano, 1965).

Modern Scholarship and Sources

Abel, Félix-Marie, *Géographie de la Palestine,* ii (Paris: Librarie Lecoffre, 1938).

Abrahams, Israel, 'Professor Schürer on Life Under the Jewish Law,' *JQR* 11 (1899): 626–42.

Abu-Rabia, Aref, *Folk Medicine among the Bedouin Tribes in the Negev* (Sede Boqer: Social Studies Center, The Jacob Blaustein Institute for Desert Research, 1983).

——*A Bedouin Century: Education and Development among the Negev Tribes in the 20th Century* (New York: Berghahn Books, 2001).

Adam, Alfred, *Antike Berichte über die Essener,* 2nd ed. (Kleine Texte für Vorlesungen und Übungen 182; Berlin: Walter de Gruyter, 1972).

Adler, Yonatan, 'Ritual Baths adjacent to Tombs: An Analysis of the Archaeological Evidence in Light of the Halakhic Sources,' *JSJ* 40 (2009): 55–73.

Al-Eisawi, Dawud M. H., *Field Guide to Wild Flowers of Jordan* (Amman: Jordan Press Foundation, 1998).

Alexander, Philip, 'Notes on the "Imago Mundi" of the Book of Jubilees,' *JJS* 38 (1982): 197–213.

—— 'Incantations and Books of Magic,' in Emil Schürer, with Geza Vermes, Fergus Millar, and Martin Goodman (eds), *The History of the Jewish People in the Age of Jesus Christ (175 B.C.E–A.D. 135),* (Edinburgh: T & T Clark, 1986), iii/i, 342–79.

——'The Parting of the Ways from the Perspective of Rabbinic Judaism,' in James Dunn (ed.), *Jews and Christians: The Parting of the Ways, A.D. 70 to 135, The Second Durham-Tübingen Research Symposium on Earliest Christianity and Judaism, Durham, September, 1989* (Tübingen: Mohr Siebeck, 1989), 1–26.

——'Physiognomy, Initiation, and Rank in the Qumran Community,' in Hubert Cancik, Hermann Lichtenberger, et al. (eds), *Geschichte—Tradition—Reflexion: Festschrift fur Martin Hengel zum 70. Geburtstag: Band I: Judentum* (Tübingen: Mohr Siebeck, 1996), 385–94.

——'The Demonology of the Dead Sea Scrolls,' in Peter W. Flint and James C. VanderKam (eds), *The Dead Sea Scrolls after Fifty Years: A Comprehensive Assessment* (Leiden: Brill, 1998–9), ii, 331–53.

—— 'Enoch and the Beginnings of Jewish Interest in Natural Science,' in Charlotte Hempel, Armin Lange, and Hermann Lichtenberger (eds), *The Wisdom Texts from Qumran and the Development of Sapiential Thought* (Leuven: Peeters/Leuven University Press, 2002), 223–43.

——'What Happened to the Jewish Priesthood after 70?' in Zuleika Rodgers, with M. Daly-Denton and A. Fitzpatrick-McKinley (eds), *A Wandering Galilean: Essays in Honour of Sean Freyne* (Supplements to the Journal for the Study of Judaism; Leiden: Brill, 2009), 3–34.

——and Alexander, Loveday, 'The Image of the Oriental Monarch in the Third Book of Maccabees,' in Tessa Rajak, Sarah Pearce, James Aitken, and Jennifer Dines (eds), *Jewish Perspectives on Hellenistic Rulers* (Berkeley: University of California Press, 2007), 92–109.

Allan, Nigel, 'The Physician in Ancient Israel: His Status and Function,' *Medical History* 45 (2001): 377–94.

Allegro, John, 'Further Messianic References in Qumran Literature,' *JBL* 75 (1956): 174–87.

——*The Sacred Mushroom and the Cross* (London: Hodder and Stoughton, 1970).

——*The Dead Sea Scrolls and the Christian Myth* (Newton Abbott: Westbridge Books, 1979).

Alon, Gedalyahu, *Jews, Judaism and the Classical World: Studies in Jewish History in the times of the Second Temple and the Talmud* (Jerusalem: Magness, 1977).

——*The Jews in their Land in the Talmudic Age (70-640 CE)* (Jerusalem: Magnes, 1980).

Alter, Robert, *The Art of Biblical Narrative* (New York: Basic Books, 1981).

Amar, Zohar, 'The Balsam Wood in the Temple Incense,' *Tehumin* 17 (1997): 473–9 (Heb.).

——'The Ash and the Red Material from Qumran,' *DSD* 5 (1998): 1–15.

——'The Production of Salt and Sulphur from the Dead Sea Region in the Tenth Century According to at-Tamimi,' *PEQ* 130 (1998): 3–7.

Amit, David and Adler, Yonatan, 'The Observance of Ritual Purity after 70 CE: A Reevaluation of the Evidence in Light of Recent Archaeological Discoveries,' in Zeev Weiss, Oded Irshai, Jodi Magness, and Seth Schwartz (eds), *'Follow the Wise': Studies in Jewish History and Culture in Honor of Lee I. Levine* (The Jewish Theological Seminary of America and Hebrew University of Jerusalem; Winona Lake: Eisenbrauns, 2010), 121–43.

——and Magness, Jodi, 'Not a Settlement of Hermits or Essenes: A Response to Y. Hirschfeld, "A Settlement of Hermits above 'En Gedi",' *Tel Aviv* 27 (2000): 273–85.

Appelbaum, Shimon, 'The Zealots: The Case for Revaluation,' *JRS* 61 (1971): 155–70.

Arbel, Daphna, 'Divine Secrets and Divination,' in April D. De Conick (ed.), *Paradise Now: Essays on Early Jewish and Christian Mysticism* (Atlanta: SBL, 2006), 355–79.

Argall, Randal A., 'A Hellenistic Jewish Source on the Essenes in Philo, Every Good Man Is Free 75-91 and Josephus, Antiquities 18.18–22,' in Randal A. Argall, Beverly A. Bow, and Rodney A. Werline (eds), *For a Later Generation: The Transformation of Tradition in Israel, Early Judaism and Early Christianity* (Harrisburg, PA: Trinity Press International, 2000), 13–24.

Atkinson, Kenneth, and Jodi Magness, 'Josephus's Essenes and the Qumran Community,' *JBL* 129 (2010): 336–40.

Audet, Jean-Paul, 'Qumrân et la notice de Pline sur les Esséniens,' *RB* 68 (1961): 346–87.

Avi-Yonah, Michael, *A History of Israel of the Holy Land* (London: Macmillan, 1969).

——*The Jews under Roman and Byzantine Rule: A Political History of Palestine from the Bar Kokhba War to the Arab Conquest* (Jerusalem: Magnes, 1984).

Bacon, B. W., 'Pharisees and Herodians in Mark,' *JBL* 39 (1920): 102–12.

Baillet, Maurice, Milik, Józef T., and de Vaux, Roland, *Les 'Petites Grottes' de Qumran* (DJD 3; Oxford: OUP, 1962).

Bar Adon, Pesach, 'Another Settlement of the Judean Desert Sect at `En el-Ghuweir on the Shores of the Dead Sea,' *BASOR* 227 (1977): 1–26.

——'Excavations in the Judean Desert,' `Atiqot 9 (1989): 1–88 (Hebrew).

Bar-Nathan, Rachel, 'Qumran and the Hasmonaean and Herodian Winter Palaces of Jericho: The Implication of the Pottery Finds on the Interpretation of the Settlement at Qumran,' in Katharina Galor, Jean-Baptiste Humbert, and Jürgen Zangenberg (eds), *Qumran, the Site of the Dead Sea Scrolls: Archaeological Interpretations and Debates* (Leiden: Brill, 2006), 264–77.

Barag, Dan, 'Alexander Jannaeus—Priest and King,' in Aren M. Maeir, Jodi Magness, and Lawrence Schiffman (eds), *'Go Out and Study the Land' (Judges 18: 2): Archaeological, Historical and Textual Studies in Honor of Hanan Eshel* (Leiden: Brill, 2011), 1–5.

Barclay, John, *Flavius Josephus: Against Apion: Translation and Commentary* (*Josephus* 10; Leiden: Brill, 2006).

Barton, T. S., *Power and Knowledge: Astrology, Physiognomics and Medicine under the Roman Empire* (Ann Arbor: University of Michigan Press, 1994).

Battles, Matthew, *Library: An Unquiet History* (New York: W. W. Norton, 2003).

Bauckham, Richard, *Jesus and the Eyewitnesses: The Gospels as Eyewitness Testimony* (Grand Rapids: Eerdmans, 2006).

Baumback, Gunther, 'The Saducees in Josephus,' in Louis H. Feldman and Gohei Hata (eds), *Josephus, The Bible and History* (Leiden: Brill, 1988), 173–95.

Baumgarten, Albert I., 'Josephus and Hippolytus on the Pharisees,' *HUCA* 55 (1984): 1–25.

——'Josephus on Essene Sacrifice,' *JJS* 45 (1994): 169–83.

——'The Temple Scroll, Toilet Practices and the Essenes,' *Jewish History* 10 (1996): 9–20.

——*The Flourishing of Jewish Sects in the Maccabean Era: An Interpretation* (Journal for the Study of Judaism Supplement Series 55; Leiden: Brill, 1997).

——'Who Cares and Why Does it Matter? Qumran and the Essenes, Once Again!' *DSD* 11 (2004): 174–90.

Baumgarten, Joseph M., 'Sacrifice and Worship among the Jewish Sectarians of the Dead Sea (Qumran) Scrolls,' *HTR* 46 (1953): 141–59, repr. in id. *Studies in Qumran Law* (Leiden: Brill, 1977), 39–56.

——'The Essenes and the Temple: A Reappraisal,' in id. *Studies in Qumran Law* (Leiden: Brill, 1977), 59–62.

——'The Pharisaic-Sadducean Controversies about Purity and the Qumran Text,' *JJS* 31 (1980): 157–70.

——'The 4Q Zadokite Fragments on Skin Disease,' *JJS* 41 (1990): 153–65.

Baur, Ferdinand C., *De Ebionitarum origine et doctrina, ab essenis repetenda* (Tübingen: Hopferi de l'Orme, 1831).

Beagon, Mary, *Roman Nature: The Thought of Pliny the Elder* (Oxford: OUP, 1992).

Beall, Todd S., *Josephus' Description of the Essenes Illustrated by the Dead Sea Scrolls* (Cambridge: CUP, 1988).

Bélis, Mirielle, 'Des Textiles: Catalogues et Commentaires,' in Jean-Baptiste Humbert and Jan Gunneweg (eds), *Khirbet Qumrân et 'Ain Feshkha II: Études d'anthropologie, de physique et de chemie* (Novum Testamentum et Orbis Antiquus, Series Archaeologica 3; Academic Press, Éditions Saint-Paul, Fribourg, Suisse/Vandenhoeck & Ruprecht, Göttingen, 2003), 207–76.

——'Les manuscrits de Qumrân: Comment se sont-ils conservés?' *L'Archéo-thema: Revue d'archéologie et d'histoire* 2 (May–June, 2009), 41–5.

——'The Workshops at 'Ein Feshkha: A New Hypothesis,' in Galor, Humbert, and Zangenberg, *Qumran*, 253–6.

Ben Ezra, Daniel Stökl, 'Old Caves and Young Caves: A Statistical Re-evaluation of a Qumran Consensus,' *DSD* 14 (2007): 313–33.

——'Further Reflections on Caves 1 and 11: A Response to Florentino García Martínez,' in Hempel, *Dead Sea Scrolls*, 211–20.

Ben-Dov, Jonathan, 'Scientific Writings in Aramaic and Hebrew at Qumran: Translation and Concealment,' in Katell Berthelot and Daniel Stökl Ben Ezra (eds), *Aramaica Qumranica: Proceedings of the Conference on the Aramaic Texts from Qumran in Aix-en-Provence, 30 June–2 July 2008* (Leiden: Brill, 2010), 379–402.

Bennett, W. J., 'The Herodians of Mark's Gospel,' *NT* 17 (1975): 9–14.

Benoit, Pierre, Milik, J. T., and de Vaux, Roland, *Les Grottes de Murabba'at* (2 vols; DJD 2; Oxford: OUP, 1960).

Bergmeier, Roland, *Die Essener-Berichte des Flavius Josephus: Quellenstudien zu den Essenertexten im Werk des judischen Historiographen* (Kampen: Kok Pharos, 1993).

Bergsma, John, 'The Relationship between Jubilees and the Early Enochic Books (Astronomical Book and Book of the Watchers),' in Gabriele Boccaccini and Giovanni Ibba, with the collaboration of Jason von Ehrenkrook, James Waddell, and Jason Zurawski (eds), *Enoch and the Mosaic Torah* (Grand Rapids: Eerdmans, 2009), in 36–51.

Betz, Hans Dieter (ed.), *The Greek Magical Papyri in Translation, including the Demotic Spells* (Chicago: The University of Chicago Press, 1986).

Bhayro, Siam, *The Shemihazah and Asael Narrative of 1 Enoch 6–11: Introduction, Text, Translation and Commentary with reference to Ancient Near Eastern and Biblical Antecedents* (Münster: Ugarit-Verlag, 2005).

Bickerman, Elias J., 'Les Hérodiens,' *RB* 47 (1938): 184–97 reprinted in id. *Studies in Jewish and Christian History* (Leiden: Brill, 1976), 22–34.

——'The Name of Christians,' *HTR* 42 (1949): 109–24.

Bieringer, Reimund, Pollefeyt, Didier, and Vandecasteel-Vanneuville, Frederique (eds), *Anti-Judaism and the Fourth Gospel* (Louisville, KY: Westminster John Knox Press, 2001), 121–40.

Bijovsky, Gabriella, 'A Hoard of Coins of Mattathias Antigonus from 'Ein Feshkha,' *IEJ* 54 (2004): 75–6.

Bilde, Per, 'The Essenes in Philo and Josephus,' in Frederick H. Cryer and Thomas L. Thompson (eds), *Qumran between the Old and New Testaments* (Journal for the Study of the Old Testament Suppl. Series 290; Sheffield: JSOT Press, 1998).

Binns, John, *Ascetics and Ambassadors of Christ: The Monasteries of Palestine 314–631* (Oxford: OUP, 1994).

Birnbaum, Ellen, 'A Leader with Vision in the Ancient Jewish Diaspora: Philo of Alexandria,' in Jack Wertheimer (ed.), *Jewish Religious Leadership: Image and Reality*, I (New York: Jewish Theological Seminary, 2004), 57–90.

Black, C. Clifton, *Mark: Images of an Apostolic Interpreter* (Columbia: University of South Carolina Press, 1994).

Black, Matthew, 'The Account of the Essenes in Hippolytus and Josephus,' in William D. Davies and David Daube (eds), *The Background of the New Testament and its Eschatology* (Cambridge: CUP, 1956), 172–82.

——*The Scrolls and Christian Origins: Studies in the Jewish Background of the New Testament* (London: Thomas Nelson, 1961).

——'The Patristic Accounts of Jewish Sects,' in id. *The Scrolls and Christian Origins* (Edinburgh: Nelson, 1962).

Bloch, R. M., 'Red Salt and Grey Salt,' *Mad`a* 6 (1962): 3–8.

Block, Daniel, *The Book of Ezekiel, Chapters 25–48* (Grand Rapids: Eerdmans, 1998).

Boccaccini, Gabriele, *Beyond the Essene Hypothesis: The Parting of the Ways between Qumran and Enochic Judaism* (Grand Rapids: Eerdmans, 1998).

Bonner, Campbell, *Studies in Magical Amulets, Chiefly Graeco-Roman* (Ann Arbor: University of Michigan Press, 1950), 208–21.

Borgen, Peder, Kåre Fuglseth and Roald Skarsten, *The Philo Index: A Complete Word Index to the Writings of Philo of Alexandria* (Grand Rapids: Eerdmans, 2000).

Bousset, Wilhelm, *Die Religion des Judentums im neutestamentichen Zeitaiter* (Berlin: Reuther, 1903).

Boyarin, Daniel, *Carnal Israel: Reading Sex in Talmudic Culture* (Berkeley: University of California Press, 1993).

——*Border Lines: The Partition of Judaeo-Christianity* (Philadelphia: University of Pennsylvania, 2004).

Brandt, Wilhelm, *Die Judischen Baptismen oder das religiose Waschen und Baden im Judentum mit Einschluss der Judenchristentums* (Giessen: Topelmann, 1910).

Braun, Willi, 'Were New Testament Herodians Essenes? A Critique of an Hypothesis,' *RQ* 14 (1989): 75–88.

Brayer, Menahem M., 'Medical, Hygienic and Psychological Aspects of the Dead Sea Scrolls,' *Harofe Haivri: The Hebrew Medical Journal* 37 (1964): 1, 9–118 (Heb.), 298–285 (Eng.); 2: 125–35 (Heb.), 272–61 (Eng.); 38 (1965) 1: 156–69 (Heb.), 254–48 (Eng.).

——'Psychosomatics, Hermetic Medicine and Dream Interpretation in the Qumran Literature,' *JQR* 60 (1969): 112–27; 213–30.

Bregman, Jay, *Synesius of Cyrene: Philosopher-Bishop* (Berkeley: University of California Press, 1982).

Brenk, Frederick, '*With Unperfumed Voice': Studies in Plutarch, in Greek Literature, Religion and Philosophy and in the New Testament* (Potsdamer Altertumswissenschaftliche Beiträge 21; Stuttgart: Franz Steiner, 2007).

Brooke, George, 'The Deuteronomic Character of 4Q252,' in John C. Reeves and John Kampen (eds), *Pursuing the Text: Studies in Honor of Ben Zion Wacholder on the Occasion of his Seventieth Birthday* (Sheffield: Sheffield Academic Press, 1994), 121–35.

——'The Thematic content of 4Q252,' *JQR* 85 (1994): 33–59.

——'Langues, sciences et techniques,' in Farah Mebarki and Emile Puech (eds), *Les manuscrits de la mer Morte* (Rodez: Rouergue, 2002), 142–8.

Brooke, George, *Qumran and the Jewish Jesus: Reading the New Testament in the Light of the Scrolls* (Cambridge: Grove Books, 2005).

Broshi, Magen, 'Date Beer and Date Wine in Antiquity,' *PEQ* 139 (2007): 55–9.

——'Essenes at Qumran? A Rejoinder to Albert Baumgarten,' *DSD* 14 (2007): 25–33.

——and Eshel, Hanan, 'Residential Caves at Qumran,' *DSD* 6 (1999): 285–323.

——, ——'Three Seasons of Excavations at Qumran,' *JRA* 17 (2004): 321–32.

——, ——'Qumran and the Dead Sea Scrolls: The Contention of Twelve Theories,' in Douglas R. Edwards (ed.), *Religion and Society in Roman Palestine: Old Questions, New Approaches* (London/New York: Routledge, 2004), 162–9.

Bruneau, Philippe, 'Les Israélites de Délos et la juiverie délienne,' *Bulletin de Correspondance Hellénique* (1982): 465–504.

Buckley, Jorunn Jacobson, *The Mandaeans: Ancient Texts and Modern People* (New York: OUP, 2002).

Buckley, Stephen A., Clark, Katherine A., and Evershed, Richard P., 'Complex Organic Chemical Balms of Pharaonic Animal Mummies,' *Nature* 431 (2004): 294–9.

——and Evershed, Richard P, 'Organic chemistry of embalming agents in Pharaonic and Graeco-Roman mummies,' *Nature* 413 (2001): 837–41.

Burchard, Christoph, 'Pline et les Esséniens: à propos d'un article récent,' *RB* 69 (1962): 533–69.

——'Solin et les Esséniens. Remarques à propos d'un article negligée,' *RB* 74 (1967): 392–407.

——'Zur Nebenüberlieferung von Josephus Bericht über die Essener, *Bell.* 2, 119–161 bei Hippolyt, Porphyrius, Eusebius, Niketas Choniates und anderen,' in Otto Betz, Klaus K. Haacker, and Martin Hengel (eds), *Josephus Studien: Untersuchungen zu Josephus dem antiken Judentum und dem Neuen Testament, Festschrift für Otto Michel* (Göttingen: Vandenhoeck & Ruprecht, 1974), 77–96.

——'Die Essener bei Hippolyt, REF. IX 18, 2–28, 2 und Josephus, Bell. 2, 119–161,' *JSJ* 8 (1977): 1–41.

Burckhardt, John Lewis, *Travels in Syria and the Holy Land* (London: John Murray, 1822).

Burkert, Walter, *Lore and Science in Ancient Pythagoreanism*, trans. E. Minar Jr (Cambridge, MA: Harvard University, 1972).

Burns, Joshua Ezra, 'Essene Sectarianism and Social Differentiation in Judaea after 70 CE,' *HTR* 99 (2006): 247–74.

Burrows, Millar, *The Dead Sea Scrolls* (London: Secker and Warburg, 1956).

Butí, Salvador, Salvadó, Nati, Lope, Nuria, Papiol, Emilia, Heras, Elena, and Gunneweg, Jan, 'Determination of Wine Residues in Qumran Amphora-35,' in Jan Gunneweg, Charles Greenblatt, and Annemie Adriaans (eds), *Bio- and Material Cultures at Qumran* (Papers from a COST Action G8 working group held in Israel on 22–3 May 2005; Fraunhofer IRB: Stuttgart, 2006), 71–80.

Campbell, Jonathan, 'The Qumran Sectarian Writings,' in William Horbury, W. D. Davies, and John Sturdy (eds), *The Cambridge History of Judaism* (Cambridge: CUP, 1999), 3: 813–21.

Cansdale, Lena, *Qumran and the Essenes: A Re-Evaluation of the Evidence* (Tübingen: J. C. B. Mohr, 1997).

Capper, Brian, 'The Palestinian Cultural Context of Earliest Christian Community of Goods,' in Richard J. Bauckham (ed.), *The Book of Acts in Its Palestinian Setting* (Grand Rapids: Eerdmans, 1995), 323–56.

——'Essene Community Houses and Jesus' Early Community,' in James H. Charlesworth (ed.), *Jesus and Archaeology* (Grand Rapids: Eerdmans, 2006), 472–502.

Cargill, Robert R., 'The Qumran Digital Model: An Argument for Archaeological Reconstruction in Virtual Reality and Response to Jodi Magness,' *Near Eastern Archaeology* 72/1 (2009): 28–47.

——*Qumran through (Real) Time: A Virtual Reconstruction of Qumran and the Dead Sea Scrolls* (Bible in Technology 1; Piscataway, NJ: Gorgias Press, 2009).

——'The Fortress at Qumran: A History of Interpretation,' http://www.bibleinterp.com/articles/qumfort.shtml.

Cartwright, John, *An Essay Upon the Virtues of Balm of Gilead* (London: G. Kearsly, 1760).

Casey, Maurice, *Aramaic Sources for Mark's Gospel* (Cambridge: CUP, 1998).

Charlesworth, James H., *The Discovery of a Dead Sea Scroll (4QTherapeia): Its Importance in the History of Medicine and Jesus Research* (Lubbock: Texas Tech University Press, 1985).

——'Jewish Astrology in the Talmud, Pseudepigrapha, the Dead Sea Scrolls and Early Palestinian Synagogues,' *HTR* 70 (1977): 183–200.

——(ed.), *Old Testament Pseudepigrapha* (London: Darton, Longman and Todd, 1983).

——'A Misunderstood Recently Published Dead Sea Scroll (4Q341),' *Explorations* 2 (Philadelphia: American Institute for the Study of Religious Co-operation, 1987).

Chepey, Stuart D., *Nazirites in Late Second Temple Judaism: A Survey of Ancient Jewish Writings, the New Testament, Archaeological Evidence, and other Writings from Late Antiquity* (Leiden: Brill, 2005).

Chitty, Derwas A., *The Desert a City: an Introduction to the Study of Egyptian and Palestinian Monasticism* (Oxford: Blackwell, 1966).

Christiansen, Arne Søby, *Cassiodorus, Jordanes and the History of the Goths* (Copenhagen: Museum Tusculanum Press, 2002).

Chroust, Anton-Hermann, 'The Ideal Polity of the Early Stoics: Zeno's Republic,' *The Review of Politics* 27 (1965): 173–83.

Clamer, Christa, '`Ain Ez-Zara Excavations 1986,' *Annual of the Department of Antiquities of Jordan* 33 (1989), 217–25.

——*Fouilles archéologiques de `Aïn ez-Zâra/Callirhoé, villegiature herodienne* (Beirut: Institut Français d'archéologie du Proche-Orient, 1997).

——'The Hot Springs of Kallirrhoe and Baarou,' in Michele Piccirillo and Eugenio Alliata (eds), *The Madaba Map Centenary 1897–1997. Travelling through the Byzantine Umayyad Period, Proceedings of the International Conference Held in Amman, 7–9 April 1997* (Collectio Maior 40; Jerusalem: Studium Biblicum Franciscanum, 1999), 221–5.

——'Paradies am Meeresrand,' in Zangenberg (ed.), *Das Tote Meer*, 113–24.

Clark Kee, Howard, *Medicine, Miracle and Magic in the New Testament* (Cambridge: CUP, 1986).

Clermont-Ganneau, Charles, 'The Jerusalem Researches III,' *PEFQSt* (1874): 80–4.

Cohen, Shaye, 'The Significance of Yavneh: Pharisees, Rabbis and the End of Jewish Sectarianism,' *HUCA* 55 (1984): 27–53.

——*From the Maccabees to the Mishnah*, 2nd ed. (Louisville: Westminster John Knox, 2006).

Cohn, Yehudah, 'Were Tefillin Phylacteries?' *JJS* 59 (2008): 55–79.

Collins, John J., 'Essenes,' in David Noel Freedman (ed.), *Anchor Bible Dictionary* (New York: Doubleday, 1992), ii, 619–26.

——*The Apocalyptic Imagination: An Introduction to Jewish Apocalyptic Literature*, 2nd ed. (Grand Rapids: Eerdmans, 1998).

——*Between Athens and Jerusalem: Jewish Identity in the Hellenistic Diaspora*, 2nd ed. (Grand Rapids: Eerdmans, 2000).

——'Forms of Community in the Dead Sea Scrolls,' in P. M. Shalom et al. (eds), *Emanuel: Studies in Hebrew Bible, Septuagint, and Dead Sea Scrolls in honor of Emanuel Tov* (Leiden: Brill, 2003), 97–111.

——'"The Yahad" and "The Qumran Community",' in Charlotte Hempel and Judith M. Lieu (eds), *Biblical Traditions in Transmission: Essays in Honour of Michael A. Knibb* (Leiden: Brill, 2006), 81–96.

——*Beyond the Qumran Community: the sectarian movement of the Dead Sea Scrolls* (Grand Rapids: Eerdmans, 2010).

——'Artapanus,' in Charlesworth, *Old Testament Pseudepigrapha*, ii, 897.

Collins, Nina, *The Library in Alexandria and the Bible in Greek* (Leiden: Brill, 2000).

Columba, Gaetano M., 'Le fonti di Giulio Solino,' in *Rassegna di antichità classica* 1 (1895), 7–32; 2 (1896), 105–16 (1896), reprinted id. *Richerche storiche i. Geografia e Geografi del Mondo antico* (Palermo: Trimarchi, 1935).

Conder, Claude R., *Tent Work in Palestine*, ii (London: Richard Bentley and Sons, 1878).

Cook, John Granger, *The Interpretation of the Old Testament in Greco-Roman Paganism* (Tübingen: Mohr Siebeck, 2004).

Corbo, Virgilio, 'La fortezza di Macheronte: Rapporto preliminare della prima campagna di scavo: 8 settembre–28 ottobre 1978,' *Liber Annuus* 28 (1978): 217–38.

——'La reggia-fortezza erodiana. Rapporto preliminare alla seconda campagna di scavo: 3 settembre–20 ottobre 1979,' *Liber Annuus* 29 (1979): 315–26.

——'La fortezza di Macheronte (Al-Mishnaqa). Rapporto preliminare alla terza campagna di scavo: 8 settembre–11 octobre 1980,' *Liber Annuus* 30 (1980): 365–76.

——and Loffreda, Stannislao, 'Nuove scoperte alla fortezza di Macheronte. Rapporto preliminare alla quarta campagna di scavo: 7 settembre–10 ottobre 1981,' *Liber Annuus* 31 (1981), 257–86.

Cotton, Hannah M., and Eck, W., 'Ein Staatsmonopol und seiner Folgen: Plinius, Naturalis Historia 12,123 und der Preis für Balsam,' *Rheinisches Museum für Philologie* 140 (1997): 153–6.

——and Geiger, Joseph, *Masada II: The Yigael Yadin Excavations 1963–1965 Final Reports/the Latin and Greek Documents* (Washington DC: Biblical Archaeology Society, 1989).

——and Greenfield, Jonas C., 'Babatha's "Patria": Maḥoza, Maḥoz Eglatain and Zo`ar,' *ZPE* 107 (1995): 126–34.

——and Larson, Erik, '4Q460/4Q350 and Tampering with Qumran Texts in Antiquity,' in Shalom M. Paul, Robert A. Kraft, Eva Ben-David, Lawrence H. Schiffman, and Weston W. Fields (eds), *Emanuel: Studies in Hebrew Bible, Septuagint, and Dead Sea Scrolls in Honor of Emanuel Tov* (Leiden: Brill, 2003), 113–25.

——'The Date of the Fall of Masada: The Evidence of the Masada Papyri,' *Zeitschrift für Papyrologie und Epigraphik* 78 (1989): 157–62.

——Cockle, W. E. H., and Millar, Fergus G. B., 'The Papyrology of the Roman Near East: A Survey,' *JRS* 85 (1995): 214–35.

——and Yardeni, Ada, *Aramaic, Hebrew and Greek Documentary Texts from the Naḥal Ḥever and Other Sites, with an Appendix Containing Alleged Qumran Texts, the Seiyal Collection*, ii (DJD 27; Oxford: OUP, 1997).

Crane, Eve, *A Book of Honey* (Oxford: OUP, 1980).

——*The World History of Bee-Keeping and Honey Hunting* (London: Routledge, 1999).

Cross, Frank Moore, *The Ancient Library of Qumran*, rev. ed. (New York: Anchor, 1961).

Crown, Alan D. and Lena Cansdale, 'Qumran: Was it an Essene Settlement?' *BAR* 20 (1994): 24–35, 73–4, 76–8.

Cryer, Frederic, *Divination in Ancient Israel and its Near Eastern Environment: A Socio-Historical Investigation* (JSOT Suppl. Series 142. Sheffield: JSOT/Sheffield Academic Press, 1994), 157–9, 267–72.

Daniel, Constantin, 'Esséniens, zélotes et sicaires et leur mention par paronymie dans le N.T.,' *Numen* 13 (1966): 88–115.

——'Les "Hérodiens" du Nouveau Testament sont-ils les Esséniens?' *RQ* 6 (1967): 31–53.

——'Nouveaux arguments en faveur de l'identification des Hérodiens et des Esséniens,' *RQ* 27 (1970): 397–402.

Davies, Philip R., *Qumran* (Cities of the Biblical World; Cambridge: Lutterworth Press, 1982).

——'Hasidim in the Maccabean Period,' in id. *Sects and Scrolls: Essays on Qumran and Related Topics* (South Florida Studies in the History of Judaism 134; Atlanta: Scholars Press, 1996), 5–22.

Davies, Steven L., *Jesus the Healer: Possession, Trance and the Origins of Christianity* (London: SCM, 1995).

Davila, James, *Descenders to the Chariot: the People behind the Hekhalot Literature* (Leiden: Brill, 2001).

de Hoop, Raymond, *Genesis 49 in its Literary and Historical Context* (Leiden: Brill, 1999).

de Jonge, Henk Jan, '"The Jews"' in Bieringer, Pollefeyt, and Vandecasteel-Vanneuville, *Anti-Judaism*, 121–40.

de Rossi, Azariah, *The Light of the Eyes*, trans. from the Hebrew, with an introduction by Joanna Weinberg (New Haven: Yale University Press, 2001).

de Vaux, Roland, 'Post-Scriptum: La Cachette des Manuscrits Hébreux,' *RB* 56 (1949): 234–7.

——'Exploration de la Région de Qumran,' *RB* 60 (1953): 540–61.

——'Fouille au Khirbet Qumrân,' *RB* 60 (1953): 83–106.

de Vaux, Roland, 'Fouilles au Khirbet Qumrân,' *RB* 61 (1954): 206–36.

——'Fouilles de Khirbet Qumrân,' *RB* 63 (1956): 533–77.

——'Fouilles de Feshkha,' *RB* 66 (1959): 225–55.

——*L'archéologie et les Manuscrits de la Mer Morte* (London: British Academy, 1961).

——*Archaeology and the Dead Sea Scrolls* (The Schweich Lectures of the British Academy; Oxford: OUP, 1973).

——*Die Ausgrabungen von Qumran und En Feschcha IA Die Grabungstagebücher*, German translation and notes by Ferdinand Rohrhirsch and Bettina Hofmeir (Gottingen: Vandenhoeck & Ruprecht, 1996).

Deines, Roland, *Die Pharisäer. Ihr Verständnis als Spiegel der christlichen und jüdischen Forschung seit Wellhausen und Graetz* (WUNT 101; Tübingen: Mohr-Siebeck, 1997).

——'The Pharisees between "Judaisms" and "Common Judaism",' in D. A. Carson, P. T. O'Brien, and M. A. Seifrid (eds), *Justification and Variegated Nomism: Volume 1—The Complexities of Second Temple Judaism* (Tübingen/Grand Rapids; Mohr Siebeck/Baker Academic, 2001), 443–504.

Deming, Will, *Paul on Marriage and Celibacy: The Hellenistic Background of 1 Corinthians 7*, 2nd ed. (Grand Rapids: Eerdmans, 2004).

Desideri, Paolo, *Dione di Prusa: un intellectuale greco nell'impero romano* (Messina/Florence: G. D'Anna, 1978).

——'Dione di Prusa fra hellenismo e romantà,' ANRW 2.33.5 (1991), 3882–902.

——'City and Country in Dio,' in Swain, *Dio Chrysostom*, 93–107.

Dixon, William Hepworth, *The Holy Land*, I, 2nd ed. (London: Chapman and Hall, 1866).

Donahue, John R., 'Windows and Mirrors: The Setting of Mark's Gospel,' *CBQ* 57 (1995): 1–26.

——and Harrington, Daniel J., *The Gospel of Mark* (Sacra Pagina; Collegeville, MN: Liturgical Press, 2002).

Donceel, Robert and Donceel-Voûte, Pauline, 'The Archaeology of Khirbet Qumrân,' in Michael Wise, Norman Golb, John J. Collins, and Dennis Pardee (eds), *Methods of Investigations of the Dead Sea Scrolls and the Khirbet Qumran Site: Present Realities and Future Prospects* (New York: Annals of the New York Academy of Sciences 722, 1994), 1–38.

——'Poursuite des travaux de publication du matériel archéologique de Khirbet Qumrân: Les lampes en terre cuite,' in Z. J. Kapera (ed.), *Mogilany 1995: Papers on the Dead Sea Scrolls Offered in Memory of Aleksy Klawek* (Qumranica Mogilanensia 15; Enigma Press, Cracow, 1998), 87–104.

Donceel-Voûte, Pauline, 'Les ruines de Qumrân réinterprétées,' *Archéologia* 298 (1994): 24–35.

——'Traces of Fragrance along the Dead Sea,' *Res Orientales* 11 (1998), 93–124.

Doran, Robert, 'Pseudo-Eupolemus,' in Charlesworth, *Old Testament Pseudepigrapha*, ii, 873–82.

Doudna, Gregory L., 'The Legacy of an Error in Archaeological Interpretation: The Dating of the Qumran Cave Scroll Deposits,' in Galor, Humbert, and Zangenberg, *Qumran*, 147–57.

Driver, Godfrey R., *The Hebrew Scrolls from the Neighbourhood of Jericho and the Dead Sea* (London: OUP, 1951).

——*The Judaean Scrolls: The Problem and a Solution* (Oxford: Blackwell, 1965).

——'Myths of Qumran,' *The Annual of Leeds University Oriental Society* 6 (1966–68): 23–48.

Droz, E. and Sharples, R.W., 'Alexander of Aphrodisias: Scholasticism and Innovation,' *ANRW* 2.36.2 (1987), 1176–243.

Dueck, Daniela, *Strabo of Amasia: A Greek Man of Letters in Augustan Rome* (London New York: Routledge, 2000).

Duling, Dennis C., 'Solomon, Exorcism and the Son of David,' *HTR* 68 (1975): 235–52.

——'Testament of Solomon,' in Charlesworth, *Old Testament Pseudepigrapha*, ii, 944–56; id. 'The Legend of Solomon the Magician in Antiquity: Problem and Perspectives,' in *Proceedings: Eastern Great Lakes Biblical Society* 4 (1984): 1–23.

——'The Eleazar Miracle and Solomon's Magical Wisdom in Flavius Josephus' *Antiquitates Judaicae* 8.42–49', *HTR* 78 (1985): 1–25.

Dupont-Sommer, André, 'On a Passage of Josephus relating to the Essenes (Antiq. XVIII, 22),' *JSS* 1 (1956): 361–6.

——*The Essene Writings from Qumran*, trans. by Geza Vermes of *Les Écrits esséniens découverts près de la Mer Morte* (Oxford: Blackwell, 1961).

Dvorjetski, Estée, 'Medicinal Hot Springs in Eretz-Israel and in the Decapolis during the Hellenistic, Roman and Byzantine Periods,' *ARAM Periodical*, 4, 1 & 2 (1992): 425–49.

——'The Medicinal Hot Springs of Kallirrhoe,' *Ariel* 110–11 (1995): 306–8 (Heb.).

——'The Thermo-Mineral Springs and the Ships' Load in the Dead Sea According to the Madaba Map', in G. Barkai and E. Schiler (eds), *Eretz-Israel in the Madaba Map* (Jerusalem: Ariel, 1996), 82–8 (Heb.).

——'Healing Waters: The Social World of Hot Springs in Roman Palestine,' *BAR* 30, 4 (2004): 16–27, 60.

——*Leisure, Pleasure and Healing: Spa Culture and Medicine in Ancient Eastern Mediterranean* (Leiden: Brill, 2007).

Ehud, Netzer, 'Did any Perfume Industry Exist at 'Ein Feshkha?' *IEJ* 55 (2005): 97–100.

Eisenman, Robert, *James the Brother of Jesus: The Key to Unlocking the Secrets of Christianity and the Dead Sea Scrolls* (New York: Penguin, 1998).

Eisenmenger, Johan Andreas, *Entdecktes Judenthum* (Schierferl: Dresden, 1893).

Eissfeldt, Otto, 'Der gegenwärtige Stand der Erforschung der in Palästina . . . Handscriften,' *Theologische Literaturzeitung* 74 (1949): cols. 595–600.

Elior, Rachael, *The Mystical Origins of Hasidism*, trans. Shalom Carmy (Portland, OR: Littman Library of Jewish Civilization, 2006).

——*Memory and Oblivion: The Secret of the Dead Sea Scrolls* (Jerusalem: Van Leer Institute and Kibbutz haMeuchad, 2009) (Heb.).

Elledge, Casey D., *Life after Death in Early Judaism: The Evidence of Josephus* (WUNT II/208; Tübingen: Mohr Siebeck, 2006).

Eshel, Esther, 'The *Imago Mundi* of the Genesis Apocryphon,' in L. R. LiDonnici and A. B. Liber (eds), *Heavenly Tablets: Interpretation, Identity and Tradition in Ancient Judaism* (Leiden: Brill, 2007), 111–31.

Eshel, Hanan, *The Dead Sea Scrolls and the Hasmonean State* (Grand Rapids: Eerdmans, 2008).

——*Qumran: Scrolls, Caves, History* (Jerusalem: Carta, 2009).

——'On the Ongoing Research of the Refuge Caves in the Judean Desert,' in Eshel and Porat, *Refuge Caves of the Bar Kokhba Revolt*, 1–9 (Heb.).

——and Amit, David, *Refuge Caves of the Bar Kochba Revolt*, i (Jerusalem: Israel Exploration Society, 1998) (Heb.).

——Broshi, Magen, Freund, Richard A., and Schultz, Brian, 'New Data on the *Cemetery* East of Khirbet Qumran,' *DSD* 9 (2002): 135–65.

——and Porat, Roi, *Refuge Caves of the Bar Kokhba Revolt*, ii (Jerusalem: Israel Exploration Society, 2009) (Heb.).

Evans, Elizabeth C., 'Galen the Physician as a Physiognomist,' *Transactions and Proceedings of the American Philological Association* 76 (1945), 287–98.

Fagan, Garrett G., *Bathing in Public in the Roman World* (Ann Arbor: University of Michigan Press, 1999), 85–103.

——'Bathing for Health with Celsus and Pliny the Elder,' *The Classical Quarterly* 56 (2006): 190–207.

Fagen, Ruth, 'Phylacteries,' in David Noel Freedman (ed.), *Anchor Bible Dictionary* (New York: Doubleday, 1992).

Falk, Daniel K., *Parabiblical Texts: Strategies for Extending the Scriptures Among the Dead Sea Scrolls* (London/New York: T & T Clark, 2007).

Feldman, Louis H., 'Josephus' Portrait of Moses,' *JQR* 82 (1992): 285–328.

——'Josephus' Portrait of Moses, Part Two,' *JQR* 83 (1992): 7–50.

——'Josephus' Portrait of Moses, Part Three,' *JQR* 83 (1993): 301–30.

——'Parallel Lives of Two Lawgivers: Josephus' Moses and Plutarch's Lycurgus,' in Jonathan Edmundson, Steve Mason, and James Rives (eds), *Flavius Josephus and Flavian Rome* (Oxford: OUP, 2005), 209–43.

Feliks, Y., 'The History of Balsamon Cultivation in the Land of Israel,' in Shimon Dar and Zev Safrai (eds), *The Village in Ancient Israel* (Tel Aviv: ERETZ—Geographic Research and Publications Project for the Advancement of Knowledge of Eretz-Israel, 1997), 275–96 (Heb.).

Ferguson, John, *Utopias of the Classical World* (London: Thames and Hudson, 1975).

Fine, Stephen, 'On the Development of a Symbol: The Date Palm in Roman Palestine,' *JSP* 4 (1989): 105–18.

Finkbeiner, Douglas, 'The Essenes according to Josephus: Exploring the Contribution of Josephus' Portrait of the Essenes to his Larger Literary Agenda,' unpublished University of Pennsylvania Ph.D. dissertation (2010).

Fischer, Moshe, Gichon, Mordecai, and Tal, Oren, '*En Boqeq: Excavations in an Oasis on the Dead Sea: Volume II, The Officina: An Early Roman Building on the Dead Sea Shore* (Mainz: Verlag Philipp von Zabern, 2000).

Fleischer, Alexander, and Fleischer, Zhenia, 'The Fragrance of Biblical Mandrake,' *Economic Botany* 48 (1994): 243–51.

Foakes-Jackson, Frederick J., and Lake, Kirsopp, *The Beginnings of Christianity: Part 1: The Acts of the Apostles* (London: Macmillan, 1920).

Fokkelman, Jan, *Reading Biblical Narrative: an Introductory Guide* (Louisville: Westminster John Knox, 1999).

Forbes, R. J., *Studies in Ancient Technology* (Leiden: Brill, 1964).

Forster, Gideon, *Masada V, The Yigael Yadin Excavations 1963–1965, Final Reports, Art and Architecture* (Jerusalem: Israel Exploration Society, 1996).

Foucault, Michel, *The History of Sexuality 3: Care of the Self* (trans. by Robert Hurley; New York: Random House, 1988).

Franklin, Clare, 'To what Extent did Posidonius and Theophanes record Pompeian ideology?' in 'Romanization?' *Digressus, The Internet Journal for the Classical World, Digressus Supplement* 1 (2003): 99–110, at 102–4: www.digressus.org.

Freeman, David L., and Judith Z. Abrams, *Illness and Health in the Jewish Tradition: Writings from the Bible to Today* (Philadelphia: Jewish Publication Society, 1999).

Frendo, Anthony J., *Pre-Exilic Israel, the Hebrew Bible, and Archaeology: Integrating Text and Artefact* (New York: T & T Clark, 2011).

Freyne, Sean, *Galilee from Alexander the Great to Hadrian 323 BCE to 135 CE: A Study of Second Temple Judaism* (Wilmington: Glazier, 1980).

——'The Galileans in the Light of Josephus' *Life*,' in id. *Galilee and Gospel: Collected Essays* (Tübingen: Mohr Siebeck, 2000), 27–44.

Friedenwald, H., 'The Bibliography of Ancient Hebrew Medicine,' *Bulletin of the Medical Library Association* 23/3 (1935): 124–57.

Friedman, Shamma, 'The Holy Scriptures Defile the Hands—the Transformation of a Biblical Concept in Rabbinic Theology,' in Marc Brettler and Michael Fishbane (eds), *Minḥah le Naḥum: Biblical and Other Studies Presented to Nahum M. Sarna in Honour of his 70th Birthday* (Sheffield: Sheffield Academic Press, 1993), 117–32.

Fröhlich, Ida, 'Demons, Scribes, and Exorcists in Qumran,' in Kinga Dévényi and Tamás Iványi (eds), *Essays in Honour of Alexander Fodor on His Sixtieth Birthday* (The Arabist: Budapest Studies in Arabic 23; Budapest: Eötuös Loránd University Press, 2001), 73–81.

Fröhlich, Ida, '"Invoke at Any Time": Apotropaic Texts and Belief in Demons in the Literature of the Qumran Community,' *Biblische Notizen* 137 (2008): 41–74.

——'Medicine and Magic in the Genesis Apocryphon. Ideas on Human Conception and its Hindrances,' *RQ* 25/98 (2011): 177–98.

Gabba, Emilio, 'True History and False History in Classical Antiquity,' *JRS* 71 (1981): 50–2.

Gagé, Jean, 'Du culte thrace de Pleistoros à la secte dace des "Pleistoi", à propos d'une dédicace épigraphique à Diana Plestrensis,' *Noul Album Macedo-Roman* 1 (1959): 15–26.

Gager, John G., *Moses in Greco-Roman Paganism* (New York: Abingdon Press, 1972).

Galor, Katharina, Humbert, Jean-Baptiste, and Jürgen Zangenberg (eds), *Qumran, The Site of the Dead Sea Scrolls: Archaeological Interpretations and Debates* (Leiden: Brill, 2006).

——'Winterpaläste in Jericho,' in Zangenberg, *Das Tote Meer*, 53–62.

Geller, Mark J., 'Look to the Stars: Babylonian Medicine and Magic, Astrology and Melthesis,' in *Max Planck Institute for the History of Science* 401 at http://www.mpiwg-berlin.mpg.de/en/resources/preprints.html.

Gershonson, Daniel, and Guispel, Gilles, 'Meristae,' *VC* 12 (1958): 10–26.

Gibson, Shimon, 'Suggested Identifications for "Bethso" and the "Gate of the Essenes" in the Light of Magen Broshi's Excavations on Mount Zion,' in Joseph Patrich and David Amit (eds), *New Studies in the Archaeology of Jerusalem and its Region. Collected Papers* (Jerusalem: Israel Antiquities Authority, 2007), 25–33.

——*The Final Days of Jesus: The Archaeological Evidence* (New York: HarperOne, 2009), 96–102.

Gichon, Mordecai, *'En Boqeq I, Ausgrabungen in einer Oase am Toten Meer: Band I: Geographie und geschichte der Oase. Das spätrömisch-byzantinische Kastell* (Mainz: Philipp von Zabern, 1993).

Gill, Christopher, and Wiseman, Timothy P. (eds), *Lies and Fiction in the Ancient World* (Exeter: University of Exeter Press, 1993).

Ginsburg, Christian D., *The Essenes: Their History and Doctrines; The Kabbalah: Its Doctrines, Development and Literature* (reprint of *The Essenes: Their History and Doctrines* [London: Longman and Green, 1864]; London: Routledge and Paul, 1955).

Gleason, Kathryn L., 'Garden Excavations at the Herodian Winter Palace in Jericho, 1985–7,' *BAIAS* 7 (1986–7): 21–39.

Golb, Norman, *Who Wrote the Dead Sea Scrolls? The Search for the Secret of Qumran* (New York: Scribner, 1995).

——'Who were the Magariya?' *JAOS* 80 (1960): 347–59.

Goodenough, Erwin, *The Politics of Philo Judaeus: Practice and Theory* (New Haven: Yale University Press, 1938).

Goodenough, Erwin R., *The Jurisprudence of the Jewish Courts in Egypt: Legal Administration under the Jews under the Early Roman Empire as described by Philo Judaeus* (New Haven: Yale University Press, 1929).

Goodman, Martin, *State and Society in Roman Galilee, AD 132–212* (Totowa, NJ: Rowman & Allanheld, 1983).

——*The Ruling Class of Judaea: The Origins of the Jewish Revolt against Rome A. D. 66–70* (Cambridge: CUP, 1987).

——'Sacred Scripture and "Defiling the Hands",' *Journal of Theological Studies* 41 (1990): 99–107.

——'A Note on the Qumran Sectarians, the Essenes and Josephus,' *JJS* 46 (1995): 161–6.

——'Josephus and Variety in First-Century Judaism,' *The Israel Academy of Sciences and Humanities Proceedings* 7/6 (2000): 201–13.

——'The Function of Minim in Early Rabbinic Judaism,' in id. *Judaism in the Roman World: Collected Essays* (Leiden: Brill, 2007), 163–74.

——'The Place of Sadducees in First-Century Judaism,' in id. *Judaism in the Roman World: Collected Essays* (Leiden: Brill, 2007), 123–36.

——*Rome and Jerusalem: The Clash of Ancient Civilizations* (New York: Alfred A. Knopf, 2007).

——'Sadducees and Essenes after 70 CE,' in id. *Judaism in the Roman World* (Leiden: Brill, 2007), 153–62.

Goranson, Stephen, 'Posidonius, Strabo, and Marcus Vipsanius Agrippa as Sources on Essenes,' *JJS* 45 (1994): 295–8.

——'Others and Intra-Jewish Polemic as Reflected in Qumran Texts,' in Peter W. Flint and James C. VanderKam (eds), *The Dead Sea Scrolls after Fifty Years: A Comprehensive Assessment*, ii (Leiden: Brill, 1999), 534–51.

Gottwald, Norman, *The Hebrew Bible: A Socio-Literary Introduction* (Philadelphia: Fortress, 1985).

Grabbe, Lester L., *An Introduction to First Century Judaism: History and Religion of the Jews in the Time of Nehemiah, the Maccabees, Hillel and Jesus* (Edinburgh: T & T Clark, 2010).

Graetz, Heinrich, *Geschichte der Juden: Von den ältesten Zeiten bis auf die Gegenwart. Aus den Quellen neu bearbeitet*, 11 vols (Leipzig: Leiner, 1853–75).

——*Sinaï et Golgotha, ou Les origines du judaisme et du christianisme, suivi d'un examen critique des eívangiles anciens et modernes*, trans. by Maurice Hess (Paris: Michel Levy, 1867).

——*History of the Jews*, 5 vols, trans. by Bella Lowy, with Phillipp Bloch (Philadelphia: Jewish Publication Society of America, 1891–98).

Graf, David, 'The Pagan Witness to the Essenes,' *BA* 40/3 (1977): 125–9.

Gray, Rebecca, *Prophetic Figures in Late Second Temple Jewish Palestine: The Evidence from Josephus* (Oxford: OUP, 1993).

Grossman, Maxine, 'Affective Masculinity: The Gender of the Patriarchs in *Jubilees*,' *Henoch* 31 (2009): 91–7.

Haaland, Gunnar, 'What Difference does Philosophy Make? The Three Schools as a Rhetorical Device in Josephus,' in Zuleika Rogers (ed.), *Making History: Josephus and Historical Method* (Leiden: Brill, 2007), 262–88.

Hachlili, Rachel, *Ancient Jewish Art and Archaeology in the Land of Israel* (Leiden: Brill, 1984).

Hadas, Gideon, 'Stone Anchors from the Dead Sea,' *'Atiqot* 21 (1992): 55–7.

——'Where was the Harbour of En Gedi Situated?' *IEJ* 43 (1993): 45–9.

——'A Stone Anchor from the Dead Sea,' *International Journal of Nautical Archaeology* 22 (1993): 89–90.

——'Dead Sea Sailing Routes during the Herodian Period,' *BAIAS* 26 (2008): 31–6.

—— Lifschitz, Nili, and Bonani, Georges, 'Two Ancient Wooden Anchors from Ein Gedi, on the Dead Sea, Israel,' *International Journal of Nautical Archaeology* 34 (2005): 307–15.

Hakola, Raimo and Reinhartz, Adele, 'John's Pharisees,' in Jacob Neusner and Bruce Chilton (eds), *In Quest of the Historical Pharisees* (Waco, TX: Baylor University Press, 2007), 131–48.

Halperin, David, 'The Book of Remedies, the Canonization of the Solomonic Writings, and the Riddle of Pseudo-Eusebius,' *JQR* 72 (1982): 269–92.

Hammond, Philip C., 'The Nabataean Bitumen Industry at the Dead Sea,' *BA* 22 (1959): 40–8.

Harding, G. Lankester, 'The Dead Sea Scrolls,' *PEQ* 81 (1949): 112–16.

Hardwick, Michael E., *Josephus as an Historical Source in Patristic Literature through Eusebius* (Atlanta: Scholars Press, 1989).

Har-El, Menahem, 'The Route of Salt, Sugar and Balsam Caravans in the Judaean Desert,' *GeoJournal* 2/6 (1978): 549–56.

Harold Remus, *Jesus as Healer* (Cambridge: CUP, 1997).

Harris, B. F., 'Dio of Prusa: A Survey of Recent Work,' in *ANRW* 2.33.5 (1991), 3853–81.

Hay, David, 'Putting Extremism in Context: The Case of Philo, De Migratione 89–93,' *SPA* 9 (1997): 126–42.

Healy, John, *Pliny the Elder on Science and Technology* (Oxford: OUP, 1999).

Hegedus, Tim, *Early Christianity and Ancient Astrology* (Frankfurt am Maim/New York: Peter Lang, 2007), 318–27.

Heid, Stefan, *Celibacy in the Early Church: The Beginnings of a Discipline of Obligatory Continence for Clerics in East and West* (San Francisco: Ignatius Press, 2000).

Heinz, Werner, 'Antike Balneologie in späthellenistischer und römischer Zeit, zur medizinischen Wirkung römischer Baäder,' in *ANRW* (1996), 2.37.3, 2411–32.

Hempel, Charlotte, *The Damascus Texts* (Sheffield: Sheffield Academic Press, 2000).

——'The Essenes,' in Dan Cohn-Sherbok and John M. Court (eds), *Religious Diversity in the Graeco-Roman World. A Survey of Recent Scholarship* (The Biblical Seminar 79; Sheffield: Sheffield Academic Press, 2001), 65–80.

——(ed.), *The Dead Sea Scrolls: Texts and Context* (Leiden: Brill, 2010).

Hendel, Ronald, Kronfeld, Chana, and Pardes, Ilana, 'Gender and Sexuality,' in Ronald Hendel (ed.), *Reading Genesis: Ten Methods* (Cambridge: CUP, 2010).

Hengel, Martin, and Roland Deines, 'E. P. Sanders' "Common Judaism", Jesus and the Pharisees,' *JTS* 46 (1995): 1–70.

Hepper, F. Nigel, *Planting a Bible Garden* (London: Lion Hudson, 2000).

——and Joan E. Taylor, 'Date Palms and Opobalsam in the Madaba Mosaic Map,' *PEQ* 136 (2004): 35–44.

Higham, Tom, Taylor, Joan E., and Green, Dennis, 'New Radiocarbon Determinations from Khirbet Qumran from the University of Waikato Laboratories,' in Humbert and Gunneweg, *Khirbet Qumrân*, 197–200.

Hirschfeld, Yizhar, *The Judean Desert Monasteries in the Byzantine Period* (New Haven: Yale University Press, 1992).

——'Early Roman Manor Houses in Judea and the Site of Khirbet Qumran,' *JNES* 57 (1998): 161–89.

——'The Architectural Context of Qumran,' in *The Dead Sea Scrolls: Fifty Years after Their Discovery. Proceedings of the Jerusalem Congress, July 20–25, 1997*, ed. Lawrence H. Schiffman, Emanuel Tov, and James C. VanderKam (Jerusalem: Israel Exploration Society in cooperation with the Shrine of the Book, Israel Museum, 2000), 673–83.

——'A Community of Hermits above En Gedi,' *Cathedra* 96 (2000): 8–40 (Heb.).

——'A Settlement of Hermits above En Gedi,' *Tel Aviv* 27 (2000): 103–55.

——'Qumran in the Second Temple Period. Reassessing the Archaeological Evidence,' *Liber Annuus* 52 (2002): 247–96.

——'Excavations at 'Ein Feshkha, 2001: Final Report,' *IEJ* 54 (2004): 35–54.

——*Qumran in Context: Reassessing the Archaeological Evidence* (Peabody, MA: Hendrickson, 2004).

——'Qumran in the Second Temple Period: A Reassessment,' in Katharina Galor, Jean-Baptiste Humbert, and Jürgen Zangenberg (eds), *The Site of the Dead Sea Scrolls: Archaeological Interpretations and Debates. Proceedings of the Conference*

Held at Brown University, November 17–19, 2002 (Studies on the Texts of the Desert of Judah 57; Leiden: Brill, 2005), 223–39.

—— 'The Archaeology of the Dead Sea Valley in the Late Hellenistic and Early Roman Periods,' *Geological Society of America Special Papers* 401 (2006): 215–29.

—— 'Fortified Manor Houses of the Ruling class in the Herodian Kingdom of Judaea,' in Nikos Kokkinos (ed.), *The World of the Herods* (Stuttgart: Franz Steiner Verlag, 2007), 197–226.

Hoade, Eugene, *Western Pilgrims* (Jerusalem: Franciscan Printing Press, 1952).

Hoehner, Harold W., *Herod Antipas* (Cambridge: CUP, 1972).

Hogan, Larry, *Healing in the Second Temple Period* (Göttingen: Vandenhoeck, 1992).

Hübner, Ulrich, 'Baaras und Zeus Beelbaaros,' *Biblische Zeitschrift* 39 (1995), 252–5.

Hudaib, Mohammad, Bustanji, Yasser, Tayyem, Rabab, Yousef, Mohammed, Abuirjeie, Mustafa, and Aburjai, Talal, 'Ethnopharmacological Survey of Medicinal plants in Jordan, Mujib Nature Reserve and Surrounding area,' *Journal of Ethnopharmacology* 120/1 (2008): 63–71.

Humbert, Jean-Baptiste, 'Reconsideration of the Archaeological Interpretation,' and 'Arguments en faveur d'une résidence pré-Essénienne,' in Jean-Baptiste Humbert and Jan Gunneweg (eds), *Khirbet Qumrân et Ain Feshkha: études d'anthropologie, de physique et de chimie* (Qumran ii; Fribourg/Göttingen: Editions universitaires Fribourg Suisse/Vandenhoeck & Ruprecht, 2003), 419–44, 467–82.

—— 'The Chronology during the First Century B.C.: De Vaux and his Method: A Debate,' in Humbert and Gunneweg, *Khirbet Qumrân*, 425–38.

—— and Chambon, Alain, *Fouilles de Khirbet Qumrân et de Ain Feshka I: Album de photographies. Répertoire du fonds photographiques. Synthèse des notes de chantier du Père Roland de Vaux* (Novum Testamentum et Orbis Antiquus, Series Archaeologica 1; Fribourg: Editions universitaires, 1994).

Humbert, Jean-Baptiste and Gunneweg, Jan, *Khirbet Qumrân et Ain Feshkha: études d'anthropologie, de physique et de chimie* (Qumran ii; Fribourg/Göttingen: Editions universitaires Fribourg Suisse/Vandenhoeck & Ruprecht, 2003).

Hyksell, Ira David, *A Study of the Latinity of Solinus* (Chicago: Chicago University Libraries, 1925).

Inowlocki, Sabrina, *Eusebius and the Jewish Authors: His Citation Technique in an Apologetic Context* (Ancient Judaism and Early Christianity 64; Leiden: Brill, 2006).

Isaac, Benjamin, 'Judaea after 70,' in id. *The Near East under Roman Rule: Selected Papers* (Leiden: Brill, 1998), 112–21, originally published in *JJS* 35 (1984): 44–50.

—— *The Near East under Roman Rule: Selected Papers* (Leiden: Brill, 1998).

—— and Roll, Isaac, 'Judea in the Early years of Hadrian's Reign,' in Isaac, *Near East*, 182–97, originally published in *Latomus* 28 (1979): 54–66.

Isser, Stanley J., *The Dositheans: A Samaritan Sect in Late Antiquity* (Leiden: Brill, 1976).

Jackson, F. J. Foakes and Lake, Kirsopp, *The Beginnings of Christianity*: Part 1, *The Acts of the Apostles* (London: Macmillan, 1920).

Jacob, Irena and Jacob, Walter (eds), *The Healing Past – Pharmaceuticals in the Biblical and Rabbinic World* (Leiden: Brill, 1993).

Jacobson, David, 'Palestine and Israel,' *BASOR* 313 (1999): 65–74.

Jacobus, Helen, '4Q318: A Jewish Zodiac Calendar at Qumran,' in Charlotte Hempel (ed.), *The Dead Sea Scrolls. Texts and Context* (STDJ 90; Leiden: Brill), 365–95.

Janowitz, Naomi, 'Rabbis and their Opponents: The Construction of the "Min" in Rabbinic Anecdotes,' *Journal of Early Christian Studies* 6 (1998): 449–62.

Jaradat, Nidal A., 'Ethnopharmacological Survey of Natural Products in Palestine,' *An-Najah National University Journal of Research* 19 (2005): 13–67.

Jeffers, Ann, *Magic and Divination in Ancient Palestine and Syria* (Leiden: Brill, 1992), 125–43.

Jeremias, Joachim, *Jerusalem in the Time of Jesus*, 3rd ed. (London: SCM Press, 1969).

Jones, Christopher P., *The Roman World of Dio Chrysostom* (Cambridge, MA: Harvard University Press, 1978).

Jones, F. Stanley, 'The Martyrdom of James in Hegesippus, Clement of Alexandria, Christian Apocrypha including Nag Hammadi, a Study of the Textual Relations,' *SBL Seminar Papers* (Atlanta: Scholars Press, 1990), 328–31.

——'Hegesippus as a Source for the History of Jewish-Christianity,' in Mimouni, Simon-Claude (ed.), *Le Judéo-christianisme dans tous ses états: actes du colloque de Jérusalem, 6–10 juillet 1998* (Paris: Cerf, 2001).

Kallner-Amiran, David H., 'A Revised Earthquake-Catalogue of Palestine,' *IEJ* 1 (1950–1): 223–46.

Kamesar, Adam, Review of *The Essenes According to the Classical Sources*, ed. Geza Vermes and Martin D. Goodman (Sheffield: JSOT Press, 1989), in *Journal of the American Oriental Society* 111 (1991): 134–5.

Kampen, John, 'A Reconsideration of the Name "Essene" in Greco-Jewish Literature in Light of Recent Perceptions,' *HUCA* 57 (1986): 61–81.

——*The Hasideans and the Origin of Pharisaism: A Study in 1 and 2 Maccabees* (SBL Septuagint and Cognate Studies Series 24; Atlanta: Scholars Press, 1988).

——'The Cult of Artemis and the Essenes in Syro-Palestine,' *DSD* 10 (2003): 205–20.

Karcz, Iaakov, 'Implications of Some Early Jewish Sources for Estimates of Earthquake Hazard in the Holy Land,' *Annals of Geophysics* 47 (2004): 759–88.

Kasher, Ariyeh, *Jews, Idumaeans and Ancient Arabs: Relations of the Jews in Eretz-Israel with the Nations of the Frontier and the Desert during the Hellenistic and Roman Eras (332 BCE–70 CE)* (Tübingen: Mohr Siebeck, 1988).

Katz, Amitai, Starinsky, Avraham, Taitel-Goldman, Nurit, and Beyth, Michael, 'Solubilities of Gypsum and Halite in the Dead Sea and in Its Mixtures with Seawater,' *Limnology and Oceanography* 26/4 (July 1981): 709–16.

Kee, Howard Clark, *The Community of the New Age: Studies in Mark's Gospel* (Philadelphia: Westminster, 1977).

——'Medicine and Healing,' in *The Anchor Bible Dictionary* 4 (New York: Doubleday, 1992), 659–64.

Kelhoffer, James A., *The Diet of John the Baptist: 'Locusts and Wild Honey' in Synoptic and Patristic Interpretation* (Tübingen: J. C. B. Mohr/Paul Siebeck, 2005).

Kelso, James L., and Powell, Alfred R., 'Glance Pitch from Tell Beit Mirsim,' *BASOR* 95 (1944): 14–18.

Klawans, Jonathan, *Impurity and Sin in Ancient Israel* (New York: OUP, 2000).

——'Josephus on Fate, Free Will and Ancient Jewish Types of Compatibilism,' *Numen* 56 (2009): 44–90.

Klotz, Alfred, *Quaestiones Plinianae geographicae* (Berlin: Weidmann, 1906).

Klutz, Todd, *The Exorcism Stories in Luke–Acts: A Sociostylistic Reading* (Society for New Testament Studies Monograph Series 129; Cambridge: CUP, 2004).

Knohl, Israel, *The Messiah before Jesus: The Suffering Servant of the Dead Sea Scrolls* (Berkeley: University of California Press, 2000).

Kohler, Kaufman, 'Essenes,' *The Jewish Encyclopedia* (New York: Funk and Wagnalls, 1901–6), 5: 224–32.

Kokkinos, Nikos, 'The City of "Mariamme": an Unknown Herodian Connection?' *Mediterraneo Antico* 5/2 (2002): 715–46.

——'The Foundation of Bethsaida-Julias by Philip the Tetrarch,' *JJS* 59 (2008): 1–16.

——'The Location of Tarichaea: North or South of Tiberias,' *PEQ* 142 (2010): 7–23.

Kottek, Samuel S., 'The Essenes and Medicine,' *Clio Medica* 18 (1983): 81–99.

——*Medicine and Hygiene in the Works of Flavius Josephus* (Leiden: Brill, 1994).

——'Hygiene and Healing among the Jews in the Post-Biblical Period: A Partial Reconstruction,' and 'Selected Elements of Talmudic Medical Terminology with Special Reference to Graeco-Latin Influences,' *ANRW* (1996), 2.37.32843–65 and 2912–32.

——and Horstmanshoff, H. F. J. (eds), *From Athens to Jerusalem: Medicine in Hellenized Jewish Lore and in early Christian Literature* (Rotterdam: Erasmus, 2000).

Kraft, Robert A., 'Pliny on Essenes, Pliny on Jews,' *DSD* 8 (2001): 255–61.

Kreiger, Barbara, *The Dead Sea: Myth, History and Politics*, 2nd ed. (Hanover, NH: Brandeis University Press/University Press of New England, 1997).

Kuefler, Matthew, *The Manly Eunuch: Masculinity, Gender Ambiguity, and Christian Ideology in Late Antiquity* (Chicago: University of Chicago Press, 2001).

Langlois, Michael, 'Shemihazah et compagnie(s). Onomastique des anges déchus dans les manuscrits araméens du Livre d'Hénoch,' in Katell Berthelot and Daniel Stökl Ben Ezra (eds), *Aramaica Qumranica. Proceedings of the conference on the Aramaic texts from Qumran in Aix-en-Provence, 30 June–2 July 2008* (Leiden: Brill, 2010), 145–80.

Laperrousaz, Ernest- Marie, ' "Infra hos Engadda", notes à propos d'un article récent,' *RB* 69 (1962): 369–80.

——'Brèves remarques archéologiques concernant la chronologie des occupations esséniennes de Qoumran,' *RQ* 12 (1966): 199–212.

——*Qoumran, l'etablissement essénien des bords de la Mer Morte, histoire et archéologie du site* (Paris: Picard, 1976).

——'Problèmes d'histoire et d'archéologie Qoumraniennes: a propos d'un souhait de précisions,' *RQ* 10 (1980): 269–91.

Lefkovits, Judah K., *The Copper Scroll—3Q15: A Reevaluation* (Leiden: Brill, 1999).

Lev, Efraim, and Amar, Zohar, *Practical Materia Medica of the Medieval Eastern Mediterranean according to the Cairo Genizah* (Leiden: Brill, 2008).

Levey, Martin, 'Gypsum, Salt and Soda in Ancient Mesopotamian Chemical Technology,' *Isis* 49/3 (1958): 336–42.

Levine, Amy-Jill, 'Luke's Pharisees,' in Jacob Neusner and Bruce Chilton (eds), *In Quest of the Historical Pharisees* (Waco, TX: Baylor University Press, 2007), 113–30.

Lewis, Naphtali (ed.), The Documents from the Bar Kochba Period in the Cave of Letters: Greek Papyri (Jerusalem: Israel Exploration Society, 1989).

Lichtenberger, Achim, *Die Baupolitik Herodes des Grossen* (Wiesbaden: Harrassowitz, 1999).

Lichtenberger, Herman, 'Spirits and Demons in the Dead Sea Scrolls,' in James D. G. Dunn, Graham Stanton, and Stephen C. Barton (eds), *The Holy Spirit and Christian Origins* (Grand Rapids: Eerdmans, 2004), 14–21.

Lidzbarski, Mark, *Mandäische Liturgien* (Berlin: Weidmann, 1920, repr. Hildesheim: Olms, 1971).

Lierman, John, *The New Testament Moses: Christian Perception of Moses and Israel in the Setting of Jewish Religion* (Tübingen: Mohr Siebeck, 2004).

Lightfoot, Joseph B., 'On Some Points Connected with the Essenes,' in id. *The Epistles of St. Paul iii. The First Roman Captivity. 2. The Epistle to the Colossians, 3. Epistle to Philemon* (London: Macmillan, 1875).

Lightstone, Jack, 'The Pharisees and Sadducees in the Earliest Rabbinic Documents,' in Jacob Neusner and Bruce Chilton (eds), *In Quest of the Historical Pharisees* (Waco, TX: Baylor University Press, 2007), 255–90.

Lillie, Arthur, *Buddhism in Christendom or Jesus the Essene* (London: K. Paul, Trench and Co, 1887).

Lim, Timothy M., 'The Defilement of the Hands as a Principle Determining the Holiness of Scriptures,' *Journal of Theological Studies* 61 (2010): 501–15.

Lim, Timothy, 'The Wicked Priests of the Groningen Hypothesis,' *JBL* 112 (1993): 415–25.

Lippert, G. F. W., *Jesus der Essener-Meister dargestellt nach dem Traumgesicht seiner Mutter Maria bei Matth. Cap. IV, V. 1–11* (Nuremberg: Wilhelm Schmid, 1857).

Lipschitz, Nili, and Bonani, Georges, 'Wild and Cultivated Date Palm from Qumran Cave 24,' *Tel Aviv* 28 (2001): 305–9.

Lönnqvist, Minna, and Lönnqvist, Kenneth, 'Parallels to Be Seen: Deir el-Medina Jars Containing Manuscripts,' in Armin Lange, Emanuel Tov, and Matthias Weigold (eds), *The Dead Sea Scrolls in Context: Integrating the Dead Sea Scrolls in the Study of Ancient Texts, Languages, and Cultures: An International Conference Organized by the University of Vienna and the Hebrew University of Jerusalem*, Vienna, 11–14 February 2008, 2 vols (Leiden: Brill, 2011), ii, 471–87.

Lopez, Davina C., 'Before Your Very Eyes: Roman Imperial Ideology, Gender Constructs and Paul's Inter-Nationalism,' in Todd Penner, and Caroline Vander Stichele (eds), *Mapping Gender in Ancient Religious Discourses* (Leiden, Brill, 2007), 115–62, at 123.

Lozovan, E., and Haddad, Safia F., 'Dacia Sacra,' *History of Religions* 7 (1968): 209–43.

Luce, T. James, 'Ancient Views on the Causes of Bias in Historical Writing,' *Classical Philology* 84 (1988): 16–31.

Lucia, Salvatore P., *A History of Wine as Therapy* (Philadelphia: Lippicott, 1963).

Lynch, William F., *Narrative of the United States' Expedition to the River Jordan and the Dead Sea*, 7th ed. (Philadelphia: Lea and Blanchard, 1850).

Machiela, Daniel A., '"Each to his own Inheritance": Geography as an Evaluative Tool in the Genesis Apocryphon,' *DSD* 15 (2008): 50–66.

—— *The Dead Sea Genesis Apocryphon: A New Text and Translation with Introduction and Special Treatment of Columns 13–17* (Leiden: Brill, 2009).

Mack, Burton, *A Myth of Innocence: Mark and Christian Origins* (Philadelphia: Fortress, 1988).

Maeir, Aren M., Magness, Jodi, and Schiffman, Lawrence H. (eds), *'Go Out and Study the Land' (Judges 18: 2): Archaeological, Historical and Textual Studies in Honor of Hanan Eshel* (Leiden: Brill, 2011).

Magen, Yitzhak, and Peleg, Yuval, *The Qumran Excavations 1993–2004: Preliminary Report* (Judaea and Samaria Publications 6; Jerusalem: Israel Antiquities Authority, 2007).

——,—— 'Back to Qumran: Ten Years of Excavation and Research, 1992–2004,' in Galor, Humbert, and Zangenberg, *Qumran*, 55–113.

Magness, Jodi, 'Why Scroll Jars?' in Douglas R. Edwards (ed.), *Religion and Society in Roman Palestine* (New York/London: Routledge, 1994), 146–61.

—— 'What Was Qumran? Not a Country Villa,' *Biblical Archaeology Review* 22 (1996): 40–7, 72–3.

—— 'The Chronology of Qumran, Ein Feshkha, and Ein El-Ghuweir,' in Zdzislaw Jan Kapera (ed.), *Mogilany 1995: Papers on the Dead Sea Scrolls Offered in Memory of Aleksy Klawek* (Kraków: Enigma Press, 1998), 55–76.

—— 'Two Notes on the Archaeology of Qumran,' *BASOR* 312 (1998): 37–44.

—— 'Qumran Archaeology: Past Perspectives and Future Prospects,' in *The Dead Sea Scrolls after Fifty Years: A Comprehensive Assessment*, ed. Peter W. Flint, and James C. VanderKam, 2 vols (Leiden: Brill, 1998–9), i: 47–77.

—— *The Archaeology of Qumran and the Dead Sea Scrolls* (Grand Rapids: Eerdmans, 2002), 79–89.

—— *Debating Qumran: Collected Essays on its Archaeology* (Interdisciplinary Studies in Ancient Culture and Religion 4; Dudley, MA: Peeters, 2004).

—— 'Qumran, the Site of the Dead Sea Scrolls: A Review Article,' *RQ* 22/4 (2006): 642–64.

—— *Stone and Dung, Oil and Spit* (Grand Rapids: Eerdmans, 2011).

—— 'A Reassessment of the Excavations of Qumran,' in Schiffman, Tov, and Vander-Kam, 708–19.

—— 'Scrolls and Hand Impurity,' in Hempel, *Dead Sea Scrolls*: 89–97.

—— and Kenneth Atkinson, 'Josephus's Essenes and the Qumran Community,' *JBL* 129 (2010): 317–42.

Maier, Johann, *The Temple Scroll* (Sheffield: JSOT Press; 1985).

Mansfeld, Jaap, 'Resurrection Added: The *interpretatio christiana* of a Stoic Doctrine,' *VC* 37 (1983): 218–33.

Marcovich, Miroslav, *Studies in Early Greco-Roman Religions and Gnosticism* (Leiden: Brill, 1988).

Marcus, Joel, 'The Jewish War and the *Sitz im Leben* of Mark,' *JBL* (1992): 441–62.

Marcus, Ralph, 'Pharisees, Essenes and Gnostics,' *JBL* 63 (1954): 157–61.

Marrou, H.-I., 'Synesius of Cyrene and Alexandrian Neoplatonism,' in Arnaldo Momigliano (ed.), *The Conflict of Paganism and Christianity in the Fourth Century* (Oxford: OUP, 1963).

Martínez, Florentino García, 'Cave 11 in Context,' in Hempel, *Dead Sea Scrolls*: 199–209.

—— 'Qumran Origins and Early History: A Groningen Hypothesis,' *Folio Orientalia* (1988), 113–36.

Martínez, Florentino García, *The Dead Sea Scrolls Translated: The Qumran Texts in English*, 2nd ed. (Leiden/Grand Rapids: Brill/Eerdmans, 1996).

Mason, Steve, 'Was Josephus a Pharisee? A Reconsideration of *Life* 10–12,' *JJS* 40 (1989): 31–45.

——*Flavius Josephus on the Pharisees: A Composition-Critical Study* (Studia Post-Biblica 29; Leiden: Brill, 1991).

——'Chief Priests, Sadducees, Pharisees and Sanhedrin in Acts,' in Richard Bauckham (ed.), *The Book of Acts in its Palestinian Setting* (Grand Rapids: Eerdmans, 1995, 115–77.

——'*Philosophiai*: Graeco-Roman, Jewish and Christian,' in John S. Kloppenborg and Stephen G. Wilson, *Voluntary Associations in the Graeco-Roman World* (London/New York: Routledge, 1996), 31–58.

——*Life of Josephus: Translation and Commentary* (Leiden: Brill, 2000).

——'What Josephus Says about Essenes in his Judean War,' in Stephen G. Wilson and Michel Desjardins (eds), *Text and Artifact in the Religions of Mediterranean Antiquity: Essays in Honour of Peter Richardson* (Waterloo, Ontario: Wilfrid Laurier University Press, 2000), 434–67.

——'Essenes and Lurking Spartans in Josephus' *Judean War*: From Story to History,' in Zuleika Rodgers (ed.), *Making History. Joseph and Historical Method* (Leiden: Brill, 2007), 219–61.

——'Excursus I: The Essenes of Josephus' War,' in id. with Honora Chapman, *Flavius Josephus: Translation and Commentary*, Vol. 1b: *Judean War 2* (Leiden: Brill, 2008).

——'Josephus and the Authorship of War 2: 119–161 (on the Essenes),' *JSJ* 25 (1994): 207–21.

——'Josephus's Pharisees: The Narratives,' in Jacob Neusner and Bruce Chilton (eds), *In Quest of the Historical Pharisees* (Waco, TX: Baylor University Press, 2007), 3–40, 429–33.

——'Josephus's Pharisees: The Philosophy,' in Jacob Neusner and Bruce Chilton (eds), *In Quest of the Historical Pharisees* (Waco, TX: Baylor University Press, 2007), 41–66, 433–6.

——'What Josephus Says about the Essenes in his Judean War,' http: orion.mscc.huji. ac.il/orion/programs/Mason00-1.shtml / orion.mscc.huji.ac.il/orion/programs/Mason00-2.shtml.

Masterman, E. W. G., 'Hygiene and Disease in Palestine in Modern and Biblical Times,' 3 parts, *PEQ* 50 (1918): 13–20, 56–71, 112–19.

Matthews, Kenneth A., 'John, Jesus and the Essenes: Trouble at the Temple,' *Criswell Theological Review* 3 (1988): 101–26.

Mazar, Benjamin, 'En-Gedi,' in Ephraim Stern (ed.), *New Encyclopedia of Archaeological Excavations in the Holy Land* (Jerusalem: Israel Exploration Society/Carta, 1993), 399–405.

McDonald, Myles A., *Roman Manliness: Virtus and the Roman Republic* (Cambridge: CUP, 2006).

Mébarki, Farah, and Puech, Emile, *Les manuscrits de la Mer Morte* (Rodez: Rouergue, 2002).

Medico, Henri del, *L'Énigme des manusrits de la Mer Morte* (Paris: Plon, 1957).

——'L'État des manuscrits de Qumran I,' *Vetus Testamentum* 7 (1957): 127–38.

Meeks, Wayne, *The Prophet King: Moses Traditions and Johannine Christology* (NT Suppl. 14; Leiden: Brill, 1967).

Meier, John P., 'The Historical Jesus and the Historical Herodians,' *JBL* 119 (2000): 740–6.

Mendels, Doron, 'Hellenistic Utopia and the Essenes,' *HTR* 72 (1979): 207–22.

Metzger, Bruce, *A Textual Commentary on the Greek New Testament* (New York: United Bible Societies, 1994).

Migowski, Claudia, Agnon, Amotz, Bookman, Revital, Negendank, Jorg F. W., and Stein, Mordechai, 'Recurrence pattern of Holocene Earthquakes along the Dead Sea transform revealed by Varve-counting and Radiocarbon Dating of Lacustrine Sediments,' *Earth and Planetary Science Letters* 222 (2004): 301–14.

Mildenberg, Leo, with Patricia Erhart Mottahedeh (ed.), *The Coinage of the Bar Kokhba War* (Typos: Monographien zur antiken Numismatik, 6; Aarau, Frankfurt am Main, Salzburg: Verlag Sauerländer, 1984).

Milgrom, Jacob, 'Purification Rule (4Q514=4QOrd^c),' in James H. Charlesworth (ed.), *The Rule of the Community and Related Documents* (Louisville: J. C. B. Mohr/Paul Siebeck/Westminster John Knox Press, 1994), 177–9.

Milik, J. T., 'Tefillin, Mezuzot et Targums,' in DJD 6 (Oxford: OUP, 1977).

Milikowsky, Chaim, 'Reflections on Hand-Washing, Hand-Purity and Holy Scripture in Rabbinic Literature,' in M. J. H. M. Poorthuis and J. Schwartz (eds), *Purity and Holiness: the Heritage of Leviticus* (Leiden: Brill, 2000), 154–9.

Millar, Fergus, *The Roman Near East: 31 BC to AD 337* (Cambridge, MA: Harvard University Press, 1993), 367–75.

Miller, Stuart S., 'Stepped Pools, Stone Vessels and Other Identity Markers of "Complex Common Judaism",' *JSJ* 41 (2010): 214–43.

Milright, Marcus, 'The Balsam of Matariyya: An Exploration of a Medieval Panacea,' *Bulletin of the School of Oriental and African Studies* 66 (2003): 193–209.

Mimouni, Simon, 'Qui sont les Jesseens dans la notice 29 du Panarion d'Epiphane de Salamine?' *NT* 43 (2001): 264–99.

Mizzi, Dennis, *The Archaeology of Khirbet Qumran: A Comparative Approach*, D.Phil. thesis (Oxford), forthcoming, Brill.

Montefiore, Claude G., 'Jewish Scholarship and Christian Silence,' *Hibbert Journal* 1 (1902–3): 335–46.

Moore, George Foot, *The History of Religions: II: Judaism, Christianity and Mohammedism* (New York: Charles Scribners, 1919).

——'Christian Writers on Judaism,' *HTR* 24 (1921): 197–254.

——*Judaism in the First Centuries of the Christian Era: The Age of the Tannaim*, Vol. 1 (Cambridge, MA: Harvard University Press, 1927).

——'Fate and Free Will in the Jewish Philosophies according to Josephus,' *HTR* 22 (1929): 371–89.

Moore, Stephen D., and Anderson, Janice Capel, 'Taking it Like a Man: Masculinity in 4 Maccabees,' *JBL* 117 (1998): 249–73.

Moraux, Joseph, *Alexandre d'Aphrodise: exégète de la noetique d'Aristote* (Liège/Paris: Faculté des Lettres, 1942).

Morris, Jenny, 'The Jewish Philosopher Philo,' in Emil Schürer, with Geza Vermes, Fergus Millar, and Martin Goodman (eds), *The History of the Jewish People in the Age of Jesus Christ (175 BC–AD 135)*, III/2 (Edinburgh: T & T Clark, 1987), 809–70.

Moss, Gloria A., 'Religion and Medicine: The Case of Qumran,' *Faith and Freedom* 51, no. 146 (1998): 44–61.

——'Historical Perspectives on Health Medicine 2000 Years Ago: The Case of Qumran and other Biblical Sites,' *The Journal of the Royal Society for the Promotion of Health* 120 (2000): 255–61.

——'Qumran Coverup,' *The Fortean Times* 131 (March 2000): 40–4.

Murphy, Trevor, *Pliny the Elder's Natural History: The Empire in the Encyclopaedia* (New York: OUP, 2004).

Naveh, Joseph, 'A Medical Document or a Writing Exercise? The So-Called 4QTherapeia,' *IEJ* 36 (1986): 52–5.

——and Shaked, Shaul, *Amulets and Magic Bowls* (Jerusalem/Leiden: Magnes, 1985).

——,——*Magic, Spells and Formulae* (Jerusalem: Magnes, 1993).

Nawash, Oraib S., and Al-Horani, Ahmad S., 'The Most Important Medicinal plants in Wadi Araba Desert in South West Jordan: A Review Article,' *Advances in Environmental Biology* 5(2) (2011): 418–25.

Neander, August, *Allgemeine Geschichte der christlichen Religion und Kirche* (Gotha: Friedrich Andrens Berthes, 1825), 24.

Neev, David and Emery, K. O., *The Dead Sea: Depositional Processes and Environments of Evaporites, State of Israel, Ministry of Development, Geological Survey Bulletin* 41 (Jerusalem: Ministry of Development, 1967).

Negev, Avraham, and Gibson, Shimon (eds), *Archaeological Encyclopedia of the Holy Land* (New York/London: Continuum, 2001).

Nesbit, Edward Planta, *Christ, Christians and Christianity: Jesus the Essene* (London: Simpkin, Marshall, Hamilton and Kent, 1895).

Netzer, Ehud, *Masada III, Buildings, Stratigraphy and Architecture* (Jerusalem: Israel Exploration Society, 1991).

——*Hasmonean and Herodian Palaces at Jericho* (Jerusalem: Israel Exploration Society, 2001).

——*The Palaces of the Hasmoneans and Herod the Great* (Jerusalem: Yad ben Zvi Press, 2001), 1–29.

——'Did any Perfume Industry Exist at `Ein Feshkha? *IEJ* 55 (2005): 97–100.

——*The Architecture of Herod, the Great Builder* (Tübingen: Mohr Siebeck, 2006).

Neuburger, Max, *Die Medizin in Flavius Josephus* (Bad Reichenhall: Buchkunst, 1919).

Neusner, Jacob, *The Rabbinic Traditions about the Pharisees before 70*, 3 vols (Leiden: Brill, 1971).

——'Varieties of Judaism in the Formative Age,' *Formative Judaism. Second Temple* (Chico: Scholars, 1983), 59–83.

——and Chilton, Bruce (eds), *In Quest of the Historical Pharisees* (Waco, TX: Baylor University Press, 2007).

Newman, Hillel, *Proximity to Power and Jewish Sectarian Groups of the Ancient Period: A Review of the Lifestyle, Values and Halakhah in the Pharisees, Sadducees, Essenes and Qumran* (Leiden: Brill, 2007).

Newmyer, Stephen T., 'Talmudic Medicine and Graeco-Roman Science. Cross-currents and Resistance,' *ANRW* (1996), 2.37.3, 2895–911.

——'Asaph the Jew and Greco-Roman Pharmaceuticals,' in Jacob and Jacob, *The Healing Past*, 107–20.

Nickelsburg, George, 'Abraham the Convert,' in Michael E. Stone and Theodore A. Bergren (eds), *Biblical Figures Outside the Bible* (Harrisburg, PA: Trinity Press International, 1998), 151–75.

——*1 Enoch: A Commentary on the Book of 1 Enoch Chapters 1–36, 81–108* (Minneapolis: Fortress, 2001).

Nissenbaum, Arie, 'Life in a Dead Sea—Fables, Allegories and Scientific Search,' *Bioscience* 29/3 (1979): 153–7.

Nissenbaum, Arie, Rullkötter, Jürgen, and Yechielli, Yoseph, 'Are the Curative Properties of "Black Mud" from the Dead Sea due to the Presence of Bitumen (Asphalt) or Other Types of Organic Matter?' *Environmental Geochemistry and Health* 24 (2002): 327–35.

Norrie, P. A., 'A History of Wine as Medicine,' in Merton Sandler and Roger Pinder (eds), *Wine: A Scientific Exploration* (Boca Raton, Florida: CRC Press, 2003).

Notley, R. Steven and Safrai, Ze'ev, *Eusebius' Onomasticon* (Leiden: Brill, 2005).

Nutton, Vivian, 'The Chronology of Galen's Early Career,' *The Classical Quarterly* 23 (1973): 158–71.

Osborne, Catherine, *Rethinking Early Greek Philosophy: Hippolytus of Rome and the Presocratics* (London: Duckworth, 1987).

Oudshoorn, Jacobine G., *The Relationship between Roman and Local Law in the Babatha and Salome Komaise Archives: General Analysis and Three Case Studies on Law of Succession, Guardianship and Marriage* (Leiden: Brill, 2007).

Palmer, Bernard (ed.), *Medicine and the Bible* (Exeter: Paternoster Press, 1986).

Patrich, Joseph, 'Khirbet Qumran in Light of New Archaeological Explorations in the Qumran Caves,' in Michael O. Wise, Norman Golb, John J. Collins, and Dennis G. Pardee (eds), *Methods of Investigation of the Dead Sea Scrolls and the Khirbet Qumran Site: Present Realities and Future Prospects* (ANYAS 722; New York: New York Academy of Sciences, 1994), 73–95.

——'Agricultural Development in Antiquity: Improvements in the Cultivation and Production of Balsam,' in Katharina Galor, Jean-Baptiste Humbert, and Jürgen Zangenberg (eds), *Qumran, the Site of the Dead Sea Scrolls: Archaeological Interpretations and Debates* (Leiden: Brill, 2006), 241–8.

——and Arubas, Benny, 'A Juglet containing Balsam Oil (?) from a Cave near Qumran,' *IEJ* 39 (1989): 43–59, also publ. in *Eretz Israel* 20 (Yadin volume) (1989): 321–9 (Hebrew).

Payne Smith, Robert, *A Compendious Syriac Dictionary* (Oxford: OUP, 1903).

Peduto, V. A., 'The Mandrake Root and the Viennese Dioscorides,' *Minerva Anestesiologica* 67/10 (2001): 751–66.

Pfann, Stephen, 'The Wine Press (and Miqveh) at Kh. Qumran (loc. 75 and 69),' *RB* 101 (1994): 212–14.

——'A Table Prepared in the Wilderness; Pantries and Tables, Pure Food and Sacred Space at Qumran,' in Katharina Galor, Jean-Baptiste Humbert, and Jürgen

Zangenberg (eds), *Qumran, the Site of the Dead Sea Scrolls: Archaeological Inter-pretations and Debates* (Leiden: Brill, 2006), 159–78.

Pfann, Stephen, 'Reassessing the Judean Desert Caves: Libraries, Archives, Genizas and Hiding Places,' *BAIAS* 25 (2007): 147–70.

——'Cryptic Texts 249a–z, 250a–j and 313–313b,' in Stephen Pfann, Alexander, Philip, et al., *Qumran Cave 4 XXVI. Cryptic Texts and Miscellanea, Part 1* (DJD 36; Oxford: OUP, 2000), 515–701.

——'The Mount Zion Inscribed Stone Cup: Preliminary Observations,' *Bible and Interpretation*, http://www.bibleinterp.com.

Piccirillo, Michele, 'Le monete della fortezza di Macheronte (El-Mishnaqa),' *Liber Annuus* 30 (1981): 403–14.

Pickup, Martin, 'Matthew's and Mark's Pharisees,' in Jacob Neusner and Bruce Chilton (eds), *In Quest of the Historical Pharisees* (Waco, TX: Baylor University Press, 2007), 67–112.

Pixner, Bargil, 'The History of the "Essene Gate" Area,' *ZDPV* 105 (1976): 96–104.

——'An Essene Quarter on Mount Zion,' in *Studia Hierosolymitana in onore di P. Bellarmino Bagatti* (Jerusalem: Franciscan Printing Press, 1986), 245–87.

——'Jerusalem's Essene Gateway: Where the Community Lived in Jesus's Time,' *BAR* 23/3 (1997): 23–31, 64–6.

——D. Chen, and S. Margalit, 'The "Gate of the Essenes" Re-Excavated,' *ZDPV* 105 (1989): 85–95.

Pococke, Richard, *A Description of the East and Some Other Countries* (London: W. Bowyer, 1745).

Politis, Konstantinos, 'Khirbet Qazone,' *American Journal of Archaeology* 102.3 (1998): 596–7.

——'Rescue Excavations in the Nabataean Cemetery at Khirbat Qazone 1996–1997,' *Annual of the Department of Antiquities of Jordan* 42 (1998): 611–14.

——'Khirbet Qazone: une nécropole nabatéene à la mer Morte,' *Le Monde de la Bible* 121 (September–October 1999): 95.

——'The Nabataean Cemetery at Khirbet Qazone,' *Near Eastern Archaeology* 62: 2 (1999): 128.

——'Chirbet Qazone. Ein nabataischer Friedhof am Toten Meer,' *Welt und Umwelt der Bibel* 16 (2000): 76.

Poole, Henry, 'Report of a Journey in Palestine,' *Journal of the Royal Geographical Society* 26 (1856): 55–70.

Popović, Mladen, *Reading the Human Body: Physiognomics and Astrology in the Dead Sea Scrolls and Hellenistic-Early Roman Period Judaism* (Leiden: Brill, 2007).

——'Roman Book Destruction in Qumran Cave 4 and the Roman Destruction of Khirbet Qumran Revisited,' in Jörg Frey, Carsten Claussen, and Nadine Kessler (eds), *Qumran und Archäologie—Texte und Kontexte* (Tübingen: Mohr Siebeck, 2011), 239–91.

Portier-Young, E., 'Sweet Mercy Metropolis: Interpreting Aseneth's Honeycomb,' *JSP* 14 (2005): 153–7.

Powell, Mark Allan, ' "Do and Keep What Moses Says" (Matthew 23.2–7),' *JBL* 114 (1995): 419–35.

Preuss, Julius, *Biblical and Talmudic Medicine*, trans. by Fred Rosner of *Biblisch-talmudische Medizin* (Berlin: S. Karger, 1911, repr. Jerusalem: Ktav, 1970), (New York: Sanhedrin Press, 1978).

Price, Randall, 'New Discoveries at Qumran,' *World of the Bible News and Views* 6/3 (2004) (online edition).

——'Qumran Plateau,' *Hadashot Arkheologiyot: Excavations and Surveys in Israel* 117 (2005) (online edition).

Puech, Emile, 'The Necropolises of Khirbet Qumran and Ain el-Ghuweir and the Essene Belief in Afterlife,' *BASOR* 312 (1998): 21–36.

——'Les psaumes davidiques du rituel d'exorcisme (11Q11),' in Daniel K. Falk (ed.), *Sapiential, Liturgical and Poetical Texts from Qumran* (Leiden: Brill, 2000), 160–81.

Pummer, Reinhard, *The Samaritans in Flavius Josephus* (Texts and Studies in Ancient Judaism 129; Tübingen: Mohr Siebeck, 2009).

Rabin, Ira, Hahn, Oliver, Wolff, Timo, Masic, Admir, and Weinberg, Gisela, 'On the Origin of the Ink of the Thanksgiving Scroll (1QHodayot^a),' *DSD* 16 (2009): 97–106.

Rahmani, L. Y., 'The Byzantine Solomon Eulogia Tokens in the British Museum,' *IEJ* 49 (1999): 92–104.

Rajak, Tessa, *Josephus: The Historian and his Society* (London: Duckworth, 1983).

——'Ciò che Flavio Giuseppe Vide: Josephus and the Essenes,' in Fausto Parente and Joseph Sievers (eds), *Josephus and the History of the Greco-Roman Period. Essays in Memory of Morton Smith* (Leiden: Brill, 1994), 141–60; reprinted in ead. *The Jewish Dialogue with Greece and Rome. Studies in Cultural and Social Interaction* (Leiden: Brill, 2002), 219–40.

Rankov, N. B., 'M. Oclatinius Adventus in Britain,' *Britannia* 18 (1987): 243–9.

Rasmussen, Kaare, Gunneweg, Jan, van der Plicht, Johannes, Kralj Cigic, Irena, Bond, Andrew D., Svensmark, Bo, Balla, Marta, Strilic, Matija, and Doudna, Greg, 'On the Age and Content of Jar-35—A Sealed and Intact Storage Jar found on the Southern Plateau of Qumran,' *Archaeometry* 53/4 (2011): 791–808.

Reed, William, 'The Qumran Caves Expedition of March 1952,' *BASOR* 135 (1954): 8–13.

Regeffe, A., *La Secte des Esseniens. Essai critique sur son organization, sa doctrine, son origine* (Lyons: Emmanuel Vitte, 1898).

Reinhardt, E. G., Goodman, B. N, Boyce, J., Lopez, G., Hengstum, P., Van Rink, W. J., Mart, Y., and Raban, A., 'The Tsunami of 13 December A.D. 115 and the Destruction of Herod the Great's Harbor at Caesarea Maritima, Israel,' *Geology* 34/12 (2006): 1061–4.

Reisner, Rainer, 'Josephus' "Gate of the Essenes" in Modern Discussion,' *ZDPV* 105 (1989): 105–9.

Rengstorf, K. H., *Hirbet Qumran und die Bibliothek vom Toten Meer* (W. Stuttgart: Kohlhammer, 1960).

——*Hirbet Qumran and the Problem of the Dead Sea Caves* (Leiden: Brill, 1963).

Rhoads, David M., *Israel in Revolution 6–74 CE: A Political History Based on the Writings of Josephus* (Philadelphia: Fortress, 1979).

Riaud, Jean, 'Les Thérapeutes d'Alexandrie dans la tradition et dans la recherche critique jusqu'aux découvertes de Qumran,' *ANRW* 2: 20: 2 (1987), 1189–295.

Richardson, Peter, *Herod: King of the Jews and Friend of the Romans* (New York: Continuum, 1999).

Ritschl, Albrecht, *Die Entstehung der altkatholischen Kirche. Ein kirchen- und dog-mengeschichtliche Monographie*, 2nd ed. (Bonn: Marcus, 1857).

Rivkin, Ellis, *The Hidden Revolution: The Pharisees' Search for the Kingdom Within* (Nashville: Abingdon, 1978).

——'Who Were the Pharisees?' in Alan J. Avery Peck and Jacob Neusner, (eds), *Judaism in Late Antiquity, Part 3* (Leiden: Brill, 2000), 1–30.

Robinson, Edward, 'A Brief Report of Travels in Palestine and the Adjacent Regions in 1839 undertaken for the Illustration of Biblical Geography,' in *The American Biblical Repository* (New York: Gould, Newman and Saxton, 1838), II, 418.

——Smith, Eli, *Biblical Researches in Palestine* (Boston: Crocker and Brewster, 1856).

Robinson, James M., 'The Discovery of the Nag Hammadi Codices,' *BA* 42/4 (1979): 206–24.

——(ed.), *The Nag Hammadi Library in English*, (rev. ed. San Francisco: Harper One, 1988).

Rocca, Samuel, *Herod's Judaea* (Tubingen: Mohr Siebeck, 2008).

Rochberg, Francesca, *The Heavenly Writing: Divination, Horoscopy, and Astronomy in Mesopotamian Culture* (Cambridge: CUP, 2009).

Röhrer-Ertl, Olav, 'Facts and Results Based on Skeletal Remains from Qumran Found in the Collectio Kurth: A Study in Methodology,' in Galor, Humbert, and Zangenberg, *Qumran*, 181–93.

Roller, Duane, *The Building Program of Herod the Great* (Berkeley: University of California Press, 1998).

Romm, James S., *The Edges of the Earth in Ancient Thought: Geography, Exploration and Fiction* (Princeton: Princeton University Press, 1992).

Roos, Bengt-Arne, *Synesius of Cyrene: A Study in His Personality* (Lund: Lund University Press, 1991).

Rosenson, J., 'What were the Ships sailing on the Dead Sea in the Map of Madaba carrying?' *Halamish* 3 (1986): 16–20.

Rosner, Fred, 'Pharmacology and Dietetics in the Bible and Talmud,' in Irene Jacob (ed.), *The Healing Past: Pharmaceuticals in the Biblical and Rabbinic World* (Leiden: Brill, 1993), 1–26.

Rosner, Fred, *Medicine in the Bible and the Talmud* (Jerusalem: Ktav, 1995).

Roth, Cecil, *The Historical Background of the Dead Sea Scrolls* (New York: Philosophical Library, 1959).

——*The Dead Sea Scrolls: A New Historical Approach* (New York: Norton and Co., 1965).

Rowland, Christopher, and Morray-Jones, Christopher, *The Mystery of God: Jewish Mysticism and the New Testament* (Leiden: Brill, 2009).

Rowley, H. H., 'The Herodians in the Gospels,' *JTS* 41 (1940): 14–27.

Russell, Kenneth W., 'The Earthquake Chronology of Palestine and Northwest Arabia from the 2nd through the Mid-8th Century A.D.,' *BASOR* 260 (1985): 37–59.

Safrai, Shemuel, Stern, Mordecai, and Flusser, David with van Unnik, Willem C., *The Jewish People in the First Century: Historical Geography, Political History, Social, Cultural and Religious Life and Institutions*, 2 vols (Assen: Van Gorcum, 1974–6).

Safrai, Ze'ev, *The Economy of Roman Palestine* (London: Routledge, 1994).

Saldarini, Anthony, *Pharisees, Scribes and Sadducees in Palestinian Society* (Edinburgh: T & T Clark, 1989).

Sallon, Sarah, Solowey, Elaine, Cohen, Yuval, Korchinsky, Raia, Egli, Markus, Woodhatch, Ivan, Simchoni, Orit, and Kislev, Mordechai, 'Germination, Genetics, and Growth of an Ancient Date Seed,' Science 320/5882 (13 June 2008): 1464.

Sanders, E. P., *Paul and Palestinian Judaism* (Philadelphia: Fortress, 1977).

——*Jewish Law from Jesus to the Mishnah: Five Studies* (London: SCM Press, 1990).

——*Judaism: Practice and Belief 63 BCE–66 CE* (London: SCM Press, 1992).

——*The Tendencies of the Synoptic Tradition* (Cambridge: CUP, 2006).

Sanders, James A., 'A Liturgy for Healing the Stricken (11QPsAp^a–11Q11),' in James H. Charlesworth and H. W. L. Rietz (eds), *The Dead Sea Scrolls: Hebrew, Aramaic and Greek Texts with English Translations Vol. 4A: Pseudepigraphic and Non-Masoretic Psalms and Prayers* (Tübingen/Louisville: J. C. B. Mohr/Paul Siebeck/Westminster John Knox Press, 1997), 216–33.

Satlow, Michael L., '"Try to Be a Man": The Rabbinic Construction of Masculinity,' *HTR* 89 (1996): 19–40.

Schäder, H. H., 'Ναζαρηνός/Ναζωραῖος,' in Gerhard Kittel (ed.), *Theological Dictionary of the New Testament* (Grand Rapids: Eerdmans, 1964–76), iv: 874–9.

Schäfer, Peter (ed.), *Geniza-Fragmente zur Hekhalot-Literatur* (TSAJ 16; Tübingen: Mohr Siebeck, 1984).

——*The Hidden and Manifest God: Some Major Themes in Jewish Mysticism* (New York: SUNY Press, 1992).

——*The Origins of Jewish Mysticism* (Tübingen: Mohr Siebeck, 2009).

Schalit, A. (ed.), *Namenwörterbuch zu Flavius Josephus* (Leiden: Brill, 1968).

Schaub, Thomas, and Rast, Walter E., *Bab edh-Dhra': Excavations in the Cemetery Directed by Paul Lapp* (Winona Lake: Eisenbrauns, 1989).

——,——*Bab edh-Dhra': Excavations at the Town Site (1975–1981)* (Winona Lake, IN: Eisenbrauns, 2003).

Schechter, Solomon, *Documents of Jewish Sectaries, edited from Hebrew MSS. in the Cairo Genizah collection, now in the possession of the University Library, Cambridge,* 2 vols (Cambridge: CUP, 1910); rev. ed. with prologomen by Joseph A. Fitzmyer, edited by Anan ben David (Jerusalem: Ktav, 1970).

——and Adler, Elkan N., 'Genizah,' in *Jewish Encyclopaedia* (ed. Isidore Singer; New York: Funk & Wagnalls, 1901–6), vol. 4, 612–13.

Schiffman, Lawrence H., 'The New Halakhic Letter (4QMMT) and the Origins of the Dead Sea Sect,' *BA* 53 (1990): 64–73; id. 'The Sadducean Origins of the Dead Sea Scroll Sect,' in Hershel Shanks (ed.), *Understanding the Dead Sea Scrolls* (London: SPCK, 1993).

——*Reclaiming the Dead Sea Scrolls: The History of Judaism, the Background of Christianity, and the Lost Library of Qumran* (Philadelphia: Jewish Publication Society, 1994).

——'Phylacteries and Mezuzot,' in Lawrence H. Schiffman and James VanderKam (eds), *Encyclopedia of the Dead Sea Scrolls* (New York: OUP, 2000).

Schiffman, Lawrence H., and Swartz, M. D., *Hebrew and Aramaic Incantation Texts from the Cairo Genizah: Selected Texts from Taylor-Schechter Box K1* (Semitic Texts and Studies 1; Sheffield: JSOT Press, 1992).

——Tov, Emanuel, and VanderKam, James C. (eds), *The Dead Sea Scrolls: Fifty Years after Their Discovery. Proceedings of the Jerusalem Congress, July 20–25, 1997* (Jerusalem: Israel Exploration Society in cooperation with the Shrine of the Book, Israel Museum, 2000).

Schmidt, Peter Lebrecht, 'Solinus Polyhistor in Wissenschaftsgeschichte und Geschichte,' *Philologus* 139 (1995): 23–35.

Schofield, Malcolm, *The Stoic Idea of the City* (Cambridge: CUP, 1991).

Schonfield, Hugh, *The Essene Odyssey: The Mystery of the True Teacher and the Essene Impact on the Shaping of Human Destiny* (Tisbury: Element Books, 1984).

Schürer, Emil, *Geschichte des judischen Volkes im Zeitalter Jesu Christi*, 5 vols (Leipzig: Hinrich, 1885–91).

——*History of the Jewish People in the Time of Jesus Christ*, 5 vols (New York: Charles Scribner, 1900).

——with Geza Vermes, Fergus Millar, and Matthew Black (eds), *The History of the Jewish People in the Age of Jesus Christ*, revised edition, 3 vols (Edinburgh: T & T Clark, 1973–9).

Schult, Heinrich, 'Zwei Häfen aus römischer Zeit am Toten Meer: Rujum el-bahr und el-beled (ez-Zara),' *ZDPV* 82 (1966): 139–48.

Schwartz, Daniel, 'The Messianic Departure from Judah (4Q Patriarchal Blessings),' *Theologische Zeitschrift* 37 (1981): 257–66.

——'Josephus and Nicolaus on the Pharisees,' *JSJ* 14 (1983): 157–71.

——'Hasidim in 1 Maccabees 2: 42,' *Scripta Classica Israelica* 13 (1994): 7–18.

Seetzen, Ulrich Jasper, *A Brief Account of the Countries Adjoining the Lake of Tiberias, the Jordan and the Dead Sea* (Bath: Meyler and Son, 1810), 43.

——*Reisen durch Syrien, Palästina, Phönicien, die Transjordan-Länder, Arabia Petraea, und Unter-Aegypten*, 4 vols, ed. and comm. Fr. Kruse (Berlin: G. Reimer, 1854).

Sellars, John, 'The Aristotelian Commentators: A Biographical Guide,' in Peter Adamson, Han Baltussen, and Martin Stone (eds), *Philosophy, Science and Exegesis in Greek, Arabic and Latin Commentaries* (*Bulletin of the Institute of Classical Studies*, supplementary volume 83.2; London: Institute of Classical Studies, 2004), 239–68.

Shamir, Orit, and Sukenik, Naama, 'Qumran Textiles and the Garments of Qumran's Inhabitants,' *DSD* 18 (2011): 206–25.

Shutz, Adolph S., *The Essenes: A Brief Historical Review of the Origin, Traditions and Principles of the Order* (New York: Occult Press, 1897).

Sievers, Joseph, 'Josephus, First Maccabees, Sparta, the Three Hairesis—and Cicero,' *JSJ* 32 (2001): 224–51.

Silverstein, Arthur J., 'Censorship of Medical Works: Hezekiah and "The Book of Remedies",' *Dine Israel: An Annual of Jewish Law and Israel Family Law* 7 (1976): 151–7.

Simon, Marcel, 'Les sectes juives d'après les témoinages patristiques,' *Studia Patristica* 1 (1957).

——*Jewish Sects at the Time of Jesus*, trans. by James H. Farley of *Les sectes juives au temps de Jésus* (Philadelphia: Fortress Press, 1967), 49–50.

Small, David B. (ed.), *Methods in the Mediterranean: Historians' and Archaeologists' Views on the Use of Texts and Archaeology* (Leiden: Brill, 1995).

——'The Tyranny of the Text: lost social strategies in current historical period archaeology in the classical Mediterranean,' in Pedro Paulo A. Funari, Martin Hall, and Siân Jones (eds), *Historical Archaeology: back from the edge* (London: Routledge, 1999), 122–35.

Smith, Morton, 'The Description of the Essenes in Josephus and the Philosophumena,' *HUCA* 29 (1958): 273–313.

Smith, Robert Payne, *A Compendious Syriac Dictionary* (Oxford: OUP, 1903).

Sorabji, Richard (ed.), *Aristotle Transformed: The Ancient Commentators and their Influence* (London: Duckworth, 1990).

Stacey, David, 'Some Archaeological Observations on the Aqueducts of Qumran,' *DSD*, 14/2 (2007): 222–43.

——'Seasonal Industries at Qumran,' *BAIAS* 26 (2008): 7–30.

——'Was there a Synagogue in Hasmonean Jericho?' article on the Bible and Interpretation site, http://www.bibleinterp.com/articles/Hasmonean_Jericho.shtml.

Steckoll, Solomon, 'Preliminary Excavation Report in the Qumran Cemetery,' *RQ* 23 (1968): 323–52.

——Goffer, Z., Nathan H., and Haas, Nathan, 'Red Stained Human Bones from Qumran,' *Israel Journal of Medical Sciences* 7/11 (1971): 1219–23.

Stegemann, Hartmut, *The Library of Qumran: On the Essenes, Qumran, John the Baptist and Jesus* (Grand Rapids: Eerdmans, 1998).

——'The Qumran Essenes—Local Members of the Main Jewish Union in Second Temple Times,' in Juan T. Barrera and Luis V. Montaner (eds), *The Madrid Qumran Congress. Proceedings of the International Congress on the Dead Sea Scrolls, Madrid, 18–21 March*, I (Leiden: Brill, 1992), 83–166.

——*Die Essener, Qumran, Johannes der Täufer und Jesus* (Freiburg im Breisgau: Herder, 1993).

——*The Library of Qumran: On the Essenes, Qumran, John the Baptist and Jesus* (Grand Rapids: Eerdmans, 1998).

Stemberger, Günther, 'The Sadducees: Their History and Doctrines,' in William Horbury, W. D. Davies, and John Sturdy (eds), *The Cambridge History of Judaism 3: The Early Roman Period* (Cambridge: CUP, 1999), 428–43.

Sterling, Gregory E., 'Universalizing the Particular: Natural Law in Second Temple Jewish Ethics,' *Studia Philonica Annual* 15 (2003): 64–80.

Stern, Menahem, *Greek and Latin Authors on Jews and Judaism*, 2 vols (Winona Lake: Eisenbrauns, 1974, 1980).

Stone, Michael, *Ancient Judaism: New Visions and Views* (Grand Rapids: Eerdmans, 2011).

Strobel, August, 'Zur Ortslage von Kallirhoe,' *ZDPV* 82 (1966): 149–62.

——'Das römische Belagerungswerk um Machärus. Topographische Untersuchungen,' *ZDPV* 90 (1974): 128–84.

——and Clamer, Christa, 'Excavations at ez-Zara,' *Annual of the Department of Antiquities of Jordan* 30 (1986): 381–4.

Strobel, August, and Wimmer, Stefan, *Kallirrhoë (`En ez-Zara): Drittes Grabungskampagne des Deutschen Evangelischen Instituts für Altertumswissenschaft des Heiligen Landes und Exkursionen in Süd-Peräa* (Wiesbadan: Harrassowitz, 2003).

Stutchbury, Howard E., and Nicholl, George R., 'Khirbet Mazin,' *Annual of the Department of Antiquities of Jordan* 6/7 (1962/3): 96–103.

Sukenik, Eleazer, *Megilot Genuzot mitokh Genizah Kedumah shenimtse'ah beMidbar Yehudah* [Hidden Scrolls from the Genizah Found in the Judaean Desert], 2 vols (Jerusalem: Bialik Institute, 1948/1949) (Heb.).

——*The Dead Sea Scrolls of the Hebrew University* (Jerusalem: Magnes, 1955).

Sussman, Yaakov, 'Babylonian Sugiyot to the Orders Zera'im and Tohorot' (unpubl. Ph.D. dissertation, Hebrew University of Jerusalem, 1969), 310–13 (Heb.).

——'The History of Halakha and the Dead Sea Scrolls: Preliminary Observations on Miqsat Ma'ase Ha-torah (4QMMT),' *Tarbiz* 59 (1990): 11–76 (Heb.).

Swain, Simon, *Hellenism and Empire: Language, Classicism, and Power in the Greek World AD 50–250* (Oxford: OUP, 1996).

——(ed.), *Dio Chrysostom, Politics, Letters and Philosophy* (Oxford: OUP, 2000).

——(ed.), *Seeing the Face, Seeing the Soul: Polemon's Physiognomy from Classical Antiquity to Medieval Islam* (Oxford: OUP, 2007).

——'Dio's Life and Works,' in Swain (ed.), *Dio Chrysostom*, 1–10.

Talmon, Shemaryahu, 'Three Scrolls they found in the Temple Court,' in Jehoshua M. Grintz and Jack Liver (eds), *Sefer Segal: M. H. Segel Festschrift* (Jerusalem: Kiryat Sefer, 1964), 25–37.

Taylor, Joan E. (ed.), with Greville Freeman-Grenville (trans.) and Rupert Chapman, *The Onomasticon by Eusebius of Caesarea: Palestine in the Fourth Century A.D.* (Jerusalem: Carta, 2003).

——*Christians and the Holy Places: The Myth of Jewish-Christian Origins* (Oxford: OUP, 1993).

——*The Immerser: John the Baptist Within Second Temple Judaism* (Grand Rapids: Eerdmans, 1997).

——'A Second Temple in Egypt: The Evidence for the Zadokite Temple of Onias,' *JSJ* 29 (1998): 1–25.

——'The Cemeteries of Khirbet Qumran and Women's Presence at the Site,' *DSD* 6 (1999): 285–323.

——'Khirbet Qumran in the Nineteenth Century and the Name of the Site,' *PEQ* 134/2 (2002): 144–64.

——*Jewish Women Philosophers of First-Century Alexandria: Philo's 'Therapeutae' Reconsidered* (Oxford: OUP, 2003).

——'Ain Feshkha,' *Encyclopaedia Judaica*, 2nd ed. (Farmington Hills, MI: Thomson Gale, 2006): vi, 255–6.

——'Pontius Pilate and the Imperial Cult in Roman Judaea,' *NTS* 52 (2006): 555–82.

——'Philo of Alexandria on the Essenes: A Case Study on the Use of Classical Sources in Discussions of the Qumran-Essene Hypothesis,' *SPA* 19 (2007): 1–28.

——'The Dead Sea in Western Travellers' Accounts from the Byzantine to the Modern Period,' *Strata: The Bulletin of the Anglo-Israel Archaeological Society* 27 (2009): 9–29.

——'On Pliny, the Essene Location and Kh. Qumran,' *DSD* 16 (2009): 129–49.

——'"Roots, Remedies and Properties of Stones": The Essenes and Dead Sea Pharmacology,' *JJS* 60 (2009): 226–44.

——'Dio Chrysostom and the Essene Landscape,' in Charlotte Hempel (ed.), *The Dead Sea Scrolls: Texts and Contexts* (Leiden: Brill, 2010), 467–86.

——'Buried Manuscripts and Empty Tombs: The *Genizah* Hypothesis Reconsidered,' in Aren Maeir, Jodi Magness, and Lawrence Schiffman (eds), *'Go out and study the Land' (Judg 18:2): Archaeological, Historical and Textual Studies in Honor of Hanan Eshel* (Supplements of the Journal for the Study of Judaism; Leiden: Brill, 2011).

Taylor, Joan E., 'Aus dem Westen ans Tote Meer: Frühe Reisende und Entdecker,' in Zangenberg, *Das Tote Meer*, 149–64.

——'The Classical Sources on the Essenes and the Scrolls Communities,' in Timothy Lim and John J. Collins (eds), *The Oxford Handbook of the Dead Sea Scrolls* (Oxford: OUP, 2011), 173–99.

——'Kh. Qumran in Period III,' in Galor, Humbert, and Zangenberg, *Qumran*, 133–46.

——'The *Nazoraeans* as a "Sect" in "Sectarian" Judaism? A Reconsideration of the Current View via the Narrative of Acts and the Meaning of *Hairesis*,' in Sacha Stern (ed.), *Sects and Sectarianism in Jewish History* (Leiden: Brill, 2011), 87–118.

——and Doudna, Greg, 'Archaeological Synthesis of the New Radiocarbon Datings from Qumran,' in Humbert and Gunneweg, *Khirbet Qumrân*, 201–5.

——and Gibson, Shimon, 'Qumran Connected: The Paths and Passes of the Northwestern Dead Sea,' in Jörg Frey, Carsten Claussen, and Nadine Kessler (eds), *Qumran und Archäologie—Texte und Kontexte* (Tübingen: Mohr Siebeck, 2011), 163–209.

——,——'Qumran in the Iron Age,' in Sidnie White Crawford (ed.), *Qumran* [tba] (forthcoming).

——,——'Qumran in the Iron Age in Comparison with the Hasmonean to Early Roman Periods: A Cross-Temporal Study,' Sidnie White Crawford (ed.), *Qumran Archaeology*, forthcoming.

Taylor, Justin, 'The Community of Goods among the First Christians and Among the Essenes,' in David Goodblatt, Avital Pinnick, and Daniel R. Schwartz (eds), *Historical Perspectives: From the Hasmoneans to Bar Kokhba in Light of the Dead Sea Scrolls* (Leiden: Brill, 2001), 147–64.

——*Pythagoreans and Essenes. Structural Parallels* (Collection de la Revue des Études Juives 32; Louvain: Peeters, 2004).

Telfer, William, 'Was Hegesippus a Jew?' *HTR* 53 (1960): 143–53.

Thiering, Barbara, *Jesus and the Riddle of the Dead Sea Scrolls* (London: HarperCollins, 1992).

Thomas, Joseph, 'Les Ebionites baptistes,' *Revue d'historie ecclesiastique* 30 (1934): 270–96.

——*Le Mouvement Baptiste en Palestine et Syrie* (Gembloux: Duculot, 1935).

Thomsen, Peter J., '"Jews" in the Gospel of John as compared with the Palestinian Talmud, the Synoptics and some New Testament Apocrypha,' in Bieringer, Pollefeyt, and Vandecasteel-Vanneuville, *Anti-Judaism*, 176–221.

Torijano, Pablo A., *Solomon, the Esoteric King: From King to Magus, Development of a Tradition* (Leiden: Brill, 2002).

Torrey, Charles C., 'James the Just, and His Name "Oblias",' *JBL* 63 (1944): 93–8.

Tov, Emanuel, *The Texts from the Judaean Desert. Indices and an Introduction to* The Discoveries in the Judaean Desert *Series* (DJD XXXIX; Oxford: OUP, 2002).

——*Hebrew Bible, Greek Bible, and Qumran: Collected Essays* (Tübingen: Mohr Siebeck, 2008).

Trafton, Joseph L., 'Commentary on Genesis (4Q252),' in James H. Charlesworth (ed.), *The Dead Sea Scrolls: Volume 6b: Pesharim, Other Commentaries, and Related Documents* (The Princeton Theological Seminary Dead Sea Scrolls Project; Louisville, KY: Westminster John Knox, 2002), 203–19.

Trever, John, 'Completion of the Publication of Some Fragments from Qumran Cave 1,' *RQ* 5/18 (1965), 323–44.

——*The Untold Story of Qumran* (Westwood, NJ: F. H. Revell, 1965).

Tsafrir, Yoram and Magen, Yitzhak, 'The Desert Fortresses of Judaea in the Second Temple Period,' *The Jerusalem Cathedra* 2 (1982): 120–45.

Twelftree, Graham H., *Jesus the Exorcist: A Contribution to the Study of the Historical Jesus* (Tübingen: J. C. B. Mohr/Paul Siebeck, 1993).

Tzoref, Shani, 'Realism, Nominalism, Subjectivism, and Gynephobia: Qumran Texts and Josephus on the Faithlessness of Women,' paper read at the International Society of Biblical Literature Conference, London, 4–6 July 2011.

Ullman-Margalit, Edna, *Out of the Cave: A Philosophical Enquiry into the Dead Sea Scrolls Research* (Cambridge, MA: Harvard University Press, 2006).

van der Horst, Pieter, *Chaeremon: Egyptian Priest and Stoic Philosopher* (Leiden: Brill, 1987).

van der Plicht, Johannes, Rasmussen, Kaare L., Glastrup, Jens, Taylor, Joan E., and Doudna, Gregory, 'Radiocarbon Datings of Material from the Qumran Excavation,' in Humbert and Gunneweg, *Khirbet Qumrân*, 193–6.

van der Ploeg, J. P. M., 'Le Psaume XCI dans une recension de Qumran,' *RB* 72 (1965): 210–17.

Van der Velde, C. W. M., *Memoir to Accompany the Map of the Holy Land* (Gotha: Justus Perthes, 1856).

van der Woude, Adam S., 'Wicked Priest or Wicked Priests? Reflections on the Identification of the Wicked Priest in the Habakkuk Commentary,' *JJS* 33 (1982): 149–59.

——'Once Again: The Wicked Priests in the Habakkuk Pesher from Cave 1 of Qumran,' *RQ* 17/90 (1996): 375–84.

van Henten, Jan W., 'The Two Dreams at the End of Book 17 of Josephus' Antiquities,' in J. U. Kalms and F. Siegert (eds), *Internationales Josephus-Kolloquium Dortmund 2002* (Münsteraner Judaistische Studien 14; Münster: Lit, 2003), 78–93.

van Unnik, Willem C. '"Tiefer Friede" (1. Klemens 2,2),' *VC* 24 (1970): 261–79.

VanderKam, James, *Textual and Historical Studies in the Book of Jubilees* (Missoula, MT: Scholars Press, 1977): 230–58.

——*Enoch and the Growth of an Apocalyptic Tradition* (Washington, DC: Catholic Biblical Association of America, 1984), 161–3.

——*The Dead Sea Scrolls Today*, rev. ed. (Grand Rapids: Eerdmans, 2010).

——'Who Were the Sadducees? The Sadducees of Jerusalem and Qumran,' in Isaiah M. Gafni, Aharon Oppenheimer, and Daniel R. Schwartz (eds), *The Jews in the*

Hellenistic-Roman World. Studies in Memory of Menahem Stern (Jerusalem: Zalman Shazar Center and the Historical Society of Israel, 1996), 393–411.

——'Identity and History of the Community,' in Peter Flint and James C. VanderKam (eds), *The Dead Sea Scrolls After Fifty Years: A Comparative Assessment* (Leiden: Brill, 1999), 2: 487–533, at 490–9.

——and Flint, Peter, *The Meaning of the Dead Sea Scrolls* (London: T & T Clark, 2002).

Vermes, Geza, 'The Etymology of "Essenes",' *RQ* 2 (1960): 427–43.

——'Jewish Studies and New Testament Interpretation,' *JJS* 31 (1980): 1–17.

——*The Dead Sea Scrolls in English*, rev. 4th ed. (Harmondsworth: Penguin, 1995).

——and Martin Goodman (eds), *The Essenes according to the Classical Sources* (Sheffield: JSOT Press, 1989).

von Martels, Zweder, 'Between Tertullian and Vincentius Lirinensis: On the Concept Constantia Veritatis and other "Christian" Influences on Solinus,' in Alasdair A. MacDonald, Michael W. Twomey, and G. J. Reinink (eds), *Learned Antiquity: Scholarship and Society in the Near East* (Groningen Studies in Cultural Change 5; Leuven: Peeters, 2003), 63–80.

von Wahlde, Urban C. 'The Johannine Jews: A Critical Survey,' *NTS* 28 (1982): 33–60.

——'The Relationships between Pharisees and Chief Priests: Some Observations on the Texts in Matthew, John and Josephus,' *NTS* 42 (1996): 506–22.

Wacholder, Ben Zion, *Nicolaus of Damascus* (Berkeley: University of California Press, 1962).

——'Pseudo-Eupolemus' Two Fragments on the Life of Abraham,' *HUCA* 34 (1963): 83–113.

——*Eupolemus: A Study of Judaeo-Greek Literature* (New York: Hebrew Union College, 1974).

——*The Dawn of Qumran: The Sectarian Torah and the Teacher of Righteousness* (Cincinnati: Hebrew Union College Press, 1983).

——'Josephus and Nicolaus of Damascus,' in Louis Feldman and G. Hatas (eds), *Josephus, the Bible and History* (Leiden: Brill, 1989), 147–72.

Wagemakers, Bart, and Taylor, Joan E., 'New Photographs of the Qumran Excavations from 1954 and Interpretations of L.77 and L.86,' *PEQ* 143 (2011): 134–56.

Wagner, Siegfried, *Die Essener in der wissenschaftlichen Diskussion vom Ausgang des 18. bis zum Beginn des 20. Jahrhunderts* (Berlin: Töpelman, 1960).

Walsh, Joseph, 'Galen Visits the Dead Sea and the Copper Mines of Cyprus (166 A.D.),' *Geographical Club of Philadelphia Bulletin* 25 (1924), 92–110.

Walter, Hermann, *Die 'Collectanea rerum memorabilium' des C. Julius Solinus. Ihre Entstehung und die Echtheit ihrer Zweitfassung* (Hermes. Einzelschriften, 22; Wiesbaden: Franz Steiner, 1969).

Waserman, M., and Kottek, Samuel S., *Health and Disease in the Holy Land: Studies in the History and Sociology of Medicine from Ancient Times to the Present* (New York: Edwin Mellen, 1996).

Weber, Ferdinand, *System der altsynagogalen palästinischen Theologie aus Targum, Midrasch und Talmud* (Leipzig: Dörfling und Franke, 1880).

Weber, Max, '"Kirchen" und "Sekten" I,' *Frankfurter Zeitung* (13 April 1906).

Weber, Max, *Gesammelte Aufsätze zur Religionssoziologie, Band 3: Das antike Judentum* (Tübingen: Mohr-Siebeck, 1921).

——*Ancient Judaism*, trans. and ed. by Hans H. Gerth and Don Martindale (Glencoe, Illinois: The Free Press, 1952).

Wells, Louise, *The Greek Language of Healing from Homer to the New Testament* (BZNW 83; Berlin/New York: Walter de Gruyter, 1998).

Werrett, Ian, 'A Scroll in One Hand and a Mattock in the Other: Latrines, Essenes, and Khirbet Qumran,' *RQ* 23 (2008): 475–89.

Wexler, Lior (ed.), *Surveys and Excavations of Caves in the Northern Judean Desert (CNJD) – 1993*, 2 vols ('*Atiqot* 41; Jerusalem: Israel Exploration Society, 2002).

White, K. D., *Agricultural Implements of the Roman World* (Cambridge: CUP, 2010).

Wilkinson, John, *Jerusalem Pilgrimage 1099–1185* (London: Hakluyt Society, 1988).

Williamson, G. A. (ed. and trans.), *Eusebius, The History of the Church from Christ to Constantine* (Harmondsworth: Penguin, 1962).

Wilson, Edmund, *The Scrolls from the Dead Sea* (London: W. H. Allen, 1955).

Winn, Adam, *The Purpose of Mark's Gospel. An Early Christian Response to Roman Imperial Propaganda* (WUNT II, 245; Tübingen: Mohr Siebeck, 2008).

Winston, David, 'Iambulus: A Literary Study in Greek Utopianism,' Ph.D. thesis (Columbia University, New York, 1956).

——, 'Iambulus' *Islands of the Sun* and Hellenistic Literary Utopias,' *Science Fiction Studies* 3 (1976): 219–27.

Winston, David, 'Philo and the Rabbis on Sex and the Body,' *Poetics Today* 19 (1998): 41–62.

Wise, Michael O., Golb, Norman, Collins, John J., and Pardee, Dennis G. (eds), *Methods of Investigation of the Dead Sea Scrolls and the Khirbet Qumran Site: Present Realities and Future Prospects* (ANYAS 722; New York: New York Academy of Sciences, 1994).

Wisen, Ed, *And You shall Surely Heal: The Albert Einstein College of Medicine Synagogue Compendium of Torah and Medicine* (Jerusalem: Ktav, 2009).

Woodman, Anthony J., *Rhetoric in Classical Historiography. Four Studies* (London and Sydney: Croom Helm, 1988).

Wortley, John (ed. and trans.), *The Spiritual Meadow of John Moschus* (Kalamazoo, MI: Cistercian Publications, 1992).

Wouters, Helena, et al., 'Archaeological Glass from Khirbet Qumran: An Analytical Approach,' in Jan Gunneweg, Charles Greenblatt, and Annemie Adriaans (eds), *Bio- and Material Cultures at Qumran* (Papers from a COST Action G8 working group held in Israel on 22–23 May 2005; Fraunhofer IRB, Stuttgart, 2006), 171–89.

——'Antique Glass from Khirbet Qumran: Archaeological Context and Chemical Determination,' *Bulletin of the Institut Royal du Patrimonie Artistique, Brussels* 28 (2002): 9–40.

Yadin, Yigael, *Tefillin from* Qumran *(XQPhyl 1–4)* (Jerusalem: Israel Exploration Society, 1970).

——'The Gate of the Essenes and the Temple Scroll,' in Yigael Yadin (ed.), *Jerusalem Revealed: Archaeology in the Holy City 1968–1974* (Jerusalem: Israel Exploration Society, 1976), 90–1.

Yardeni, Ada, 'A Note on a Qumran Scribe,' in *New Seals and Inscriptions, Hebrew, Idumean and Cuneiform* (ed. Meir Lubetski; Sheffield: Sheffield Phoenix Press, 2007), 287–98.

Yardley, John, *Justin and Pompeius Trogus: A Study in the Language of Justin's Epitome of Trogus* (Toronto: University of Toronto Press, 2003).

Yegül, Fikret K., *Baths and Bathing in Classical Antiquity* (Cambridge, MA: MIT Press, 1992).

Zangenberg, Jürgen, 'Das Tote Meer in neutestamentlicher Zeit,' in E. A. Knauf, U. Hübner, and R. Wenning (eds), *Nach Petra und ins Königreich der Nabatäer: Festschrift Manfred Lindner* (Bonner Biblische Beoiträge 118; Bodenheim: Beltz Athenäum, 1998), 49–59.

——'Wildnis unter Palmen? Khirbet Qumran in regionalen Kontext des Toten Meers,' in Bernard Mayer (ed.), *Jericho und Qumran: Neues zum Umfeld der Bibel* (Regensburg: Friedrich Pustet, 2000), 129–63.

——'Opening Up our View: Khirbet Qumran in Regional Perspective,' in Douglas R. Edwards (ed.), *Religion and Society in Roman Palestine: Old Questions, New Approaches* (New York/London: Routledge, 2004), 170–87.

——'Die hellenistisch-romische Zeit am Toten Meer,' in Jürgen Zangenberg (ed.), *Das Tote Meer: Kultur und Geschichte am Tiefsten Punkt der Erde* (Mainz: Philipp von Zabern Verlag, 2010): 39–52.

Zeitlin, Solomon, 'The Account of the Essenes in Josephus and the Philosophoumena,' *JQR* 29 (1958–9): 292–9.

Zeuner, Frederick E., 'Notes on Qumran,' *PEQ* 92 (1960): 27–36.

Zias, Joe E., Tabor, James D., and Harter-Laiheugue, Stephanie, 'Toilets at Qumran, the Essenes, and the Scrolls: New Anthropological Data and Old Theories,' *RQ* 22 (2006): 631–40.

Zissu, Boaz, 'Field Graves at Beit Zafafa: Archaeological Evidence for the Essene Community,' in Avraham Faust (ed.), *New Studies on Jerusalem* (Ramat Gan: Bar Ilan University, 1996), 32–40 (Heb.).

——'"Qumran Type" Graves in Jerusalem: Archaeological Evidence of an Essene Community,' *DSD* 5 (1998), 158–71.

Zohary, Michael, *Flora Palaestina*, with Naomi Feinbrun-Dothan, 3 vols (Jerusalem: Israel Academy of Sciences and Letters, 1966–79).

——*Plants of the Bible* (Cambridge: CUP, 1982).

Index of Ancient Sources

Numbers in italic indicate material found in Tables

Subject Index

Numbers in italic indicate illustrations and material found in Tables